ARTHURIAN STUDIES XLI

KING ARTHUR IN AMERICA

ARTHURIAN STUDIES

ISSN 0261–9814

Previously published volumes in the series
are listed at the back of this book

KING ARTHUR IN AMERICA

Alan Lupack
and
Barbara Tepa Lupack

D. S. BREWER

First published 1999
D. S. Brewer, Cambridge

ISBN 0 85991 543 3

D. S. Brewer is an imprint of Boydell & Brewer Ltd
PO Box 9, Woodbridge, Suffolk IP12 3DF, UK
and of Boydell & Brewer Inc.
PO Box 41026, Rochester, NY 14604–4126, USA
website: http://www.boydell.co.uk

A catalogue record for this book is available
from the British Library

Library of Congress Cataloging-in-Publication Data

Lupack, Alan.
  King Arthur in America / Alan Lupack and Barbara Tepa Lupack.
  p. cm. — (Arthurian studies, ISSN 0261-9814 ; 41)
  Includes bibliographical references and index.
  ISBN 0-85991-543-3 (hc. : alk. paper)
  1. American literature—History and criticism. 2. Arthurian
romances—Adaptations—History and criticism. 3. American
literature—Celtic influences. 4. Knights and knighthood in
literature. 5. Kings and rulers in literature.   I. Lupack, Barbara
Tepa, 1951– . II. Title. III. Series.
PS169.A9L86 1999
813.009'351—dc21   98-51847

This publication is printed on acid-free paper

Printed in Great Britain by
St Edmundsbury Press Ltd, Bury St Edmunds, Suffolk

Contents

Illustrations

In Memory of
George W. Tepa
and
Edna Boitano Lupack

Acknowledgments

We gratefully acknowledge the support of our colleagues, especially Russell Peck, who provided encouragement throughout this project and who assisted in the preparation of the illustrations; Kevin Harty, who generously allowed access to Arthurian films and other materials in his collection; and Norris Lacy, who offered good advice and whose *New Arthurian Encyclopedia* and *Arthurian Handbook* were invaluable resources. Our thanks to Donna Bell and Ian Peddie, graduate students at the University of Rochester, who served as research assistants. The staff of the Interlibrary Loan Department at Rush Rhees Library at the University of Rochester provided invaluable assistance in finding many of the books and articles needed for this project. We also want to thank McIntosh and Otis, Inc., agents for the estate of John Steinbeck, for permission to obtain a copy of portions of Steinbeck's "Arthur" manuscript and Ms. Barbara Smith-LaBorde of the Harry Ransom Humanities Research Center at the University of Texas at Austin for her assistance in acquiring the copy.

Portions of some of these chapters or ideas found in them have appeared in essays we have published in *Studies in Medievalism*, *Avalon to Camelot*, and *Arthuriana*, and in *Vision/Revision: Adapting Contemporary American Fiction by Women to Film*, ed. Barbara Tepa Lupack; in *Retelling Tales*, ed. Thomas Hahn and Alan Lupack; in *The Arthurian Revival: Essays on Form, Tradition, and Transformation*, ed. Debra N. Mancoff; in *Cinema Arthuriana*, ed. Kevin J. Harty; and in *Popular Arthurian Traditions*, ed. Sally Slocum. We would like to thank the editors and publishers of these publications for their support of our work.

Preface

This book has grown out of an attempt to resolve a paradox: the tremendous appeal of the Arthurian legends in America, where they are even more popular than in Britain. Yet those legends are seemingly at odds with American ideals and values. The social order of Camelot, after all, is based on inherited rank rather than advancement by merit. The appropriate American response to such an order would appear to be that of Hank Morgan, Mark Twain's Connecticut Yankee, who sought to undermine the aristocratic system he found in Arthur's kingdom by giving opportunity to the talented. While Twain indeed parodied aspects of the Arthurian world, many others have found ways to Americanize and democratize the Matter of Britain and to incorporate aspects of it into America's own mythologies; and ultimately even Twain discovered that Arthur's Britain and his own late nineteenth-century America had a good deal in common.

Evident in the earliest examples of American Arthuriana is a perspective, not to mention a rewriting of the traditional stories, that is different from that of European models. In "The Vision of Sir Launfal," for instance, a poem frequently reprinted and routinely read, studied, and memorized by several generations of Americans, James Russell Lowell created an original version of the Grail story. Lowell not only made the Grail knight someone other than those chosen few who are traditionally blessed with success in the quest but also radically reinterpreted the nature of the quest itself. Launfal achieves the Grail by learning charity towards his fellow human beings, something that is possible, though not easy, for anyone to attain.

Surprisingly, one of the greatest influences on nineteenth- and early twentieth-century American Arthuriana was the British laureate, Alfred, Lord Tennyson. Like Twain in *A Connecticut Yankee in King Arthur's Court*, a number of American writers responded to Tennyson's lofty idealism with satire or parody. Edgar Fawcett, for instance, in his delightful and parodic play *The New King Arthur*, offered a thoroughly new – and a New-World – view of Camelot. Tennyson's *Idylls* and other poems, however, were even more influential in providing a view of knighthood that Americans enthusiastically adopted. Particularly important in this regard was Tennyson's "Sir Galahad," whose well known lines, "My strength is as the strength of ten, / Because my heart is pure," echo through American popular culture, in large part because they support a notion of moral knighthood that allowed Americans to identify with Arthurian heroes who otherwise might seem quite foreign or remote. If purity of heart – rather than the wealth necessary to buy horses and arms, or the strength and skill necessary to use those tools effectively – was the primary requirement of knighthood, then anyone could be a knight, even the crippled boys who are referred to as "Little Sir Galahads" in two different works of early twentieth-century American popular fiction.

The notion of moral knighthood led William Byron Forbush, a minister, to create clubs, initially for boys and later for girls as well, modeled on the ideals of chivalry and a bowdlerized reading of the Arthurian tales. Forbush's clubs, called the Knights of King Arthur, were organized into Castles, each with an adviser called a Merlin and each with its own King Arthur, *elected* by the boys to lead them. These highly popular clubs, which urged the boys to emulate a knight of Arthur's court or some other hero, influenced the Boy Scouts and other smaller groups and were imitated by a program called the Knighthood of Youth, run through the public schools. Hundreds of thousands of children were members of Forbush's clubs or participated in the Knighthood of Youth. They read numerous versions of the tales of Malory and Tennyson written specifically for them, and they re-enacted the legends in their own lives. Moreover, as these youngsters grew to be adults, they continued to be interested in Arthuriana and passed that interest on to their own children, thus increasing even more the popularity of the legends in America.

Between the publication of Twain's book and the twenties, even as the youth groups were flourishing, another phenomenon occurred in American Arthuriana. Scholarly research influenced the creation of new Arthurian literature. Study of early sources provided material for the writing of the first American Arthurian historical novel, William H. Babcock's *Cian of the Chariots*, while the work of scholars like Joseph Bédier led others to reinterpret the story of Tristan and Isolt. But the most influential scholarly study by far was Jessie Weston's *From Ritual to Romance*, which inspired T. S. Eliot's *The Waste Land*, a poem that introduced the Grail, wasteland, and Fisher King motifs to a generation of novelists, who, in turn, influenced succeeding generations.

Ernest Hemingway, F. Scott Fitzgerald, and William Faulkner were all inspired by Eliot's poem, which shifted the focus of the Grail story from the quester and his achievement to the wounded king and his ravaged land, images in which Hemingway in particular found perfect symbols for the post-World War I world and the disillusioned and scarred soldiers who returned to a new society. This less romantic view of the Grail quest also made its way into the works of Fitzgerald, who was himself fascinated with things medieval and who saw in the Gothic buildings of Princeton and its football team a re-creation of the medieval world and its chivalric tournaments. His Great Gatsby, among other of his characters, is depicted as a Grail quester, but Gatsby's Grail is the shallow Daisy Fay, who chooses old wealth over knightly devotion. Gatsby's quest becomes a comment on the American

Dream, a quest that is often doomed to failure. Faulkner too found a rich source of imagery in Eliot's poem, and in his early short Arthurian piece *Mayday,* and in later major novels like *Absalom, Absalom!* and *The Sound and the Fury,* he made it clear that he was inclined to the medievalism of Eliot and other contemporaries like James Branch Cabell.

Another writer who devoted much of his career to exploring the Arthurian legends was John Steinbeck, one of the most American of novelists. Steinbeck said that his feeling for the oppressed and against the oppressor grew out of his childhood reading of a version of Malory, a book that colored all of his works, even those of social protest. Steinbeck's very specific uses of Arthurian material are apparent in a novel like *Tortilla Flat,* in which a group of poor *paisanos* is ennobled by an overlay of Arthurian allusion, as well as in his unfinished and posthumously published *Acts of King Arthur and His Noble Knights,* which began as a straightforward modernization of Malory but evolved into a new and innovative work that anticipated some of the developments in later Arthurian fiction.

Influenced by Eliot, by the Arthurian motifs in the writers of the Lost Generation, and by their own Arthurian reading and interests, new generations of novelists have found inspiration in the Arthurian legends. Writers as diverse as Bernard Malamud, Ken Kesey, Jerzy Kosinski, William Styron, Walker Percy, and Bobbie Ann Mason have created modern and often distinctly American versions of the Grail quest. In *In Country,* for example, Mason uses the Grail as an analogue for the meaning of the Vietnam War. Other novelists have given new vitality to the Arthurian world by making it postmodern, as Donald Barthelme does; by adding uniquely modern twists to the story of Arthur's reign, as Thomas Berger does; or by updating the legend of Tristan and Isolt, as John Updike does.

A final but essential aspect of American Arthuriana is the widespread infiltration of the legends into the many forms of American popular culture, from street to business names, from commercial products to advertising, from toys and games to CD-ROMs, from art to architecture. Arthurian characters and themes are regularly featured in cartoons, comic books, and television shows, as well as in cinema from the days of silent film to the present. Arthurian images abound in detective novels, fantasy and science fiction, juvenile literature, romance novels, and other popular literature. Clearly influenced by earlier American reinterpretations of the material and by the youth groups, which were themselves a popularizing of the stories of King Arthur, the prevalence of the Arthurian legends in American popular culture attests to the continuing interest in the tradition and is, in fact, that tradition's ultimate democratization.

1

Arthurian Literature in America before Twain

Nineteenth-century American writers, struggling to overcome the cultural dominance of England, found their own literary voices in remarkable ways: by looking to the Puritan past, as Hawthorne did; by creating thoroughly American yet universally recognizable characters, as Melville did; by looking minutely at the world around them or expansively at the universe and finding in the small or large canvas a metaphor for the self, as Dickinson and Whitman did. Some of the most important and influential American authors as well as many minor figures, however, turned to the Arthurian legends for their sources and inspiration – surprisingly, perhaps, since Americans in search of their identities would seem more likely to reject Old-World stories with a theme so innately British and so dominated by giants like Malory and Tennyson than to embrace them. This, in fact, appears to be the point of one of Nathaniel Hawthorne's tales.

Hawthorne's "The Antique Ring" tells of a minor writer named Edward Caryl who gives an antique ring to Clara Pemberton, his fiancée. Clara asks Edward to create a legend to accompany the gift, a romantic story that need not be "too scrupulous about facts" (107); and he obliges with a legend tracing the ring's lineage to Merlin. That ring, Edward says, had once been the property of the British wizard, who presented it to the lady he loved. Merlin's "art had made [its] diamond the abiding-place of a spirit, which, though of a fiendish nature, was bound to work only good, so long as the ring was an unviolated pledge of love and faith, both of the giver and receiver. But should love prove false, and faith be broken, then the evil spirit would work his own devilish will, until the ring were purified by becoming the medium of some good and holy act, and again the pledge of faithful love" (111).

Handed down to Queen Elizabeth through her Tudor ancestors, the ring was given to the Earl of Essex, who, after being imprisoned in the Tower to await execution, asked the Countess of Shrewsbury to convey it to the Queen as a reminder of her former affection. But the Countess betrayed Essex and the ring never reached Elizabeth. Later, one of Cromwell's soldiers stole it from the ancestral vaults of the Shrewsburys; and, after being used as a pledge in a series of faithless relationships, it arrived in the New World: "the legend now crosses the Atlantic" (119), Edward tells his auditors. The ring turns up in a collection box in a New England church where the charity of the giver purifies it and makes it once again a symbol of "faithful and devoted love" (123), and so a fitting engagement gift for Edward to offer Clara.

The device of the story within a story which Hawthorne employs in "The Antique Ring" permits him to relate the legend of Merlin's ring at the same time that he distances himself from the very tale that he creates. This distance is a significant element; without it, the tale can be misread, the way at least one critic has, as a story about a ring that is "an emblem of the human heart. And the truth about the human heart which the two legends [of Merlin and Essex] embody is that it has, inherent within it, falsehood" (Folsom 80). The simplistic point about falsehood, however, is made not by Hawthorne but by Edward Caryl, who is "somewhat of a carpet knight in literature," that is, one who has not entered the fray or undertaken the quest for a truly original (or, more specifically, a truly native) literature. He has written "stanzas of Tennysonian sweetness, tales imbued with German mysticism, versions from Jean Paul, criticisms of the old English poets, and essays smacking of Dialistic philosophy" (108). His lack of depth and focus is demonstrated by the fact that when Clara first proposes his making a legend for the ring, he asks, "Shall it be a ballad? – a tale in verse? . . . Enchanted rings often glisten in old English poetry" (109). Thus he proposes imitating the very old English poets whom he has criticized. Clara steers him away from this notion, insisting that he "tell the legend in simple prose" (109). But the legend he ultimately recites is no more than a prosaic version of the story to which he referred. Clara, who is a better critic than Edward, passes final judgment: "believe me, whatever the world may say of the story, I prize it far above the diamond which enkindled your imagination" (124). It is almost as if she is recognizing that the world will not think much of the story, that it is a story only a fiancée could love. What is actually wrong with the story is that it does not embody *any* truth to the human heart, as Hawthorne would use the phrase. Clara realizes, "It is really a pretty tale, and very proper for any of the Annuals. But, Edward, your moral does not satisfy me. What thought did you embody in the ring?" (124). Edward replies that he "can never separate the idea from the symbol in which it manifests itself" and then goes on to do just that by explaining that the gem is the human heart, and the Evil Spirit is Falsehood.

As interesting as it might be that Hawthorne writes about Merlin, the structure of "The Antique Ring" further indicates that he is rejecting such stories. As Chaucer did in his Tale of Sir Thopas, Hawthorne presents a tale that is deliberately flawed in order to comment on the nature of the tale itself. The fantastic legends of the old English poets, legends like those about Merlin, Hawthorne seems to be suggesting, are not a fruitful area for those, like Edward Caryl, who seek to assist in "the growth of American Literature" (108).

Hawthorne, then, brings an Arthurian legend to the New World in order to employ it against itself, to show the danger of its use by a young writer trying to define himself and his young country in literature. In a sense, "The Antique Ring" is analogous to Hawthorne's "My Kinsman, Major Molineux," a story that depicts another young American, a boy whose coming of age requires him to reject, on a personal and political level, the dominance of his kinsman who is a colonial governor appointed by the King of England. Just as Robin must learn to make his own way in the world, so must Edward Caryl learn to make his own way in literature, free from the dominance of British authors.

Quite a few nineteenth-century authors, however, ignored Hawthorne's warning and looked to the matter of Britain; but they adapted the legends in strikingly original ways – even before Mark Twain reacted to British cultural snobbism by satirizing chivalry and kingship in his *Connecticut Yankee in King Arthur's Court*. In fact, it appears to be the rule and not the exception for American writers to change traditional settings and symbols, to create new stories and characters, and to downplay the role of Arthur – and thus to offer a more democratic approach to the legends.

One way in which American authors accomplish this democratizing is by associating the Dream of Camelot with the American Dream and the related notion of the American Adam, perhaps America's only truly native mythology. For the Dream of Camelot, like the American Dream, is a glorious ideal, the envisioning of which is an inspiration for much that is good. But for all its glory, the American Dream – especially since the Civil War and the rise of realism in literature – has too often been seen as a nightmare that leads to disillusionment, if not doom, when it comes into contact with practical considerations and harsh realities. Similarly, the Arthurian world, with its focus typically on the Grail quest or the character of Merlin, is perceived as one in which the dream of perfection is impossible to achieve because of its distance from the actual and the practical, or, more simply, because of the demands of the real world. Yet, though ultimately doomed to failure, the vision of Camelot, like the American Dream, is so noble that its failure is not pathetic but tragic.

The power of Merlin and the quest for the Holy Grail are the earliest and most common motifs in American Arthurian literature. This may well be because Merlin, like the mythic American, has the potential to create a new world and because the quest for the Grail is like the quest for Edenic perfection that is such a common metaphor for the American Dream. As they appear in American literature prior to Twain, these two motifs demonstrate the originality, the Americanness, with which the legends are treated by American authors – an originality that makes these versions interesting foreshadowings of later interpretations of the Arthurian stories and therefore worthy of notice even when they themselves do not rise to the level of great literature.

Merlin as prophet inspired one of the earliest American Arthurian works, a pamphlet with a blatantly political purpose written in 1807 by Joseph Leigh, a Welsh-born American. Although *Illustrations of the Fulfilment of the Prediction of Merlin* imitated the prophecies of Merlin as found in Geoffrey of Monmouth and other authors, Leigh created his own prophecy, which speaks about a lion that wounds a "Virgin true." The prophecy is a commentary on the relationship between Britain, represented by the lion, and the United States, represented by the Virgin, symbolic of "injured innocence" (10–11) both because of the events leading to the Revolution and because of a specific later incident, the attack by the British ship *Leopard* on the American frigate *Chesapeake*. This attack, occasioned by a British demand to be allowed to search the *Chesapeake* and remove four members of the crew considered to be deserters from the British navy, was part of a pattern of British impressment of members of the crews of American vessels. Tensions between the two countries were greatly increased by what the United States saw as an assault on its sovereignty.

Leigh's prediction, written in appropriately cryptic language and later explained in detail, is a reminder of the consequences for Britain the last time it tested the United States and its ally France. It is also a warning that a similar fate awaits if Britain does not make reparations for the attack. In the terms of the prediction: "When the Cock [France] and Dove [the United States] the Lion [Britain] shall fight, / The Lion shall crouch beneath their might" (12). The final line states bluntly that "The Lion's might shall be undone" (18). The prediction is clearly proudly patriotic; and in it Leigh appropriates Merlin not to glorify the British monarchy, as some earlier prophecies had done, but rather to lend the supernatural weight of prophecy to the claims of a young nation.

Merlin serves a different purpose in Lambert A. Wilmer's *Merlin: A Drama in Three Acts*, a short play, first published in the *Baltimore North American* in 1827. As Thomas Ollive Mabbott, the play's editor, has noted, *Merlin* was a response to Edgar Allan Poe's unhappy love for Sarah Elmira Royster. Their engagement had been broken off by Sarah's parents, who considered Poe an unpromising prospect (v–vi). The relationship, treated poetically in Poe's *Tamerlane* (1827), apparently left the poet so despondent that his friends worried about the possibility of his suicide. Wilmer, an acquaintance of Poe's brother, wrote *Merlin* as a way of suggesting that Poe should avoid despair because the seemingly hopeless situation might actually turn out for the best.

In the play, which makes obvious allusions to Poe's passion, Alphonso loves a woman named Elmira. Elmira's father, however, demands that Alphonso seek his fortune before wooing his daughter; and Alphonso complies. In his absence, Merlin overhears Elmira's complaint and her fears, and with the help of attendant spirits, acts as a *deus ex machina*: he frustrates the wrath of the furies when they shipwreck Alphonso, has the treasure that would have been lost in the wreck restored to him, and ultimately reunites the lovers. The message, clear enough from the action of the play, is made even more specific in the spirits' final song:

> And O thus forever
>   Shall true love be blest,
> Then lovers be constant,
>   And fear not the rest.
>
> Tho' clouds of misfortune
>   May threaten awhile,
> Be patient and trust that
>   Kind Heaven will smile.   (23)

At the end of the play, in a bow to the traditional character, Merlin says that

> With charms of force, a brazen wall I'll rear
> Around Cairmardin, that in future there
> Unharm'd by foes, I may pursue that lore
> Which erst hath been the source of all my power.
> Those dark, mysterious volumes that contain
> The scrolls of fate, I will peruse again . . .   (24)

The action of the play takes place on the banks of the Hudson River. Even stranger, however, than the New-World setting is the choice of Merlin for the task of bringing together Alphonso and Elmira, since the wizard's traditional record in arranging happy love affairs is hardly exemplary. Wilmer's Cupid-playing Merlin is unconventional in other ways as well: he is a Prospero figure who commands both the spirits and the elements and in whom the play's Arthurian, Shakespearean, and classical influences blend.

Although radically at odds with Arthurian tradition, Wilmer's *Merlin* remains an important and instructive document that suggests the willingness of American dramatists to disregard whatever features of the legend they find inconvenient and to create new ones as they need them. Wilmer takes what seems a thoroughly American practical approach to the earlier material, using Merlin as a character because his plot demands a readily recognizable figure of power but ignoring most of the traditional associations because they are not suitable to his intentions in writing the play.

As the first to combine a major Arthurian character with an American setting, Wilmer is the precursor of modern fantasy writers like H. Warner Munn and Sanders Anne Laubenthal. Yet Wilmer's work is also of interest for the way in which he democratizes the legend: Merlin's craft is used not to help a king solidify his power and establish his authority but merely to help a common man and woman. Its emphasis on the individual, its lack of references to king and kingdom, and its American locale all mark *Merlin* as very different from British Arthurian literature of the nineteenth century.

Although not especially influential, Wilmer's play is nevertheless an appropriate beginning for American Arthurian drama.

Perhaps the first poem to Americanize the legends and the first American Arthurian work by a woman – the author identifies herself only as "a daughter of Eve" (467) – is one that appeared anonymously in *The Democratic Review* in May, 1844. "The Ylle Cut Mantell" purported to be "A Romaunt of the Tyme of Gud Kynge Arthur Done Into English from an Authentic Version." The authentic version referred to is "The Boy and the Mantle," a ballad which Bishop Thomas Percy included in his *Reliques of Ancient English Poetry* in 1765 and which describes a test of faithfulness: putting on a mantle that "shall never become that wiffe, / That hath done amisse" (2: 107). Guinevere, of course, fails the test, as does Sir Kay's wife. Only the wife of Sir Craddocke, after confessing to the fault of having kissed her husband before their marriage, can wear the garment. While Guinevere, out of malice, accuses Craddocke's loyal wife of infidelity, two other tests, one with a carving knife and one with a drinking horn, ultimately confirm the mantle's judgment.

The American poem transforms the ballad collected in Percy's *Reliques* in some fascinating ways. Considerably longer than the earlier ballad, it presents the mantle as the only test of fidelity. As in the ballad, Guinevere fails the test; but in a departure from its source, the wife of "Caradois," here called Ella, also fails: the robe is too short on her "by half an ell." This is because "she had been faithless and untrue" (471). There is no mitigating explanation, as in the ballad, that she had merely kissed her future husband. Following Ella's discomfiture, another character, Genelas, who "had lovers many a one" (472), also fails; so do two hundred other ladies, all the women of Arthur's court, save one. That young woman, Coralie, had been brought to court to marry a lord named Hubert before "envious lips and lying tongue" had poisoned his mind against her. The remarkable thing is that Coralie is "a Norman peasant's child" (473), a point emphasized when the handsome young knight who brings the mantle to Arthur's court announces that "the magic robe was woven / for the poor Norman peasant girl" and proclaims her "of maids the pride and pearl" (475).

In this way, "The Ylle Cut Mantell," the earliest of American Arthurian poems, rejects worth based on birth. As does much of the American Arthurian literature of the nineteenth and early twentieth centuries, it underscores the notion that virtue is more important than rank or wealth, a lesson Hubert appears to learn when he weds Coralie in her native village rather than "amid regal pomp and show" (476). The anonymous author of "The Ylle Cut Mantell," by reworking the earlier English ballad, makes her poem more democratic and therefore more suitable to the readers of *The Democratic Review*.

Some writers more famous and influential than Leigh or Wilmer or the author of "The Ylle Cutt Mantell" find equally intriguing ways to make the Arthurian material their own. In his Merlin poems, "Merlin I," "Merlin II," and "Merlin's Song," Ralph Waldo Emerson, for example, ignores all of the narratives associated with the wizard and presents him as a type of bardic power and vision. Rather than a character in a story, Merlin becomes, in effect, a symbol for the visionary, self-reliant individual that Emerson sees as an ideal. In none of these poems is there a suggestion of or allusion to any specific incidents from Malory or other Arthurian romances. Instead, Emerson is concerned almost solely with Merlin's symbolic value as a poet and a prophet (see Adkins 662–67).

In "Merlin I," Emerson describes the "kingly bard" who:

> Must smite the chords rudely and hard,
> As with hammer or with mace;
> That they may render back
> Artful thunder, which conveys
> Secrets of the solar track,
> Sparks of the supersolar blaze.   (*Poems* 120)

The power of the bard's song results from his vision, which puts him in tune with nature. Kenneth Walter Cameron has observed that "The song which Merlin sang or taught is the voice of the Divine indwelling Reason or Oversoul" (28). This song echoes the balance of Nature that "Made all things in pairs," as Emerson says in "Merlin II" (123), a poem that demonstrates how the order of art reflects the order of the universe.

Merlin's bardic chords seem also to predict – almost to control or direct – the secrets of the universe. In "Merlin I" and "Merlin II," his song is associated with fate. In the former, Emerson says explicitly that "Merlin's blows are strokes of fate" (*Poems* 120), and in the latter he observes that:

> Subtle rhymes with ruin rife,
> Murmur in the house of life,
> Sung by the Sisters as they spin;
> In perfect time and measure they
> Build and unbuild our echoing day.   (*Poems* 124)

The prophetic nature of Merlin's vision and its link to the mystic vision of the Transcendentalist ideal, the self-reliant individual, is suggested by a journal entry Emerson made in 1848: "The boy Merlin laughs three times," writes Emerson, "and, in each instance, because he foresees or second-sees what is future or distant. We are always on the edge of this, but cannot quite fetch it" (XI, 43).

Unlike Wilmer, whose plot and purpose require a Merlin who is a wonder-worker, Emerson depicts a Merlin whose power lies in his poetic and prophetic abilities. Such an interpretation of the character was peculiar to Emerson, who lauded "the old lays in which Merlin and Arthur are celebrated" (XI, 42) but demonstrated in his own writings that the romance traditions were incompatible with his personal philosophy. For example, he praised an incident from the *Morte d'Arthur* that recounts "Sir Gawain's

parley with Merlin in his wonderful prison," calling the scene "a height
which attracts more than other parts, and is best remembered."[1] But perhaps
what most attracted Emerson was the following exchange:

> "How, Merlin, my good friend," said Sir Gawain, "are you restrained so
> strongly that you cannot deliver yourself nor make yourself visible unto
> me; how can this happen, seeing that you are the wisest man in the world."
> "Rather," said Merlin, "the greatest fool; for I well knew that all this would
> befall me, and I have been fool enough to love another more than myself,
> for I taught my mistress that whereby she hath imprisoned me in such
> manner that none can set me free."

Whereas the Merlin of medieval romance ultimately surrenders his self-
reliance, Emerson escapes this contradiction of his own romantic philosophy
and of the symbolic meaning he intends for Merlin by using the alternative
bardic tradition in his poems.

Another Arthurian work written prior to *Connecticut Yankee* provides an
unusual variation, this time on the Grail quest theme. *Arteloise* by J. Dunbar
Hylton, a New Jersey physician and writer of epic poems, does not mock the
story of the Grail and the Grail knight; yet, like so much of this early
Arthurian literature in America, it introduces elements not found in any
previous tradition.

The hero of *Arteloise* is a knight named Beau de Main in whom are
combined the valor of Lancelot and the purity of Galahad. Beau de Main is
led on a series of quests by a guide, a character more typical of a romance by
Hawthorne than of an Arthurian romance. The guide, none other than the
Wandering Jew, leads the valiant knight on a series of adventures that
include the slaying of a dragon, the freeing of the castle Arteloise from the
power of the evil prophet who controls it, the obtaining of superhuman arms
and armor from Vulcan, and the freeing of Merlin's daughter Ursula from
the enchantment placed on her by Polar spirits.

Clearly, in his poem Hylton conflates medieval and nineteenth-century
popular motifs with little regard for historical accuracy or literary tradition –
though neither the medieval nor the contemporary motifs account for his
innovative and surprisingly feminist handling of the Grail theme. In the
course of his adventures, Beau de Main meets a woman named Griselda. She
is "a maiden knight" (139), who boasts of her prowess:

> Oft on my gallant steed I ride,
> Scour the country far and wide.
> All clad like knight in gleaming mail,
> I wear a helm, I bear a shield,

---

1 There is some doubt about the exact source of the passage that follows (quoted on pp.
   54–55 of the first edition of *Letters and Social Aims* [1876]), which is clearly not from
   Malory. For a discussion of this question, see Adkins, p. 673.

The spear I lift, the sword I wield,
  Although my hand seems small and frail;
And ne'er to foeman did I yield,
  Nor at grim danger quake nor quail;
I meet my foemen on the field –
  All who would me with wrong assail,
I pierce their steel, my blows they feel,
  To earth doth steeds and riders reel,
  And I o'er all their might prevail.   (140)

Not only does Griselda ride and fight as a knight errant but she is also in quest of the Grail. And, contrary to any tradition, she actually achieves it: an angel brings the sacred vessel to her and Beau de Main after they have demonstrated their courage and have, despite their love for each other, remained chaste.

Griselda is still clutching the Grail in the final scene when the Wandering Jew, by his power as a Rabbi, joins her and Beau de Main in wedlock. This happy ending follows the final battle with the Romans, a battle that – though itself quite unconventional – is entirely consistent with Hylton's treatment of the Grail theme in elevating the female characters to an unprecedented position of prominence.

The Wandering Jew has informed Clotilda, a maiden freed by the Grail-bearing Griselda from yet another enchantment, that according to prophecy only a maiden knight can overcome Terentius Arlus, the leader of the Romans attacking Arthur's realm. Clotilda therefore attacks Terentius, only to be slain herself. With her dying words she proclaims her willingness "To give my life in freedom's cause" (259).

After her failure, Arthur and Beau de Main and Pellinore all try to slay Terentius; but none of them succeeds. Despite their failure, the day is not yet lost. A third maiden knight, clad in snow-white armor, attacks the Roman commander, pierces his heart and lungs with her lance, cuts off his head, and tosses it in the air for all to see. This maiden knight, who is Merlin's daughter Ursula, is herself slain before the final defeat of the Romans.

The motif of a female Grail knight and of a female warrior who succeed where Arthur and his greatest knights fail is certainly noteworthy. Hylton was not alone in taking liberties with tradition; even some non-American nineteenth-century authors exercised a similar license. Bulwer-Lytton, for instance, set part of his epic *King Arthur* in the same Polar regions as Hylton did – though Bulwer-Lytton used the locale for a different effect. (His Gawain escapes being eaten by Vikings as a sacrifice to the goddess Freya, while his Arthur fights attacking walruses!) Nevertheless, Hylton's departures from earlier accounts of the Grail quest were quite radical; and his innovations, such as the climactic battle, indicate that he not only elaborates on tradition but in many instances disregards it entirely.

This disregard for tradition is apparent again in what is perhaps the most interesting and important example of American Arthurian literature before Twain, James Russell Lowell's *The Vision of Sir Launfal*. This poem, so popular in its day, is generally dismissed by critics as "one of the worst constructed poems in English" (*Literary History of the United States* 604), or as "the most disorganized poem ever written" and "the extreme example of Lowell's disregard for form" (Stauffer 186), or as a poem that seems "to moralize its subject too easily" (Waggoner 60). Some of these criticisms are warranted. After all, the "prelude" to the first of the poem's two parts is seventeen lines longer than the first part itself (ninety-five lines as opposed to seventy-eight). And the poem does have an overtly moral purpose – though not necessarily a simplistic one. But whatever the ultimate judgment on Lowell's poem as a work of art, it remains an excellent example of how early nineteenth-century American authors treated the Arthurian legends.

As in all of the works thus far considered, the departure from the medieval traditions is significant – so significant that it extends even to the genre of the poem. In Lowell's telling, Launfal falls asleep in the first stanza of part one; and all of the poem's action, including the entire quest and the learning of the true meaning of the Grail, occurs in the vision that comes to him as he sleeps. Since the reader sees Launfal only as he is setting out on the quest and then returning, the poem is not really a narrative. Nor is it a romance, particularly in the medieval sense. Were it a romance, it would in fact be quite deficient and poorly constructed – a sort of *Sir Gawain and the Green Knight* without the temptations and the hunts and the beheading contest. *The Vision of Sir Launfal* is most reminiscent of the dream vision, in which a lesson is learned – though the lesson is not about love, as in Chaucer's *Book of the Duchess*, or about spiritual happiness, as in *Pearl*, but rather about the true meaning of charity.

Even as a dream vision, however, *Launfal* suffers from structural problems, since Lowell tries to combine the medieval form (which has never been employed before for an Arthurian tale) with the style and description of an American romantic nature poem. As one critic has pointed out, "the castle in the north country of England is surrounded by a New England country; the famous day in June is all New England June; and the little December brook is a New England brook in winter" (Maynadier 381).

Such Americanizing of the Arthurian world may well be a reason for the poem's popularity among its nineteenth-century audience, just as the anachronisms in Chaucer and other medieval writers made their poems more accessible to contemporary readers. But Lowell's use of natural description is more than a superficial updating. As so often occurs in nineteenth-century America, Nature becomes a teacher. The charity and generosity that Launfal must learn are paralleled by the freely-given bounty of nature and of nature's God. The point is made early in the prologue to the first part:

> Earth gets its price for what Earth gives us;
>   The beggar is taxed for a corner to die in,
> The priest hath his fee who comes and shrives us,
>   We bargain for the graves we lie in;
> At the devil's booth are all things sold,
> Each ounce of dross costs its ounce of gold;
>   For a cup and bells our lives we pay,
> Bubbles we buy with a whole soul's tasking:
>   'Tis heaven alone that is given away,
>   'Tis only God may be had for the asking;
> No price is set on the lavish summer;
> June may be had by the poorest comer.   (4)

The following line – "And what is so rare as a day in June?" – has become such a cliché that its original importance to the poem is easily overlooked. The glory of a June day, the rarest and therefore the most valuable thing possible, is freely bestowed upon men. The lesson Launfal must learn is to bestow his charity just as freely and as lovingly on others.

If the approach of combining American themes and motifs with the medieval structure of the dream vision does not raise Lowell's poem to the level of greatness, at least it makes *Launfal* seem a less disorganized work, a good poem worthy of further consideration for the liberties an American author is willing to take with Arthurian matter. Lowell's originality with the material extends beyond his experimentation with structure, however, to the character of Sir Launfal himself. Like Hylton, Lowell presents a most un-traditional Grail knight – a Grail hero to be found nowhere else in Arthurian legend. Though Launfal appears in other works, he is usually little more than one of the members of Arthur's court. Brewer and Taylor observe that Marie de France's *Lanval* and the Middle English *Sir Launfal* "describe the knight's liaison with a fairy mistress rather than a Grail quest," though both "emphasise Launfal's largesse" (167), which is precisely the virtue that Lowell's Launfal acquires.

Yet, more than largesse, Lowell's hero learns a true charity that allows him not simply to toss a coin to a beggar but to empathize with his fellow man so fully that his castle becomes home to any other person who wants or needs it. And, while any one of the traditional Grail knights might have acquired this virtue, the fact that Lowell chose such a relatively minor knight to become his Grail hero is important, both in itself and as a departure from Arthurian tradition.

Lowell's choice of Launfal is even more surprising given his own fascina-tion with another Arthurian knight, Perceval. At one point Lowell was so intrigued by that character that he even considered changing his name to Perceval Lowell (Howard vii). And surely as a poetical work *The Vision of Sir Perceval* would have been as acceptable as *The Vision of Sir Launfal* – but in his choice of Launfal and not Perceval as Grail hero Lowell was deliberately

Figure 1. Sir Launfal scorns a beggar in Sol Eytinge's illustration for an edition of
The Vision of Sir Launfal (Boston: Ticknor and Fields, 1867).

attempting to distance himself from tradition. This is clear from the note Lowell placed at the beginning of his poem. He writes: "The plot (if I may give that name to any thing so slight) of the following poem is my own, and, to serve its purposes, I have enlarged the circle of competition in search of the miraculous cup in such a manner as to include, not only other persons than the heroes of the Round Table, but also a period of time subsequent to the date of King Arthur's reign." This note is instructive not only because its remark on the slightness of the plot recognizes that the poem is different from traditional narratives, but also – and perhaps especially – because it deliberately divorces the Grail legend from Arthur (though no part of the poem dates it outside of Arthur's reign). So what Lowell offers is a comment specifically saying the poem is not set in Arthur's time – even though there is no narrative imperative for doing so, even though Grail stories traditionally are set in that period, and even though Launfal is a knight typically associated with Arthur's court.

Why then does Lowell deliberately establish *The Vision of Sir Launfal* as a non-Arthurian Arthurian poem? The answer can only be that he wants to disassociate the Grail from its connections to nobility, even the admirable nobility of Arthur. Such disassociation allows Lowell to make the north country where Launfal's castle is located a world unto itself, a world that can become a sort of new Eden as a consequence of the natural charity that Launfal learns from his vision. It also implies that the achieving of the Grail – that is, the acquiring and practicing of this transforming charity – is not something limited to Arthur's time and place or to the few good men whom Arthur gathered about him. Rather, the achieving of the Grail comes within the reach of all men, surely a democratic notion appropriate to an American poem.

Lowell's reinterpretation of the legend obviously struck a chord with the American public. *The Vision of Sir Launfal* became one of the most beloved and best known American poems of the second half of the nineteenth century, a new edition or a reprint of an earlier edition appearing on the average of once a year from the time of its publication in 1848 until the turn of the century; and its popularity remained high into the early twentieth century. The de-emphasis of nobility and the emphasis on simple morality not only turned the world of Arthurian romance into a model for the common man; it also made the Grail a symbol and a concept accessible to vast numbers of Americans – one reason the Grail legend remains even today the subject of continuing interest in American literary and popular culture.

The downplaying of nobility and of King Arthur himself is consistent with the treatment of Arthurian material in other early American Arthurian works. Arthur, after all, does not even appear in Wilmer's play or Hawthorne's story or Emerson's poems; and, in Hylton's poem, he is unable to win the day without the intercession of a maiden knight. This diminution of

Arthur's role is therefore one way that nineteenth-century authors before Twain adapted an old monarchic legend to a young country with democratic ideals; another way was to disregard the traditions surrounding the Arthurian legends to create new characters, adventures, genres, and symbolism. The legends themselves may have been borrowed from the Old World, but nineteenth-century American authors shaped them into something very new.

The same adaptability of traditional Arthurian material to contemporary concerns is evident in the works of two nineteenth-century women writers, Sallie Bridges and Elizabeth Stuart Phelps. Bridges, though virtually unknown today and apparently little recognized in her own day, wrote a sequence of Arthurian poems that is of considerable interest in the context of American Arthuriana, largely because of the ways in which she recast the material that she borrowed, clearly and admittedly, from Malory. The sequence "Legends of the Round Table," which appears in her collection entitled *Marble Isle, Legends of the Round Table, and Other Poems*, contains fourteen poems that tell Arthur's story from the pulling of the sword from the stone to his resting in Avalon ("Avilion" in Bridges's poem). Bridges says pointedly that she got the ideas for many of her poems "several years before reading a line of Tennyson" when she "met with the old romance of 'Prince Arthur' translated from the French" (158), by which she means Malory's *Morte d'Arthur*.

The sequence opens with a poem called "Excalibur," which is a fairly traditional retelling of the story of the sword in the stone. Kay forgets his sword and Arthur, unable to get access to the quarters where Kay's sword was left, pulls the sword from the stone so his "brother shall not go unarm'd / To battle" (160). As is usual, the sword is the sign of kingship and Arthur is recognized as heir to the throne. "Excalibur" is followed by another fairly straightforward narrative, "The Death of Lanceor," which tells the story of Lanceor, the son of the King of Ireland, who is killed in battle by Sir Balin, whereupon Colombe, Lanceor's beloved, uses his sword to commit suicide. This poem suggests one of the thematic concerns of Bridges's poems, the relationship between men and women, and also exemplifies a stylistic trait found in several poems from her Arthurian sequence, the tendency to insert aphorisms or morals that sum up the essence of the tale she has recounted. In commenting on the love of Colombe for Lanceor, Bridges says:

> Oh matchless love of Woman! Sure thou art
> The only flower of Eden left to bloom
> Amid the thorny thistles of real life,
> Scenting the wayside with thy rich perfume,
> Brightening with beauty common spots of earth! (163)

While out of favor in modern poetry, such blunt authorial statements were common and almost expected in much nineteenth-century American verse and are often found in the works of better known and more widely published poets, like James Russell Lowell. And, for both Lowell and Bridges, the attraction of the Arthurian stories seems to have been in part the truths they saw embedded in them.

From the tomb of Lanceor and Colombe at the end of "The Death of Lanceor," the sequence moves to "The Tomb of the Twelve Kings." After briefly recounting the death of Lot and the other rebellious monarchs in battle against Arthur, the poem describes the magnanimity of the victor in providing an honorable and elaborate burial for his fallen foes. Above their tombs is a kind of eternal flame: "Twelve gilded figures, night and day, / Held burning tapers bright alway" (166), though the figure of Arthur triumphant stands above them all. In its closing image, the poem suggests a pending evolution in the Arthurian realm:

> For years before the Sancgreal came,
> Above each quaintly sculptured name,
> Like living bursts of golden flame,
>   Their light the tapers shed.   (167)

The light representing the slain in battle will soon be replaced by the light of the Grail, which figures prominently in a couple of the subsequent poems.

Before treating the Grail quest, however, Bridges introduces the love of Lancelot and Guinevere in "The First Meeting of Sir Launcelot and Queen Guinevere." A simple poem, it describes a beautiful and regal Guinevere receiving for the first time the fealty of Arthur's knights. But as Launcelot approaches to do homage to his queen, their eyes meet and she blushes. In a moment, "the spell was o'er: / The woman was a queen once more" (168); but that moment is frozen in two of the poem's six stanzas.

The tomb motif in Bridges's poems combines with her concern for male–female relationships in the poem "Merlin's Grave," which tells of the infatuation of the wizard with "the Ladye of the Lake." To learn his magic, the Lady feigns love for him. When she has the knowledge she seeks, she wants to get rid of him and so seals him in a cave with a huge stone held in place by sorcery. An aphorism suggests her motivation and the moral of the poem: "ladies laugh at lovers gray-bearded and three-score" (170). But she pays a price for her deception: "forever kept the Ladye the secret of the stone, / As she sat beneath the waters and wrought her spells alone" (171).

The two poems following "Merlin's Grave" are simple, straightforward narratives lacking even the morals of some of the other pieces in the sequence. In "Sir Launcelot's Slumber," love is again the subject. The poem tells of Launcelot's being made captive by four queens but resisting their advances because he dreams of Guinevere; "Beaumain's Vow" describes Gareth's arrival at Camelot and his request for three boons. His first request is for food and drink for the coming year. With no account of the events of that year, the poem takes up the next two requests, "a perilous quest," the nature of which is not spelled out, and knighting by Launcelot. The purpose of both of these poems seems to be merely to versify a passage from Malory.

The nature of the poems makes the next one in the sequence all the more surprising. In "The King and the Bard," Arthur offers a minstrel gold in return for singing a lay, but the minstrel remains silent. The reason, as he explains, is that "true song cannot be sold!" (178). Arthur agrees with the minstrel's reasoning and extends the moral: "Monarchs cannot rule men's *spirits*," he proclaims, "By the might of law or gold!" (178). The poem closes with a toast by Arthur

> To the bard who freely renders
>   The gift he has been given,
> And sings but when his strain exalts
>   His hearers nigher heaven!   (179)

The poem is in conformity with other American works that downplay the power of the Arthur as king. He rules but he cannot rule men's spirits. His request is ignored by the bard, who uses his moral authority to lecture the king. Yet, unlike the preceding poems in the sequence, this one has no source in Malory. As in some of Bridges's other poems, though, there is a moral; but it is one that grows from a situation of her own construction rather than being imposed on a scene she has retold from the *Morte d'Arthur*.

In her treatment of the Tristan story, "The Love-Drink," Bridges returns to a poem of love that contains a moral. In a compression of the traditional story, Tristan, who is depicted as the epitome of the loyal knight, is wounded in combat while defending Cornwall against a demand for "truage" even as he is on his way to obtain Isoude as a bride for his uncle King Marke. Despite the grievous wound, Tristan says, "Duty could not wait / Because a man should bleed!" (179–80). This moral comes early in the poem and is consistent with other material that precedes the drinking of the love potion. When he falls in love with Isoude, for example, Tristan reminds himself that she is to be "my uncle's wife" (182) and suppresses his passion. When he teaches her to play the lute, he sings "mostly battle-songs" or "lays / Of sunny France, the harvest hymns," or, in what seems a particularly American touch, "plaints / Of captured slaves," but he "never sang of love" (181). Only when they find the love-drink given to Governale, Tristan's squire (since Brangwain, who traditionally receives the drink, does not appear in the poem), do they yield to passion: "one long kiss seal'd their eternal troth" (184).

It is interesting that the next poem, "The Best Knight," which tells of Launcelot's healing of Sir Urre, falls where it does in Bridges's sequence – immediately before the poem describing the quest for the Holy Grail. This reverses the order in Malory, who allows his Lancelot to work a miracle as a blessing and a sign of his great nobility despite the fact that at this point he has not succeeded in the quest for the Grail. Bridges seems to be doing two things with her poem. First, she presents a picture of Guinevere as a real woman. The queen suggests postponing a tournament so the knights can try to heal Sir Urre and relieve his pain and his mother's grief. When Launcelot rides up after all the other knights have failed, she drops the royal sceptre in the dust, an act for which she is chided by Arthur. Second, the poem shows Launcelot as humble before God. He prays that God will heal Sir Urre; and when he searches the knight's wounds, his prayers are answered. In response to Guinevere's question about what spell he used to achieve this miracle, he says merely, "I pray'd to God" (189). These simple words, the last in the poem, seem to epitomize the point of the poem, that God answers prayers, even the prayers of sinners. They also set the tone for the following poem, "The Quest of the Sancgreal."

Bridges's Grail poem is the longest in her sequence. Much of it retells, fairly closely, incidents from Malory, including such scenes as the pulling of a sword from the stone by Galahad, Galahad's sitting in the Siege Perilous, an appearance of the Grail at Camelot, the vowing to undertake the quest by knights ill suited for the task, Galahad's obtaining of the shield with the red cross, Launcelot's being struck down as he attempts to enter the Grail Chapel, and the achievement of the Grail by Galahad. But there are some significant differences from Malory's version. The most noteworthy of these is the characterization of Galahad, which at times seems more influenced by the Wordsworth of "Intimations of Immortality" or the Blake of "Songs of Innocence" than by Malory. Bridges says her Galahad's

> . . . heart was tender yet with dreams of youth,
> And, as his life was nearer to his birth,
> His soul was closer to his God than theirs
> Who had forgotten heaven in the heat
> Of earthly conflicts mid the light of fame.
> He look'd on nature with such earnest love
> His rapturous delight to worship soar'd.   (200)

As he rides on his quest, he "turn'd aside / His courser's hoofs lest they should heedless tread / To dust and death a daisy in the grass" (200). And he is more concerned about the suffering of his horse than about his own pains. He smooths the horse's mane, pulls its weary head onto his shoulder, and washes its "bleeding limbs and panting sides"; when he reaches a castle, he enters it "more because his courser was so maim'd / Than that himself was tempted at the sight" (202–03). But he also displays a work ethic that is defined as a necessary quality for success:

> . . . Yet still he onward toil'd;
> For this, the monks had told him, was the road
> Alone could forward him upon his quest.
> Sometimes he long'd to throw aside his arms
> And rest his weary limbs; but evermore

> He saw some work to do, some goal to win
> That brought him nearer to the end, nor dared
> To slumber, lest he should be stung to death
> By creeping creatures, or waste precious hours.   (202)

In keeping with Bridges's recurring use of love as a theme, her Galahad even feels love, which of course he must resist in order to succeed in his quest.

Though the poem ends anticlimactically with Galahad's dying statement that the Grail was "God's own Eternal Truth" (212), Bridges nevertheless creates an interesting picture of the Grail knight. Despite the traditional nature of much of what is found in her poem, her Galahad is an original combination of Romantic and American qualities.

Ignoring Mordred's plot to catch Launcelot and Guinevere, the final battle, and the slaying of Mordred and the wounding of Arthur, Bridges proceeds to "The Last Meeting of Launcelot and Guinevere," a poem that follows naturally from the Grail poem. In "The Last Meeting," she describes Launcelot's arrival – by chance – at Almesbury where he happens upon the queen. Guinevere resists the temptation to rekindle her love for Launcelot and represses the desire she clearly feels. On the verge of yielding, she hears "the vesper-hymn," and their love "Seem'd to grow dim before the cross of Christ." Then

> Her agony was o'er; the thorns upon her brow
> Became a crown of light through passion slain!
> She found the Sancgreal in that trial-hour!
> A vision of unspoken glory fill'd
> Her raptured view, and, when it died away,
> It left her face as 'twere the face of one
> Who might have talk'd with God!   (216)

As in Lowell's *Vision of Sir Launfal*, the Grail becomes something that anyone, even the formerly fallen queen, can achieve because it requires only moral fortitude to do so.

Launcelot himself is redeemed in "Launcelot's Vigil," the next poem in the sequence. After a vision of Guinevere's death, he returns to Almesbury to arrange her burial. Melodramatically, Launcelot is shown to be in agony when he learns that Guinevere's last wish was that she not see him while she lived. His redemption comes in an equally melodramatic moment. Lancelot prays that

> . . . if so be he yet should win
> A place in paradise, it might be where,
> In Christ's wide heaven, she ne'er might see his face!
> For, as he cast such sorrow on her life,
> He would not shadow her immortal bliss
> Even by memories he would cherish still
> Through all eternity apart from her!   (222)

Perhaps it is this selfless act that allows the poem to end with Ector's eulogy declaring Launcelot a worthy example for men to hold up to their sons (223).

The final poem in the sequence is the most original of all. Called "Avilion," its narrator tells of her sorrow that her work will soon be forgotten and wishes she could go to rest in the Happy Isle, as Arthur did. The action of the poem begins with a striking image:

> And so I closed my tired eyes, that press'd
> Two tears between the lids, that, as they touch'd
> The level ground, into a wonder grew;
> For, lo! a lake that spread its waters up
> Nigh to my feet, while through the sunset glow
> A black barge hove in sight, like one that came
> For wounded Arthur, only now it bore
> No fair, crown'd queens, no hooded, weeping dames!
> Only a pallid steersman stood at helm,
> With white garb stirless as a statue's robe
> That seem'd to sweep adown o'er folded wings.   (225)

The Avilion she reaches is an idyllic place where she is aware of the meaning of "earth's great riddle" and realizes "What grand significance e'en evil took" (227). She meets there "one that I knew" but who had died before her and awaited her arrival, finding even the joys of Avilion incomplete without her.

In the Happy Isle, the narrator also meets Arthur, Guinevere, and Launcelot. The former lovers are purified of their passion for one another. And Arthur is the ideal ruler. He is "grand in his presence" and yet had "Such courteous, kindly mien, that one who begg'd / Might call him 'brother' " (229). Thus the Arthur of Bridges's poem is like many other American Arthurs and Arthurian characters in that he is no different from the common person. He is also one who realizes that he must serve those who trust in him. When Arthur asks if men still hope for his return "To do my best to win for them the right," he is touched by the narrator's response. She gives him "a picture of the times, / And how the nations groan'd because was found / No strong, true leader pure in life and aim" (230). So he decides "The time is ripe" for him to return "To lead the way to truth through seas of blood!" (231). The poem ends after Arthur announces to his knights who would join him that he must go alone. And then something, perhaps the flapping of the barge's sail in the wind, breaks the spell and she finds herself:

> . . . once more within this world,
> On which the shades had gather'd into night,
> And mid the throng that wait the Coming King!   (238)

"Avilion" is a remarkable poem for its depiction of Avalon but also for its call for Arthur to return. Though no specific allusion is made to contemporary events, one cannot help but feel the poem is really a comment on the events surrounding the Civil War.[2] This seems a plausible interpretation since, in the same volume, there appears a poem entitled "The Question of the Day in 1860." The question of the day is the "dissolution of the Union," which Bridges clearly thinks would be a great tragedy. She writes:

> Dissolve this Union, and dear hope dies out
> In all the eager souls that watch its stars
> Rise steadfast o'er the earth with growing light.   (115)

And she calls her "young and lovely land" that is "Throned on two seas" the "Queen of nations." Perhaps it is the threat to this queen that causes the "nations" to groan in "Avilion"; and perhaps when Arthur says the time is ripe for him to return "To lead the way to truth through seas of blood!" it is to the bloodshed of the Civil War and the truth of maintaining the Union that he is alluding.

Like Sallie Bridges, another nineteenth-century American woman, Elizabeth Stuart Phelps (1844–1911), author of fifty-seven volumes of fiction, poetry, and essays, wrote a number of Arthurian poems and stories. Yet now she, too, for the most part, is forgotten or overlooked. In her own day, however, Phelps's writing was thought to have "vividness," "spiritual passion," and "the power to strike the human note"; and it was praised by prominent literary figures (Halsey 290). Though much of her work focused on social problems, "it was as a religious writer," observes Lori Duin Kelly, "that Phelps was best known to her own contemporaries, and it is largely for her religious writings that Phelps is remembered at all today. Yet what is perhaps most interesting about this aspect of Phelps's work is its intimate connection with her interest in women, for this interest not only motivated her to write her first religious work, it also directly affected her religious views – shaping her theology and ultimately coloring her vision of the afterlife" (7–8). Thus, in effect, her religious writing had a strongly social agenda.

As Perry D. Westbrook noted in his *Literary History of New England*, Phelps is also important as "a pioneer in her realistic accounts of the degradation of labor as society became more and more industrialized and an ardent and tireless champion of women's rights" (245). Phelps "had been roused to a sense of the wrongs of the factory-workers by the great mill fire in Lawrence [Massachusetts] in 1859, when scores of New England girls were burned to

---

2   Bridges is not the only American author to link the Arthurian legends and the Civil War. Frank O. Ticknor, a Georgia physician and poet, wrote a poem called "Arthur, the Great King," which was addressed to Jefferson Davis and made an analogy between Davis and King Arthur. A Northern work, a pamphlet called *Excalibur: A Tale for American Boys*, constructs a bizarre history of Excalibur and its uses in the fighting of oppression from the time Bedivere casts it into the mere until it reaches America: having been given to George Washington by Frederick the Great, it comes to be used by John Brown in his fight against slavery and then is passed on to Abraham Lincoln. Finally, upon Lincoln's death, it passes to Andrew Johnson, who the anonymous author hopes "may never blunt its fine edge" (24).

death" (Brooks 99). And her decision to tackle social issues in her fiction must have been reinforced when "The Tenth of January," the story she wrote about the Lawrence incident, gave her "the first recognition which [she] received from literary people" (Phelps, *Chapters* 92), such as Thomas Wentworth Higginson and John Greenleaf Whittier, both of whom wrote letters of unsolicited praise when it appeared in *The Atlantic Monthly*. Personal experience in combination with a strong belief in social equality also led her to write about the problems and treatment of women.

Given Phelps's surprisingly prescient social and feminist concerns, the poems and stories she published on Arthurian themes at first seem hardly to be of a piece with her numerous other publications – though, in fact, they are. The manner of her retelling of the Arthurian tales shows them to be altogether consistent with her other work. In her fiction, for instance, she translates the inhabitants of medieval Camelot into a nineteenth-century setting. Phelps's Lady of Shalott (in "The Lady of Shalott") is a sickly seventeen-year-old girl living in a slum and supported by her sister who earns a poverty wage doing piece-work. When the mirror through which she views the world is broken by street urchins throwing rocks, she succumbs to her harsh environment and dies. Phelps's Galahad (in "The Christmas of Sir Galahad") is a man who, despite his love for another woman, remains faithful to his wife, even though she is erratic and addicted to narcotics. Only after her death does he marry the woman he really loves. And Phelps's Arthur, Guenever, and Launcelot (in "The True Story of Guenever") are a carpenter, his wife, and their boarder.

Phelps was certainly capable of presenting these characters in their traditional settings. She does just that in her three Arthurian poems, "The Terrible Test," "Elaine and Elaine," and "Guinevere," all of which were reprinted in her collection *Songs of the Silent World* (1891). But even in these poems there is a twist to the familiar material that suggests the originality with which Phelps constructed her stories. "The Terrible Test" describes Galahad "whose strength was the strength of ten" and who is recognized as "the eidolon of holiness" because he is "pure in deed, and word, and thought." But Phelps closes her poem with the comment that it is "Enough, to know that once the clay / Hath worn the features of God," that is, in the person of Christ. The implication is that only one perfect model is necessary. Galahad's "test" is terrible not because of its difficulty but because it has cost him his humanity:

> . . . no man thou wast;
> No human pulses thine could be;
> With downcast eyes we read – and sigh;
> So terrible is purity!

"Elaine and Elaine," despite its title, deals with only one Elaine, the Lily Maid who dies for love of Lancelot. Like the title, the poem itself is somewhat cryptic: it seems to argue paradoxically for silence in the face of the tragedy. The two sections of the poem end with questions about whether we should speak about Elaine if the steersman of her barge "speaketh not a word" and whether "If she [Elaine] / Sayeth nothing, how should we?" It may be that Phelps wishes her readers to be silent so they can reflect on the fact that Elaine's position is representative. Her penultimate stanza – "Oh! the river floweth fast. / Who is justified at last?" – implies that all people are in the position of ending their journeys through life without any ultimate justification for what they have, or have not, done.

Phelps's third Arthurian poem, "Guinevere," which was originally published with the title "Afterward," anticipates her story about Arthur's queen. Both are concerned with Guinevere in the nunnery and with the guilt ascribed to her. While the story is more radical in its reinterpretation of Guinevere's betrayal of Arthur and refuses to accept her groveling before a sternly moral king, the poem is also unwilling to condone the Tennysonian view of the queen's guilt. In "Guinevere," the queen also grovels, but

> When, kneeling as she was, her limbs
> Refused to bear her, and she fell afaint
> From weariness and striving to become
> A holy woman, all her splendid length
> Upon the ground, and groveled there, aghast
> That buried nature was not dead in her,
> But lived, a rebel through her fair, fierce youth . . . .   (61)

Thus Guinevere grovels not because she is overwhelmed by her guilt but because she falls from weakness caused by her striving to repress her irrepressible nature. It is evident from Guinevere's actions that Phelps is deliberately challenging the traditional view that blames the woman for the failings of the Arthurian world. Again, this is a less radical challenge than that found in her story, wherein Phelps actively "rebels" against the male tellings. In the poem, however, Phelps explains that Guinevere's wishing God to "listen while / I sing, as well as while I pray" (62) comes from a text that

> Was written in the story we have learned,
> Between the ashen lines, invisible,
> In hieroglyphs that blazed and leaped like light
> Unto the eyes.   (59)

Phelps's poems, though set in the Arthurian world, demonstrate the same willingness to rework traditional versions of the legend that is found in her fiction, where she consciously reinterprets the romantic tales into a realistic world. In her story "The Christmas of Sir Galahad," she spells out her rationale: "It would be found, so it is said, had we eyes that see or ears that hear either signs or sounds of such a matter, that certain of the old romances which we have been accustomed to regard as finished and fated for all times arc, in fact, re-enacting and repeating themselves with a timidity amounting almost to stealth, in the chilling and alien climate of our modern civilization: that steam has not scorched out valor, nor the telegraph overtaken chivalry, nor universal suffrage extinguished loyalty; that the golden years did not go dumbly to their graves, as we are wont to think." As a result, the "Blameless King" and the "Mismated Queen" may be found somewhere on earth; and the Knights of the Round Table may appear "in strange guise": Percivale as a Pennsylvania coal-miner, Launcelot as a street preacher, and Arthur himself as an official in Washington. Her conclusion is that "a Romance never died, nor ever will, but is adjudged to be the only immortal thing on earth, save the soul of man" (1).

Phelps believes so strongly in the immortal nature of romance that in *Beyond the Gates*, one of the books in which she describes the afterlife, among the pleasures she imagines is the ability to speak with "those creations of the human intellect which had acquired immortality," including "the great creatures of our imagination known to us below." She asks, "Was it incredible that Helen, and Lancelot, and Sigfried, and Juliet, and Faust, and Dinah Morris, and the Lady of Shalott, and Don Quixote, and Colonel Newcome, and Sam Weller, and Uncle Tom, and Hester Prynne and Jean Valjean existed? Could be approached by way of holiday, as one used to take up the drama or the fiction, on a leisure hour, down below?" (184–85).[3]

If the characters of literature are so real as to secure an immortal existence in a heavenly theme park, surely they are real enough to provide the basis for characters in a realistic story. And this is precisely the use that Phelps makes of them: as commentary on real-life problems, not as typically romantic versions of the tales of Camelot.

As Mary Angela Bennett, author of the first book-length study of Phelps and her writing, observed, Phelps "preached even in her poetry, and her stories are never without their lesson, direct or implied" (109). Phelps herself was aware of the didactic element in her writing and was unapologetic about it. She noted that "If I am reminded how many of my stories have been written with an ethical purpose, that is quite another accusation, and one which I have not, from any point of view, the wraith of a wish to deny" (*Chapters* 257). She even took issue with William Dean Howells' statement that the writings of New England authors were marred by the "intense ethicism" of the New England mind. Her rebuttal of his view was based on her own understanding of realism and of morality. She and Howells agreed that "the province of the artist is to portray life as it is," but for Phelps, life, in addition to being many other things, "was steadily and sturdily and always moral responsibility" (*Chapters* 263). Thus it is not surprising that Phelps

---

3   It is interesting that Phelps also imagines conversing with Arthur in the afterlife, but she groups him with historical figures like Joan of Arc and Luther (182) rather than with the "figments of fancy" who achieved immortality.

retells the Arthurian stories in the particular way she does, that is, by translating them into the real world of the nineteenth century and by making them a vehicle for social and moral commentary.

Her first two Arthurian stories, "The Christmas of Sir Galahad" and "The Lady of Shalott," were both published originally in the *Independent* in 1871, and the third, "The True Story of Guenever," appeared there in 1876. The *Independent*, which began as a religious newspaper, not only printed articles advocating liberal attitudes towards religion but also became a forum for those espousing social reform, including the anti-slavery movement before the Civil War and women's suffrage and the plight of the poor after the war (see Kelly 49–50). While such a publication might seem a strange place to retell Arthurian tales, it was actually a natural venue for Phelps's stories because of their liberal attitudes towards women and social change. Phelps refers to herself in her autobiography as a "born rebel" (*Chapters* 33), and her Arthurian stories, like most of her writing, show a rebel's concern with ameliorating social conditions and the plight of the underprivileged and of women.

Perhaps the most didactic and melodramatic and the least successful of Phelps's stories is "The Christmas of Sir Galahad." The title character is "Sir Galahad Holt," a worker in an organ factory who returns from his labor with "grimy, princely hands." He is in love with Rebecca Rock, who works in a necktie factory "cutting 'foundation' into strips for the public neck, eleven hours a day" (1) and whom the narrator calls "Lady Rebecca." Rebecca shares his feelings, but Galahad is married to Mery Ann, a woman who is "crazy" and who "takes opium." Though Mery Ann left him six years earlier and returns only occasionally to his apartment, Galahad does not feel free to become involved with Rebecca. And so they wait four long years until Mery Ann finally dies.

The nobility of these characters, for Phelps, lies in their restraint. They never meet for a lovers' tryst, never kiss, never even hold hands. In the romance terms that Phelps overlays onto their lives, Rebecca "had not even offered to embroider him a banner, nor to net him a silken favor, nor to fringe so much as a scarf for the next tournament to be held in Primrose Court." The only sign of affection between them is Rebecca's act of darning Galahad's socks – and even that occurs after they ask the landlady if it is proper. This innate nobility of character raises them to the level of legendary figures. The narrator notes that "if Di Rimini had worked beside Rebecca at the neck-tie factory, she would have learned a royal lesson. And Abelard might well have sat at the feet of Galahad, making organs with his grimy hands. And if Eve or Isaac had wandered into the first floor front, or second back corner of 16½, on a lonesome, rainy evening, they would have wept for pity, and smiled for blessing, and mused much" (1).

While Phelps's Arthurian works generally seem to be based on Tennyson's versions of the Arthurian tales, "The Christmas of Sir Galahad" has few links to either the *Idylls* or the shorter poem "Sir Galahad" other than the notion that Galahad's nobility is in his virtue, a notion that echoes the well known lines, "My strength is as the strength of ten, / Because my heart is pure." But since the short story ends with the marriage of Galahad to Rebecca on Christmas Day, obviously Phelps makes no attempt to follow Tennyson's story of the pure knight. She may, however, be alluding in her story to another Victorian poem, Morris's "Sir Galahad, A Christmas Mystery," since both Morris's poem and her own story refer to Christmas in their titles. But a more important connection lies in the type of trial that Galahad endures in each. The Galahad of the story, as well as the woman he loves – for women are always a concern to Phelps – must live a lonely life until his first wife dies. During this time, "the Lady Rebecca had lain sick of a deadly fever, and Sir Galahad had lost six months' wages in a strike; and the man's face had grown gaunt, and the woman's old, and his had pinched and hers had paled: – yet their hands had never met since they stood by the pump in the starlight; nor had Sir Galahad's knightly foot once crossed the croaking stairs which bore the regular calm feet of the Lady Rebecca to the solitary second back corner of 16½; nor had he said, God bless her! when she sung at the little church, lest, indeed, his whole soul should rise up perforce, and choose cursing for blessing and death for life" (1). In Morris's poem Galahad knows that Palomides, riding alone in search of the questing beast, can dream of Iseult and that Lancelot can think of Guenevere's arms, "round / Warm and lithe about his neck, and shout / Till all the place grows joyful with the sound." But he fears riding alone, with no one to dream of or return to, until he dies and is found "Dead in my arms in the half-melted snow" by some carl and people lament for his "poor chaste body."

Though it seems that Phelps had Morris in mind when she wrote "The Christmas of Sir Galahad," her story diverges from his poem in that her Galahad is relieved from the pangs of loneliness not by a vision of Christ and saints but by a woman. It is, in fact, the woman who is Galahad Holt's Grail. When the narrator meets

> Sir Galahad at the meat-stall, buying steak for dinner, and saw the eyes and smile he carried in the sight of God and Christmas Day, I bethought me of the Spotless Knight: how he – tired, stainless, and alone – was found worthy to be the guardian ("pure in thought and word and deed") of the blessed cup from which our Lord drank the last wine which should touch his lips till he drank it new in the kingdom of the Father; how his mortal eyes beheld it, palled in red samite, treasured by "a great fellowship of angels; how his mortal hand laid hold of it and Heaven, and his mortal name grew to be a holy thing upon the lips of men forever; and how since then 'was there never one so hardy as to say that he had seen the Sangreal on earth any more.' "

But more than that, she reveals his nobility. The narrator asks, "Did you

ever know a lost knight to be found until a woman tracked Him? Is it, therefore, surprising that if it had not been for Rebecca Rock, Sir Galahad Holt
would have escaped recognition completely, and the modest number of men
and women now admitted to the secret of the discovery have gone the
hungrier and the sadder for the loss?" (1). Even in this story of a male hero
who traditionally achieves his fame in part because he is so chaste that he
rejects women totally, Phelps manages to make a woman central to the plot.
Thus she transforms her source material in two ways: first by casting
characters from the lower classes in terms of the Arthurian legends, thereby
ennobling them, and then by transforming the Grail story so that a woman
becomes both the Grail and the discoverer of the nobility of the Grail
knight.

Phelps's concerns for women and for the working classes combine even
more successfully in "The Lady of Shalott," which translates Tennyson's
poem of that name into a nineteenth-century context and which has been
accurately described as a "pathetic tale of unrelieved misery" (Bennett 59). It
is the story of a young woman, now seventeen, who was crippled at the age
of five when "her mother threw her down-stairs by mistake, instead of the
whisky-jug." This bit of information, the author adds, is one "fact which I
think Mr. Tennyson has omitted to mention in his poem" (48). In this manner
Phelps sets her story up as a more complete and more realistic – one might
contend more relevant – version of the one told by Tennyson. In Phelps's
retelling, the alcoholic mother dies a few years later, leaving the Lady of
Shalott with only her sister to support her. The title character's life becomes
still more pathetic because her immobility prevents her from weaving – or
from doing anything else. In Tennyson's poem, weaving implies artistic
creativity, and while it cannot alone provide fulfillment, it does offer some
happiness: "But in her web she still delights / To weave the mirror's magic
sights," wrote Tennyson. In Phelps's story, the weaver becomes the title
character's sister Sary Jane, who "made nankeen vests, at sixteen and three-
quarter cents a dozen" (49). Sary Jane must work hunched over under the
eaves looking out on repulsive slum conditions from a window in the small
garret room in the building where the two young women live, and the
earnings from her piece-work barely allow the two to subsist.

Their apartment, described ironically as a palace, is another point of
contrast between Tennyson's Lady and Phelps's character. The former lives
in "Four gray walls, and four gray towers," which "Overlook a space of
flowers." The palace in the story

> measured just twelve by nine feet. . . . There were two windows and a loose
> scuttle to the palace. The scuttle let in the snow in winter and the sun in
> summer, and the rain and wind at all times. It was quite a diversion to the
> Lady of Shalott to see how many different ways of doing a disagreeable
> thing seemed to be practicable to that scuttle. Beside the bed on which the
> Lady of Shalott lay, there was a stove in the palace, two chairs, a very

ragged rag-mat, a shelf, with two notched cups and plates upon it, one pewter teaspoon, and a looking-glass. . . . (50)

Phelps's Lady of Shalott is trapped by her disability in a tower of sorts, for "her room opened directly upon a precipice. The lessor of the house called it a flight of stairs." Lacking a bannister, these stairs are so steep that in times of emergency they become a death trap rather than an escape route: "Once, when there was a fire-alarm, the precipice was very serviceable. Four women and an old man went over. With one exception (she was eighteen, and could bear a broken collar-bone), they will not, I am informed, go over again" (50–51).

Phelps's narrative strategy here is obvious: looking to the traditional story, she offers analogous but more pathetic and oppressive details. Like the castle tower of Tennyson's Lady that becomes a slum apartment at the top of a dangerous flight of stairs, the river that flows past the tower in Tennyson's poem becomes "a dirty hydrant in the yard, four flights below, which supplied the Lady of Shalott and all her neighbors" (50). And whereas the tower in the poem overlooks "a space of flowers," the only flowers in the life of Phelps's character are those provided by "the Flower Charity" that almost hide the odor of the slum. "You can 'most stand the yard with them round," says the Lady of the story (56). But when Sary Jane brings her sister the flowers, the pathos of their situation is highlighted by the fact that, having gone out to obtain dinner for the two, Sary Jane returns with only one lemon, all that she can afford (56).

The primary correspondence between the poem and the story is the mirror through which Phelps's character sees her surroundings and the doctor, her Lancelot figure, who might have been her salvation. The smallness of her world is symbolized by the size of her mirror: "All the world came for the Lady of Shalott into her little looking-glass, – the joy of it, the anguish of it, the hope and fear of it, the health and hurt, – ten by six inches of it exactly" (51–52).

The mirror is also used as a device for social commentary. Emphasizing the drastic inequalities in society, the narrator comments that "the Lady of Shalott would have experienced rather a touch of mortification than of envy if she had known that there was a mirror in a house just around the corner measuring almost as many feet. But that was one of the advantages of being the Lady of Shalott. She never parsed life in the comparative degree" (51).

Sometimes the mirror provides the Lady of the story with views that disturb her. But when she is half sick of these shadows, her only recourse is to tip her mirror so they do not come within its scope, as she does when she sees the joyless, hungry children locked in the garret apartment across from hers (52). As in Tennyson's poem, the cracking of the mirror is a foreshadowing of the Lady of Shalott's death. In Tennyson's poem, the mirror cracks when the Lady sees Lancelot, and her world of shadows is no longer sufficient to sustain her. In Phelps's story, the mirror is cracked by a rock thrown by street urchins just after the Lady has seen in it the image of a doctor who is visiting the slum. In response to her cry, the doctor rushes to her room and takes pity on the sickly young woman. Declaring her curable, he offers to tend to the terrible conditions outside the window in which Sary Jane sits and sews. Although those conditions are not described in detail, they are gruesome enough to force the doctor to turn "away from the window, with a sudden white face" (60). He promises to remediate them "directly," but it is two days before the Board of Health arrives. They are met by "another board," a pine board on which the body of the Lady is carried from her room. This Lady of Shalott does not rest in a wooden boat singing her last song but is carried, silent, on a plain wooden slab. Nor is there even the final compliment from her Lancelot figure – Tennyson's Lancelot says: "She had a lovely face; / God in his mercy send her grace"; but all the doctor can say when he sees the body is: "We're too late, I see" (63).

The plight of Phelps's Lady of Shalott is caused by a variety of social ills – her mother's alcoholism, the labor laws that allow her sister to be paid so little, the lack of adequate health care for the poor, and the slum conditions in which they live. Phelps's purpose undoubtedly is to call attention to these ills by means of analogy to Tennyson's familiar poem and by deromanticizing one of the most romantic and most recognizable images of the nineteenth century – that of the Lady of Shalott floating down to Camelot. There is nothing romantic about the pine board or the steep flight of stairs down which Phelps's Lady is carried.

Whereas "The Christmas of Sir Galahad" works by allusion and "The Lady of Shalott" by analogy, Phelps's third and most interesting Arthurian story, "The True Story of Guenever," in effect enters into a debate with its source. Instead of using that source, Tennyson's "Guinevere" idyll, for purposes of comparison or contrast, Phelps actively rejects Tennyson's telling of the story and retells it in a manner more consistent with her sympathies for the woman she called "the mismated queen."

There is a hint of this sort of rebelling against the story in her version of "The Lady of Shalott" when she speaks of Tennyson's failure to mention that the Lady's mother threw her down a flight of stairs. In another passage in the same story, Phelps argues with a different author. She observes that

> The Lady of Shalott lay quite still in her brown calico night-gown [I cannot learn, by the way, that Bulfinch's studious and in general trustworthy researches have put him in possession of this point. Indeed, I feel justified in asserting that Mr. Bulfinch never so much as *intimated* that the Lady of Shalott wore a brown calico night-dress]. . . . (58)

But Phelps does not enter into the wholesale rejection of the narrative as she does in "The True Story of Guenever."

The narrator of "The True Story of Guenever" explicitly "rebel[s] against the story" because she "cannot bear to leave her [Guenever] there upon the convent floor." Phelps is, of course, responding to the passage in Tennyson's "Guinevere" in which Arthur visits his wife in the convent before the final battle:

> ... She sat
> Stiff-stricken, listening; but when armed feet
> Thro' the long gallery from the outer doors
> Rang coming, prone from off her seat she fell,
> And grovell'd with her face against the floor.   (234)

This scene becomes for Phelps a symbolic icon of the distorted relationship between man and woman: Guinevere groveling and yearning for forgiveness before the masterful, royal, almost divine Arthur.[4] In the image of Guinevere, she writes, "we see a delicate, high-strung, impulsive creature, a trifle mismated to a faultless, unimpulsive man. We shudder to discover in her, before she discovers it for or in herself, that, having given herself to Arthur, she yet has not given all; that there arises now another self, an existence hitherto unknown, unsuspected, – a character groping, unstable, unable, a wandering wind, a mist of darkness, a chaos, over which Arthur has no empire, of which he has no comprehension, and of which she – whether of Nature or of training who shall judge? – has long since discrowned herself the Queen" (65).

The mismated woman is a figure who appears frequently in Phelps's work. As Lori Duin Kelly notes, "Phelps detailed the frustrations and difficulties often found in the married state, putting particular emphasis on the toll marriage could exact on a woman's personal growth and happiness" (Kelly vii). Her best novel, *The Story of Avis* (1877), recounts the problems of another mismated woman, an artist named Avis, who is truly a rare bird in the nineteenth century – a woman who wishes to pursue a career as an artist rather than to become a housewife. Unfortunately for her, she agrees – partly out of love and partly out of sympathy – to marry a man named Philip

---

4   How deeply the scene affected Phelps is demonstrated not only by the fact that she wrote "The True Story of Guenever" but also by her reworking of the icon in her play *Within the Gates*. In this play a husband verbally and emotionally mistreats his loving wife just before he is killed in a buggy accident. After death, he realizes his error and cannot partake of the joys of Paradise because his wife is not there with him. When she dies and appears before him in heaven, she seems "tall and glorious. ... Her expression is radiant" (142–43). She is to him "like a goddess" (144). He, like Tennyson's Guinevere, is "prostrate at his wife's feet" yearning for forgiveness, which she grants when she approaches him "not royally, like a wife who was wronged; but like the sweetest woman in the world, who loves him because she cannot help it, and would not if she could" (143–44). This scene clearly inverts the dynamic of Tennyson's characters, with the husband groveling before the wife who forgives magnanimously the wrong done to her and who, despite her royal and near divine position in the relationship, acts like a loving partner.

Ostrander, who is wounded in the Civil War. Though Philip recognizes his wife's dedication to art and promises her that she will not have to worry about running a household, he of course never keeps that promise. Philip's physical weakness, not to mention the flaws in his character, the birth of two children, his ultimate concern for his own career over hers, and the death of their son, make the creative life Avis had hoped for impossible. Only through her daughter can Avis in any way resolve her own plight.

The novel opens with the epigraph "Now, all the meaning of the King was to see Sir Galahad proved," a quotation from Bulfinch's *The Age of Chivalry*. The significance of such a strange epigraph for a work about a female artist – something from *Aurora Leigh*, from which Avis reads in the novel, would seem far more appropriate – is realized at the end when Avis, now with no hope of fulfilling her potential as an artist, reads to her daughter an account of the Grail story. She quotes an abstracted passage that puts two separate scenes from Bulfinch's text into conjunction. The first is a scene of Lancelot's failure; in the second, Galahad is brought into Arthur's court by a hermit, who reveals the writing on the Siege Perilous, which proclaims "This is the seat of Sir Galahad the good knight" (*Story of Avis* 250). The implication is that though Avis has been unable to pursue a fulfilling career, her daughter will, just as Lancelot failed in the quest that was to be achieved by his son Galahad.

If in *The Story of Avis* Phelps appropriates the story of the male heroes to present the Grail of female fulfillment for a mismated woman, so in "The True Story of Guenever" she appropriates to the female voice a traditionally male story. In so doing, she provides a resolution that prevents her Guenever from groveling on the floor but only by accepting a less than satisfactory marriage; and, in the end, the appropriation of the story is more interesting and makes more of a feminist statement than the narrative resolution. Phelps's true story of Guenever, she says, came to her through her washerwoman, not from any of the number of male authors who tell of the queen's shame. This rejection both of the male voice and of class privileging is in itself a comment on the original story and a means of achieving truth about female characters. Phelps writes:

> Who can capture the where, the how, the wherefore of a train of fancy? Was it because I thought of Guenever that I heard the story? Or because I heard the story that I thought of Guenever? My washwoman told it, coming in that bitter day at twilight and sitting by the open fire, as I had bidden her, for rest and warmth. What should *she* know of the Bulfinch and Ellis and Tennyson and Dunlop that had fallen from my lap upon the cricket at her feet, that she should sit, with hands across her draggled knees, and tell me such a story? Or were Dunlop and the rest untouched upon the library shelves till after she had told it? Whether the legend drew me to the fact, or the fact impelled me to the legend? Indeed, why should I know? It is enough that I heard the story. She told it in her way. I, for lack of her fine, realistic manner, must tell it in my own. (67)

In Phelps's version, which she declares to be "the true story of Guenever the Queen" (80), Arthur is called "the blameless king" (65). But obviously Phelps lays some of the blame for Guenever's actions upon him, for he fails to understand that she is "a delicate, high-strung, impulsive creature, a trifle mismated to a faultless, unimpulsive man" (65).

Phelps's view of Arthur seems tied up with her notions of the chivalric and the feudal. In her autobiography she gives high praise to publisher James T. Fields by observing that he "was a man of marked chivalry of nature, and, at a time when it was not fashionable to help the movements for the elevation of women, his sympathy was distinct, fearless, faithful" (*Chapters* 146). And in her novel *The Gates Ajar* (1869), the narrator's beloved deceased brother is said to have had a "pretty chivalry . . . which developed afterwards into that rarer treatment of women, of which every one speaks who speaks of him" (25). In an essay for the *Independent* in 1873, Phelps writes of a code "as old as the first tournament and as misty as the Round Table," which implies that women are weak and men strong, that women live through men and men "deprive life of its thorns" for women (417). In that essay, called "The New Knighthood," she describes the code in practical terms: "Mend our stockings, and we will tip our hats to you. Cook our dinners, and we will shawl you for an evening party. Vote – and you shall stand in the cars. Preach – and you carry your own bundles. Rival us in trade – and you may get over a mud-puddle as best you can" (417). Phelps claims no right of women to special treatment but instead attempts to point out the hypocrisy of the new knighthood, which seeks to keep women in their traditional place without extending to them even the courtesies of the old code. She writes that though women do not have "the ghost of a right to complain that a man does not sacrifice his convenience to her because he is a man and because she is a woman," the denial of those of the new order that they have "such obligations is no longer a misty threat, but is becoming a fixed fact, and this before women have acquired that position upon the yielding of which he has made the code of his devotion contingent. He cannot wait till he may bully us at the ballot-box. He will inaugurate the new system of suppression while we are still out shopping for Berlin wools and baby edgings. He will don the order of the new knighthood while as yet we are taxed to support his colleges and compelled to 'petition' from him as a privilege, rather than to vote away from him as a right, the repeal of such laws of his making as that recent enactment known as the shame of St. Louis" (417).[5] Elsewhere Phelps refers to this sort of an unenlightened attitude towards women as "feudal" rather than "chivalric." In her autobiography, for example, she speaks of the "rather feudal views" of her father (*Chapters* 60), and later in the same work she says that the best of Andover's "good men

5   "The shame of St. Louis" refers to a law passed by the City Council of St. Louis in 1870 which "legislated regulated prostitution by using a loophole in a state law" (Pivar 52).

were too feudal in their views of women in those days, to understand a life like Mrs. Stowe's" (*Chapters* 134).

The Arthur of "The True Story of Guenever" may not be as offensive a character as some of those referred to in "The New Knighthood," but he certainly leans more towards the feudal than the chivalric. The story itself is couched more in personal than in political terms – though for Phelps the two were closely related. The position of women in their relationships with their husbands was a reflection of the role that society prescribes for them, as *The Story of Avis* and other of her writings make clear.

Phelps's Arthur is translated into a master carpenter, just as her Launcelot, "as all scholars of romantic fiction know, was the young bricklayer to whom Arthur and Guenever had rented the spare room when the hard times came on, – a good-natured, inoffensive lodger as one could ask for" (68–69). Of her nineteenth-century translation of the blameless king, Phelps says, "To tell the truth, Arthur was often dull of late, what with being out of work so much, and the foot he lamed with a rusty nail" (69). Arthur's dullness extends to his understanding of his wife's needs. At times he cannot be more mistaken about what she wants. When Guenever has a toothache, Arthur's advice is merely to "Take some drops." But, as Phelps writes,

> There was nothing Guenever wanted to take. She wanted, in fact, to *be* taken; to be caught and gathered to her husband's safe, broad breast; to be held against his faithful heart; to be fondled and crooned over and cuddled. She would have her aching head imprisoned in his healthy hands. And if he should think to kiss the agonizing cheek, as *she* would kiss a woman's cheek if she loved her and she had the toothache? But Arthur never thought! Men were so dull at things. Only women knew how to take care of one another. Only women knew the infinite fine languages of love. A man was tender when he thought of it, in a blunt, broad way. (69–70)

Phelps's Guenever is mismated not, as in Tennyson, because Arthur is so far above the average man that he is unable to understand human needs and desires, but rather because he is typical of the average man who, for Phelps, is unable to understand a woman's needs and desires. Arthur "supposed, if she had the toothache, she would n't want to be touched. He knew he shouldn't. So, not knowing what else to do, he just limped royally about and got the supper, like a dear old dull king as he was" (71). Launcelot, by contrast, is more active in trying to help her. He goes to the druggist and gets her laudanum to deal with the pain. Unfortunately, Guenever cannot tolerate laudanum and so the medication is useless. Arthur differs from Launcelot in another way. He is unable to give even a simple compliment. "Secretly he liked to see Guenever in the bird-of-paradise chair, with the moody firelight upon her; but he had never said so – it was not Arthur's 'way.' Launcelot, now, for instance had said something to that effect several times" (68).

In Phelps's "true story," when Guenever departs with her lover, she hears an old gossip saying, "Guenever has fled with Launcelot. The Queen has left the King. All the world will know it by to-morrow" (75); and immediately she feels pangs of guilt. There comes to her "a revelation awful as some that might shock a soul upon the day of doom . . . that she was no longer a bewildered or a pitiable, but an evil creature" (74). She finds herself in a stormy wilderness with no one but Launcelot: "It was a desolate spot in which she and Launcelot stood. They had left the safe, sweet signs of holy human lives and loves behind them. They were quite alone. A wide and windy moor stretched from them to a forest, on which a horror of great darkness seemed to hang" (76). But even Launcelot is no comfort to her. When she hears a voice telling her she can never be clean, she is unsure whether it is the voice of Launcelot or "the deathly wind" (76). When she says "Perhaps I have been dreaming or have been ill. Let me go home at once to the King!" the voice, "which seemed neither of Launcelot nor of the wind, but yet akin to both," tells her that "there is no mistake," and that "you are not dreaming and you can never return to the King. The thing that is done is done. Sorrow and longing are dead to help you. Agony and repentance are feeble friends. Neither man nor Nature can wash away a stain" (77).

But then another vision appears to her:

> It seemed suddenly to the kneeling woman, that He whose body and blood were broken for tempted souls appeared to seek her out across the deso-lated moor. The Man whose stainless lips were first to touch the cup of the Holy Grael, which all poor souls should after Him go seeking up and down upon the earth, stood in the pure white snow, and smiling, spoke to her.
>
> "*Though your sins,*" he said, "*are scarlet, they shall be white.*" (77)

Having begged divine forgiveness, Guenever has apparently received it. But in a striking reversal, almost as if the word of Christ cannot be trusted, she finds no redemption. She is in the same position towards Christ that she is towards Arthur in Tennyson's *Idylls*: "she groveled on the ground where the sacred Feet had stood, which now were vanished from her. Wretched woman that she was! Who would deliver her from this bondage to her life's great holy love? If Arthur would but open the door for her in the fair distance, where the palace windows shone; if he would take a single step towards her where she kneeled within the wilderness." But "the King took no step toward the wilderness. The King was mute as death and cold as his own white soul. On Arthur's throne was never more a place for Guenever" (78). Guenever remains groveling on the ground, wretched because she must depend on Christ, who seems to deceive her, or on another man, Arthur, who is cold and uncaring, to deliver her from her bondage. And neither does so. It is left to the narrator, or the washerwoman who is her source, to give the Guenever of the tale what little relief she can obtain. Despite the statement of Launcelot, another unreliable male voice – if indeed it is his voice – that what has

happened is no dream, Guenever wakes to find herself in Arthur's sheltering
arms. She has been redeemed by the storyteller's suggestion that her running
off with Launcelot occurred in a nightmare induced when the Queen mistakenly took laudanum for a toothache. Thus she can wake, morally unblem-
ished, to a loving Arthur.

This ending raises Guenever from the convent floor. She is not left groveling or in "disgrace, exile, and despair" (66). But neither has she attained a
totally fulfilling life. As Carol Farley Kessler observed, Phelps's fiction
"would never show a married woman happy" (36); but Phelps also felt that
women had a need, "above all, for loving concern in a stable relationship,
even though this last be available only at the price of subordination" (Kessler
43). Guenever is better off in such a relationship with her husband, as the
washerwoman, the female narrator, and Phelps all seem to be saying. The
price, however, is certainly high: she must accept the limitations that that
relationship with a man with typical nineteenth-century attitudes implies.
Guenever has attained a modicum of peace and respectability, but she has
not achieved the Holy Grail of female fulfillment. Phelps's fiction suggests
that this ideal is not yet something women can achieve in this world.
Perhaps the appeal of her books depicting life after death lies largely in their
vision of a place that offers "to women what earth lacked – namely, men
prepared as adults to nurture the lives of women and children, and oppor-
tunities for women to experience pleasure, self-fulfillment, and the com-
panionship of equals" (Kessler 36).

2

Reaction to Tennyson: Parody

Although there is a surprising variety of Arthurian literature in America before the appearance of *A Connecticut Yankee in King Arthur's Court*, Mark Twain's novel is in many ways the central text in American Arthuriana. *Connecticut Yankee* is important for many reasons: it lacks the acceptance of romantic ideals typical of much nineteenth-century literature; it rejects the notion of the knights of Camelot as models of virtue, an approach that is common in both literature and social organizations influenced by Tennyson; and it deliberately deflates what Twain regards as the literary and moral pretensions of the *Idylls of the King*. At the same time, however, Twain recognizes in *Connecticut Yankee* (as he does in other of his works) that there can indeed be some nobility – not of birth but of character – even in the people he chooses to mock. And Twain appreciates the fact that some of those who preach democracy and capitalism are little better – and, perhaps sometimes, even worse – than Arthur's legendary benighted knights.

Twain was not, of course, the only author to dislike or to poke fun at the Tennysonian version of the Arthurian world; nor was he the first. On both sides of the Atlantic, there were those who found the British laureate's poems too pompous and his moralizing too tempting a target. In Britain, Swinburne had written "Tristram of Lyonesse" (1882) in reaction to Tennyson's disparagement of the love affair of Tristan and Isolt; and even before the *Idylls* were completed, they were being parodied in the anonymously published *The Coming K-: A Set of Idyll Lays* (1873).

In America, where Tennyson's poems were almost as well known as in England, they were even more frequently parodied. One of the most clever of the American parodists was Edgar Fawcett, a forerunner of Twain in his deliberate mockery of the chivalric ideals of Tennyson's Camelot. In the mock dedication of his burlesque play *The New King Arthur* to Tennyson, Fawcett says:

> Take, Alfred, this mellifluous verse of mine,
> Nor rank too high the honor I bestow,
> Howe'er it thrill thy soul with grateful pride.
> For thou hast sung of Arthur and his knights,
> And thou hast told of deeds that they have done,
> And thou hast told of loves that they have loved,
> And thou hast told of sins that they have sinned,

And I have sung in my way, thou in thine.
I think my way superior to thine,
Yes, Alfred, yes, in loyal faith I do . . . .   (iii)

As the dedication suggests, Fawcett's intention in *The New King Arthur* is to strip all of the grandeur, heroic or tragic, from Tennyson's characters. Fawcett's Merlin, for instance, is someone who "has lived ten spans / Of usual life, and dies but when he will" (33). Yet Merlin's primary power lies not in his worldly wisdom or magic but in his possession of two cosmetic products, which Lancelot describes to Guinevere in terms that might be suitable for the billboards carried by Twain's knights, who use their errantry to advertise. One of the products is a "face-wash that shall lend those blooming cheeks / A pearlier beauty than of mortal tint"; the other is a "hair-dye that shall stain each silken strand / Of those rich tresses into sunnier sheen."

Just as the pearly whiteness and the sunny brightness of the face-wash and hair-dye suggest the persuasiveness of a contemporary ad, Lancelot's hawking of the two products is about as far from the realm of traditional chivalry as a knight can get. Even more unchivalric is Lancelot's motive: he tempts Guinevere with the cosmetics in order to induce her to steal Excalibur from Arthur. Lancelot's scheme is simple: the fairy sword gives Arthur control over Merlin. Once Excalibur is his, Lancelot will use it to force Merlin to give Guinevere the cosmetics she covets; and then Lancelot and Guinevere will run off together. Not only does Lancelot get Guinevere to agree to this plan, but he also enlists the cooperation of Merlin, who – convinced by Lancelot that Arthur considers him little more than a mountebank or charlatan – jumps at Lancelot's offer to become Prime Minister (42).

If Fawcett transforms Merlin, the architect of Camelot, into a traitor, he degrades Galahad, Tennyson's Grail knight, even more. Presented as haughty and pompous, Galahad at one point admits, "Myself I love, and virtue – which are one" (69). When Arthur, who is himself "drenched and steeped in arrogant egotism" (135), says to Galahad, "We both are almost, in our separate ways, / Pre-eminently perfect, yet not quite," the knight's response is "It seems to me, my liege, that I am quite" (145). And when Galahad learns of Vivien's love for him, he is sure that she is "only one of many maids / Who bear me this devout idolatry" (94).

Vivien does indeed love Galahad, and she too covets the magic cosmetics because she wants to become more like the vision of an angelic woman with golden hair that Galahad once described to her (cf. p. 77). By changing herself from a brunette to a blonde, Vivien believes she can persuade Galahad to return her affection. But Modred, who in turn loves Vivien and wants the hair-dye to tempt her, plans to steal Excalibur from Guinevere after she has stolen it from Arthur. Thus, all of the betrayals in the play revolve not around courtly love triangles or dynastic contentions but around

Merlin's cosmetics. The final irony is that Dagonet the Fool, the one person true to Arthur, steals Excalibur from Guinevere before Modred does. Dagonet is then accused of the crime by all of the conspirators. His punishment is confinement in a monastery as a lunatic.

In the general chorus that closes the play, Fawcett notes that "no King Arthur / One bit of authenticity may hold / In his apocryphal and mythic mould" (164). Fawcett therefore deliberately creates a new King Arthur, one who, like Merlin and Galahad and almost all the other inhabitants of the legendary kingdom, has human failings. In the new Camelot – one might say the New-World Camelot – people are motivated by something as mundane as a hair-dye. Fawcett's play thus foreshadows Twain's novel not only by departing radically from any traditional version of the Arthurian legends but also by introducing some everyday reality and some everyday morality into Camelot.

Oscar Fay Adams, in his *Post-Laureate Idyls*, responds to Tennyson in a similarly mocking tone. Adams's "idyls" appeared in two volumes, ten of them in *Post-Laureate Idyls and Other Poems* (1886) and four more in a sequence called "Post-Laureate Idyls, Second Series" in the volume *Sicut Patribus and Other Verse* (1906). As Taylor and Brewer observe, the poems "offer a pastiche of lines from the *Idylls* but tell original stories and introduce characters not in Tennyson's narratives" (168). The poems, in fact, are a strange conglomeration of forms, themes, influence, and originality. Imposing upon himself the demands of Tennysonian blank verse, Adams not only weaves into his idyls lines from the *Idylls* themselves but also begins each idyl with a verse from a nursery rhyme, which he calls an "Argument" for the poem and which appears to be a driving force for its plot. The combination of material from Tennyson (and occasionally from other Arthurian sources) and from nursery rhymes would seem to make for disjointed and silly poems, initially funny perhaps but soon cloying. But Adams's idyls are actually very interesting and engaging. Although – even in combination – they do not retell the whole Arthurian story, they treat some of the story's more sad and human elements, including the romance of Tristan and Isolt, the passing of Arthur, Guinevere in the nunnery, and the aftermath of the final battle. Typical of American Arthurian literature, they also shift the focus to everyday concerns, frequently to the tragedy behind seemingly simple events and to characters not central to the tales.

The first poem in *Post-Laureate Idyls* brings Sir Gawain, on the morning he and Ettarre have awakened with Pelleas's sword across their throats, to the palace of King Mark; there Isolt, having been brought back from the forest where she and Tristram had lived in bliss, is baking pastries. The argument for this poem is "The Queen of Hearts, / She made some tarts . . ."; and the baking becomes integral to the plot when Gawain pilfers the fresh tarts. After Gawain is apprehended, Isolt overlooks his thieving on the condition that he never steal from her kitchen again and that he stay to eat with her. She is forgiving because "a goodly man he seems / Since Tristram is not by" (16). Adams thus de-emphasizes the tragic story of Tristan and Isolt and of Pelleas and Ettarre and highlights instead the pilfering of pastries and the encounter between two legendary Arthurian characters rarely associated with each other. The slight subject matter of the poem serves merely to put Isolt and Gawain on the same level as the average person. The theft of the tarts has no serious repercussions: the dalliance does not lead to any romantic feelings; Gawain leaves as soon as he hears that Mark is returning to the castle; and there is no confrontation. Whereas the idylls of Tennyson all depict heroic deeds and tragic love, the events of "The Rape of the Tarts" lead to nothing of any real consequence. Even the tone of the idyl is deliberately not mock-heroic, as its title, recalling Pope's "Rape of the Lock," might suggest it should be. And this seems to be precisely Adams's point: not that the heroic is lost in the ordinary, but that the romantic and heroic world of Tennyson is simply not real.

Other of Adams's poems are likewise steeped in the mundane, even as the Arthurian tragedy lurks in the background. In "At the Palace of King Lot," the king who has not yet fought against Arthur would prefer to be out hunting but must instead receive bills from the butcher, baker, chandler, and host. And Lot's queen, named Bellicent, as in Tennyson, feels an inexplicable sorrow, whose cause she does not know. Perhaps it is prescience of the tragic events that will befall her family – Lot's death in the war with Arthur; the death of her sons, particularly of innocent Gareth, at the hands of Lancelot. But these issues are neither raised nor discussed in the poem. Only when Bellicent finds "a wheaten loaf" and "a jar of amber honey" in her kitchen (21) is her sorrow dispelled. Her very ordinary hunger – relieved by the loaf and the honey – and not the more romantic and heroic events of Arthurian legend is apparently the reason for her sadness. As Bellicent eats, she becomes:

> Forgetful wholly of her lord the King,
> Forgetful of the honey on her gown,
> Forgetful of the dinner to be cook'd.
> Forgetful of the swift-approaching noon,
> Forgetful of her kitchen and its cares.
> And this forgetfulness was pleasant to her.   (21–22)

The anaphora echoes Tennyson's in the "Marriage of Geraint" idyll, but the very banality of the matter that Bellicent forgets puts the poem at odds with its source. This banality carries through the remainder of Adams's idyl: in an incident unrelated except in its ordinariness, a young Modred gets a black-bird to nip the rosy nose of Edith the washerwoman and then trips her with a cord as she runs from her attacker. The concluding line sums up the hurtful behavior of the child: "in the heart of Modred joy was lord" (24). Adams's subject is thus the wickedness of a mischievous boy and not the wickedness that brings down kingdoms.

A similar account of ordinary evil is found in the poem "Thomas and Vivien." Thomas, another mischievous boy, is the son of Sir Guy, who counsels Arthur after Merlin's departure. Although wise, Guy is evidently not wise enough to rule his own son. But it is not Thomas who represents the banal evil in the poem; rather, it is Vivien. After seeing Thomas steal a pig and bring it to his friend, the palace cook, Vivien tells Arthur of the theft. Because this is not the boy's first infraction, the king condemns the boy to twelve stripes with a birch rod. Meanwhile, in the same way that she charms Merlin in Tennyson's idyll, Vivien charms the cook, who has not yet learned of her wickedness.

> For breath of scandal soiling Vivien's name
> Had not so far as palace kitchen blown,
> And therefore deem'd he still the damsel pure.   (43)

The infatuated cook promises to prepare the pig and then serve it to Vivien in her private bower. And she enjoys it all the more because "high above the tumult of the streets / Below, in direful anguish, rang the shrieks / Of Tom" (43), who is being whipped for stealing the very pig on which she dines.

Unlike Tennyson, whose poems focus on the exceptional and the extra-ordinary, Adams writes about that which is unexceptional and ordinary. He even demystifies and deromanticizes much of the legendary material on which he draws. In the poem "The Vision of Sir Lamoracke," for example, Lamoracke's vision is neither the one that his sister saw, which "Sent half the court in quest of Holy Grail" (45), nor the transforming dream of Sir Launfal, whose vision is surely echoed in the title of Adams's poem. Lamoracke, by contrast, has failed in the quest, and consequently has "the fire / Of zeal and holy purpose quite burnt out" of him (47). His only consolation is the advice of Sir Sagramour that "failure is not crime" (48). His "vision" thus derives not from the Holy Grail but from the nursery rhyme "argument" for the poem: "As I was going to Saint Ives / I met seven wives." Lamoracke recalls how he came to St. Ives in Cornwall and saw St. Michael's Mount, which rose "like a vision fair" from the Cornish sea (48). He also sees seven fisher-wives, who possess little of the romantic beauty usually associated with the Arthurian tales:

> Small trace had these of brow may-blossoms, cheek
> Of apple blossom or the eye of hawk,
> And clumsily the wrinkl'd nose of each,
> Tip-tilted, like a thirsty duckling's bill
> After much guzzling in the pool, did seem
> To point the way.   (49)

Developing further the "argument," the poem recounts how each of the seven wives has seven sacks, each of which has seven cats, each of which has seven kittens. When Lamoracke asks how many kittens, cats, sacks, and wives were going to St. Ives, Sagramour is puzzled and spends the night trying to count their number on his fingers, a task he still has not accomplished by the time Lamoracke leaves in the morning. The poem thus descends into triteness, a triteness not offset by any account of success in the quest for the Grail or by any realization that comes to Lamoracke or to those who observe him because of his failure. Even in the next idyl in the volume, "The Return from the Quest," there is no triumph, no suggestion of achievement by any of the knights. Bors, Lancelot, and Percivale are mentioned by name, but the implication is that none of them has succeeded in the quest; and Galahad is neither mentioned nor alluded to at all. The poem's tone is set by Dagonet, who sings about "glory past away" (55), and the knights are said to come back like "beggars from their bootless quest" (57). Only Gawain does not return in rags, and that is because "pleasant was the Quest for him who made / So sure the holy Quest was not for him" (57). Similarly, in another vision poem, "The Vision of Sir Lionel" in the second series of "Post-Laureate Idyls," Lionel rides through a "wide waste land" (94) that reflects his mood after the death of Lancelot. But it is not an achieving of the Grail that brings renewed life to Lionel or to the land. Instead, it is something much less exceptional: the natural cycle, the coming of spring.

Other of the poems in the volume *Post-Laureate Idyls* develop the ideas of "The Vision of Sir Lionel" by suggesting that the events of daily life contain enough sorrow and tragedy of their own without having to be aggrandized by exaggerated valor or love. "The Water Carriers" tells of Lavaine, who – besides Bedivere – is the only survivor of the final battle. Lavaine recovers from his battle wounds but ten years later becomes seriously ill. His daughter Gillian believes that water from a spring on top of a particular hill will cure him. The "argument" is "Jack and Gill went up the hill / To draw a pail of water"; and in the poem Gillian and her brother Jack do indeed obtain some of the healing water, but on their return they fall. Both perish, as Sir Lavaine himself does shortly afterward. The only hint of something beyond life's ordinary calamity, however, is the statement that Jack and Gill were of "the fated house / Of Astolat" (72), Lavaine of course being the brother of Elaine of Astolat. Even Arthur's final battle in this poem is treated in much the way the Grail quest is in other poems in the series: without the romance and the mystery. The heroic deeds of the final battle are not even described. Lavaine's survival, in fact, assures that his death will be unheroic and ordinary.

Although the "Post-Laureate Idyls" from *Post-Laureate Idyls* and from *Sicut Patribus and Other Verse* do not tell a complete or consistent story of the Arthurian world, together they are fairly consistent in their presentation of a very un-Tennysonian world. Adams does not dwell on aristocracy or even on the morality of which Tennyson is so fond – though there are hints of that morality in "Gawain and Marjorie," a poem in the second series, in which Arthur "bent / A brow of gloom on Gawain" when his royal nephew returns to Camelot to find dead the maiden whom he left behind and who grew fatally ill while searching for him. But generally the deeds and the deaths, the visions and the quests are as simple and ordinary, as untinged with romance and heroism, as the nursery rhymes that serve as the epigraphs to each of the idyls.

Perhaps Adams's purpose can best be understood by reference to an essay he wrote in 1886 for the *North American Review* on a subject far removed from both poetry and the Arthurian legends. Called the "Aristocratic Drift of American Protestantism," the essay criticizes the Protestant religions in the United States for the class distinctions that they establish. Adams writes: "The whole fabric of American Protestantism is inwrought with the notion that class distinctions must exist, must be intensified in fact, in the houses it erects to the worship of a Divine Being who is supposed to care nothing for such distinctions and whose Son, when on earth, consorted with fisherman and 'the lower classes' generally in preference to the company of 'nice people' " (196). Later in the same essay Adams complains that "the Protestant communion has from the beginning fostered an aristocratic, exclusive spirit, which has resulted in making its churches but too often religious clubhouses, and in deepening the caste distinctions which practically deny the brotherhood of man" (197). This is the same sort of distinction that Tennyson's Arthurian poetry, with its inherent sense of aristocracy, invites. And although many Americans found a way to democratize the notions contained in Tennyson's poems, Adams seems to reject the laureate idylls and offers an Americanized, post-laureate answer to them that focuses on the ordinary man and the ordinary events of life. Just as Fawcett writes a new version of the story of King Arthur to deflate what he saw as the pretensions of Tennyson's poetry, so Adams writes post-laureate idyls, poems deliberately after Tennyson – in other words, based on Tennyson's works and chronologically later than Tennyson's works, but also beyond the aristocratic ideals that Adams sees in Tennyson's verse.

As the works of Fawcett and Adams confirm, Twain did not write his satiric *A Connecticut Yankee in King Arthur's Court* in a vacuum. Whether Twain was familiar with them or not, these other literary efforts are indicative of the interest in the Arthurian legends that the *Idylls* created among American authors, an interest in large part inspired by the popularity of Tennyson's poems in the United States. Twain's novel is undoubtedly a response to Tennyson as well as to Matthew Arnold's criticism of American culture; but it is also part of the rich tradition of American humor – a tall tale applied to Arthurian Britain rather than the Wild West. Yet even this humorous aspect of Twain's novel had a predecessor in American fiction, the story called "The Fortunate Island" by Max Adeler (a pseudonym for Charles Heber Clark [1841–1915]).

Well known in his day, Adeler was considered a humorist of the first rank. In his book on *American Humourists: Recent and Living*, Robert Ford claimed that "For real, hearty, healthy, honest, side-splitting humour . . . there is not one of all the large crowd of American funny men that excels" Adeler (137). In *Famous Funny Fellows*, Will M. Clemens observed that Adeler's "fun is the most rollicking kind, and ranks him along with Mark Twain and Artemus Ward" (35). But Adeler's link to Twain is not limited simply to the type of humorous stories he wrote. As Edward F. Foster first noted in an article in 1968, "Seven years before the appearance of *A Connecticut Yankee* . . . the humorist Max Adeler published a novelette, *The Fortunate Island*, which contains an identical theme and numerous interesting parallels" to Twain's novel (73).

More properly a long story than a novelette, "The Fortunate Island" (1882), originally titled "Professor Baffin's Adventures,"[1] is the tale of Professor E. L. Baffin and his daughter Matilda. As Baffin is on the way to lecture in England and Scotland, he and Matilda are shipwrecked. Rather than trusting the ship's lifeboats, the Professor inflates "a patent india-rubber life-raft, which [he] was carrying with him to Europe, with the hope that he could sell certain patent rights in the contrivance" (9). As they drift away from the other boats, Baffin and Matilda sight land sooner than expected. As it turns out, that land is an island that "in the time of King Arthur" was "separated from the rest, and drifted far out upon the ocean" with hundreds of inhabitants (24). At the time of the Baffins' arrival, the population of the island is about 100,000 people, who are under the rule of eleven kings. The Professor is delighted to have "an opportunity to study the middle ages on the spot" (26) since the island's residents "reverence the past"; as Father Anselm the hermit, the first resident whom the Baffins meet, confirms, "it is a matter of pride among us to preserve the habits, the manners, the ideas, the social state which our forefathers had when they sundered from their nation" (25).

As in Twain's novel, there are some obvious discrepancies between the values and customs of the inhabitants of the island and the newcomers; there is also some of the same kind of humor. In a notebook entry in December of 1884 (cited by Henry Nash Smith 41), Twain describes the problems that Hank experiences with his armor. Similarly, in Adeler's story, Baffin, forced into a joust just as Hank was, tries to kiss his daughter, "but he merely succeeded in injuring her nose with the visor of his helmet" (66). And when

---

1   On the change of title from "Professor Baffin's Adventures" to "The Fortunate Island," see Ketterer, "The Fortunate Island . . ." 29.

  We are grateful to Elizabeth Sklar, who presented a paper on "The Fortunate Island" at a conference of the Popular Culture Association, for first bringing this story to our attention.

Baffin's poor horsemanship causes him to turn his mount in the wrong direction and to strike a tree with his lance, he winds up bleeding on the ground and unable to reach his handkerchief, a detail Twain also recorded in his notebook.

As in Twain's novel and in all the literary and cinematic remakes and updates of *A Connecticut Yankee*, Adeler uses modern inventions and gadgets to generate humor and interest. Baffin, for instance, amazes Father Anselm with his umbrella and his watch and with talk of modern inventions; and after Baffin lights a match, the surprised hermit wonders if he is a wizard. When his hostess, Lady Bors, is ill, the Professor gives his daughter the necessary "plasters and a soothing drug or two" (51) to cure her. Baffin also rigs up a phone line so Ysolt can converse with her lover Bleoberis, from whom she is separated by her disapproving father. When Ysolt finally escapes from her father, she is carried off by another suitor, Sir Dagonet; but Bleoberis cannot give chase because his armor is stuck to a metal box, magnetized by the battery used to power the phone. In order to defend himself against Bleoberis's accusations of betrayal, Baffin then plans a rescue mission that requires making a small steam engine and a boat with a propeller to traverse the lake surrounding Dagonet's castle.

Also like Twain, Adeler pokes fun at medieval customs, values, and superstitions; and he contrasts them with American attitudes. One target of Adeler's satire is courtly love. Sir Dinadan, for example, asks Matilda to marry him as they take a walk just minutes after they meet. And "While Sir Dinadan was protesting that he should love her for ever and for ever," the two return to the hermit's cell where Matilda meets Sir Agravaine, whose first question is whether or not she is married. When Agravaine learns that she is unattached, he immediately proposes to her (43). Other subjects of satire are the medieval attitudes that are at odds with nineteenth-century science. When Agravaine asks if he can "cast a lover's horoscope," Professor Baffin tells him that "there is no such foolery as a horoscope" (45). And when the Professor shows King Brandegore "a number of experiments, chiefly electrical," they "so affected" the king that "he ordered the regular court magician to be executed as a perfectly hopeless humbug" (though, at the Professor's request, Brandegore relents).

The difference between Twain and Adeler is that the satire of the latter is fairly mild. As Edward Foster has noted, "Unlike Twain, Adeler does not venture on any criticism of medieval politics and religion" (74). Similarly, David Ketterer observed that "Whereas the focus of *A Connecticut Yankee's* often bitter satire is the oppressive role of superstitions, the church, and nobility in King Arthur's England, the much milder satire and humor of 'Professor Baffin's Adventures' is artfully directed at the romantic side of medieval life and the absurd practice of duelling – both matters present in *A Connecticut Yankee* but of peripheral concern" (Ketterer, " 'Professor Baffin's Adventures' . . ." 27).

Despite this significant difference in the approach of the two works, they do share some often striking qualities. Like Hank, the Professor advocates modern (that is, nineteenth-century) American values. And both Hank and Baffin value the self-made man. Hank tries to encourage advancement by merit rather than birth, and of course he himself wants to make his fortune based on his talent and his superiority to the sixth-century Britons. One of his first acts after pretending to bring back the sun is, after all, to ask for a piece of the action, a percentage of the increased revenues he will bring to Arthur's realm. Baffin too sees hard work and the seizing of opportunity as the keys to success. When Ysolt's father prevents Bleoberis from courting her because the young knight is too poor, Baffin says to him, "Can't you go to work, go into business, start a factory, speculate in stocks, or something of that kind?" (40). But as Bleoberis observes, people of his class do not work. The Professor's solution to this dilemma is to invite Bleoberis to help him "revolutionize" the island by means of "the telegraph, the phonograph, the photograph, and other modern inventions" (40) and to reap the resulting entrepreneurial rewards.

While the similarities between Adeler's story and Twain's novel are clear, perhaps the most important element of "The Fortunate Island" that foreshadows Twain's tale is Baffin's betrayal of his own principles as he attempts to deal with a culture radically different from his own. Baffin is the first vice president of the Universal Peace Society. Nevertheless, when he is challenged to a joust, he does not hesitate to accept. As Adeler comments, "It is melancholy to think what would have been the sorrow of the members of the Universal Peace Society . . . if they could have observed the eagerness with which the good man seemed to long for the fray, and the fiery rage which beamed from his eyes until the sparks almost appeared to fly from his spectacles" (64). When Matilda questions how a member of the Society can bring himself to fight, Baffin says, "You may omit to note this extraordinary occurrence in your journal. The Society may as well remain in ignorance of it. But I must conform to the customs of the place" (65).

Later, Baffin proves even more false to the pacificist values he has espoused. He constructs a steam engine and a small boat with a screw propeller in order to effect the rescue of Ysolt, who has been carried off by Dinadan to his castle elsewhere on the island. After rescuing her and returning to shore, Baffin stokes the engine's fires and ties down the safety valve. Dagonet and two of his men soon approach by boat; but, as they stop to inspect the Professor's craft, the engine explodes and they are blown up along with it. Baffin rationalizes the unnecessary murder: "It is dreadful . . . but self-preservation is the first law of nature, and then he [Dagonet] had no right to run away with Ysolt, at any rate" (93). Yet it is obvious that Baffin's actions are reprehensible by any standards and completely contrary to his own principles.

Figure 2. Sir Bleoberis's armor is magnetized in an illustration for Max Adeler's "The Fortunate Island." From *The Fortunate Island and Other Stories* (Boston: Lee and Shepard, 1882).

This explosion scene seems to define a problem that Adeler does not develop in his account of a contemporary American in a world with the values of Arthurian Britain. Adeler, in fact, obviates the need for any real consideration of the concerns that arise from the increase in technology in the nineteenth century by turning the entire adventure of Professor Baffin into a dream. But one cannot help but remember the gratuitous death of Dagonet and his men when reading about the final confrontation between Hank and the assembled chivalry of Britain. For in that scene – discussed below – there is also an abandonment by the central character of the democratic and humanitarian principles he has advocated earlier in the book.

An examination of the similarities between Adeler's and Twain's stories led Ketterer to the reasonable conclusion that "'Professor Baffin's Adventures' inspired *A Connecticut Yankee in King Arthur's Court*" (" 'Professor Baffin's Adventures' . . ." 31). While there is indeed a good chance that Twain knew Adeler's story and that he got from it some ideas for his own book, it is also obvious that Twain made much better comic and serious use of the juxtaposition of the nineteenth and sixth centuries. Twain, for example, is more adept at using for comic effect the differences in language between the two periods, a device at whose possibilities Adeler merely hints in his story. In one scene, Baffin says that he has some scientific instruments in his trunks, meaning his luggage; the response from the baron to whom he addresses the comment is, "You do not wear trunks as we do" (55). Twain, by contrast, has many more (and more humorous) instances of this kind of inter-cultural punning. In addition, he uses long passages of Malory to contrast with modern narrative style and to provide a means for Hank to comment on what he perceives as the shortcomings of sixth-century storytelling. Twain's superiority in using language for comic purposes is typical of his approach: when Twain sees the potential of a device, a motif, or a character trait, he cannot resist a magnificent effect; like his own protagonist Hank Morgan, he plays the situation for all it is worth. Consequently, Twain contrasts far more effectively the values of the two historical periods just as he highlights the flaw in Hank's character and his failure to adhere to the principles Hank himself defines as important. Though, as Foster noted, "Professor Baffin, unlike Hank Morgan, is an intellectual," both of them "share one important trait with equal force: the American zeal for progress, self-improvement, and getting ahead" (74). But Twain turns Hank's zeal into zealotry and creates a much more complex character and, ultimately, a more interesting and complex narrative.

A Connecticut Yankee in King Arthur's Court has occasionally been criticized for its lack of focus. One explanation for this apparent structural flaw – an explanation advanced by Howard G. Baetzhold in his article "The Course of Composition of *A Connecticut Yankee*: A Reinterpretation" (1961) and elaborated on by Henry Nash Smith in his excellent study *Mark Twain's Fable of*

Progress (1964) – may be found in the manner of the book's development: from a burlesque inspired by the thought of a practical nineteenth-century American finding himself in the midst of a society that is socially, technologically, and morally backward by his standards into a critique of modern society. Twain's novel, to be sure, has various levels of meaning. Besides burlesque, there is satire of both medieval and modern Britain as well as satire of nineteenth-century America, which at its extreme presents a disturbing picture of American and human ideals. At the same time, however, there is a level of respect for some aspects of the medieval and modern worlds that adds to the apparent disjunction in the novel.

Despite some disagreement as to the extent to which Twain intended to criticize contemporary England,[2] all of these elements – of burlesque; of satire of America, England, and humanity; and of ambivalence about the very things that are satirized – contribute to what is sometimes perceived as the novel's lack of focus. But it is also the conjunction of these numerous elements and levels of meaning that makes *A Connecticut Yankee* such a fascinating and such a pivotal book in the American Arthurian tradition.

Surely the inspiration for the story of a modern American in Camelot was the comic possibilities of such an incongruity. Twain's notebook entry from December 1884 shows the kind of comedy he imagined:

> Have the notions & habits of thought of the present day mixed with the necessities of that. No pockets in the armor. No way to manage certain requirements of nature. Can't scratch. Cold in the head – can't blow – can't get at handkerchief, can't use iron sleeve. Iron gets red hot in the sun – leaks in the rain, gets white with frost & freezes me solid in winter. Suffer from lice & fleas. Make disagreeable clatter when I enter church. Can't dress or undress myself. Always getting struck by lightning. Fall down, can't get up. See Morte DArthur. (III: 78)

Some of these very incidents are introduced into the novel and into the illustrations completed by Dan Beard. These illustrations are crucial to the feel of the original edition and indicate the way that the book was perceived by a sympathetic contemporary reader. They are also, to a certain extent, a key to the way that Twain envisioned his story of the Connecticut Yankee. Twain, after all, was delighted with Beard's illustrations and believed that they captured perfectly the spirit of his work. In his autobiography, *Hardly a Man Is Now Alive*, Beard quotes a letter in which Twain wrote to him: "Hold me under everlasting obligations. There are a hundred artists who could have illustrated any other of my books, but only one who could illustrate

2   In her study of *Mark Twain as a Literary Artist*, Gladys Carmen Bellamy noted that "most critics now agree that *Connecticut Yankee* was written to point up the injustices both of Victoria's England and of Mark Twain's America" (312). James D. Williams objects to this statement in his article on "Revision and Intention in Mark Twain's *Connecticut Yankee*." He feels that Twain "seems to have had more trouble *including* satire of England in his novel than in toning it down or eliminating it" (297).

this one. It was a lucky day I went netting for lightning bugs and caught a meteor" (337–38).

One of the levels of meaning that Beard captures is the burlesque. For instance, he illustrates the scene in which Sandy pours water down Hank's overheated suit of armor. Beard also captures other comic moments, as when he depicts Lancelot on a bicycle with a large front wheel, racing to rescue Hank and the king. In a companion illustration, called "Galahad Takes a Header," Galahad's bicycle strikes a rock, and the fully-armored fabled knight flies over its handlebars. This conjunction of armor and bicycle suggests the conjunction of medieval and modern that Twain employs throughout the book to evoke humor. The conjunction occurs even in the use of language: Hank's Yankee accent and American slang is juxtaposed with the language of Malory, sometimes quoted directly and sometimes reconstructed by Twain. When Clarence, for example, says he is a page, Hank's response is "you ain't more than a paragraph" (34).[3]

The humorous if occasionally heavy-handed contrast between archaic diction and nineteenth-century speech is a verbal reflection of the way Twain creates humor – and interest for American readers – in his text. He commercializes the sacred Siege Perilous into a seat on the stock exchange, depicts the knights playing baseball, and further deromanticizes the "knight in shining armor" by Americanizing the image into a hawker for various products. In Beard's illustration (192), not only is Sir Cote Male Taile wearing a sandwich board, but the trappings of his horse and even the banner on his lance advertise Persimmon's Soap. Hank remarks that this was "a furtive, underhand blow at this nonsense of knight errantry . . . . I had started a number of these people out – the bravest knights I could get – each sandwiched between bulletin-boards bearing one device or another, and I judged that by and by when they got to be numerous enough they would begin to look ridiculous; and then, even the steel-clad ass that *hadn't* any board would himself begin to look ridiculous because he was out of the fashion" (190). The ever-practical Hank cannot resist killing two birds with one stone by advertising his products and undermining knighthood through the same device. Appalled by the waste of energy he sees in the devoutly bowing monk in the Valley of Holiness – "it was his way of praying," Hank observes – Hank calculates the potential energy: "I timed him with a stop-watch, and he made 1244 revolutions in 24 minutes and 46 seconds. . . . It was one of the most useful movements in mechanics, the pedal movement." So Hank resolves to "apply a system of elastic cords to him and run a sewing machine with it," from which he clears a considerable profit, producing tow-linen

---

3   It is significant, however, as Dennis Berthold points out in his article on "The Conflict of Dialects in *A Connecticut Yankee*," that "The novel is framed by Hank Morgan's use of the medieval dialect, underscoring his failure to replace Arthurian English with Hartford English," and that this failure underscores his larger ethical failure (58).

shirts to sell to pilgrims. He even works the monk "Sundays and all" because the monk kept up his bowing on Sundays and "it was no use to waste the power" (281). This bringing together of the naive devotion of the medieval monk and the opportunism of the practical Yankee is wonderfully comic. Yet the comedy is disconcerting. It is not enough of a justification of Hank's actions to recognize, as Joseph R. McElrath rightly does, that in this scene Twain clearly differentiates "the Protestant-American consciousness from the less work- and production-oriented attitude of a Catholic culture" (McElrath 43). Hank's profit comes at the expense of the religious beliefs of the monk, beliefs that Hank feels justified in exploiting and undermining, just as he does with the chivalric values of the knights. Even Sunday, the holiest day for the monk, is just another work day for Hank. The monk's bowing is to Hank a waste of power unless it is put to some practical use, yet Hank's channeling of that energy into his sewing machine is at the same time an abuse of power. Although it would be a mistake to be too moralistic about this comic scene, it certainly reflects other abuses of power by Hank in more serious parts of the book. While in the end there is a line between the bur-lesque and the more bitingly satiric elements of the book, sometimes that line is very fine. And both elements can derive from the same source, as is the case with the contrast between the medieval and the modern American or capitalistic values.

In the notebook entry cited above, Twain writes that he first conceived of the story of a modern man in Arthurian Britain as a "Dream of being a knight errant in armor in the middle ages" (as, in fact, Adeler's "The Fortu-nate Island" turns out to be). But for the satiric purposes of his book, Twain found the dream device to be too facile and unrealistic, so he abandoned that idea and substituted as an explanation the "transposition of epochs – and bodies" (18), thus making the shift in time more like science fiction than like fantasy.

The more realistic approach also affects the presentation of the central character Hank Morgan. Hank is in many ways a larger-than-life superhero who can "make anything a body wanted – anything in the world, it didn't make any difference what; and if there wasn't any quick new-fangled way to make a thing, I could invent one – and do it as easy as rolling off a log" (20). But he is also "practical" to a fault and "nearly barren of sentiment, I suppose – or poetry, in other words" (20). It is precisely this lack of sentiment or poetry that is Hank's fatal flaw, a flaw that is not immediately apparent because Hank's ability and his espousal of democratic ideals make him seem like the prototypical American democrat at odds with tyranny and social codes that deny equality of opportunity.

On one level Hank fulfills this latter role. There is undeniable satire of advancement by birth rather than by talent in *Connecticut Yankee*, and Hank at times speaks and acts nobly in defense of a more just system. He establishes Man Factories to train those who could not otherwise rise to

"HELLO-CENTRAL!"

Figure 3. Hank Morgan as Uncle Sam in one of Dan Beard's illustrations for the first edition of Mark Twain's *Connecticut Yankee in King Arthur's Court* (New York: Charles L. Webster, 1889).

positions of power in the rigidly structured political, military, and social hierarchy of Arthur's Britain; and he recognizes that "there is nothing diviner
about a king than there is about a tramp" (252–53). Hank also seems genuinely concerned about the plight of the poor. He observes that England is like
"a corporation where nine hundred and ninety-four of the members fur-
nished all the money and did all the work, and the other six elected themselves a permanent board of direction and took all the dividends." His hope
is to change the situation so that the "nine hundred and ninety-four dupes"
get "a new deal" (85). The idea seems so democratically fair that Franklin
Roosevelt took the phrase and applied it to his plans for economic recovery
because, he wrote, "I felt the same way about conditions in America as the
Yankee did about those in ancient Britain" (quoted in Cyril Clemens 19–20).
In certain ways, in fact, Hank seems such a representative of American ideals
that in the first edition of the book Dan Beard portrayed him, in a couple of
illustrations, dressed like Uncle Sam. (See p. 525 for the clearest example and
p. 575, where the Uncle Sam figure astride Thomas Paine's *Common Sense*
uses a quill pen to joust with an overweight nobleman.) Hank can even be
magnanimously fair to Arthur, the supreme representative of the monarchical system that he despises. In the smallpox hut, when Arthur ignores the
danger to himself in order to carry the young girl dying of the disease down
to her mother, Hank sees the act for what it is, "heroism at its last and loftiest
possibility," because Arthur "was challenging death in the open field
unarmed, with all odds set against the challenger, no reward set upon the
contest . . ." (206).

There is, however, another side to this champion of democracy and the
common man. While it may be going too far to say, as one critic does, that
Hank's "only genuine characteristic is his egomania" (Zurlo 60), he does
seem to identify himself as the perfect despot. After suggesting that "unlim-
ited power *is* the ideal thing when in safe hands" (64) and that despotism
would be the best form of government except that a perfect despot must die
and be succeeded by someone less perfect, Hank declares that his "works
showed what a despot could do with the resources of a kingdom at his
command" (64–65). In the final analysis, this statement is highly ironic.
Hank's actions do indeed show what a despot can do: he can destroy a world
and turn an Eden into a wasteland.

The two elements of Hank's character, his democratic leanings and his
despotic nature, blend in a disturbing way and reflect a recurring dilemma
for American protagonists as well as for historical American figures who
achieve power through wealth or politics. On one level, Hank represents the
classic dilemma of democracy, a dilemma spoken about, for example, by
James Fenimore Cooper in *The American Democrat*: equality of opportunity
does not lead to equality of achievement, suggested Cooper, and therefore
there are differences in status among "equal" citizens. On another level,
Hank represents the American Adam who is presented with a new world

but who inevitably suffers a fall. As Henry Nash Smith has pointed out, Twain's Yankee is "an avatar of the American Adam dwelling in the Garden of the World" (67). Hank himself says early in the book, "I stood here, at the very spring and source of the second great period of the world's history; and could see the trickling stream of that history gather, and deepen and broaden, and roll its mighty tide down the far centuries . . . I was a Unique; and glad to know that that fact could not be dislodged or challenged for thirteen centuries and a half, for sure" (53). Given the opportunity to make of the world what he will, Hank decides he can "boss the whole country inside of three months" (23); and his rise to power, like those of other American Adams, is phenomenal. But, as it does for other American Adams – F. Scott Fitzgerald's Gatsby, for example – the American Dream turns into a nightmare, which leads the Adam to his fall.

Hank's problem is that he recognizes, quite rightly, that he has more knowledge, at least of a certain sort, than those around him. This knowledge gives him power, the power to control the whole nation; and such nearly absolute power, which he seizes and uses unabashedly, magnifies the flaws in his character until he is almost absolutely corrupted. Hank is aware that he possesses a "crying defect" (268), but he is mistaken when he characterizes it as his desire to find the "picturesque" rather than the simple way to accomplish a goal. In fact, his flaw is really that he is, as he said early in his story, "practical" and "nearly barren of sentiment" (14). This unsentimental practicality leads him to act in ways that are designed to achieve an end without consideration of the consequences. By overriding the values in which he purports to believe, it leads him to justify his own abuses of power because of the end towards which he thinks he is working. Hank has fallen because he has eaten of the tree of knowledge – the knowledge of technology and science and the knowledge, which parallels Merlin's, that people can be forced to submit to what they perceive as more powerful than themselves. As a result, Hank behaves in a manner that solidifies his power or enhances his status even when such behavior requires that he, for practical purposes, ignore his own allegedly democratic and social ideals.

The contradiction between Hank's stated ideals and his true feelings is demonstrated in numerous ways. An offhand observation of his is particularly telling. When he notes that priests had told him of the distress an executioner had caused a young woman and urged Hank to punish the offender, he is troubled that "something of this disagreeable sort" keeps happening – that is, "episodes that showed that not all priests were frauds and selfseekers, but that many, even the great majority, of these that were down on the ground among the common people, were sincere and right-hearted, and devoted to the alleviation of human troubles and sufferings." Such priests seem exactly the type Hank should be encouraging as he attempts to give the common people a new deal. They work for the good of those who have no political power and even recognize and oppose the abuses of those, like the executioner, who do have power. But Hank is concerned that the very virtue of these men will "keep people reconciled to an Established Church" and thus, as he says, "I did not like it" (113).

It is possible to argue that Hank's fear of the oppressive power of established religion and its support of the monarchical system outweighs the little good that the priests do. But other incidents in the novel make unmistakable the discrepancy between Hank's stated values and his actions. His treatment of the blacksmith Dowley is an indisputable example of his willingness to use his money, power, and knowledge to destroy a common man. Hank is calculating in his display of wealth to humiliate the blacksmith. (The chapter relating these events is titled "Dowley's Humiliation.") He spends the tremendous amount of "thirty-nine thousand one hundred and fifty milrays" (230) for a meal so lavish that it makes the material success of which Dowley is so proud seem insignificant. When Hank receives the bill, he tells the clerk to keep the nine cents in change, a gesture that amazes all the dinner guests. As a result "the blacksmith was a crushed man" (231). While conspicuous consumption is a time-honored American means of certifying and announcing one's success, Hank is not just trying to keep up with or even surpass the Joneses (or the Smiths); he is trying to put Dowley in his place. His deliberate crushing of the blacksmith demonstrates that Hank is willing to use the power of his wealth for his own aggrandizement.

What makes Hank's actions so despicable is that Dowley is just the type of man who deserves the admiration of those who espouse democratic values. Dowley's is a rags-to-riches story – as close to the American Dream as a commoner in the sixth-century Britain of Twain's novel could come. His biography chronicles his rise:

> He told how he had begun life an orphan lad without money and without friends able to help him; how he had lived as the slaves of the meanest master lived; how his day's work was from sixteen to eighteen hours long, and yielded him only enough black bread to keep him in a half-fed condition; how his faithful endeavors finally attracted the attention of a good blacksmith, who came near knocking him dead with kindness by suddenly offering, when he was totally unprepared, to take him as his bound apprentice for nine years and give him board and clothes and teach him the trade – or "mystery" as Dowley called it. That was his first great rise, his first gorgeous stroke of fortune; and you saw that he couldn't yet speak of it without a sort of eloquent wonder and delight that such a gilded promotion should have fallen to the lot of a common human being. (226–27)

This rise from poverty, recognizable to anyone who has read a Horatio Alger tale, is a pattern that is basic to the American experience, a pattern that is found in American literature as early as the *Autobiography of Benjamin Franklin*. Not only is Dowley a man who has earned success through his own hard work, but he is also someone who has not been spoiled by that success.

Although he is proud of what he has accomplished, he does not have an exaggerated opinion of his own worth or see himself as better than those less fortunate. Dowley says that he remains a man who is "willing to receive any he as his fellow and equal that carrieth a right heart in his body, be his worldly estate howsoever modest," and, offering his hand to the king, whom he believes to be of a lower class, says "we are equals – equals" (228).

Whereas Dowley expresses sincerely democratic sentiments, Hank – in his actions towards Dowley and elsewhere in the book – shows himself to be anything but democratic. Hank's true nature comes out again in his debate with Dowley over the relative worth of money. Dowley and his friends do not recognize the principle that it is the buying power and not the actual amount of money that is important. Hank demonstrates his point in an argument that he calls "a crusher" (236); but Dowley, who values high wages over buying power, is neither crushed nor convinced. Furious at being bested by a man he considers his intellectual inferior, Hank responds angrily: "And to think of the circumstances: the first statesman of the age, the capablest man, the best informed in the entire world, the loftiest uncrowned head that had moved through the clouds of any political firmament for centuries, sitting here apparently defeated in argument by an ignorant country blacksmith" (236). Then Hank deliberately strikes "below the belt to get even" (237), making Dowley fear for his life because he has inadvertently admitted that he paid a worker more than the allowable wages. Hank's purportedly democratic ideal thus yields to his offended sense of superiority as he uses his intellectual power to destroy the blacksmith.

Hank blames his action on "human nature" and claims that "*anybody* would have done it" (237), but more should be expected of "the capablest man, the best informed in the entire world" than this least-common-denominator approach to morality. The very premise of Hank's defense is questionable. Hank had crushed Dowley earlier, but the blacksmith did not respond with the kind of low blow that Hank calls not a love tap but a "lifter" (237). Insofar as Hank is a representative of enlightened nineteenth-century attitudes over those of the hierarchic British of the sixth, and by extension the nineteenth, century, he is lacking. His conduct therefore adds another level to the humor of the book and the satire of British society: criticism of modern American values.

It is sometimes difficult to separate the humorous from the more bitingly satiric levels in *Connecticut Yankee*. For example, Hank is horrified by the cruelty of Morgan le Fay, whose callous disregard for human life and liberty he has vowed to punish some day (see p. 115). He prevents her from hanging an old woman who has cursed Morgan le Fay for killing her grandchild. Then when Morgan wants to hang a composer, Hank listens to his music and gives Morgan "permission to hang the whole band." While the incident is comic, it nonetheless must give us pause, especially when Hank justifies the action by appealing to the practical consideration that "a statesman gains little by the arbitrary exercise of ironclad authority upon all occasions that offer, for this wounds the just pride of his subordinates, and thus tends to undermine his strength. A little concession, now and then, where it can do no harm, is the wiser policy" (107). Hank chooses to solidify his power and position as a statesman at the expense of the lives of all the members of the band. Of course, such humorous hyperbole might not even be considered a serious indicator of a flaw in Hank's character were it not for the fact that it is of a piece with other actions; and, in retrospect, it seems an ominous pre-figuring of Hank's slaughter of the assembled chivalry of England at the end of the book.

Hank is willing to destroy all those who disagree with him and who would be a danger to his political plan. It is no wonder that one critic refers to Hank's disregard for the lives of his opponents as his "final solution" (Robert Keith Miller 131). In preparation for the Battle of the Sand Belt Hank tells his fifty-two faithful followers that they should not be concerned about the upcoming battle because, although the whole of England is marching against them, they will have to fight only the thirty thousand armed knights and then "the civilian multitude in the war will retire" (307). The undemo-cratic sentiment underlying this statement is striking. While admitting that everyone in England opposes him and rejects his authority, Hank neverthe-less is willing to resist them all in order to advance his plans for the kingdom. Stephen Knight's observation that Hank's "democratic values only operate to any extent when he is a passive observer: when he is active he is quite dictatorial" (196) is surely borne out by Hank's disregard for majority rule in the final battle.

Hank's cold-blooded side is also demonstrated in the battle. He plans to give the knights of Britain a collective "lifter," an unexpected blow so devas-tating that it will destroy the very institution of knighthood. As he prepares for the encounter, Hank proves just how cheaply he has come to regard life. In checking the electrified fences that will slaughter the knights, he is primar-ily concerned that Clarence has set up the electrical connections in a way which will waste energy:

> It's too expensive – uses up force for nothing. You don't want any ground connection except the one through the negative brush. The other end of the wire must be brought back into the cave and fastened independently and *without* any ground connection. Now, then, observe the economy of it. A cavalry charge hurls itself against the fence; you are using no power, you are spending no money, for there is only one ground wire; the moment they touch it they form a connection with the negative brush *through* the ground, and drop dead. Don't you see – you are using no energy until it is needed, your lightning is there, and ready, like the load in a gun; but it isn't costing you a cent till you touch it off. Oh, yes, the single ground connection – (302)

This is surely as much an abuse of Hank's intellectual power over the people of the sixth century as it is an abuse of electrical power. Ultimately, Hank shows himself to be much worse than those whose policies he has decried: he is more dictatorial than any of the nobles he has encountered; he has less regard for human life than Morgan le Fay; and he uses his technological wizardry of electric wires and Gatling guns more ruthlessly than Merlin, from whose cave Hank directs the slaughter at the Battle of the Sand Belt, ever used his phony magic.

Hank's final act of destruction helps to explain why Twain changed his protagonist's name from its original form. Howard Baetzhold has noted that, in its earliest stages, Twain's tale was created merely to have fun with the contrast between two ages and was not designed for satire; and the protagonist was called Bob Smith. The change of the name to Hank Morgan, writes Baetzhold, is symbolic: "Just as the British Henry Morgan skillfully, but brutally, harassed Spanish authority in the New World, so the Yankee Hank sought to destroy Old World British authority vested in monarch, aristocracy, and an Established Church" ("The Autobiography of Sir Robert Smith of Camelot" 460). Stephen Knight expands on this idea by observing that the name Hank Morgan suggests not only "the notorious pirate" but also "makes him kin with Morgan le Fay" and identifies him with J. P. Morgan, "one of the great monopolists" (197–98).

In the same account, Knight also observes that Bob Smith is "an everyman's name." And surely the change *from* Bob Smith is as important as the change *to* Hank Morgan. Bob Smith is a name for a common man, for someone who is typical of the American Dream. Of course, Hank – "the self-made man, the man who has risen from poverty to riches" (Douglas 187) – might have been such a person. But as Chadwick Hansen argues in his article on "The Once and Future Boss: Mark Twain's Yankee," Hank also has a "lust for absolute power" and is "capable of the most callous mass slaughter" (72). Thus, as Twain developed the concept of his character, he needed a name that was less representative of democratic ideals. After all, Smith, the commonest of names in the English-speaking world, links a person to a profession that demands hard, honest labor. Earlier in American literature, the village blacksmith was idealized by Henry Wadsworth Longfellow as the embodiment of certain basic values, a strong man whose "brow is wet with honest sweat" and who "looks the whole world in the face, / For he owes not any man." Longfellow's blacksmith teaches the typical American "lesson" that "at the flaming forge of life / Our fortunes must be wrought," that is, that people must make their way in the world through their own hard work.

Hank seems to have violated the spirit of the blacksmith in many ways, not the least of which is that he, like his father before him, was a blacksmith; but he abandoned the smithy for the "great arms factory" (14), where, instead of being his own boss, he could boss thousands of men. It is interesting to note and relevant to the discussion of Hank's name and profession that in one of the cinematic versions of *Connecticut Yankee*, the 1949 production directed by Tay Garnett and starring Bing Crosby, Hank is named Martin, not Morgan, and he is in fact a blacksmith. While one must be wary of reading too much into it, the film does seem to reflect the values of its age and to present a simpler view of Hank as an American hero by avoiding all the darkness of Twain's book. Although the Hank of the movie is a victim of Merlin's plotting, he is not forced to slaughter the assembled chivalry of Britain. He rides alone for the noble purpose of rescuing Sandy, a damsel in distress. Hank is also less of an acquiring capitalist. In return for not using his supposed magic to blot out the sun, he asks not for a percentage of the profits he brings in, as the Hank of the book does, but only for "a little black-smith shop."[4] Garnett's Hank is thus a figure much like Longfellow's blacksmith, a simple man who prefers the smithy to the factory, whereas Twain's Hank is a businessman and ultimately a dictator.

In the final analysis, Dowley, the "ignorant country blacksmith" who has a touch of pride but is not power-hungry like Hank, is better deserving of the name Smith than the Connecticut Yankee is. By changing Hank's name from Bob Smith, Twain seems to have given a clear indication that his hero was no longer a representative of the common man. Hank had evolved into a character who has the Yankee ingenuity to boss the nation but not the simple values and the "sentiment" that would allow him to avoid being corrupted by the power he thus achieves.

An important development in the American Arthurian tradition, Twain's *Connecticut Yankee* has often been reproduced or reinvented, not only in the 1949 Bing Crosby movie but also in a host of other retellings: in a 1920 silent film, a 1931 movie starring Will Rogers, several made-for-television movies, and a Rodgers and Hart musical (1927), which was revived in 1943 with the Yankee as a naval officer. In addition, there have been a Walt Disney version (*The Spaceman and King Arthur*), a Bugs Bunny cartoon (*Bugs Bunny in King Arthur's Court*), and a *National Lampoon* parody called "A New York Yankee in King Arthur's Court," in which Reggie Jackson, the New York Yankee, is hit with an empty whiskey bottle hurled from the stands, wakes up in Arthur's time, and comes into conflict with "Billy Merlin." The retellings usually focus on the comic aspect of the novel and create much of their fun by updating the technology that Hank employs to include airplanes, boom boxes, and even lunar rovers and lasers.

---

4   Tay Garnett also directed another Arthurian movie in which a blacksmith is the protago-nist. In *The Black Knight*, he creates an exemplar of the American Dream in Arthurian Britain. John the blacksmith uses his skill, hard work, and courage to save Arthur's realm from invaders. As a reward he is knighted and given the hand of the woman he loves, the daughter of an earl. For further comments on the way this movie Americanizes the Arthurian world, see Lupack, "An Enemy in Our Midst," as well as the last chapter of this book.

But more significant than such retellings is the approach Twain takes to the Arthurian material. That approach has a thematic analogue in a number of later Arthurian works which question the possibility of achieving the glorious dream of Arthur's kingdom or of remaining an innocent in a world that, however Edenic it may seem, always has a serpent in the garden (or, as Twain might have put it, a snake in the grass). The Americanizing of Arthurian themes has, to be sure, analogues earlier than Twain; but Twain's novel most clearly and literally brings Arthurian values together with American concerns and characters. The association of Arthur's dream with the American Dream and of Arthur, attempting to create a new order, with the American Adam paves the way for writers like Edwin Arlington Robinson, who removes the magic from the legend to present a realistic exploration of its characters, and T. S. Eliot, who uses the Grail motif that he finds in Jessie Weston's *From Ritual to Romance* to comment on modern values.

3

Reaction to Tennyson: Visions of Courageous Achievement

As American writers like Mark Twain (in *A Connecticut Yankee in King Arthur's Court*), Edgar Fawcett (in *The New King Arthur*), and Oscar Fay Adams (in *Post-Laureate Idyls*) satirized Tennyson's lofty view of certain Arthurian heroes, other Americans were translating idyllic notions of knight-hood into an American setting. Their strategy was much the same as that of James Russell Lowell, who in *The Vision of Sir Launfal* obviated the basic democratic objection to knighthood – raised, for example, in Twain's novel – by opening the most exclusive of knightly clubs, achievers of the Grail, to any person willing to be charitable. Like Lowell, these American authors re-defined knighthood in terms of moral achievement rather than nobility of birth, inherited wealth, and physical prowess.

In his book *Twentieth Century Knighthood: A Series of Addresses to Young Men* (1900), Louis Albert Banks succinctly defined the notion of symbolic, moral knighthood. Banks observed that "We do not all have splendid physiques, and some deeds of hardihood in which the old knights rejoice are beyond our power, but the higher deeds of the loftier chivalry, of upright thinking, of pure conduct, of self-denying devotion, are within the reach of every one of us" (129). The highly idealized notion of knighthood that lies behind such a statement is, of course, based on literary rather than historical examples. Banks obviously could not have been thinking of actual feuding barons or struggles for the throne when he wrote: "Chivalry during its golden days made the world a much pleasanter place in which to live. It did away with low suspicions and jealousies and filled the land with an atmosphere of noble hospitality and courtesy" or that "no spirit of discord or peevishness was ever allowed in these knights toward one another" (9).

Much of Banks's book is a catalogue of chivalric virtues coupled with exempla illustrating how those virtues have been demonstrated in the modern world. Knightly simplicity of character, for instance, is demon-strated by an anecdote about Abraham Lincoln's carrying a trunk for a little girl so that she would not miss her train. But it is not only the famous or powerful like Lincoln, a Congressman at the time of the story, who can act like the heroes of medieval romance. Banks also finds chivalric qualities in the common man. He tells of a sailor who is asked what he was doing when

Commodore Winfield Scott Schley was "pulverizing Cervera" (that is, Admiral Pascual Cervera y Topete) near Santiago, Cuba, in the Spanish–American War. The sailor's response that he was "shoveling coal down yonder" in the "lower regions of the ship" prompts Banks to comment that "everybody knows that it was the knightly loyalty of the coal shovelers and engineers down in the smothering and sweltering furnace rooms that made the victory possible" (50–51). Other knightly virtues are exemplified by stories about Americans as famous as Ulysses S. Grant, who showed compassion by allowing Lee to keep his sword after his surrender, and as ordinary as a train inspector who refused to be provoked by a rude passenger. The point is that "the real gentleman, of the old knighthood or the new, is not to be judged by his employment, but by the personal honor evinced in his character and conduct" (95).

Since "chivalry emphasized the theory that it is natural for youth to be courageous, and that it is the greatest shame for a young man to lack courage," it provided, in Banks's view, a fine model for modern youth. "I am profoundly convinced," he wrote, "that our own age would be greatly improved, and the outlook of civilization distinctly brightened, if there might be a wide stimulation of manly courage in the hearts of American youth. I do not mean physical courage only, but the courage to face the great moral and social and political problems of our time, and ride them down with the dauntless valor of youth. It is as natural now as it was in the days of chivalry for young men to dream dreams and see visions of courageous achievement" (14).

A contemporary of Banks whose ideas had much greater influence also believed chivalry to be important in the development of American youth. In 1901, a minister named William Byron Forbush (1868–1927) wrote a book whose title, *The Boy Problem*, reflects a serious concern of its age. Forbush divided the stages of a boy's life into infancy (until the age of six), childhood (from six to twelve), and adolescence (from twelve to manhood) (9), a scheme altogether consistent with the psychological theory of his day. (G. Stanley Hall, sometimes referred to as the "father of American psychology," for example, not only wrote a brief introduction to Forbush's book, but also outlined similar stages in the development of boys in his own two-volume study of *Adolescence*, published in 1904.) According to Forbush, it is in the last of these stages that the boy problem arises because the boy "has become endowed with the passions and independence of manhood while still a child in foresight and judgment. He rushes now into so many crazy plans and harmful deeds" (23). In addition, "the very sensitiveness, longing and overpowering sense of the new life . . . is often so concealed by inconsistent and even barbarous behavior that one quite loses both comprehension and patience" (24).

The moral dangers of this stage in a boy's growth are balanced by great potential, for this is "the time for shaping ideals" (11). This notion of shaping ideals aligned Forbush once again with contemporary theory, especially with

Figure 4. A Castle of the Knights of King Arthur. From *The Knights of King Arthur* by William Byron Forbush (Oberlin: The Knights of King Arthur, 1916).

Banks, who saw the manly courage of knighthood as a model to be imitated by youngsters who need to deal with societal problems, and with Hall, whose assessment of the condition of youth in America is that "our young people leap rather than grow into maturity." This "leap" occurs largely because, as America is "conquering nature" and "achieving a magnificent material civilization . . . our vast and complex business organization . . . absorbs ever more and earlier the best talent and muscle of youth . . . [and] we are progressively forgetting that for the complete apprenticeship to life, youth needs repose, leisure, art, legends, romance, idealization, and in a word humanism" (I, xvi–xvii). Referring again to the importance of such legends later in his study, Hall says that "some would measure the progress of culture by the work of reinterpreting on ever higher planes the mythic tradition of a race, and how this is done for youth is a good criterion of pedagogic progress" (II, 444).

Interestingly, it was in the stories of King Arthur and the Knights of the Round Table that Hall saw "perhaps the very best ideals for youth to be found in history" (I, 532). Hall's singling out of the Arthurian legends is no doubt based in part on his knowledge of and admiration for an organization founded by Forbush to put into practice some of Forbush's own theories about the development of adolescent males. In 1893 Forbush established the first of what was to become a network of clubs for boys called the Knights of King Arthur. These clubs, felt Hall, captured "the spirit of fealty and piety" that made the medieval legends in general and "the literature of the Arthuriad and the Sangrail" in particular so wholesomely appealing to young boys; and he spoke of the clubs as "an unique order of Christian knighthood for boys" (I, 442–44).

Of course, there were many societies for young boys in addition to Forbush's Knights of King Arthur, some of them based on chivalric virtues and some not. Hall refers to groups such as "the Captains of Ten," which promoted "a spirit of loyalty to Christ"; "the Agassiz Association," which encouraged "personal work in natural science"; and "the Princely Knights of the Character Castle," which tried to inculcate "the principles of heroism" in boys (418–19). The most successful and long-lasting was the Boy Scouts, whose founder, Sir Robert Baden-Powell, modeled his club largely on Forbush's Knights of King Arthur and on another American group, the Woodcraft Indians (cf. Girouard 254). Scouts, in fact, were encouraged to read stories of chivalry; and many of the virtues espoused by the Scouting movement derived from Baden-Powell's notions of chivalry (Girouard 255).

After the Scouts had been founded, Forbush himself advised the adults who guided each of his Castles, as the local clubs were called, to "buy the manual of the Boy Scouts" (Forbush and Forbush, *The Knights of King Arthur: How to Begin and What to Do* 20). But he made a clear distinction between the two: "While the Knights may use and should use scouting and camp methods, its appeal is a higher one than that of the Scouts. It deals with the fraternal, the emotional and the intellectual, with a constant emphasis on the spiritual. The very ideals of the two movements show the difference; the ideal product of the Scouts is the scout, the agile frontiersman; the ideal product of the Knights is the knight, the Christian gentleman. The Scout movement may do this latter, the Knights can do nothing less or else" (21).

Forbush founded his organization originally for boys between the ages of thirteen and sixteen, a time when they "are said by psychologists to be in the knightly period, and it is just then that they respond to the ritual, regalia and the glamor of exclusiveness" (*The Coming Generation* 352). The general plan, outlined by Forbush in a pamphlet called *Knights of King Arthur: How to Begin and What to Do*, was fairly simple and flexible. Each Castle, he wrote, is "a fraternity, private but not secret, self-governing and under the control of the local church. It is based upon the oldest English Christian legend, that of the Round Table. It is a revival of the nobler side of medieval chivalry. The thought is to fulfill the prophecy of King Arthur that he would return to re-establish a kingdom of righteousness, honor and service." Such clubs were seen as ways of channeling what was believed to be the instinctive tendency in adolescent males to form gangs into a means of doing good deeds and developing character. Hall discussed "the propensity of boys from thirteen on to consort in gangs" (II, 396) and concluded that "Every adolescent boy ought to belong to some club or society marked by as much secrecy as is compatible with safety" (II, 429).

In the course of his membership in Forbush's clubs, a boy progressed through the stages of Page, Esquire, and finally Knight (Forbush and Forbush, *The Knights of King Arthur: How to Begin and What to Do* 4). In order to help him focus on particular virtues, "Each boy takes the name of some ancient knight or some hero, ancient or modern, and tries to represent his knightly traits" (4). The fact that the heroes the boys emulate need not be knights of Arthur's court – or even knights at all – implies that for Forbush, as for Banks, the force of the example was more important than consistency with the Arthurian stories. In a book called *The Boys' Round Table*, which Forbush co-authored, he suggested that boys adopt the name of such Arthurian heroes as Launcelot, Gawain, Bedivere, Percivale, Bors, and Gareth; but the boys might also choose names of saints such as Luke, George, and Francis, or of other heroes such as Alfred, Roland, Ivanhoe, Ulysses, Luther, Christopher Columbus, or even Thor (55–56). Forbush was determined that the boys "actually live out the knightly life together, and their 'gang' spirit, instead of tending, as is usual, towards the ideals of the noisiest or most dominant boy, which are probably lower than the average, are lifted toward the ideal of the best manhood" (*The Coming Generation* 352–53). If consistency suffered because of the eclectic models allowed, Forbush and the others who organized Castles were unconcerned, so long as the proper models were followed and the proper ideals were fostered.[1]

Since Forbush's conception of the Arthurian stories was based largely on Tennyson, he conceived of Merlin as "the venerable counsellor of Arthur." Therefore, in each of his clubs, the adult responsible for guiding the boys was known as the Merlin. By taking the role of Merlin rather than of the king himself, the adult leader would be seen as an advisor rather than a ruler so that the Castle would "feel that it is self-governing." The Merlin was to take a seat "before and below the throne" to emphasize that "what he gives the Castle is his wisdom and not his authority" (Forbush and Forbush, *The Knights of King Arthur: How to Begin and What to Do* 7).

The Merlin could help the boys organize "tournaments," which were "usually athletic," and "quests," which were "co-operative deeds of kindness" (Forbush, *The Coming Generation* 352). Among the good deeds performed by

---

1   The same impetus is behind books such as *Heroes Every Child Should Know* (1907), ed. Hamilton Wright Mabie, which provided models for youth, including such diverse personages as King Arthur and Sir Galahad, Daniel and David, St. George and King Alfred, George Washington and Abraham Lincoln. Another book of tales with a more specifically religious purpose, Basil Mathews' *The Splendid Quest: Stories of Knights on the Pilgrims' Way* (1929), also combines, as two of its thirteen stories of quest, the tales of Abraham Lincoln's abolition of slavery and Galahad's achieving of the Grail.

Figure 5. A Court of the Queens of Avalon. From *The Queens of Avalon* by William Byron Forbush (Boston: The Knights of King Arthur, 1911).

some of the Castles, Forbush cites such things as cleaning up and beautifying parts of town, providing lunch and hot coffee for policemen on Halloween, earning money to place a King Arthur memorial window in a church (in Rutland, Vermont), sending magazines to a church mission in Alaska, and giving King Arthur Flour to the poor (Forbush and Forbush, *The Knights of King Arthur: How to Begin and What to Do* 23).[2]

A particular honor was reserved for exceptional service performed by one of the members. That boy would be allowed for one evening to adopt the name of Sir Galahad and to sit in the Siege Perilous. Each Castle was to have such a seat, and the honor of occupying it could only be conferred by the unanimous consent of the members (Forbush and Masseck 35). It is some indication of the kind of ritual the clubs promoted that the Siege Perilous, usually covered with a red cloth, was "to be treated reverentially" and that

2   The gift was appropriate to the aims of the club. The *King Arthur Flour 200th Anniversary Cookbook* (actually the 200th anniversary of Sands, Taylor and Woods, the parent company, and only the 100th anniversary of King Arthur Flour) recounts the origin of the name: "The 1890's were a time when the Arthurian romances were having a renaissance. While Sands, Taylor and Wood were trying to decide on a name for their new and exceptional flour, George Wood attended a musical in Boston called *King Arthur and the Knights of the Round Table*. He came away feeling that the values inherent in the Arthurian legends, purity, loyalty, honesty, superior strength, and a dedication to a higher purpose, were the values that most closely expressed their feelings about their new flour. So it was decided that King Arthur would be its symbol" (I–12).

"in some Castles it is almost a superstition that it shall not be uncovered even by accident" (Forbush and Forbush, *The Merlin's Book* 30). This sense of ritual was enhanced by the fact that the boys generally wore some sort of costume, ranging from simple sashes to tunics or more elaborate dress, including shields decorated with heraldic emblems and swords or spears. Pins and badges identifying them as members could be purchased and worn when the boys were not in uniform. In addition, there were formulaic ceremonies not only for granting the right to sit in the Siege Perilous but also for the installation of the officers of the Castle, such as the Chamberlain, the Heralds, and the Seneschal.

Although boys were seen as more problematic than girls, a female parallel to the Knights of King Arthur known as the Queens of Avalon (originally Queens of Avilion) was established in 1902, nine years after the Knights. Whereas the boys' clubs were directed by a Merlin, the girls were guided by a Lady of the Lake. As did the Knights, the Queens of Avalon strove to revive medieval values. The society "represents itself as the revival of the group of royal ladies, who, in the Arthurian legends, lived on the magic island of Avalon, the land of flowers and fruit, of peace and purity, of wholesomeness and healing, and ministered to humanity with graciousness and beauty. It is the Kingdom of Ideal Womanhood" (Forbush, *The Queens of Avalon* 7).[3] Forbush chose Avalon as the group's controlling symbol because he believed that the isle, "bright though misty, may correspond in the idealism of girls to what the Holy Grail does in the idealism of boys; that, a vision to be won by the chivalrous; this, a social condition to be earned by the pure in heart. And the ideal is truly feminine – woman the nurse and healer of mankind, in youth and age, rules by her virtue the kingdom where all men live in peace and purity" (11).

Forbush's clubs continue to be of interest and importance not only in the study of the history of pedagogy and adolescent psychology; they also bear on American cultural and literary history in two important ways. First, they were a means of democratizing the Arthurian legends by making them accessible to anyone willing to live a morally noble life. And second, they were a way of spreading knowledge of and interest in the Arthurian legends.

Arthurian books were suggested for reading and Arthurian illustrations

---

3 Forbush's view of Avalon is no doubt based on the description in Thomas Wentworth Higginson's *Tales of the Enchanted Islands of the Atlantic* (1898), a book Forbush recommends to the girls who join the Queens of Avalon. Higginson describes Arthur's resting place as a "green and fertile island which each year is blessed with two autumns, two springs, two summers, two gatherings of fruit, – the land where pearls are found, where the flowers spring as you gather them – that isle of orchards called the 'Isle of the Blessed.' No tillage there, no coulter to tear the bosom of the earth. Without labor it affords wheat and the grape. There the lives extend beyond a century. There nine sisters, whose will is the only law, rule over those who go from us to them. The eldest excels in the art of healing, and exceeds her sisters in beauty. She is called Morgana, and knows the virtues of all the herbs of the meadow" (92).

for viewing, though, like the names of persons to be imitated and the names of Castles, readings went far beyond the strictly Arthurian. In *The Boys' Round Table*, Forbush and co-author Frank Masseck provided a reading list (128–32) that included various retellings of the legends, such as *The Boy's King Arthur* by Lanier; the *Idylls of the King* and other Arthurian poems (like "Sir Galahad," which presented an idealized model of virtue) by Tennyson; Bulfinch's *Age of Chivalry*; and the Arthurian ballads from Percy's *Reliques of Ancient English Poetry*. In the manual on *How to Begin and What to Do* to start a Castle, the novice Merlin was instructed to have available for the boys a "library of books of King Arthur and other heroic stories" as well as reproductions of Edwin Austin Abbey's Holy Grail paintings for the Boston Public Library (22). And in his *Queens of Avalon* guide, Forbush recommended, among other books, Mary MacLeod's *The Story of King Arthur and His Noble Knights* (26). He noted that one Court of girls read regularly from Tennyson's *Idylls* (24); and he made it a requirement that any girl chosen as a Queen of a Court must have read all of the *Idylls* (33), just as to advance to the degree of Knight a boy had to memorize the lines from Tennyson's "Guinevere" which begin "In that fair Order of my Table Round" (*The Merlin's Book* 27), the lines that contain the impossible vows to which Arthur makes his knights swear.

The emphasis placed on Tennyson is due, of course, to the conception of the *Idylls* as a morally appropriate example. The spiritual ideal, after all, was foremost in Forbush's clubs, which is why sitting in the Siege Perilous was deemed the highest honor and why Abbey's Grail images were recommended for viewing. Forbush also suggested that each Castle "be adorned with beautiful pictures" and that "the most familiar and easily obtained is Watts' Sir Galahad." He even advised that a copy of Watts' painting be given to every member of the Castle (Forbush and Masseck 139).

The very extent of the clubs is noteworthy as an indicator of increasing interest in the Arthurian legends. Writing in *The Knights of King Arthur: The Merlin's Book of Advanced Work* in 1916, Forbush observed that "there have been over 3,000 Castles. There have been over 350 Courts of Queens and over 200 Camps of the Brotherhood of David.[4] It is believed that over 125,000 young people have been identified with the King Arthur movement" (55). And the entry on Forbush in *The National Cyclopædia of American Biography* estimates that the Knights of King Arthur had 130,000 members by 1922. Though the movement extended to Canada, Mexico, England, Jamaica, and New Zealand (cf. Forbush and Masseck 18), its spread throughout the United

---

4   The Brotherhood of David was an organization for boys younger than those admitted to the Knights of King Arthur. The ideal was to make use of "entirely different legendary material from that of the Round Table" so as not to "take the edge off the King Arthur idea when the time comes for it"; but since there was "some demand for a preparatory stage for boys from ten to thirteen in which the King Arthur stories are used in very simple fashion," Forbush established a group called the Yeomen of King Arthur (Forbush, *The Knights of King Arthur: The Merlin's Book of Advanced Work*, 43).

States, where it was not limited to any one region of the country, was by far the most impressive. In his various publications, Forbush referred to Castles of the Knights of King Arthur and Courts of the Queens of Avalon in such places as Bangor, Maine; Milford, New Hampshire; Boston, Massachusetts; Hartford, Connecticut; Columbia, Pennsylvania; Otterbein, Indiana; Versailles, Ohio; Estherville, Iowa; Lincoln, Nebraska; Fargo, North Dakota; Telluride, Colorado; Cheyenne, Wyoming; Marshall, Texas; Seaside, Oregon; and San Francisco, California. Equally impressive is the longevity of the clubs. As late as 1940, the Knights of King Arthur and Queens of Avalon were still being recognized as organizations that could help young people (cf. Colby 272); and, in isolated cases, Castles lasted much longer. And so in cities and towns all over America for a period of more than fifty years, boys and girls were playing at being Arthurian heroes and heroines and participating in basketball game "tournaments" and "quests" to beautify towns or feed the poor.

When dealing with any sort of American Arthurianism, we must always ask why a legend based on a hierarchical system headed by a monarch is attractive in a land where such things are alien to our national values. Forbush seems to answer this question by translating the hierarchy from a social to a moral realm. A youngster advanced in the peerage of the Knights of King Arthur or the Queens of Avalon not by being wealthier or from a nobler family than the average person but by being better and by doing more of the kind of good deeds that anyone can do. The clubs' compatibility to American values was enhanced by the fact that some of those boys and girls, as members of an Arthurian Castle or Court, could take names such as Roosevelt or Edison (Forbush and Masseck 56) or Clara Barton, Dorothea Dix, or Louisa Alcott (Forbush, *Queens of Avalon* 12).

This notion of the legends as suitable to American youth was embedded in Forbush's understanding of the Arthurian material and of the clubs he founded. In *The Boys' Round Table*, the manual for the Knights of King Arthur, Forbush and his co-author Masseck noted that "Although the framework of the order is a monarchy, there is nothing dictatorial about its management" (18) and also that "the most cogent reason yet given for the roundness of the [i.e., Arthur's] table is that at a round table there is no head, and so there can be no jealousy. Thus we have, in a democracy under leadership, the ideal form of organization for boys" (29). The democratic and patriotic nature of the clubs was evident also in the two banners that each Castle was to have, "the Castle flag and the American flag" (Forbush and Forbush, *The Knights of King Arthur: How to Begin and What to Do* 7). And in his book on the *Queens of Avalon*, Forbush observed that those who are attracted by the poetry of legends such as those surrounding Avalon and dreams of places like Utopia and the New Atlantas (Forbush's spelling) "may even think it fair to place the real Avalon on the shores of the New World, toward which all such dreams have tended" (11).

Forbush's notion of Arthur's returning through his organization and of Avalon's being located on the shores of the New World may have been romantic enthusiasms, but in a very real sense Arthur, or at least the stories surrounding him, did indeed have a rebirth through the Knights of King Arthur and related groups. After all, some 130,000 youngsters – not to mention the Merlins and Ladies of the Lake guiding them – were taught to read and to dream about and to imitate in their daily lives the legends of Camelot.

Forbush's was not the only group to increase interest in the Arthurian tales and knowledge of the texts in which they were treated as a way of dealing with the boy problem in America. In *The Boys' Round Table*, Forbush and Masseck mentioned "several imitations" of their order and "a number of independent societies having the main features of our order . . . without acknowledgment to their parent organization" (18). One man, a minister named Perry Edwards Powell, founded a strikingly similar organization that he described in a book called *Knights of the Holy Grail: A Solution to the Boy Problem*. Though he claimed his "new order is original" and that it "evolved independently" (20), borrowing from Forbush is evident both in the title of his book and in the structure of the organization itself.[5]

Powell's Knights went through two of the three degrees that Forbush's did, Esquire and Knight, and were led by a Merlin. Like Forbush's Knights, Powell's clubs were designed to deal with the boy problem by channeling the "gang spirit" (20) and appealing to the "mystic, private, clannish, chivalrous, and . . . religious" instincts of boys (9). One of the few differences between the groups is that Powell's was a little more openly religious and so the Merlin was usually a pastor who was to be "in supreme charge and his will obeyed." Such authoritarianism might make the Knights of the Holy Grail appear less democratic and less well suited to an American setting, yet Powell looked to James Russell Lowell's very American poem *The Vision of Sir Launfal* as a model. Of the two poems that Powell believed set forth the story of the Grail "in epic measure," Tennyson's idyll "The Holy Grail" and Lowell's poem (15), he considered the latter to embody particularly American values: "The Britisher is aristocratic and can not free himself from his pedigree and environment. But the American voices all the traditions of his favored Republic, and we find Lowell's Sir Launfal a social Knight" (17). The co-importance of Galahad's chastity and Launfal's charity was emphasized in Powell's ritual of initiation into the order of knighthood, in which there were four lectures. The first was on confessing Christ before the world; the second was on chastity, for which Galahad was the model; and the third discussed charity, as exemplified by Launfal. In the fourth, on the Holy Grail, the candidate was told: "The Holy Grail is in the world to-day, and is in the

5   Powell even includes Forbush's *The Boy Problem* in a list of recommended readings for his Merlins (83).

Church as of old. Galahad saw it within the shrine at the holy altar, and there can you, in the Holy Supper of our Lord. Sir Launfal saw it in the sweet works of love and there you may ever behold it" (74). This final lecture was followed by a reading from Lowell's poem of the lines which state that the Holy Grail is the cup that Launfal filled at a stream for the leper who is actually Christ.

Powell's Knights of the Holy Grail seems to have remained relatively small and not to have achieved the national membership that Forbush's Knights or another similar organization called the Knighthood of Youth did. "Directed by the National Child Welfare Association and intended primarily for school children from 7 to 12 years old" (Haviland 36), the Knighthood of Youth program had enrolled "more than a hundred thousand boys and girls in various parts of the United States" (Williams 9) by 1930. And in 1934 the *New York Times* reported that there were "now 370,000 children enrolled in the 'Knighthood of Youth' clubs" ("370,000 in Child Clubs" 24:2).

The Knighthood of Youth was designed to provide moral training in a manner analogous to the training in health habits offered in the schools, that is by "a definite, concrete program which the child can pursue and by which he can measure his improvement"; but character training was also meant to "fire the imagination, and arouse the will power of the child at the habit-forming age" (Haviland 36). One of the principal ways of doing this was through stories of King Arthur and his knights. One book written "to captivate the imagination and hold the attention of every boy and girl reader in the upper elementary grades" at the same time that it aids and encourages "character building by giving the child an example . . . of the highest development of individuals" was a series of stories "based on Malory's *Morte d'Arthur* and the *Mabinogion*" (Hoben iii) called *Knights Old and New*. In an introduction to this book, John H. Finley observed that the author "has given careful consideration to the Knighthood [of Youth] program and has included text material and activities that make the volume especially useful for the pupils in schools that have adopted the program" (Hoben v).

Classes enrolled in the program devised codes of conduct and charts with questions about their behavior, such as "Did I knowingly break any law of the class code? Did I brush my teeth today, both night and morning? Did I meet difficulties or defeat in a sportsmanlike manner?" etc. A chart was labeled "A List of Daily Adventures" and each question was called either a "dragon" or an "adventure"; and the list was said to contain "reminders of the adventures which young knights may undertake" (Williams 9). In these and other ways, the moral and democratic concept of knighthood underlying the Knighthood of Youth was apparent. Though the children were told stories about King Arthur and his knights and about the crusaders, they also discussed men and women who might be considered "modern knights," people like Thomas Edison, who could be called "the *knight of electricity*," or Charles Lindbergh, "a *knight of the air*" (Williams 9).

To understand the impact of clubs such as the Knighthood of Youth, the Knights of King Arthur, and the Knights of the Holy Grail, one must imagine the members of these groups, nearly half a million in all, thinking of themselves and of those they admired – not only heroes like Edison or Lindbergh but also policemen, firemen, politicians, inventors, nurses, and the other common men and women who do their jobs well out of a sense of duty – as knights of the modern world. The concept of knighthood was thus absorbed into the popular culture and transformed from something attainable only by the nobility to a state expected of the moral youth or adult.

The scope and cultural significance of this transformation are evident in the literature that was influenced either specifically by the youth groups or generally by the notion of moral knighthood and that, in turn, was another way of spreading knowledge of the Arthurian legends in America. There were, for example, the rituals designed to initiate members into the various ranks of the respective organizations. Such rituals made use of Arthurian stories while being themselves a new form of Arthurian drama. In addition, plays and pageants were written specifically for the groups. In *The Boys' Round Table*, there is an advertisement for " 'The Young Knight, or How Gareth Won His Spurs,' a dramatization of Tennyson's 'Gareth and Lynette,' for castle use, by the Rev. James Yeames" (179). There must have been many other local productions. Forbush himself compiled a collection called *Songs of the Knights of King Arthur* that contained original verses intended to be sung to traditional tunes. And the Knighthood of Youth groups "wrote and encouraged others to write stories and poems relating to knighthood of all times" (Williams 10).

Many Arthurian works written about or for children also used notions of symbolic knighthood similar to those fostered by the youth groups. One novel called *The Gang of Six: A Story of the Boy Life of Today* (1906) is clearly an outgrowth of such clubs. In an introductory note the author, Horace M. Du Bose, refers to the three stages of childhood outlined by Forbush and others and even quotes Forbush on the "possibilities of danger or help" that the gang spirit presents (8). Du Bose's didactic novel is the story of Harry Wilmot, a young man who sets about to reform six street urchins by organizing them into a club modeled on the Round Table that meets in a cave they call a "castle."

In *The Gang of Six*, as in the groups formed by Forbush and Powell, Tennyson is an obvious influence. At one point, Wilmot warns his boys that "The tempter will come every day" and describes the statues in Arthur's palace "that showed beasts overcoming men; there were also statues showing men overcoming beasts; then there were statues showing men in armor with their swords in their hands; and above all, there were statues showing men with wings starting from their shoulders and with flames of fire on their brows. These were to show how men must fight to overcome evil, and after overcoming how they must continue to use the sword of truth to win the highest glory" (84). The descriptions of these statues are obvious paraphrases of the four zones of statuary in Camelot as described by Tennyson in the "Holy Grail" idyll:

> And four great zones of sculpture, set betwixt
> With many a mystic symbol, gird the hall;
> And in the lowest beasts are slaying men,
> And in the second men are slaying beasts,
> And on the third are warriors, perfect men,
> And on the fourth are men with growing wings .... (187)

What Du Bose omits, of course, is the statue of the nearly godlike king that Tennyson places "over all." Perhaps this omission indicates a deliberate avoidance of the monarchical setting of the British Arthurian stories. A similar democratizing of the legends seems to be at work elsewhere in the novel.

Almost as if he were following Forbush's injunction to his Merlins to inspire boys "with the poetry of the King Arthur Plan" (*The Knights of King Arthur: How to Begin* 4), Wilmot relates the story of Yarkin, "a shepherd boy who desired to become a knight" (42). After Yarkin tells Arthur that he was instructed in knighthood by the voice of one who claimed to be the sister of Purity and Faith, a voice he heard under a hawthorn tree, Arthur makes him a squire to Sir Christopher and changes his name to Hermas. Young Hermas then follows his lord for a year and a day, all the time learning obedience. He also serves the king by capturing two caitiff knights; and, for his faithful and obedient service, he is made a knight. But when Sir Hermas goes to the castle of Purity and Faith seeking the sister whose beautiful voice inspired him, he finds that there are just two daughters. The third, Obedience, only seemed to be a sister, for "how should Purity and Faith be without *Obedience*?" Hermas "had heard the voice of obedience calling him, and it was this obedience whom the squire had worthily loved and whom the knight had sought to woo. He could not be sad, therefore, because he had lost an unseen bride, but rejoiced because he had gained forever the favor of one whom he knew" (48).

The story is noteworthy because of the use of an Arthurian context to promote a virtue appropriate to young boys. But it is also significant that the hero of the story is a shepherd boy who becomes a knight. The shepherd boy is not, as it might turn out in a medieval romance, someone who is sired by a knight or nobleman and whose nobility is ultimately discovered. He is actually a commoner whose nobility is moral rather than hereditary. Thus Yarkin, who becomes Hermas, is a perfect model for the American urchins that Harry Wilmot is trying to rehabilitate and for other boys who will be inspired with the poetry of the Arthurian plan.

The symbolic interpretation of knighthood seen in *The Gang of Six* and indeed in all the clubs based on the Arthurian legends contributes to the

creation of thoroughly original uses of Arthurian material in works designed
to exemplify how the concept of knighthood can be utilized to instruct
children. This is not to say that tradition is wholly ignored, for the concept of
knighthood and often of a particular character or characters frequently
comes from earlier sources. Such is the case with Du Bose's view of the
stages of knighthood, which provide the moral framework for instruction
even though the novel is otherwise totally nontraditional.

Two didactic novels, each with the same title *Little Sir Galahad*, take a
similar approach. The earlier of the two (1904), by Lillian Holmes, is the
story of a crippled boy named David. David's friend Arthur Bryan plays at
being King Arthur (18) and laments to his mother that David cannot play
knight because of his disability. But Mrs. Bryan offers the example of
Galahad and quotes from Tennyson's poem "Sir Galahad": "My strength is
as the strength of ten, / Because my heart is pure." As in the vision of Sir
Launfal, the Grail that Holmes's little Sir Galahad can achieve is not a
material object but a spiritual quality. Mrs. Bryan says that the knights other
than Galahad "thought they were looking for the cup out of which Christ
drank at the Last Supper. What is really meant and what they wanted, was
the presence of Christ, their King" (22–23).

David proves his worthiness by doing good deeds such as not becoming
angry with a three-year-old who breaks his slate (27–28) and, after regaining
his ability to walk, by carrying books for a girl whose brothers unchivalrously make her carry their books as well as her own (35–36). When he
cheats in school and so fails to live up to the knightly code, David confesses
and then "instead of feeling like a coward, he again had the strength of ten,
because his heart was pure from dishonor" (34). Ultimately David recovers
his health and finds wealthy relatives who provide for his education and the
employment of his poor aunt, the woman who cared for him in his illness.
But "whenever he seems inclined to be exultant about his returning strength,
she reminds him of the better strength which the years of lameness taught
him" (64).

The second of the *Little Sir Galahad* novels was written by Phoebe Gray in
1914. As in Holmes's story, there is a strong didactic bent, one of the chief
messages being the dangers of alcohol. Also as in Holmes's story, the little Sir
Galahad of the title is crippled, a condition that occurred when his "jovially
stimulated" father dropped him. Charlie, the title character, is enrolled by a
young friend, Mary Alice Brown, in a group called the Galahad Knights.
Mary Alice is herself the victim of a father who beats her and her mother
when he drinks. And the young boy who founded the Galahad Knights,
Francis Willett, falls in with the wrong crowd at college and is expelled
because he gets drunk and steals a car. Having forgotten the ideals of the
group he founded, Francis loses his reputation and almost his life because of
alcohol.

It is Charlie who remains true to his quest and is dubbed "little Sir

Galahad" by the renowned doctor who saves Francis's life. The doctor finds Charlie's "fidelity to his quest for the Grail . . . infinitely fine and touching" and observes, in a sentiment reminiscent of the inspiration for the Arthurian clubs of Forbush and Powell, that "the development of these rare little souls is the vital problem of our country" (222). The doctor himself ultimately joins the Galahad Knights as reformed by Charlie and goes to help "the wounded, the suffering, the poverty-stricken people of prostrate Belgium," where he enlists soldiers for the organization (372–74).

The crippled son of a poor farmer can be the exemplar of Grail Knighthood because, as in the clubs and in much of the American Arthurian literature, knighthood is symbolic. Charlie himself defines that noble concept as it occurs in the novel: "Well, us fellers are pledged, just like Sir Galahad, to do everythin' to help and purtect folks that's weaker'n us. Our sword is Brotherly Love, and our shield is made of Faith, Courage, Symp'thy, and Willin'ness," and the Grail "stands for Perfect Manhood" and is "full of a dullicious drink, called Unselfishness" (193).

Symbolic notions of the Grail and of knighthood also play a part in a novel in the "Little Colonel" series by one of the most popular turn-of-the-century American authors of juvenile literature. In her epigraph (a passage from the novel [116]) to the tale of *Two Little Knights of Kentucky* (1899), Annie Fellows Johnston sets the tone for her Americanization of chivalry: "Knighthood has not passed away. The flower of Chivalry has blossomed anew in this New World, and America, too, has her 'Hall of the Shields.' "

The New-World chivalry is exemplified by Keith and Malcolm MacIntyre when they befriend a boy named Jonesy, who is abandoned by the tramp with whom he has been travelling. To raise money so Jonesy can stay in the care of a kindly but poor old professor, the two boys want to organize a benefit. Their Aunt Allison pleads with her mother, the boys' grandmother, to allow them to hold the benefit by pointing out that it is a way for them to learn the lesson of *The Vision of Sir Launfal* that what is important is "Not what we give, but what we share, / For the gift without the giver is bare." The grandmother agrees because she feels that "If this little beggar at the gate can teach them where to find the Holy Grail, through unselfish service to him, I do not want to stand in the way" (96–97). The benefit itself is to take the form of a pageant in which "the old days of chivalry" will live again through readings from *The Vision of Sir Launfal* and Tennyson's *Idylls*, accompanied by tableaux in which the children don the garb of knights and ladies.

The boys exhibit the New-World chivalry not by dressing up as knights but by performing an act of charity. The professor tells Keith that because of his good intentions, "thy shield will never be blank and bare. Already thou hast blazoned it with the beauty of a noble purpose, and like Galahad, thou too shalt find the Grail" (109). And when Keith says that if he and Malcolm could keep Jonesy from growing up to be a tramp, that would be "as good a deed as some the real knights did," their aunt calls them "my dear little Sir Galahads" (120–21). Later she tells them of Tennyson's Sir Galahad "whose strength was as the strength of ten because his heart was pure" (121). The symbolic nature of their knighthood is underscored when Aunt Allison gives the boys a badge of knighthood, a white enamel flower with a small diamond in the center. Though they "can't wear armour in these days," wearing "the white flower of a blameless life," like the badges Forbush's Knights of King Arthur wore, is meant to remind them that they "are pledged to right the wrong wherever you find it, in little things as well as great" (121–22).

In addition to the fact that two little boys with good hearts can be knights of the New World, the Americanization of knighthood is apparent in another way in *Two Little Knights of Kentucky*. When the boys, forgetting the chivalry they are supposed to represent, taunt their cousin Ginger because she cannot be a knight, she asserts that she can be a patriot, which is "lots better." Aunt Allison responds that "they ought to mean the same thing exactly in this day of the world" (222) and then gives Ginger a badge appropriate for the patriot knight, "a little flag whose red, white, and blue was made of tiny settings of garnets, sapphires, and diamonds." The flag is to be a reminder to her of the values espoused by the boys in the code they have adopted from Tennyson: "Live pure, speak truth, right the wrong, follow the king; else wherefore born?" Aunt Allison explains the connection between the American flag and modern knighthood: "there is the white for the first part, the 'live pure,' and the 'true blue' for the 'speak truth,' and then the red, – surely no soldier's little daughter needs to be told what that stands for, when her own brave father has spilled part of his good red life-blood to 'right the wrong' on the field of battle" (123).

The link between the American flag and knighthood strengthens the reading of another tale by Johnston as an Americanization of the concept of knighthood. In a short prose work called *Keeping Tryst: A Tale of King Arthur's Time* (1906), she tells the story of a page boy named Ederyn who asks a minstrel if it is possible for him to become a knight. Told that some win knighthood by slaying dragons or giants or by going on crusades, Ederyn is advised to "forget thy dreams of glory, and be content to serve thy squire. For what hast such as thou to do with great ambitions? They'd prove but flames to burn away thy daily peace" (8–9). A year later the minstrel returns to say that "there *is* a way for even such as thou to win the honours thou dost covet." The opportunity arises because Arthur wishes to establish "round him at his court a chosen circle whose fidelity hath stood the utmost test. Not deeds of prowess are required of these true followers, . . . but they must prove themselves trustworthy, until on hand and heart it may be graven large, '*In all things faithful*' " (12–14). Ederyn must undergo and pass a series of tests of his faithfulness by keeping tryst despite obstacles and temptations. Since he answers each call to keep tryst without neglecting his duty, first as a page and then as a squire, he is finally knighted by the king.

The notion that a young person becomes a knight of the Round Table because of moral integrity rather than prowess or nobility of birth is the very basis for the Arthurian clubs and for the symbolic knighthood in the other literature under discussion. Ederyn is much more like American knights from Sir Launfal to the Black Knight of the 1954 movie of that name than he is like the heroes of medieval romance. He is no dragonslayer or giant killer or crusader. Like the twentieth-century knight of whom Banks wrote, he does not have a splendid physique, and some "deeds of hardihood in which the old knights rejoice" are beyond his power; "but the higher deeds of the loftier chivalry, of upright thinking, of pure conduct, of self-denying devotion, are within his reach" (129). Johnston's message is that any person of character can possess this moral strength. And because it is not a condition of birth or wealth, it becomes an appropriate model for American youth and a means by which the hierarchical realms described by Malory and Tennyson can be made compatible with American ideals.

The model of moral knighthood that was influenced largely by Tennyson and adapted in the American Arthurian youth groups and in related popular literature was no doubt behind the interest in the latter part of the nineteenth century and the early twentieth century in retellings of the Arthurian legends for young people, especially young boys. Even before the youth groups boosted the readership for Arthurian stories, Sidney Lanier's *The Boy's King Arthur* had become popular. First published in 1880 with illustrations by Alfred Kappes, *The Boy's King Arthur* was reissued in 1917 with illustrations by N. C. Wyeth, a student of Howard Pyle (whose own retelling of the Arthurian stories in words and pictures is discussed below). For the first edition, Kappes provided a dozen illustrations; for the later edition, Wyeth provided fourteen, although only nine appear in some editions. (The 1917 reissue is pared down considerably, chiefly by the omission of the tale of Balin and other episodes.) Only two illustrations in the different editions treat the same subject (though in very different styles): Arthur receiving Excalibur from the Lady of the Lake and the final battle between Arthur and Mordred. Of the remaining illustrations, five of Wyeth's focus on Lancelot and three of Kappes's on the Grail story. Wyeth's color illustrations, however, form an intricate part of the book in a way that Kappes's black and white illustrations do not; and they have stirred the imaginations of generations of readers. How vividly they make the story come alive and how effective they are can be seen in the comments of one contemporary novelist who was influenced by them. In a letter dated February 14, 1987, Walker Percy noted that his novel *Lancelot* was inspired by Lanier's book and "most importantly [by] the marvellous illustrations – most especially the one of Lancelot bloodied up in his chain mail and leaning on his broadsword and saying to Sir Turquine, who has just said to him, what manner of man are

Figure 6. Sir Galahad is brought to the Siege Perilous in Alfred Kappes's illustration for the first edition of Sidney Lanier's *The Boy's King Arthur* (New York: Charles Scribner's Sons, 1880).

you to have fought me for hours: 'I am Sir Lancelot du Lake – ' etc. – plus the hand coming out of the misty lake holding Excalibur – plus the last: Mordred facing Arthur . . . in a battle to death in a bloodred sunset." Percy adds that his recollections are "60 years old and fallible" and even puts a question mark after the name "Wyeth," but obviously he remembers the illustrations very clearly.

The Boy's King Arthur is basically an abridged edition of Malory with modernized spelling. Lanier notes that, with the exception of words used to explain unfamiliar or archaic terms (like "hight" or "mickle") and connective passages to "preserve the thread of a story which could not be given entire," "every word in the book . . . is Malory's, unchanged except that the spelling is modernized" (1880 ed., xxii). Using Malory's words is not, however, the same as telling Malory's story.

As is common with retellings for young people, certain elements of the story are omitted or glossed over. Lanier comments in his introduction to another of his books for boys, *Knightly Legends of Wales or The Boy's Mabinogion*, that he has preserved the original narrative in all his books for boys, including *The Boy's King Arthur*, except where the narrative tends to slow and he needs to "hasten the long-lagging action" and where "the demands of modern reserve required excision" (xix). Uther's rape of Igraine, for example, has no place in an edifying tale, so Lanier's story begins with the birth of Arthur, who is delivered, without explanation, to Merlin. Other elements of sexual impropriety are similarly disregarded, and new explanations are created for matters that would otherwise require some tarnishing of the knights who are meant to be models for the young readers. For instance, Lanier obviously deems the true account of Launcelot's madness unsuitable. He does not want to relate the facts as described by Malory: that Lancelot has been deceived by Brisen's sorcery into sleeping with Elaine, as a result of which Guinevere thinks him unfaithful to his adulterous love for her; that Guinevere berates and banishes him from her presence; that the loss of her affection causes Lancelot's madness. To avoid the sordid details, Lanier concocts an excuse that makes the queen's anger seem a misunderstanding: "it happened that Queen Guenever was angered with Sir Launcelot, yet truly for no fault of his, but only because a certain enchantress had wrought that Sir Launcelot seemed to have shamed his knighthood" (1880 ed., 79). Elements of Malory's story are there – the enchantress, the queen's anger, her perception that Launcelot has shamed himself – but the explanation clearly makes it a no-fault situation: Launcelot is maligned through no failing of his own, and Guenever is not the jealous lover she appears to be in Malory but a queen rightly concerned with knightly honor. Later, when Guenever does not go to the tournament at Winchester, there is no suggestion that Launcelot wants to stay behind to be with her. She remains, and in the next paragraph Launcelot sets off for the tournament. Why he is so eager to fight disguised is not explicitly stated, but Lanier implies that Launcelot will win more honor this way. And when Elaine of Astolat inevitably dies from unrequited love, there is no scene in which Guenever expresses her jealous anger before the barge reaches Camelot.

The whole relationship between queen and knight and even the notion that their love is a contributing factor in the destruction of Arthur's kingdom are obscured. The way Lanier explains the final calamity is especially fascinating. He resorts to an explanatory footnote to the scene in which the queen is accused by Sir Mador of poisoning the apple that his cousin Sir Patrice eats at the queen's feast. Ultimately, Launcelot returns in time to fight for the queen and to prove that she is innocent. In Malory, this is one of three times that Lancelot fights for Guinevere. On the second occasion, he is only technically fighting for the truth. Accused by Meliagrant of sleeping with one of the wounded knights, the queen has in fact spent the night with Lancelot, who has cut his hand getting to her. When Lancelot fights to prove that Meliagrant's claim is false, he is technically correct. In the third instance, Lancelot must save the queen from the fire after she has been caught with him in her chamber. As Lanier begins the account of the incident with the poisoned apple, in which Guenever is falsely accused, he adds a note saying that "We have here the beginning of that series of quarrels which presently arrays Sir Gawaine and King Arthur (who with many protests allows himself to be guided by Sir Gawaine) on one side, against Queen Guenever and Sir Launcelot (who has taken the queen's part) on the other, and which ends with the great battle in which Arthur is slain and the Round Table broken up forever" (1880 ed., 307).

The second accusation of the queen is presented in innocuous terms. Lanier says only that Sir Meliagrance "appealed the queen of treason" (1880 ed., 349) – with no explanation of the specifics of the charge. Lancelot, of course, slays Sir Meliagrance and clears the name of the queen once again; and in Lanier's vague version of the events there is none of the uneasy feeling that Malory's readers must have felt because of the technicality on which the queen is found not guilty. When the queen is accused of treason at Camelot and is condemned to be burnt, Lanier's abridgement once again avoids the issue of adultery: "But ever in those days the enemies of Sir Launcelot and Queen Guenever lay in wait to do them harm, in especial Sir Mordred and Sir Agravaine. So it befell that the queen was again appealed of treason and was condemned to the fire while Sir Launcelot was away. But when Sir Launcelot heard thereof, he came suddenly with his kindred and attacked them that guarded about the queen whereas she stood at the stake about to be burnt" (359).

One could easily multiply the examples of Lanier's bowdlerizing of Malory's text.[6] In his account of Sir Gareth's adventures, Lanier omits the young knight's attempts at pre-marital sex; in the story of Tristram and Isolde, he obscures the true nature of the relationship between them; in the tale of Elaine of Astolat, he does not reveal the real reason why Launcelot cannot return her affection.

On the other hand, there is little or no attempt to downplay the violence of the Arthurian world. Gareth, for instance, is praised when he slays six thieves, one after another (1880 ed., 105–06). Many knights are also slain in the course of the book, and there are numerous examples of less than ethical or noble action, most taken directly from Malory and again indicating the selective censorship that Lanier practices. These include, to name just a few, Kay's mocking of Gareth and Lynet's scorning him; the throwing of turfs at the mad Launcelot by a group of young men; Mark's hostility towards and his eventual slaying of Tristram (which have even less motivation than in Malory's version of the story); and the slaying of Sir Lamorak by Gawaine and his brothers – again without the explanation of the brothers' hostility towards him, the fact that Lamorak had been the lover of their mother.

But these examples of uncourtly actions are balanced by numerous examples that are suitable models of behavior for the boys who are the book's intended audience. Gareth stoically endures Lynet's mockery and even uses it as a spur to his knightly valor: "all the missaying that ye missayed me furthered me in my battle, and caused me to think to show and

6 For a summary of some of the ways in which Lanier avoids unwholesome elements in Malory and the sources of his other books for boys, see Starke 382–84.

prove myself at the end what I was" (1880 ed., 115). Sir Tristram asks mercy for his stepmother even though she tried to poison him. He also selflessly asks for the hand of the woman he loves for his uncle King Mark. Sir Launcelot does numerous chivalrous deeds, not the least of which are his miraculous healing of Sir Urre[7] and his refusal to let Bors slay King Arthur, even though the king has ravaged Launcelot's lands and besieged his castle. And of course, Galahad achieves the Holy Grail through his piety and devotion.

It is noble deeds such as these that make the Arthurian stories as retold by Lanier a model for young boys to emulate. Lanier offered a typically American comment on this aspect of the book in his introduction:

> No book ever needed less pointing-out of its intrinsic faults and beauties than this frank work of a soul so transparent that one is made to think of the Wakulla Spring in Florida where one can see a penny on the bottom at a hundred feet depth. I will but ask you to observe specially the majestic manhood of Sir Launcelot during those dolorous last days when King Arthur, under the frenzied advice of Sir Gawaine, brings two great armies in succession to besiege Joyous Gard. Day after day Gawaine, and sometimes Arthur, call out the vilest taunts and dares and accusations over the walls; but ever Sir Launcelot, though urged even by his own indignant followers within, replies with a grave and lordly reasonableness which shames his enemies beyond measure: twice he fights a great single-handed battle with Sir Gawaine, and, although Gawaine is miraculously helped, wounds him sorely, yet spares his life; he charges his knights to be still loyal to King Arthur, and to do the king no hurt, upon pain of death; and one day in a general engagement when King Arthur is unhorsed Sir Launcelot himself flies to the rescue, places the king on horseback again, and sees him safe, with perfect tenderness and loyalty. Larger behavior is not shown us anywhere in English literature. (xxi)

Launcelot's large or greatly generous and chivalric behavior is precisely the point of the story for Lanier. It is a lesson in how one should act in times of adversity. It is an example of a great spirit, which is precisely why writers like Lanier and others concerned with educating youth, like Forbush, turned to the Arthurian legends as a way of teaching youngsters how to conduct themselves. In fact, Lanier seems to have seen the world of Malory's *Morte d'Arthur* as singularly exemplary and instructive. In his introduction to *Knightly Legends of Wales or The Boy's Mabinogion*, Lanier contrasts the world

---

7   It is curious that the healing of Sir Urre is not included in the 1917 edition of *The Boy's King Arthur*. Perhaps as the narratives were tightened, this tale, which is of tremendous significance in Malory's portrayal of Lancelot as his hero, seemed less important to the straightforward development of the events that is presented particularly in the 1917 edition. It may also be that the near-saintly action made Lancelot seem almost otherworldly and therefore inappropriate as a model for young boys to imitate.

of the Welsh tales with that of Malory: "If we compare these [the wild tales of the *Mabinogion*] with the wildest flights in Malory's *King Arthur*, nothing can be clearer than the constant presence in the latter of a certain reasonable restraint, a sober proportion, a sense of the supreme value of law, even in the most apparently lawless excursions" (x–xi). The suggestion seems to be that even when Malory is describing reprehensible acts, there is a value system at work that makes it obvious that those acts are indeed reprehensible; therefore even those stories that describe wickedness are instructive.

Lanier may have had a Southerner's interest in the chivalric and the courtly. Surely the chivalric code appealed to his southern temperament, just as it did later for writers like William Faulkner and Walker Percy. As Jack De Bellis has noted, early in his career Lanier "would turn to a general tradition so rife in the South on which to harness his effulgent Romantic inclinations – the chivalric tradition, or what Mark Twain called 'Sir Walter Scottism.' It offered the young poet ready models in diction, setting, symbolism, and, most importantly, morality" (32). But it is also apparent that *The Boy's King Arthur* shares with many other American works the transformation of knighthood into something that may be imitated by anyone because it is, for these writers, based on moral rather than social qualities. How fully a part of this tradition Lanier is can be seen in a passage that he added to Malory. Although he has said that his only additions to Malory's text are explanatory words or connective passages, both of which are put into brackets, Lanier inserts an original passage into his text. Ostensibly addressed to "mighty and pompous lords" and "fierce and mighty knights," it is actually addressed to the boys who, the title of the volume makes clear, are the readers of the book. The passage is significant because it marks Lanier's book as being in the tradition of those writers who see the moral aspects of knighthood and the Arthurian realm as the truly important ones – and the ones that make the story applicable to Americans. He, or more precisely his narrative voice, says that it seems to him that "this present book is right necessary often to be read, for in it shall ye find the most gracious, knightly, and virtuous war of the most noble knights of the world, whereby they gat praising continually. Also me seemeth, by the oft reading thereof, ye shall greatly desire to accustom yourself in following of those gracious knightly deeds, that is to say, to dread God, and to love righteousness, faithfully and courageously to serve your sovereign prince; and the more that God hath given you the triumphal honor, the meeker ye ought to be, ever fearing the unstableness of this deceitful world" (1880 ed., 398–99).

Of even more significance than Lanier to the American Arthurian tradition is Howard Pyle (1853–1911). Recognized as one of the greatest illustrators America has produced, Pyle was well known in his day as an illustrator of articles on American history for magazines such as *Scribner's* and *Harper's*, and he made his reputation as an illustrator and writer of children's books with his version of the story of Robin Hood (1883). Moreover, he was prolific, illustrating more than 400 magazine articles or stories (nearly half of which he wrote himself), writing and illustrating more than twenty books, and contributing illustrations to more than a hundred books by other authors.[8]

No less a figure than N. C. Wyeth (writing in the Introduction to Charles D. Abbott's *Howard Pyle: A Chronicle*) felt that among all this work "the pen drawings which adorn the pages of the Arthurian legends" are "Pyle's most important contribution to the world of art." In four books that he wrote and illustrated, Pyle retold the Arthurian stories from Arthur's birth to his death: *The Story of King Arthur and His Knights* (1903), *The Story of the Champions of the Round Table* (1905), *The Story of Sir Launcelot and His Companions* (1907), and *The Story of the Grail and the Passing of Arthur* (1910). (He also illustrated an 1881 edition of Tennyson's "Lady of Shalott." This early attempt at color illustration was not to Pyle's liking, although the book as a whole is quite beautiful.)

Pyle's tetralogy has in common with Lanier's book the fact that it is a version of the Arthurian legends for children, that it is based primarily on Malory, and that it is illustrated; but the similarities do not extend beyond these superficial points. Perhaps the most important difference is that Pyle makes no attempt to derive every word of his text (and thus the subject of every illustration) from Malory. What Pyle did with Malory (and his other sources) may best be understood by means of an analogy to his philosophy of teaching art. Henry Pitz records that Pyle "introduced his students to the posing model in this way: 'Here is your model – make a picture of him! You will have to scrutinize him sharply to find his proportions, how his weight is supported, how each joint is functioning. Watch for the presence of the body under the clothes, how the folds and wrinkles tell the story. Look for the color and tone and texture of the garments. See how the light falls on the figure especially on the face. But above all, this is an opportunity to make a picture – a picture more than a copy!' " (Pitz 134). In a letter dated June 22, 1905, to W. M. R. French of the Chicago Art Institute, Pyle expands on this philosophy:

> suppose an artist were called upon to paint a picture of a man running away from his enemies along the shores of a sea, with a gray sky overhead, and a strong wind blowing over the landscape. You see, he could not pose a model in the required position, for not only could no model hold such a position as that of a man running, with a center of gravity projected far beyond the point of impact; but even if the model were suspended in the air in such a position, yet he would not convey the idea of running. Apart from this it would be very difficult to find exactly the seascape to fit the

8   For a complete listing, see the bibliography in Henry C. Pitz's study, *Howard Pyle: Writer, Illustrator, Founder of the Brandywine School.*

picture, and exactly the landscape. For all this, the man must draw, not upon the facts of nature, but upon his imagination.

If I have expressed myself at all clearly, you will see that what a man needs to paint an imaginative picture of such a sort, is not the power of imitation, but the knowledge to draw a figure from imagination. (Quoted in Abbott 225–26)

These statements, the latter of which seems couched in terms of the typical conflict between a classical and a romantic theory of art, help to explain his handling of the Arthurian legends. Just as an artist must begin with but go beyond his model to make a picture that is more than just a copy, must add imagination to the technical skill of the imitator, so Pyle in approaching the Arthurian legends went beyond his model.

Unlike Lanier, who edited Malory with a good deal of abridging and bowdlerizing, Pyle was not an editor. Nor was he even a reteller in the sense of one who merely simplifies an old story for young readers. Pyle created a new version of the legends, a version clearly intended for children, but one that does not patronize them (though it often preached to them). He took the basic form from Malory but changed it to suit his purposes, combined material from other sources, and added scenes and characters from his own imagination – much as Malory and the other great interpreters of the Arthurian legends had done before him. This is not to suggest that Pyle is on a par with such figures as Malory or Tennyson or that the quality of his written work compares to theirs. He is, after all, writing with a different purpose and for a different audience. But his approach to the Arthurian legends is essentially the same as theirs.

While Malory is his primary model, Pyle also borrows from the *Mabinogion*, from some French versions of the legends, and probably from ballad material. And he goes beyond all of his models in several ways. Perhaps the most obvious, and yet also the most skillful, way is by the interplay of text and illustrations.[9] This interplay takes several forms. In many instances the visual and the literary are complementary. This is obvious in the treatment of the characters, of whom there is generally very little description. Of Mordred, for example, Pyle writes that "he hath ever had a dark and gloomy spirit" (*The Story of the Grail* [hereafter *Grail*] 218). But we get no extended description of his appearance. There is, however, a depiction of Mordred that captures his evil nature (*Grail* 222). Pyle uses such portraits – thirty-one of them in all – throughout his tetralogy as a means of describing the major characters and some of the minor ones, including Arthur, Guinevere, Launcelot, Merlin, Gawain, Galahad, Elaine, Tristram and Isoult. (There are

---

9   Lucien L. Agosta, in the preface to his book *Howard Pyle*, mentions the "interdependence of text and illustration" in Pyle's Arthurian books, but in his discussion of those books he does not analyze the nature of that interdependence.

ten portraits in the first book, nine in the second, eight in the third, and four in the fourth.)

Another way in which Pyle uses text and illustrations to complement one another is in the presentation of natural description. In the illustration titled "Sir Mellegrans Interrupts the Sport of the Queen" (*The Story of Sir Launcelot* [hereafter *Launcelot*] 2), for example, Guinevere and her attendants are seen on a grassy plain with a few flowers on the ground; but the image conveys little sense of the springtime beauty that led to the maying party. Such description is reserved for the text:

> So when the next morning was come they all rode forth in the freshness of dewy spring-tide; what time the birds were singing so joyously, so joyously, from every hedge and coppice; what time the soft wind was blowing great white clouds, slow sailing across the canopy of heaven, each cloud casting a soft and darkling shadow that moved across the hills and uplands as it swam the light blue heaven above; what time all the trees and hedgerows were abloom with fragrant and dewy blossoms, and fields and meadow-lands, all shining bright with dew, were spread over with a wonderful carpet of pretty flowers, gladdening the eye with their charm and making fragrant the breeze that blew across the smooth and grassy plain. (*Launcelot* 4)

The dew, the clouds, the birds – all are absent from the illustration.

Later in the same book, as Percival and Ector seek Launcelot, they approach the island where he is residing with Elaine and are amazed by the beauty of the scene before them, which is described in great detail (see *Launcelot* 281). The illustration titled "Sir Percival and Sir Ector Look upon the Isle of Joy" (278) shows little of this detail. The written description adds color and a degree of specificity to the black and white of the drawing, in which one cannot find the daffodils or even the long grass of which Pyle writes.

This emphasis on the natural world, indicative of Pyle's basically romantic approach to the Arthurian legends, is also an essential element in the picture-beyond-the-model that he creates. After another lengthy description of natural beauty in *The Story of Sir Launcelot and His Companions*, Pyle comments on his own inclination to dwell on such scenes: "All this Sir Percival and Sir Sagramore beheld and they took such joy in it that so I cannot forbear to tell you of it as I have done because of the joy that I also take in what they beheld. Wherefore I pray you to forgive me if I have recounted more of those things than need be, who am writing a history of chivalry and of knightly daring" (265).

But of course Pyle is doing more than writing a history of chivalry. He is providing a model for behavior and in the process Americanizing – or at least democratizing – the medieval legends. The apology for extended natural description is a literary device, as insincere as Chaucer's apology for the vulgarity of his pilgrims. It is actually Pyle's way of linking himself to the knights and presumably to his readers, who cannot help but be drawn into the story by those descriptions that offer some of the best writing in the four Arthurian books.

Just as Pyle and his readers are like Percival and Sagramore in their love of nature, so too can they be like the other great knights and even King Arthur himself if they live the right way. In fact, a pattern of moralizing, particularly strong in the first of Pyle's Arthurian books, suggests that anyone can achieve the moral equivalent of knighthood or kinghood. The spirit of these comments is reminiscent of James Russell Lowell's *The Vision of Sir Launfal*, in which Launfal learns that the Grail is not some precious object that is found by searching distant places. Rather, it is in his own castle – indeed, in his own heart. It exists in the spirit of charity that prompts him to share lovingly with those in need and, as such, it is obtainable by any man.

Moreover, in Pyle's version, it is not the Grail but nobility itself that is democratized. Early in *The Story of King Arthur*, just after Arthur has drawn the sword from the anvil, Pyle writes: "Thus Arthur achieved the adventure of the sword that day and entered into his birthright of royalty. Wherefore, may God grant His Grace unto you all that ye too may likewise succeed in your undertakings. For any man may be a king in that life in which he is placed if so he may draw forth the sword of success from out of the iron of circumstance. Wherefore when your time of assay cometh, I do hope it may be with you as it was with Arthur that day, and that ye too may achieve success with entire satisfaction unto yourself and to your great glory and perfect happiness" (35). Later, when Arthur, acting as the champion of Leodegrance of Cameliard, defeats the Duke of Umber and then rides off without waiting for the gratitude of the king or his people, Pyle notes that:

> When a man is a king among men, as was King Arthur, then is he of such a calm and equal temper that neither victory nor defeat may cause him to become either unduly exalted in his own opinion or so troubled in spirit as to be altogether cast-down into despair. So if you would become like to King Arthur, then you shall take all your triumphs as he took this victory, for you will not be turned aside from your final purposes by the great applause that many men may give you, but you will first finish your work that you have set yourself to perform, ere you give yourself ease to sit you down and to enjoy the fruits of your victory.
>
> Yea, he who is a true king of men, will not say to himself, "Lo! I am worthy to be crowned with laurels;" but rather will he say to himself, "What more is there that I may do to make the world the better because of my endeavors?" (97–98)

The conclusion to the final adventure in *The Story of King Arthur*, a retelling of the story of Gawaine and the loathly lady, provides a similar link between the reader and the inhabitants of Camelot. Pyle advises: "when you shall have become entirely wedded unto your duty, then shall you become equally worthy with that good knight and gentleman Sir Gawaine; for it needs not that a man shall wear armor for to be a true knight, but only that he shall do his best endeavor with all patience and humility as it hath been ordained for him to do. Wherefore, when your time cometh unto you to display your knightness by assuming your duty, I do pray that you also may approve yourself as worthy as Sir Gawaine approved himself in this story which I have told you of as above written" (312).

Pyle's interest in things American and in creating an American art is well attested. Even his obituary in the *New York Times* (Friday, 10 Nov. 1911: 11) commented on his "intense Americanism." A frequent illustrator of American historical scenes, Pyle even rewrote the story of Christ's crucifixion in an American setting – in the novel *Rejected of Men*, which tried to imitate the realistic style of William Dean Howells and which (though written earlier) was published in 1903, the same year as Pyle's first Arthurian book. While it may therefore seem unusual that Pyle chose to write four books based on the Arthurian legends, Lucien Agosta points out the contradiction: "A determined advocate of all things American, Pyle ironically chose to feature European folk heroes like Robin Hood and King Arthur in his most ambitious works for children, even at a time when America was claiming or creating its own native folk heroes such as Daniel Boone, Davy Crockett, Pecos Bill, Slue-foot Sue, and Paul Bunyan" (19).

But, as the passages quoted above demonstrate, if the heroes are not American, at least the manner in which they are treated is wholly consistent with Pyle's Americanism. Arthur and his knights are not ideals from another time and place for which there are no parallels in the modern world; they are examples of certain virtues that can be translated into the modern world, as Pyle translates the story of the crucifixion. But the translation is to be accomplished by the reader in his or her personal life, not by the writer.

This democratization, the notion that it is not the armor that makes the knight but rather his virtuous and dutiful action, is supported in a number of ways by the illustrations and the text of Pyle's tetralogy. The very code of Arthur's knights and the manner in which it is presented emphasize Pyle's ideal. Pellias, riding towards Ettard's castle with her maiden, Parcenet, comes upon a haggard old woman who asks the knight to take her across a river on his horse. Parcenet scolds the hag, saying "Who art thou to ask this noble knight for to do thee such a service as that?" But Pellias is displeased with Parcenet, not with the hag. He says to her: "Damsel, thou dost not speak properly in this matter, for that which beseemeth a true knight is to give succor unto anyone soever who needeth his aid. For King Arthur is the perfect looking-glass of knighthood, and he hath taught his knights to give succor unto all who ask succor of them, without regarding their condition" (*King Arthur* 210). The code formulated by Arthur in Malory does not go

nearly so far. It advises the knights to avoid murder and treason and other
excesses and to give mercy to knights who request it and to succor ladies,
damsels, gentlewomen, and widows (see Vinaver's 2nd edition, p. 75). But it
says nothing of withered hags with eyes red with "rheum," cheeks and chin
covered with "bristles," and face with a "multitude of wrinkles" (*King Arthur*
210). The fact that the hag turns out to be the Lady of the Lake in disguise
and that she rewards and later assists Pellias does not diminish the force or
the sincerity of the principle that he espouses.

Pyle's democratization of the legends takes other forms as well. He tells a
number of tales in which knights take on the duties or the appearance of
the lower classes or associate with them; and he introduces characters from
the lower classes into both his text and his illustrations. Pyle treats some of
the well-known stories, such as Gareth's working as a kitchen servant and
Launcelot's riding in the cart; but he gives these two stories prominence –
and he seems to associate them – by making them the first and second tales
in *The Story of Sir Launcelot and His Companions*. It is especially interesting
that Launcelot responds to the jeers of those who think it unseemly for a
knight to ride in a cart by saying that "the adventure which I have undertaken just now to perform is in itself so worthy that it will make worthy any
man who may undertake it, no matter how he may ride to that adventure"
(*Launcelot* 21). Launcelot's statement echoes the notion that one does not
need armor to be noble. The chivalrous act itself defines nobility – not the
trappings of chivalry, the horse and armor that made knighthood a matter of
class because only the wealthy could afford them.

Pyle adds to the model these traditional stories provide by recounting a
tale in *The Story of King Arthur* about how Arthur won Guinevere as his
queen. Pyle says specifically that the addition is his own, that he does not
think "the whole story of those adventures by the which King Arthur won
her good favor hath ever yet been told" (*King Arthur* 77). In his version of the
wooing, Arthur disguises himself as a gardener's boy so he can be close to
Guinevere and observe her. In the course of the story Guinevere makes four
knights serve a meal to the disguised king, a scene that Pyle emphasizes by
illustrating (*King Arthur* 112). Naturally, Arthur's royalty saves him from
retribution by both the gardener and the knights; but the lesson once again
seems to be that a person's worth cannot be judged by what he wears – the
symbolic equivalent of the statement that it is not the armor that makes for
nobility.

Of course, the characters in these stories are knights or even the king
himself. The model on which Pyle draws – the medieval versions of the
Arthurian legends – has certain conventions. But it does not demand that so
much emphasis be given to stories about noblemen disguised as peasants. Nor
does it demand that the illustrations give prominence to the owner of the cart
that Launcelot rides in, that they portray the minstrels Launcelot dines with as
he rides errant (in *Launcelot* 18 and 106) or the king's physicians (in *Grail* 58),

or that Lamorak be seen as a swineherd and Launcelot as a madman un-
horsing Kay, with an audience of peasants (*The Story of the Champions of the
Round Table* [hereafter *Champions*] 208 and 230). These pictures of Lamorak
and Launcelot and the stories they illustrate offer two more dramatic repre-
sentations of the notion that nobility does not reside in the trappings of
knighthood and give further indications of how Pyle goes beyond his
models to create a new picture of the Arthurian world.

Another of Pyle's innovations is his treatment of the relationship between
Launcelot and Guinevere. While some redactors, like Lanier, gloss over the
affair in order to make their tales suitable for children, Pyle does not avoid
the issue but chooses to see it in the best possible light. He says: "I am aware
that there have been many scandalous things said concerning that friendship, but I do not choose to believe any such evil sayings. Yet though it is not
to be denied that Sir Launcelot never had for his lady any other dame than
the Lady Guinevere, still no one hath ever said with truth that she regarded
Sir Launcelot otherwise than as her very dear friend. For Sir Launcelot
always avouched with his knightly word, unto the last day of his life, that
the Lady Guinevere was noble and worthy in all ways, wherefore I choose
to believe his knightly word and to hold that what he said was true"
(*Champions* 23). Pyle even uses the beauties of nature as an excuse for
Launcelot's lack of desire to serve any other woman but Guinevere. Pyle
explains that when Launcelot emerged from the realm of the Lady of the
Lake, who raised him, into the real world, it seemed wonderful. As he says,
"methinks that I love every blade of grass upon the fields, and every leaf
upon every tree; and that I love everything that creepeth or that flyeth, so
that when I am abroad under the sky and behold these things about me I am
whiles like to weep for very joy of them. . . . meseems that because of my joy
in these things I have no room in my heart for such a love of lady as thou
speakest of, but only for the love of knight-errantry, and a great wish to
make this world in which I now live the better and the happier for my
dwelling in it" (*Champions* 59).

As Pyle's treatment of Launcelot and Guinevere develops, however, he is
forced – perhaps by his plot as much as anything else – to create a relationship, though not a sexual one, between the two. Launcelot does have another
dame for his lady, that is, Elaine, who is a combination of the two Elaines
from Malory. But while the queen's champion marries Elaine, he is ever
drawn to Guinevere. After he and his wife return to court, Elaine is soon sent
away by Guinevere, at whose command Launcelot remains behind even
though Elaine is "in exceeding tender health" (*Launcelot* 307). Some time
afterwards, Elaine gives birth to Galahad and dies. Even after Mordred and
Agravaine trick Launcelot into visiting Guinevere's chamber, Pyle insists that
"the Queen was ever as honorable and as pure as she had been when first
she came to Camelot." There is, however, a kind of fatal attraction at work.
Guinevere is "fascinated" by Launcelot's having come from the lake and by

Figure 7. Howard Pyle's depiction of Launcelot's decorous service to Queen Guinevere. From *The Story of the Champions of the Round Table* (New York: Charles Scribner's Sons, 1905).

his greatness as a knight (*Grail* 185). And Launcelot is ever torn between his duty and his love (though Pyle does not call it that) for Guinevere: "his soul was dragged this way and that way. And whether he had gone away from the court or whether he had stayed as he did, in either case he would have been most unhappy. Yet to his present unhappiness was added many pangs like to the pangs of remorse. For he could not tell whether he did altogether ill or somewhat well in remaining at the King's court as he did" (*Launcelot* 308).

Perhaps even this flaw in Launcelot is meant to be part of the pattern of democratization of knighthood. It is the human failing that helps the reader identify with the great hero and allows him or her to hope to imitate Launce-lot's virtues. This seems to be the point Pyle is making when, in the preface to *The Story of the Champions of the Round Table*, he writes:

> if Sir Launcelot of the Lake failed now and then in his behavior, who is there in the world shall say, 'I never fell into error'? And if he more than once offended, who is there shall have hardihood to say, 'I never com-mitted offence'?
>
> Yea, that which maketh Launcelot so singularly dear to all the world, is that he was not different from other men, but like other men, both in his virtues and his shortcomings; only that he was more strong and more brave and more untiring than those of us who are his brethren, both in our endeavors and in our failures. (vi)

Perhaps Pyle finds in Launcelot the same quality that Steinbeck commented on in one of his letters. Steinbeck writes that a novelist puts himself into each of his characters but that there is always one who can be called a self-character or a spokesman for the author (even when that character is not the narrator). He continues: "Now it seems to me that Malory's self-character would be Lancelot. All of the perfections he knew went into this character, all of the things of which he thought himself capable. But, being an honest man he found faults in himself, faults of vanity, faults of violence, faults of dis-loyalty, and these would naturally find their way into his dream character" (*Acts* 304). Yet for Pyle the flawed perfection provides not (or not only) an expression of the author's honest ideal but rather an example for the reader, not a saint or even a perfect knight, but a human being striving for excel-lence, someone that each of us is or can be like.

The notion of flawed perfection plays a vital part in Pyle's vision of the Arthurian world. Pyle, like other American writers such as Twain and Robinson, employs the Arthurian legends as a vehicle for the Edenic theme so common in American literature. One critic has suggested that "In his Arthuriad Pyle repeatedly demonstrates, especially in his treatment of Launcelot, the dangers of attempting to remain in the youthful Arcadian realm of freedom from adult responsibilities . . ." (Agosta 24). But it is not quite as simple as that. Launcelot, after all, wants to make the world better, a desire that implies the world is imperfect. And yet the desire for perfection is enhanced by the beauties of the natural world that provide intimations of Eden. In one of those frequent passages commenting on the beauties of nature, Pyle observes that in the fall:

> when you look into the cold blue shadows of the wayside bank, there you behold everywhere the sparkling of many myriads of bright points of light where the thin frosts catch the shining of the early and yet slanting sun. Then do the birds cry with a wilder note as though heralding the approach of dreary winter. Then do the squirrels gambol in the dry, dead foliage in search of their winter store of food. Then is all the world clad very gloriously in russet and gold, and when the bright and jolly sun shines down through the thin yellow leaves of the woodland, all the earth appears to be illuminated with a wonderful splendor of golden light, so that it may be that even the glory of Paradise is not more wonderful than that unusual radiance. (*Launcelot* 311–12)

To be sure, the garden of this world is one with a serpent – perhaps many serpents – in it. Yet there are numerous images of light in Pyle's Arthurian books. These images are concentrated most heavily in the last two-thirds of the fourth book, the parts that tell the story of the Grail and the fall of Arthur. The radiant light of the Grail (reflected in picture as well as text – cf. *Grail* 100) is but another symbol for the perfection that can be envisioned. But the light is counterbalanced by darkness – the darkness of Mordred's soul and of the tragic passing of Arthur (a darkness that Pyle also represents visually [cf. *Grail* 222 and 236]). Even Arthur's dream of his fall is presented in terms of light and dark. When he is on top of the Wheel of Fortune, "he beheld the sun shining in all his glory." But the wheel soon begins to descend "below the rim of the world, and so the sunlight had left the King." At its lowest point there is a large pool "filled with blackness and with blood, and behold there was no bottom to that pool" (*Grail* 228–29). Pyle gets the image of the Wheel of Fortune from Malory. Even the dark water – in Malory, it is "an hydeous depe blak watir" filled with serpents and dragons and hideous wild beasts – comes from the *Morte d'Arthur* (3: 1233). But in Malory's description there is no mention of the sun that Pyle emphasizes. For Pyle, that sun recalls the Paradisal sun that gladdens the knights of the Arthurian world as much as it gladdens Pyle himself.

The fall that is foreshadowed by such light and dark imagery is caused by Mordred's evil and by Launcelot's flaw. And yet, Pyle's optimistic and romantic view of the Arthurian world (and the modern world that it stands for) does not allow him to leave Launcelot or Guinevere in the darkness of that fallen world. Launcelot and some of his followers become hermits and, Pyle says, "they dwelt in great peace and concord. And they disturbed none of those things that were living within the forest, so that the wild creatures of the forest presently grew tame to them. For they could lay their hands upon the haunches of the wild doe of the forest and it would not flee away from them, for the wild thing wist that they meant it no harm" (*Grail* 253). Though Guinevere does not share this idyllic existence with him, she too leads a holy life, and the final vision of her places her in a Paradisal light, which is the culmination of the images of light throughout the tetralogy. When she dies, Launcelot dreams that he sees her "standing before him, and her face smiled and was very radiant as though a bright light shone through her face from behind. For her face was translated by that light so that it was all of a glorious and rosy pink in its color. And the Queen was clad all in a very straight robe of cloth of gold and that robe shone with a very singular lustre. And around her neck and her arms were many ornaments of gold and these also shone and glittered as she moved or breathed" (*Grail* 253). It is interesting that, once again, Pyle adds details to Malory's account. In the *Morte d'Arthur*, Lancelot becomes a hermit, but there is no mention of the Edenic detail of the tame beasts; and Malory's vision of Guinevere's death contains none of the images of light that Pyle uses. For Pyle, even the prediction of Arthur's return, which according to tradition will be at a time of great need for the people of Britain, is a sign of the return of a golden age. There is, however, none of Malory's ambiguity about the return of Arthur. The king lies in Avalon, which Pyle describes in terms that seem a cross between Lerner and Loewe's description of Camelot and a Renaissance Arcadia:

> There in that pleasant country is no snow and no ice; neither is there the scorching heats and droughts of summer, but all forever and for aye is the tepid warmth of vernal springtime.
>   And the people of Avalon are always happy, for never do they weep and never do they bear enmity to one another, but all live in peace and tranquillity [sic] watching their flocks, which are as white as snow, and their herds, whose breath smelleth of wild thyme and parsley. (*Grail* 246)

The pattern of democratizing the Arthurian legend continues even to the point of Arthur's return when "all shall be peace and concord amongst men." Everyone can play a part in that return by living "at peace with other men" and wishing them well and doing them well: "then will King Arthur awake from his sleep." Pyle sees this time as "nigh at hand" because "less and less is there war within the world, and more and more is there peace and concord and good will amongst men" (*Grail* 246).

In the preface to the fourth of his Arthurian books, Pyle says that he has adapted the Arthurian legends "from the ancient style in which they were first written so as to fit them to the taste of those who read them to-day" (*Grail* viii). At first, this seems a strange remark. Pyle, after all, uses an unvaryingly archaic style in retelling the tales. Medieval words appear frequently without even the parenthetical explanations that Lanier provides; and the illustrations are conscious imitations of Dürer, perhaps a deliberate device to make the visual style coincide with the textual. So it seems appropriate to raise the question: in what sense have they been adapted to the taste of young Americans? The answer must lie in the optimistic, romantic, and democratic nature of Pyle's treatment. By instilling the legends with an early-twentieth-century optimism expressed through the images of an Edenic world that seem to speak to American dreamers in every century, and especially by providing direct and indirect examples of how young people of the time could be like the knights of Arthur's court and even like Arthur himself, Pyle has gone beyond his models and transformed the legends of Camelot into a story that reflects and speaks to his own age.

4

From Twain to the Twenties

The period from Twain to the twenties was a very active time in the development of the American Arthurian tradition. Arthurian youth groups were founded, reached their peak, and influenced the production of some classics of Arthurian literature for the young. But many other things were also occurring, under the influence both of Twain and of the literary and scholarly trends in America and in Europe.

Whereas the movement towards realism in American literature was reflected in Twain's novels, Twain himself was an impetus towards the realistic treatment of Arthurian material by Americans. His approach not only allowed for parody but also suggested possibilities for less romantic treatments of the Arthurian stories than Tennyson's. Consequently, new attitudes towards some of the characters and new interpretations of some of the events of the legends appeared in the works of poets, dramatists, and novelists. The scholarly interest in medieval texts also began to send out shock waves that could be felt in the world of creative writers. The work of certain scholars, like Joseph Bédier, who explored the Tristan legend, and Jessie Weston, who studied the myths of the Grail and the wasteland, provided inspiration for American as well as European writers and influenced contemporary poetry and drama. And finally, much of the period's best Arthurian fiction and poetry was written by authors who were themselves scholars of medieval literature.

The influence of medieval scholarship is obvious in William H. Babcock's *Cian of the Chariots* (1898), a book that is of particular interest because it is the first American historical novel to deal with the Arthurian legends. The novel's long subtitle – *A Romance of the Days of Arthur Emperor of Britain and His Knights of the Round Table, How They Delivered London and Overthrew the Saxons after the Downfall of Roman Britain* – gives some idea of the author's subject matter and approach. Like more recent historical novels, *Cian of the Chariots* attempts to capture the chaos and the intrigues that resulted from the Roman withdrawal from Britain, the subsequent Anglo-Saxon invasions, and the conflicts between Christian and pagan religions as well as among Romano-British, Celtic, and Saxon cultures.

Babcock takes the name of his title character from Nennius, who included Cian among such figures as "Neirin, et Talliessin" as poets who recounted British bravery against the invaders (78). Indeed, Babcock portrays Cian as both a poet and a warrior – although the one example of his verse that

Babcock creates sounds more like the work of Poe than of an ancient Celtic
bard:

> Where is the woodland city,
> The city beside the sea,
> White from her ramparts towering,
> Queen of the Andred lea?
>
> Lovely her courts were, and woven
> With rainbows her palace walls;
> The voice of her many fountains
> Was the song of the waterfalls.
>
> But ever a threatful shadow
> Grew from the eastward haze,
> Out of the bath of burning,
> Dawn of the evil days
>
> And ever a wordless horror
> Deepened in heart and eye,
> Till the noisome breath was o'er her,
> And the coils were winding nigh.   (74)

While the poem, which continues in this style for two more pages, sounds
more American than Welsh, it does serve to identify Babcock's hero with the
figure mentioned in Nennius.

In fact, much of what Babcock presents is an elaboration on the few
details Nennius and Gildas provide rather than a recounting of the narrative
of Geoffrey, who is the primary source for most of the recent historical novelists who treat Arthurian themes. Not that Geoffrey was unknown to
Babcock, who in a volume he wrote called *The Two Lost Centuries of Britain*
lists his sources for that work, including "the early Welsh poetry of
Llywarch, Aneurin, Taliessin, Merddin, and lesser bards"; Geoffrey of Monmouth and Henry of Huntington (though he recognizes that in their work
"fancy and real tradition are interwoven"); other medieval works in modern
editions or translations, such as " 'The Mabinogion' of Lady Guest,"
"Florence of Worcester," Malory's "History of King Arthur," Dr. Child's first
six volumes of "English Ballads," and Taylor's "Ballads and Songs of
Brittany"; scholarly journals such as the *Journal of the Archæological Society*,
the *Archæological Journal*, the *Archæologia Cambrensis*, the *Cambro-Britain*, and
the *Proceedings of the Archæological Institute*; and a long list of other scholarly
publications, including "Mr. Skene's 'The Four Ancient Books of Wales' and
'Celtic Scotland;' Professor Pearson's 'History of the Early and Middle Ages
of England;' Professor Rhys's 'Celtic Britain;' Dr. Guest's 'Origines Celtica'
and scattered papers; Mr. Whittaker's 'History of Manchester;' Mr. Stephens's
'Literature of the Cymry;' Dr. Freeman's various histories and addresses; Mr.
Wright's 'The Celt, the Roman, and the Saxon;' Mr. Coode's 'The Romans in

Britain;' and Mr. Green's 'The Making of England' " as well as numerous other sources dealing with Arthurian and Anglo-Saxon topics (5–6).

This long list of sources is significant for two reasons. First, it shows the wealth of material available to scholars and students of early Britain at the end of the nineteenth century. Second, it bears directly on the historical novel written by Babcock, in which he availed himself of the information contained in much of this source material. The epigraphs to the chapters in *Cian of the Chariots*, in fact, are taken from some of these same sources – from Welsh poets like Aneurin, Taliessin, Llywarch, Merddyn; from the Anglo-Saxon poem "The Ruin"; from the *Black Book of Carmarthen* and the *Red Book of Hergest*; and even from a "Note to Gunn's *Nennius*."

The setting for much of the action of Babcock's novel is the time between the sixth and seventh of Arthur's battles as listed by Nennius, that is, between the battle on the River Bassas and the battle in Celydon Forest. Babcock proceeds to chronicle the subsequent battles, leading up to the climactic battle at Camelot. Like many later historical novelists, Babcock uses the sparse accounts of the medieval chronicles as a frame on which to build his story. Almost inevitably, there is a nod to Tennyson: Arthur has the "poise and air" of a "warrior archangel" (310); Guinevere is assigned the epithet "luxuriant" (292 and 305); and the Britain of the time is troubled by wild beasts (packs of wolves) and pagans. The romance tradition also figures in the novel, in the repeated allusions to the relationship between Lancelot and Guinevere. But this relationship never becomes a major motif in the novel and has little significance in the real conflict developed in Babcock's story.

The backdrop for the novel is, as one would expect, the Anglo-Saxon invasions, and the battles are the testing ground for most of the important characters. In addition, Babcock focuses on the religious conflicts between the native Celtic religion, represented by the title character, Cian, and the Christian religion that Arthur adopts and to which he gives preference. When a priest presents Arthur with a cameo depicting the Virgin Mary, Arthur has it set into his shield as a boss, and when he wins his next battle, he decides that "It was Mary, Queen of Heaven, . . . who had saved him, and won the victory." Cian, however, finds Arthur's interpretation "well-nigh insufferable" (326) since it was Cian's timely arrival with his charioteers that assured the victory. The religious rift between the two increases when Cian absents his forces from the battle "on the strand of Trath Tribuit" (341) because Arthur insists that those fighting with him renounce any non-Christian beliefs. Interestingly, it is the non-Christian who makes the moral argument for following his conscience. "There are powers above emperors," Cian argues, "and mandates from of old" (243). When Cian says in Arthur's presence, "I value truth. I value justice. Our Emperor is giving us neither" (344), Arthur's reaction is surprising:

> Arthur shook with passion, but the assured fortitude and quiet exaltation of the other compelled him to think as well as feel. Also, these words

"THEY BORE TOKENS WITH THEM, AND CHARMS OF MIGHTY EFFICIENCY."

Figure 8. George Foster Barnes's depiction of Druid ritual in William H. Babcock's *Cian of the Chariots* (Boston: Lothrop Publishing Co., 1898).

had ever been the strongest appeal, outside of religion, which any man could make to him; and the part of the persecutor was both ill-suited and new. (344)

In the battle at Camelot, however, Cian swallows his pride and rides to the rescue. The fight is going badly for Arthur, but Cian and his charioteers break through the Saxon ranks. This time, though, there is no question about credit for the victory: it clearly belongs to Cian. As a result, the good will between Arthur and Cian is restored "with no compulsion of faith" (388), and the friendship and tolerance last until the end of Arthur's reign. Cian, we are told, fought with Arthur at "Mount Baden" and was with his emperor at "the utter disaster of Camlan" (395).

Aside from its significance as the first American historical novel to depict Arthur, *Cian of the Chariots* is a fascinating addition to American Arthuriana because of its unusual treatment of the religious conflict. Particularly surprising is the fact that in the late nineteenth century a novel would present as flawed an attempt by Arthur to compel the people of Britain to become Christians. Perhaps it is a sign of the Americanness of the book that it turns the historical account of Arthur's battles into an argument for freedom of religion.

Babcock's novel was not followed by another American historical Arthurian novel until Farnham Bishop and Arthur Gilchrist Brodeur's *The Altar of the Legion* in 1926. Brodeur was himself a medieval scholar who later wrote a piece on the historical Arthur called *Arthur: Dux Bellorum* (1939) as well as studies devoted to Old English and Old Norse topics.[1] Bishop and Brodeur's novel is actually set in the time just after Arthur's death. The only one of his warriors left alive is an aging Owain, who still leads a band of horsemen known as the Ravens. And even though Owain is killed in battle with the Saxons halfway through the novel, his memory, like the memory of Arthur, continues to inspire the people of Britain. As Nathan Comfort Starr observed in *King Arthur Today*, "Bishop and Brodeur's novel . . . emphasizes sixth-century rather than medieval chivalric warfare and the resounding fame of Arthur as a leader. It comes closer than any previous work to suggesting the presence of the *dux bellorum*" (90).

A good portion of the action of *The Altar of the Legion* is set in the fabled land of Lyonesse, whose "soft-sounding name," "the time-worn remnant of a bit of soldiers' Latin: Legionis Asa, the Altar of the Legion" (ix), explains the title. Although Lyonesse may seem an inappropriate setting for a historical novel, the authors recount the story of Tristram and note that "if such a fair lost land there were, the peaks of the Scilly Isles rise above its ocean grave, and the mighty granite walls of Land's End mark its eastern boundary"

---

1   Brodeur's best known work is his book *The Art of Beowulf*. He also translated the *Prose Edda*.

(viii). They conclude that "it may well be that Lyonesse the Fair was once the farthest outpost of Roman power and Roman grandeur" (viii).

Despite the legendary setting, Bishop and Brodeur do a good job of describing the struggle for independence of the last outposts of free Celtic people in Britain. The novel chronicles the constant warring with the Saxon invaders, the shifting fortunes as now one side, now the other gains the strategic advantage, and the political intrigues among Saxons and Celts that contribute to victory or defeat. Because of the importance of Legionis Asa in the story, the historical details create a better picture of Roman Britain than of Celtic Britain; and initially it seems strange to have the land of Celtic legend presented as such a Roman region. While it is easy to imagine the Roman-ized soldier Drusus, the heroic warrior who carries on the struggle against the Saxons after the deaths of Arthur and Owain, coming from such a place, it is more difficult to see a Romanized Legionis Asa as the homeland of Tristan, whom the authors invoke in their "Foreword." But readers able to suspend their disbelief over this detail are rewarded with a rich historical description of the sophisticated Romanized city Bellerium in Legionis Asa, a city that is highly civilized and defended from external threat by legions and from internal ones by a police force and firefighters.

A strength of the novel, in fact, is its depiction of a society that has become complacent and allowed corruption to creep in. Perhaps as a way of making the novel more interesting for modern readers or of making it seem more realistic, the authors portray political figures and policemen who have become dishonest; they recount how a commoner complains about "brutal police hired by rich oppressors" (88) and how others fear "the laying off of honest workers" (79) as a result of a politically manipulated decision by the Senate. The most corrupt of the senators, for example, becomes the villain who sells out his city to the Saxons; tries to force Gwenliuan, the daughter of Owain, into marriage; and abducts her when that scheme fails and his plotting is exposed. Other realistic touches include scenes showing Drusus, after he has been proclaimed Dictator by the people, taking care of adminis-trative chores, and elaborate descriptions of the ships, siege engines, and artillery he employs against the Saxons. In fact, it is the use of the *carroballista* or "cart catapult"[2] by the new "horse artillery" (249) that allows Drusus to breach the shield wall of the Saxons and win a crucial battle against them.

The beginning of *The Altar of the Legion* is the weakest part of the book. Owain's daughter is ill, so his son Meriaduc takes her place in a delegation to Legionis Asa to request help fighting the Saxons. Since Meriaduc dresses and poses as his sister, when she finally is well and able to travel, she dresses

2   There is almost too scholarly a discussion of these machines: "Each *carroballista* or 'cart catapult' was a huge crossbow mounted on a light field carriage drawn by two mules or horses and served by two men. Its likeness can be seen to-day on Trajan's Column. Most legions of the Middle Empire had a number of these weapons and used them as field artillery. Later, their very existence was forgotten" (249).

and poses as him, gratuitous examples of cross-dressing that do little for the plot. At first, Meriaduc, unlike his famous father, is appalled by the thought of killing and is sickened by the sight of blood. His feelings change after his father is slain and his sister abducted. In the end, Meriaduc dies fighting heroically in defense of Legionis Asa when the treacherous Ventidius leads the Saxons by a secret passage into the city. The implication is that this newfound Celtic identity is responsible for the Celtic legends surrounding Lyonesse.

In contrast to the opening, the ending, which encompasses this battle, is the strongest part of the book. As Saxon and Celt battle for the crucial region, a force larger than either intervenes: an earthquake and the resultant tidal wave devastate the city. Legionis Asa with all its Roman splendor sinks into the sea to be remembered as the legendary land of Lyonesse. A handful of survivors, including Drusus and Gwenlian, head to North Wales, the land of Owain, to continue the struggle against the Saxons, with Drusus declaring himself no longer a Roman but a Celt committed to the protection of his motherland.

Another Arthurian author, John Lesslie Hall, was a scholar who collaborated on an *Anglo-Saxon Reader* and who translated *Beowulf*. His *Old English Idyls* (1899) reflects his interest in Old English literature. In the poems in that volume he assumes "the rôle of an English gleeman of about A.D. 1000" and therefore writes in "the spirit" and "the metre" of Old English verse. To tell the history of the establishment of the Germanic tribes in Britain, Hall adopts an alliterative line, though with more internal rhyme than an Anglo-Saxon scop would ever have used, and fills his poems with kennings and compound nouns and adjectives as well as motifs adapted from Anglo-Saxon poetry, such as gift-giving, descriptions of mead halls and sea journeys, named swords, boar images on helmets, the beasts of battle theme, and barrows for dead heroes.

The first poem in the volume, "The Calling of Hengist and Horsa," tells of the embassy Vortigern sends to seek help protecting Britain from invaders. Though Hengist feels it would be better

> That your king grapple and gird on his weapons,
> His armor and arms, his excellent falchion,
> And lead out his loyal liegemen and vassals
> To fight for their home, than hide in his palace
> In shameless deeds, shaking with terror,
> Meek 'mid his maidens . . .   (7)

he nevertheless agrees to make the journey, which is described in the next poem, "The Landing of Hengist and Horsa." As soon as they land, Hengist asks to be given the Isle of Thanet before he will fight in Vortigern's cause, a request the British king readily grants.

The story of Vortigern and Hengist continues in the poem "The Lady

Rowena," which opens with a rebellion against the British king by his own people. When the "Woe-begone king, the womanish, white-livered / Liege-lord of Albion" (20), learns of the rebellion, he calls once again on Hengist who enlists even more Germanic warriors from the continent. But the central theme of the poem, which makes clear its Anglo-Saxon perspective, is Vortigern's lust for Rowena. When Hengist uses Rowena to elicit a rash promise from Vortigern that Kent will pass to him in return for Rowena's hand, he is described as "most artful of athelings" (30).

The picture of Rowena herself is unusual. In the chronicles, Rowena is described as a treacherous poisoner. Geoffrey of Monmouth reports that she was egged on by the devil to destroy Vortimer: "She, calling to her aid all the sleights of witchcraft, gave him by a certain familiar of his own, whom she had corrupted with bribes innumerable, a draught of poison" (128). But in Hall's poem she is "the peerless, precious princess Rowena" (31). She and Vortigern live together happily for six years, and then, as told in the poem on "The Death of Horsa," "hot-hearted Kentmen . . . cruelly vexed her" by saying that she has robbed Vortigern of his "metal and valor" (34).

"Cerdic and Arthur," the final poem dealing with material from the Arthurian legends,[3] tells of the time after Hengist's death when a new Saxon leader, Cerdic, comes to Britain. Though Arthur's name is said to be "far-reaching" (50) and, like Beowulf, Arthur is "eager for glory" (51), he is only temporarily favored by Wyrd. Able for a time to delay "that sturdy, mighty / Invincible march" of the Saxons through Britain (52), he ulti-mately dies, in a manner not explained in the poem – though there is an allusion to the involvement of a foul "traitor, hated of heroes" (52). But the focus of the poem is on Cerdic rather than Arthur. The final section is devoted to an account of how Cerdic slew a dragon and found in its treasure trove the sword that he used for "sixty of winters." Now he passes the sword, and thus symbolically the kingdom he has won with it, on to his son Cynric. Even more noteworthy than the shift in focus from Arthur to Cerdic and the talk of Cerdic's heroic exploits is the praise of Cerdic both as the "Father of England" (54) and as the "founder of freedom" who is said to have "builded his kingdom / As a bulwark of freedom" (52). The rewrit-ing of Arthurian history and pre-history from a Saxon perspective is, finally, not just an academic exercise by a professor of Old English but rather a means of glorifying the heritage of laws and the defense of freedom that Hall sees as descending from the Anglo-Saxon rulers of England and that is, of course, the tradition upon which the American system of justice is based.

Yet another academic who also wrote Arthurian verse is Charlton Miner Lewis, a professor of English literature at Yale whose scholarly books include

---

3   Hall's volume contains three poems after the Arthurian sequence: "Augustine," "Alfred," and "Edgar the Peaceable."

The Principles of English Verse and a survey of *The Beginnings of English Literature*. In the latter book, Lewis describes *Sir Gawain and the Green Knight* as "one of the best of the Arthurian romances" and observes that it "differs from most poems of its class in being profoundly moral in spirit and in purpose." He explains that "The difficulties Gawayne encounters are temptations rather than dangers, and the reader is led to admire him more for his integrity than for his prowess." He also finds in the poem "some humor, and some elements of pathos, and an admirable vividness of natural description," which make it "altogether a delightful poem" (106). In his own rendition, so radically different from the medieval poem that it must be considered inspired by but not a translation of its namesake, Lewis attempts to capture these qualities. But he adds a tone of parody, not to mention new plot elements and a new character.

In a nod to its American origin and to the literary taste of the time, Lewis notes that his poem is "a plain, straightforward man's unvarnished word" and says that it is "part sad, part sweet, – and part of it absurd" (64). A "plain, straightforward man" might indeed classify some elements of the story as absurd: the fairies that Lewis introduces, for example, or the Green Knight who can walk away after being decapitated. But the tone and the similes and metaphors also contribute to the spirit of absurdity. When Gawayne chops off the Green Knight's head, the author struggles to describe the flowing blood:

> The head dropped off; out gushed the thick, hot blood
> Like – I can't find the simile I want,
> But let us say a flood of *crème de menthe*!   (31)

Moreover, when the Green Knight leaves the castle, his green horse's hoofs strike the floor and produce green sparks. And when Gawayne arrives at the Green Chapel, its inhabitant offers to brew him "a cup of hot green tea" (100).

The exaggerated greenness of the knight and his trappings is merely an extension of the description found in the medieval poem. But Lewis takes even greater liberties with his source. He subtitles his *Gawayne and the Green Knight* "A Fairy Tale," a phrase that is to be taken literally since Lewis's major innovation in his rendition is a subplot involving the young woman Elfinhart. After her mother, widowed in "the dark days before King Arthur came," makes her way to the shore of "the Murmuring Mere, in Fairyland" (38) and dies there, the infant Elfinhart is taken in by the fairies, who raise her. Elfinhart becomes a good and beautiful woman, and as she matures she outgrows the "mad cap antics" (42) of the fairies who age much more slowly than she; and "a half unconscious yearning / For humankind stirred in her gentle heart" (44). Elfinhart's wish "to share man's burden in this world of duty" prompts the poet to proclaim that just when he convinced the reader of the lightness of his tale, the "story threatens to be moral," a quality without which "I can't be realistic" because although in verse morals are generally avoided, "in life we somehow can't get on without them" (45). But in the poem, which proceeds to tell of Gawayne's love for Elfinhart, the moral element is nonetheless light.

It is this love that prompts the testing by the Green Knight, who is sent by the fairies to prove Gawayne's courage and his affection for their charge. For of all the dangers to Elfinhart in the world of humans, it is love that the fairies fear the most. So the exchange of blows and the temptations by the lady of the castle not only are a reflection of the whimsical nature of the fairies but also are designed to determine if Gawayne is a fit protector and husband for Elfinhart. As in the medieval poem, the hero lacks only a little – "Your fault was small," the Green Knight tells him (104) – and the poem ends with the union of Gawayne and Elfinhart and the suggestion that, as in a fairy tale, they will live happily ever after.

Like Lewis's poem, a number of plays written in the period between Twain and the twenties reflect a fresh approach to Arthurian literature. While these plays maintain, as Lewis's poem does, many of the elements found in more romantic treatments, there is nevertheless a new spirit to them that marks them as clearly different from the earlier, more romantic material. One of these plays is *Excalibur: An Arthurian Drama*, written in 1893 (though not published until 1909) by Ralph Adams Cram. While Cram was not a literary scholar like Brodeur or Hall, he was a student of Gothic architecture and the author of a number of books on the subject as well as a prominent practicing neo-Gothic architect. But whether or not his study of medieval architecture influenced his *Excalibur*, a play that itself might be described as neo-Gothic, he presents his material in a way that is consistent with the more realistic literary taste of his time. This is evident especially in two themes that are obvious departures from the medieval stories. The first is Arthur's doting love for Guenever. While Arthur typically ignores Merlin's warning about his proposed marriage to Guenever, Cram's version of the triangle that undoes Camelot is unprecedented. Lancelot expresses his love before Guenever has become queen and, when he discovers her with Arthur, goes so far as to accuse her of betraying him. This accusation leads to a fight between knight and king, which is stopped only when Merlin intervenes, against Arthur's will. Later in the play, Arthur's love blinds him to the dangers to his kingship and causes him to lose Excalibur to a scheming Morgan. Instead of being oblivious to the love between his wife and his knight and of paying more attention to his kingdom than to his queen, as is traditional, Arthur is so deeply enamored of Guenever that he risks losing his kingdom. Consequently, Lancelot and Arthur are presented as squabbling, jealous rivals rather than as courtly lovers.

While the conflict between Arthur and Lancelot may be seen as a variation, though a radical one, on the common theme of the love triangle, the role and character of Merlin are unquestionably innovations that reflect Cram's American outlook and inspiration. Merlin is ordinarily presented as a guide who sets Arthur on the path to kingship but not as one who controls Arthur's destiny, a relationship clearly represented in Malory's *Le Morte d'Arthur* through the early disappearance of Merlin from the story. In the British tradition, in fact, Merlin plays a secondary role while Arthur is essential to the fated events. Cram's Merlin, on the other hand, says of himself:

> . . . I am he
> That God has made His deputy on earth.
> I am incarnate will, and I abide
> Forever scathless.   (52)

Unlike Malory's Merlin, who is a tool of fate, Cram's Merlin sees himself as assuming the role of fortune or destiny in creating the king and the realm (cf. p. 49). Later, Merlin separates the dueling rivals in love. When Arthur, wishing to continue, asks, "Am I the king, or thou, bold sorcerer?" Merlin chides that no king "sits on a steadfast throne unless he learn / The wisdom that God gives not with a crown" (99). And when Arthur suggests that such subordination makes his rule "but a pageant," Merlin offers him no consolation or face-saving. His metaphor is even harsher than Arthur's:

> Ring thyself with knights
> And daunt the world with show of dreadful arms,
> Thou art a crownèd jester, if thou lack'st
> The prop of wisdom for thy majesty.   (99)

And, of course, it is Merlin who is that prop of wisdom. Merlin's dominance continues to the end of the play. In the final scenes, Arthur is willing to give up his crown in order to have his lover. Deceived into thinking he is meeting Guenever, he in fact meets and yields his sword to Morgan. Yet even at this point, Arthur appeals to Merlin as the controlling agent. "Give me back my lady and I do thy will" (155), he says.

This unusual relationship between Arthur and Merlin deviates fairly radically from the normal dynamic between the two. Merlin is obviously directing events, and Arthur seems little more than a tool he uses to achieve his end. Cram's Merlin is less the beneficent guide and more the frustrated artist or creator, annoyed with the lack of understanding of his higher purpose that Arthur epitomizes. The upshot is that, in Cram's play, Merlin is the focal point. He is the moral center, intent on establishing order, a function performed by Arthur in some medieval romances and in many later works, of which Tennyson's *Idylls* is the prime example. Cram's emphasis on Merlin demonstrates a typically American discomfort with the concept of a king as the sun that provides spiritual light.

As Cram did, Richard Hovey rewrites the relationship among the three principals. Hovey intended to write a sequence of nine plays, collectively titled *Launcelot and Guenevere, A Poem in Dramas*. The nine projected plays were to be divided into three groups, each consisting of a masque "foreshadowing the events to follow," a tragedy, and a third play that provided a "reconciliation and solution." But only four of these works were completed, two masques (*The Quest of Merlin* [1891] and *Taliesin* [1900]) and the two plays of the first part (*The Marriage of Guenevere* [1899] and *The Birth of Galahad* [1898]).

As Lambert Wilmer did, Hovey felt free to combine the Arthurian legend with non-Arthurian mythological characters. In *The Quest of Merlin*, seeking knowledge about the results of the upcoming marriage between Arthur and Guenevere, Merlin goes to a cavern in the bowels of the earth where he compels the Norns to predict the future. Their predictions are dire: one foresees "Woe to the maiden, for her doom is dark"; another, "Woe to the knight! His thread is stained with blood"; and the third, "Woe to the Prince! For a witless fault great woe!" A series of classical characters, including dryads, fauns, Pan, and Bacchus, assume a lighter tone. The god of wine, for instance, takes a *carpe-diem* approach to life as a counterpoint to the somber fate foretold by the Norns:

> Let the future brood and bode
> Let the past go spinning!
> Pluck the roses by the road,
> You'll find them worth the winning.   (27)

Among other mythological creatures, angels appear and sing of night and dawn, which they proclaim – like the tiger and the fawn – to be two parts of creation (31).

The point of whisking through the various mythologies and the philosophical approaches to life that they represent is revealed at the end of the masque in monologues by "three forms like unto the Angels," who predict a harmonious outcome to the strife caused by the love triangle, as Launcelot "will prevail" and Guenevere "will leave a name beyond Time's scorn" (78, 79). Hovey seems to be employing the Arthurian legend as a central point in the world's development and in his own world view, which is a harmonizing of the earlier philosophies. The dire fate of the Arthurian dream does not negate the love of Launcelot and Guenevere, a joy that should be seized while it can be. Both the destructive and the creative aspects of their love are parts of the created world. From Hovey's more cosmic perspective, that love, despite the initial destruction that it causes, can be seen as a positive force.

As Hovey's sequence progresses, he adds to this blending of mythologies and idiosyncratic vision of the Arthurian world other radical deviations from received tradition. In *The Marriage of Guenevere*, Launcelot tells of how, at the point of death, he traveled without food through rough terrain on his way to

Camelot and was rescued by a lady, whom he later learns to be the queen.
The fact that their love began at this time, before her marriage to Arthur, represents to them a prior commitment so that Guenevere considers her true
(though not legally recognized) husband to be Launcelot. Such justification
of a love that transcends the restrictions of society was essential not only to
Hovey's view of the legend but also to him personally because he himself
had an affair with a married woman, Henrietta Russell, who later divorced
her husband and married him.[4] It is no doubt due in part to his identification
of his and Mrs. Russell's affair with that of Launcelot and Guenevere that his
Guenevere "is the personification of the 'new woman' " who complains
about the restrictions put on women by society (Linneman 81) and about the
roles women are expected to play.[5] In this reinterpretation of the queen's
affair, Hovey ascribes to her the kinds of feelings and beliefs that a "new
woman" of his times might have. Just before her marriage to Arthur, she
complains that from the time she is a girl, a woman

> . . . must be quiet,
> Demure – not have her freedom with the boys.
> While they are running on the battlements,
> Playing at war or at the chase, she sits
> Eating her heart out at embroidery frames
> Among old dames that chatter of a world
> Where women are put up as merchandise.
> – Oh, I have slipped away a thousand times
> Into the garden close and scaled the wall
> And fled from them to freedom and the hills.
> And I have passed the women in the fields,
> With stupid faces dulled by long constraint,
> Bowing their backs beneath the double burden
> Of labor and unkindness – all alike,
> Princess and peasant, bondslaves by their sex!   (41–42)

Later in the same monologue, she observes that by marrying Arthur, "I have
ordered a new pair of manacles." This use of Guenevere to reflect new attitudes towards women marks a development in the Arthurian story and illustrates a strategy that other writers, particularly women, adopt as they
reinterpret the legends for their own times. Sara Teasdale, for example, in her
poem "Guenevere" (which appeared in her collection *Helen of Troy and Other
Poems* [1911]), allows the queen to complain that the people "only asked that I
should be right fair, / A little kind, and gownèd wondrously" (27–28). The

4   On the affair with Mrs. Russell, see Macdonald 61–79.
5   See Cecilia Tichi, "Women Writers and the New Woman," for a survey of some of the
    major American New Woman literature. For a survey of British New Woman literature,
    see the chapter on "New Woman Fiction" in Kate Flint's book *The Woman Reader
    1837–1914*. On New Woman drama, see *The New Woman and Her Sisters*, ed. Vivien
    Gardner and Susan Rutherford.

accented *e* in "gownèd" emphasizes the artificiality of the role Guenevere is expected to play. And she must pay dearly for her attempt to stop being the doll on display that others insist she be. She has learned that "A queen should never dream on summer nights" (28). It is precisely this outdated attitude concerning social role and Guenever's resentment of it that Hovey has incorporated into his play.

Hovey's other two completed plays also depart from tradition to develop his notion of a new world view. *The Birth of Galahad* portrays Launcelot as the Grail knight's father, as is usual; however, it makes his mother not Elaine (or Ylen, as she is called in the play) but Guenevere. This is a significant alteration: in no earlier work does Guenevere bear Launcelot's child. Of course, this device is essential for Hovey's purpose in his sequence: the glorification of love and the presentation of a new world order based on the harmony of which true love is a symbol. As Hovey's wife noted in her introduction to the fragments of his uncompleted plays:

> In the "Poem in Dramas" we have the creation of a Galahad who could be to the thought of our time what the Galahad of the legend was to the knightly or to the new-come Christian thought of the Middle Ages. He was no witchcraft-engendered abnormality. He was a spirit engendered in the highest love, and his purity was ultimation, not elimination. He is to the modern mind what the Galahad of Malory or the Parsifal of Eschenbach and Wagner is to the medieval-minded Christian. The immaculate conception, an idea which Christianity brought to our Western world, *is here held an ideal of every conception.* Galahad's pure soul grew as the form of blessing which only "the miracle," the mystic love, can bring to earth. It belongs to the realms that are above the laws of social order. (13) (Emphasis added.)

The use of Galahad as a model for every birth and the creation of a new image of the world are motifs perfectly consistent with the democratization and reinterpretation of the Arthurian legend that is typical of American authors.

Hovey's sequence of plays was supposed to lead up to the death of Arthur; but this was not to have been Hovey's final statement on the legend. In *The Holy Graal and Other Fragments by Richard Hovey*, Mrs. Hovey observed that "the evolution of mythologies running through the masques makes it seem likely that all the people of [Hovey's] earth-world and his unreal world as well should have assembled, each making some essential part of the completed harmony" (127), which was to be presented in the final play, *Avalon: A Harmonody.* Hovey apparently regarded Avalon as a spiritual symbol. In his wife's words, "Somewhere in eternity, not regarding place, all stages of the human race must coexist regardless of their place in time, and their relation or absence of relation or their experiences. This condition he uses as a place, and calls Avalon" (128). Thus Hovey's Arthurian world was to be transformed into an Avalon where everyone lived in harmony.

Like Hovey and Cram, Southern playwright and poet Stark Young drama-
tized the relationship between Launcelot and Guenevere. While his play
Guenevere (1906) can hardly be deemed an example of literary realism, it
nevertheless partakes of the spirit of its age by focusing on Guenevere and
making her internal struggle the centerpiece of the drama. As John Pilkington has observed, although Young gets much of the plot of his play from
Malory, he "clearly intended to subordinate this material to the analysis of
the queen's feelings" (18).

At her trial, Young's Guenevere tells Arthur that since he is "ideal, they
that love thee love / Thee as a mystic symbol" and that he tries her for no
"husband's / Nor no lover's jealousy" but because of "the jealous eye the
king bends on the crystal / Perfectness of his long-dreamed-of court" (59).
Moreover, she admits that while she loves him "as men love saints" (58), she
also loves Launcelot in a more romantic way:

> . . . All the pomp
> And glory of this world, of sights and sound,
> Of summer air and downs of May, of stars
> And white dawn leaping over dewy fields,
> Of life and love and the little moods men know
> And bossèd arms, and chivalry, and jousts
> Of blood and wild, unquenchable revenge,
> Of bowers drunk with music and sweet sound,
> All this my woman's heart hath found to love
> In him, Sir Launcelot.   (59)

Even in the convent Guenevere feels the pull of two worlds. Having given up
the world of the court, she still dreams of a tournament at Camelot, a dream
that makes her fear that she can "be neither / Spiritual nor fleshly, saint nor
queen" (66). When Arthur visits her, she wishes to leave with him and return
to Camelot, a situation that is impossible because of the events that she has
helped to cause. She is so torn that her body can no longer take the strain.
The result is her fatal illness.

Although she never returns to Camelot, in the end Guenevere is for
Launcelot a symbol for its glory, a reminder, as he says, of "the peerless
ventures and sweet courtesy / Of this the summer of all time" (76). But she is
also a woman destroyed by the clash between her spiritual and her physical
desires.

Another group of American plays focuses not on the love of Lancelot and
Guinevere but rather on that of Tristan and Isolt. Much of the interest in this
pair of lovers resulted from the work done by Joseph Bédier to reconstruct
the original story – and for the English-speaking world, especially from the
translation of Bédier's reconstruction by English poet Hilaire Belloc, which
was first printed in 1903. Between the appearance of Belloc's translation and
1930, sixteen Tristan plays in English were written, three of which were by

Americans.[6] In one of them, *Tristram and Iseult* (1930), the author Amory Hare (pseudonym of [Mary] Amory Hare Hutchinson) acknowledges her debt to Bédier by saying that she owes "the greater portion of my play" to his rendition and to other medieval sources – except that, in the more realistic spirit of the day, she has omitted "the supernatural elements" (8–9). Unfortunately, her derivative and unfocused play has little to recommend it over other dramatic versions of the story. *Tristan and Isolde: A Tragedy* (1904) by Louis K. Anspacher, on the other hand, is not as much a slave to the medieval story. Anspacher introduces a subplot in which Isolde's maid Isabel is wooed by two suitors. Yet while the obvious intent is to parallel the tragic triangle of the major action of the play, the device achieves little. Anspacher also tries to constrain the action to one day. This attempt at a unity of time requires a good deal of exposition, which gives the sense that there is more talk than action in the play, but it also directs attention to the tragic outcome of the interactions of the characters.

The third play, in some ways the furthest from Bédier and the medieval sources, is also the most successful, perhaps because it best integrates the romantic medieval material with realism and best adapts it to its American audience. Don Marquis brings an American to a realm haunted by the spirit of the Arthurian world in his *Out of the Sea: A Play in Four Acts* (1927). Marquis (who also wrote poems called "Tristram and Isolt" and "Lancelot and Guinevere") retells the Tristan story in a modern setting. On the coast of Cornwall near the spot where the mythic land of Lyonnesse sank into the sea, a group of characters reenacts the tragedy of Tristan and Isolt. The modern counterpart of Tristan is John Harding, an American poet, who is taken with the romance of Cornwall, where, he says, the ghosts from Lyonnesse speak to him *out of the sea*. The Isolt character is Isobel Tregesal, who, as a child, was found in an open boat with a bronze bodkin beside her. Having come out of the sea originally, she comes from it again when her husband Mark Tregesal sails out into a fierce storm and his yawl breaks up.

Mark, who is compared to the ancient giants of Cornwall, is like his original in the Tristan legend in that he is jealous and cruel, crueler "than the old king was to them other lovers," as one of the characters says (62). As Mark begins to suspect that his wife and Harding are lovers, he taunts them, trying to make them wonder about the extent of his real knowledge. His deliberate cruelty to his wife convinces Harding and Isobel that they must run away together, a decision that is supported by her foster-father and by Arthur Logris, the owner of the house in Cornwall where much of the action takes place. Logris, who is on one level a modern King Arthur, is also in love

6   Bédier himself wrote a play on the theme in 1929, *Tristan et Iseut: Pièce en trois actes, un prologue et huit tableaux*. On the plays in English, see Alan Lupack's article, "Acting Out an Old Story: Twentieth-Century Tristan Plays."

with Isobel, so much so that he puts her chance for happiness with Harding above his own desires.

When Mark discovers Isobel in a cave where the lovers have met before, he is aware of their plan and attempts to force her to remain with him. She is defiant, telling him "You have no power over me" (114). But, as Mark observes, like her, he himself is "elemental" (112). Not only does he try to stop her, but he also proclaims his desire for a son and attempts to rape her in the cave. Isobel resists and finally stabs him with the bodkin. Logris wants to take the blame for the murder so Isobel can live with the man she loves, but she will not allow this. All she asks is to see Harding one more time. Confronted with the violent deed, the American poet reveals that he has none of the elemental force of Isobel or Mark or Logris or the Tristan of legend. He says, "I never thought . . . that it would come . . . to bloodshed" (130). When Isobel, now "free even of love" (131), ultimately leaps into the sea, Harding says that he should follow her. But Logris, recognizing that Harding lacks the age-old passion that is bred into those who have lived on the coast of Cornwall and in the presence of the legend of Lyonnesse, replies "You won't, though. You'll write a poem about it" (133).

Logris's comment is an indictment of the American Tristan and an indication of the transformation that one of the greatest romantic heroes has undergone. Harding's poetry is neither a sign of his accomplishments nor an expression of passionate intensity. Rather, it is a substitute for passionate living and loving. Yet, although Marquis depicts a Tristan incapable of tragic stature, his play is a tragedy – the tragedy of Isobel, whose return to the sea is a tragic victory over both the cruelty of Mark and the pusillanimity of Harding.

The fact that the American poet suffers by comparison to the characters who inhabit Cornwall does not lessen his importance to the drama or to Marquis's theme. There is, at least on one level, something incompatible between the ancient legends and the values of a modern American. Harding is romantic, but only to a point. When it comes to acting on his passion, he defers to his practical side, a flaw that allies him with Twain's Hank Morgan.

Even in this age of literary realism and of the reshaping of the Arthurian legend in America, there are, of course, some writers who take a romantic approach to the material. A poet such as Sophie Jewett, writing a Grail poem in 1905, seems a direct descendent of James Russell Lowell and not a precursor of Eliot and Robinson. Jewett, who, like a number of the other authors who produced Arthurian works in this period, was an academic, had translated the Middle English poem *Pearl*, and had written about medieval English literature.

In her poem "The Dwarf's Quest," Jewett retells the story of the Grail quest in a typically American way by placing the focus on a character outside the usual circle of Grail knights. Jewett's protagonist is Dagonet the dwarf, King Arthur's fool. The object of derision and even physical abuse by knights such as Sir Kay – "The foot and fist of rude Sir Kay / He bore with jest and sneer" (53) – Dagonet believes that the quest is not for someone such as himself. But a divine voice gentler than Queen Guinevere's and "kinglier than the King's" informs him that "There waits one vision of the Cup / For thee and Galahad" (55). This injunction to seek the Holy Grail comes despite the fact that Dagonet, feeling as if he were excluded from the quest, had earlier "cursed" the Holy Grail (53, 55). Yet the King of Heaven, like the King of Camelot, seems able to forgive the biting words of the jester.

How different Dagonet is from the usual Grail knight is made clear in the poem. In addition to being "an impish, mocking thing" (53), he is "crooked and weak" (54). By contrast, Galahad has a face "like a star" (55); and Galahad and Percivale ride in the "shining mail" (53) that marks them as traditional heroes of romance. But Dagonet is deemed worthy of the quest by the divine voice because of his "heart's prayer" (56). His physical deformity becomes less important than his inner qualities, qualities that are demonstrated in the poem when he comes upon Lancelot seriously wounded and stops to care for him.

As Dagonet tends to the unconscious Lancelot, he sees a bright light and then four maidens, one of whom bears the Holy Grail. His response to the vision highlights his moral qualities. He tries to awaken Lancelot because he thinks it is Lancelot for whom the vision has appeared. And when Dagonet cannot wake him, his "answered prayer [seeing the Grail] is punishment / Since my lord might not see!" (58). While Lancelot is cured by the Grail, he does not achieve the quest because he has not witnessed the Grail's appearance, as Dagonet has. When Dagonet returns to Camelot, he is mocked again for setting out on the quest, "Till something in the rider's eyes / Silenced the merry jest" (59).

In "The Dwarf's Quest," Galahad and Percivale also achieve the Grail. It is, however, unprecedented for the third successful quester to be Dagonet the fool. Usually when there are three, the third is Bors, as in Malory. By substituting Dagonet, Jewett redeems the character who initially curses the Grail, and she allows for a new kind of Arthurian hero, one who is not noble by birth and who is not skillful or strong but who has moral qualities that have been enhanced by his own suffering, by the scorn and jibes of those who felt themselves superior to him. Thus Jewett's Grail knight is in the tradition of Sir Launfal and of the Little Sir Galahads of the literature inspired by the Arthurian youth groups and numerous other characters in the American Arthurian tradition who imitate the denizens of Camelot not because of status or birth but because of their innate virtues.

Quite prolific and highly regarded in his day, Madison Cawein (1865–1914) is another poet who used Arthurian material, which was for him a subject of continuing interest. An account in the Louisville *Courier-Journal* reports that "his study of Milton made him resolve ere he had read Tennyson, to throw the Arthurian legends into verse. He accomplished one,

'Parsifal.' . . . Before going on, Mr. Cawein read Tennyson and at once burnt all his efforts" (cited in Rothert 99). Apparently, however, Cawein recovered from his feeling of inadequacy before the achievements of Tennyson since he ultimately wrote a long poem of some sixteen hundred lines, *Accolon of Gaul*, as well as a dozen shorter poems on Arthurian themes.

Accolon of Gaul (1889) retells Malory's story of the affair between Morgane (to use Cawein's spelling) and Accolon and the treachery of Morgane in duping Arthur with a copy of Excalibur while she gives the original sword to her lover when Arthur and Accolon fight as the champions, respectively, of Damas and Ontzlake. In broad outline Cawein follows Malory, but the few changes he makes are significant. Nimue, who rescues Arthur in Malory's version and uses her magic to force Accolon to drop Excalibur, does not appear in Cawein's. Instead, Arthur, who realizes after his counterfeit blade shatters that Accolon has the true sword, picks up "the truncheon of a bursten lance" (48) and strikes Accolon on the wrist as he seizes Excalibur. Since Cawein is telling the story of Morgane and Accolon and not the intricate, extended story that Malory recounts, his exclusion of Nimue seems to be for purposes of narrative compression. Nevertheless, the change makes this climactic moment in the struggle ordinary and almost comic. A similar effect occurs at the point of Accolon's death. Arthur forces Accolon to recognize him as the king and then Accolon "clashed and died" (52).[7] While the clashing of the falling knight's armor may be a realistic detail, it is in this instance the wrong one.

Another innovation introduced by Cawein is the motivation of Morgane, who appears intent on having a passionate love affair. She falls in love first with Urience (Malory's Uriens), who saves her from a wild boar and then brings her water from a well in his "deep casque" (60). As a result of his brave deed and tender act, Morgane "felt she'd loved him" until she hears of the

> Fame of the love of Isoud, whom from home
> Brought knightly Tristram o'er the Irish foam,
> And Guenevere's for Launcelot of the Lake.
> And then how passion from these seemed to wake
> Reflex of longing; and within her wake
> Longing for some great gallant who should slake –
> And such found Accolon. (61)

Morgane's desire for passionate love suggests a reason for her betrayal of Arthur. She would have Accolon crowned so that the emphasis of the kingdom will shift from war to love (cf. pp. 55–56). The love motif not only seems imposed on the tale but also fails to explain the ending of the poem,

---

7 In the version of *Accolon of Gaul* that appears in the 1907 edition of Cawein's *Poems*, the word is "crashed" rather than "clashed"; but this change, like the other changes in that version, does little to improve the poem.

when two knights drop the dead body of Accolon at Morgane's feet and tell her that it comes from the king. Morgane flees to Avalon and is not heard of again until she comes to bear "The wounded Arthur from that last fought fight / Of Camlan in a black barge into night" (64). Given Morgane's "morbid hatred" (54) of her brother, there is no reason why she should perform this final act. This inconsistency, however, is not the most serious flaw in a work marred by unfortunate details and poor verse. Cawein surely had not matched the achievement of Tennyson, whose spectre must still have haunted him as he wrote his own poem.

Despite Cawein's opinion that *Accolon of Gaul* was "my best piece of narrative work" (Letter to Eric Pape, cited in Rothert 248), it is in some shorter lyric poems on Arthurian themes that Cawein made most effective use of the legendary material and demonstrated the talent that made him so widely published even in some of the foremost and most innovative magazines of his day, including *Poetry*. In the short poem "In the Forest," he suggests that the magic of the legend might be recovered in a deep forest, reminiscent of "Broceliande and Dean," which he calls "Forests of the Holy Grail." In such a place one "Might think he hears the laugh of Vivien / Blent with the moan of Merlin" in the murmuring of a brook, and in "the clouds that loom above the glen, . . . Might dream he sees the towers of Camelot" (3: 344). The romance of the legend comes into the modern world again in the poem "A Guinevere," one of several works of this period to cast Arthur's queen as a model of a new woman, in this case a woman who is married to a "gouty gray one" merely because "he had gold" and who finds love in her Lancelot (1: 154–55).

In the lyric mode, Cawein can be successful even in poems that not only allude to but are actually set in the Arthurian world. Cawein's "Dream of Sir Galahad," for example, describes the Grail knight's vision of three angels who command him to know and to see and who then instruct him, "What thou art arise and be!" (1: 339). The vision allows Galahad's soul to be "new-born" and prepares him for the achieving of the Grail. The poem also becomes a metaphor for any sort of rebirth that must come from knowledge and vision. In another poem, "After the Tournament," Cawein describes a dying Sir Lionell who finds solace in his beautiful beloved as he asks that she let her hair, "a golden wonder, fall" and her "fair / Full throat bend low" and her last kiss "be hot / With love, not dry / With anguish" (1: 341). The brief image of the dying knight longing for a last view of the beauties of his lady and a final kiss is a better picture of and comment on love than the more elaborate treatment of the theme in *Accolon of Gaul*, just as Cawein's short poem "Morgan Le Fay" evokes a more vivid and terrifying portrait of Morgan than does the longer narrative.

In lyrics such as these, Cawein produced some of his best poetry; and, while he has never been considered one of the major figures of his age, he did occasionally write poems worthy of this innovative period in American verse. It has even been suggested that Cawein's poem "Waste Land," which appeared in *Poetry* in 1913, may have influenced the creation of one of the most influential works of the twentieth century, T. S. Eliot's *The Waste Land*. In an essay in the *Times Literary Supplement*, Robert Ian Scott notes similarities between Eliot's imagery and Cawein's. Scott believes that Cawein "provided the emotional geography on which Eliot's poem, its effect and much of his fame are based" (14), and points out that many of Cawein's images are mirrored in Eliot. One stanza, which seems very Eliotic in tone and imagery, suffices to demonstrate the kinds of connections that can be made between the two poems:

> The cricket's cry and the locust's whir,
> And the note of a bird's distress,
> With the rasping sound of the grasshopper,
> Clung to the loneliness
> Like burrs to a trailing dress.   (104)

The use of images such as the crickets and the distressed bird to suggest a moral state and even the final simile that brings together the elegant world of society and an image of desolation seem to support Scott's contention that Eliot may have known Cawein's poem. At the very least, unlike most of his other Arthurian poems, Cawein's "Waste Land" is similar in spirit to Eliot's masterpiece.

While some writers of this period persisted in presenting romantic, if somewhat Americanized, visions of the Arthurian world, the ravages of World War I gave great impetus to the deromanticization of the Arthurian legends. The brutal slaughter with modern weapons of destruction ended the innocence not only of Americans but of the entire world and made Twain's vision of destruction at the Battle of the Sand Belt seem prophetic. The new awareness wrought by the destructive power of modern technology, reflected in postwar Arthurian literature, was especially evident in two major poets, T. S. Eliot and Edwin Arlington Robinson, who changed the dominant mode of treating the Matter of Britain.

T. S. Eliot's *The Waste Land* responded directly and immediately to the plight of the postwar world by describing the wasteland of contemporary society. What makes Eliot's poem interesting and still meaningful three-quarters of a century later is that he found a way to see in the condition of the world a reflection of the human condition and of rampant spiritual decline. And what allowed him to make this connection was the myth he found in Jessie Weston's *From Ritual to Romance*. Weston had a wide-ranging knowledge of texts and was more conversant with medieval romance than almost any other scholar; and, although many of the conclusions of her book have subsequently been rejected, in its day *From Ritual to Romance* was a monument of research. Eliot would surely have been drawn to the cultural fluency displayed in the book and would have seen in its use of myths and texts from different periods and cultures a paradigm for the use of imagery and allusion in *The Waste Land*.

Despite Weston's influence on Eliot's poem, some critics have gone astray by trying to tie *The Waste Land* too closely or too literally to the Grail story. One such critic, Grover Smith (72–98), has, in fact, attempted to link almost every aspect of *The Waste Land* to one incident or another in some version of the Grail legend, a practice that produces an ingenious reading for which Ian Hamilton has branded Smith the "explicator-in-chief" of Eliot's poem (103). Another critic, Christine Froula, bases her analysis of the poem heavily on "the one version of the Grail romance that Eliot cites in *The Waste Land*, Paul Verlaine's sonnet 'Parsifal' " (239). While each of these readings adds some insights, their authors seem to have followed false paths on the quest for the meaning of *The Waste Land*.

Eliot himself is responsible for much of the misdirection. In his notes to the poem he says that "Not only the title, but the plan and a good deal of the incidental symbolism of the poem were suggested by Miss Jessie L. Weston's book on the Grail legend: *From Ritual to Romance* (Cambridge). Indeed, so deeply am I indebted, Miss Weston's book will elucidate the difficulties of the poem much better than my notes can do: and I recommend it (apart from the great interest of the book itself) to any who think such elucidation of the poem worth the trouble" (47).[8] This and the other notes Eliot wrote to explain various allusions in the poem led to a search for all of the sources upon which the poet drew to put together the suggestive structure that critics have explained by analogy to Cubist painting (Korg 88–90) and to a "musical organization" (Leavis 27). Because of the abundance of critical attention to its web of allusions, *The Waste Land* has been called "the supreme puzzle poem" (Hamilton 102). And while the explanation of the sources of the allusions of the poem was an important step in the understanding of *The Waste Land*, it was only a step. As F. B. Pinion recognized, even Eliot came to realize he had misled many readers: "Unfortunately he had 'stimulated the wrong kind of interest among the seekers of sources'. He was justified in acknowledging his indebtedness to Jessie Weston, but regretted sending 'so many enquirers off on a wild goose chase after Tarot cards and the Holy Grail' " (139).

Weston's account of the wasteland nevertheless offers some important insights into the meaning of Eliot's poem. In her study, Weston observed that "the 'Waste Land' is really the very heart of our problem; a rightful appreciation of its position and significance will place us in possession of the clue which will lead us safely through the most bewildering mazes of the fully developed tale" (63–64). Eliot no doubt recalled this statement or at least the concept behind it, the centrality of the wasteland to a series of myths, for

8   Our citations of *The Waste Land* will be from *The Waste Land and Other Poems* since this text is more readily available than the 1922 Boni & Liveright first edition.

which the idea of the wasted land and the need for its restoration serves as a unifying motif.

Eliot, moreover, surely adopted the approach suggested by this notion as a means of consolidating a host of otherwise disparate stories, characters, and images. As George Williamson observed, "The most important idea for Eliot in Miss Weston's scheme was that the Grail story subsumes a number of myths; this provided him with both a central myth and a basic system of metaphor" (119). Thus Eliot had a complex of stories and ideas, a multi-layered system of suggestion and metaphor, or as Williamson calls it, a "sub-sumptive myth" (120), to provide material and meaning for his poem. The system is in some ways analogous to the complex of metaphors available to Elizabethan writers (and analyzed in Tillyard's *The Elizabethan World Picture*). What Eliot is using is a world view in which the king and the land are identi-fied, though he is using it in a more consciously literary way than the Eliza-bethan writers did when they incorporated their notions of levels of being reflecting one another in their poems and plays.

Through this method, Eliot brings together a wealth of allusion that allows him to contrast the rich intellectual and emotional life of past ages with the sterile and passionless people of the present. As Elizabeth Drew notes, "The structure of the poem is built up of contrasts, of which the most obvious and ironically dramatic are the series of 'scenes' from modern life, set against the memories of the myths related in *From Ritual to Romance* and *The Golden Bough*, and supported by the suggestions evoked by Eliot's vast store of literary remi-niscence. But interwoven with these, so that the two constantly 'melt into' one another, are the passages of drama on the psychological level, the conflicts and contrasts of mood, which again in their turn interpenetrate and interfuse" (67). As a result, the Grail myth can be all-important to the poem without having *specific* Grail allusions occupy much of the text. It is worth commenting, in fact, that although *The Waste Land* is one of the most influential Arthurian poems in America, the actual Arthurian content of the poem is slight. Aside from the use of the Grail story as a "subsumptive myth," *The Waste Land* contains only a few references to the Fisher King, the general symbol of the wasteland, and a couple of allusions to the story of Tristan and Isolt. But the symbolism of the wasteland and the Fisher King resonated with writers, par-ticularly novelists, who saw in the myth Eliot had adapted the perfect symbol for modern society and its ills.

Following Weston's lead, Eliot placed the Fisher King at the center of the poem. Since the basic premise of the theory that links the Fisher King to vegetation and fertility rituals is that the king and the land are bound together and the fate of one is dependent upon the other, a wounded king means a wounded land, the land that is wasted until, in terms of the ritual, the new season brings new growth, or, in terms of the romance, the Grail knight cures the king and thus restores the land. The link between king and land allows both geography and character to reflect the same condition.

There is sterility of all kinds in the wasteland of modern society, which Eliot emphasizes in both the form and the content of his poem. In the section, for example, describing the typist's rendezvous with "the young man carbuncular," Eliot demonstrates the lack of passion between the two in a number of ways. He employs a series of negatives and terms implying the mechanical rather than the elemental: "unreproved," "undesired," "no defence," "no response," "indifference," "patronising kiss," "half-formed thought," "automatic hand" (38–39). All of these occur in a passage of twenty-eight lines (beginning with "The time is now propitious, as he guesses" and ending with "And a clatter and a chatter from within") that comprise metrically two Shakespearean sonnets, though each has one flaw, a rhyme required by the form but never completed. The form itself, traditionally associated with the great statements of passion found in Shakespeare's verse, is ironic in this context and is one of many ways that Eliot emphasizes the disjunction between the world of the past and the state of things in the present.

The condition of the typist and the young man, two typical inhabitants of the modern wasteland, is part of the general mythic framework of the poem because the myths "have a common meaning, which permits their union; and this fact testifies to something permanent in human nature, which may be repeated in individual experience" (Williamson 119). And just as all of the people in the poem partake of the sterility of the wasteland, so all the male characters share the metaphoric wound of the Fisher King. The typist's young man is carbuncular, but that physical condition, like the wound of the Fisher King, hints at a more serious affliction that affects him and results in his passionless lovemaking. It also affects his land, the modern city of London. When Eliot alludes to the Fisher King, his picture bespeaks a languid and debilitated world that is far from either ritual or romance:

> A rat crept softly through the vegetation
> Dragging its slimy belly on the bank
> While I was fishing in the dull canal
> On a winter evening round behind the gashouse . . . .   (36)

The reference to the "dull canal" reflects an attitude towards water that makes the presentation of the wasteland image so unusual in this poem: "At the beginning of *The Waste Land*," notes Williamson, "we notice a fundamental, indeed instrumental, difference in Eliot's use of the vegetation myths. In these myths the appropriate attitude towards the renewal of life, or spring, is one of rejoicing; here it is the reverse" (125). In Eliot's poem, "April is the cruellest month" (29), not the month of hope for renewal and the return of spring. What traditionally makes April the beginning of a season of hope is the coming of the spring rains that bring life to dormant vegetation and as a result to those who depend on that vegetation for life. But Eliot has Madame Sosostris, his "famous clairvoyante," advise her client to "Fear death by water" (30–31). And the fourth section of the poem is called "Death by Water."

This paradox raises the question of whether any redemption is possible: if water, the life-giving force in vegetation myths, is to be feared, what then offers hope? The overriding pessimism arising from this attitude towards water is perhaps reflected as well in the lack of a Grail knight in the poem. Though there is one line from Verlaine's "Parsifal" quoted in the poem – *"Et O ces voix d'enfants, chantant dans la coupole"* – the line does not refer in any substantive way to the Grail knight himself. And although Eliot alludes to the Chapel Perilous, there are no references to Galahad or to another Grail knight enduring the trials the Chapel traditionally presents. Weston observes that the hero of the Grail romance often "meets with a strange and terrifying adventure in a mysterious Chapel, an adventure which, we are given to understand, is fraught with extreme peril to life. The details vary: sometimes there is a Dead Body laid on the altar; sometimes a Black Hand extinguishes the tapers; there are strange and threatening voices, and the general impression is that this is an adventure in which supernatural, and evil, forces are engaged" (175). But in *The Waste Land*, "There is the empty chapel, only the wind's home. / It has no windows, and the door swings, / Dry bones can harm no one" (44). With the Chapel divested of its dangers and trials, there is no chance for a hero to prove his courage and virtue, and thus to prove himself worthy of achieving the Grail – if there were a hero, that is. But there is not. And without the Grail knight, what hope is there that the wounded king will be healed and his land restored?

Eliot presents the Fisher King as a type of "the many dying, sacrificed gods mentioned by Frazer in *The Golden Bough*, figures that reiteratively enable regeneration of the land" (Abdoo 54). Although the Fisher King's rebirth or regeneration is crucial to the restoration of life and fertility, Eliot's poem ends on a note of ambiguity as to whether there is going to be a rebirth of the dead god and thus a revitalization of the land. As Elizabeth Drew has summarized the situation, "at the end the Fisher King, though the arid plain is *behind* him, is still fishing, still questioning if any achievement is ahead" (84). That image and the final fragments of the poem provide no clear resolution to the problem of the poem, just as the barrage of quotations at the end merely raises other questions, which are unresolved by the explication of the sources. It may be that the questions are a mad gibberish that indicates the mental as well as the physical collapse of the Fisher King and his land, a position taken by George Williamson, who considers "the repetition of the Sanskrit commands, supported by the Upanishad ending," to sound like "the mad talk of Hieronymo, and hallucinative vision appears to end in madness" (154). On the other hand, it may be, as D. C. Fowler has noted, that these quotations, following the Fisher King's question, "Shall I at least set my lands in order?" are "nothing more than a charm, the purpose of which is to break the spell of the waste land." Fowler explains that "the foreign-language quotations provide the *abracadabra* element. Just as the hero of the Grail romances was expected to speak the proper words (usually in the form of a question) before the wounded king and his land could be restored, so the protagonist in *The Waste Land*, as both hero and king, utters an incantation designed to bring about the restoration of life in himself and his environment" (35). The only hope is offered by the final two lines with their suggestion of a formula for spiritual renewal in the Sanskrit injunctions: "Datta. Dayadhvam. Damyata." The result of following this formula – Give, Sympathize, Control – may be "shantih," which Eliot's note translates as "the Peace which passeth understanding." If so, though, it is a peace that is gained, the poem suggests, by cultural tradition and individual spirituality, by personal trial and triumph, not by those of a rescuer or Grail knight. One of the most important things that Eliot found in Jessie Weston's book may have been the notion that "The shift toward an emphasis on the Quester, his guilts and inadequacies, displaces the King from the centering role he had played in a legend of wonderous recuperation. To Weston, then, 'the dependence of the Curse upon the Quester reduces the story to incoherence.' So her book is written to reduce this latter heretical narrative of guilt and belatedness, in which the motif of impotence and castration is shifted to the Quester and tied to his ability to speak or use a wordy weaponry, to a position of heresy relative to the primacy of what Weston considers to be the 'original' myth" (Jay 32, who cites Weston 17). Perhaps this is why Eliot puts the emphasis on the Fisher King and not on the Grail knight as earlier authors, such as James Russell Lowell, did. The Fisher King, who merges with many of the other characters in the poem, is a kind of Everyman or at least Every Modern Man, for whom, Eliot's poem seems to say, redemption must come from within.

Eliot's treatment of the wasteland and of the figure of the wounded Fisher King was to have a tremendous impact on future writers. The novelists of the Lost Generation found in these images a symbol for the troubles of their age and incorporated them into some of the most significant novels they wrote. Writers like Fitzgerald, Hemingway, and Faulkner, were, in turn, major influences on the novelists of the succeeding generations, who also adapted and further Americanized the imagery Eliot had appropriated from Jessie Weston. Yet even as Eliot was transforming the use and interpretations of the Grail and other Arthurian imagery from the romantic approach taken by James Russell Lowell and others, writers like Edwin Arlington Robinson and John Erskine were finding new ways to modernize, Americanize, and de-romanticize traditional Arthurian story.

Edwin Arlington Robinson wrote three unusual book-length Arthurian poems: *Merlin* (1917), *Lancelot* (1920), and *Tristram* (1927).[9] Neither romances

---

9   A fragment cut from *Lancelot* was published in a limited edition under the title *Modred*. In this poem Robinson describes how Modred uses Colgrevance's best qualities, his sense of justice and desire for a kingdom run by law, to manipulate him into taking part in the plot to catch Lancelot and Guinevere together in the queen's chamber.

in the medieval sense nor even poems of the same narrative type, "Robinson's poems are in their very essence drama" (Pipkin 7). Indeed, they consist of essentially dramatic confrontations between characters and contain much more dialogue than action. Robinson's characters, especially some of his female characters, at times seem more modern than medieval or Victorian. Conrad Aiken has described quite well the denizens of Robinson's Arthurian world: "Mr. Robinson turns his Arthurian heroes and heroines and brooding villains into such figures as could not conceivably exist anywhere else. They are as signally and idiosyncratically stamped, as invariably and unalterably Robinsonian, as the characters of Henry James are Jamesian. These Merlins and Tristrams and Isolts and Lancelots are modern and highly self-conscious folk; they move in a world of moral and emotional subtlety which is decidedly more redolent of the age of Proust than of the age of Malory; they take on a psychological reality and intensity which would have astonished, and might have shocked, either Tennyson or William Morris" (26). Despite knowing and drawing heavily on medieval versions of the Arthurian story,[10] Robinson strips his poems of those elements of the supernatural that form such a basic part of the medieval stories. In his *Tristram*, for instance, Robinson felt strongly that the medieval love potion should play no role in explaining the love between his Tristram and Isolt. Robinson observed that "much as I despise the Eighteenth Amendment, I'm a strict prohibitionist when it comes to potions" (*Edwin Arlington Robinson's Letters to Edith Brower* 189). And in his treatment of the Grail, he eliminated the marvelous and the miraculous so that it "has become merely a symbol of a light that leads men on, luring them to ideals as yet ill-defined, but clear enough to make them dissatisfied with the existing social order" (Pipkin 14).

Of Robinson's three Arthurian poems, *Tristram* generally received the most critical praise when it first appeared[11] and won for him the Pulitzer Prize. It is, however, the least interesting and ultimately the least successful, and later criticism of the poem has been considerably less favorable than the initial reviews. One of the few critics who sees significant accomplishment in the work, Frederic Ives Carpenter, feels that "from a tale of lawless passion, treachery, and revenge, the story has become one of a passion purified by suffering, of joy beyond sorrow, and of the slow growth of wisdom" (82) and

---

10 On Robinson's sources, see Laurence Perrine's "The Sources of Robinson's *Merlin*"; John Hurt Fisher's "Edwin Arlington Robinson and Arthurian Tradition"; and Charles T. Davis's "Robinson's Road to Camelot." Though Bédier's version of the Tristan story is not a direct source for Robinson, Charles T. Davis feels that he must justify his claim that Malory was a principal source for *Tristram* "because of the popularity of Joseph Bédier's reconstruction of the celebrated romance" (90). And it was no doubt in part the popularity of Bédier's version and the subsequent dramatic treatments that led Robinson to take up the story of the tragic lovers and to treat it in the highly dramatic form that he employed.

11 On the reactions of the critics, see Frederic Ives Carpenter's "Tristram the Transcendent" 75–76.

that "in this one poem, Robinson realized, for the first and perhaps the only time, the positive implications which had lain implicit in the transcendental philosophy from the beginning. Transcending 'time,' Tristram gained wisdom without sacrificing the fullness of life in this world" (89). Whether the poem was meant to present such a transcendental view of the way one should live in the world or merely a modernized picture of a passionate love, the poem seems flawed in design and in execution.

One of the main defects of the poem comes from Robinson's rejection of the traditional endings of the story. Although, like Matthew Arnold's "Tristram and Iseult," the poem opens with a view of Isolt of Brittany,[12] it is not she who brings about Tristram's death by lying about the color of the sail (a device Robinson shuns) and thus causing Tristram to give up hope. In fact, although the poem ends as it begins, with Isolt of Brittany looking out to sea, she seems too resigned. Clutching melodramatically an agate that Tristram had given her years before, an agate that is worth more to her than a fleet of ships with a "golden cargo" (209), she muses that "He had been all, / And would be always all there was for her"; and though "he had not come back to her alive," her response is:

> . . . It was like that
> For women, sometimes, and might be so too often
> For women like her. She hoped there were not many
> Of them, or many of them to be . . . .   (209)

Having little of the passion needed for great tragedy, Isolt of Brittany becomes at best a pathetic figure who does not even elicit the sympathy that her counterpart in Arnold's poem – a woman broken down in "the gradual furnace of the world" and destroyed in spirit – does.

Nor does Robinson allow Mark's jealousy to be the cause of Tristram's death, as happens in Malory, who is the major source of Robinson's poem. *Tristram's* Mark appears to be of a villainous and passionate enough nature to do the deed: he is arrested and imprisoned for forging the Pope's name on a document instructing Tristram to go "to fight the Saracens / And by safe inference to find a grave" (107), a device that seems as "clumsy beyond credence" in the plot as Gawain claims it to be in the poem (108). Nevertheless, the imprisonment removes Mark long enough for the lovers to enjoy an Edenic retreat at Joyous Gard, where Tristram is said to be "Like a man lost / In paradise" (157). As soon as Mark is free – with no explanation of how or why he is freed – he sends his men in a small boat to capture Isolt as she walks on the coast near Lancelot's castle and to carry her off to Cornwall. When he has her, he experiences a sudden and unexplained change of heart,

---

12 Emery Neff believes that "By representing Isolt of Brittany, left to suffer, as more pitiable than the tragic lovers, it begins and ends quietly, like Arnold's poem, in the manner of Greek drama" (225).

shows Isolt kindness, and even allows her to see Tristram.

Tristram is prompted to travel to Cornwall by a letter he receives from Morgan, not called "le Fay" because of the general demystification of the story that Robinson intends. The letter urges Tristram to go to Isolt, who is "alone and sore bestead" (174); but when he arrives, he is killed by Andred at the instigation of Morgan. Mark wonders "How much there was of Morgan in this last / Unhappy work of Andred's" (199), and it is clear from her letter to Tristram that she has plotted his death. A minor figure in the poem, Andred is compared to a "reptile" (60), a "lizard" (63), and a "serpent" (81). Earlier, he had his skull cracked against the castle wall by Tristram, on whom he had been spying. Presumably that incident provided Andred's motivation for slaying Tristram. But the roles of Morgan and Andred seem removed from the love triangle that is central to the action of the poem. For Robinson, the tragic force is not the great love between Tristram and Isolt; in fact, that love is diminished all the more by Andred's "worse than insane love" for Isolt (179). And, as Ellsworth Barnard has commented, Morgan "seems not to belong in *Tristram*" (95). Yvor Winters also believed that "Robinson's poem would have been more successful had she not been employed in it" (88). Moreover, Winters felt that the use of Andred to bring about the death of Tristram is "unfortunate" (93): "Robinson employs Andred, who is of no importance in the poem and could easily be dropped, and makes of him the tool of Morgan, who could just as easily be dropped," while "Isolt of Brittany and Mark, the wronged wife and the wronged husband, remain as passive bystanders" (94).

Even granting that it is meant to be dramatic rather than narrative, *Tristram* suffers more than Robinson's other two Arthurian poems from excessive use of dialogue. As a result, the lovers' "folk-tale simplicity is metamorphosed into ultrasophisticated intellectualism. . . . Passion is vaporized into speech, and although this is periodically interrupted by breathless embraces, we begin to question whether a love that is so much talked about but so rarely evident in real action is as overpowering as it is declared to be" (Barnard 151). There are, to be sure, moments of lyric beauty in the poem. The sea and things related to the sea, such as sea birds and ships, provide a pattern of imagery that Robinson skillfully uses as a unifying device. Many of the dramatic moments, such as Isolt of Brittany's looking to the ocean at the beginning and the end of the poem and Isolt of Ireland's abduction on the shore, are set near the sea. And some of the finest metaphors and similes relate to the sea. For example, Isolt says that "Were it not for love, / Poor life would be a ship not worth a launching" (181); and Isolt of Brittany observes that "Wisdom is like a dawn that comes up slowly / Out of an unknown ocean" (206). The "changefulness and irrationality" of the medieval versions of the legend "are at every turn symbolized by the sea – unpredictable, uncontrollable, calm or frenzied on its surface, mysterious in its depths" (Barnard 86). Thus, there is enough lyric beauty, enough powerful imagery and dramatic confrontation, enough of the mystery and intensity of the original stories in which the sea also plays a part, to explain why early critics were so taken with *Tristram*. Unfortunately there is not enough of any of these elements to outweigh the poem's flaws.

In a letter written on January 1, 1930, Robinson noted that while there is no "symbolic significance in *Tristram* . . . there is a certain amount in *Merlin* and *Lancelot*, which were suggested by the world war – Camelot representing in a way the going of a world that is now pretty much gone" (*Selected Letters* 160). One of the reasons that *Lancelot* and *Merlin* are more successful than *Tristram*, which he wrote later in his career, is that Robinson was closer to his own sensibility in the earlier poems. Nowhere, in fact, was Robinson's New England heritage more evident than in *Lancelot*, which has a moral tone that rivals Lowell's in *The Vision of Sir Launfal*. And by using Camelot, at one level, as an image for the modern world, Robinson was able to comment on war and destruction and the end of personal dreams with an obvious modern application. At the same time, in the first two poems he retold the Arthurian stories in ways that made them clearly Americanized versions of the medieval and Victorian tales that preceded them.

In *Lancelot*, the most important thematic element is the Light that haunts Lancelot. A motif that also appeared in *Merlin*, the Light is, in terms of the traditional story, the light of the Grail; but in Robinson's interpretation the Light is demystified, though still difficult to attain. As one critic has observed, "It is not even clear that the 'Light' which Lancelot follows into the sunset is a religious symbol. Lancelot's light represents some sort of higher truth to be sure, but its associations with Lancelot's visions of Galahad seem only to stress a purity of character, singleness of purpose, and ability to persevere that Lancelot lacks" (Cox 497). On the quest for the Grail, Lancelot was "blinded" by the Light (9) and now feels "There is no place for me save where the Light / May lead me" (9–10). And yet, as Guinevere perceptively comments, "There is a Light that you fear more today / Than all the darkness that has ever been" (31). What Lancelot fears is the total commitment and single-minded resolution that following the Light requires.[13] He himself realizes that it would have "blinded me / To death, had I seen more" (133).

In addition, as in Malory, following this light means abandoning his love for Guinevere. As she says to him, "Another light, a longer time ago, / Was living in your eyes, and we were happy" (31). This lower-case "light" is, of

---

13 Yvor Winters felt that "the recurring use of the terms *Vision* and *Light* to represent that for which Lancelot is turning from the world is very weak; the effect is that of a somewhat sentimental cliché, partly because the words themselves are stereotyped, partly because their use represents an evasion of exact statement" (78). While the terms, especially "Light," do appear frequently, the lack of specificity is not much different than that found in the Grail in medieval stories, where the concrete object represents an ideal that is not clearly defined.

course, the light of his love for her, which distracts him from his pursuit of the loftier ideal. It is a sign of how divided Lancelot is – "a person of divided loyalties," E. Edith Pipkin has called him (13) – that ultimately, despite his near obsession with the Light, Guinevere must make the decision that allows him to pursue the spiritual goal. Even when she enters the convent at Almesbury, Lancelot goes to her and asks her to journey with him to France. She is the one who must decline. "I shall not come / Between you and the Gleam that you must follow, / Whether you will or not," (174), she tells him.[14] Though Guinevere is compared by Lancelot to a flower (132), she is actually far more decisive than he is. As Christopher Brookhouse notes, "At last Lancelot follows his vision, but less by his own will, which wavered between the old and the new, than by Guinevere's" (128). Similarly, of Lancelot and Guinevere, Hoyt C. Franchere says, "it is her wisdom that brings him to the full realization of the world he is losing. In his darkness comes the Light" (125).

Lancelot is a study of an individual who has had a glimpse of a way of life that he recognizes as a good higher than anything he has achieved or can achieve by pursuing any other goal. It is, to be sure, an account of "a private, spiritual salvation" (Brookhouse 128). But there is another dimension to the poem. *Lancelot*, like its companion piece *Merlin*, also implies a less private, more universal spiritual salvation. Just as "Robinson clearly used Arthur, Camelot, and the Round Table as symbols of his own civilization – one that also, even if for different reasons, stood on infirm and rotten foundations" (Franchere 121) – he also suggests in both poems a formula for the improvement or advancement of the world. It is one of Robinson's innovations that he looks on Camelot not as an ideal but as a stage in the development of the world.

Robinson said that the most significant line in the two poems (*Merlin* and *Lancelot*) "is, perhaps, 'The world has paid enough for Camelot' – in *L. & G.*" (*Selected Letters* 113). Clearly, then, Robinson's Camelot is not the idyllic place of the musical based on T. H. White's *The Once and Future King*. Not only is Lancelot unable to find the ideal he is seeking through Guinevere; he cannot find it at all in Camelot. As Bors tells Lancelot,

> . . . The Light you saw
> Was not for this poor crumbling realm of Arthur
> Nor more for Rome; but for another state
> That shall be neither Rome nor Camelot,
> Nor one that we may name.   (85)

And the notion is repeated by Guinevere, who confirms that the Light

14 The notion of "following the Gleam" is an obvious echo of Tennyson. Though Robinson diverges radically from Tennyson's versions of the stories of the Arthurian characters he treats, he was nevertheless greatly influenced by the *Idylls* and by Tennyson's Arthurian poems, as the discussion of Robinson's *Lancelot* and *Merlin* in this chapter makes clear.

Lancelot saw was "not the Light of Rome, / Or Time" (92), that is, of any kingdom in time, including Camelot. This is not to say that Camelot is the "black nest of rats" (205) that the disillusioned Pelleas of the *Idylls* calls it. Robinson's Gawain tells Lancelot, "you might have had no Gleam had I been King, / Or had the Queen been like some queens I knew" (151). As in Tennyson's *Idylls*, there is a sense that in some ways Arthur's kingdom took the world a step beyond where it was, but that step was surely not a final one.[15] Robinson, looking beyond the Middle Ages to the modern world, saw a democratic country like the United States as an improvement over monarchy. But he felt that even the most enlightened monarchy seems benighted in comparison to the Light that Lancelot pursues. Early in the poem Lancelot asks

> . . . how much longer are there to be kings?
> When are the millions who are now like worms
> To know that kings are worms, if they are worms?
> When are the women who make toys of men
> To know that they themselves are less than toys
> When Time has laid upon their skins the touch
> Of his all-shrivelling fingers? When are they
> To know that men must have an end of them
> When men have seen the Light and left the world
> That I am leaving now.   (43)

Although there are two ways to read the "they" and "them" in the last lines, the reference seems to be back to "kings" rather than to "women" – a reading consistent with the ideas in this passage and elsewhere in the poem. Shortly after this passage, Bedevere tells Gawaine that he has had a dream "Of a sword over kings, and of a world / Without them" (55).

At the very end of the poem Lancelot hears a voice within him saying, "Where the Light falls, death falls; a world has died / For you, that a world may live." The cryptically paradoxical nature of these lines is reminiscent of the end of the *Idylls*, where Tennyson writes that "The old order changeth, yielding place to the new, . . . Lest one good custom should corrupt the world" (251). In both cases, there is a sense that something passes but that what is born in its place is an improvement. The alternative, after all, is stagnation. For Robinson, if Camelot does not pass, there can be no advancement in the condition of the world.

Robinson seemed to have had a similar idea in *Merlin*, which he said "was written in anticipation of" *Lancelot* and also "to complement its various incompletenesses." For those reasons, he advised that "the two should be read together" (*Selected Letters* 113). In *Merlin*, as in *Lancelot*, Camelot is

---

15 In "Tennyson and the Passing of Arthur," John D. Rosenberg has said that "Perhaps the surest road to Tennyson's Camelot is via another great Victorian epic that appeared in the bookshops alongside the *Idylls* in 1859, Darwin's *Origin of the Species*" (232).

undeniably a world that is passing. And in the earlier poem Robinson surely had in mind some of the same notions about the evolution of society. Though the final line of *Merlin* seems to leave the world in gloom and with little hope, Robinson said in a letter to Edith Brower, "I wish you wouldn't call the poem 'sad' for I'm ---- if it is anything of the kind. There is nothing especially sad about the end of kings and the redemption of the world, and that is what Merlin seems to be driving at" (*Edwin Arlington Robinson's Letters to Edith Brower* 169).

This vision of a future without kings is not the only way that Robinson modernizes and Americanizes his version of the Merlin and Vivian story. *Merlin* is the most effective of his Arthurian poems because it best adapts an aspect of the legend to his own day. In the process, Robinson also creates the most interesting characters in any of his Arthurian poems. Although he alludes to the rumors that call him the son of a devil (65), Merlin says he does not believe them and there is no cause for the reader of the poem to do so either. Merlin is not the mystical figure, not the prophet or magician or shape-shifter that he is in earlier versions of the story. As Yvor Winters has noted, Merlin's "prophetic power appears to be mainly the clear foresight of great intelligence, but it is given a supernatural air by the fatalism which is central to the theme" (63).

Even Merlin's confinement in Broceliande is divested of the magical element it has in earlier versions. Merlin remains with Vivian of his own free will; her natural charm, not any supernatural one, keeps them together. As Nathan Comfort Starr noted, Vivian "is a believable and intelligently con-ceived woman, no vulgar wanton as in Tennyson, no ambitious amateur in magic as in Malory, but an unusually fascinating and capable person, entan-gled in a difficulty far more troublesome than a love affair between a young woman and an older man. Vivian is no longer simply a seductress, finally extracting the secrets of Merlin's magic and condemning him to a perpetual imprisonment" (Starr, "The Transformation of Merlin" 111).

Robinson sets his poem in a time when Arthur's kingdom is crumbling, a clear echo of the world war. Yet, even more than *Lancelot, Merlin* must be seen in a larger context than that of a world ravaged by war. Of the "two actions" Yvor Winters has identified in the poem (62) – "on the one hand Merlin's love affair with Vivian, and on the other the disintegration of Arthur's kingdom" (63) – Winters correctly observes that "such unity as *Merlin* attains . . . resides in the character of Merlin and in the collapse of his two worlds" (70). Though Winters sees the two actions as "only loosely connected" (63), it is, in fact, the interplay between the actions that is the crux of the poem.

Broceliande, where Merlin and Vivian live happily for a time, is described as an "elysian wilderness" (60) And when Merlin first approaches it:

> The birds were singing still; leaves flashed and swung
> Before him in the sunlight; a soft breeze

Made intermittent whisperings around him
Of love and fate and danger, and faint waves
Of many sweetly-stinging fragile odors
Broke lightly as they touched him; cherry-boughs
Above him snowed white petals down upon him,
And under their snow falling Merlin smiled
Contentedly; as one who contemplates
No longer fear, confusion, or regret
May smile at ruin or revelation.   (56–57)

Merlin is obviously entering an Edenic place, but even in this idyllic description there is a hint of the eventual, inevitable fall. Later in the poem,
Robinson makes it explicit that Broceliande is Merlin's Eden. As Merlin
prepares to leave because of his concern for Arthur and Camelot, Vivian says
to him that Eden is a better name for their retreat because it has been inhabited by a man and a woman and now there is "a Tree of Knowledge"
(126–27). Merlin's departure from Broceliande is thus prompted by his inability to ignore the concerns of the real world, represented by the fate of
Camelot. But although he returns to Camelot, he is unable to save the
doomed kingdom.

Whatever Robinson may have thought about the need for the passing of
monarchies, his Arthur and Merlin see Camelot as an ideal. Merlin makes
Arthur king "Thereby to be a mirror for the world" (102). What Merlin
created at Camelot was to be an ideal world in a broader, but no more
important, sense than Broceliande was to be. Yet the pull between the political and the personal makes it impossible for Merlin to be totally happy in
either realm. Thus, there is a double fall in Robinson's poem: Arthur's ideal
kingdom collapses and Merlin's own happiness is destroyed because he
cannot ignore the larger political situation that, Robinson's poem suggests,
necessarily overrides, or at least overshadows, personal considerations.
Though Merlin is not trapped in the way he is in medieval story, what he
"could never escape from was the 'wilderness' of his dual obligations" (Starr,
"The Transformation of Merlin" 114). The historical and social forces that
affect men's lives make Broceliande and Camelot, the two Edens of
Robinson's poem, fallen worlds. And they turn Robinson into as much of a
pessimist about the possibility of achieving an ideal as Twain was. Merlin
imagines Vivian saying late in the poem:

Time called him home,
And that was as it was, for much is lost
Between Broceliande and Camelot.   (163)

Lost in the pull between the personal Eden and the ideal society is Merlin's
ability to achieve perfect contentment in either sphere.

The notion of creating a perfect world is supported by various patterns of imagery in the poem, including the numerous references to "specks," which Valerie Lagorio has explained as "standing for moral and spiritual imperfections" (167). The notion of specks as an image of imperfection is surely one of the many elements that Robinson borrowed from Tennyson. In the "Merlin and Vivien" idyll, when the wily Vivien is trying to convince Merlin to trust her and impart to her the secret charm that she will use against him, she sings the song that implores that he "trust me not at all or all in all"; one of the images used to make this point is that of the "little pitted speck in garner'd fruit / That rotting inward slowly moulders all" (125). Robinson's Vivian introduces the concept when she pours wine for Merlin and says, "I fear there may be specks." Merlin picks up the theme. "There are specks everywhere. I fear them not," he tells her and goes on to say that were he the king in Camelot he would "Fear more than specks" (90–91). Later Vivian quotes these words back to him when he is about to return to "a speckled king" (123) who, Vivian believes, Merlin made king "To be a moral for the speckled ages" (120). Vivian, who is trying to create a world free of change for her and Merlin in Broceliande, admits that she will never like the king because "There are specks / Almost all over him" (125). Grouping Arthur with Guinevere, Lancelot and Modred, she calls all four "speckled like a merry nest / Of addled eggs together" (126).

Of course, Vivian's attempt to shut herself off from the world of change and to create an idyllic place in Broceliande is doomed to failure. Seeing everyone as "speckled with imperfection" necessarily isolates Vivian from the world, just as it does Young Goodman Brown in Hawthorne's classic story. Ultimately it denies human nature, which may be improved but never perfected. How bent Vivian is on preventing the intrusion of the outside world into her Eden is suggested by another recurring image in the poem, Merlin's beard. One of the first things Vivian, who "abhors / Mortality in all its hues and emblems" (73), asks of Merlin when he comes to Broceliande is that he shave off his beard, which, she tells him, brought her terror night and day (84). When Merlin leaves Broceliande for good, a sign that he has returned to the world of change is that he is "Made older with an inch of silver beard" (148).

The change symbolized by Merlin's beard is, with all its implied imperfections, inevitable. But *Merlin* is not just a lament that things pass: the notion of the evolution of society redeems change. Crucial to an understanding of this aspect of the poem is an explanation of the two lights that Robinson refers to as "the torch / Of woman" and "the light that Galahad found." These two lights "Are some day to illuminate the world" (155). Asked the meaning of these symbols, Robinson explained that "Galahad's 'light' is simply the light of the Grail, interpreted universally as a spiritual realization of Things and their significance." Less clear about the second part of this phrase, Robinson said merely that "the 'torch of women' is to be taken literally" (*Selected Letters* 113). Hoyt C. Franchere has commented that "The expression 'the torch of woman' – that is, woman as a torch – must, in its connotative force, turn in two directions: woman as an inspirer, as a producer of enlightment, knowledge; and as a producer of that flame of love or passion that moves even the mightiest of men" (122).[16] In the poem Dagonet repeats the phrase and adds the fact that the torch of woman and the light that Galahad found "Will some day save us all, as they saved Merlin" (158). What actually saved Merlin was the combination of attempting to create an ideal world where moral goals are important and at the same time finding, if not inspiration, at least solace and personal happiness in the world that Vivian has created for him. She is a civilizing force, making his personal life something of significance so that he is not wholly absorbed by the speckled machinations of politics and power. In *Merlin*, there is the hope that these two forces will become more and more vital and will combine "to light the world" (166). This explains why, although the last line of the poem is "And there was darkness over Camelot," Robinson could say that the ending of *Merlin* was not sad. For Robinson, the darkness will one day be dispelled by the two lights that Merlin predicts.

A writer who approaches the Arthurian stories in a realistic manner similar to Robinson's is John Erskine. Like a number of the other Arthurian authors of the period, Erskine was an academic, a professor of English Literature at Columbia University. His knowledge of the medieval sources, particularly Malory, about whom he wrote an essay in his study *The Delight of Great Books*, is obvious in his two novels *Galahad: Enough of His Life to Explain His Reputation* (1926) and *Tristan and Isolde: Restoring Palamede* (1932), but both depart radically from their medieval precursors. As he re-creates their stories, Erskine reinterprets the principal characters. Therefore, while the novels are quite different from each other in subject matter, they are nonetheless comparable in tone and theme. Both adopt an urbane, somewhat ironic view of the Arthurian material; and both use that material to explore a quest for perfection and the consequences thereof, a common theme in American literature.

The tone of Erskine's "The Tale of Sir Galahad and His Quest for the Sangreal," one of seven stories that he wrote for the *The American Weekly* in 1940,[17] is similar to that of his Galahad novel. Lancelot, for example,

16 In another explanation, Frederic Ives Carpenter finds the "realization" of this "cryptic and seemingly un-puritan prophecy" in *Tristram* "where the dark Isolt points to salvation through passionate love (the torch of woman), while Isolt of the white hands realizes the ideal of purity, which Galahad found" (84).

17 The other stories are "The Tale of King Arthur's Sword 'Excalibur,' " "The Tale of Sir Tristram and the Love Potion" (referred to below in the discussion of Erskine's *Tristan and Isolde*), "The Tale of the Enchantress and the Magic Scabbard," "The Tale of Launcelot and the Four Queens," "The Tale of Merlin and One of the Ladies of the Lake," and "The Tale of How Sir Launcelot Slew Sir Agravaine." The seven stories appeared in *The American Weekly* from February 4 to March 17, 1940. They have been reprinted in *The Camelot Periodicals: Arthurian Fiction from Magazine Appearance*.

confesses his sins to a hermit, who is really an angel, and says he repents, if repenting means he is sorry that what he did is a sin; when the angel explains that repenting means he must be sorry that he and Guinevere loved each other, Lancelot realizes that he cannot repudiate the affection and therefore can not achieve the Grail. But, as Erskine tells in very abbreviated form the story of Galahad's achieving of the Grail, he does not overlook the legendary elements of the story. He recounts how five angels and Joseph of Aramathie appear to Galahad, Percival, and Bors; Joseph gives them his blessing; and then he reveals the Grail to them.

In the novel *Galahad: Enough of His Life to Explain His Reputation*, however, Erskine takes an altogether different approach to the story of the Grail knight. "We say nothing here," he explains, "of the Grail, nor of Joseph of Arimathea, nor of the Round Table, nor of Excalibur; we confine our report to the first causes, as it were, of these famous dreams." Like Robinson, Erskine deliberately eliminates the legendary elements that he sees as the elaborations of poets and minstrels. Choosing instead to focus on realistic events, he tells "the story as it happened in our world, to people like ourselves or only a little better" (16). The people who are most like "ourselves," that is, the people of the nineteen-twenties, are the women of the story. Erskine says that "the plot is composed of three women and one coincidence" (16), the coincidence being that two of the women who play major roles in the story are named Elaine, the first Elaine of Corbin, the daughter of Pelles, and the second Elaine of Astolat. The third woman is, of course, Guinevere. Elaine of Astolat, in fact, plays a rather minor part in the novel and contributes more to the picture of the relationship between Lancelot and Guinevere than to the explanation of Galahad's reputation.

The other two women are much more integral to this story. Neither is the typical courtly lady of medieval romance. In the world created by Erskine, there are, as Lancelot tells Galahad, no ladies in distress (164). Even more than the Guenevere of Hovey's plays or the Vivian of Robinson's *Merlin*, the women of this novel, particularly Guinevere and the Elaine who gives birth to Galahad, are representative of the "new woman" who "had an enhanced sense of self, gender, and mission. Vigorous and energetic, she was likely to be involved in institutions beyond the family" (Woloch 269). In both England and America, a considerable body of literature, particularly fiction and drama, was beginning to explore the position of women and alternately expose the societal limitations placed on intelligent and talented women and to present new images of women who resisted those limitations.

At the start of the novel, Elaine of Corbin is a model new woman. A free-thinking and bold-speaking individual, she finds "the whole matrimonial program" to be "unattractive" (21); she tells her father that he can "give orders for dinner" better than she can (46); she considers jousting "out of date" (22); and she engages in what her father calls "flippant discussion of King Arthur" (28). The fact that she names her overfed spaniel Arthur after

the king demonstrates that she is not a slave to social convention. Elaine has
a respectable suitor, Sir Bromel, but deplores "the sort of home you think I
ought to long for – you presiding over me and the children, telling us what
thoughts to have" (19). When she falls in love with Lancelot, she determines
to give him a child although the thought of giving birth out of wedlock
shocks Sir Bromel and ultimately makes that very child, Galahad, turn away
from her.

When Elaine does offer herself to Lancelot in the Castle Case, there is no
Dame Brisen with her magical sense-dulling potion. Though Lancelot and
Elaine disagree about whether or not she tricked him into coming to the
castle, there is no doubt that he knows with whom he is sleeping; and while
he recognizes that he might hate her afterwards (96), he yields to her arguments and her charms. Since Lancelot ignores his son and Elaine and since
Galahad then desires to leave her for Camelot, she feels that her life has been
a "total failure" (172) but that Galahad "has it in him to be a great man, if
some one can bring it out" (176). In this novel named after a male knight but
whose plot, says the author, is composed of three women, two of those
women are indeed essential for explaining Galahad's reputation. It is Elaine's
independence and determination that lead to the birth of Galahad, and it is
the task of Guinevere to bring the greatness out of Galahad.

Guinevere is a woman of vision. She can say as a new woman would that
"I thought we had got beyond the doctrine that women are here just to
increase the population" (290). She describes her marriage to Arthur as one
in which her wishes were not consulted. She was taken "as a sort of payment
on a debt" because of the service Arthur had done for her father (298); but
she married him because she knew that as a woman she "can't do stirring
things" and so wanted to assist Arthur, who she thought would achieve
greatness. When she saw him become complacent with what he had accomplished, she turned to Lancelot, hoping, she tells Arthur, that he would
complete Arthur's work and "encouraged him – all I could" (104). She
explains her hope to Lancelot: "My one excuse is that through our love you
became the best of living men – or so I thought. With this result, our life
together might be said to have a reason, to be almost holy. Otherwise, we are
only two traitors, concealing a sin, and I'll have no more to do with you"
(71). Too devoted to the king, Lancelot not only shares Arthur's values but
also follows him even in matters that Guinevere considers trivial rather than
reserving his knightly skills for weightier things. Her conclusion is that
neither Arthur nor Lancelot "will do anything more of importance" (105).

In Galahad, Guinevere sees the potential for greatness of which Elaine
spoke, and she takes it upon herself to mold him in a way that she could not
do with her husband or her lover. What Guinevere is striving for is something beyond what ordinary people can achieve. Arthur and Lancelot are
both good men, though neither is perfect; and it is clear that Guinevere
assists both of them in establishing a peaceful kingdom at Camelot, which in

this book is not a place riddled with evil. As Taylor and Brewer observe, "The chief problem at Camelot is not that it is corrupt; this is not the fallen world of Tennyson's later idylls. It is simply the imperfect world of men and women" (199).

Galahad seems to be of a piece with this world. In his early years he is a spoiled, self-centered, and difficult child who blackens the eyes of his nurse. But when he comes to Camelot he is filled with visions of courageous achievement. Guinevere, who once thought of "Lancelot's noble work and his splendid name" as her "children" (134), adopts Galahad so she can make of him the "masterpiece" (198) that she could not make of Arthur or Lancelot. The content of the masterpiece is to be a kind of American Adam, "an absolutely new kind of man, an original type. In the first place, he will be spiritually strong and physically clean. He won't even have an impulse to regret or be ashamed of, and he'll never love a woman, except as your boy is fond of me" (198). To the end of creating this "new kind of man" (236), Guinevere teaches Galahad to resist the charms of women, to fight only in defense of what is right, to "have some passion or vision" in his life (216) and, when he has chosen "one dream," to "be faithful to that" whatever the cost (218–19).

It is indicative of how successful Guinevere is in inspiring Galahad to pursue this new kind of life that when he learns that he was conceived out of wedlock he rejects both of his parents and has no desire to see them again. But the ultimate test of Guinevere's success comes when she tells her protégé about her affair with Lancelot. Earlier she had made Galahad promise that "if ever I do anything unworthy of me, of you and me," he would abandon her "then and there, absolutely, forever!" (249). Upon her admission, Galahad, true to his principles and his promise, disappears from the court, an event that Guinevere sees as "a masterpiece of character-training" (304). His rejection of his mentor, of the one who inspired him to his vision, is a sign that he has achieved the single-minded devotion to an ideal that Guinevere recognizes as the sign of greatness.

The pursuit of this ideal comes at a cost. It requires Galahad to reject anyone who loves him – in the noblest sense, as Elaine does, or even in a less noble way, as Ettard does. In rejecting his parents, he cuts himself off from "bigger people" than himself, as Arthur tells him (263). But it is precisely this single-mindedness that made his reputation. When he disappears from court, people say that he is "devoting his life . . . to the search for the holiest treasure in the world" (339). In one sense this is true: the purity he seeks is beyond what is reasonable to expect in the real world and so is worthy of description in the superlative degree. Such talk is also, as Lancelot says, "how stories grow" (339), tales like that of the quest for the Holy Grail. The rumor that grew into Galahad's storied success in this quest thus explains his reputation.

The idea behind Erskine's second Arthurian novel, which is dedicated to

Arthurian scholar William Nitze,[18] is similar to that found in another of the seven Arthurian short stories he wrote for the *American Weekly* in 1940. In this story, "The Tale of Sir Tristram and the Love Potion," which is much closer to the medieval sources in narrative detail – though not in style – than the novel, Erskine includes the love potion. In the longer treatment, Erskine tells of "two young things getting ready for trouble" (63) who have a natural attraction to each other. He observes that "The minstrels made much of a magic draught which Brangain, according to them, poured in the cup when Isolde was crossing the sea to marry King Mark. . . . The minstrels were always singing about magic drinks! No, the doom of these lovers came upon them there, as I have just told you, under the open sky, in the glade by the sea. They were what they were, and they were young" (64).

The primary innovation in this novel is the shift in focus from the trials, triumphs, and tragedy of the lovers to the quest of Palamede, a young man who, like Galahad, is seeking an ideal. Palamede hears from a Christian slave, a captured Crusader named Jaafar, idealized stories of his homeland, stories that are like the medieval romances in that "all the women became beautiful, and their admirers beyond reproach" (20). The world of his own parents seems pedestrian by comparison, so Palamede, who is "a dreamer, but of the dangerous kind" for whom "the world had to be as he saw it, not as God made it" (22), sets out to find the wondrous world of Jaafar's stories and in particular a woman worthy of his devotion.

Of course, the world he finds is very different from that of Jaafar's stories. When Palamede arrives at a port city, he is greeted by commoners and merchants who sell him defective equipment. Put off by the discourteous reception at Pharamont's castle, Palamede strikes Meliant, with whom he has been asked to joust, harder than is necessary, and he is accepted because of the display of prowess. Ironically, "An angry blow had got him into noble society." It is understandable that this "was not the initiation he had dreamt of" (79). The first "castle" he encounters is not the many-towered, penanted structure that he has heard of but rather "a fortress, inviting you chiefly to stay out" (76). "As in *Galahad*, much of the book's irony and humour arises from the conflict between a naïve young man's conception of chivalry and the realities of men and women" (Taylor and Brewer 201). Most of all, Palamede is disappointed in the people he meets.

Mark, who is mentioned in Jaafar's stories, hardly fits the image of a courtly ruler that Palamede has formed. At their first meeting, Mark greets Palamede with a rudeness that was "spontaneous, an instinctive reaction to strange faces and new ideas" (164). Palamede finds him to be crude and is amazed that being married to Isolde neither makes him happy nor ennobles

---

18 Nitze wrote a study titled *Arthurian Romance and Modern Poetry and Music*, in which he mentions Erskine in his list of the "competent and gifted authors" who treat the story of Tristan and Isolt (19).

him. He is particularly offended by Mark's attraction to other women, like Phenice, the wife of Sir Segurade.

Tristan is little better. He is boorish, hardly the picture of courtesy that medieval romance makes him out to be. When given a room not to his liking in Mark's castle, Tristan takes it upon himself to change it for a better one. When seated at the end of the table, he moves up higher. But more offensive is the fact that he, like Mark, is unfaithful to Isolde. He makes love to Phenice and excuses the deed to Isolde by saying "A man's a man" (213); then he marries Isolde of Brittany. The actions of Mark and Tristan lead Palamede to the conclusion that "but for him Isolde would not have known what courtesy was" (196).

The reason Palamede is so upset by the treatment of Isolde is that it threatens his ideal view of women and of love. His father and his mother tried to warn him that physical attraction was an important element of love, but he refused to believe them. Brangain, who looks so much like Isolde that they could be twins and who herself loves Palamede, also tries to warn him that love is not the ideal that he would make it. But throughout most of the book Palamede is a courtly lover who loves at first sight. When he sees Isolde, he knows instantly that she is "what his youth had sought, a perfection challenging yet unattainable, commanding worship, imposing adoration" (165). Believing her to be "the woman he was born to worship" (171), he offers her love even if there is no hope that he will be loved in return. When he tells Isolde that he asks "nothing but for a while to be near you, and afterwards to remember!" she reacts very casually and encourages him to think of Brangain. His response is that Isolde "might have estimated at its proper value the dream of perfection which he had brought out of the east and laid at her feet!" (180). Like the courtly lover, he feels that a noble love should be secret. At one point he blames himself for having talked to Brangain about Isolde since "If you really loved, you did not talk!" (227).

Palamede's idealized view of love is subjected to a number of tests. Initially he tells Isolde that he could not "admire" her if she did not love her husband (180), but he comes to realize that she loves Tristan. Believing Mark to be unworthy of her love, he accepts her affection for Tristan. But when Tristan gives Isolde an ultimatum in front of Mark by threatening to go to Phenice unless she leaves with him at that moment, Palamede concludes that "Tristan was, in fact, no better than Mark" (226). In part because he is prodded by the words of Brangain and of the hermit he met on the way to Cornwall to accept that it is less than manly not to do whatever he can to win the woman he loves and in part because of his own desires, Palamede determines to take her from Tristan. The hermit told Palamede that "Since you are unbaptised, no woman of consequence will risk her soul in your company" (94); so the first step in winning Isolde is to have the hermit baptize him. He then goes to Tristan in Brittany and tells him that he will take Isolde from her husband. As a counter to Tristan's argument that Isolde loves him and not

Palamede, he suggests that he will inform her that Tristan has wed the other Isolde and that this will offend her "maiden soul," which is "a wall between you and her!"[19] (319). But Tristan says she is a maiden soul who is "at home in the world" (320). As proof, he tells of her asking Brangain to sleep with Mark on the night of Isolde's and Mark's wedding, a charge that Palamede finds so offensive that he calls Tristan a liar. In the ensuing fight, Palamede gives Tristan a fatal wound but then agrees to return to Cornwall and to bring Isolde to her dying lover.

When Palamede learns from Brangain that Tristan's account of Isolde's wedding night is true, he realizes that "Tristan was not a liar, after all, and I've murdered him!" (334). While Palamede's faith in himself and in the world of Jaafar's stories is undermined – and even as he is about to leave this land and return to the home that he once considered inferior to the marvelous western world but no longer does – he still can say "I did not come in vain! I have seen one woman, noble beyond hope, one flawless love, not for me!" (344). Palamede remains a dreamer and an idealist. He believes he has seen the kind of love he thought he would be capable of. It is not in the end his love for Isolde that supports his faith in an ideal love; rather it is Isolde's love for Tristan. Her willingness to sacrifice anything and anyone for her love and her single-minded devotion to Tristan, like Galahad's to his ideal of purity, is what makes the love of Isolde and Tristan the stuff of legends.

In this period from Twain to the twenties, the movement from romance to realism took various forms: the historical novel, the treatment of the legends filtered through scholarship, realistic and modernized presentations of characters, and the use of a "new woman" figure. With the exception of Robinson and Eliot, most of the Arthurian authors in this period – from Babcock to Erskine – are minor literary figures. Yet the abundance and vitality of Arthurian material, in addition to being an important phenomenon in its own right, provides a context for the use of Arthurian themes by some of the major writers of the first half of the twentieth century.

---

19 The number of exclamation points following Palamede's remarks is a sign of his idealized view of life. He is up until shortly after this point sure – too sure – of things.

5

Beyond The Waste Land: *Fitzgerald, Hemingway, and Faulkner*

The Arthurian legends appealed not only to Eliot, Robinson, and other American poets and dramatists of the early twentieth century but also to some of the most prominent American novelists. F. Scott Fitzgerald, the great chronicler of America's Jazz Age, Ernest Hemingway, the popular novelist whose economical prose redefined contemporary American fiction, and William Faulkner, the lyrical voice of the American South, all found vitality and contemporaneity in the legends. Yet, while they reinterpreted the Arthurian legends in distinctly American ways, each was inspired by different aspects of them: Fitzgerald, by the Grail quest, which became for him a metaphor for modern man's search for meaning; Hemingway, by the Fisher King, whose story provided an analogue for a modern society so bereft of values that it seemed a type of the wasteland in need of revival; and Faulkner, by the chivalric virtues of questing knights like Gawain and Tristram, which recalled the increasingly-forgotten values of his traditional and beloved South: "courage and honor and pride" ("The Bear," *GDM* 297) and love of the land.

Drawn to traditional elements of Arthurian mythology, F. Scott Fitzgerald often reinterpreted those elements in untraditional ways in his fiction. The wasteland, for instance – a concept popularized by Eliot's *The Waste Land* – afforded Fitzgerald a powerful image for the deterioration of social values and the resulting emphasis on materialism and gaudy excess in the first half of the century, particularly the years between the two world wars. The related and recurring image of the Grail quest became a paradigm for contemporary man's search for honor – though, in Fitzgerald's shorter fiction and in his novels, his characters generally failed to fulfill their quests because they abandoned their ideals or perverted and debased the notion of the Grail itself.

Fitzgerald's fascination with medievalism, particularly with Arthurian myth and the romance of chivalry, began early. As a child, he imagined himself to be the son not of his parents but "of a king, a king who ruled the whole world" (Fitzgerald, "Author's House," cited in Turnbull 28). Even his own family's snobbery had its origins in a nostalgia for the romantic values of a by-gone era threatened by the encroaching materialism of the twentieth century (a theme that – recast – becomes prominent in his most significant work, *The Great Gatsby* [1925]). Fitzgerald's forebears, after all, were patrician. His ancestors included Francis Scott Key, for whom Fitzgerald was named; and, as André Le Vot demonstrates, their "moral heritage, reviewed and revised by [F. Scott's] romantic imagination, can be summed up as an idealistic attitude contrasting with America's postwar materialism – the Southern aristocracy's traditional panache, inherited from the English Cavaliers and sharply different from the down-to-earth mercantilism of the Puritans' descendants" (6). It is therefore unsurprising that Fitzgerald admired his father's distinctly Southern courtesy, courtliness, and romantic love of the past or that, even after the elder Fitzgerald's financial failure adversely affected the family's social standing, Scott still found him to be a sympathetic figure ("of tired stock" perhaps, but nevertheless "his [son's] moral guide" [Piper 9, 11], like Reverend Diver in *Tender Is the Night*).[1]

Fitzgerald's whole life had romantic overtones. It was, as Matthew J. Bruccoli observed, "a quest for heroism" (*Grandeur* xx); and Fitzgerald's commitment to and sense of a personal chivalric code continued even as his own life and behavior grew increasingly more unheroic. "I feel very strongly about you doing [your] duty" (*Letters* 15), he wrote to his young daughter Scottie; and he urged her to establish certain resolves (similar to the "General Resolves" outlined by the youthful Gatsby) that would encourage her to pay attention to scholarship, to her ability to understand and get along with people, and to her own body as "a useful instrument." Such a basic code of behavior was important, he explained with paternal concern, because "My generation of the radicals and the breakers-down never found anything to take the place of the old virtues of work and courage and the old graces of courtesy and politeness" (*Letters* 50).

Fitzgerald was acutely aware of his own breaches of that code, as his voluminous correspondence with family and friends reveals. After one of his wife Zelda's numerous hospitalizations, he wrote to Dr. Carroll, her physician, that – despite his recent "slip off the wagon" – he recognized his responsibility to help Zelda stabilize her health. At the same time, he explained in familiar chivalric terms that any real reconciliation with her would constitute an impossible quest: "There is simply too much of the past between us. When that mist falls . . . no knight errant can transverse its immense distance" (*Correspondence* 487). In a note written shortly before his death to his mistress Sheilah Graham, he apologizes for yet another episode of rude and drunken behavior. His unfitness "for any human relations" was, he contends, in marked contrast to her conduct, which he praised as "fine and chivalrous" (Graham 300–01). This awareness and acknowledgement of chivalric conduct served to inform Fitzgerald's fictional characters as well, who, as Sy Kahn observed, are variously undone by an idealism much like Fitzgerald's own, an idealism "bravely asserted but doomed" (47); and such

1 Piper quotes from Fitzgerald's fragmentary manuscript, "The Death of My Father" (1931). That handwritten manuscript is reproduced on pp. 177–82 of *The Apprentice Fiction of F. Scott Fitzgerald*.

conduct became one significant measure of his code hero, much the way that "grace under pressure" did for Hemingway's code hero.

Fitzgerald's interest in the medieval was also evident in other aspects of his life. As a boy, he read *Scottish Chiefs, Ivanhoe*, and action-based historical stories for young men; and by high school he progressed to Tennyson, Chesterton, and Twain.[2] Fitzgerald's earliest writings, according to his *Ledger* entry for June, 1909, included an imitation of *Ivanhoe* called "Elavo" and "a complicated story of some knights," both unfinished (Bruccoli *Grandeur* 20, 28; Kuehl, *Apprentice Fiction* 17).

Years later, in an epilogue to Matthew Bruccoli's biography of Fitzgerald, Scottie Fitzgerald recalled her father's "annoyance when I kept falling asleep during his detailed background briefings on *Ivanhoe*." She remembered, too, the charts of the Middle Ages and other "Histomaps" which hung on the walls of his workroom in Baltimore and his collections of miniature soldiers, "which he deployed on marches around our Christmas trees" (Scottie Fitzgerald Smith in *Grandeur* 496). Scottie herself played "Knights of the Round Table" with paper dolls that had been elaborately painted by Zelda (*Grandeur* 262) – "coats-of-mail of Galahad and Lancelot . . . [and other] proud members" of the court of King Arthur (*Bits of Paradise* 3) – in a doll-house described by Fitzgerald in "Outside the Cabinet-Maker's." (In that poignant story, written when the Fitzgeralds were living at Ellersie in Wilmington and Scottie was six, a father buys an expensive doll's house for his young daughter. Though he knows it is only a costly piece of cabinet-making and not a fairy's castle, he imagines for her mysteries "whose luster and texture he could never see or touch any more himself" [140].)

It was during Fitzgerald's years at Princeton University (1913–17) that his fascination with the medieval deepened and his vision of the questing romantic hero, which became the basis for all of his fictional characters, crystallized. The Gothic splendor of the campus provided a fertile environment for the young Fitzgerald's preoccupation with chivalric tradition: at the time he attended, Princeton was not simply a top-ranked college but an academic and social community so organized that it resembled an order of chivalry, with its various heroes, ceremonies, and cults (Le Vot 42, 46). The very architecture of the venerable institution evoked in him "a deep and almost reverent liking for the gray walls and gothic peaks and all they symbolized in the store of the ages of antiquity" ("The Spire and the Gargoyle" 106). As he rambled down the shadowy lanes whose names he later recited with devotion in his stories and novels or as he explored the imposing buildings on the campus, Fitzgerald felt that he had crossed into a different world and time. Like the "mediævalist" Amory Blaine, who feels a "reverent

2   Among the courses Fitzgerald took at Princeton was one on "Chaucer and His Contemporaries" (1916). Nancy Y. Hoffmann, in *"The Great Gatsby: Troilus and Criseyde* Revisited?,"* suggests that "Gatsby's grail quest is influenced directly or indirectly by the tradition of Troilus" (156).

devotion" to Princeton's architecture, symbolic of "lofty aspiration" (*TSP* 105, 53–54), Fitzgerald viewed it all with the awe of the outsider who is offered a privileged glance into the secrets of the aristocracy, a perspective on which he later drew in some of his best fiction.

Among the most important of Princeton's cults was the football team: they were champions, in the medieval sense, defending the community's prestige and honor in perilous tournaments. Fitzgerald – who revered the football players for their skill, intelligence, and prowess – considered them to be modern-day knights; in "The Bowl," he described them as questing heroes, "bewitched figures in another world, strange and infinitely romantic, . . . consecrated and unreachable – vaguely holy" (97). Hobey Baker, captain of the football team during Fitzgerald's freshman year, was one of the greatest athletes in Princeton's history; Bruccoli notes that to Fitzgerald and his classmates Baker seemed like "a Galahad figure on and off the field" (*Grandeur* 44).

Although Fitzgerald himself failed to qualify for the team – a disappointment matched only by his inability a few years later to see action during World War I – he followed Princeton football fervently throughout his college years and beyond; at the time of his fatal heart attack in 1940, in fact, he was readying an article about the current football season for the *Princeton Alumni Weekly*. His interest in the game that he termed symbolic of the "essential and beautiful" ("Princeton," *Afternoon of an Author* 72) persisted because he saw football in chivalric terms – as an act of faith, intensely personal, on the one hand; as an expression of communion, ritually collective, on the other. Even in his fiction, football assumed a critical place, as a romantic longing for all that is best in youth and idealism,[3] in much the same way that sports like bullfighting and baseball did in Hemingway's code work. In *The Great Gatsby*, for example, Tom Buchanan's only real personal claim to fame – apart from his family's money – is that he used to be "one of the most powerful ends that ever played football at New Haven – a national figure." But Tom betrayed that promise and became an arrogant, supercilious man with "a cruel body," a man who, having reached such "an acute limited excellence at twenty-one that everything afterward savors of anticlimax,"

---

3 Bruccoli (*Grandeur* 228) notes that the second story that Fitzgerald ever wrote, "Reade, Substitute Right Half," published in the February 1910 *Now and Then*, was "a perfect example of fiction as wish-fulfillment. . . . a small boy comes off the bench to lead his football team to victory."

   Fitzgerald's interest in football persisted throughout his lifetime. In numerous letters to Scottie (for instance, November 2, 1940, in *Letters* 114), Fitzgerald writes that he is listening to Princeton football games on the radio. His companion Sheilah Graham remembers that he would often doodle football plays in her books (*The Real F. Scott Fitzgerald* 147).

   And Turnbull (*Scott Fitzgerald* 211–12) recalls playing football with Fitzgerald, who gave him football books and introduced him to the *Football Annual*. Fitzgerald also took the young Turnbull to a Navy game at Princeton. Turnbull was "struck by his uncanny familiarity with the Princeton team. He knew so many details about each player that I suspected him of having memorized the programs of previous contests."

wistfully drifts on forever seeking "the dramatic turbulence of some ir-recoverable football game" (6).

As he ultimately did with his fictional characters, Fitzgerald cast himself in the role of romantic hero. The various honors and successes that he achieved at Princeton – making the prestigious Cottage Club, becoming president of Triangle Club, and holding other offices – were, to him, "badges of pride, medals" (Milford 29, citing Fitzgerald). With those tokens he hoped to earn the admiration of his peers and, perhaps even more importantly at the time, to prove himself worthy of his first love, a rich and wildly popular young woman from Chicago with the almost improbably Arthurian name of Ginevra King. But, just as Daisy left Gatsby for Tom, the moneyed scion of a prominent Midwestern family, Ginevra eventually terminated her relation-ship with Fitzgerald and married another man, William Mitchell, "the current catch of Chicago" and heir to an extremely wealthy family associated with Chicago banking (Lehan 67).[4] Fitzgerald was crushed by the break-up. As Andrew Turnbull writes, "Ginevra had been the princess for whom he sought fame and honors at Princeton in the spirit of the knight errant" (72),[5] and he never really got over losing her. In fact, his longing for Ginevra, the rich, beautiful girl he could never possess, finds its way into much of his work, especially in Gatsby's expressions of his undying love for Daisy.

The loss of Ginevra was only one of many setbacks that Fitzgerald suffered during and soon after his Princeton years. A malaria-like illness forced him to move back temporarily to the Midwest, and a record of undis-tinguished academic achievement upon his return to college required him to repeat a year; eventually he left altogether without graduating. By then the war was being fought in Europe, and Fitzgerald managed to get a commis-sion as an infantry 2nd lieutenant. Envisioning himself a "hero in the field" (Turnbull 80), he expected to be posted overseas; instead, he was sent to Kansas and afterwards to Alabama, where he met and courted Zelda Sayre, the popular Montgomery belle whose wit and antic behavior he later appro-priated as the stuff of his fiction.

After several months of courtship, however, Zelda grew "nervous" about Fitzgerald's elusive career success (as Daisy later reacts to the young Gatsby's), broke off their engagement, and returned to the gay world of parties and dances. The episode reminded Scott of the failure of his quest for

4 "The current catch of Chicago" is how Fitzgerald described Gordon Tinsley in "A Woman with a Past," one of the Josephine stories based on Ginevra King. Ginevra later married another wealthy Midwesterner, John Pirie.
5 Turnbull also comments upon Fitzgerald's sense of "corruption in the rich": " 'That was always my experience,' he wrote near the end of his life, ' – a poor boy in a rich town; a poor boy in a rich boy's school; a poor boy in a rich man's club at Princeton. . . . I have never been able to forgive the rich for being rich, and it has colored my entire life and works.' He told a friend that 'the whole idea of *Gatsby* is the unfairness of a poor young man not being able to marry a girl with money. This theme comes up again and again because I lived it' " (150).

Ginevra, and he recorded his disappointment in his *Ledger* in typically romantic fashion: "Failure. I used to wonder why they locked princesses in towers" (Milford 45; Le Vot 69). He repeated that sentiment in at least six letters to Zelda, who finally replied that she had heard enough from him about towers. Later, plagiarizing their lives as Fitzgerald so often did, Zelda included the episode in her autobiographical novel, *Save Me the Waltz* (1932). David Knight, the male protagonist obviously based on Fitzgerald, writes to his beloved Alabama: "Oh, my dear, you are my princess and I'd like to shut you up forever in an ivory tower for my private delectation" (55). And the self-assured Alabama replies that she does not want him to mention the tower ever again.

Back again, and alone, in Saint Louis, Fitzgerald – still trying to prove his worthiness to Zelda and her parents – returned to a manuscript that had earlier been rejected for publication. Revised and expanded, the novel was soon published to considerable acclaim. A history of Amory Blaine, a "romantic egotist," from his indulged childhood with his eccentric mother through prep school and Princeton, *This Side of Paradise* (1920) culminates in an unhappy love affair and a "renewed quest for values upon which to erect a fulfilling life" (*Grandeur* 124). Concluding that he is "capable of infinite expansion for good or evil" (*TSP* 18), Amory – a projection of the youthful Fitzgerald – formulates "a code to live by . . . a sort of aristocratic egotism" (as Gatsby, another romantic dreamer, would later do as well) and undertakes a regimen of self-improvement, part of which includes the reading of certain biographical novels that he christens "quest books," books about heroes who "set off in life armed with the best weapons" but who discover that "there might be a more magnificent use" for their talents than simply pushing "selfishly and blindly" ahead (120).

In the course of Fitzgerald's first novel, Amory acts much as the questing heroes he reads about do: pushing ahead, at first selfishly and finally a little less blindly, he comes of age and begins to metamorphose.[6] Sergio Perosa considers this period of Amory's development, of his preparation for the new trials to come, "typical [of] Celtic heroes from Parsifal to Tristan" (20). Amory leaves behind some of his earlier egotism and tries to reshape himself as a man "spiritually unmarried [who] continually seeks for new systems that will control or counteract human nature" (272).

By novel's end, he has not yet become that "personage" to which he aspires, but at least he has attained the ground from which he may begin to work. As Robert Sklar notes, Amory "has given up a passive but secure place in the social order for an active and problematic role in creating constructive social change. He has turned his back on a system of values which exalts the

---

6   Bruccoli (*Grandeur* 51) notes that, in this instance, fiction certainly imitated life. "The strongest influences" on Fitzgerald as a young man, notes Bruccoli, "were the novels he called 'quest books.' "

individual will in theory but in practice constricts it. Now he must make a direct confrontation with the capacity of his will to create values for himself" (56).

In a point of view for the first time distinctly his own, Amory starts to free himself from both genteel social conventions and the extremes of romantic despair. A quest hero of sorts, he is left to embark on a new quest. "Even if, deep in my heart, I thought we were all blind atoms in a world as limited as a stroke of a pendulum," he admits, "I and my sort would struggle against tradition; try, at least, to displace old cants with new ones. . . . faith is difficult. One thing I know. *If living isn't a seeking for the grail it may be a damned amusing game*" (278).[7]

That important line about living as a seeking for the Grail provides perhaps the best explanation for the earlier self-directed and sometimes silly behavior of Amory and of the other characters in Fitzgerald's novels: without noble aspirations (epitomized by "a seeking for the grail"), they lead purposeless lives, at best amusing, but at worst fatuous and despairing. In *The Beautiful and Damned* (1922), for instance, Gloria and Anthony Patch become, as their name suggests, little more than a colorful swatch on the fabric of American social life in the decade between 1910 and 1920.[8] Anthony – obsessed with "a self-absorption with no comfort, a demand for expression with no outlet, a sense of time rushing by, ceaselessly and wastefully . . . assuaged only by that conviction that there was nothing to waste, because all efforts and attainments were equally valueless" (93) – is no more than a pathetic dilettante who rationalizes his indolence, a wastelander with little hope of ameliorating his sorry plight. His beautiful, manipulative wife Gloria provides him with some distraction and occasionally some direction, but their climb up the social ladder is followed by their inexorable slide into depression, alcoholism, and madness. From the beginning, theirs is no noble quest; and in the end, even the inheritance from Anthony's grandfather that they have coveted for years cannot obliterate their unhappiness. Ultimately, their good financial fortune affords them a more lavish lifestyle but no escape from the inherent meaninglessness of their lives. Similarly, in *Tender Is the Night* (1934), Dick and Nicole Diver are the stuff of a Jazz Age wasteland, hollow people in a hollow land, whose very name echoes their declining fortunes.[9]

---

7   The emphasis in the quote is ours, not Fitzgerald's. In *The Beautiful and Damned* (305), Fitzgerald expressed a similar sentiment: "If living was not purposeful it was, at any rate, essentially romantic!"

8   Like Fitzgerald's other novels, *The Beautiful and Damned* contains various medieval images and allusions. For instance, Anthony expresses his intention to write "a history of the Middle Ages" (15); he speaks of creating a character called the Chevalier, a sentimentalist and romantic who was exiled "in the late days of chivalry" (89); and he refers to the need for a chivalric code ("a clear code of honor" [226]).

9   Kim Moreland, in fact, suggests that, just as Eliot's *The Waste Land* stands behind Gatsby's "waste land," the valley of the ashes, "it stands even more insistently behind the sterile modern world of *Tender Is the Night*." She argues that the wasteland motif is evident in the psychiatric hospitals, the mental illnesses of the characters, and their aberrant sexual roles

It is in Fitzgerald's third and best-known novel *The Great Gatsby*, though, that both the idea of living as a seeking for the Grail and the whole quest motif find their fullest expression. Gatsby, the novel's title character, is a more developed questing hero than the romantic and egotistical Amory Blaine, or the spiritually spent Anthony Patch, or even the broken Dick Diver – though, as "brother" to those other protagonists, he wins sympathy because he clings to a romantic, Platonic image of himself in spite of his dis-illusioning pilgrimage (Kahn 47). Gatsby is, in fact, a contemporary Grail knight who undergoes numerous trials in order to become worthy of the precious object he desires. That object is the "excitingly desirable" (148) Daisy Fay Buchanan, a woman with such extraordinary "star-shine" (which Fitzgerald describes as a "bought luxury" of the affluent [149]) that she blinds others to her irresolute carelessness and facile cynicism. From their first meeting five years earlier, Gatsby had "felt married to her, that was all." And so, with the unattainable Daisy ever drawing him on, over the years "he found that he committed himself to the following of a grail" (149).

To earn Daisy's love, he observes a regimen as disciplined and purposeful as any knight errant's, transforming himself into what he believes she wants him to be. Earnest Jimmy Gatz, a young army officer so poor that he must borrow a uniform in order to go courting, becomes handsome, mysterious Jay Gatsby, a man so affluent that he can afford to hold his own court on the shore of West Egg. But, despite his best efforts to ingratiate himself, he remains an outsider to Daisy's world, a parvenu whose lack of social standing distinguishes him from the careless rich across the bay.[10]

As the story of a contemporary romantic questing knight errant who has journeyed east from his home in North Dakota in search of a larger experi-ence of life, Gatsby's tale takes on a special – and mythic – significance that, at least initially, reverses the old formulas of west and east in American fiction and ultimately re-examines the notion of the American dream. The once limitless western horizon that attracted Gatsby's mentor Dan Cody and other pioneering entrepreneurs had, by Gatsby's generation, been circum-scribed by the "bored, sprawling, swollen towns beyond the Ohio, with their interminable inquisitions which spared only the children and the very old" (177); the locus of opportunity had shifted from a once glamorous and

and practices. "Normal sexuality," she concludes, "is also a casualty of war" (130–31).

Moreover, according to Moreland, "Tender is the knight indeed in the modern world, which offers an inhospitable environment for courtly behavior and unsuitable objects for courtly admiration." Dick cannot be "a true courtly knight": he is "caught between the medieval world of the courtly knight, which endows the romantic relationship with tran-scendent significance, and the modern world, which accepts meaninglessness as a given and celebrates all sexual activity as a simple marker of existence" (148).

10 Bruccoli (*Grandeur* 25) observed that Fitzgerald was very self-conscious about his own breeding. "If I were elected King of Scotland tomorrow after graduating from Eton, Magdelene the Guards with an embryonic history which tied me to the Plantagenets," Fitzgerald wrote, "I would still be a *parvenue*."

golden West, now a dull and settled land of conformist, respectable towns,[11] to the big cities of the East. For those reasons, after some nomadism immediately following their marriage, the Buchanans settle "permanently" on Long Island because Tom would be "a God damned fool to live anywhere else" (10); Nick, for whom the Middle West "seemed like the ragged edge of the universe" (3), heads for New York with a dozen volumes on finance which promise "to unfold the shining secrets that only Midas, Morgan and Maecenas knew" (4); and even the green light on which Gatsby fixates shines in just one direction – from the East across the continent, beckoning him to its coast; from the East across the bay to his mansion in West Egg, beckoning him to Daisy. Only those too deeply mired in the wasteland to make any movement – George Wilson, who wants to "go West" (123) to start a new life with his wife, and Myrtle Wilson, who expects to divorce George, marry Tom, and go "West for a while until it blows over" (34) – still find promise in the West.

For Fitzgerald, though, the lure of the East was false and represented "a profound displacement of the American dream, a turning back upon itself of the historic pilgrimage towards the frontier which had, in fact, created and sustained that dream" (Ornstein 63).[12] That dream, after all, had once been, as Milton Stern suggests, a dream of self "at the golden moment of emergence from wanting greatness to being great" (166, 190) – a dream shared by all of Fitzgerald's characters beginning with Amory Blaine – but it had deteriorated into the irresponsible actuality of American wealth, complete with the deceit and superficiality of its appearances. Promising an "orgiastic future," it had instead "borne back" (182) the transcendent expectations of Gatsby and other youthful dreamers. Thus, only the irresponsible, perpetually adolescent Buchanans eventually resettle in the East. A more sober and mature Nick, fed up with the artificiality of New York society, instead returns to the Midwest. And Gatsby dies, destroyed as much by the provincial squeamishness that makes all Westerners in the novel "unadaptable to Eastern life" (177) as by his own "small-time notions of virtue and chivalry" (Ornstein 65).

In portraying the limitations of the orgiastic future inherent in the new American Dream, *The Great Gatsby* mourns the emptiness and hollowness of America in the Jazz Age. Implicating America itself, which measures its heroes not by their morality but by their material success (Whitley 18), Fitzgerald expresses a certain disenchantment with the post-World-War-I era in which ideals are corrupted and love, like faith, is impossible. But, while in its portrait of contemporary life *Gatsby* is a singularly American romance, in

11 Milton R. Stern (151–288) analyzes at some length Fitzgerald's use of East and West as symbols in *The Great Gatsby*. (See especially pp. 191, 198–213, 241–250.)
12 Stern adds that "The West had become a dull and settled place, and the Middle West had, by 1925, come to represent Babbitt on Main Street in his repressive Winesburg, Ohio" (198).

its imagery and its structure it harks back to earlier romantic tradition. As Jerome Mandel notes, there are numerous similarities between "the Arthurian – [and] the American – Way of Life" (547), beginning with Fitzgerald's depiction of the aristocratic class in American society as a modern version of the medieval nobility, presided over by powerful lords like Tom Buchanan in "white palaces" (5–6); privileged ladies like Daisy Fay, "the king's daughter, the golden girl" (120), safely distant from the struggling poor; and noble knights like Nick Carraway, whose family is "descended from the Dukes of Buccleuch" (2). Fitzgerald himself recognized the similarities: he characterized the New York society of the Buchanans as "a silly, pretentious, vicious mockery of a defunct feudal regime . . . [with] violently selfish and unchivalric standards" (Bruccoli, *Fitzgerald in His Own Time* 190).

In telling his very contemporary romance, Fitzgerald borrows various important elements from medieval romance, such as the existence of two distinct worlds in which the action occurs – one public, a world of political concerns and accepted laws, where the ordinary rules of proper behavior normally prevail; the other private, a lovers' world inhabited by only two, where the ordinary rules that govern society are suspended in the service of courtly love (Mandel 547). In *Gatsby*, the public world is typified by the lavish parties that Gatsby throws, parties to which come all manner of socially pretentious and sycophantic guests with names like Leech, Civet, Beaver, Fishguard, Whitebait, Beluga, Catlip, Belcher, Smirke.[13] Each weekend, Gatsby's lawn is manicured by an extra crew of gardeners; his house is lit up like "a Christmas tree"; his Rolls-Royce becomes an omnibus, bearing guests to and from the city; and his station wagon "scampers like a little yellow bug to meet all trains" (39). With fruiterers and caterers abounding, the parties resemble medieval banquets: "On buffet tables, garnished with glistening hors-d'oeuvre, spiced baked hams crowded against salads of harlequin designs and pastry pigs and turkeys bewitched to a dark gold" (39–40).

But once Daisy makes clear her distaste for such spectroscopic affairs, Gatsby abandons them, deferring, as a courtly lover would, to the wishes of his beloved. His "elaborate road-house" (64) becomes a bower of bliss, a private world in which the servants are sent away; the house goes dark; and "Daisy comes over quite often – in the afternoons" (114). Even in more extreme circumstances, as Mandel suggests, the lovers attempt to re-create their own private world (548). For instance, as partying guests take over his mansion one weekend, Gatsby steals away for half an hour with Daisy; ignoring the noise and distractions of the revelers, they take refuge together on the steps of Nick's cottage as Nick stands guard in the garden. And on the

13 Ironically, even Tom Buchanan recognizes the animalistic, atavistic tendencies of Gatsby's invited and uninvited guests, which reflect on the nature of his own society. "I suppose," utters Tom to Gatsby, "you've got to make your house into a pigsty in order to have any friends – in the modern world" (131).

trip to New York, to which the summer-weary Buchanans and their friends escape for the day, Daisy and Gatsby create another private moment for themselves by arranging to drive alone in Tom's coupé.

Nick senses the lovers' intimacy almost immediately. After facilitating Gatsby and Daisy's first meeting in his home,[14] he feels so much like an intruder in their private world that he runs off and sits on the lawn gazing in the rain at the architecture of the sprawling white mansion next door. When he returns a half hour later, he tries loudly to announce his presence. "But I don't believe they heard a sound," he says. "They were sitting at either end of the couch, looking at each other as if some question had been asked, or was in the air, and every vestige of embarrassment was gone" (90).

Tom Buchanan and his mistress Myrtle Wilson have also established a private lovers' world of sorts; they keep an apartment in New York, at a safe remove from the garage apartment Myrtle shares with her husband, George. But Tom and Myrtle's carnal, violent relationship, which provides a worldly foil to Gatsby's more idealized and spiritual love for Daisy, perverts any notion of courtly love; and even their apartment reflects the perversion. It is garish and grotesque, the oversized furniture decorated with large tapestries of palatial scenes from Versailles. Moreover, instead of being private (as Gatsby's house becomes after he and Daisy become lovers), it is public: Myrtle invites her neighbors and her sister in for a party so raucous that it ends in a fight during which Tom breaks Myrtle's nose, a foreshadowing of the deadly violence – also at Tom's hands (albeit more indirectly) – that soon claims Myrtle's life. As Mandel notes, "the idealized values and spiritual concerns of medieval authors never exist in Tom and Myrtle's private world, which is characterized by increasingly drunken conversations about people and feet and appendicitis" (548). In fact, the apartment scene in the second chapter is almost a parody of the private, idyllic Cave of Lovers to which Iseult, Tristan, and the handsome hound Hudein retreat. Tom and Myrtle's place is a perverse cave into which they bring a mongrel dog, purchased for the exorbitant sum of $10 from a street vendor who bears "an absurd resemblance to John D. Rockefeller" (27).

The most enduring of the lovers' worlds in *Gatsby*, however, is neither Tom and Myrtle's nor Gatsby and Daisy's; it is the Buchanans'. Bound together in their disregard of the consequences of their actions, Tom and Daisy are "careless people . . . [who] smashed up things and people and then retreated back into their money or their vast carelessness, or whatever it was that kept them together, and let other people clean up the mess they had made" (180–81). The night of Myrtle's death, as Gatsby the Grail knight

---

14 Elizabeth Morgan points out that Gatsby, in preparation for Daisy's visit, makes elaborate arrangements, even to the point of "dress[ing] for the rendez-vous in a seeming semblance of shining armor" (167).

watches over Daisy's home with "the sacredness of a vigil," Nick spies the Buchanans at their kitchen table, holding hands and talking earnestly over cold chicken and ale. "There was," Nick remarks, "an unmistakable air of natural intimacy about the picture, and anybody would have said that they were conspiring together" (146). The next day, when Nick calls to tell Daisy of Gatsby's death, he learns the nature and extent of that conspiracy: she and Tom had gone away earlier that afternoon. They had taken baggage but left no word of where they were heading or when they would return, withdrawing into the protected world of money and lack of conscience in which they were so inutterably wed. Indeed, Nick realizes, Gatsby had been "watching over nothing" (146); the Grail he had followed for so long and held so sacred was a mere illusion.

If the various lovers' private worlds provide, at least for a time, some solace and consolation from the vicissitudes of the outside world, there is one place that provides no solace or consolation whatsoever: the wasteland that Fitzgerald calls the Valley of the Ashes. Located between the privileged world of the Long Island Eggs and the corrupt world of New York, the valley is a "fantastic farm where ashes grow like wheat into ridges and hills and grotesque gardens; where ashes take the form of houses and chimneys and rising smoke and . . . ash-gray men who move dimly and already crumbling through the powdery air" (23). It is a place whose physical deterioration mirrors the moral despair of its few remaining inhabitants, who are bereft not only of hope but also of vitality. Like Eliot's wasteland, it is an "arid plane," a "dead land" strewn with "dry bones" (*WL* lines 425, 2, 391).

The valley is presided over by the eyes of Dr. Eckleburg, an oculist long since gone from the borough. Peering down from a solitary signpost, those huge eyes, simultaneously unseeing and all-seeing, mock the misery of the wastelanders below and serve as a reminder that God, too, has turned a blind eye to their suffering. Letha Audhuy, who draws extensive parallels between *The Waste Land* and *The Great Gatsby*, suggests that, in the wasteland of Gatsby's world, Eckleburg is himself a godlike figure, the false new god of "commercialism or materialism . . . in America in the 1920's." She points to "the line from 'Gerontion' (a poem so closely related to *The Waste Land* that Eliot wanted to use it for a prologue): 'Signs are taken for wonders,'" and concludes that in *Gatsby* "Fitzgerald's joke is to make an actual sign (board) into a wonder" (43). Similarly, John W. Bicknell, who sees in the grotesque image of Eckleburg "a symbol of what God has become in the modern world . . . indifferent, faceless, blank," draws the comparison to the lines from *The Waste Land*, which he notes Fitzgerald "knew by heart": "What are the roots that clutch, what branches grow / Out of this stony rubbish? Son of man, / You cannot say, or guess, for you know only / A heap of broken images, where the sun beats / And the dead tree gives no shelter . . ." (68).

No one in Eckleburg's view seems to suffer more than George Wilson, owner of a grimy garage, one of only two shops left on "a small block of yellow brick sitting on the edge of the waste land" (24). A blond, faintly handsome man, George is as spiritless as his surroundings. When he appears in the door of his office to greet Tom and Nick, he is "wiping his hands on a piece of waste" (25). So poor that he had to borrow a suit in which to wed Myrtle (just as Gatsby had to borrow clothing in which to court Daisy in Louisville), George wants only to please his wife, who – unbeknownst to him – is smitten with Tom and who prefers Tom's brand of vulgarity.

There is, to be sure, a certain symmetry in the fact that both George and Gatsby die in the service of the women they love, women who are taken from them in a kind of *droit de seigneur* by Tom.[15] Both men, moreover, are condemned as cowards for their inability to hold on to the objects of their desire; and both die oblivious to the actual forces that destroy their illusions and their lives. When Daisy, driving Gatsby's yellow Rolls-Royce through the Valley of the Ashes, kills Myrtle, Gatsby assumes the blame, a gesture he as the chivalrous, courtly lover gladly makes to protect his beloved. After keeping a vigil outside her window that evening, the next day he dies awaiting word from her, unaware that she has betrayed him, and, by her betrayal, conspired in his death. Similarly, incited by Tom to avenge what he believes to be Gatsby's gutlessness and carelessness (a revenge Tom is not courageous enough to exact directly), the griefstricken George kills Gatsby and then turns the gun on himself. Tom is thus as complicitous in George's death as he is in Gatsby's. Milton Stern summarizes the major plot action even more succinctly: "Tom," he writes, "cuckolds Wilson, indirectly causes Myrtle's and Gatsby's death; Daisy betrays Gatsby, directly causes Myrtle's and indirectly causes Gatsby's death" (240).

Daisy herself is amoral and adulterous; she shares Tom's moral corruptness, as is apparent in her encouraging of promiscuity between Nick and her close friend Jordan, a golf champion who cheats to win and who, like the Buchanans, drives recklessly (a metaphor in the novel for other careless behaviors). Inherently insincere, Daisy merely plays with Gatsby's affections, perhaps out of her own romantic nostalgia, perhaps as retribution for Tom's infidelities, perhaps – as Bicknell suggests – more "as a relief from boredom" (69); and she even repudiates Tom briefly, until her fear of possible reprisals

---

15 In "Handle with Care," one of the three articles that Edmund Wilson edited as *The Crack-Up*, Fitzgerald wrote of how his own love for Zelda was almost "doomed for lack of money": "The man with the jingle of money in his pocket who married the girl a year later would always cherish an abiding distrust, an animosity toward the leisure class – not the conviction of a revolutionist but the smouldering hatred of a peasant. In the years since then I have never been able to stop wondering where my friends' money came from, nor to stop thinking that at one time a sort of *droit de seigneur* might have been exercised to give one of them my girl" (Stern 164).

for her criminal actions sends her back to him, and to the protection of his good family name.

Only Nick, the novel's true moral center, fully grasps both Buchanans' duplicity. Feeling as uncomfortable in their home as he does initially at Gatsby's parties, he chooses after Gatsby's death to return to the Middle West, whose fertile wheatfields contrast sharply with the valley's aridness and barrenness and the spiritual emptiness of the neighboring Eggs. Interestingly, Nick's final act before leaving New York is to visit Jordan. Wanting "to leave things in order and not just trust that obliging sea to sweep my refuse away," Nick confronts her about her carelessness and hypocrisy; it is something he must do, he claims, because "I'm . . . too old to lie to myself and call it honor" (178–79). His deliberate gesture is as diametrically opposed to the Buchanan's careless "smash[ing] up" of things and letting "other people clean up the mess they made" (180–81) as the natural fecundity of the Midwest is to the artificial splendor of East Egg.

If Nick is able to see realistically, Gatsby sees only romantically. And, like earlier romantic heroes, particularly the heroes of Arthurian medieval romance, Gatsby appears to be unbound by time.[16] (By contrast, most of the other characters, like Eliot's aimless and sterile wastelanders, feel restricted by or unable to handle chronological time: Daisy, for instance, wearily repeats the question, "What'll we do with ourselves this afternoon . . . and the day after that, and the next thirty years?" (118), much the way Eliot's lady asks "What shall we do tomorrow? What shall we ever do?") Convinced that he can adjust time or at least set it askew by simply erasing the last five years, Gatsby insists that Daisy admit that she never really loved Tom, not even on their wedding day – an admission Daisy makes but quickly retracts. By pushing Daisy to repudiate Tom, Gatsby tries to legitimate his own unsacramental "marriage" to her, which in his eyes invalidates her subsequent marriage to Tom. And when Daisy responds that she did, at one time, love her husband, Gatsby dismisses those feelings as "just personal," thus distinguishing Tom and Daisy's affection from his own spiritual and ideal love.

Likewise, Gatsby replies with astonishment to Nick's observation that one cannot repeat the past: "Why of course you can!" And that is what he proceeds to try to do, beginning with his intention to take Daisy, "after she was free, . . . back to Louisville and be married from her house – just as if it were five years ago" (111). Significantly, at Nick's home during his first encounter with Daisy, Gatsby leans against the mantelpiece upon which rests

---

16 It is interesting to note that the brewer who built the house in West Egg that Gatsby purchases felt, in odd ways, similarly unbound by time. Fitzgerald writes that, in a sort of throwback to feudal times, "he'd agreed to pay five years' taxes on all the neighboring cottages if the owners would have their roofs thatched with straw." When they refused, the brewer went into "an immediate decline" and – ominously for Gatsby – "his children sold his house with the black wreath still on the door" (*GG* 89).

a clock, old and defunct but nonetheless dangerous as it tilts at his head. "I'm sorry about the clock" (87), he says, oblivious to the irony. Only Nick makes the connection: later, after Tom denounces Gatsby as a common thug and exposes his vulnerability, Nick realizes that Gatsby "was running down like an overwound clock" (93).

In his disregard of chronological time, Gatsby is reminiscent of the hero of medieval romance, who exists outside of time. Moreover, as Jerome Mandel (554) notes, he is also like Parzifal, who fails to ask the questions at the Grail castle and then searches again for the castle to rectify the original error. Unlike Parzifal, however, Gatsby merely repeats his error as he single-mindedly attempts to recreate his month of love with Daisy, the only idyllic part of his youth. Whereas Gatsby's humble origins prevented him from winning Daisy's hand years before, the ignoble past that haunts him again ruins his effort to claim her. The wealth he acquired through bootlegging and other illicit enterprises, rather than obliterating his low birth, gives him a history that Tom exploits, a history that Gatsby cannot ultimately explain or wish away, as he does with the five years of lost time apart from Daisy.

But if Gatsby's unconventional background makes him a less heroic Grail seeker, Daisy, in turn, is an even less worthy Grail. Unlike the priceless cup that justifies and completes the seeker's quest, she proves to be more like "a loving cup that goes hand to hand" (*BD* 182), an image that Gloria uses to describe herself in *The Beautiful and Damned*. Common dross, Daisy eventually tarnishes Gatsby and most of those around her. Superficial and remorseless – all gilt and no guilt – she lives in an "artificial world redolent of orchids and pleasant, cheerful snobbery and orchestras which set the rhythm of the year, summing up the sadness and suggestiveness of life in new tunes," a world in which "a hundred pairs of golden and silver slippers shuffled the shining dust" (151) – a dust that, despite its shine, originates in the wasteland.

While Gatsby professes not to comprehend what compelled Daisy to marry Tom, he in fact is overwhelmingly aware of "the youth and mystery that wealth imprisons and preserves, of the freshness of many clothes, and of Daisy, gleaming like silver, safe and proud above the hot struggles of the poor" (150). That is why, in order to reclaim her affection, he knows he must amass a fortune greater than Tom's. But that fortune is important to Gatsby only as a means to an end; for him, it is but one more test of worthiness in the pursuit of his personal Grail, one more proof of his courtly love. As Gatsby takes Daisy through his estate for the first time, Nick observes that "Gatsby revalued everything in his house according to the measure of response it drew from her well-loved eyes"; it was "as though in her actual and astounding presence none of it was any longer real" (92).

But, for Daisy, what matters is precisely the reality of it; unlike Gatsby, who lives for the seeking, she delights in the having. When faced with the choice between a letter of love from Gatsby, who is absent and whose future is uncertain, and the $350,000 pearl necklace from Tom, who is very much present and whose future is lavishly certain (Stern 245), she opts not for Gatsby's vision but for Tom's money. At West Egg, Daisy admires "with enchanting murmurs . . . this aspect or that of the feudal silhouette [of Gatsby's ostentatious home] against the sky" (92), but the towered mansion becomes tangible to her only when she can actually handle its pricey contents. After seeing in Gatsby's bedroom "the toilet set of pure dull gold," she grabs the brush "with great delight" (93), and, as if to confirm that it is real, strokes her own hair – a scene which Mandel likens to Lancelot's finding Guinevere's comb in *Le Chevalier de la Charrette* and the medieval tradition of holding sacred the hair of a lover.[17] Later, in another scene with possible medieval and Arthurian analogues,[18] Daisy is moved to tears by the amplitude of Gatsby's closets. Lost in the rich heaps of his expensive silk, linen and soft flannel shirts, she begins to sob and "to cry stormily" (93). It is during the orgiastic emptying of Gatsby's closets in the bedroom of the great castle-like home he has purchased and maintained for her that the two achieve their greatest intimacy. Yet this strange consummation of their relationship involves no actual lovemaking – fittingly so, perhaps, since Daisy represents for Gatsby a spiritual, not a physical ideal, and Gatsby represents for Daisy the satisfaction not of any sexual need but rather of her lust for material excess.

Virtually every description of Daisy, even those unwittingly provided by Gatsby, hint at her vulgarity. Daisy's voice, though it sings to him "a deathless song" (97), is nonetheless "full of money" (120). Even her name, Daisy, suggests not an exotic hothouse orchid but a common, almost weedlike flower – as common as Myrtle, the rival whom she eventually destroys. Just as the daisy's white petals sometimes obscure its golden center, Daisy uses her genteel manners and expensive tastes to mask her baseness. It is with some irony, therefore, that she, herself so skilled in duplicity, fails to appreciate the unspoiled sentimentality that underlies Gatsby's occasional coarseness

---

17 Mandel (554) writes: "the hair of the beloved is sacred to the medieval lover. Soredamors sews a strand of his own hair into a shirt that Guenevere gives to Alexander; when he discovers the secret of the shirt, 'all night he presses the shirt in his arms, and when he looks at the golden hair, he feels like the lord of the whole wide world.' When Lancelot in *Le Chevalier de la Charrette* finds Guenevere's comb on a stone, he discovers a few 'strands of the Queen's hair . . . clinging in the teeth of the comb.' He removes the hair 'so carefully that he tears none of it' and 'lays [it] in his bosom near his heart . . . He would not exchange [it] for a cartload of emeralds.' "

18 Mandel (547 n.10) notes that medieval romance is flush with splendid descriptions of gorgeous clothes: "Erec's coronation robes, Isolde's clinging robe when she enters the judgment hall in Ireland, Culhwch's clothes on his spectacular ride to Arthur's court are only among the most obvious examples of this medieval love of splendor and display." He concludes that "they may well be the folkloric source of Gatsby's splendid display of shirts."

and unsavory associations. But she survives, even thrives, while Gatsby dies precisely because of her reluctance to look below the surface; her lack of sentimentality becomes part of the "hard malice" that not only drives her but also saves her from engagement and accountability.

Daisy is every bit as false, or fey, as her maiden name suggests. Yet that name, Fay, hints at more than her duplicity: it also suggests her kinship to another Fay, Morgan le Fay, the evil enchantress of Arthurian myth.[19] Daisy's magic is as powerful, and as malicious, as her namesake's. The "enchanting murmurs" (92) of Daisy's whispery voice cast spells on those around her. To Nick, she boasts of her sophistication. But "the instant her voice broke off," Nick remembers, "ceasing to compel my attention, my belief, I felt the basic insincerity of what she had said. It made me uneasy, as though the whole evening had been a trick of some sort . . ." (18). Even Nick's first impression of Daisy suggests a certain witchcraft: her dress is rippled and fluttery, as if she "had just been blown back in after a short flight around the house" (8), and she herself seems to be floating above her living room couch. For Gatsby, Daisy works the strongest magic of all: she creates an illusion of innocent beauty that endures virtually until his death. The bewitched Gatsby includes Daisy in his "count of enchanted objects" (94); and his last thoughts are of "the pale magic of her face" (153), images that suggest her dual role as Grail and as enchantress.

Despite Daisy's repeated abuses of his devotion, he remains captive to that magic and to his wishful remembrance of past affection. In the Plaza Hotel suite parlor, where he is humiliated first by Tom and then by Daisy, Gatsby still continues to cling to the "colossal vitality of his illusion" (97). He does not realize, as Nick already has intuited, that his happiness is doomed. In a fine bit of foreshadowing that also underscores the contrast between Nick's realism and Gatsby's romanticism, Gatsby completely ignores the portent upon which Nick comments: en route to New York City, Nick recalls, "a dead man passed us in a hearse." The juxtaposition of gaiety and sorrow makes Nick aware that "anything can happen now that we've slid over this bridge" (69).

Only Gatsby's "romantic readiness" and "extraordinary gift for hope" (2), writes Fitzgerald, kept his dream of Daisy alive so long; and in the end Gatsby "paid a high price for living too long with a single dream" (162). The "shining dust" of silver and gold slippers from Daisy's world which Gatsby so admired and by which he was so entranced becomes the "foul dust float[ing] in the wake of his dreams" (2) and extinguishes his quest for the life-affirming Grail, for the green light at the end of the dock that suggests promise and vitality, for the "fresh green breast of the new world" in which

19 The relationship between Daisy and Morgan le Fay is discussed by Barbara Tepa Lupack in "F. Scott Fitzgerald's 'Following of a Grail' " and subsequently by Kim Moreland (143–44).

Gatsby so fervently believed. After Gatsby's death, even his palatial home –
"a huge incoherent failure" (181), now overgrown and empty, an obscenity
scrawled on its white steps – begins to resemble the wasteland from which
the foul dust emanates. As surely as Daisy tarnishes Gatsby's ideals, the dust
of the wasteland sullies his dreams and reverberates in a number of finely-
honed images throughout the novel, from the conspiratorially silent careless
world of the Buchanans, whose actions are reminiscent of the rote movements of the lovers in Eliot's poem, to the sly corruption of Jordan Baker and
Meyer Wolfsheim, Jordan's practices being only superficially more genteel
than Meyer's while ethically just as culpable.

The inspiration for the wastelands of *Gatsby* was clearly Eliot, whom
Fitzgerald regarded, with profound admiration, as "the greatest living poet
in any language" (*Letters* 221) and in whose vision of deadening decadence
and cultural malaise he found a theme which, while universal, was especially
topical and symbolically appropriate to the material excesses and the
spiritual paucity of his time. Fitzgerald explored that theme not only in
Gatsby (published a mere three years after Eliot's poem) but also in his other
novels. The wasteland is evident in the parched European beaches, places
that his well-heeled characters in *The Beautiful and Damned* "invented" and
"perverted to the tastes of the tasteless" (*BD* 280) and to which they retreat to
escape their shallow lives; in the "waste acres" (*BD* 175) of the suburbs
outside New York City that the Patches visit; in the physical illnesses that
mirror spiritual malaise; in the mechanical lovemaking and the disintegrating marriages; in the incessant bickering and abominable drunken sprees
that "decay and coarsen" (*BD* 424). From the "smothery" rooms (*BD* 150) in
which Anthony hides to avoid the ghastly sounds of "the business of life"
below him to the insane asylums in *Tender is the Night*, where the inmates are
saner than their doctors, Fitzgerald chronicles "the drought in the marrow of
his [characters'] bones" (*TN* 190). The theme recurs even in his unfinished
novel *The Last Tycoon*. Monroe Stahr, "the last of the princes" (*LT* 27), a man
more "royal" (*LT* 65) – and powerful – than most kings, whose crashing
death is a metaphor for the fates of many of Fitzgerald's protagonists[20] and of
the Fitzgeralds themselves, for a time rules Hollywood, a place so barren and
soulless that it is perhaps the biggest wasteland of all. A land of "jerky hopes
and graceful rogueries and awkward sorrows" (*LT* 20), it not only thrives on
the superficial but it creates the artifice by which men and women gauge the
hollowness of their lives.

The image of the wasteland also occurs in many of Fitzgerald's short
stories, from "One Trip Abroad" and "The Swimmer" to "The Ice Palace" and
"The Diamond as Big as the Ritz"; and it finds particularly rich expression in

---

20 Kim Moreland notes that Monroe Stahr is "a kind of falling star" (125). Like Amory
    Blaine, Anthony Patch, Jay Gatsby, and Dick Diver, he ultimately comes crashing back to
    earth in a decline and fall that Fitzgerald recounts in painful detail.

"Babylon Revisited" (1931), probably Fitzgerald's best and most frequently anthologized short story. Charlie Wales, haunted by his dissolute past in the postwar wasteland and his youthful carelessness that contributed to the death of his wife and to the loss of custody of their daughter, returns to Paris. But, unsuccessful in his attempt to regain "Honoria," Charlie is left to ponder his fate at the Ritz Bar, the scene of some of his earlier debauches; his resulting sense of personal loss is part of a larger loss – of values, of honor, of meaning – in his society and his culture. For Fitzgerald, honor was an especially appropriate if not always attainable quest. In his *Notebooks*, he observed: "As a novelist I reach out to the end of all man's variance, all man's villainy – as a man I do not go that far. I cannot claim honor – but even the knights of the Holy Grail were only striving for it, as I remember" (*Notebooks* 324).

While the Grail and the wasteland are the predominant Arthurian images in Fitzgerald's work, others appear as well. The Lady of Shalott, for example, figures prominently in the story, "The Spire and the Gargoyle" (later incorporated as a chapter in *This Side of Paradise*) – both implicitly, in the tower of one of the Princeton buildings that becomes for the protagonist "the symbol of his perception" ("There was something terribly pure in the slope of the chaste stone, something which led and directed and called" [*TSP* 106]); and more explicitly, in the description of his college preceptor (a "gargoyle" among the hallowed spires because he cannot appreciate the magnificence that surrounds him or the intelligence of his young charges, a man whose view is so distorted that he sees only through his "two 'Mirrors of Shallot'" [*TSP* 110]).

Even more important is the character of Merlin, whom Fitzgerald makes the subject of an entire story, "O Russet Witch!," one of the contemporary "fantasies" in *Tales of the Jazz Age*. In the story, originally entitled "His Russet Witch," a modest bookstore clerk, Merlin Grainger, becomes infatuated with a beautiful, mysterious young woman, Alicia Dare ("all is a dare" [Lehan *Short Stories* 9]), an enchantress whose voice is "full of sorcery" (239). But rather than succumb to her magic, Merlin assumes domestic responsibilities and settles for a drab, mundane life with his wife, appropriately named Olive, and their ungrateful son, Arthur. He sacrifices for them, putting their interests above his own; yet, in the end, he recognizes that both "used him for their blind purposes" (272). Olive had nagged and coerced him into ignoring Alicia's attractive presence over the years and Arthur, showing no interest in his father's business, had chosen instead to sell bonds on Wall Street. "Let Old Merlin get what magic he could from his books," Merlin scornfully remarked; "the place of young King Arthur was in the counting house" (262).

When, at the end of the story, Merlin again sees the "russet witch" – now a grandmother – who, for four decades, had embodied his "romantic yearning" for the beautiful, he realizes that she was never possessed of any special magic; it was only Merlin's imagination that had turned a flamboyant, silly socialite into such a bewitching figure. Left with no illusions, "He knew now that he had always been a fool. . . . But it was too late. He had angered Providence by resisting too many temptations" (272).

The tale is not one of Fitzgerald's most successful, but in it he seems to be using the elements of Arthurian myth to suggest that fantasy, though it inevitably disrupts solid middle class respectability, is necessary to give color to drab lives (Sklar 90). He had expressed a similar sentiment while writing *Gatsby*, which shares some plot similarities to "O Russet Witch!": "That's the whole burden of [*The Great Gatsby*]," Fitzgerald noted to a friend, "the loss of those illusions that give such color to the world so you don't care whether things are true or false as long as they partake of the magical glory" (Stern 165).

At the same time, however, in "O Russet Witch!" Fitzgerald appears to be utilizing the framework of the Arthurian story to comment in some ways favorably on the Jazz Age, a period during which people flaunted conventional notions of respectability and protested stupid laws like Prohibition by breaking them. Merlin, locked so solidly into his marriage and his position in the bookshop, fails to avail himself of the kinds of distractions that might have brought an element of pleasure to his life. For example, he notices "Alicia" dancing atop a round table in a restaurant but tries not to glance her way because it would upset Olive. Such distractions may ultimately prove fleeting; but Merlin's failure to risk or to dream proves even more debilitating. In the end, Merlin's life is a flimsy construct, less real and substantive than the fantasies in which he refused to indulge.

From his early short stories on, Fitzgerald demonstrated an interest in the medieval and in medievalism that persisted throughout his lifetime. ("Tarquin of Cheepside" [1917], for instance, makes repeated mention of the legend of Britomartis in *The Fairie Queene*; a later story, "Six of One – " [1931], contrasts over the course of a decade a half dozen poor boys with the sons of wealth, six "young knights" and "six young princes in velvet.") In fact, among the projects that Fitzgerald had outlined for himself shortly before his death was a continuation of "The Count of Darkness," a series begun in 1934 about a medieval knight named Phillipe – modeled on Hemingway – whose life spanned the founding of France as a nation and the consolidation of the feudal system. Those stories, which Scottie called his "most abysmal failure" (Bruccoli, *Grandeur* 496) but which Max Perkins thought profitable enough to consider publishing, had originally been planned to be part of *The Castle*, a novel set entirely in medieval times. And in his best work, most notably *The Great Gatsby*, Fitzgerald used specifically Arthurian themes and motifs, which he reinterpreted in topical and distinctly American ways. His literary career would therefore indicate that, like the characters about whom he wrote, F. Scott Fitzgerald had indeed "committed himself to the following of a grail."

Like his contemporary and sometime friend Scott Fitzgerald, Ernest Hemingway was born at the turn of the century and raised in the Midwest.

Like Fitzgerald, who imagined himself to be the son of a king, Hemingway told his first wife Hadley that he "would have liked to be a king" (Baker 166). Hadley, after all, of the many women in his life, "best understood his romantic streak, his admiration of Chaucer's medieval knight" (Reynolds, *Paris Years* 20). Like Fitzgerald, who modeled his heroes upon his romantic notions of himself, Hemingway "loved to dramatize everything, continuing his boyhood habit of making up stories in which he was invariably the swash-buckling hero" (Baker 15). His first actual experience on the stage, notes Carlos Baker, was, if not Arthurian, at least medieval; it "came in March of 1912, when he appeared in the seventh-grade play, *Robin Hood*, wearing high buckled boots, a wig, a velvet cap, and a long soutane, and carrying a homemade bow through the simulated glades of Sherwood Forest" (15). And, as Michael S. Reynolds demonstrates, much of his adolescent reading – *Old English Ballads*, Chaucer's "General Prologue" and "Knight's Tale," the first two books of *The Faerie Queene*, and Tennyson's *Idylls of the King* – had as its focus one particular hero: the medieval knight.[21]

Like Fitzgerald, whose interest in football persisted throughout his lifetime, Hemingway found in sports like fishing, bullfighting, and boxing a metaphor for heroism in action; around those sports, notes Kim Moreland, he "elaborated a set of codes, obedience to which enabled him in a limited way to function as a knight in the modern world" (180). Like Fitzgerald, Hemingway read T. S. Eliot's *The Waste Land* (in Hemingway's case, from a copy lent him by Ezra Pound, who had given Eliot tremendously valuable editorial advice on the poem), admired Eliot's "fine talent," and found his poetry to be "perfect"[22] – although Hemingway eventually disparaged Eliot, as he did the many other writers with whom he felt competitive (Fenton 179).[23] And, like Fitzgerald, Hemingway saw in Eliot's contemporary

---

21 Michael S. Reynolds posits that critics have largely ignored the element of "the medieval knight" in Hemingway's work because the chivalric influence, while pervasive, "will not be found on the fiction's surface" (*Hemingway's Reading* 26).

22 "All of Eliot's poems are perfect," Hemingway wrote in 1925, "and there are very few of them. He has a very fine talent and he is very careful of it. He never takes chances with it and it is doing very well thank you" (cited in Newman, "Hemingway's Grail Quest" 295, and elsewhere).

23 Carlos Baker, in *Ernest Hemingway: A Life Story* (107), observes that Hemingway, who was lent a copy of Eliot's *The Waste Land* by Pound himself, was "unable to take [the poem] seriously, though he echoes it" in "Cat in the Rain," a story eventually included in *In Our Time*. Other critics disagree with Baker and argue that Hemingway took Eliot's work quite seriously. For example, John Rohrkemper and Karen L. Gutmann (61) suggest that for Hemingway, as for his contemporaries Fitzgerald and Faulkner, *The Waste Land* served as "a model for the emerging modernist literature" they sought to create. Rohrkemper and Gutmann, in their article "The Search for Control: Eliot, Hemingway, and *In Our Time*," show how *The Waste Land* and *In Our Time* "share the basic assumption of the Edenic myth in the American consciousness" and "juxtapose that mythic image with the waste land reality of the modern world" (60). Roger Casey (190–93) sees echoes of Eliot throughout *In Our Time*, particularly in "Cat in the Rain," "Cross Country Snow," "Big Two-Hearted River," and "Mr. and Mrs. Elliot." Mr. Elliot (which is how Hemingway was known to misspell Eliot's name), a Harvard-educated poet "with an income"

recasting of the Arthurian mythology an appropriate frame for his own distinctive chronicle of the postwar malaise of a lost generation.[24] But whereas
Fitzgerald focused quite explicitly on the redemptive possibilities inherent in
the Grail quest, Hemingway was more fascinated with the story of the
wounded Fisher King, whose health is tied to the fertility of the land; and he
incorporated details of that aspect of the Arthurian legends into several of
his works.[25]

Hemingway's interest in the Fisher King had no doubt been piqued "in
the early twenties," during which, according to Paul B. Newman, "Hemingway was a good friend of Ezra Pound, at a time when the latter had just

who "wrote very long poems very rapidly" and "was going to bring out [a book of
poems] in Boston" (*IOT* 109–10; 113), seems, according to Casey, to suggest personally
T. S. Eliot and his then recent publication of *The Waste Land*. Jackson Benson has noted
structural and stylistic similarities between *The Waste Land* and *In Our Time*, even down to
the vignettes Hemingway placed between his stories. Paul B. Newman, in "Hemingway's
Grail Quest," attempts to call attention to the influence of the work of Jessie Weston and
the concepts of Eliot on Hemingway, particularly on *The Sun Also Rises*, and "to suggest
an affinity between the current interest in the breakdown of individualism and the preoccupation of a number of writers with the legend of the Holy Grail" (295). And Richard
Adams, in "Sunrise Out of the Waste Land," discusses in considerable detail strong
stylistic and thematic similarities between Eliot's poem and Hemingway's poetry and
fiction throughout the twenties.

24 Apparently, Hemingway was influenced not only by Eliot's recasting of the Arthurian
mythology but also by Fitzgerald's. Richard Adams demonstrates how, under the surface
of Hemingway's novel, "lay the same solid structure of traditional myth that had made
The Waste Land a great and enduring work" (57–58). Michael S. Reynolds, in "Signs,
Motifs, and Themes in *The Sun Also Rises*," argues convincingly that the parallels between
The Great Gatsby and *The Sun Also Rises* "are not coincidental." He writes: "As several
commentators have noted, there is more than a passing similarity between the two books.
Indeed, when twenties historians quote from fiction, they almost always draw from both
books, for each indicts a sick society that has lost its moral bearings. Fitzgerald's narrator,
Nick Carraway, contributes to the formation of Jake Barnes. The two are both seemingly
minor-character narrators who think that they are less important than the story they are
telling. Both men are bewitched by a woman with whom they cannot have sexual relations: Nick by Daisy Buchanan, his cousin and a married woman; Jake by Brett Ashley.
Both men act as procurers: at Gatsby's request, Nick arranges for him a clandestine
meeting with Daisy; Jake . . . arranges for Brett her meeting with Pedro Romero. Both narrators are left alone at the end of their stories to clean up after careless main participants."
Moreover, continues Reynolds, between the two of them, Hemingway and Fitzgerald
"anatomized the moral condition of America in the mid-twenties. Fitzgerald at home
and Hemingway in Paris were taking the same pulse, hearing the same sick wheezing in
the national respiration" (152). And both used images from Eliot's *Waste Land* – failed
sexual relationships as metaphors for the postwar condition, rituals that no longer work,
etc. (159) – to convey their themes to their readers.

25 Hemingway, however, in his literature as in his life, was generally reluctant to acknowledge his sources; he preferred to give the impression that he *created* his legends rather
than borrowed or reworked them – a tendency reflected by a number of critics and
scholars, who recognize Hemingway's obvious borrowings from Eliot but downplay
their significance. Malcolm Cowley, for example, in his Introduction to the Viking
Portable *Hemingway*, acknowledged that *The Sun Also Rises* "dealt with the same legend
that Eliot had discovered by scholarship," but argued vaguely – and, ultimately, incor-
rectly – that Hemingway had somehow succeeded in "discovering it for himself, I think,
by a sort of instinct for legendary situations" (Cowley in Weeks 50).

finished editing 'The Waste Land.' Eliot himself was an occasional visitor to Paris and the story of the Fisher King may well have been a topic of discussion in the evenings of Gertrude Stein" (295). Richard P. Adams, however, suggests that above all it was Fitzgerald's arrival in Paris in May, 1925, that focused Hemingway's attention on the "mythical method" popularized by Eliot in his classic poem. *"The Great Gatsby,"* writes Adams, "had appeared on April 10, and copies had been sent to Gertrude Stein and to Eliot, both of whom were highly pleased with it. Eliot had a personal reason to be, for *The Great Gatsby* has the same theme, uses the same imagery, and is based on the same myth as *The Waste Land*. Fitzgerald certainly knew what he had done, for he was a great admirer of Eliot, and Hemingway was certainly a good enough reader to see the point for himself, if Fitzgerald did not explain it. The two struck up a warm friendship and spent a good deal of time together that summer; and by July Hemingway was at work on *The Sun Also Rises"* (57), his first novel (eventually published on October 22, 1926, by Scribner's, Fitzgerald's publisher, and edited by Max Perkins, Fitzgerald's editor).[26] In a jesting letter written in April, 1926, just after Hemingway had finished a revised typescript of *The Sun Also Rises*, he wrote Fitzgerald that his novel "followed the outline of *Gatsby"* and that, apart from a few details gotten from Dreiser, "practically everything else in the book was his own or Fitzgerald's." And later, in a letter of December, 1926, Hemingway proposed that as a token of his gratitude he would ask Scribner's to insert a new subtitle after the eighth printing, which would read:

> THE SUN ALSO RISES (LIKE YOUR COCK IF YOU HAVE ONE)
> A Greater Gatsby
> (Written with the friendship of F. Scott Fitzgerald,
> Prophet of the Jazz Age)   (Reynolds in Noble 119)

The Sun Also Rises was not, however, the first occasion on which Hemingway had used traditional mythic material. The image of the Fisher King actually appears as early as Hemingway's first collection of short stories. In that book, entitled *In Our Time* (1925), Nick Adams, the hero of most of the stories, goes to war, is wounded, and returns to a home and to a society into which he no longer fits. Nothing, he realizes, is as it used to be. The familiar countryside near the town of Seney "was burned over and changed" (134–35); even the grasshoppers "had all turned black from living in the burned-out land" (136).

The wound that Nick Adams suffers is both physical and psychological. The physical injury is explicitly described in the interlude that precedes "A Very Short Story": "He had been hit in the spine. . . . Both legs stuck out

---

26 In a 1934 letter to Max Perkins, Fitzgerald feared that Hemingway's interest in chivalry might cause him to appropriate another of Fitzgerald's themes. Fitzgerald wrote: "Needless to say I am highly curious about the setting of his novel. I hope to God it isn't the crusading story that he once had in mind, for I would hate like hell for my 9th-century novel [*Philippe, Count of Darkness*] to compete with *that"* (*Dear Scott* 212).

awkwardly" (81). The even greater psychological injury is inflicted much
earlier; evident already in his childhood (in his mother's attempts to demor-
alize and emasculate both her husband and her son, as Hemingway's own
mother had done – events described in "The Doctor and the Doctor's Wife"),
it continues throughout his adolescence (by – among others – the brakesman
in "The Battler" who kicks the boy off a moving train onto the "sand and
cinders" [65]) and into his early manhood (by the nurse in "A Very Short
Story" who treats his war wounds, agrees to marry him, but then throws him
over for another man and by the wife in "Cross-Country Snow" who forces
him to leave the freedom of the mountains and the pleasure of skiing to
return to the middle-class American lifestyle he considers hypocritical and
abhorrent). Moreover, Nick's wound is mirrored in the wounds, both spiritual and physical, of others around him. The Indian father in "Indian Camp,"
for instance, has injured his foot and lost his ability to work as well as – it is
implied – his potency; unable to relieve his wife's pain as she gives birth in
the bunk below his and unable to endure her cries, he commits suicide by
slashing his throat. Harold Krebs, in "Soldier's Home," has returned from
the war; but he is too late for the celebrations and "the greeting of heroes"
(89). All that awaits him is the same dysfunctional family he left behind,
including his henpecked father and his overbearing mother, who insists on
infanticising him and forcing him to pray with her the prayers in which he
no longer has any faith. Ad Francis, the embattled "Battler," has little to
show for his lifetime of fights besides a mutilated face and a brain addled
from too many punches to the head; his success in the ring has only begotten
more violence, including the regular beatings Ad receives from his homosexual companion. Even the mules left behind by their Greek owners in "On
the Quai at Smyrna" are not spared violence or injury: unable to take them as
they escape and unwilling to leave them for the invading Turks, the Greeks
break the animals' forelegs and push them into the shallow waters of the
harbor to die in pain, near the dead and dying women and children on the
pier. In this way the mules' plight reflects Nick's own, since he too is hostage
to his past, unsure of his future, and certain only of his current pain.

The sole consolation for Nick lies in returning to nature, to the spots
where he had hunted and fished and come of age.[27] Yet the very places to
which Nick has always retreated in order to rediscover himself are as
wounded as he: his youthful haunt, Horton's Bay, which had once seemed
"like a castle" (36), is now desolate. Its "one-story bunk houses, the eating

---

27 The same is true of other Hemingway protagonists. The unnamed American volunteer in
the Italian Army in "Now I Lay Me," for example, could easily be mistaken for Nick.
Afraid to sleep at night "ever since I had been blown up at night," he lies awake
"think[ing] of a trout stream I had fished along when I was a boy." He "fish[es] its whole
length very carefully in his mind; fishing very carefully under all the logs, all the turns of
the bank, the deep holes and the clear shallow stretches, sometimes catching trout and
sometimes losing them."

house, the company store, the mill offices, and the big mill itself stood deserted in the acres of sawdust that covered the swampy meadow by the shore of the bay" (35). And even the area near the "Big Two-Hearted River" has become a wasteland, a "burned-over stretch of hillside" (177) marked by cinders and chipped stones. Nick must travel far into the woods to find land that resembles the unblighted natural terrain of his youth; but before he is ready to fish the river, he must prepare himself by performing certain rituals akin to those of the knight errant. With great deliberation and concentration, he levels his campsite, pitches his tent, and lays out his blanket for the solitary night ahead of him; with each ritual movement, from eating to undressing, he strives for order and control. "There had been this to do," he notes. "Now it was done. . . . Nothing could touch him" (187). Interestingly, the journey that Nick, the Fisher King, takes into the heart of the woods is signalled by the appearance of a bird – a kingfisher – that "flew up the stream" [178] away from the town.

On the next morning, Nick continues his rituals. He catches fifty medium brown grasshoppers, still wet with dew, and then replaces the log under which they nest so that he can come back for more bait each day; he secures his familiar equipment; and, with patient thrusts of his rod, he manages to regularize his actions. As Roger Casey writes, "The ritual of fishing provides promise of rejuvenation, a return to a primitive state of serenity in contrast to the destruction he has seen in Seney or, more so, the war" (192). Even though Nick loses the big trout on his line, he starts fishing again and this time catches several smaller fish. His effort is satisfying; and, while the deep swamp water down the river promises both excitement and "tragic adventure" (211), he is content to go no further that day. Unlike the henpecked husband in "Out of Season," whose fishing trip to the "brown and muddy" river on whose bank "there was a dung heap" (131) is foiled, Nick knows that "there were plenty of days coming when he could fish the swamp" (212). He is happy to sit, as Eliot's Fisher King does, fishing on the river bank "with the arid plain behind" him, knowing that he will indeed "set [his] lands in order" (lines 424–25). It is only through such actions, at once real and symbolic, that Nick – as Charles G. and A. C. Hoffmann have noted – "can achieve the needed balance and control to hold his own steadily in the stream of life as the trout do in the river and face the more dangerous, treacherous cross-currents of the swamp" (106).

In his adherence to certain elemental rituals, Nick is both a prototype of his creator and a typical Hemingway hero, who observes a strict code of "proper" behavior and of "grace under pressure."[28] The code also serves to reinforce the notion of him as representing not only the Fisher King but also

28 "Proper" was a word which Hemingway, like his father before him, often used. As most of Hemingway's biographers have noted, it was important to both "to do things properly."

a "knight-questor making a perilous journey to the good place,"[29] a contemporary knight errant traversing the wasteland in search of his own healing, since in the modern wasteland the wounded hero must find his own cure. And there are reverberations from Nick's quest throughout Hemingway's later stories and novels – particularly *A Farewell to Arms*, in which the wounded Frederic Henry's disillusionment with "glory" and "sacrifice" represents the disillusionment of his postwar generation; *For Whom the Bell Tolls*, in which Robert Jordan – described by Leland as "a man on a quest" whose actions partake of game rules and ritual (49) – initially perceives himself to be a crusading knight fighting with other knights in a great cause ("a feeling of consecration to duty . . . an absolute brotherhood with the others who were engaged in it" [235]) and ultimately as a lone modern knight waging a more solitary war; even *The Old Man and the Sea*, in which the aged fisherman Santiago unsuccessfully battles the elements yet emerges renewed, and healed, by the experience. As Kim Moreland notes, Santiago's fishing trip "is a pilgrimage – or more accurately, a quest. Like the Fisher King of ancient vegetation myths . . . Santiago is identified with 'a fishless desert,' a sterility that awaits redemption. His one-on-one victory over a worthy antagonist, whose 'sword was . . . tapered like a rapier,' enables him to prove himself via a chivalric test and thereby to bring back knowledge that will result in potency and fertility after a dry spell of eighty-four days" (180–81).[30]

But it is in *The Sun Also Rises* that Hemingway most comprehensively treats his Arthurian theme. Philip Young contends, in fact, that *The Sun Also Rises* "is Hemingway's *Waste Land*" (59). And indeed, as most critics from Malcolm Cowley and Philip Young to Carlos Baker and beyond have observed, *The Sun Also Rises* is based on the same structural principles as Eliot's poem, including the sterility of the modern city and the meaninglessness of relations, especially sexual ones. Yet *The Sun Also Rises* is no more a simple expression of despair than is *The Waste Land*. "It does," as Richard P. Adams demonstrates, "embody the feeling Hemingway shared with Eliot

29 Hoffman and Hoffman demonstrate that Nick, the knight-questor, emerges as "The Fisher King who is reborn" (106). They also suggest numerous other parallels between *The Waste Land* and "Big Two-Hearted River," including the emphasis on fire as purgation (e.g., fire's destructiveness as "associated on the macrocosmic level with the conflagration of the war which destroyed the symbolic landmarks of an entire pre-war civilization and on the microcosmic, personal level more directly with the scars and wounds of Nick's experience") and water as a "paradoxical element of death and rebirth" (as in the violent birth and death in "Indian Camp," the dead marriage in "Cat in the Rain," the death of first love in "End of Something," and the malaise of postwar life in "Out of Season"). See especially pp. 106–109 for a discussion of these parallels.
30 Moreland also writes that Santiago's frequently-noted identification with Christ, whose Passion he replicates in his three-day voyage, "aligns him with the Christian version of such vegetation myths." Yet she concludes that Santiago's end is "more equivocal than the ultimately optimistic conclusion of Christ's Passion in Resurrection – in this regard more like Eliot's equivocal conclusion to his modernist *Waste Land*" (182). Bickford Sylvester, in "Hemingway's Extended Vision: *The Old Man and the Sea*," also discusses Calvary allusions and ritualism in *The Old Man and the Sea*.

and others that Western civilization was dying. But that feeling was not so naively entertained by these writers as it has been by some of their disciples." Rather, "the Waste Land imagery of *The Sun Also Rises* is a more complex and ambiguous web of sterile and creative, good and evil, cheerful and desperate implications than has generally been seen" (58–59).[31]

If *The Sun Also Rises* is Hemingway's *Waste Land*, Jake Barnes is the novel's Fisher King. Rendered impotent by a shell wound during the war, Jake finds himself in a world as sterile as he is, a world as impoverished spiritually as he is sexually. Young characterizes that world as one in which "prayer breaks down and fails, a knowledge of traditional distinctions between good and evil is largely lost, copulation is morally neutral and, cut off from the past chiefly by the spiritual disaster of war, life has become mostly meaningless. 'What shall we do?' is the same constant question, to which the answer must be, again, 'Nothing.' To hide it, instead of playing chess one drinks, mechanically and always" (59–60).

Though there is constant movement throughout the novel – from Paris to Burguete, Pamplona, San Sebastian, Madrid, and ultimately back again to Paris – there is, as in Eliot's *Waste Land*, also constant boredom among the characters. That boredom, observes Arthur Waldhorn, coupled with the characters' hysteria and agony, "mirror[s] the chaotic past of the war experience and the cynical or hedonistic masks that later disguise disfigured or mutilated dreams and illusions" (96). In Hemingway's land of waste, the altar is a bar, the Grail a glass of absinthe. Unable to find adequate diversion despite the lively Parisian nightlife in the Quarter or the raucous, boisterous Spanish fiesta being celebrated around them, the characters move rather mechanically from club to pub, from restaurant to bodega, until – exhausted by drink and by their own cynicism – they fall into bed, sometimes alone, sometimes with each other, but even then in a succession of generally quick and meaningless copulations. Ironically, love is possible only for the emasculated Jake and the defeminized Lady Brett Ashley, the two who cannot love, and that is so perhaps *because* they cannot love: the impossibility of their consummating the relationship is precisely what sustains it. Brett, after all, is Jake's female counterpart: she too has been wounded by the colossal violence of war. A former nurse, she no longer gives succor to the injured and the ill; it is she who now is injured and requires succor. Her first husband had died of dysentery; her second husband has been sent home in a dangerous state of shock; and her postwar lovers offer only a moral and emotional vacuum that echoes society as a whole. For Brett, these blows are the equivalent of Jake's emasculation; as Mark Spilka observes, "they seem to release her from her womanly nature and expose her to the male

31 Paul B. Newman similarly observed that "the influence of Eliot's work on Hemingway is perhaps deeper than has been generally appreciated," as revealed by an examination of "the current of symbolic overtones [owing much to Eliot and Jessie Weston] . . . beneath the surface of *The Sun Also Rises*" (295).

prerogatives of drink and promiscuity" (130). In fact, even her surname, Ashley, suggests the sterile, ashen wasteland of which she and Jake have become a part.

Book I of the novel finds Jake in the heart of that wasteland, amidst the expatriate crowd in Paris – "the Fisher King," as Paul B. Newman calls him, "of a Waste Land whose inhabitants are in the same disastrous condition as himself" (297). The artists, writers and derelicts who surround him are sexual cripples: all have, in some figurative manner, also been rendered impotent by the war. Jake feels a kinship with the few who bear their sickness well. The prostitute Georgette, for instance, whom Jake picks up one evening so that he will not have to eat alone and whom he later introduces to friends as his fiancée, reduces love to a simple exchange of money and is sterile and "sick"; but, as Spilka notes, "like Barnes, she manages to be frank and forthright and to keep an even keel among the drifters of Paris. Together they form a pair of honest cripples, in contrast with the various pretenders whom they meet along the Left Bank" (30), like Robert Cohn, a persistent romantic (Arthur Mizener calls him "a high-school Lancelot" [138]) who loves the pose of manhood,[32] and his steely mistress Frances Clyne.

When one of Brett's band of homosexual friends spies Georgette at the Bal Musette and begins to dance with her, the others – in a deliberate parody of normal love – follow suit. Brett also participates in the distortion of sexual roles: she keeps her boyishly bobbed hair covered with a man's felt hat; addresses the men around her as fellow "chaps"; and introduces to Jake her friend, the wealthy, wounded Count Mippipopolous, who is, she contends, "one of us."

But this moral wasteland is too much for even the stoic Jake to bear. Anxious to escape the hollow men and women who have cut themselves off from conventional society, he decides to leave Paris – as he does each year – to return to the trout stream at Burguete and the bull ring at Pamplona. Leo Gurko writes that Jake must "refresh himself at the source of the one enduring reality in Hemingway's universe. . . [the place where] the sun also rises and the earth always abides" (Gurko, *Pursuit of Heroism* 60).[33] Like "the sun that rises every morning, makes its journey across the heavens, sets, only to rise again the next day," Jake's annual excursion from France to Spain back to France leaves him "recharged" and able to "resume his struggle for

32 For a fuller description of Robert Cohn as a romantic and quixotic figure, see Martin Light, "Sweeping Out Chivalric Silliness: The Example of *Huck Finn* and *The Sun Also Rises*." Paul B. Newman, in "Hemingway's Grail Quest," also discusses Cohn as a "collapsed Byronian romantic" (296–97).

33 Gurko notes, in "Hemingway and the Magical Journey," that Jake's trip beyond the hills of Burguete is a journey to "the unspoiled earth, suggested by the wine-drinking peasants in the bus, the secluded country inn, the sun-filled woods dotted with wild strawberries, and the Irati River teeming with fish. . . . [Jake] is refreshed. He has gone back to the beginning of things. Sun, woods, earth, heat, river – unspoiled and all but untouched – release him from the complexities of civilized life" (70).

survival" (Gurko in Noble, 73) – in other words, renewed and reborn, like the legendary Fisher King.

So Book II finds Jake fishing with his friend Bill Gorton, and the particulars of their adventure are treated with the same reverence of detail as Nick's in "Big Two-Hearted River." They travel through "barren" country, in which "rocks struck up through the clay" and where "there was no grass," until they reach "a rolling green plain, with dark mountains beyond" (108, 120). "Like Nick Adams," notes Spilka, "these men have left the wasteland for the green plains of health; they have traveled miles, by train and on foot, to reach a particular trout stream. The fishing there is good, the talk free and easy" (132), and even the usually insomniac Barnes is able to sleep well after lunch, a meal that itself is handled like a mock religious ceremony. The whole ritualistic exercise proves therapeutic for Jake, who describes himself as a "rotten Catholic"[34] and speaks briefly to Gorton of his abortive love for Brett before acknowledging that, with religion defunct and love no longer possible, happiness can only be found through private and imaginative means. "Thus," concludes Spilka, "he now constructs a more positive code to follow: as with Nick Adams, it brings him health, pleasure, beauty and order, and helps to wipe out the damage of his troubled life in Paris" (132).

Soon Jake decides to move on to Pamplona, which stands roughly to Burguete as the swamp in "Big Two-Hearted River" stands to the trout stream (Spilka 132–33). There he participates in the annual fiesta (a seasonal ritual, the whole experience of which harks back to ancient rites discussed by Frazer and Weston – sources for Eliot and other contemporary writers – and suggests the cleansing and purging of emotion); enjoys the bullfights, another ritualistic celebration, that vicariously help to restore his potency;[35] and

34 "Almost the first thing Jake does when he gets to Pamplona," writes Adams, "is to go into the cathedral and pray, at the same time regretting that he is 'such a rotten Catholic . . . I only wished I felt religious and maybe I would the next time. . . .' The monastery of Roncevalles is a feature of the Burguete interlude, and perhaps has some analogy to the Chapel Perilous" (61). Brett, by contrast, feels "damned nervous" in church; instead of going to confession, she visits a gypsy camp and has her fortune told.
  H. R. Stoneback, however, rejects the notion that Jake's admission that he is a "rotten Catholic" suggests "the failure of prayer and religion in the Wasteland" (143). Instead, he sees Jake not as a skeptic but as "a pilgram [sic] seeking a deeper participation in grace through the careful practice of ritual and discipline" (145) – a reading certainly consistent with Stoneback's thesis that the novel is a "quest, or pilgrimage" (138). Moreover, Stoneback finds special significance in Jake's proselytizing to Brett about prayer, "for religion as for the bullfight" are the ways in the novel by which "one may best come to know the 'values' " (149).
35 In *The Golden Bough*, Frazer describes the *taurobolium*, the ceremonial baptism in bull's blood, which was supposed to insure rebirth to eternal life. Used in the ritual were bull's testicles, which were considered powerful charms in promoting fertility and hastening new birth.
  For Hemingway, the bullfights had another important ritual significance. In *Death in the Afternoon*, he described the sport as "well ordered and . . . strongly disciplined by ritual" (8) and later likened bullfighters to "the crusaders in the middle ages" (265). Bullfighting thus became a form of modern chivalric ritual for Hemingway, the equivalent of the medieval tournament at which knights were challenged and tested.

meets Pedro Romero, the courageous young bullfighter who ultimately serves as a foil for him. And there too Jake finds his own stoicism tested, when Brett and the spoilers who have followed her from Paris ruin his brief idyll: Brett's fiancé Mike Campbell, resentful of Brett's infidelities, baits Robert Cohn, one of Brett's former lovers; and Cohn – "ready to do battle for his lady" (178) in a pointless show of chivalric silliness – fights Jake, Mike, and ultimately Romero.

The unfortunate episode forces Jake to contrast his own lack of heroism with Romero's bravery. The young bullfighter, though severely beaten by Cohn, in turn disgraces Cohn by refusing to yield in the fight, an act of dignity that he repeats the next day in the bullring with his skillful, controlled performance. Like the virtuous knight victorious in battle, Romero therefore emerges as an exemplum of the highest code of sportsmanship, which holds that a man's dignity depends on his own resources and inner strength. Jake, on the other hand, is reduced to a dazed adolescent by Cohn; and he is reduced yet again – this time to a slavish pimp – by Brett, who solicits his help in seducing Romero. Like a sick romantic steer (an image Hemingway also applies to Cohn) rather than a proud bull, Jake allows himself to be used as a go-between, to be disgraced with his friend Montoya, to be made a party to Romero's corruption.

This confluence of events in Book II – Cohn's empty romantic sense of chivalry, Romero's real heroism as a modern day knight tested by his participation in the contemporary tournament of the bullring, Brett's lust for Romero that requires Jake's help to bring about – thus provides "a peacetime demonstration, postwar style, of the meaning of Jake's shell wound" (Spilka 135–36). The demonstration continues at Pamplona, where Romero presents Brett with the ear of a bull he has slain. Since that bull had earlier gored a man during the ceremonial run through the streets, Romero's killing of it provides a kind of communal, if primitive, triumph. For Brett, however, the ear – itself a token of communal strength – has no larger significance. She considers it simply a private trophy, sticks it in the drawer of her night table alongside some cigarette butts, and quickly forgets about it.[36] Brett's careless actions effectively rob the community of its triumph and ruin the fiesta for Jake. Having despoiled the celebration's symbol of integrity and manhood, Brett leaves with Romero for Madrid; and Jake's "good place" is good no more.

In Book III, Barnes tries to purge himself of the damage done in Pamplona. He swims in the ocean waters, as if to cleanse himself of Brett (something he had tried to do at the Hotel Montoya, where "the water would not run" in the stone tub [195]), and relaxes in a café in San Sebastian. But his solace is

---

36 This incident is apparently based on an actual experience of Hadley's. Hemingway, like Fitzgerald, obviously borrowed details not only from his own life but also from his wife's.

short-lived: Brett telegraphs him from Madrid to ask for help. Going to her rescue, Jake finds Brett alone and learns the reason for Romero's departure: the young bullfighter had tried to change her, had insisted that she grow her hair long. The "purifying transformation" of Brett that Romero sought but could not achieve, according to Gurko, was his attempt to make her a whole woman again (560).[37] Yet, her normal sexual role having been robbed by the war and the society that created it, Brett can no sooner let her hair grow than Jake can recover his manhood. So, Brett tells Jake, she has sent Romero away.

If Brett's transformation is incomplete,[38] however, Jake's is not. He realizes that, even had he not been wounded so grievously, Brett and he could never really have been lovers; love, for their generation, is dead. The novel's closing lines reveal that he has no more illusions. As the two approach a mounted policeman[39] who has raised his baton to direct traffic – an ironic, symbolic reminder of their own sterility and impotence – and are pressed together by the motion of the slowing car, Brett says to Jake, "we could have had such a damned good time together." And Jake replies, "Yes. . . . Isn't it pretty to think so?"

It is easy to misread Jake's stoicism as weakness; but, in fact, his stoicism is at the heart of his heroism. And in the end he is every bit as heroic as his friend Romero – perhaps even more so, in the face of the greater burden he must bear. Jake's rejection of Brett's romantic posturing, which mirrors Romero's rejection of Brett's traditionally unfeminine guises, shows that he has acquired a measure of control in his relationship with her, "gained in self-mastery" (Daiker 74), and grown emotionally as well. Even Brett comes to appreciate his quiet strength. After telling Romero to leave, she calls on Jake to rescue and support her, thus supplanting one "hero" with another.

Moreover, in his role as the Fisher King, Jake brings what little meaning or moral authority exists to the wasteland of his postwar society. As Leo Gurko notes, not only does he rescue Brett; he also "befriends Cohn, listens patiently to Harvey Stone, accompanies Bill, calms Mike, appreciates Count Mippipopolous, attracts Harris, and admires Romero for the right reasons. He links Robert Cohn, a Jew, to the Christian world. Through his contact with Montoya and Romero, he is the liaison between his non-Spanish friends

37 Delbert E. Wylder takes issue with this familiar reading. Citing the Victorian attitude that "long hair . . . was the symbol for woman" (93), Wylder dismisses as Victorian and stereotypical the notion of contemporary critics that Brett's short hair suggests her lack of femininity. Wylder, moreover, urges a reassessment of Brett "in the role of the new woman."

38 Linda Patterson Miller holds a different view. She suggests – quite persuasively – that Brett is indeed transformed by her experiences, that she ultimately finds herself, and that she alone has "the potential for the clearest vision" in the novel. Miller concludes that, "in the themes of appearance and reality, and of personal growth and self-realization, *The Sun Also Rises* is very much her novel, and she stands at the center of it, beautiful, vulnerable, and finally herself" (182).

39 The mounted policeman, his baton held high, is not only an emblem to Jake of his physical impotence; the officer's uniform is also a reminder of the war, which was the cause of Jake's injury.

and the Spaniards. Without being able to live wholly himself, he is a catalytic agent who releases life in others" (59). Despite his physical impotence, Jake is capable of unusually deep emotion; bullfighting is for him a true passion, or *aficion*, as Montoya recognizes.[40] Although Jake never actually enters the ring as a bullfighter the way Romero does, he becomes something just as good: someone who understands the sport thoroughly and reacts to it with the exquisite sensitivity of the connoisseur. Jake's kind of passion, according to Gurko, "the passion of knowledge rather than the passion of the act itself, the emotion of the spectator instead of the participant, . . . [is] wholly authentic, meaningful, and pure," and is typical of Jake's many "efforts in the direction of life and the heightening of his human faculties" (Gurko, *Pursuit of Heroism* 57–58). All of those efforts demand an understanding of the elemental rituals inherent in moral actions; and in his cyclical return to nature for healing, Jake is again reminiscent of the legendary Fisher King.

Brett, too, while not qualified to be a Grail maiden, has – as Richard P. Adams has observed – some relations to the older fertility myths. "One is her interest in fortune-telling, which, according to Miss Weston's account of the Tarot cards, was originally the art of predicting 'the rise and fall of the waters which brought fertility to the land.' Her bathing, which is frequent and obsessive, also associates her with the life-giving water" (59),[41] as does her becoming "an image to dance around" in the wine shop, where she is seated on a cask and decorated with a garlic wreath.

Other characters in the novel also have connections, though sometimes oblique, to the Grail legends. Robert Cohn is a kind of Grail knight who, like Percival, fails to ask the right questions. Mike Campbell, suggests Adams, "is perhaps another unworthy knight" (60). And Bill Gorton, Montoya, and Count Mippipopolous, while they do not participate in any quest directly, serve as wise guides who help to point Jake towards his goal; in a novel that H. R. Stoneback characterizes thematically and structurally as a "quest, a desperate crusade . . . to find action and behavior that will signify" (138), even these minor characters are significant in helping the questing Jake "to know the 'values' " (149).[42]

---

40 Richard P. Adams writes, "Richard Ford, whose book on Spain Hemingway mentions favorably in *Death in the Afternoon*, associates modern bullfights with 'the *taurobolia* of antiquity,' in which 'those who were sprinkled with blood were absolved from sin.' Miss Weston mentions the *taurobolium* in connection with Mithraism, which was spread throughout the Western Roman Empire, and with the cult of the *Magna Mater*, the Attis cult, which she says is the primitive origin of the Grail legend" (60–61). Adams also suggests other connections between bullfighting and other rites of sacrifice and renewal, a knowledge of which enhances "our appreciation of the bullfighting scenes" in Hemingway's novel.

41 For a fuller description of Brett's obsession with bathing and of the other water imagery in the novel, see George D. Murphy, "Hemingway's *Waste Land*: The Controlling Water Symbolism in *The Sun Also Rises*."

42 Stoneback, who reads the novel as a journey through a "paysage moralisé," attempts to demonstrate the spiritual nature of Jake's quest "to know the 'values' " (149) through "the careful practice of ritual and discipline" (145).

While *The Sun Also Rises* offers Hemingway's most sustained and comprehensive treatment of the Grail legends, his interest in the medieval[43] and especially the Arthurian is also apparent in other areas of his work – for instance, in the collection of short stories he was contemplating as he worked on *The Sun Also Rises*, a collection that he considered calling *A New Slain Knight* (Baker *EH* 166). ("A New-Slain Knight" is also the title he initially gave to a later novel, *Across the River and into the Trees*, whose protagonist, Colonel Cantwell, becomes – as do so many of Hemingway's other protagonists – a kind of chivalric knight battling the technological horrors of modern warfare.[44]) That interest is apparent as well in "The Road to Avallon," a poem published in 1949. Written when the Hemingways were still living in France, the poem describes a journey to a town in Yonne, about 200 kilometers southeast of Paris. Most immediately evident in the poem are its racist language, in phrases such as "nigger ric" (line 1), and its otherwise unremarkable verse, such as "Dogs must shit as well as men" (line 12); but, as Nicholas Gerogiannis has observed, Hemingway may well have had Avalon, "the island sanctuary where King Arthur was taken after he has been mortally wounded" (156), in mind. Arthur's journey for healing thus corresponds to Nick's and to Jake's and to that of other of Hemingway's wounded heroes, like the fisherman Santiago in *The Old Man and the Sea*.

Furthermore, the code of honor implicit in the Arthurian knightly traditions was in many ways similar to the code of honor and grace under pressure that Hemingway defined for himself in his own life. His first wife Hadley Richardson seemed especially aware of his chivalric propensities. In a 1921 letter written during their courtship, she observed that he "would have been an alchemist in the Middle Ages, or a Galahad"; and in another letter written that same year she dubbed him "a verry, perfect, gentile knight" (Griffin, *Youth* 191, 154, cited in Moreland 173). Hemingway, too, defined himself in chivalric terms. In a 1925 letter to Fitzgerald, he cast himself, perhaps somewhat parodically, "in the role of the quester for truth, the Red Cross Knight" (Griffin 108). Hemingway's self-imposed knightly

43 Hemingway, like Fitzgerald, had a lifelong interest in medievalism and romance. Baker notes that in 1953, when Hemingway made the trip from Paris through Chartres south to the Basque country, he "amused himself by imagining that he was a medieval knight riding his horse along the riverbank" (648). Even in his last years, as late as 1959, he revisited the "magical region" around Roncevaux and dreamed one more time in what he called "the last great forest of the Middle Ages" (693).

Stoneback discusses at some length the importance of the actual Roncevaux to the overall symbolism of *The Sun Also Rises* and suggests that Roland, a hero with whom Hemingway must have been familiar, "is type and paradigm for Jacob Barnes who wrestles courageously with the angel of his fate in the country around Roncevaux" (137). He also offers some interesting insights into Hemingway's medievalism, as does Kim Moreland in *The Medievalist Impulse in American Literature*.

44 See Moreland's chapter on "Ernest Hemingway: Knighthood in Our Time," pp. 161–200 (but especially pp. 174–76), for a discussion of Hemingway's "late incarnation of the medieval knight" as a modern soldier.

role, writes Kim Moreland, was also manifest in "his exaggerated sense of protectiveness toward ladies": reportedly, he was ready to slug anyone who so much as jostled his companion Ada MacLeish at prizefights or bike races, and years later he was ready to fight a duel for Ingrid Bergman, who played Maria in the screen version of *For Whom the Bell Tolls* (229). Adriana Ivancich, another young woman with whom Hemingway was infatuated, served both as a kind of muse for him late in his life and as the object of his courtly devotion. Jeffrey Meyers notes that, in a letter to Adriana, Hemingway recognized that he could not marry her but "wished only to serve her well, like a chivalric knight" (*Hemingway* 443, cited in Moreland 192).

But Hemingway did not always live up to his own code of knightly standards. For instance, after a particularly unpleasant meeting with his third wife, Martha Gellhorn, from whom he was seeking a divorce, Hemingway was full of morning-after remorse. Using chivalric behavior as an appropriate model, he wrote Martha a note of apology in which he likened his boorish treatment of her to "spitting upon the Holy Grail" (Lynn 519). That boorish behavior was soon repeated, though: after disparaging Martha publicly, he returned to her hotel, stripped down into his long underwear, and grabbed a mop and bucket from a utility closet; with the bucket on his head and the mop clutched like a lance, he tried – not only unchivalrously but also unsuccessfully – to batter down her door (Lynn 521).

Throughout his lifetime, Hemingway admired as well as envied other questers, especially daring, courageous men like Philip Percival, the great white hunter who led him on a quest for kudu ("a knight's quest," according to Michael S. Reynolds [*Hemingway's Reading* 27]). That quest is chronicled in the autobiographical *Green Hills of Africa*, in which Percival appears as "Pop."[45] As John Leland observed, Percival, "like the original Grail keeper . . . in the Grail Legend . . . was a symbol of all that is worthy and pure"; and, though Hemingway aspired to match or displace him, "like a Galahad . . . in later legends," he ultimately realized that he was "no pure knight" and thus was "unworthy of becoming the Grail keeper" (52–53) himself. He could only hope to follow Percival into the restored wasteland – or, as in *Green Hills of Africa*, to the banks of the Sea of Galilee, the once edenic and still Holy Land.[46]

---

45 Percival served as a model for other Hemingway characters. Carlos Baker (*Life Story* 284) notes that "Robert Wilson, white hunter to the Macombers [in "The Short Happy Life of Francis Macomber"], was based on Philip Percival, with his rubicund face, cool blue eyes, laconic speech habits, and his enviable combination of courage and judgment." Hemingway also attributed the epigraph of "The Snows of Kilimanjaro," which he later called "part of the metaphysics of the story" (Baker 289), to Percival.

46 John Leland (52) suggests that, just as the quest for Eden informs much of Hemingway's work, the stories of the wasteland and the Fisher King underlie *Green Hills of Africa*. In the book's "Foreword," Hemingway wrote that *Green Hills of Africa* was "an absolutely true book . . . [that can] compete with a work of the imagination"; and Leland concurs, offering as explanation that "both fact and fiction partake of the pattern of myth." In his essay, Leland goes on to explore that "pattern" in terms of the wasteland and the Grail quest.

Just as Hemingway kept revisiting Philip Percival throughout his lifetime, he kept returning to the wasteland and to the wounded Fisher King in his fiction; and, as Fitzgerald had done, he effectively used that central image to reflect the wounds of postwar men and women mired in their societal and cultural wastelands. It is, in Malcolm Cowley's words, this "instinct for legends, for sacraments, for rituals, for symbols appealing to buried hopes and fears, that helps to explain the power of Hemingway's work" (50). And it is especially his ability to take a legend popularized by Eliot and to "recover it for himself" that places Hemingway in the forefront of the American Arthurian tradition in the first half of the twentieth century.

William Faulkner, the great and lyrical voice of the American South, was affected not only by Eliot's notion of the wasteland but also by the ways in which Fitzgerald and Hemingway reinterpreted it in their fiction;[47] and he reflected a similar postwar disillusion – and appropriated similar images – in several of his earliest works. His first novel,[48] *Soldier's Pay* (1926), whose atmosphere Frederic J. Hoffman describes as "pseudo-Eliotic" (40), is the story of another wounded soldier's homecoming.[49] Donald Mahon, Faulkner's Everyman, returns injured, blinded, dying, to Charlestown, Georgia. His fiancée Cecily Saunders, who – like Daisy Fay in *The Great Gatsby* – had been captivated by the romance and glamour of the soldier's promise, cannot accept the end of that fantasy; repulsed by Donald's scars, she runs away to marry the sophomoric but unscarred George Farr. Mrs. Powers, the young war widow who accompanies Mahon on his journey home, had predicted Cecily's reaction: "all the old bunk about knights of the air and the romance of battle," she said, "[is] outgrow[n] soon as the excitement is over and uniforms and being wounded ain't only not stylish anymore, but it is trouble-some . . . [especially for] one of them flighty-looking pretty ones with lots of hair. Just the sort who would have got herself engaged to him" (*SP* 35). And after Cecily indeed rejects Donald, it is Margaret Powers who marries him, in part to expiate her own guilt over her first marriage, into which she

---

47 Before *The Sun Also Rises* was published, apparently on the basis of *In Our Time* and what-ever short stories Faulkner had seen in the little magazines (for example, *The Double Dealer*, where he had been published in the same number as Hemingway), Faulkner felt that "Ernest Hemingway is so far the greatest American fictionist." *The Sun Also Rises*, which Faulkner admired, certainly reinforced this opinion. Faulkner's experience and preoccupation, moreover, from the time of World War I to the time of writing *Flags in the Dust* (later revised and published in 1929 as *Sartoris*), prepared Faulkner to find the concerns and the spirit of Hemingway's first novel very congenial indeed – in fact, amazingly close to Faulkner's concerns and spirit (Stoneback 157–58).

48 *Soldier's Pay* was Faulkner's first novel but his second book. The first was a volume of poems, *The Marble Faun*, published in 1924.

49 There are intimations of this same theme in other Faulkner works. "Ad Astra" (1931; reprinted in *These Thirteen*, 1931), for example, suggests the waste and futility of war by showing that those who have been in the war come out of it morally and spiritually dead. Another story, "Crevasse" (first published in *These Thirteen*), evokes "the desolation of war through the sterility of the landscape and the seemingly benumbed condition of the characters" (Tuck 164).

entered for much the same reason Cecily had initially entered into her engagement to Donald. The marriage, however, in no way improves the dying Donald's condition; it serves only to reinforce the fact that in the postwar wasteland Faulkner describes, there are no means to heal the wounded or restore their loss.

The satyr-like Januarius Jones acts "as the epitome of civilian indifference to the reality of war" (Tuck 126) and tries to usurp Donald's place with the various women in his life: Cecily, Mrs. Powers, even the serving girl Emmy, who – believing "I could have cured him!" (301) – tries to re-create her brief romantic experience with the pre-war Donald by giving herself to Jones on the night of Donald's death. Yet, more than any other character in the novel, Jones recognizes the emptiness of romantic attitudes. He pointedly asks Margaret and her friend, Private Joe Gilligan, whom he addresses as a romantic "Mr. Galahad," a rhetorical question: "You had expected great things from marriage, hadn't you? Sort of a miracle rejuvenation?" (294).

There is, of course, no rejuvenation for Mahon, who is as alienated from his former self as he is from the rest of the world and who knows only an "imminent nothingness more profound than any yet" (299), an "unseen forgotten spring, of greenness neither recalled nor forgot" (297). In a semi-comatose state that leaves him unconcerned about his surroundings and unaware of the circumstances of his injuries, he finally dies in the spring, the very season of rejuvenation. For Faulkner's Mahon, as for Eliot's men, April indeed becomes the cruellest month, and May brings little relief.

In *Soldier's Pay*, there are numerous other images reminiscent of *The Waste Land* and of Fitzgerald's and Hemingway's recasting of it in their novels: from the grey "towns like bubbles of ghostly sound beaded on a steel wire" (19) to the impersonal "fornication with a beautiful woman who chews gum steadily all the while" (188); from the ungathered and now "withered rose" to the "mummied hyacinth bulb"[50] that the rector picks up and that "crumbled to dust in his hand" (62); from the dreams "reft, restored, reft again" and "nightmares" (307) to the "bitter ashes" (164), "cinders" (313), and "dust in their shoes" (the novel's final words [326]).

Just as Faulkner uses the wounded Mahon as a realistic reminder of war to combat the idealized, romantic notions people have of the war and its heroes, in his second and even less successful novel *Mosquitoes* he focuses on a group of vacuous, world-weary party guests aboard a pleasure yacht who epitomize the hollowness of a society that has become morally and spiritually paralyzed. The guests talk – and talk – about sex and art without ever really performing sexual or artistic acts of any significance. Words "substitute . . . for things and deeds, like the withered cuckold husband that

50 There are numerous other hyacinth references as well. See, for example, pp. 50 ("April busy in a hyacinth bed"), 102 ("Donald's things . . . a girl's undie and a hyacinth bulb he carried with him in France"), 295 ("hyacinths swung pale bells, waiting for another day . . . a dream of arrested time"), and 322 ("the ruined hyacinth bed").

took the *Decameron* to bed with him every night" (210). But their words are nothing more than "a kind of sterility" (210). And, in the end, the guests demonstrate that they are unable to survive for long outside the rarified atmosphere of the boat's artificial world.

Like *Soldier's Pay*, the novel draws heavily on Eliot's themes and images, especially in lines such as "Spring and the cruellest months were gone, the cruel months, the wantons that break the fat hybernatant dullness and comfort of Time" (10).[51] And, in an almost dreamlike passage in the novel's final pages, Ernest Talliaferro, *Mosquitoes'* most Eliotic character, finds himself wandering the dark streets of the city, "rich with decay" (335), and pondering the meaning of beauty and genius. Those verities, he realizes, often result from a "passive state of the heart[; and] . . . the hackneyed accidents which make up this world – love and life and death and sex and sorrow – brought together by chance in perfect proportions, take on a kind of splendid and timeless beauty. Like Yseult of the White Hands and her Tristan with that clean, highhearted dullness of his" (339–40). As do his pretentious companions in the novel, Talliaferro alludes to legends, Arthurian and otherwise; and, by means of their allusions, they draw attention precisely to the heroic qualities and values that they lack in their own lives.

Faulkner returns to the familiar territory of the wasteland in other novels such as *Pylon* (1935). "Created out of the Waste Land" reads the sign on the new Feinman Airport, where much of *Pylon's* action occurs. The novel's characters include a family of air circus people – Roger, Jack, Laverne (who, though legally married to Roger, is their mutual "wife"), and little Jackie, her son by one of the men, though neither knows which – and a nameless reporter infatuated with Laverne who helps Roger, at times illicitly, acquire a plane to fly in the big Trophy Race. While rootless and pastless, the family of fliers have a kind of commitment to each other and to their work; they alone maintain "the still white glare of honor" (119) and consequently provide a contrast to the mindless, joyless merrymakers at the New Valois Mardi Gras. As Dorothy Tuck observes, "the Reporter, as a representative of the city, is repeatedly described as corpselike, cadaverous, skeletal – one of the spiritually dead who populate the 'Unreal City' of Eliot's *Waste Land*" (134). The fliers, to whom the Reporter is drawn, however, have in a sense escaped the dehumanization and the death of the city by repudiating the way of life of modern society. They are, as Faulkner later put it, "ephemera on the face of the contemporary scene" (Gwynn and Blotner 36). Recognizing no ties of geography or kin, they place

---

51 Joseph Blotner suggests that even the protagonist of *Mosquitoes*, widower Ernest Talliaferro, "suggested Eliot." A buyer of woman's clothing, he "was cut from the same pattern as Prufrock. Aging, worried about his attire and thinning hair, he was excited by women but unsuccessful despite a self-regenerating faith in the ultimate success of stratagems of seduction which were mainly verbal. The [novel's] prose was full of echoes of Eliot, not just from 'The Love Song of J. Alfred Prufrock' but from other poems such as 'The Waste Land' " (514).

the airplane at the center of their family unit and anoint the man who flies it as their leader; yet, "within this anomalous structure," writes Tuck, "they have a kind of integrity, and show themselves, especially Roger, capable of a degree of responsibility for the preservation of the group. They have, on the whole, a discipline and vitality – even a strange but coherent morality – that the Waste Land, the dead city of New Valois [based on New Orleans, another emblem of the modern mechanized wasteland] lacks" (134).

Roger, especially, is a "knight of the air."[52] The airfield, decorated with "gold-and-purple pennons" (17; description repeated on 30, 140, and 247), "looped bunting" (247; also 87, 267) caught "from post to post by cryptic shields" (87), and tunic-clad gatesmen (29), is his field of battle. His quest to prove himself worthy of the cup (specifically, in this case, the Trophy Cup) fails only because his craft is faulty.[53] Yet even his failure is noble: after the fuselage of his plane collapses under strain, he uses what minimal control is left to get out of the other fliers' way and to crash into the lake, away from the spectators in the grandstand.

After Roger's death, however, there is little hope for the rejuvenation of the land or the redemption of the other fliers, who "become merely May flies flitting over the corpse of a dead world, powerless to save even themselves" (Tuck 135). It is the reporter who most fully recognizes their spiritual barrenness; after Laverne decides to leave Jackie with Roger's parents to go off with Jack, thereby destroying their family group, the reporter drives out to the airfield, where (in the chapter Faulkner titles "Lovesong of J. A. Prufrock") he finally recognizes "the illusion" (283) he had embraced.

Faulkner's descriptions of the city and especially of the Mardi Gras – from the glitter to the litter, from the excrement to the deaths (Lieutenant Burnham's by fire, Shumann's by water), from the noise to the sex – evoke the sights, sounds, and smells of Eliot's *The Waste Land*; and the recurring images of time, clocks, and newspapers suggest the "cryptic staccato crossection of an instant crystallized and now dead" (53) in which the characters are trapped. But, as several critics have observed, Faulkner's heavy – and heavily derivative – load of symbolism is precisely what contributes to *Pylon's* ultimate failure. In contrast to more successful novels like *Absalom, Absalom!* or *The Sound and the Fury*,[54] in which the wasteland and quest

52 "Knight of the air" is how Margaret Powers describes Donald Mahon and the other young fliers in *Soldier's Pay*. It is, however, an accurate description of the fliers in *Pylon* as well.
53 Clearly, though, it is not the actual cup that Roger seeks. Even the reporter realizes that: "Yair," he says. "Ord talking about how he would be disqualified for the cup, the prize, like that would stop him, like that was what . . ." (ellipsis original, 229).
54 Hyatt Waggoner, among others, likens *Absalom, Absalom!* to Eliot's "Waste Land" (see Warren 175), while Robert Penn Warren sees similarities between *The Waste Land* and *The Sound and the Fury* (Warren 269). Warren suggests, however, that "if *The Sound and the Fury* is Faulkner's *Wasteland* [sic], it is a wasteland that, unlike Eliot's, ends in Easter" (269). Cleanth Brooks, in *William Faulkner* (105–06), also compares *The Waste Land* to Sartoris. See his chapter "The Waste Land: Southern Exposure," *William Faulkner* 100–15.

symbolism becomes a dynamic and integral element in the novel's structure, *Pylon's* Eliotic symbolism generally seems pasted on.[55]

Faulkner's most comprehensive treatment of Arthurian myth, however, occurs not in the later novels but in an early work, a forty-eight page novelette entitled *Mayday* that he wrote, hand-lettered, illustrated (with images influenced by Aubrey Beardsley's designs for the *Morte d'Arthur*), and bound as a courtship gift for Helen Baird in early 1926.[56] In *Mayday* (which had been the original title of *Soldier's Pay*), the protagonist is another of Faulkner's wounded soldier-heroes, Sir Galwyn of Arthgyl, whom Joseph Blotner characterizes as "a quester-knight" (511). The name Galwyn, writes Michael Salda, is "apparently Faulkner's Englishing of . . . 'Galvanus,' one of the earliest recorded forms of Gawain's name." And " 'of Arthgyll,' though meaning nothing in itself, suggests both 'Arthur' – Gawain's uncle and king – and 'Argyll' in northwestern Scotland – as good a location as any for a knight believed by many medievals and moderns to be a highlander" (366).

Although *Mayday* has been dismissed by most critics as a "little tale . . . in itself of minor literary importance" (Brooks, "The Image of Helen Baird . . ." 226), it has not only intrinsic merit but also interesting implications for the development of later Faulkner heroes, including Quentin in *The Sound and the Fury*.[57] And, while its adaptation of Arthurian themes and characters is certainly unusual, *Mayday* draws on several popular and well-known American Arthurian works as sources. One of those sources is James Branch Cabell's 1919 parodic romance *Jurgen*, which became the subject of a highly publicized censorship trial in the early 1920s.

Faulkner undoubtedly had read *Jurgen*; Januarius Jones, in fact, quotes from it in *Soldier's Pay*. Moreover, as Carvel Collins notes, "many of the elements of *Jurgen* and of *Mayday* are alike: the settings, the sardonic ironies, the joking anachronisms, that each protagonist is 'nothing' except a 'shadow,' that lives are possibly only dreams, the protagonists' loves of even legendary women (Guenevere for Jurgen, Yseult for Sir Galwyn) which bring only sighs of boredom when the women are no longer available, the protagonists'

---

55 Dorothy Tuck argues that *Pylon's* overreliance on imagery from Eliot's *Waste Land* is its most significant flaw, but she adds that "part of Faulkner's difficulty with *Pylon* might be explained as a result of his leaving Yoknapatawpha for an urban setting; Faulkner is not a novelist of cities" (133).

56 Carvel Collins, in his Introduction to *Mayday*, notes that elements of Faulkner's romantic yet frustrated love for Helen are apparent in the presentation of Patricia in *Mosquitoes* (Faulkner's second novel, dedicated – as was *Mayday* – to Helen Baird) and, more extensively, in the final scenes of Charlotte Rittenmeyer and Harry Wilbourne in *The Wild Palms* (1939).

57 James G. Watson also links *Mayday* and *The Sound and the Fury*, especially in a "line of development" that is "overtly self-critical" (51). Gail Moore Morrison writes that *Mayday*, "this important precursor of Faulkner's first masterpiece [*The Sound and the Fury*], deserves to be better known." Morrison is one scholar who disagrees with Collins' assertion, which she suggests "distort[s] the relationship of the novel not only to *Mayday* but to the canon as a whole" (338).

uncertainties about what it really is which they desire, . . . the return at the end of each book to the place of beginning where Jurgen and Sir Galwyn have brief recapitulatory final meetings with women they have known, and the similarity of the opening phrases of the two books as well as the complete identity of their closing sentences: 'Thus it was in the old days' " (21–22). Cleanth Brooks sees still other similarities between *Jurgen* and *Mayday*, including the carefully archaic language, the constant undercutting of romantic expectations, the thematic regarding of man as a victim of his illusions, and even specific details, such as "the time of day in which the story proper begins" – although he finds decisive differences in the endings (Brooks, "The Image of Helen Baird . . ." 223–24).

At the same time that it draws deeply from Cabell's work, *Mayday* differs from it in several significant ways. Not only does it lack the pornographic element – such as the repeated references to the protagonist's penetrating lance – of *Jurgen*; it also eschews any optimistic compromises in its ending. In *Jurgen*, as in his novel *The Cream of the Jest* (1917; rev. 1922)[58] and in other of his fiction, Cabell ends with a somewhat optimistic resolution of the protagonist's problem: after many magical years of youth, Jurgen once again becomes the middle-aged man he was; but, disillusioned by idealized romantic love and continually emphasized sensuality, he is able to settle down with his wife, with whom he now realizes he has much in common. In *Mayday*, Faulkner offers Galwyn no such pleasant middle ground; instead he sends Galwyn, as a suicide, into the river. Carvel Collins links *Mayday's* distinctly different and unhappy ending to the portions of *The Sound and the Fury* that Collins maintains Faulkner was writing at the same time (a point other scholars have disputed). Collins notes the similarities between *Mayday* and Quentin Compson's monologue: each protagonist, Sir Galwyn and Quentin, has spent the night prior to the opening of the story in solitary vigil; each fiction begins with the arrival of day beyond the protagonist's window; each protagonist has a girl on his mind (for Galwyn it is Little sister Death,[59] for Quentin it is his sister Caddy, who in a sense is the death of him); each travels restlessly throughout the narrative, towards death; each has an encounter with Saint Francis of Assisi (Quentin thinks about him, Galwyn actually speaks to him, twice); each has similar traveling companions (Benjy

---

58 In *The Cream of the Jest*, Kennaston, Cabell's twentieth-century protagonist, dwells in a dream in which his beloved ideal woman is the unattainable Ettarre; at the end of the novel, he is simultaneously elated and terrified when Ettarre's hands reach toward him and "the universe seemed to fold about him." He thinks, in that final dream, that possibly it is as death that Ettarre is coming to him (Collins 21).

59 Little sister Death and St. Francis are recurring characters in Faulkner's work: the former is a character who had appeared as a symbolic vision at the end of Faulkner's short gangster story, "The Kid Learns," published in the *Times-Picayune* [May 31, 1925]); the latter was one of the main characters in Faulkner's amusing, magical children's tale, *The Wishing Tree* [1927].

and Jason for Quentin, Hunger and Pain for Galwyn);[60] and each ultimately drowns himself in a river (Collins 27–28).

Whereas many of the themes and characters of Faulkner's novelette derive from Cabell's *Jurgen*, the narrative structure derives from an even more widely read work, James Russell Lowell's *Vision of Sir Launfal*. As Michael Salda writes, although "Faulkner probably found little in the moralistic themes of Lowell's 'Vision' that he could use in *Mayday*, he did find there the dream-vision frame that he needed to hold together the diverse elements he planned to include in his own Arthurian tale" (353). Like Lowell's poem, Faulkner's *Mayday* opens just as a quest is about to begin; like Lowell's vision, Faulkner's dream vision reveals to the seeker-knight the true object of the quest that he must seek, and it offers finally the lesson that the object need not be sought at all because it is already available to him. Moreover, both "are circular tales in which the knight returns to his starting point, and both employ while fundamentally altering a traditional Arthurian character" (Salda 354). The preface to *Launfal*, in which Lowell admits to "enlarg[ing] the circle of competition in search of the miraculous cup in such a manner as to include, not only other persons than the heroes of the Round Table, but also a period of Time subsequent to the supposed date of King Arthur's reign," may even have granted Faulkner the poetic license he needed to try his first story with an explicitly Arthurian character. Like Lowell's Launfal, who shares scarcely more than the name of a knight drawn from the Arthurian world, Faulkner's Galwyn of Arthgyl is similarly not the Gawain of *Sir Gawain and the Green Knight* or Malory. Yet, as Salda argues, "Faulkner does have good reasons for choosing Gawain as his model rather than many possible other knights – Gawain is young, untried as the story begins, 'glib,' attracted to and pursued by women, sexually and morally tempted/compromised in the course of the story, easy to anger, rash in his actions, and wiser by the end of the tale – but all these things do not make Galwyn and Gawain identical. In fact, the contrary is true: Galwyn is *not* Gawain, a point that Faulkner will take some trouble to demonstrate in *Mayday*. Faulkner does something different with the old materials; Lowell's preface authorizes such a departure from tradition," (354) as do the many other contemporary American recastings of Arthurian themes in works as diverse as Booth Tarkington's *Penrod* (1914), Floyd Dell's *King Arthur's Socks* (1916), Edwin Arlington Robinson's *Lancelot* (1920), and Heywood Broun's "The Fifty-First Dragon" (1921).

Furthermore, Faulkner's dream vision differs from Lowell's in at least one critical way: for whereas Launfal easily discerns what portion of his experience has actually occurred and what is merely a dream, Galwyn cannot

60 Carvel Collins admits that the "connection [between Quentin's companions, Benjy and Jason, and Galwyn's companions, Hunger and Pain] requires here some background and discussion," which he provides in his Introduction, pp. 28–39.

separate his dreams from reality.[61] Faulkner's *Mayday*, in fact, is the story of a dream "in which further nested dreams are possible, but there exists no dreamer 'outside' the action" (Salda 357) to distinguish the dream from reality. As if to underscore the deliberate confusion, the novelette even begins *in medias res*, without a clear beginning: "And the tale tells how at last one came to him" (47).

The vision ("the one") that comes to Galwyn is of the shadows Hunger and Pain, who show him a dark stream that undergoes a series of transformations before his eyes. Galwyn wonders what all of this signifies, to which his companions reply merely, "Wait." As Galwyn continues to watch the metamorphosing stream, he sees the faces of Fortitude ("more beautiful than death") and Ambition ("a tall bright one like a pillar of silver fire") leading a procession of knights. Recognizing himself among the knights, he is taken aback by his own puniness: "tiny in mock battle with quarter staff and blunt lance and sword, and Hunger lay in his belly like fire and Pain lay in all his limbs" (50).

---

61 Another interesting comment on the relationship between dream and reality appears in a work by Cabell that appeared the year after *Mayday* was written. In Cabell's episodic novel *Something About Eve*, Gerald Musgrave, a young writer, allows a devil to take over his earthly body so he can seek Antan, a land where he believes he will find perfect happiness. Along the way, he has many experiences and meets many characters who make him question and ultimately abandon the journey. One of these is Merlin, who explains the notion of chivalry that he gave Arthur and his knights "to play with." This notion was "very beautiful" and for a time "created beauty everywhere"; and the knights "discharged their moral and constabulary duties quite picturesquely." But it was also "a rather outrageous notion upon which all was founded" (230–31). After a while, his "toys . . . began to break one another. Dissension and lust and hatred woke among them. They forgot the very pretty notion which I gave them in their turn to play with. The land was no longer an ordered realm. My toys now fought in the land's naked fields and they murderously waylaid one another in its old forests." This continued until Arthur was dead and the Round Table dissolved. Merlin, who had left behind his "toys" so that he could dwell with Nimue, found a measure of domestic bliss with her, but no variety. And so he left her to seek Antan.

Gerald's encounter with Merlin (and other characters in the book) convinces him of something that even wise Merlin did not learn from his own experiment with chivalry – that "the one way for a poet to appreciate the true loveliness of a place is not ever to go to it" (339). Merlin's wisdom, which substitutes one ideal for another, is not the answer. In fact, the wisdom of Cabell's Merlin, like that of Twain's, is illusory because it is not based on and cannot deal with the real and the practical.

So, instead of continuing his journey to Antan, Gerald goes back to Lichfield, his hometown, and reoccupies his now old body. In the end, he returns to his writing, to be always a man who finds "one or another beautiful idea to play with and who must remain, so long as life remained, a poet whose one real delight was to play with puppets" (363). Like the Merlin of the book, Gerald Musgrave creates beautiful notions, but since he does not try to make actual his dream of Antan, "it must remain . . . whatever I choose to imagine it" (338). Thus *Something About Eve* has a comic ending, but the tragic implications are as clear as they are in *Connecticut Yankee*, which is also on one level a comic book. Cabell suggests that dreams and ideals remain beautiful only until they come in contact with reality. Cabell presents Merlin's chivalry as illusory because it maintains its perfection only as long as it is the toy of men's minds and only as long as there is no attempt to realize – i.e., to make real – the dream.

Hunger and Pain then lead Galwyn to an image of the face of a young girl who makes him think of "young hyacinths in the spring, and honey and sunlight" (50); he soon realizes that she is the object of his quest. As the girl's image recedes into the water of the stream, Galwyn – with his companions at his side – departs in search of her. After passing through an enchanted forest, he encounters a hermit-philosopher identified as Time who tells him little about the mysterious woman he is seeking. So Galwyn rides on, into Faulkner's Arthurian world, where he meets – and slays – both King Mark's man-at-arms, who has been assigned the task of keeping strangers away from Yseult as she bathes in the stream, and Tristram himself, who is "lying in yonder shade and writhing in love for the maiden" (64).

The flirtatious Yseult had been waiting to be ravished by Tristram; but, upon learning of Tristram's death, she is even happier to be ravished by Galwyn. Almost immediately after they make love, however, Galwyn "began to be restlessly aware that young hyacinths were no longer fresh, once you had picked them" (68). He is quickly bored by Yseult's silly chatter about hair and clothing; and, when she leaves to get dressed, he abandons her. With Hunger and Pain again at his side, Galwyn rides on, to experience amorous but equally disappointing encounters with Elys and Aela, respectively the evening and morning stars, and to an even more cataclysmic meeting at the stream with the Lord of Sleep, who forces him to "choose": Galwyn can either relive any of the "various phases of all life" (83) – a shadow existence, at best, since he could not return as Galwyn of Arthgyll and would thus lose his whole identity – or "be submerged in these waters" (83) like so many before him, to be a sight for others who follow to see. This second choice, according to Sleep, "is Fame" (84). Displeased with both choices, Galwyn ultimately chooses Fame; and he enters the stream to accept the embrace of "Little sister Death," the girl he had seen there at the beginning of *Mayday*. As Salda observes, Galwyn *seems* to have accepted death by water rather than pass through the circuit once again; but Faulkner's meta-commentarial running head for the novelette's final pages reads "MEETS ONE HE HAD SEEN IN HIS DREAM AND / HE ENTERS HIS DREAM AGAIN." Galwyn's cycle, then, will inexorably continue: "A choice to die while dreaming is not a choice to die. It is *all* a vision, from first to last, and we have been gazing into Galwyn's dream" (Salda 365).

The ways in which Faulkner departs from tradition in *Mayday*, especially in the second major narrative movement, the Yseult episode, are particularly interesting. While the Isolt of medieval story is wise in the ways of love and a master of the arts of healing, Faulkner depicts his Yseult as a mindless young maiden who, upon being discovered bathing naked in the stream, covers herself by "putting her two hands before her eyes" (66). Learning that the "impossible Sir Tristram" (67) is dead, she expresses no grief; she is distressed only that Galwyn "should have seen me with my hair done like this." (*Mayday*'s Tristram, in this respect, is reminiscent of the "clean, highhearted

[but] dull" Tristan to whom Faulkner alludes at the end of *Mosquitoes* [340].) And, following sex with Galwyn, Yseult starts "comfortably making [plans] for hers and young Sir Galwyn's future" (68).

Faulkner also gives his Gawain character, typically depicted as both a ladies' man and a fierce fighter, an unusual twist: in no other version does he employ his amorous skills on Yseult or his martial skills to kill Tristram. Yet in *Mayday*, deciding to "waste no time arguing with this unmannerly brute . . . and a would-be adulterer, also!" (65), Galwyn slays Tristram, after which "young Sir Galwyn's glib tongue wove such a magic that the Princess Yseult purred like a kitten" (68). Even the manner in which Galwyn achieves his knighthood is distinctly *un*-Arthurian: like Tristram, who is knighted by Uther Pendragon rather than by King Mark of Cornwall, Galwyn is knighted "at the hand of the Constable du Boisgeclin" (66). "There are indeed Arthurian touchstones," as Salda correctly concludes, "but Faulkner has done more to *prevent* this from becoming [traditionally] Arthurian than he has done to make it so" (361). Like Lowell in *The Vision of Sir Launfal*, then, Faulkner has adapted the legend to suit the specific story he wishes to tell – a story, James G. Watson suggests, Faulkner intended to be allegorical as well as biographical: "Galwyn is Faulkner, the ideal woman more beautiful than Yseult and her lustful sisterhood is Helen Baird, and Galwyn's suicide symbolizes the threatened end to unrequited love" (51). And there is another important distinction to be made between the traditional Gawain and Faulkner's Galwyn. As Gail Moore Morrison notes, "Sir Gawain's succumbing to the sexual temptation offered by the Green Knight's lady, for instance, testifies to his basic humanity – to his involvement with rather than his withdrawal from the inevitable complications of human relationships" (349). By contrast, the more cynical Galwyn is quick to embrace the "bottomless sleep" (*Mayday* 87) and the release from time and memory that such submersion offers.

Allegorical or autobiographical, Sir Galwyn nevertheless is an intriguing and appropriate antecedent for some of Faulkner's later questing heroes, like Ike McCaslin. In "The Bear," the central and longest story in *Go Down, Moses*, 21-year-old Ike discovers that part of his inheritance, the "silver cup filled with gold pieces and wrapped in burlap and sealed with his godfather's ring in the hot wax" (301) to be passed "down from hand to hand" (304), is a curiously empty Grail; it contains instead only a handful of copper coins and IOUs, "a collection of minutely-folded scraps of paper sufficient almost for a rat's nest" (306). Yet, unlike Galwyn, whose choices are limiting, Ike finds his circumstances liberating. Renouncing the property bequeathed to him by Lucius Quintus Carothers McCaslin, which constitutes the rest of his inheritance, Ike repudiates the corruptness and hypocrisy of his forebear and endures the scorn of his wife; choosing to pursue a more humble existence as a carpenter, he looks to the "doomed wilderness" (321) for the proper values in his own life. Ike's quest is both paralleled and highlighted by others in the book, including Lucas Beauchamp's hunt for riches in "The

Fire and the Hearth," which culminates in Lucas's realization – similar to that of Lowell's Launfal – that his greatest wealth is to be found in his own home.

Just as Faulkner returns to the theme of the quest – albeit a less specifically Arthurian quest – in other of his novels after *Mayday*, he also returns in some of his later works to the character of Gawain.[62] In *The Town* (1957), for example, Gavin (like Galwyn, another variant of Gawain) Stevens is the exemplum of chivalric virtue: he defends "with blood the principle that chastity and virtue in women shall be defended whether they exist or not" (76), and acts honorably and in the best romantic tradition by loving another man's wife, Eula Varner Snopes, from afar, even to the point of refusing her when she offers herself to him out of pity for his devotion. Gavin, Eula, and Manfred De Spain (Eula's longtime lover), in fact, are viewed in an essentially romantic and tragic light; and, as Olga Vickery observes, the fact that they enter the timeless world of pure legend is attested to by the frequency of allusions to medieval as well as classical literature. Eula and De Spain "re-enact what is almost a modern version of courtly love" (Vickery, *Novels* 190) while even Gavin finds a place in the archetypal pattern "Because there was more folks among the Helens and Juliets and Isoldes and Guineveres than jest the Launcelots and Tristrams and Romeos and Parises" (*Town* 101).

In "Go Down, Moses," the title story of the 1942 collection, Gavin again acts honorably – and with Southern chivalric courtesy – by assisting Miss Worsham in the return of the body of Molly Beauchamp's grandson, Butch. Gavin contributes his own money to cover the funeral expenses and tries to persuade his editor not to print the story of Butch's death by execution for murder, thereby sparing the women further grief. And in *Requiem for a Nun* (1951), Gavin forces Temple Drake to assume responsibility for the death of her baby and, in this way, to be afforded some small measure of redemption for her actions, which have brought suffering to many, especially to her friend Nancy, who has been sentenced to hang for the infant's death.

Gawain (Gavin/Galwyn), however, is only one of several Arthurian characters whom Faulkner weaves into his work. Launcelot "Lump" Snopes is a principal player in the parody of medieval romance that constitutes Part III of *The Hamlet* (1940), the first novel of Faulkner's Snopes Trilogy. In that parody, the idiot Ike Snopes – the only innocent member of the large and avaricious Snopes clan that includes Flem Snopes, an impotent Fisher King who rules the wasteland – is presented as a courtly lover who "lie[s] in the drenched myriad waking life of grasses and listen[s]" for the approach of his beloved (*Hamlet* 188); he is, as Olga Vickery demonstrates, a lover so deep and intense in his emotions that he "give[s] expression to all that is most permanent in human nature, [projecting his love] beyond the world of space

---

62 Brooks, in "The Image of Helen Baird . . ." (26), suggests, for instance, that "Horace Benbow is a kind of Sir Galwyn."

and time into the timeless world of legend that is recreated by the use of rhetoric and allusion" (*Novels* 178–79).[63] Ike's coy mistress, however, is no ordinary maiden but a cow he has spirited away from its original owner, Jack Houston (who recognizes that Ike's love in effect "transcends questions of moral or social propriety" [Vickery, *Novels* 180]). Lump, one of Ike's many cousins, becomes the spoiler who salaciously exploits – and ultimately helps to destroy – their highly romanticized relationship. It is Lump who rips a plank from the stable wall so that he and others can observe the lovers' intercourse (I. O. Snopes describes it as "stock diddling"); and it is Lump's continued exploitation of the affair that forces a "family conference," after which the decision is made to "take and beef the critter the fellow has done formed the habit with, and cook a piece of it and let him eat it. . . . Then he'll be all right again and wont want to chase nothing but human women" (231). Ike's infatuation is thus brought to a rude conclusion; his "devastated eyes . . . remembering," Ike is left in the empty stall with only "the battered effigy of a cow such as children receive on Christmas" (305). By his selfish and rapacious actions, Lump – like his namesake Launcelot, who helps to destroy Arthur's beloved fellowship – succeeds in ruining the one pure, natural, affectionate relationship in the novel.

Lump again shows himself to be ethically bankrupt when he urges his cousin Mink Snopes to steal from the man whom he has just killed over a disputed pasturage fee, and yet again, in Part IV of *The Hamlet*, when he perjures himself by swearing that he saw Flem Snopes return Mrs. Armstid's money to the Texan horse auctioneer before the man left town. (The Texan, in fact, had promised Mrs. Armstid that Flem would give back her hard-earned five dollars; but Flem never does.)

Lump's unnamed mother, Faulkner reveals, had had much higher hopes for her son. Having brought into her marriage "a belief that there was honor and pride and salvation and hope too to be found for man's example between the pages of books," she had borne "one child and named it Launcelot, flinging this quenchless defiance into the very jaws of the closing trap, and died" (*Hamlet* 226). But those lofty aspirations die along with her; and the young Launcelot inherits only the corrupt Snopes' legacy of his father. The Snopeses, in fact, so thoroughly invert the natural order of things that they manage to transform his mother's idealism into a burden of which they must rid the boy. As Ratliff relates, "Launcelot! . . . Just think of the shame and horror when he got big enough to realise what his ma had done to his family's name and pride so that he even had to take Lump for folks to call him in place of it" (*Hamlet* 226).

In Faulkner's early drafts of the novel, however, the boy had a different name. Joseph Blotner notes that Lump was originally called "Maud," short

---

63 Vickery concludes that "Ike as a lover is absurd, but there is no absurdity in his love" (*Novels* 178).

for Mordred – certainly more appropriate for the exploiter the boy soon becomes. But apparently in Launcelot/Lump, Faulkner found a sharper and even more powerful symbol than in Mordred/Maud for the lack of heroic idealism in the modern world and for the degree to which such legendary ideals have been perverted or debased. Like the self-absorbed, vamping Yseult in *Mayday*, Faulkner's Launcelot Snopes is no noble character but rather is thoroughly deromanticized.

Arthurian elements also figure in other of Faulkner's works. In *The Sound and the Fury*, for example, Quentin tries to preserve the moral code of the Old South by equating his family's honor with his beloved sister Caddy's chastity. But Caddy, after being seduced and impregnated by Dalton Ames, agrees to marry Sydney Herbert Head, whom Quentin detests; and, soon afterwards, Quentin decides to kill himself so that Caddy's dishonor will die along with his memory of it. Within a year, Herbert indeed proves as morally bankrupt as Quentin believes him to be: he divorces Caddy, breaks his promise to establish Quentin and Caddy's younger brother Jason in business, and thereby disgraces the Compson family yet again. Nevertheless, even during their first meeting, Herbert is astute enough – and realistic enough – to recognize the foolishness of Quentin's overly romantic postures; he dismisses him as a "half-baked Galahad" (136–37). And Herbert's assessment is at least partly correct: for Quentin makes his concept of virginity, which he associates so completely with virtue and honor, the center of his world. But his ethical order is based not on actions but on words, on "fine, dead sounds," the meaning of which he has yet to learn. So, as Vickery demonstrates, he has "separated ethics from the total context of humanity" to such a degree that the order he builds around Caddy "is as rigid and inflexible as [his idiot brother] Benjy's and it shares Benjy's fear of change and his expectation that all experience should conform to his pattern" (37). Unlike Galahad's purity, which allows him to achieve the Grail, Quentin's half-baked notion of purity causes him to withdraw, even to take his own life (much as Galwyn chooses to embrace Little sister Death in *Mayday*) when his fantastic world collides with the real.

Absalom, Absalom!, perhaps Faulkner's finest novel, also treats the collision of the worlds of dream and reality, and it does so by translating portions of the Arthurian story into the nineteenth- and twentieth-century South. Thomas Sutpen, the son of a poor-white Virginia mountaineer, grew up believing in the equality of men and in possession as a matter of luck rather than of superiority; but after being snubbed at the home of a wealthy plantation owner, he reacts by adopting the aristocratic Southern code as his guiding principle. In particular, he decides to create his own dynasty. After purchasing a hundred square miles of land in Jefferson, he builds a mansion and even orders a throne-like chair hewn out of a half barrel so that, like a feudal lord, he can sit on the porch of his home and survey his property. Faulkner describes Sutpen as a bombastic madman "who creates within his very coffin walls his fabulous immeasurable Camelots" (160).

Like Camelot, however, the very dynasty Sutpen tries to create is soon destroyed; and, like Camelot, it is destroyed not from without but from within. After marrying the respectable Ellen Coldfield and becoming the father of Henry and Judith, Sutpen is shocked to discover that Henry's closest friend and Judith's betrothed is Charles Bon, Sutpen's son by the first wife he divorced thirty years earlier upon learning that she had black blood. In response to Sutpen's objections to Charles's marriage to Judith, Henry renounces his birthright and returns with his friend to the university, where the two men eventually join an infantry regiment and fight side by side for most of the war. Yet, on returning together to Sutpen's Hundred, Henry shoots Charles to prevent him from going through with the forbidden marriage. Later, when Sutpen returns from the war, he finds his dynasty in ruins: his wife is dead, his son is a fugitive, and his daughter is a spinster. Trying to beget a male heir to replace Henry, Sutpen becomes engaged to his sister-in-law, whom he offends by suggesting that "they try it first and if it was a boy and lived, they would be married" (284); then he seduces the granddaughter of Wash Jones, his poor-white handyman. When the girl gives birth to a daughter rather than a son, Sutpen rejects both mother and child, an act that provokes Jones into killing all of them. After Sutpen's death, Judith and her mulatto half-sister Clytie bring Charles Etienne Saint-Valery Bon, Charles Bon's son by his octoroon mistress, back from New Orleans; but Etienne and Judith die after a bout of yellow fever and Sutpen's grand home falls into ruin. Years later, Rosa Coldfield, Sutpen's former betrothed, visits the house to find Clytie still there and caring for the sick fugitive Henry. When Rosa summons an ambulance, Clytie thinks Henry is being charged for the murder he committed more than fifty years before, and she sets fire to the house, killing herself as well as Henry. Left howling in the ashes is Sutpen's only descendant, the idiot Jim Bond, Etienne's son by his very black wife.

Though Faulkner describes Charles Bon as a "silken and tragic Lancelot" (320), he in fact is more of a Mordred figure in the novel: the unacknowledged son who introduces discord into Sutpen's kingdom and who causes the deaths of those closest to his father and, ultimately, of his father himself. And Rosa Coldfield, the "Southern Guinevere" (174), also watches the dissolution of that kingdom and the killings, both accidental and deliberate, of the fathers, sons, and boon comrades; apart from Jim Bond and her young listener Quentin Compson (who narrates the longest portion of the novel to his Harvard roommate, Shreve McCannon), she alone survives to tell the Sutpen tale.

By introducing such Arthurian elements and motifs into *Absalom, Absalom!* and other of his novels, Faulkner recalls the chivalric virtues of his traditional and beloved South at the same time that he illustrates the degree to which such legendary ideals have been tarnished or debased in the modern world. And, by giving the legends a contemporaneity and vitality, Faulkner successfully employs them much the way Fitzgerald and Hemingway did: as a frame for the modernist literature he sought to create.

6

Steinbeck and the Arthurian legend

Like Hemingway, Fitzgerald, and Faulkner, the other great American novelist of the first half of the twentieth century, John Steinbeck, drew extensively on Arthurian themes and images. Steinbeck was so taken by the Arthurian legends that he even attempted a modern version of Malory, a book that – although never completed – had the potential of becoming one of the high-points of Arthurian literature with the stature and significance of Tennyson's *Idylls* and T. H. White's *The Once and Future King*. But long before he began working on that version, which was posthumously published in 1976 as *The Acts of King Arthur*, Steinbeck was incorporating Arthurian themes into other works. In his first novel *Cup of Gold* (1929), in fact, he depicted a rather unusual quest for the Grail. "It is this search for the holy cup which Christ passed at the Last Supper," remarked Warren French, "that links John Steinbeck, generally thought of as one of the emerging 'poets' of the depressed of the 1930s, with the 'waste land' artists of the 1920s" ("Steinbeck's Use of Malory" 4).

Moreover, like those "waste land artists," Steinbeck used T. S. Eliot's poem to provide an underlying pattern of myth in one of his novels – not, however, in an early novel but rather in *The Winter of Our Discontent*, pub-lished in 1961. "*The Waste Land*," as Donna Gerstenberger writes, "provides a general pattern as well as an ironic frame of meaning for *The Winter of Our Discontent*. Ethan Allen Hawley, the novel's hero, is the quester, a Knight Templar, whose hat has a symbolically yellowing plume, for the white plume of honor would be inappropriate as he seeks corruption in the moral waste-land of a small New England town" (Gerstenberger 59). The story begins on a "fair gold morning of April" (5), and this April becomes the cruellest month. The novel also contains, as does Eliot's poem, a series of allusions: to literature, to history, to the main character's family history. Ethan is fond of quoting snippets of texts and sometimes playing with and changing the wording of those texts. Yet the title alone suggests that there is more going on than just a pattern of references to the Grail legend and *The Waste Land*; and, in the context of the novel, the allusion to Shakespeare's *Richard the Third* takes on a highly ironic meaning, especially as it is combined with the complex of allusions to Eliot's poem. The winter of Ethan's discontent with his financial and social position changes to a glorious summer in terms of his elevated status in his hometown, New Baytown. But because of the unethical means by which this new status is achieved, the turning point, the symbolic April, becomes the cruellest month since it marks the beginning of Ethan's moral decline; and the glorious summer is glorious only when viewed superficially by those who do not know of the inner struggle and sense of failure that he experiences.

Ethan Allen Hawley comes from an old New England family that lost its fortune in part because of a code of ethics that has prevented them from engaging in the cutthroat business tactics Steinbeck presents as typical of American society. Ethan's father had lost a sailing ship – and his wealth – in a fire deliberately set by his partner, whose son is now the town banker. When Ethan says, or actually pleads with his father to confirm, that "There must be some difference" now from the way it was then, his father replies "Only in a single man alone – only in one man alone. There's the only power – one man alone. Can't depend on anything else" (55). Following his own code, Ethan's father refuses to carry his estrangement from his corrupt partner over to the next generation: "he didn't carry it to his son, Mr. Banker Baker. He wouldn't do that any more than he would burn a ship" (55–56). His father imparts to Ethan the need for an individual code of ethics, which makes of him an errant and lonely knight in the modern world. And for a time, Ethan, a Mason or modern Knight Templar, follows his own code, gaining in the process a reputation for honesty that is his true accomplishment. But he falls prey to the many voices that say how out of touch he is with the modern world and particularly with the world of business.

His decline begins when Margie Young-Hunt tells his wife Mary's fortune with tarot cards. The Madame Sosostris of the novel, Margie predicts that Ethan will make a fortune, and he sets about to make the prediction come true. In order to do this, however, he betrays two of the people who are closest to him. He reports Marullo, the Italian owner of a grocery store and his longtime employer, to the Department of Immigration for having come to America illegally many years before. Marullo is deported but, to reward his honest and loyal employee, he gives Ethan the store. Marullo thinks that by allowing Ethan some measure of economic freedom, he can assure that "the light won't go out" (256). The "light" is, of course, the idealism that Marullo believes Ethan represents.

The other betrayal is even more despicable. Ethan's friend Danny, a man who was like a brother to him in his youth, has become an alcoholic. When Ethan learns that a plot of land that Danny owns is sought after as a site for a new airfield, he gives Danny a thousand dollars, ostensibly to get him into a treatment program but actually so Danny will drink himself to death and leave to Ethan, his only friend, the valuable land. This is precisely what happens.

Ethan realizes that he has sold his honor for the worldly gain that has replaced the "light" as the Grail for most of those in the modern world and that in doing so he no longer makes the difference that "one man alone" can make. What drives home to him the depth to which he has sunk is seeing in his own son Allen not the positive values of his father but the greed and pride that have led to his own downfall. Allen enters a contest in which he must write an essay on why he loves America: when he wins honorable mention, he is scheduled to appear on television, which he sees as the beginning of a great career. Ethan is pleased but surprised, since he knows that his son is neither a very good writer nor a good thinker. But both their illusions are shattered when an official from the contest shows up to inform Ethan that Allen had plagiarized much of his essay from the speeches of Henry Clay and other great American rhetoricians, a fact that eluded the contest officials until they received an anonymous tip – actually from Allen's sister Ellen.

In the final scene of the novel Ethan visits a special place to which he goes when he needs to be alone, a hole not large enough to be a cave in the rock by the ocean. He climbs in and is about to slit his wrists as the water begins to fill the opening. His planned death, by water and razor blade, is interrupted when he realizes that he has taken with him a family heirloom, "a kind of mound of translucent stone, perhaps quartz or jadeite or even soapstone" that was "carved on its surface" with "an endless interweaving shape" (143). Ethan recognizes this object as a talisman, defined in the novel as a "stone or other object engraved with figures or characters to which are attributed the occult powers of the planetary influences and celestial configurations under which it was made, usually worn as an amulet to avert evil from or bring fortune to the bearer" (228). The talisman, which has been many things to Ethan as he grew up and has, he believes, brought him some luck in business as an adult, is a "magic mound" analogous to the Grail in that it seems to fulfill the desires of the one who possesses it. But Ethan knows that while it may avert a certain kind of evil or bring a certain kind of fortune, it cannot protect him from himself. Ethan has betrayed the talisman and the family tradition it represents. As he is about to seek redemption through suicide, however, he realizes that though his "light is out," he must return the talisman to his daughter Ellen, "its new owner," who in her sleepwalking has been drawn to it. Perhaps because she was unwilling to let her brother's cheating be rewarded, Ethan sees her as the one to carry forward the honor that his family once stood for – even though her act may not have been totally noble, may have mixed spite with honesty. He feels he must return the talisman to her "Else another light might go out" (311).

In *The Winter of Our Discontent*, Steinbeck seems very interested in American values. The New England heritage of the main character, whose roots go back to the Mayflower, makes him an emblem of the development – and in some ways the decline – of American values. As John H. Timmerman has observed, at the time of the writing of this novel, Steinbeck was very concerned with "moral manhood," which "meant the strength to stand by convictions and to act according to them. . . . The glory of Camelot as a shimmering beacon of moral rectitude in a world blasted and darkened by moral perfidy grew in his mind as an analogy to America" (255).

Among the books in Ethan's attic where his son found the tomes from which he plagiarized the material for his essay is one of particular note. It is a copy of Malory's *Morte d'Arthur*, a book "of majesty." But this particular edition is not a children's version such as that which inspired Steinbeck himself; it is the one "with drawings by Aubrey Beardsley, a sickly, warped creature, a strange choice to illustrate great, manly Malory" (80). The contrast between the decadent illustrations by Beardsley and the "manly" romance, which Steinbeck considered to be infused with values and idealism, is symbolic of the uneasy blend of modern values and old-fashioned idealism in the novel.

The cameo appearance of Malory's book is also important because the *Morte d'Arthur* had a special place in Steinbeck's thinking and writing. Whereas *The Winter of Our Discontent* shows that Eliot's poem provided Steinbeck with some Arthurian material and Twain's *Connecticut Yankee* suggested to Steinbeck the possibilities of bringing together Arthurian themes and modern concerns (as he did in the story "Saint Katy and the Virgin," his only work set in the Middle Ages[1]), the influence of Malory is present in many of his works, from his earliest novel to the posthumous *Acts of King Arthur and His Noble Knights*. As he noted in the Introduction to the *Acts of King Arthur*, it was a version of Malory designed for youngsters from which he developed "my sense of right and wrong, my feeling of noblesse oblige, and any thought I may have against the oppressor and for the oppressed" (4). Thus Malory's *Morte* helped to shape all of Steinbeck's novels. Even in books like *The Grapes of Wrath*, which are more dependent on Biblical than Arthurian themes, the overriding sympathy for the downtrodden results from the author's early reading of that version of Malory. In addition, though, a number of Steinbeck's novels and stories show the specific influence of the *Morte*, especially in the use of the Grail quest (which sometimes reflects the influence of Eliot's poem as well as of Malory's romance) and of the bond that unites a group of characters in some common purpose.

The Arthurian influence is evident in Steinbeck's first novel, *Cup of Gold* (1929). The focus on the Grail legend is clearly signaled by the shift from the working title of the novel, *The Pot of Gold*, to a title that is suggestive of the Holy Grail. The novel's symbolism and structure and the characterization of the protagonist are all governed by the Grail theme. As John H. Timmerman

---

1   Sydney Krause has also noted that it is "with their parallel interest in history and the Middle Ages that one finds the most relevant literary comparisons [between Twain and Steinbeck]: to wit, the fact that both men specifically wrote a formally planned parody of Malory's *Morte d'Arthur*, cast in the tradition of 'folk humour,' which would have social implications for their own times" (147). In "Saint Katy and the Virgin," a mean pig is converted to Christianity, does good works, and is ultimately canonized; Sanford E. Marovitz has said that the story is perhaps "derived in part from the hilarious pig/maiden rescue episode in Mark Twain's *A Connecticut Yankee*" (73).

remarks, "Apparent everywhere in the novel, finally, is the influence of the Grail quest of Malory's *Morte D'Arthur*. The story functions as a plot motif and a thematic complement to the individual-social tension in *Cup of Gold*" (53–54).

The cup of gold that Henry Morgan seeks is Panama, a city of great wealth and the ultimate prize of pirate plundering. But besides its fabled wealth, Panama contains another treasure, a woman of such beauty that "men fall before her as heathen kneel before the sun." Though none of the pirates has ever seen her, they all dream of "La Santa Roja" and address prayers to her. As her legend grows, "She became to every man the quest of his heart, bearing the image of some fair young girl left on a European beach to be gloriously colored by the years. And Panama was to every man the nest of his desire" (123). Like the Holy Grail that provides everyone with the sustenance he most desires, La Santa Roja becomes the woman every man idealizes in his memory. And for Morgan himself she becomes "the harbor of all my questing," a woman whom he thinks of not "as a female thing with arms and breasts, but as a moment of peace after turmoil, a perfume after rancid filth" (175).

To take Panama, Morgan leads his men on an arduous overland journey reminiscent of the questers' struggles in search of the Holy Grail. Although they suffer various trials, including fatigue, hunger, and thirst, ultimately they take the prize. But when Morgan finds himself conqueror of Panama, he is not filled with peace; in fact, he has lost more than he has gained. Although he is the captor of La Santa Roja, his dream of winning her love proves illusory: she recognizes that he does not "carry a torch" for her and that she does not "burn" with love for him.

Therefore, instead of finding the ultimate reality at the end of his quest, he realizes that he had gone "sailing and sailing looking for something – well, something that did not exist, perhaps" (241). The achieving of his Grail turns out to be an ironic reversal of the traditional motif. After taking the Cup of Gold and being rejected by La Santa Roja, he experiences a spiritual and emotional dryness of the sort that success in the traditional Grail quest would have eradicated. And ironically, he loses the obsessive drive and desire that allowed him to succeed in taking the Cup of Gold in the first place. "I have not lusts and my desires are dry and rattling" (222), Morgan says in a line that seems to echo the sterility (and the language) of Eliot's *Waste Land*.[2] Instead of achieving perfection through the quest, Morgan becomes much worse than he was before. Although he was ruthless and single-minded in pursuing his dream, he now grows so cold that he kills his only friend Coeur de Gris.

2   Richard Astro says of Morgan that "Eventually, he completes his Grail quest by capturing the city of Panama and the beautiful woman known throughout the Caribbean as La Santa Roja. But Morgan's golden cup proves counterfeit when he finds that his successes give him little pleasure" ("Phlebas Sails the Caribbean" 220).

In another reversal of traditional Grail motifs, Morgan becomes a fool after his success. Unlike Perceval, an innocent fool who must learn empathy before he can cure the wounded king, Morgan is wise in the ways of the world when engaged in his quest. But afterwards he is referred to as a "dear fool" by La Santa Roja; and later he is branded a fool by both King Charles II and John Evelyn. In addition, Morgan becomes a knight literally only after his quest is completed. And he is knighted not because of any innate nobility or worth but only because he has betrayed all of the pirates who sought the Cup of Gold with him by stealing their booty and then buying his way into the favor of the crown.

In the end, what Henry Morgan has achieved on his quest is wealth and status, a perversion of what the Grail quest should bring, as is symbolized nicely by an actual golden cup that Morgan lifts from a mound of loot from the sack of Panama: "It was a lovely, slender chalice with long curved handles and a rim of silver. Around its outer edge four grotesque lambs chased each other, and inside, on the bottom, a naked girl lifted her arms in sensual ecstasy" (205). Instead of the innocent lamb, often a symbol of Christ, the animals on this cup are "grotesque," and the lascivious woman depicted inside the cup suggests the perversion of the quest, for which chastity and purity are requirements.[3] Warren French has observed that "Steinbeck's cynical philosophy when he wrote his apprentice novel was that the purity and integrity demanded by a grail quest are incompatible with success as measured by a materialistic culture" ("Steinbeck's Use of Malory" 5).

In thus using the Grail motif to comment on modern society, Steinbeck – as critics have noted – is akin to writers like Hemingway and Fitzgerald. In *John Steinbeck's Fiction Revisited*, for instance, French correctly sees a connection to *The Great Gatsby*. Observing that *Cup of Gold* "generically, despite the fancy dress and pseudo-seventeenth-century conversation, is a modernist tale of alienation and disenchantment," French concludes that Henry Morgan resembles "not the swashbuckling Captain Blood" – and even less, we might add, the Galahad or Perceval of medieval story – "but a more recent romantic pirate who lived flamboyantly while secretly preying on a complacently trusting society, F. Scott Fitzgerald's Jay Gatsby" (39).[4]

A pathetic figure in part because his "exploits are utterly divorced from the traditions of his native Wales that might once have given them mythic

3   Peter Lisca has commented on the significance of this cup and its relation to the other Grails in the novel: "Panama, the treasure city known as 'the Cup of Gold,' is thus itself a kind of Grail symbol, but this profane cup of gold contains a Red Saint, *La Santa Roja*, whom Morgan fails to possess, thus symbolically failing to attain his worldly Grail. Again Steinbeck constructs a paradigm of this failure in Morgan's discovery, among the loot, of a real gold cup, curiously inscribed with a frieze of four lambs; but these lambs are 'grotesque,' and the cup is a false Grail, for inside, Morgan discovers and is mocked by a naked girl with arms lifted 'in sensual ecstasy' " (32).
4   Kiyohiko Tsuboi also compares Gatsby and Morgan as Grail seekers in "Steinbeck's *Cup of Gold* and Fitzgerald's *The Great Gatsby*"; see especially p. 44.

shape and meaning" (Prindle 28), Henry Morgan as a modern Grail knight may seem far removed from the world of Malory. There is, however, another character in the book who is more obviously Malorian: the bard to whom the young Henry Morgan is sent by his father before he sets off on his new life. That bard, who is named Merlin, cannot be the Merlin of Arthur's court; and yet, as one reads the passages in which he appears, it is easy to forget the chronological impossibility. Steinbeck's Merlin, a poet who had won first prize several times at the Eisteddfod and would have been named First Bard were it not for an apparently political decision to select someone from the House of Rhys instead, had, as a young man, "shut up his song in the stone house on Crag-top and kept it a strict prisoner there" (20). About Merlin there arose legends; and when he grew old, "There was much about him of an ancient Druid priest with clear, far-seeing eyes which watched the stars" (21). In the Crag-top, the "tower" (21) in which he has imprisoned his song and himself, Merlin tries to appeal to the "love of the wild Cambria" that traces its origins back to the Trojan race and that boasts of "great Arthur" who conquered Rome and "sailed away undying to dear Avalon" (25).

Though Merlin sees "a million mysteries" in his native Cambria – "Have you found out the Chair of Arthur or the meaning of the circling stones?" he asks – the young Morgan quotes the local Curate's unromantic explanation that "Arthur was an unimportant chieftain" and Merlin "a figment of the mad brain of Geoffrey of Monmouth" (26). This discussion between the boy and the bard illustrates clearly the contrast between the Old World and the New. In the end Henry cannot be swayed because his "dream is over the sea" (25) in the unknown new world of adventure and opportunity.

Merlin realizes that it is pointless to preach to Henry because he can offer nothing to counter the spell of the irresistible dream, which is like the call of the Grail. "You want the moon to drink from as a golden cup," Merlin tells him, "and so, it is very likely that you will become a great man – if only you remain a child" (27). Indeed, Henry does remain a child throughout the pirate adventures that win him fame, throughout his planning to capture the fabled city, and throughout his years of dreaming of and desiring La Santa Roja. It is only when he achieves the quest and learns the hollowness of what he sought that he grows up. And it is then that whatever greatness he has achieved turns into mediocrity. He becomes a bureaucrat; appointed Lieutenant-Governor of Jamaica by the King, he is charged with eradicating piracy and, to that end, he condemns to death some of his former associates.

Merlin's role in the action of the novel is relatively small: he appears briefly in the beginning of the book and again in the middle when Henry's father visits him and tells him of Henry's exploits, which leads Merlin to comment that "He is still a little boy and wants the moon" (147). But his prophecy about Henry Morgan, which provides insights into the structure, characterization, and symbolism of the novel, is crucial – so crucial that as astute a commentator on Steinbeck's writing as Warren French has suggested that "The hero of *Cup of Gold*" is not Henry Morgan but rather "Merlin, the ancient Welsh magician who advised King Arthur . . . Merlin escapes splitting by civilization by hiding away from it and continuing to make his songs" (*John Steinbeck's Fiction Revisited* 40). In his rocky tower, Merlin avoids the commercialism of the world, avoids the quest for wealth that consumes Morgan without fulfilling him. Merlin's significance is highlighted by the fact that he appears again in Morgan's dying vision at the very end of the novel. Morgan believes he sees Elizabeth, the young Welsh woman whom he loved before leaving on his quest but to whom he never spoke of his feelings. Although he romanticized and aggrandized his relationship with her throughout the novel, in his final vision, she appears once again as the real person that his stories had falsified. After hearing from her that his father is "happily dead," Morgan asks about Merlin. "If only I could find him," he pleads. The vision ends with her response: "Merlin? You should know of him. Merlin is herding dreams in Avalon" (269). Even on his death bed, Morgan's unkept promise to return to his native Cambria haunts him. In his vision, the innocent woman who might have made him happier than the fabled Santa Roja did is there with him in his homeland; and the dream of new worlds to conquer, which in the end reversed the pattern of the Grail quest and made him empty and sterile, is supplanted by the dreams of Avalon, which are ancient and legendary but more real and satisfying than anything Henry Morgan has achieved.

As Michael Sundermeier has observed, "*Cup of Gold* makes obvious, if unsystematic, use of Arthurian materials" (38), a strategy that Steinbeck followed in a number of his other novels as well. In *Tortilla Flat* (1935), for example, Steinbeck translates the Arthurian realm into the modern world. Though he "avoided the dangers of too close a parallel" to Malory's account of the Arthurian world (Kinney, "The Arthurian Cycle in *Tortilla Flat*" 46),[5] Steinbeck nevertheless creates an overlay of Arthurian allusion to ennoble the lower-class characters of the novel. Steinbeck himself said that *Tortilla Flat*, "has a very definite theme. I thought it was clear enough. I have expected that the plan of the Arthurian cycle would be recognized, that my Gawaine and my Launcelot, my Arthur and Galahad would be recognized. Even the incident of the Sangreal in the search in the forest is not clear enough I guess. The form is that of the Malory version, the coming of Arthur and the mystic quality of owning a house, the forming of the round table, the adventure of the knights and finally, the mystic translation of Danny" (*Steinbeck: A Life in Letters* 96–97). These comments, written in a letter in 1934, prior to the book's publication, reflect Steinbeck's concern that those reading the manuscript were missing the Arthurian theme in the book. To make the link

5   In "*Tortilla Flat* Re-Visited," Kinney suggests that Steinbeck shares with Malory a "discomforting medley of tones" (14) and that the recognition of this fact will lead us to "a sharper appreciation for Steinbeck's discordances," which Kinney sees as more important than "exact correspondences for Steinbeck's characters and episodes in Malory" (18).

more obvious, therefore, Steinbeck added chapter headings that imitated those in the Caxton edition of Malory (see Fontenrose 24–25). For example, the sixth chapter is headed "How three sinful men, through contrition, attained peace. How Danny's Friends swore comradeship"; and the last chapter is headed "How Danny's sorrowing Friends defied the conventions. How the Talismanic Bond was burned. How each Friend departed alone." Interestingly, in these headings, the words "Friend" and "Friends" are always capitalized to indicate the special nature of these characters whom Danny has gathered around him. Steinbeck also added a sentence to the preface to make the Arthurian connection more explicit. He wrote: "For Danny's house was not unlike the Round Table, and Danny's friends were not unlike the knights of it" (9). Perhaps such blatant devices were necessary because the characters of Tortilla Flat are in many ways just the opposite of our idealized view of Arthur and the knights of the Round Table.[6] The main concern of each of Steinbeck's "knights" seems to be obtaining a bottle of wine; and having obtained such a treasure, he is not eager to share it, even with his Friends, the symbolic companions of the Round Table.

And yet the comparisons to the Arthurian legends are unavoidable. Arthur F. Kinney has detailed the correspondences between Danny and Arthur: "Danny often functions as Arthur; he begins the book as a young soldier discharged from service and comes to Monterey. Like Arthur, he comes to his homeland about to found a kingdom; like Arthur, he is young and has just survived some major battles. Arthur's talisman was the precious sword Excalibur . . . This is an inherited greatness, a legacy predicted by Merlin which makes Arthur leader and king. Danny is presented his legacy – two houses – which were the property of his grandfather . . . Danny and his followers, who feel a deep kinship to him, . . . are the subjects of several episodic adventures, as loosely strung together as Malory's knightly tales. As Malory ends with the death of Arthur, and the final breaking up of his followers, so Steinbeck ends with the death of Danny and the dissolution of his band of *paisanos*" (37).[7] Danny, who shelters his friends, takes on the role of Arthur in medieval romance by providing a focal point for his followers and a starting point for all their adventures. Late in the book, when Danny becomes weary with life, the narrator speaks of him as of a king: "Thy life is not thine own to govern, Danny, for it controls other lives. See how thy friends suffer! Spring to life, Danny, that thy friends may live again!" (287).

Whereas Danny is an Arthur figure, his companion Pilon seems to be the

---

6   There is also "an interminable list of dissimilarities" between Steinbeck's book and Malory's romance (Timmerman 138). This does not, however, diminish the importance of the Arthurian tales as a framework for *Tortilla Flat*.

7   Although it has been argued that there is no Arthur figure in *Tortilla Flat* because Steinbeck tells us that *Arthur* Morales died in the war (Owens 205), it seems clear, as others such as Joseph Fontenrose have observed, that "Danny corresponds to Arthur" (25).

story's Merlin. Pilon is the one who advises Danny about his kingdom – that is, the houses he has inherited. Of course, Pilon's advice is that Danny should rent out one of the houses – even though, once Danny agrees, Pilon rents it himself (without ever actually paying any rent) and, with the others whom he allows to live with him, eventually burns it down. But even this apparent tragedy is a boon to Danny, who is relieved not to have the responsibility of the second house. Pilon also has the knowledge and wisdom of Merlin: "There were few things going on in Tortilla Flat that Pilon did not know. His mind made sharp little notes of everything that his eyes saw or his ears heard" (167–68). Later in the story, Pilon is again said to have a "sharp mind" (239) and to be generally aware of "everything that happened" (242). His most unusual quality is his ability to think of new things. In telling a story about an old man, Jesus Maria Corcoran says that "he was not a man to invent anything. He was not like Pilon. He could not think of anything new" (255).

The correspondences between characters, however, are never exact. Kinney, who demonstrates how Danny is analogous to Arthur, also sees Danny's madness as comparable to Lancelot's in Malory (40). Similarly, though Pilon is the novel's Merlin figure, he is also at times more like Galahad than Merlin. He is said to be "a lover of beauty and a mystic" (38), and he has a near mystical experience as he watches gulls returning to their nests among the rocks by the ocean in the crepuscular light. Speaking to the gulls, he says, "I love you all. Your slow wings stroke my heart as the hand of a gentle master strokes the full stomach of a sleeping dog, as the hand of Christ stroked the heads of little children." And, as he prays the "Ave Maria," "the loveliest words he knew," he is transformed. The "bad Pilon" ceases to exist, and "There was, nor is, nor ever has been a purer soul than Pilon's at that moment" (39). Though fleeting, the moment is nonetheless real.

Pilon is also like Galahad in that he is the achiever of a kind of Grail quest. On St. Andrew's Eve, when buried treasure was believed to reveal itself with "a faint phosphorescent glow through the ground" (125), searchers "wandered restlessly, zig-zagging among the pines" (127). When Pilon finds such a light, he tells Big Joe Portagee that he and his companions have been seeking a treasure so they can repay Danny for his hospitality and friendship; and, he adds, "It is because my heart is clean of selfishness that I can find this treasure" (133). Like the Grail knight, the seekers of Tortilla Flat recognize the need for a pure heart in order to achieve the quest – and although Pilon strongly suspects that Danny might use the treasure to buy wine to share with his friends, his cleanness of heart prevents him from suggesting such a thing. That Pilon finds only an elevation marker placed by the United States Geodetic Survey, which cannot even be sold for the value of the metal because it is a crime to remove it, suggests that in Tortilla Flat, as in East Egg in *The Great Gatsby*, the Grail is not what it used to be.

Despite the use of the Arthurian material to ennoble his characters, Steinbeck never idealizes or overly romanticizes them. In fact, one of the things that makes *Tortilla Flat* such a masterly piece of writing is that its author demonstrates the worth and nobility of these characters without being sentimental and without avoiding their obvious human flaws. They are generally presented as lazy louts who will make more effort to get a bottle of wine than for almost anything else; and even Danny is far removed from the courtly king of the legends. At one point, to satisfy his thirst, he visits Mrs. Morales. "I went to her house last night," he explains. "That is a pretty woman in some lights, and not so old, either" (53). Spending the night with a woman to obtain wine is hardly a chivalrous deed; and the qualified compliment paid to Mrs. Morales hardly puts him in the ranks of courtly lovers or her in the ranks of the heroines of romance. Similarly, Big Joe Portagee is hardly an ideal lover. As the widow Tia Ignacia waits "for his gallantry to awaken" (191), he falls asleep and she beats him with a stick. It is only to stop the beating that he takes hold of her, and love "sang in his head; it roared through his body like a great freshet; it shook him as a storm shakes a forest of palms" (194). He must literally be hit in the head before he feels love. Another story, told by Jesus Maria Corcoran, describes Petey Ravanno as a courtly lover who "wanted what Gracie [Montez] had so much that he grew thin, and his eyes were as wide and pained as the eyes of one who smokes marihuana" (250). After Petey tries to commit suicide because of unrequited love, Gracie visits him, finally marries him, and becomes a good wife. The outcome makes this an exemplum, "a story for a priest to tell," and certainly one that entertains the companions who "liked a story with a meaning" (253).

Despite their shortcomings, Danny and his friends have their own code of ethics, a code to which they adhere as rigidly as if it were a sworn vow of knighthood. That code is evident in the incident involving the character called the Pirate. They know that for a long time the Pirate has been earning but never spending a quarter a day and that he must have amassed what to them is a fortune. As a means of getting the money, which is buried in the woods, they devise a plan. They invite the Pirate and his five dogs to live in Danny's house, scare him with stories of buried treasure discovered and stolen by others, and wait for him to bring the money into the house for them to watch over. When the Pirate confides that he has been saving his "two bitses" to fulfill a vow to buy a gold candlestick for St. Francis of Assisi if a sick dog would recover – "And . . . that dog got well" (119) – they realize they cannot violate the sanctity of his promise: "it was over, all hope of diverting the money. . . . There was nothing in the world they could do about it" (119). The knights of Tortilla Flat are, in fact, common men, in some ways the most common of men. Yet they follow an uncommonly noble code. When Big Joe Portagee, a newcomer to their circle, steals the Pirate's savings, the companions, led by Danny, administer a rough justice. They beat him, cut

him, and pour salt in his wounds. But when he returns the money, they
welcome him back into their company.

The characters are chivalric in other ways as well. Like knights of old,
they aid damsels in distress. The children of Señora Teresina Cortez thrive on
a diet of tortillas and beans, which they eat for breakfast, lunch, and dinner.
A doctor who visits them has "never seen healthier children" (227). Each
year, to sustain her brood, Señora Cortez gathers hundreds of pounds of
beans from what is left in the fields after the bean threshers have passed. But
one year the bean crop is ruined by rain, and the children have nothing to
eat. By some "mystical attraction between pain and humanitarianism" (230),
Jesus Maria Corcoran, the great humanitarian among the friends, visits
Señora Cortez on the very day she cooks the last of her supply of beans.
When news of the tragedy is conveyed to Danny and his companions, they
make it their "trust" that the "children shall not starve" (231), and they set
about to fulfill this trust by stealing food throughout Monterey. Though they
fill the Cortez house with fruits and vegetables and milk and fish, the
children become sick because they do not have "the proper food" (234). So
the companions undertake the quest for the beans needed to keep the
children healthy. Breaking into a warehouse, they steal four hundred pounds
of beans and deliver them surreptitiously to the troubled home for the
Señora to find and declare a "miracle" (235).

Steinbeck's novel contains other chivalrous adventures. When Jesus Maria
Corcoran rescues from a policeman a young Mexican soldier, a cáporal
whose beautiful young wife was stolen by a capitán, Danny wishes he and
his friends were in Torreón, the town where these events transpired, so that
Pilon, in his role of adviser, could "make a plan for us" (183) to right the
wrong. But the young cáporal's "adventure" (183) remains only a story and
their action a wish for the knights of Tortilla Flat. Though they are unable to
punish the offending officer or to save the young soldier's sickly baby from
death, they offer friendship and support.

Similarly, the companions are unable to prevent Danny's death. When
Danny first tires of life, he goes into the woods in a fit of madness not unlike
that ascribed to various heroes in Arthurian romance. And when he finally
comes to his senses, his friends throw him a party that involves all of Tortilla
Flat, because everyone is a friend of Danny and wants to contribute and participate. Food and drink are prepared in what seems by their standards regal
abundance: "Food appeared. Basins of rice, pots of steaming chicken, dump-
lings to startle you! And the wine came, gallons and gallons of it. Martinez
dug up a keg of potato whiskey from his manure pile and carried it to
Danny's house" (291–92). There are even the equivalents of jousts and
tournaments, as no man "came out of that night without some glorious cuts
and bruises"; there were more fights than ever before, and not just "fights
between two men, but roaring battles that raged through whole clots of
men" (296). The party is so good that "No one ever tried to give a better one.

Such a thing was unthinkable, for within two days Danny's party was lifted out of possible comparison with all other parties that ever were" (296). Like the feasts of Arthurian romance, this one rises to the superlative degree. And like the stories of Arthur, those of Danny grow and will continue to grow. Danny alone, it is reported, drank three gallons of wine. But, in a detail that is reminiscent of Arthur's being said to have slain nine hundred men in one battle in Nennius's account, the narrator reminds us that "It must be remembered, however, that Danny is now a god. In a few years it may be thirty gallons. In twenty years it may be plainly remembered that the clouds flamed and spelled DANNY in tremendous letters; that the moon dripped blood; that the wolf of the world bayed prophetically from the mountains of the Milky Way" (299).

At the party, in a drunken fury, the guest of honor seeks "the Enemy who is worthy of Danny" (300–01) and rushes off. When his friends follow, they find him dead, "broken and twisted" at the bottom of a gulch. Unable to attend the funeral because they do not have proper clothes, his companions can only watch from across the street; but they honor him by telling each other "little stories of Danny, of his goodness, his courage, his piety" (312). With Danny gone, they decide to dissolve the "talismanic bond" between them by allowing a fire accidentally started – and easily extinguishable – to burn down his house. The narrator's comment on this scene is a tribute to the nobility of the order that passed with Danny: "Thus must it be, oh, wise friends of Danny. The cord that bound you together is cut. The magnet that drew you has lost its virtue. Some stranger will own the house, some joyless relative of Danny's. Better that this symbol of holy friendship, this good house of parties and fights, of love and comfort, should die as Danny died, in one last glorious hopeless assault on the gods" (316). The friends watch the house burn and they walk away, each in a different direction. We might say, "the old order changeth."

Given the importance Steinbeck placed on Malory's book as a source of his own values, it seems natural that he should use an overlay of Arthurian allusion to transform the lives of the nearly penniless inhabitants of Tortilla Flat into something as noteworthy as the lives of the noblest of knights. Steinbeck's aggrandizement of these paisanos and his presentation of one of their number as a modern Arthur is, moreover, of a piece with the use of the legend for social purposes found in Pyle, in the Arthurian youth groups, and in Phelps's stories; and it is consistent with the image of Arthur and his power presented by Bridges, Twain, and Beard. All of these works suggest that there is an American tradition of democratizing the Arthurian legends by parodying the figure of Arthur or downplaying his power, or by suggesting that Arthur's true nobility comes from basic human qualities, not from an accident of birth. In a telling comment in a letter to Eugène Vinaver, Steinbeck notes that the knights of the Round Table, except for Galahad, have faults like those "we find in ourselves." In the same letter he observes that "those earnest scholars who search so diligently for some kind of objective reality for Arthur are trying to divest themselves of the responsibility of *being* Arthur" (July 6, 1965, cited in Mitchell 78). Particularly significant are Steinbeck's implications that what is important about Arthur is his symbolic, not his historical, reality and that anyone, even someone from the lowest class, can *be* Arthur because of what he represents symbolically.

Steinbeck's next two published novels, *In Dubious Battle* (1936) and *Of Mice and Men* (1937), also involve groups of men joined together for a common purpose. Warren French has noted a basic similarity between these novels and *Tortilla Flat*. "Despite other significant differences between the books," he writes, "both *In Dubious Battle* (1936) and *Of Mice and Men* (1937) follow the same basic pattern as *Tortilla Flat* (1935). In all three, a modern variation on the knightly band pledged to help those in distress has been formed only to be destroyed by the machinations of the irresponsible forces of a degenerate society" ("Steinbeck's Use of Malory" 7). Of the three, however, *In Dubious Battle* owes least to Steinbeck's Arthurian interests. It is the story of Communist organizers who convince a group of fruit pickers to strike. Mac, the principal organizer, takes a new recruit, Jim Nolan, on this assignment with him. Through these two characters, Steinbeck explores the notion of dedication to a cause.

Jim, who has joined the party because he wants to "work towards something" (16) and because "Nothing I ever did before had any meaning" (31), clearly represents the little man who has never had a break or even a chance. In his newfound work, however, he sees a means of providing a better life for men like his father and himself, hard workers who are unable to rise above the poverty into which they are born. Mac appreciates Jim's potential and determines to make of him a useful member of the Party. But though he espouses the same values, Mac tries to teach Jim that individuals are less important than the larger cause. Instead of championing the weak or oppressed individual as the Arthurian model that Steinbeck so admired might have called for, Mac uses individuals to promote ideology. When Jim befriends Dan, an aging worker, Mac advises him not to waste his time on the old. Only when Dan falls from a tree and is injured because of a defective ladder does Mac admit "The old buzzard was worth something after all" (107). But Dan's worth is not, in Mac's view, as a human being or even as a contributing member of society; it arises from the fact that, as Mac says, "We can use him now" (107) to stir up the other workers. Similarly, when a longtime friend and colleague named Joy is shot in the course of the strike, Mac does not grieve but wants only to use his body "to step our guys up, to keep 'em together," and to "make 'em fight" (169). Unable to "think about the hurts of one man" (207), he is consistent to the end. When Jim, with whom Mac seems to have formed a special bond, is shot, Mac picks up his body and carries him before the strikers as a way of making his speech to them more effective and moving.

Mac's view of people, even of his closest friends, is utilitarian. As such, it is totally at odds with the notions of sympathy for the oppressed that fired Steinbeck's imagination when he read the Arthurian tales as a child. Apart from the underlying motif of a band of men organized for a common purpose in this novel, the only other influence of the legends is in the depiction of the dangers of adhering too strictly to a principle. Like Arthur, whose sense of justice leads to the condemnation of his best knight and his queen, Mac is willing to sacrifice individuals to what he perceives as a higher good.

Of Mice and Men also depicts a group of men working towards a common purpose; but in this novel, the Arthurian pattern is somewhat more integral than in *In Dubious Battle*. The story focuses on the two friends George and Lennie, who, unlike most of the workers and ranchhands in the novel, travel together and look out for one another. They are also set apart by their dream of one day owning a place of their own where they can *"live off the fatta the lan'* " (15). This dream is much delayed by the fact that the slow-witted Lennie continually gets into trouble because he likes to feel soft things. As the book opens, George and Lennie have just been forced to flee the town where they were working because Lennie wanted to touch the fabric of a girl's dress. Though done in all innocence, naturally his gesture was misunderstood.

In their new job, George and Lennie form an alliance with two other misfits, Candy, an old man who lost a hand in a ranch accident and has been kept on to do menial jobs, and Crooks, a black man with "a crooked back where a horse kicked him" (22) who works in the ranch's stable. The four men join in their American Dream of having a place of their own where they will have to answer to no one but themselves. This is, as Crooks points out before he begins to believe such a dream might be possible, a kind of Holy Grail for itinerant workers: "I seen hundreds of men come by on the road an' on the ranches, with their bindles on their back an' that same damn thing in their heads. They come, an' they quit an' go on; an' every damn one of 'em's got a little piece of land in his head" (81). But Crooks becomes entranced by the dream; and with Candy's savings of three hundred dollars, it looks as if they might be able to achieve it.

One very real threat to their dream, however, is the owner's son Curley, whose flirtatious young wife makes him angry and pugnacious. When Curley picks a fight with Lennie, George tells his friend to defend himself, which he does by breaking most of the bones in Curley's hands. By threatening to make Curley a laughingstock if he tries to get Lennie fired, Slim the foreman saves the day and the dream – for a time at least. Slim is the leader of the misfits who make up the Round Table of ranchhands. Steinbeck depicts him as just, principled, and strong. Steinbeck's description marks him with the regal dignity of a "prince" among the working men:

A tall man stood in the doorway. He held a crushed Stetson hat under his arm while he combed his long, black, damp hair straight back. Like the

others he wore blue jeans and a short denim jacket. When he had finished
combing his hair he moved into the room, and he moved with a majesty
only achieved by royalty and master craftsmen. He was a jerkline skinner,
the prince of the ranch, capable of driving ten, sixteen, even twenty mules
with a single line to the leaders. He was capable of killing a fly on the
wheeler's butt with a bull whip without touching the mule. There was a
gravity in his manner and a quiet so profound that all talk stopped when
he spoke. His authority was so great that his word was taken on any
subject, be it politics or love. . . . His hatchet face was ageless. He might
have been thirty-five or fifty. His ear heard more than was said to him, and
his slow speech had overtones not of thought, but of understanding
beyond thought. (37)

Even Slim, however, cannot protect Lennie when he accidentally kills Curley's
wife while trying to feel her soft hair – although Slim is the only one of the
ranchhands who understands both what Lennie has done and the pain that it
causes George.

While Lennie's act is innocent, there is no way for him to avoid punishment. Remembering Candy's regret at not having put his old dog to death
but letting another ranchhand do the deed, George decides to be a true
friend to Lennie by ending his life rather than letting a group of strangers do
it. Putting a bullet through Lennie's head becomes a final act of friendship,
an adherence to a simple code dictating how friends should act.

More than *In Dubious Battle*, "*Of Mice and Men* is an Arthurian story"
because "the fundamental parallels – the knightly loyalty, the pursuit of the
vision, the creation of a bond (shared briefly by Candy and Crooks), and its
destruction by an at least potentially adulterous relationship – are there.
They are, however, so concealed by the surface realism of the work that one
unfamiliar with Steinbeck's previous Arthurian experiments would be
hardly likely to notice them. The one obvious Arthurian hangover is George,
who is not only remarkably loyal to his charge – the feeble-minded Lennie –
but also remarkably pure" (French, *John Steinbeck* 73). Here again, as in
Tortilla Flat Steinbeck shows the nobility in a group of common men, most of
them rejected by society, and some of them, like Crooks, rejected even by the
small realm of the ranch. Yet even these men display the qualities, the
loyalty, the vision, and the courage, of the knights of the Round Table.

With the exception of *Sweet Thursday* (1954), not much of Steinbeck's
fiction after *Of Mice and Men* makes significant use of Arthurian motifs.[8]
Though Roy S. Simmonds has commented that *Sweet Thursday* is "Steinbeck's one last attempt to revive the Arthurian myth in the Monterey
setting" ("The Unrealized Dream" 34), he does not explore the manner in

8   In the same year that *Of Mice and Men* appeared, Steinbeck also published a collection
of fiction under the title *The Red Pony*. In that collection was a story called "The Great
Mountains," which Richard F. Peterson in "The Grail Legend and Steinbeck's 'The Great
Mountains' " saw as a modern reenactment of the Grail theme.

which the myth is developed in the novel. Nor have other critics examined the ways in which this novel, never highly regarded, adapts the material that was so important to earlier works by Steinbeck.

Reintroducing many of the characters from Steinbeck's earlier novel *Cannery Row* (1945), which Peter Lisca has described as "a philosophically based and impassioned celebration of values directly opposed to the capitalist ethic dominant in Western society" (112), *Sweet Thursday* is perhaps a less philosophical novel; but it is nonetheless a more interesting book than most assume. The interest lies in large part in its relationship to the Arthurian material that so fascinated Steinbeck. Like *Tortilla Flat*, *Sweet Thursday* reenacts portions of the Arthurian story in the modern world; but instead of following the tragic pattern of Malory's romance, as the earlier novel does, *Sweet Thursday* offers a deliberate and comic reversal of that pattern.

The central figure, the Arthur figure, in *Sweet Thursday* is Doc, a biologist who makes his living gathering marine specimens and preparing them for use in research. The person to whom the residents of Cannery Row appeal when they need help, Doc is the stabilizing force in the community. All the residents of the "Palace Flophouse," an establishment whose name suggests that the men who live there are to be seen as another group of Steinbeck's modern knights of the Round Table, "hustle him a little" (77); but Doc is aware of this and is glad to participate. So when Doc, who "had always been a fulfilled and contented man," is affected by an uncharacteristic malaise and "discontent nibbles at him" (22), it is troubling to the inhabitants of Cannery Row. After all, Doc – as his friend Mack suggests – is essential to the health and well-being of his community just as the security of the royal person is linked to the health of the state. When Doc observes that he has changed, Mack responds imploringly, "Hell, Doc, you can't change. Why, what could we depend on! Doc, if you change a lot of people are going to cash in their chips. Why, we was all just waiting around for you to get back so we could go on being normal" (19).

Doc's malaise finds its objective correlative in his inability to write a scientific paper, a goal he has set for himself as a way of dealing with a kind of mid-life crisis that he is experiencing. But writer's block and thinker's block keep him from completing his project. One of the modern knights from the Palace, a man named Hazel, becomes Doc's champion and the Lancelot figure of the book. His desire to "beat the holy hell" out of Mack (77) for implying that Doc cannot write the paper galvanizes the group into trying to solve Doc's problem. In recognition of Hazel's initiative and his noble friendship, the men who live in the Palace Flophouse "stood in a circle around him [Hazel], Mack and Eddie, Whitey No. 1 and Whitey No. 2, and each one tipped the jug over his shoulder and drank to Hazel." This circle of men, a comic Round Table, drinks several more toasts until a "courtliness crept into the speech of the dwellers of the Palace Flophouse, an old-world courtesy." The result is a solemn vow, couched in mock-heroic terms that blend slang and corrupted literary allusion, to assist Doc. "Gentlemen," Mack says, "let us here highly resolve to get Doc's ass out of the sling of despond" (79).

The solution that Mack proposes and that the group endorses is to find Doc a wife. Mack's notion that left to choose his own wife, a man will almost surely find the wrong woman for him – "the only guy that shouldn't have nothing to do with picking out a wife is the guy that's going to marry her," he asserts (80) – has echoes of Arthur's selecting Guinevere as his spouse despite the warnings of Merlin in Malory's account. Determining to select Doc's wife for him, the men settle on a woman named Suzy who is new in town and who, since she has nowhere else to go, moves into the Bear Flag, the local whorehouse. Because Suzy is none too good at her new trade and because of her own fondness for Doc, Fauna, the owner of the whorehouse, participates in the plan to get the two together.

The scheme Doc and Fauna devise is a costume ball. Initially, they consider a theme with Arthurian overtones, "At the court of the Fairy Queen," but reject it in favor of "Snow White and the Seven Dwarfs" (172–73). Hazel attends as Prince Charming and wears his version of knightly adornment, a cavalry sabre and "a Knight Templar's hat with a white ostrich plume" (192) – not, it should be noted, the symbolically yellowing feather that embellishes the Knight Templar's hat of Ethan Allen Hawley in *The Winter of Our Discontent*. When Fauna, as the Fairy Godmother, presents Suzy to Doc, Suzy reads the surprised embarrassment in Doc's face. Because she loves him and mistakenly thinks he does not reciprocate her feelings, she cannot play along with the game; so she rushes off, shocked into leaving the Bear Flag and making a new and independent life for herself.

However misguided their method of bringing Doc and Suzy together, the brotherhood of the Palace is not mistaken about Doc's need for a wife or in their selection of Suzy. In a chapter ironically called "The Arming," after Fauna dresses Suzy for an arranged date with Doc, he is smitten with her; and after the disastrous party Doc admits that he is "not whole without her" (244). In fact, even before Mack devises his plan, Doc's need is obvious. While walking on the beach, Doc meets a man who has visions and is called "the seer."[9] (Although he appears only one other time in the book, the seer takes on – or rather, he shares with Mack – the role of Merlin in this modern Camelot.) The seer gets Doc to speak of his malaise, which of course has a larger cause than the inability to write a scholarly paper. Doc explains, "I want to take everything I've seen and thought and learned and reduce them and relate them and refine them until I have something of meaning, something of use. And I can't seem to do it." The seer implies that such an

---

9 Peter Lisca has noted that Merlin in *Cup of Gold* is the "original of many subsequent 'hermit' and seer figures in Steinbeck's work" (34). The seer in *Sweet Thursday* is another such figure.

undertaking might require assistance. "I wouldn't think of trying anything so big without – " he says, pausing before revealing any more. When Doc wonders just what is needed, the seer completes the thought: "Without love" (73). What this conversation suggests is that Doc is really trying to find order in his life and in the world around him, something that it is impossible to do alone. In the romantic and comedic world of *Sweet Thursday*, the missing ingredient for finding meaning in the world is love.

When love between Doc and Suzy seems impossible, it is the seer who gives the advice that ensures the novel's happy ending. Hazel realizes that Suzy's pride prevents her from renewing her relationship: only if she feels that Doc needs her will she go to him. Hazel thinks of a way to bring this about but needs confirmation that he is justified in taking the radical action that his plan requires. At Doc's request, Hazel goes to the jail where the seer is being held. Unlike Merlin, however, the seer is not imprisoned because of his desire for a woman but because of another appetite, a liking for candy bars, which he steals from the local Safeway. And unlike Merlin, the seer is easily freed from his prison when Doc pays for the stolen candy bars. The fact that Steinbeck's Merlin and his wisdom are not lost to the kingdom forever is part of the novel's comic reversal of Malory's tragedy. When Hazel asks if someone should offer help to a friend even if "it hurt like hell" and it "might maybe not work," the seer replies that "If you love him you must do anything to help him – anything"; but he urges Hazel to be sure that there is a chance of success and warns that his friend might never speak to him again (256). Hazel's plan is to force Suzy's hand by incapacitating Doc just as he is about to set out on trip to gather much-needed marine specimens to replenish his diminished stock. Encouraged by the seer's advice, Hazel breaks Doc's arm with a baseball bat. When Mack learns what Hazel did, he recognizes the deed for what it is: "You don noble stuff," Mack praises. "Wasn't nobody with guts but you" (266). Mack's words echo the narrator's comment: "No one knows how greatness comes to a man" (256).

Hazel's plan works. Suzy rushes to Doc, offering to drive him on his trip and turn over rocks for him so he can find his specimens. The reversal of Malory's tragedy is complete when Doc tells Suzy of his love for her and she responds, "Brother . . . you got yourself a girl" (270). Instead of the fatal wound that Malory's Arthur suffers, Doc receives a wound that gives his life meaning. Instead of having his closest companion betray him by loving his wife, Doc's friends bring him together with the woman he loves. And in another reversal, the knights of the Palace Flophouse rig a raffle so that Doc wins the building in which they dwell. Thus, instead of causing the destruction of Camelot, Doc's friends make him the possessor of the Palace.

The ending offers yet another inversion of the traditional story. Doc and Suzy depart after she, never having driven before, gets a quick driving lesson. Steinbeck seems to be thinking of the ending of Tennyson's *Idylls* where Bedivere, alone on the shore, watches the barge carrying Arthur and the mystic maidens becomes smaller and smaller until it disappears into the light of the dawn. Steinbeck's departure scene suggests the different tone of his novel: "Doc turned in the seat and looked back. The disappearing sun shone on his laughing face, his gay and eager face. With his left hand he held the bucking steering wheel" (273). Doc, wounded but joyful, sets out towards the water – never mind that they are heading for La Jolla rather than Avalon – with Suzy driving the car for their festive rather than funereal trip.

There is a final reversal, among the most comic in the book. Traditionally, Arthur must return Excalibur, the instrument that gives him his authority, to the mere at the end of his reign. Doc, on the other hand, has been without the instrument he needs to perform his labor, a microscope. His friends order one for him, and it arrives at the very end of the novel. Because of the great affection they have for Doc, they have bought the "[b]iggest one in the whole goddam catalogue," which turns out to be a telescope and not a microscope. But, as Doc realizes, "it doesn't matter whether you look down or up – as long as you look" (273). In fact, the gift may be symbolic in that his friends have given him a new and larger perspective on life and have perhaps helped him to achieve the macrocosmic understanding he has been seeking.

Throughout his career, Steinbeck had used Malory to give shape to a number of works of fiction; but he wanted to do even more with the book that had fired his imagination as a child. He wanted to make it accessible to contemporary readers, and so he set out to modernize Malory.[10] As a novelist, Steinbeck possessed insights into the *Morte d'Arthur* that other readers, including literary scholars, did not have. As Eugène Vinaver observed, Steinbeck "could see in Malory certain things that the so-called experts have consistently failed to see, for instance the stylistic discrepancies

10 While Steinbeck was working on *The Acts of King Arthur*, he was also writing the text for *America and Americans*. In that book, Steinbeck makes a specific connection between America and the Arthurian world. He says that "the brave and honest sheriff who with courage and a six-gun brings law and order and civic virtue to a Western community is perhaps our most familiar hero, no doubt descended from the brave mailed knight of chivalry who battled and overcame evil with lance and sword." In both legends Steinbeck recognizes a basic similarity, that "virtue does not arise out of reason or orderly process of law – it is imposed and maintained by violence." He goes on to make a link between Arthur and the image we have of the heroic lawman battling outlaws: "There must have been a leader like King Arthur; although there is no historical record to prove it, the very strength of the story presumes his existence. We know there were gunslinging sheriffs – not many, but some; but if they had not existed, our need for them would have created them" (34). Mimi Reisel Gladstein's perceptive "*America and Americans*: The Arthurian Consummation" has called attention to other less specific but in some ways more important connections between the Matter of Britain and *America and Americans*, including the recounting of an incident involving an American Indian that has resonances of the Grail quest (233–34) and the similarity of the structure of Steinbeck's book to that of Malory's *Morte d'Arthur*. What is significant here is that the Arthurian legend is so pervasive in Steinbeck's thought and sensibility that even when he is writing a study of the essence of America and the American character, he cannot avoid Arthurian overtones.

between the various parts of the work, indicative of its gradual growth" (Letter to Roy S. Simmonds, cited in Simmonds, "A Note . . ." 27). But also – and perhaps more important – was Steinbeck's ability both to see the Arthurian characters in modern men and women and to see real people in the denizens of Camelot. In Steinbeck's *Acts*, therefore, "We meet King Arthur and his court face to face, and they are we" (Dowell 72).

In fact, even as he worked on his modernization of Malory, Steinbeck could not help thinking in the same way that inspired novels like *Tortilla Flat* and *Sweet Thursday*. In a letter to Vinaver (dated July 6, 1955, cited in Mitchell 78), he says: "in all the years of fruitless exploring . . . I come back again and again to one thought, planted perhaps when I was nine years old and never far away from me. And that thought is that the Matter of Arthur is essentially a subjective matter. Geoffrey knew Arthur as belonging to his time or shortly before. Malory writes and thinks of a 15th century Arthur – Chrétien speaks of his time and I, heaven help me, can only think of the Round Table as having existed in Salinas, California around the turn of the 20th century."

Some of the changes Steinbeck made to Malory are merely editorial. "Malory removed some of the repetition from the Frensshe books," Steinbeck wrote. "I find it necessary to remove most of the repetition from Malory" (Steinbeck, *Steinbeck: A Life in Letters* 558). But though Steinbeck set out merely to modernize Malory's *Morte*, he began making other changes that went far beyond the editorial. He wanted to update and Americanize the characters and events that existed in his mind in Salinas. One of the ways he did this was by Americanizing the language. In a letter to Chase Horton, he records an epiphany that he had as he worked on the project. "My 'slight thing,' " he writes, "was about present day America. Why not write it in American? This is a highly complicated and hugely communicative language. It has been used in dialogues, in cuteness and perhaps by a few sports writers. It has been used by a first person telling a story but I don't think it has been used as a legitimate literary language. . . . And suddenly I felt as Chaucer must have felt when he found he could write the language he had all around him and nobody would put him in jail . . ." (Steinbeck, *Steinbeck: A Life in Letters* 562–63).

Steinbeck occasionally adds other touches that Americanize the tale. For example, in Malory, after his sword breaks during the fight with Pellinore, Arthur merely observes that he has no sword; then Merlin takes him to the Lady of the Lake to receive the replacement for the blade he has broken. Steinbeck's Arthur, however, complains about the loss of the sword and asks, "What is a knight without a sword? A nothing – even less than nothing." To this, Merlin replies "It is a child speaking, . . . not a king and not a knight, but a hurt and angry child, or you would known, my lord, that there is more to a king than a crown, and far more to a knight than a sword" (57). This statement that Steinbeck adds to his source reads like something out of the

literature of the youth groups or like the statements found in Howard Pyle's
reinterpretation of Malory.[11]

Steinbeck elaborates on Malory's text in other ways as well, such as by
providing more explanation and commentary than Malory did. When
Malory's Merlin tells of his own fate, Arthur advises him to use his
"crauftes" to prevent it. Merlin simply replies, "hit woll not be" (I: 125).
Steinbeck's Merlin responds that he cannot save himself "Because I am wise.
In the combat between wisdom and feeling, wisdom never wins" (122). Similarly, Steinbeck feels the novelist's need to explain changes in characters. He
transforms Kay from a brave knight to a petty, sniping critic who never sees
the true worth of others. Steinbeck has Kay explain to Lancelot how his
position as seneschal altered him:

> Granite so hard that it will smash a hammer can be worn away by little
> grains of moving sand. And a heart that will not break under the great
> blows of fate can be eroded by the nibbling of numbers, the creeping of
> days, the numbing treachery of littleness, of important littleness. I could
> fight men but I was defeated by marching numbers on a page. . . . To you
> war is fighting. To me it is so many ashen poles for spears, so many strips
> of steel – counting of tents, of knives, of leather straps – counting – count-
> ing of pieces of bread. . . . Look, sir, did you ever know a man of numbers
> who did not become small and mean and frightened – all greatness eaten
> away by little numbers as marching ants nibble a dragon and leave picked
> bones? (321–22)

Steinbeck's interest in characterization finds its most interesting expression in his Lancelot, who, he recognized, was the most important figure in
Malory and was to be the most important in his own rendition of the *Morte*.
Steinbeck saw Lancelot as the character with whom Malory identified. "A
novel may be said to be the man who writes it," he stated. "Now it is nearly
always true that a novelist, perhaps unconsciously, identifies himself with
one chief or central character in his novel. Into this character he puts not only
what he thinks he is but what he hopes to be. We can call this spokesman the
self-character. You will find one in every one of my books and in the novels
of everyone I can remember" (Steinbeck, *Steinbeck: A Life in Letters* 518).
Steinbeck believes "that Malory's self-character would be Launcelot. All of
the perfections he knew went into this character, all of the things of which he
thought himself capable. But being an honest man he found faults in himself,
faults of vanity, faults of violence, faults even of disloyalty and these would

11 There are also things in Malory that seem to support such a democratic notion without
    having to be changed at all, such as the comment made by Balin to the damsel who wears
    the sword from which she can be freed only by a knight of surpassing virtue. Since Balin
    is a prisoner, she is reluctant to let him attempt to draw the sword; but he argues that "a
    man's worth is not in his clothing. Manhood and honor are hidden inside. And some-
    times virtues are not known to everyone" (67). Though taken directly from Malory, this
    reads like an explication of moral knighthood.

naturally find their way into his dream character" (Steinbeck, *Steinbeck: A Life in Letters* 519).

Although Lancelot is the greatest knight, he is nevertheless subject to derision from the young knights of Camelot as they gather around the well outside the castle keep. When young Lyonel is asked to go on a quest with Lancelot, his friends encourage him despite his reluctance because it will provide him with entertaining stories, not about battles but about Lancelot's outdated ideas of knighthood. Lancelot's answers to the "old-fashioned questions" would be "better than a juggler" (258), Lyonel's friends assure him. One of the questions Lyonel asks Lancelot on their journey is whether his perfection in knighthood is enough for him. In response, "A black rage shook Sir Lancelot, drew his lips snarling from his teeth. His right hand struck like a snake at this sword hilt and half the silver blade slipped from the scabbard. Lyonel felt the wind of his death blow on his cheek." Then Lyonel witnesses in Lancelot "a combat more savage than ever he had seen between two, saw wounds given and received and a heart riven to bursting" (264). Lancelot soon regains control and slips his sword back into his scabbard. Shortly afterward when they stop to rest, Lyonel, watching the sleeping Lancelot, knows that "he had seen greatness beyond reason and courage that made words seem craven and peace that must be earned with agony" (265). Because of his earlier disrespect, Lyonel feels ashamed and thinks of the young knights back in Camelot who said Lancelot "was too stupid to know he was ridiculous, too innocent to see the life around him, convinced of perfectibility in a heap of evil, romantic and sentimental in a world where reality is overlord, an anachronism before the earth was born." Lyonel now realizes what those young fools do not, that Lancelot "would charge to his known defeat with neither hesitation nor despair and finally would accept his death with courtesy and grace as though it were a prize." And more importantly, recognizing the total dedication that makes Lancelot great and the tremendous struggle he undergoes to keep the control that greatness demands, Lyonel understands "why Lancelot would gallop down the centuries, spear in rest, gathering men's hearts on his lance head like tilting rings" (265).

Steinbeck takes what is a given in Malory's romance, Lancelot's greatness, and analyzes it. Not content simply to assert that greatness, Steinbeck explores it, showing both how ridiculous total dedication can be to those who do not understand it and how inspiring it can be to those who do. For when Lyonel has his realization, "He chose his side and it was Lancelot's" (265). This scene with Lyonel is one of the most significant in the *Acts* because it explains why and how someone could come to love Lancelot even above a great king like Arthur; thus, it provides probability for the love between Lancelot and Guinevere – a section which, if written, would have made clear in terms of character why the conflict with Lancelot split the kingdom and ended the fellowship of the Round Table.

Another important scene in Steinbeck's development of Lancelot's character is his capture and temptation by the four queens, which Steinbeck expands considerably. As Andrew Welsh observes, "Two pages of Malory become in his version seventeen pages of narrative, and he makes the scene central to the meaning of the entire tale" (486). Each of the queens tempts Lancelot – the queen of Northgalys offers him endlessly new sensations; the queen of the Outer Isles offers him change; the queen of Eastland offers to be like a mother to him; and Morgan le Fay, queen of Gore, offers power, which she says will allow him to obtain all that the others would give and more – so that he will choose her over the others. Since Lancelot cannot accept any of them because of his "knightly love" for Guinevere, which, as he told Lyonel, "is not a coupling of dog and bitch" but something from which she should have "only honor and joy" (261), he is left in a dungeon until the daughter of Sir Bagdemagus frees him so he can fight for her father in a tournament. But Lancelot's love is more than knightly; and part of what Lyonel witnessed earlier is Lancelot's struggle to suppress and to sublimate the more passionate love that he feels. Commenting on the encounter with the four queens, Andrew Welsh has observed that "Steinbeck rewrites that situation in a way both modern and medieval. First he gives a modern complexity to the character of Lancelot by giving him a subconscious mind, in which is located all unknown to Lancelot his love for Guinevere. Other doubts and desires contend there as well, manifesting themselves in the feelings of uneasiness, irritability, and self-questioning which dog him throughout the tale. Steinbeck wrote in a letter that in the first part of the tale 'Lancelot has not yet had to face his dual self. He is morally untested.' The dual self, Lancelot's other identity, surfaces only at the end of the tale, where Steinbeck restores the famous 'first kiss' episode of the *Prose Lancelot*, which Malory had dropped" (498–99). Whereas Malory's "Noble Tale of Sir Launcelot du Lake" is designed to show Launcelot's rise to prominence as a knight, Steinbeck's rendition is concerned more with Lancelot's inner struggle and his ultimate realization and expression of his love for Guinevere, which culminates in the passionate kiss. That kiss, which occurs as "Their bodies locked together as though a trap had sprung" (349), causes Lancelot to weep bitterly, presumably with a combination of ecstasy and guilt.

In addition to the emphasis on characterization, Steinbeck modernizes his account of Arthur's realm in the way he treats the women of the story. The expanded tale of the temptations by the four queens is just one example of his attempt to individualize some of the stock characters from Malory. Steinbeck also gives the women richer and more complex roles, and it seems likely that, had the book been finished, a character like Guinevere would have had a prominent role in the events leading to the final battle. Even in the portions of the *Acts* that were completed, Guinevere already has more influence in shaping events than she does in Malory. When Arthur worries that his young knights have no direction and that his older knights have no mission worthy of their skill and experience, Guinevere points out that there are small conflicts everywhere in the kingdom that could be resolved if the knights saw those conflicts as part of something larger. "I think that every man wants to be larger than himself," she advises Arthur, "and that he can be only if he is part of something immeasurably larger than himself. . . . We must seek a way to declare a great war on little things." And it is she who comes up with the idea that every knight will be an agent of what she calls "the King's Justice" (250). Furthermore, she suggests pairing the best knight with the worst – a notion that brings Lancelot and Lyonel together for the quest that transforms the younger knight. Steinbeck's Guinevere is, however, as unhappy with her lot as are some of the manifestations of the queen in works such as Phelps's "True Story of Guenever" and Teasdale's "Guenevere." She even wishes that she could be a man because her "only adventures are in the pictures in colored thread of the great gallant world. My little needle is my sword. That's not a very satisfying conflict" (252). Surely had her character been fully developed, she would have had a tremendous influence on the events at Camelot and in her own life.

Another example of the new direction Steinbeck was taking with his women characters can be found in the threefold quest undertaken by Gawain, Ewain, and Marhalt. The knights encounter three ladies, each knight choosing one of them to accompany him in search of adventures. Sir Gawain picks the youngest, who comes to recognize him for the vain and pompous person he is. She admits that she does not even like him and eventually rides off with another knight while Gawain is engaged in combat. The second damsel, who is paired with Marhalt, is more mature than the first; practical and skilled in the art of making questing and living in the outdoors as comfortable as possible, she is a professional at being a companion to a questing knight. And Marhalt has a more realistic and less inflated opinion of his talent and person than Gawain had about himself. After a series of adventures culminating in the slaying of a giant who had been plaguing Earl Fergus, Marhalt decides to settle with the maiden for a time in the Earl's castle. Soon, however, their domestic routine begins to grate on both of them, and they set off again.

While these first two ladies have roles much expanded over those of their counterparts in Malory, it is with the third and oldest damsel who accompanies Ewain that Steinbeck takes the greatest liberties. Named Lyne by Steinbeck, she "is almost totally a Steinbeck invention, since Malory tells us only that she is responsible for Ewain's deeds on his quest, that her age is three score winters, and Malory leaves her unnamed. But Steinbeck does name her, and he gives her a distinctive characterization. Her character serves to illustrate how power should be wisely used, and, ironically, her wise use of her limited power underscores the unwise abuses of power made by Arthur and Morgan" (Hodges, "The Personae of Acts" 26). In fact, the section in which Lyne appears indicates the type of modernization that

Steinbeck increasingly believed he should be doing – not just a modernizing or even Americanizing of the language but a modernizing of the characters that involved a wholesale reworking of the original material.

Lyne is not the typical damsel of medieval literature. In a statement that seems to foreshadow Guinevere's complaint, she says of herself, "A little girl, hating embroidery, I watched the young boys practicing and I hated the hobbles of a gown" (210). So she dresses as a boy and wrestles with young men, and fights them with staves and with sword and shield. When she kills a young knight in a fair fight, she realizes she must give up fighting with men, but she does not lose her interest in their activities. So she uses her skill and knowledge to train and mold young knights, teaching them about every aspect of combat, from the care of horses to the type of armor they should wear. Her training ground is a medieval boot camp with long days of hard work and constant practice in the arts of war. But her training is successful. After ten months under her tutelage, Ewain, like other knights before him, emerges as a skilled warrior who is able to analyze his opponent's fighting style and discover his weaknesses. In his first battle following the training, Ewain defeats two knights fighting together against him. Clearly an independent, intelligent, and free-thinking woman, Lyne envisions a time when peasants like the Welsh bowmen who guard her camp will defeat armed knights. When Ewain protests that "no peasant will stand up to a noble knight, a man born to arms," she replies, "They may learn" (220).

Though Lyne is a minor character in the *Acts*, she is both indicative of Steinbeck's willingness to make more than minor alterations to Malory's text and suggestive of his strategy of modernizing the women of the story and of giving them an identity that the medieval romance denied them. Steinbeck thus seems to have anticipated one of the major developments in the popular Arthurian novels of the latter half of the twentieth century by emphasizing the roles of the women of the Arthurian legends.

Moreover, the portion of the *Acts* that Steinbeck completed shows a progression from straightforward modernization to the creation of a new Arthurian novel. Though he recognized that "Some things must be changed, edited, arranged," that he did not immediately set out to make such wholesale change is natural, especially since he felt that reworking Malory "is like rewriting the Bible" (Letter to Eugène Vinaver, dated August 27, 1959, cited in Mitchell 73). Steinbeck may, in fact, have been prevented from completing the project because of this change in his conception: his new emphasis would have meant going back and redoing sections like the story of Gareth in accordance with his new plan. (Steinbeck completed a modernization of Malory's tale of Gareth that was not published in the *Acts*, perhaps because it was a very faithful rendition without any of the elaborations on plot or character that are found elsewhere in the book.) Even though he did not totally realize his new intention, however, the *Acts* is a significant addition to the Arthurian tradition by a major American novelist.

Steinbeck's achievement in the *Acts* is largely a result of his focus on Lancelot, a character he said, in a letter dated July 25, 1959, he loved because he "is tested, he fails the test and still remains noble." Steinbeck had come to understand Lancelot, or at least to understand how he wanted to portray Lancelot. "He's my boy," Steinbeck wrote in the same letter. "I can feel him. And I'm beginning to feel Guinevere and out of that I will get to feel Arthur" (*Acts* 437–38). What he seemed to appreciate most about Lancelot was that he was struggling toward an unachievable but ennobling perfection. Steinbeck believed that "strength and purity lie almost exclusively in the struggle – the becoming" (Steinbeck, *Steinbeck: A Life in Letters* 741). It is this quality of struggle towards an unattainable goal rather than his prowess in battle that makes Lancelot a hero for Steinbeck, a hero who is as relevant to the modern world as he was to the medieval. Steinbeck identified Lancelot with another hero, President John F. Kennedy. In a letter to Mrs. Kennedy on February 25, 1964, Steinbeck observed that "The Western World has invented only one thing of the spirit and that is gallantry. You won't find it in any Eastern or Oriental concept. And I guess gallantry is that quality which, when faced with overwhelming odds, fights on as though it could win and by that very token sometimes does." He also mentions that he is sending to her "Sir Ector's lament over the body of Sir Launcelot" (*Steinbeck: A Life in Letters* 741), obviously because he felt the lament was applicable to Kennedy as another gallant hero.

Steinbeck compared writing to the quest for the Grail and the writer to a knight (*Steinbeck: A Life in Letters* 859, 649). And Steinbeck's Grail seems to have been a version of Malory modernized and Americanized in language, character, and plot. Though, like his self-character Lancelot, Steinbeck never achieved this Grail, he did, like Lancelot, accomplish many noble deeds. He blended thoroughly American motifs with the Arthurian world in a number of his novels. He demonstrated in his work the quality that he found so inspiring in Malory, sympathy for the oppressed as against the oppressor. And, though falling short in his quest to modernize Malory's great work, he did, like Lancelot, reveal his nobility through his struggle towards that end.

7

Contemporary Novelists

Just as John Steinbeck used Arthurian motifs in several of his novels and stories, so too have the Arthurian legends influenced the work of some of the most interesting and sometimes unlikely contemporary American writers. Tennessee Williams, for instance, wrote his "first literary piece" when he was twelve years old; his teacher had assigned the class to pick out a subject for a theme, and Tennessee "chose the Lady of Shalott, drifting down the river on a boat. He read the theme in front of the class," and it had a very good reception. "From that time on," Williams realized, "I knew I was going to be a writer" (Williams and Mead 23). And, indeed, in a number of his best plays, the image of the Lady of Shalott recurs, usually in the character of the woman who is willing to sacrifice everything for love, often with tragic consequences – one of the hallmarks of Williams' drama.

Arthurian themes are explored even more extensively in the works of many contemporary American novelists. Bernard Malamud, Ken Kesey, Walker Percy, Jerzy Kosinski, William Styron, Bobbie Ann Mason, Thomas Berger, Donald Barthelme, John Updike, and others do not simply retell the Arthurian stories but rather reinterpret them and recast them, often in uniquely American ways, to reflect topical as well as timeless concerns. While a few of those writers are drawn to Tristan and Isolt or to other specific characters or events in the legends, the majority who treat Arthurian themes in their fiction focus on the stories of the Grail – hardly a surprising fact, given that many contemporary novelists came of age and learned their craft in the wake of Eliot's *Waste Land*, which had tremendous literary and social reverberations. Their literary models also included such remarkable authors as Hemingway, Fitzgerald, Faulkner, and Steinbeck, all of whom explored the wasteland and related themes in their fiction. And postwar life offered further socioeconomic and political corroboration of the reality of the wasteland – a wasteland more extreme than Eliot could ever have conceived. The fallout of the atomic bomb ushered in the nuclear age of fear, anxiety, and distrust; political scandals violated the national innocence and violence, both global and local, haunted the national conscience. Science seemed to be shifting its collective force from improving life to systematizing death, while the inhumane technology that created eminently efficient warfare and other not-so-brave new worlds became itself a symbol of the plight of modern man overwhelmed by totalitarian forces very much out of his control. Perhaps

Kurt Vonnegut expressed it best when he wrote: "I thought scientists were going to find out exactly how everything worked, and then make it work better. . . . what actually happened when I was twenty-one was that we dropped scientific truth on Hiroshima" (*Wampeters* 161).

Yet, in the Grail story, novelists found not only an enduring appeal but also a valuable perspective from which to examine contemporary life, and they began reshaping the legend accordingly. For some, like Donald Barthelme, Bobbie Ann Mason, and Kurt Vonnegut, the image of the Fisher King, a wounded man in a wounded land, became a vehicle for denouncing the violence of war, from World War II to Vietnam, and the attendant destruction of traditional notions of morality. For others, like Walker Percy and William Styron, the wasteland suggested the dearth of real values, chivalric or otherwise, and the pervasiveness of evil and immorality; they envisioned modern man as a quester in search of healing through personal salvation or redemption. For still others, like Jerzy Kosinski, the traditional Grail had become corrupted in the modern world; the new knight errant had to seek in its place something less crass and commercialized and even more elusive: a sense of self.

Contemporary writers' quests for that new Grail took them in some interesting new directions: from baseball parks, polo fields, and Wild West round-ups (as sports increasingly became a metaphor for the quest) to prison cells and mental hospitals (as modern questers – male and female – increasingly pursued nontraditional methods to heal themselves and others); from concentration camps to pink palaces in postwar Brooklyn; from London during the blitz and Berlin after the bombings to rural Kentucky during the 1980s. In each case, however, the updating and Americanizing of the Arthurian themes – a blending of the real and the mythic – afforded fresh insights into contemporary concerns as well as clever and often surprising variations of an old, familiar legend.

Whereas Fitzgerald conflated the American Dream with the Arthurian legends in *The Great Gatsby*, Bernard Malamud used the framework of the Arthurian legends to explore – and to explode – another uniquely American myth, baseball, as a metaphor for contemporary American life. Like Fitzgerald, who retold the Grail story in a distinctly modern and American way, Malamud drew on events out of baseball lore and legend, including the 1949 hotel room shooting by a crazed female fan of Philadelphia Phillies infielder Eddie Waitkus (who came back the following year to lead the Phillies to their first pennant in forty years), the infamous Black Sox scandal of 1919, the many achievements of Babe Ruth, and the fate of "Casey at the Bat" (Helterman 23), to create a familiar contemporary setting upon which he superimposed his medieval story of a heroic quest.

The Natural (1952), Malamud's first novel, is the story of Roy Hobbs, a remarkable ballplayer who at nineteen is invited to try out as pitcher for the Cubs. But en route to Chicago, he is seduced – and almost destroyed – by a dark, mysterious woman named Harriet Bird, who hunts down star athletes and shoots them with a silver bullet. Fifteen years pass before Roy's near-lethal groin wounds heal and he regains his former prowess. Now the oldest rookie player, he makes it to the big leagues again – this time, though, not with the Cubs but with the New York Knights, the worst team in the National League. Roy instantly perceives that he has a "mission": to lead his fellow Knights to victory. That mission becomes particularly urgent when the Knights' manager, Pop Fisher, makes a deal with the team's majority owner, Judge Banner: unless the Knights have a winning year, Pop stands to lose his job, his financial stake in the team, and the single dream he has ever had, to retire to a farm after winning the pennant. Roy promises to play his best for Pop, and for a while that is precisely what he does. After Bump Baily, the Knights' star player, dies while attempting the catch of his life, Roy takes over Bump's role – both on the team and in the affection of Bump's girlfriend Memo Paris (Pop's niece) – and guides the team towards its best season ever.

Roy's intimacy with Memo, however, causes the worst slump of his career, a slump that has deleterious consequences for all of the Knights. Even after the earth-motherly Iris Lemon, a woman who "hate[s] to see heroes fail" and who appreciates that "without heroes we're all plain people and don't know how far we can go" (154), helps to restore his status as a popular idol, Roy cannot seem to resist Memo. Before a crucial game near the end of the season, he attends a party in Memo's hotel room. In contrast to the obligatory fasting of the Grail knight the night before his vigil, Roy over-indulges his gluttonous appetite, just as he had indulged a different appetite years earlier in Harriet's hotel room on the eve of his tryout with the Cubs – an indulgence that had earned him his first terrible blow to the gut. He lands in the hospital, where he is visited by the Judge, who tempts him to throw the last game. Roy realizes that, by taking the bribe, he could afford the kind of life Memo desires; and it seems that he is ready to accept the money, even though it means disappointing Pop and the rest of his teammates. The next day, during his first couple of attempts at the plate, a weak Roy intentionally hits foul balls and then strikes out; but at his final try at bat, after another encounter with Iris (during which she reveals that she is pregnant with his son), he finds a fresh energy and purpose. Unfortunately, it is too little, too late: he strikes out again, on a "bad ball" from the Pirates' young replace-ment pitcher, aptly named Youngberry, who – in the cyclic pattern of the novel and of Arthurian mythology, especially the legends of the Fisher King – becomes the new hero who displaces the aging one, much as Roy did fifteen years earlier when he struck out Walter the Whammer Wambold, the leading hitter of the American League and three times Most Valuable Player.[1]

---

1   Of the scene between Whammer and Roy, Earl R. Wasserman writes that "The young
     hero's symbolic slaying of the waning baseball god [Whammer] and thus his accession to

Roy, however, is more than just an ordinary "hero" (32) in the novel; from the beginning, he is described as a "bewitched" (14) and mystical figure, a contemporary knight who, Malamud repeats, could even have been "king" (156, 237), as his name suggests (Roy = *roi*).[2] Moreover, he is a "natural" not just in the modern sense of possessing an outstanding innate talent but also in the medieval sense of being an innocent fool. As Jeffrey Helterman explains, "The natural [of the Middle Ages], touched by God, retained his Edenic nature and seemed a fool to the rest of mankind. Though armed with a natural goodness, the natural was easy prey to the worldly-wise if he strayed from his God-given intuitions" (24).[3] At the age of nineteen, Roy is good enough to strike out the legendary Whammer; but he is not sufficiently worldly-wise to keep from succumbing to the charms of the mysterious Harriet, a Morgan le Fay figure who, suggests Sidney Richman, "in the tradition of grail literature, has been sent to test the hero's worthiness and exact punishment when he fails" (32). Nor is he sufficiently self-aware to grasp that it is not enough for a hero simply to have talent; he must also have a purpose in life. When Harriet asks what he hopes to accomplish, he replies

his own potency role is simultaneously the slaying of the father image [Sam] to which he had been a servile appendage" (52). This particular pattern is repeated often in the novel: as Roy assumes Bump's role on the Knights, and – of course – as Youngberry strikes out Roy in the crucial final game.

It is important to understand the various father-son relationships in the novel, from Roy's poor relationship with his own father to his tenuous relationships with his surrogate fathers (Sam Simpson, Pop Fisher). Part of Roy's reluctance to pursue a relationship with Iris is that she is a mother and a grandmother; commitment to her would force him into a (grand)fatherly role, which he resists. When he agrees to try to hit a home run for the ailing son of a truckdriver, the man calls after him, "A father's blessing on you"; but Roy is afraid of the "responsibility." Fatherhood is nonetheless thrust upon him, with the baby Iris is carrying and with the figure of substitute son Herman Youngberry, the young farm boy who becomes the new pitching sensation (as Roy did when he struck out the Whammer en route to his Cubs' try-out). Yet, as Earl Wasserman writes, "Roy's failure to be the hero is his failure to accept the mature father role." Thus, concludes Wasserman, "it is properly a boy who ends the novel, begging hopefully in disillusionment, 'Say it ain't true, Roy' " (64).

2 Roy is already "King of the Klouters" (164), though he soon becomes "the Clown Prince" (170).

John Kimsey also provides another interpretation of Roy as king. Kimsey writes that Roy Hobbs' "name – in a narrative full of archly symbolic names – suggests a king (roi) who is lame (hobbled)" (107). Though Kimsey's inference that Roy is lame is largely inaccurate, his suggestion that Roy is injured ("hobbled") certainly offers an interesting reading.

3 Wasserman suggests another perspective on Roy as the natural. He notes that "Roy, the questing Knight, by access to the sources of life, has restored virility to his community and the vegetative process to nature. In this radical sense of the word, he is the 'natural' " (48).

Other critics have also commented on Roy as the natural. For instance, Ellen Pifer (139-40), basing her definition on listings in the *OED*, sees Roy as "a man who rejects moral knowledge and, for most of his career, remains blind to moral responsibility." And John Kimsey (106), in explaining and contextualizing Roy's "feeble-mindedness," reaches back to Locke's *Essay Concerning Human Understanding* and Shakespeare's *The Tempest*.

that he wants people to say of him, "there goes Roy Hobbs, the best there ever was in the game." Harriet assumes there must be more to the nature of his quest, "something over and above earthly things – some more glorious meaning to one's life and activities . . . perhaps if you understood that our values must derive from – " (33–34). Not understanding "what she's been driving at," Roy feels "curiously deflated and a little lost, as if he had just flunked a test" (34). Fifteen years after his disastrous encounter with Harriet, he is certainly less innocent although not much wiser. He ignores Iris's important lesson about redemption through suffering, the lesson that people have two lives, "the life we learn with and the life we live with after that" (158); persists in chasing records rather than values; and continues to be distracted from virtue (Iris) by duplicity (Memo).

Roy's first publicly heroic feat, "the inspiring sight" of his victory over Whammer, is likened to "Sir Percy lancing Sir Maldemar" (32–33). Malamud's allusion, while humorous, is not spurious, for Roy is indeed much like the Percival of Arthurian legend, the sometimes foolish but ultimately heroic knight who fails to ask the correct question of the Fisher King and therefore cannot achieve his quest – at least not until a subsequent attempt, which Percival earns through his persistence.[4] Roy, too, is both fool and hero; and Roy, too, is persistent. (As Jonathan Baumbach notes, even Roy's name – "linguistically, king rustic" – is "an analogue of Percival" [107].) Like his medieval counterpart, Roy engages in games that are "contests of skill" (26) or "tourneys" (31). Although the team to which he has been signed consists of little more than a bunch of "cripples" (55), denizens of a modern waste-land, he wears their uniform with great pride; the first time he dons it, in fact, tears come to his eyes. In uniform, Roy takes on "a warrior's quality" (152). Despite the Knights' reputation, Roy immediately determines to apply all of his "magic" (119) to winning the contemporary Grail of the pennant. His "undeniable destiny," it seems, is to "lead the Knights" (168) to victory; so "even when no enemy was visible . . . he roused himself to do battle" (190). Without him, as the Judge recognizes, "the Knights are demoralized" (209) and unable to beat even a sandlot team.

At first it seems as if nothing can distract Roy from his goal. Other teams unsuccessfully try "probing his armor" (83); but Roy refuses to let anything bother him, "not sun, shadow, nor smoke-haze. . . . [H]e was good at gauging slices and he knew when to charge" (84). At the plate, he holds his position, his bat "lifted slightly above his head" (84), his stride "smooth," and his wrists ready to "slash" out at the necessary moment. Even after he becomes physically and ethically debilitated, he still makes a powerful impression: Vogelman, the opposing pitcher, imagines an indestructible "Roy, in full armor, mounted on a black charger" (231) coming directly at him, and he

---

4   For another view of Roy as Percival, see Peter Freese's "Parzival als Baseballstar: Bernard Malamuds *The Natural*."

passes out from fright, forcing the younger, more fearless Youngsberry to replace him on the mound.

Roy's "foolproof lance" (11) is Wonderboy, a naturally white bat hewn by Roy's hands from a lightning-felled tree near his childhood home.[5] Like Arthur's Excalibur, Roy's Wonderboy does not fail him; in fact, only when he corrupts the ideal for which Wonderboy stands by trying to foul out in the final game – a particularly passive and cowardly way of keeping his bargain with the Judge – does it lose its magic and break irreparably into several pieces. Earlier, however, when Roy used Wonderboy to play with honor, it "flashed in the sun" (80), so blindingly golden that "some of the opposing pitchers complained that it shone in their eyes" (90–91). During Roy's first time at bat, Wonderboy "cracked the sky. There was a strange, ripping sound and a few drops of rain spattered to the ground" (80), delivering the first signs of life to the parched wasteland of Knights' Field. With the magical bat, Roy's "performance" is so excellent that he breaks numerous records; yet, with "nothing of value yet to show for what he was accomplishing" (91), he feels strangely unsatisfied. When Roy begins to focus more on Memo than on the game, Pop urges him to break his slump by trying a different bat. But Roy realizes that, while Wonderboy shines whenever he does, "whatever is wrong is wrong with me and not my bat" (135). And, in the final game, even after Wonderboy is broken, Roy knows that he can still "cure what ailed him" with a single hit or "truly redeem" himself with "a homer, with himself scoring the winning run" (230). (It is worth noting that, like Arthur returning Excalibur to the lake after the final battle, Roy, after the last game, carefully buries Wonderboy in the earth, "wishing it would take root and become a tree" again [234].)

Like Sir Percival and the other heroes of medieval romance – and like their contemporary counterparts, such as Jay Gatsby – Roy Hobbs is a figure very much out of time. On the novel's opening page, he is described as "having no timepiece" (9). By returning to the game as the oldest rookie baseball player, he indeed tries to erase the damage done by Harriet's bullet and by the intervening years (much the way that Gatsby tries to ignore the fact of Daisy's five-year marriage to Tom Buchanan).[6] And for most of the

5 Wasserman calls Wonderboy a talisman of Roy's male potency, just as Harriet's hatbox is a talisman of female potency. "The two objects – bat and hat – correspond to the Arthurian symbols, sword and chalice, which Jessie Weston and others have identified as talismans of male and female potency. Each has selfishly made the talisman for himself and will not relinquish it to others" (52). Wasserman also offers an excellent analysis of Harriet's role as "terrible mother" and of Roy's groping of Harriet's breast and his other acts of infantilism, especially in the absence of a father figure.
6 Robert Ducharme lists a number of other parallels between *The Natural* and *The Great Gatsby*. He suggests that the incident involving Memo, the white Mercedes, and the boy and his dog in *The Natural* is analogous to the incident of the fatal accident on Long Island in *Gatsby*. "In that book too," writes Ducharme, "the fatal woman hits someone crossing the street and does not stop. Both Gatsby and Hobbs yearn for some precious lost quality of value located in the past; both have an irresistible attraction for a woman whom both

season, at least, Roy is quite successful. During one game, he even smashes a ball into the outfield clock, shattering it and scattering time everywhere, in "a symbolic gesture" that Helterman (32) notes is ultimately as futile as his desire to achieve a certain kind of immortality by fathering a child with the barren Memo. But Roy's past soon catches up to him, in turn obliterating his present successes. He realizes that Memo is not his girl but the girl of "the dead man," Bump; he is implicated by Max Mercy not only in the earlier scandal with Harriet but in the current "sell-out"; and in the novel's final paragraphs, as Malamud suggests, he "will be excluded from the game and all his records forever destroyed" (237). Thus, what is expunged is not the past that Roy has tried to repress but rather his glorious moment in the sun of Knights Field.

Distracted too long by a false Grail, symbolized by the sterile Memo (whose "sick breast" reveals her inability to nurture the hero or bear her own offspring and makes her "inimical to life in every way" [Helterman 28]), Roy overlooks the redeeming fecundity of the true Grail, symbolized by Iris Lemon (whose very name reinforces her fertility and vitality). Nowhere is the contrast between the two women more vivid than in the scenes involving children and automobile accidents. In the first of those scenes, after Roy's abortive attempt at lovemaking, Memo takes the wheel and drives his new white Mercedes away at more than ninety miles an hour. At the side of the road, Roy glimpses what he believes to be a boy and his dog; then he hears a thud, but Memo refuses to stop to investigate. Although there is no blood on the car, Roy is convinced that they have killed the child, and he suffers tremendous guilt over his complicity in the crime. (As several critics have demonstrated, the boy is likely more symbolic than real, an emblem of Roy's lost hopes and innocence, while Memo – like Harriet before her – is an agent of that loss and destruction.[7])

By contrast, Iris is connected with Roy's first selfless act, which also

vastly over-estimate; and both rely on money, dishonestly obtained, to secure that woman for them" (12). Ducharme also claims that it was Gatsby's belief in the power of wealth "that led him to the morally shabby life of an underworld figure. Similarly Roy is snared by belief in money and desire for Memo . . . [who] strikes the reader as remarkably like Daisy Fay" (11), especially when she confesses her fear of being poor.

   Jonathan Baumbach also notes resemblances between Roy and Gatsby: "Hobbs (like Gatsby) is part Grail knight and part absurd, existential hero, whose goal, to be 'the greatest in the game,' is meaningful only in terms of a perfect (romantic) commitment to an impossible dream" (107).

7 According to Pifer, "as a figment of Roy's longing, and of Malamud's art, he [the boy by the side of the road] is real insofar as he embodies that self or being Roy once was – and perhaps may still recover." When Roy fears that they have struck and killed the boy ("I heard somebody groan"), Memo's response ("That was yourself") is, writes Pifer, "more perceptive than she realizes. If the boy 'coming out of the woods' is the imaginative embodiment of Roy's own potential for self-recovery – for his emergence from the moral wilderness and 'the dark' – then Roy's fear that Memo has killed him is especially telling" since "Memo's seductive beauty, resembling Harriet Bird's, operates on Roy like fatal ambition" (144–45).

involves a boy injured in a car accident. As Babe Ruth actually did, Roy promises to hit a home run for the hospitalized boy who has lost his will to live. It is the first time in Roy's life that he attempts to assume any responsibility for someone other than himself. But his guilt over the boy he might have killed and his frustration over his affair with Memo leave him in a terrible slump, unable to concentrate on the game. When Iris, white rose in hand, stands up in the bleachers in a symbolic show of support, Roy responds by hitting the ball so hard that it bounces between the second baseman's legs and up to the very spot where Iris is standing. It is Iris, an inspiring vision, therefore, who helps him to fulfill his promise.

Iris, it turns out, is Roy's spiritual counterpart in many ways. She too has suffered: like Roy, she was the youthful victim of an unknown assailant, a man who had "pounced like a tiger" and raped her. At thirty-three, Iris decides (just as Roy does) to begin her life again – or more literally, to resurrect it at the point at which she had abandoned it years before. When she and Roy swim by moonlight in the waters of Lake Michigan – a contrast to the stagnant pool that Roy visits with Memo – Iris offers Roy an opportunity for rebirth and regeneration through commitment. He leaps to the lake bottom and as he ascends, according to Sidney Richman, sees "the form of the frantic Iris floating beyond his head in the emblem of the Grail, luminously gold and charged with love" (38). After they make love and she admits to him that she is a grandmother, Iris appears as another archetype, "a form of the ancient hag whom the knight must marry in order to attain his goal" (Richman 38) – although, ultimately, Iris is more of a fecund vegetation goddess than a hag, and such "marriage" offers precisely the fertility that is lacking in Roy's life.

But Roy can neither see Iris's real beauty nor accept the opportunity of rejuvenation she offers; after their evening together, he neglects her and continues to pursue Memo. His moral blindness is shared by several other characters in the novel, who, as Jeffrey Helterman (32–33) and others have demonstrated, are afflicted with various disorders of the eye. "Through the Keyhole" columnist Max Mercy, who in fact shows no mercy at all, has a "one-eyed obsession with finding the worst in anyone"; the myopic Judge Goodwill Banner, whose name belies his satanic nature, prefers to sit in rooms so dark that they suggest his own spiritual state; the glass-eyed gambler Gus Sands, who manipulates events for his own greedy purposes, is indeed a magical Merlin in a kingdom of wastelanders who are blind to nobler causes.

Because of his own blindness, Roy fails both in his quest for Knightly fame and in his quest to help others, including the Fisher King, Pop Fisher.[8]

---

8   Although Pop Fisher is clearly the Fisher King figure of the novel, it is worth noting the existence of a secondary Fisher King – Happy Pellers, the groundskeeper of Knights Field.

A former ballplayer, Pop once played in the World Series against the Athletics, but as he was circling the bases in the crucial seventh game "his legs got tangled under him and he fell flat on his stomach, the living bejesus knocked out of him" (62); ever since, he has lived with the painful memory of what the newspapers called "Fisher's Famous Flop." When Roy first meets him, Pop – now the team's manager and part owner – is seated at the edge of a "dusty field" complaining, literally and metaphorically, that "it's been a blasted dry season. No rains at all. The grass is worn scabby in the outfield and the infield is cracking. My heart feels as dry as dirt" (45). And he has a wound – athlete's foot on his hands – that will not heal. As Roy begins winning games for the Knights, the rains come; Knights Field grows green again; and even Pop "got into the spirit . . . He unwound the oily rags on his fingers and flushed them down the bowl. His hands healed and so did his heart" (93). But when Roy, distracted by Memo, goes into a slump, Pop again feels the pain of his wounds and restores the bandages to "his pusing fingers" (138). Nevertheless Pop maintains his faith in Roy, believing that he alone will deliver the pennant and Pop's other lifelong dreams. During the final game, however, after Roy deliberately strikes out, "there were no Knight hits after [that;] . . . a breeze blew dust all over the place" (221); and Pop recognizes that his last hope is gone. Removing his false teeth, which felt like rocks in his mouth, Pop "swayed on the bench, drooling a little out of the corners of his puckered mouth" (228), his eyes ringed in black, his voice broken. The prospect of fulfilling the Knights' "mission" had been within Roy's reach; but Roy squanders Pop's dream along with his own, until all that remains is the foul dust of the field after yet another losing season and the dashed hopes in the eyes of the little boys who had once aspired to be Knights themselves.

Critics have commented on various aspects of Malamud's Grail story. Sidney Richman, for instance, identifies the "pattern of the grail-quest" (33) underlying the novel, especially in incidents such as the trip to the netherworld-like nightclub, the Pot of Fire. According to Richman, Roy fails because "he hides the secrets of his past from all eyes . . . unlike the grail knight who bore the evidence of his perfidy for all to see in a gesture of humility." The secrecy breeds such guilt that Roy "not only suffers on the field but must encounter, like knights in the Chapel Perilous, the visitations of bats, monsters and formless spectres" (35). Robert Ducharme, on the other hand, links each of the characters in *The Natural* to the Grail stories of Frazer, Weston, and Eliot: Roy as "a modern Sir Percival in quest of the major league pennant," Gus as Merlin, Iris as the Lady of the Lake, Memo as Morgan, and the derisive fan in the bleachers Otto Zipp "as the Arthurian dwarf who taunts and scourges the questing hero" (9). John Kimsey asserts that *The Natural* draws on Chrétien's *Perceval* and Malory's *Balin, or the Knight with the Two Swords* (allegories "of the male quest for individuation" and essays "on the meaning of heroism" [103]), while Peter L. Hays tries to find the

origins of *The Natural* and Malamud's other "medieval stories" in another of
Chrétien's works, "Lancelot, or The Knight of the Cart."[9] Jonathan Baumbach
also identifies Hobbs with Percival; he concludes, though, that while the
notion of "Sir Percival as baseball star is a witty idea," the pleasure of the
novel is not in its Arthurian allegory but rather "in the hallucinated and idio-
matic particulars of its narrative" (111). Earl R. Wasserman, however, argues
just the opposite: in perhaps the most perceptive essay of all on *The Natural*,
he writes that Malamud avoided the risk of contrived allegory that lurks in
inventing a fiction in order to carry a meaning precisely by drawing on
memorable real events; yet "the clean surface of this baseball story . . .
repeatedly shows beneath its translucency another myth of another culture's
heroic ritual by which man once measured the moral power of his human-
ness." Roy at bat "is every quester who has had to shape his own character
to fulfill his goal"; by drawing his material from actual baseball lore and yet
fusing it with Arthurian legend, "Malamud sustains his novel in a region
that is both real and mythic, particular and universal" (47).[10]

Malamud also incorporated aspects of Arthurian myth in works other
than *The Natural*.[11] Most of Malamud's novels, in fact, feature Ladies of the
Lake (many of whom swim naked, like Iris, or bathe nude, like Pauline
Gilley in *A New Life*); employ archetypal Fisher King figures (Morris of *The
Assistant*, Salzman of "The Magic Barrel," Shmuel of *The Fixer*, Fairchild in *A
New Life*); and are set in moral and/or economic wastelands (the stultifyingly
dull Lower East Side of New York City in *The Assistant*, the intellectually
sterile Cascadia College of *A New Life*, the desolate "valley of bones" over
which Tsar Nicholas II rules in *The Fixer*). And, as Max Schulz observes, all of
the novels are about maimed kings or questers and about the vegetation
rituals, nature cycles, and other myths of rebirth that underlie the Grail
stories. In *The Assistant*, for instance, after the death of Morris Bober, the
goodhearted but luckless Jewish grocer who runs a small store in a largely

9   Hays's arguments in "Malamud's Yiddish-Accented Medieval Stories" are often broad
    but nonetheless worth considering. "In Malamud's fiction," he writes, "the protagonists
    suffer predicaments like Lancelot's in Chrétien's tale. "Thus, just as Lancelot, the Knight
    of the Cart, is thoroughly reviled for the crime of love, so are Frank Alpine, Sy Levin, and
    Arthur Fidelman. As Lancelot is reproached by his lover, so Roy is by Harriet, Memo, and
    Iris; Frank is by Helen . . . . Like Lancelot, Malamud's heroes are cut to ribbons in their
    quests for love and fortune. Also like Lancelot, Malamud's heroes persist. Where the
    medieval knight went in search of glory, conquest, and approval of a beloved,
    Malamud's protagonists search for an authentic self and life-style, an identity worthy of
    commitment. Like Lancelot, they often conceal their identities – Roy Hobbs hides his
    past, Frank Alpine covers his face with a mask, Sy Levin covers his with a beard, and Bok
    becomes Dologushev" (90). Hays also identifies rebirth themes in Malamud's that are
    similar to those in Chrétien (91).
10 Similarly, Sheldon J. Hershinow suggests that "by melding the Arthurian quest with a
    baseball story, Malamud extends the quest beyond time, making Roy Hobbs's baseball
    career symbolic of the human psychological and moral situation" (21).
11 Malamud's interest in the Arthurian may have originated in his readings of the works of
    Thomas Hardy, the subject of his master's thesis.

non-Jewish part of town, Morris's assistant and adopted son Frank Alpine "almost triumphantly renews Morris' existence" (Baumbach 120–21). At Morris's burial, which occurs in the spring, Frank falls into the gravesite, not only achieving a final identification with Morris, whom he had earlier robbed and injured, an act for which he has since been compensating, but also rising from the grave as Morris himself in a symbolic resurrection. Frank converts to Judaism; is circumcised; assumes Morris's life at the store, even to the point of rising an hour earlier than he must to sell the three-cent roll to the "Polisheh," as Morris had; committing himself in marriage to Morris's daughter; and otherwise fulfilling the role of the son that Morris and Ida had lost many years earlier. And in at least one episode of *A New Life*, S. Levin, who has travelled from east to west in the hope of re-establishing his identity, takes on a specifically knightly guise. Like Sir Percival in search of the Grail, he sets off to meet one of his students in San Francisco. Before leaving, he pictures himself "speeding up hill and down in his trusty Hudson, his lance at his side, driving through a series of amorous and philanthropic adventures" (136). The episodes of Levin's journey, according to Marc L. Ratner, include pursuit by a fiendish road hog, the passage through the mountains, and the breakdown of Levin's steed, all of which "take on the attributes of a trip to the medieval Chapel Perilous. Log trucks are described as giants; he is pulled out of the ditch by a wizened elfin farmer; his journey is blocked by a nightmare white mule that he passes by means of the magic charm of a lifesaver" (673). And in "Lady of the Lake," one of the short stories collected in *The Magic Barrel*, Henry Levin (newly self-christened Henry R. Freeman) learns an important lesson about integrity and the Jewish identity he has been attempting to hide from Isabella, the "Lady of the Lake" of the story's title, who – like the traditional Lady of the Lake – is a teacher of questing knights. But it is in *The Natural* that Malamud most comprehensively reinterprets Arthurian mythology, assimilating and utilizing it to define the historical perspective of contemporary America.

A Hollywood version of *The Natural*, starring Robert Redford as Roy Hobbs, followed in 1984. Predictably, the film (directed by Barry Levinson) turned Malamud's darkly comic tale into fairly standard cinematic fare, which included a happy ending: Roy does not accept the bribe, and – although badly wounded – he bangs a home run out of the park, in the process knocking out the stadium lights as if he were shooting off fireworks. Levinson's happy Hollywood ending is reinforced by a happy beginning: unlike Malamud's Roy, the film's Roy has a sensitive, devoted father; and it is to his father's home, the family farm, that Roy, Iris, and their adolescent son ultimately return. (The film's Iris, played by Glenn Close, has just one child, the product of her youthful relationship with Roy.) In the film's last scene, in fact, Roy and his son play ball on the farm as Iris looks on, much the way that, in an earlier scene, the elder Hobbs played ball with a teenaged Roy as a young Iris watched. Like the movie as a whole, however, the ending is rather melodramatic and lacks the darker world view and many of the Arthurian and other mythic undertones that make the novel so successful and so complex.

Whereas Malamud's *The Natural* is a tale of a contemporary knight errant whose greed and selfish ambition prevent him from redeeming Pop Fisher and restoring the wasteland, Ken Kesey's first novel, *One Flew Over the Cuckoo's Nest* (1961), is the story of a decidedly unconventional Grail knight who sacrifices himself for a group of wastelanders, the inmates of a mental ward controlled by a dehumanized and dehumanizing force called the "Combine" and the robotic nurse Ratched who acts as the Combine's agent. Randle Patrick ("Mack") McMurphy, the novel's protagonist and Grail knight figure, saves the men from being swallowed up in the institution's technological horror and anonymity. He makes them aware of their own manhood, in the sense of both their masculinity and their humanity (Leeds, *Kesey* 15), and restores their individual and collective potency so that they can assert their own identities and oppose Big Nurse's mindless regimen.

A gambler and profiteer, McMurphy is an unlikely hero; by feigning madness to avoid prison, he is assigned to Ratched's ward, where he virtually explodes on the scene. Even the acute patients sense that the red-headed Irish brawler is "different from anybody been coming on this ward for the past ten years, different from anybody they ever met outside" (83). And different he is. His resonant voice and hearty laugh pierce the silent void and assail the asylum's order. Yet his very disruption of the mechanical routine is actually a restoration of normalcy. Like the Grail knight returning life to the wasteland, McMurphy's eccentric behavior generates some intense passions in a conspicuously passionless environment. Unwilling merely to bear passive witness to the other inmates' lethargy, he fills the sterile ward with sounds long unheard – ribald jokes and songs, which echo in the halls and challenge the Combine's authority as they revive the patients' saltpetered spirits. His laughter is especially welcome because it is unlike the derisive and belittling noises the inmates are used to: the snickering orderlies, "mumbling . . . and humming hate and death and other hospital secrets" (10); the falsity of "Public Relation," leading his tours through Ratched's model ward; the tight-lipped pleasantries of the hypocritical Big Nurse and her surrogates. Above all, McMurphy uses his laughter as a weapon to short-circuit Ratched's machine by turning her humorlessness against her. For instance, when the ward policy prohibits him from leaving the mess hall until exactly 7:30 a.m. even though he is finished with his breakfast long before, he uses the extra time to make bets on whether he can shoot a pat of butter onto the face of the clock and make it stick. And when Ratched puts him on latrine duty, he responds graciously that every time he swabs a crapper, he will think of her.

Unused as they are to humor, the inmates do not laugh easily at first. The institution itself prohibits it: the novel's narrator Chief Bromden says, "the

air is pressed in by the walls, too tight for laughing" (48). Indeed, the stuttering, innocent Billy "opens his mouth but can't say a thing" (92); the emasculated Harding tries to laugh but makes merely a "mousy little squeak" (158);
and Chief, his brain addled by repeated electroshock therapies, does not
speak or laugh at all. When he finally utters his first words and attempts to
laugh along with McMurphy, "it was a squawking sound, like a pullet trying
to crow. It sounded more like crying than laughing" (185). Yet, even when he
gets little reaction, McMurphy persists in engaging the men, because he
realizes that once they can laugh at themselves, they will be less likely to be
hurt by the vitriolic remarks of Ratched and her staff – and they can begin to
recover the potency they have lost.

Similarly, McMurphy makes a point of reaching out to the patients with a
friendly outstretched hand. The human touching contrasts with the cold and
sterile treatment they receive from Ratched; unlike her mechanical actions,
his is a warm, natural, spontaneous gesture. Consequently, McMurphy's big
hand, symbolizing masculinity and power, becomes the answer to Ratched's
momism and represents his ability to reverse the deadly and emasculating
monotony of her ward. As with McMurphy's laughter, however, the inmates
do not know how to respond to his touch. Harding hides his dainty white
hands between his knees; phobic Big George shies back from McMurphy's
"unsanitary" hand; while Chief contrasts McMurphy's strong hand with his
own "stick of an arm" (27). Yet throughout the novel, McMurphy refuses to
release his grip on the inmates, both literally and metaphorically. Even
though he knows he cannot succeed, he strains to lift the enormous control
panel; the attempt leaves his hands bloody and damaged. But it also embold-
ens the men to raise their own hands – for the first time – in a vote of
defiance against Ratched, who refuses to let them watch the World Series.
Then, having shown the inmates that they can function again as individuals
within the asylum walls, McMurphy decides to prove they can manage
outside as well. He takes Bromden and the other patients fishing; and when
they start landing fish and crying for his help, he stands aside, forcing them
to use their own hands, to rely on their own resources and feel responsible
for each other, to reclaim their identities as capable and functioning persons
– a victory they celebrate with a drunken party upon their return to the
ward. Yet it is a sign of how difficult the task of this Grail knight is that he
must teach Bromden, the wounded Fisher King figure in the novel, to fish,
that he must make Bromden a Fisher King before he can heal him.

From the beginning, no one benefits more from Mack's friendly hand than
Chief Bromden. Whereas others have come to take Chief's hulking silence
for granted, McMurphy pays attention to him and, with the simple offering
of a stick of Juicy Fruit gum, brings him back from his self-imposed silence.
Later, McMurphy unties the bedsheets that restrain Chief, restoring a part of
Bromden's psychological manhood, which in turn triggers his sexual
re-awakening. The next morning, when the aides hand Chief his customary

broom so that he can sweep the floor for them, he refuses. His potency regained, Chief does not need the broom's dead wood to define him ever again.

McMurphy works similar wonders on the other men trapped in the wasteland of the ward. He helps Harding to find the courage to criticize Ratched and to stand up to his emasculating wife Vera, who – like Ratched – goes straight for his "everlovin' *balls*" (57). On the fishing trip, Harding is further fortified: he volunteers to go without a life jacket on board the boat, helps reel in a prize fish, and laughs loudly at himself, acknowledging that his mental illness has given him "an aspect of power, *power*" (202). Later, after McMurphy's incapacitation, Harding assumes a role of leadership on the ward as he prepares to check himself out and return to life outside the asylum with Vera. Even the self-crucified Ellis eventually draws some strength from Mack. As the group departs on the fishing trip, "Ellis pulled his hands off the nails in the wall and squeezed Billy Bibbit's hand and told him to be a fisher of men" (198). The innocent, stuttering Billy becomes that – and a fisher of women – and for a while it seems that he too will be redeemed by McMurphy's efforts. Asserting his masculinity, Billy chooses (as Harding did) to go without a life jacket on the boat; then he imitates Mack's strong hands by drawing ink tattoos on his own; and finally he loses his virginity to McMurphy's girl before Ratched shames him into suicide.

If McMurphy's initials – R.P.M. – suggest one kind of force, his nemesis Big Nurse represents another. A mechanical marvel, she is precise, efficient, and robotlike; her cold sterility sharply contrasts with McMurphy's earthy sexuality and fertility. Ratched has "dry-ice eyes" (31); she "freezes" (88) people with her stare or blasts them with a "blizzard"-like fury; "frost forms" (89) when she moves. "It's a little cold where the nurse just went past," says Chief, "and the white tubes in the ceiling circulate frozen light like rods of glowing ice, like frosted refrigerator coils rigged up to glow white" (130) in her wake. Ratched's iciness extends to her own sexuality, which she tries urgently to repress. Her huge breasts, however, betray her vulnerability, which McMurphy exploits when he assaults and chokes her at the end of the novel. By ripping her starchy white uniform and exposing her chest in full view of all of the men – inmates, orderlies, and doctors – around her, McMurphy succeeds in asserting his dominant sexuality and forces Ratched to acknowledge the femininity – and the very humanity – she has denied. Without the sterile wrappings of her uniform to shield her any longer, Big Nurse loses her intimidating presence as well as her authority. Her only recourse is to invoke the now-diminishing power of the Combine and, in a symbolic act of castration, to have McMurphy lobotomized. Yet her victory is Pyrrhic at best: McMurphy has already passed his strength and manhood on to the other inmates so that not one new knight but several rise out of the wasteland in his stead. Chief Bromden, after suffocating McMurphy to end his suffering and to prevent Ratched from using his lobotomized shell to keep other patients in line, recalls McMurphy's earlier lesson-by-example. Chief lifts the control panel, which represents the monolithic weight of the Combine, and with a ripping crash heaves it through the asylum window – the same escape route McMurphy had planned to use for his breakout. "Like a bright cold water baptizing the sleeping earth" (271), the glass shatters and a reborn Chief vaults to freedom and to his tribal land at Columbia Gorge, leaving behind him forever the fog and the Combine and the Big Nurse's frozen smile. And as the other inmates begin to check themselves out or request transfer to other wards, Big Nurse is voiceless – and powerless – to prevent them. Silenced, Madame Sosostris can no longer rule the wasteland.

From the increasingly difficult trials that McMurphy as knight and deliverer must endure to the wasteland of the ward that he ultimately restores, Kesey's richly mythic first novel is replete with elements of the traditional Grail quest and the story of the Fisher King. Not surprisingly, Arthurian images appear as well in other of Kesey's works. *Demon Box*, for instance, opens with a short poem called "Tarnished Galahad," the name given to Kesey by the judge who sentenced him on charges of marijuana possession, from which he soon fled to Mexico.

The concept of the "tarnished Galahad" and other Arthurian motifs are also evident in Kesey's most recent novel, *Last Go Round* (1994), written with fellow Merry Prankster Ken Babbs. A combination historical novel and dime Western, *Last Go Round* tells the story of three good friends – "Nigger George" Fletcher, a popular black cowboy; Jackson Sundown, a Nez Percé Indian cowboy; and Johnathan E. Lee Spain, a fresh-faced white boy from Tennessee – who compete in the Pendleton (Oregon) Round Up of 1911, a legendary event that Kesey describes in mythic and Arthurian terms. Part of the "famous cowboy chivalry" (3) of the past, the three are likened to knights on a divine mission westward "to tame a wild land" (84). Each rides into Pendleton "shining" (10): George, as the "champion" (84) of the crowd and the "Black King of the Broncbusters, just waitin' to be crowned" (19); Johnathan as "Misteh Enchanted" (34); and Jackson as "the right full hair [heir] to the throne" (17). George, abandoned at birth and raised among the Nez Percé, and Jackson – competitors on the rodeo circuit – are brothers of sorts, both raised in a Native American tradition that in many ways parallels the Arthurian (e.g., the series of trials that the warrior must pass; the lesson of the blade in the water; the spectacular *Ko Shar* throne ["Nobody knows where it came from" (54)], a kind of Siege Perilous in which only those who speak the truth can sit). And both men occasionally engage in behavior that disappoints their naive protégé. At one point, for instance, Johnathan calls them "tarnished Galahads" and realizes that not one image from their previous night's debauchery "still shined. . . . My frontier Camelot was turning out to be infested with rats and riddled with weakness and greed" (167). Even "the fair maid Meyerhoff," described elsewhere in the novel not

only as one of the Round Up princesses but as "the *crown* princess" (85) and
for whom Johnathan is glad to ride "to glory or doom," is evidently "more
interested in racehorses than in a shining knight from Nashville" (167). But,
after "lick[ing his] wounds and rest[ing his] bones and get[ting] revitalized"
by new contests of skill, Johnathan sees that his embattled heroes had indeed
been able to "forswear whatever dark deals they'd been tenderized into"
(179, 167); and the conclusion of the Round Up, when in a surprise decision
he is crowned "the first World! Champion! All Round Cowboy" (222) while
George walks away with the actual trophy (a silver saddle), provides "a
medium-happy ending . . . with a certain amount of sadness and a twist of
irony" in which "the Bad Guys had been routed, their last low act transformed into an uplifting solution, [and] just about everybody was satisfied,
one way or another" (236).

Though both George and Jackson are generally portrayed as noble characters throughout the novel, it is Johnathan who represents the Grail knight;
like his medieval counterpart, the untried young man must overcome a
variety of trials that test his courage and resolve. "*Any* greenhorn," George
tells him, "is going to have to endure a certain amount of initiation" (104),
and both George and Jackson offer him many "valuable lesson[s] in the
course of [his] education" (97), from pointers on racing and broncobusting to
advice on romance. The more time Johnathan spends with them, the more he
realizes that he "is getting shed of everything I call my own . . . even my
given name" (62) and being transformed into a champion himself. Finally,
after the appropriate preparation and introspection, he is ready to spur his
mount "toward the jousts – a knight alone" (135) – where he achieves the
quest on which he had originally set out.

That quest includes many elements typical of medieval romance – a battle
with a giant (Frank Gotch, the wrestling ogre nicknamed "the Cruel
Crusher"); the wearing of a lady's favor into battle (the black silk from his
friend Sue Lin's bloomers); even an "enchanted chalice" (176) given by a
maiden (a cream bottle from Sarah Meyerhoff, which he must fill with milk
from a wild cow in one of the rodeo's events[12]). Similarly, the often fierce
competition among the cowboy-knights is described in terms common to
medieval romance. A contest between George and Jackson, for instance, is
"deadly serious," with both men "armed and bloodied." Jackson holds a big
twisted tree-root "like a transmogrified snake," while George wields a
jagged shard of crockery that "gleamed like a battle-ax as [he] hewed the air
in front of him" (159–60). And during the three-way tie-break that decides
the All Round Cowboy of the Round Up event, each man proves himself to

12 "One of these crystal chalices is enchanted," Sarah tells Johnathan. "If you can choose that
magic bottle from among all the others you have a chance to change your fortune. Your
cloudy past will clear up. Your murky future will open like a blossom and your sulky
nature will cheerfully pour forth fruit forever. Treasures untold will be yours. Choose
one" (176).

be worthy of the honor. Jackson rides so well and so bravely that "every watching wife is uplifted; every husband's heart made proud" (213); George rides so flamboyantly that his saddle hits the ground and scatters to pieces at the end; and Johnathan rides so gracefully that he feels the "tingling residue [of grace] in its wake" (220). Though Johnathan wins by default, the celebration of his victory is royal by any standard, even down to the "royal regalia" – the purple cape, rhinestone crown, and queenly sceptre – worn by the "queen" (223) who awards him the prize.

The notion of the quest is central to *Last Go Round*, just as it is to all of Kesey's fiction. Whether that quest takes the form of a search for a specific Grail, as in the rodeo title and trophy the three cowboys covet, or of some other attempt to find affirmation of life in the wasteland, as in McMurphy's struggle against Big Nurse and the institution, the application of Arthurian motifs to contemporary realities (e.g., the Wild West expansion of the American Dream at the end of the nineteenth century and the beginning of the twentieth, as portrayed in *Last Go Round*; the pervasive modern fear of the institution's encroachment on the individual, as portrayed in *One Flew Over the Cuckoo's Nest*) adds an important mythic dimension to Kesey's protagonists and to their adventures.

In a self-interview, "Questions They Never Asked Me (So He Asked Them Himself)" (79), another contemporary novelist, Walker Percy described the writing process rather simply: " – something opens. A miracle occurs. Somebody must have found the Grail. The fisher king is healed, the desert turns green – or better still: the old desert is still the old desert but the poet names it and makes it a new desert."

Not only did Percy "find the Grail" through the writing of his own fiction; he – like Malamud and Kesey and other prominent contemporary writers – also made the search for the Grail and the healing of the Fisher King the subject of some of his best work. From Binx Bolling in *The Moviegoer* (1961) and Will Barrett in *The Last Gentleman* (1966) and *The Second Coming* (1980), who discover the potential for redemption (Binx, in the Ash Wednesday that ends his personal Mardi Gras; Will, in the sacramental baptism that ends the first novel and in his life-affirming marriage to Allie in the second), to Dr. Tom More, a fallen version of his namesake and Percy's own knight of faith, who struggles against a wasteland of scientific and sexual secularism (Crowley and Crowley, "Walker Percy's Grail" 256) in *Love in the Ruins* (1971) and *The Thanatos Syndrome* (1987) – the protagonists of all six of Percy's novels are contemporary seekers in a modern wasteland.

Specifically Arthurian motifs appear in Percy's fiction as early as his first novel; and, as in Faulkner's work, those motifs serve as paradigms for the Southern chivalric code, especially for the southern sense of stoicism in defeat. Binx's Aunt Emily Cutrer in *The Moviegoer*, for instance, recalls her brother Alex, who had "the Rupert Brooke-Galahad sort of face" (24) and who died a hero's death in the Argonne. Emily's husband Jules also employs Arthurian imagery, albeit in a more modern way, by applying it – as Fitzgerald did – to the sport of football. He describes a Tulane University goal-line stand against LSU as "King Arthur standing fast in the bloodred sunset against Sir Modred and the traitors" (30). Later in the novel, suspecting that Binx has betrayed her code of moral behavior, Emily confronts him upon his return from Chicago. As they gaze at a small Excalibur-like letter opener, a "soft iron sword she has withdrawn from the grasp of a helmeted figure on the inkstand" (221), Emily realizes that the blade's tip is bent – bent, as Binx alone is aware, from his attempt years earlier to pry open a drawer with it. Accusing him of having broken a "sacred trust" by sexually compromising her stepdaughter Kate, she "raises the sword to Prytania Street" and claims that she has tried to "save" him by passing on to him the one significant heritage of the family: "a certain quality of spirit, a gaiety, a sense of duty, a nobility worn lightly, a sweetness, a gentleness with women – the only good things the South ever had and the only things that really matter in this life" (221, 224). Eventually Binx does find his Grail, though for him, as for so many of Percy's other characters, that Grail manifests itself not so much as provocative and legendary symbol but rather as sacrament, its ultimate incarnational meaning. J. Donald and Sue Mitchell Crowley write that Binx ends his Grail quest "not in an idealized past but rather in the present of the communal feast of fish with his mother and her family, in the Mass they attend together, in his handicapped and holy brother Lonnie's devotion to sacramental Penance and his request for last rites, and, finally, in his love for and marriage to Kate" (Crowley and Crowley, "Walker Percy's Grail" 258, 260).[13]

Percy's most dedicated Grail seeker is Lancelot Andrewes Lamar, the protagonist and narrator of Percy's fourth novel, *Lancelot* (1977). Unlike his medieval counterpart, however, who searches for a Holy Grail that he has only glimpsed, Percy's Lancelot seeks to discover an undeluded memory of his past – or, as Robert Coles observes, Percy's Lancelot "begs to remember so that once and for all he can forget" (220). After years of what he believes is a happy marriage, Lancelot learns that his beautiful, voluptuous wife has been unfaithful to him. Margot, Texas-rich but low born, had aspired to

---

13 Crowley and Crowley observe that "each work [by Percy] ends with a sacrament, Walker Percy's Grail. In *The Moviegoer* Binx follows the Mardi Gras of his life with the penitential understanding of Ash Wednesday. Like Chrétien's Percival on Good Friday, he then has the potential to see the Grail. . . . *The Last Gentleman* ends with a baptism in Sante Fe, *Love in the Ruins* with a Christmas Mass. *The Second Coming*, the novel which follows *Lancelot*, is as much about life as *Lancelot* is about death. It offers an answer to both the malaise and the old and new adulteration of love in the truly life-enhancing coming together and marriage of Will Barret [sic] and Allie, herself a sacrament for Will. The 'Space Odyssey,' the last chapter of *Lost in the Cosmos*, concludes with the ancient Abbot Liebowitz offering Mass for an extraordinarily ecumenical group of survivors as the world begins over again after the nuclear holocaust of the obscene year 2069." And *The Thanatos Syndrome* "concludes with a Mass of the Epiphany, the feast which celebrates Christ's being shown forth to the world" ("Walker Percy's Grail" 274–75).

marry up; her original attraction, in fact, was as much to Lancelot's name and ancestral property as to Lancelot himself. After their marriage, she devotes herself to renovating Lancelot's dilapidated mansion, the Joyous-Gard-like sanctuary called Belle Isle, and – when the renovation is complete – to acting in films that she helps to underwrite, films that are produced by her former lover, Robert Merlin. Although, as John Gardner noted, Margot takes on Lancelot's class as she takes on accents in her third-rate acting roles, even from the beginning there was no hope that she would be faithful. So, "out of his disappointment and jealousy – and out of his sophisticated modern sense that there are no evil acts, no good acts either, only acts of sickness, on one hand, and acts flowing from unrecognized self-interest, on the other – Lancelot turns his wife's betrayal into a central philosophical mystery" (Gardner 58). Lancelot muses that "the more we know about the beauty and order of the universe, the less God has to do with it. I mean who cares about such things as the Great Watchmaker? But what if you could show me a *sin*? a purely evil deed, an intolerable deed for which there is no explanation?" Later, he turns the question back on itself: "In times when nobody is interested in God, what would happen if you could prove the existence of sin, pure and simple. . . . If there is such a thing as sin, evil, a living malignant sore, there must be a God" (52). Thus, according to Lancelot, either good is merely an illusion, in which case there is no God, or the existence of evil can in fact be affirmed, in which case God can be glimpsed by His shadow.

It is this question concerning the existence of true evil that sets Lancelot off on his quest, which inverts the traditional quest of medieval romance. "We've spoken of the Knights of the Holy Grail," Lancelot tells his old friend Percival, who serves as both his psychiatrist and his father-confessor throughout the novel. "But do you know what I was? The Knight of the Unholy Grail. In times like this when everyone is wonderful, what is needed is a quest for evil" (138). And "so Sir Lancelot set out, looking for something rarer than the Grail. A sin" (140). To Percival, Lancelot reveals the ways he has pursued evil, beginning with voyeurism, by which he confirms what he has already suspected – that his wife and almost everyone else around him have betrayed traditional values – and ending with murder, by which Lancelot expects to learn just how evil feels. As he probes Margot's adulterous behavior, Lancelot alternates between an almost scientific dispassion and a philosophic questioning; yet the more he uncovers about the nature of her unfaithfulness – especially after he sends Elgin, the son of the black family retainer, to spy on her and his older daughter and to film their indiscretions – the more Lancelot comes alive. He tells Percival that it is strange how such a discovery, "of evil, of a kinsman's dishonesty, a wife's infidelity, can shake you up, knock you out of your rut, be the occasion of a new way of looking at things." Later, he connects his wife's infidelity to his own moment of revelation: "I discovered my own life" (51). Lancelot had indeed been drifting for

years, living without any real sense of purpose. Having abandoned his early
idealism, during which he wrote briefs for the NAACP and performed other
meaningful work, he had fallen into a pattern of almost aristocratic idleness.
Only his "peculiar quest" (137) reinvigorates him – at least for a time. But
once he actually orchestrates Margot's murder and the deaths of her colleagues, Lancelot finds that he feels little satisfaction; instead, he feels
nothing at all.

Lancelot is able to relate the details of his experiences to Percival because
he is a fellow quester seeking to fill a void in his own life and to discover his
own version of the Grail. And even though Percival is silent for most of the
novel (he utters "yes" a few times and "no" once, on the last two pages of
the text), his presence is central to the narrative. "I am reliving my quest with
you" (137), Lancelot tells his old friend. And indeed Percival, who shares
Lancelot's sense that something in contemporary life is deficient or, at best,
awry, comes to know the nature of his own quest only when he hears the
story of Lancelot's antithetical one. J. Donald and Sue Mitchell Crowley note
that "As the medieval friends Lancelot and Percival sought each other
during their Grail quests, so these two twentieth-century souls are deeply
interdependent and, in Percy's word, potentially 'intersubjective.' " Yet their
choices, especially at the end of the novel, are as opposite as the dual view
onto Lafayette Cemetery (suggestive of both revolutionary chivalry and
death) and "Annunciation Street" (evocative of new, redemptive life) from
Lancelot's cell in New Orleans' "Center for Aberrant Behavior" (Crowley
and Crowley, "Walker Percy's Grail" 260–61).

As a boy in Northumberland, near Belle Isle, Percival had earned many
nicknames: Harry Hotspur, for his pugnacity; Prince Hal, for the pleasure
he took from whorehouses; Pussy and "several other obscene nicknames in
the D.K.E. fraternity," evidently for similar affections. Most significant,
however, were "Percival and Parsifal, who found the Grail and brought life
to a dead land" (10). As a religious name, he chose Father John, after the
Evangelist – Lancelot speculates – who "loved so much" or after the
Baptist, who lived life as "a loner out in the wilderness" (10). By contrast,
Lancelot became a college football hero, a Rhodes scholar, "a Comus
knight" (213), and a lawyer; and he served briefly in the army until his discharge, "not bloody and victorious and battered by Sir Turquine but with
persistent diarrhea" (28). (The reference to Lancelot and Turquine is significant. Percy apparently was deeply affected by "the great picture of
Lancelot and Turquine" in *The Boy's King Arthur*, one of the first books he
ever read; "it made an indelible impression." Later, he wrote that "the
provenance of my Lancelot . . . is *The Boys* [sic] *King Arthur* and most
importantly the marvellous illustrations – most especially the one of
Lancelot bloodied up in his chain mail and leaning on his broadsword
and saying to Sir Turquine, who has just said to him, what manner of man
are you to have fought me for hours: 'I am Sir Lancelot du Lake' –

etc."[14]) Soon, however, Lancelot stopped practicing law and began devoting himself to certain civil rights causes, especially those that irked his acquaintances, and to publishing nostalgic essays on Civil War skirmishes in the *Louisiana Historical Journal*, a repetition of his father's own rather dilletantish efforts. His father Maury, once Poet Laureate of his small parish, had surrounded himself with works of English romantic poetry, Episcopal Church history, Southern history, and biographies of Robert E. Lee, who became for him "as legendary and mythical" as King Arthur and the Round Table. "Do you think I was named Lancelot for nothing?" Lancelot asks. "The Andrewes was tacked on by him to give it some Episcopal sanction, but what he [Maury] really had in mind . . . was Lancelot du Lac, King Ban of Benwick's son, knight of the Round Table and – here was the part he could never get over – one of only two knights to see the Grail (you, Percival, the other)" (116).

This reinterpretation (or misremembering) of Lancelot and Percival as the only two knights ever to see the Grail is unique to Percy and, in fact, is central to his retelling. In none of the other versions of the Grail story is Lancelot successful in his quest. In Malory, although Percival and Bors also achieve the Grail, it is Lancelot's son Galahad and not Lancelot who is the main Grail knight; when Lancelot himself attempts to approach the Grail, he is stunned by a light so bright it knocks him out for weeks. And, while Chrétien's tale ends before the Grail is actually achieved, in his version – as in Wolfram's – Percival is the sole Grail knight.

Yet Percy's use of Lancelot and Percival as co-equal achievers of the Grail, though by opposite means, is quite intentional. "The legend that only Percival and Lancelot saw the Grail – correct or not, it suited my purposes in the novel in establishing a final bond of hope and salvation for both characters," Percy wrote. "The last word in the novel – Percival's 'Yes' – is nothing less than an affirmation of this very hope, though no one has noticed this."[15] Moreover, Percy's choice of two seasoned knights, both of whom are more battle-hardened and worldly-wise than the virginal, almost ethereal Galahad, suggests that the quest for the contemporary Grail requires a different type of quester. After all, if, as Percy has noted, his novel "use[s the] Grail quest (turned upside down)," perhaps only a failed knight like Lancelot is capable of grasping the inversion and therefore of succeeding in the new quest.

The climax of the novel occurs as the film crew prepares to shoot a fake hurricane scene on Lancelot's property – an event that, in the manner of the best Southern Gothic novels, occurs just as a real hurricane rages nearby; no longer a cuckold, Lancelot, transformed into avenger, takes his own action.

14 Letters from Walker Percy to Alan Lupack, the first undated, the second dated February 14, 1987.
15 Letter from Walker Percy to Alan Lupack, February 14, 1987. In that same letter Percy asks, parenthetically: "Did I dream it or is there not in fact a legend which holds that only Lancelot and Percival saw the Grail?"

"Convinced," writes Gardner, "that Percival's meek Christianity and faith can have no effect and incensed, rightly, by the modern world's obscenity – summed up in the trashy illusions of the film maker, Merlin – Lancelot decides, slipping into madness, to start up, somehow, a new revolution and, like Christ Triumphant, either purify the world or destroy it utterly" (Gardner, "The Quest . . ." 60). Believing that only violence can cleanse the perverse "heart of evil" (253) exposed by Margot's betrayal, Lancelot sets off a methane gas leak that causes Belle Isle to explode, killing his wife and everyone else inside. But he soon realizes the error of his actions: left "cold," he acknowledges that there was "no 'secret' after all, no discovery, no flickering of interest, nothing at all, not even any evil . . . there is no answer. There is no question. There is no unholy grail just as there was no Holy Grail" (253). So after a year of incarceration in a hospital he chooses to make a "new beginning" in a world of his own creation with his new Eve, the mental patient Anna who has been raped back into innocence. Percival, meanwhile, commits to the pursuit of his own Grail – and his own "new beginning" – in a "little church in Alabama" (257). Yet, although the two old friends ultimately go in different directions, both find in their Grails a source of grace and redemption, a way of filling their spiritual voids, a justification for their struggles, and – above all, as Percy intended – an affirmation of their hopes.

While the quest for the Grail is certainly the central motif, other Arthurian elements abound in the novel. Lancelot's mother Lily enjoys a dalliance with "Uncle" Harry Wills, a Mardi Gras krewe knight; cuckolded Maury, Lancelot's father, thus becomes a kind of Arthur figure – and a role model for Lancelot's own cuckolding. Lily, meanwhile, is "a clear parody of the maid of Astolat" (Crowley and Crowley, "Walker Percy's Grail" 264): "like a lovebird. She lived for love. Literally. Unless she was loved, she withered and died" (212). By contrast, Lancelot's second wife Margot is a Morgan figure. A "Texas magician," she transforms Belle Isle; when she is finished, she sets her sights on creating cinematic magic with Merlin. The movie on which they collaborate is, ironically, about promiscuity as freedom; but it is also, as J. Donald and Sue Mitchell Crowley point out, a parody of the "Vegetation Ritual and the Life-Cult" that underlie Jessie Weston's *From Ritual to Romance* ("Walker Percy's Grail" 270–71) and thus another allusion to Arthurian mythology. At first, Lancelot had loved Margot with a courtly love: "Almost religious. Things she owned were like saints' relics. The place where she lived . . . became a shrine" (170). Had she remained a "Lady," Lancelot says, he would have fought for her. But she, like "Guinevere[,] didn't think twice about adultery. It was Lancelot, poor bastard, who went off and brooded in the woods" (179). And when he embarks on his night of revenge at Belle Isle, Lancelot assaults Margot as she lies in bed with Jacoby, her latest lover. Wanting "to feel the lance strike home," he wounds Jacoby with his Bowie knife.

Percy, whose cousin William Alexander Percy ("Uncle Will") also incorporated Arthurian material in some of his writing,[16] readily admits that he
turned to the Arthurian legend "because it's a good story and has the theme
of the Grail quest besides." Above all, though, in the legend he found "a convenient mythical frame for ordering certain familiar themes" (Percy, undated
letter to Alan Lupack), especially those deriving from the Southern chivalric
values he prized. Lancelot's affirmation of life and community at the end of
Percy's novel is thus Percy's own affirmation – and his confirmation of the
endurance of myth as a model, especially for modern life.

The quest for an unusual and at times unholy Grail is not unique to
Walker Percy's *Lancelot*; it also occurs in another important contemporary
novel, William Styron's *Sophie's Choice* (1979). Like the protagonists of
Styron's other novels – Peyton Loftis in *Lie Down in Darkness* (1951), Cass
Kinsolving in *Set This House on Fire* (1960), Nat Turner in *The Confessions of
Nat Turner* (1967), and Paul Whitehurst in *A Tidewater Morning* (1993) – all
three of the major characters and several of the minor characters in *Sophie's
Choice* are questers in search of their own personal Grails. Yet their Grail
quests share a common theme: all seek to restore old faiths that might lead to
their redemptions.

Sophie, the novel's title character, is the most enigmatic. At once the agent
of hatred and destruction and the passive victim of racial and male dominance, she tries to celebrate life even as her own lies and half-truths hurtle
her headlong toward doom. A beautiful but ravaged woman who has
survived the horrors of war and concentration camps in Poland, Sophie
seems content – often even radiant – in her new postwar life in Brooklyn. But
the past she has tried to bury in order to survive keeps resurrecting itself,
and she continues to be tormented by demons that refuse to be repressed,
preyed on by the dark gods to whom she once turned in prayer, and
oppressed by the cultural and social institutions she thought she had
escaped. She soon finds herself on an increasingly urgent quest: to redeem
her sins and quell her guilt over the numerous betrayals she has perpetrated.
At the same time, she struggles to regain and to maintain a sense of self,
largely destroyed by the men in her life who have in turn betrayed and
abused her.

Relegated to a subordinate status in her East European homeland, where
traditional cultural values of male dominance prevail, and in her new
country, where many of the same patriarchal patterns are repeated, Sophie
learns to live in the shadow of the men whom she is with. In fact, she loses
herself so fully in their image that she becomes a reflection of their ideas,

16 In his volume *Enzio's Kingdom and Other Poems* (1924), William Alexander Percy includes
   three Arthurian poems. "In the Cold Bright Wind" is a brief lyrical account of Merlin's
   passing to Fairyland; "The Green Bird Seeth Iseult" is a colorful impression of the drinking of the love potion; and "A Brittany Idyl" presents a modern love story in counterpoint
   to the romance of Tristan and Iseult (*NAE* 357).

prejudices, sexual tastes, even language. She assists her father, a renowned professor at the Jagiellonian University, with his venomous, anti-Semitic tracts; and though he consistently repays Sophie's diligence with disgust, her devotion with cruelty, she continues to defend him as a good and civilized man, throwing upon him "a falsely beneficent, even heroic light" (302). She marries Bieganski's witless disciple, a junior professor at the University, at whose hand she suffers similar abuses; yet she paints a rosy picture of Kazik, too, as generous, loving, and intelligent. After she is sent to Auschwitz, she trusts in Hauptsturmführer Fritz Jemand von Neimand and then in Commandant Rudolf Höss to deliver her, but both only further assault her fragile identity and send her more deeply into the contemporary hell of the camp, where she ultimately is forced to sacrifice not one but both of her children. Her experience at Auschwitz corresponds to her loss of faith in God, whom she believes has turned a deaf an ear to all of her prayers. In Brooklyn, Sophie looks to other "saviors" – her boss, Dr. Blackstock; her lover, Nathan; her friend, Stingo – all of whom unwittingly contribute to her destruction. "Quite unbeknownst to herself," Stingo realizes, Sophie "was questing for someone to serve in place of those religious confessors she had coldly renounced" (177). But she finds nothing to replace her old faith and no one to restore her losses. Thus, having failed to achieve her quest for personal redemption, she "redeems" herself in the only way she has left: by her own death.[17]

Nathan, Sophie's handsome but mad lover in Brooklyn, is also "in quest of salvation" (417). An American Jew personally untouched by the Holocaust, he is obsessed with the Nazi horrors (which, to a lesser degree, he inflicts upon Sophie as punishment for her survival). He enters Sophie's life when he rushes, like a knight in shining armor, to rescue her from the hectoring Brooklyn College librarian Sholom Weiss, who had belittled her ignorance of American literature and caused her to swoon and vomit. Back in Sophie's room, Nathan revives her with consommé and liver for her anemia and gives her delicious Château-Margaux to drink. And that night he returns, to continue ministering her back to health. In her broken English, Sophie later recounts that first meeting: Nathan, she tells Stingo, came along like Prince Charming "and he save my life. . . . like magic, as if he had a magic wand and he wave it over me, and very soon I am well" (188). "He was my savior" (190). And, indeed, like the hero of a medieval romance or the Prince Charming of a modern fairy tale, Nathan transforms Sophie. He gives her a new name ("Sophielove," "dollbaby," "sweetie"); a new identity

---

17 Years earlier, in Warsaw, before being sent to Auschwitz, Sophie had discussed *Lord Jim* with her friend Wanda, a resistance fighter who was also the sister of Jozef, Sophie's lover. Wanda tells Sophie: "I think you somehow have forgotten the ending [of the novel]. I think you've forgotten how in the end the hero redeems himself for his betrayal, redeems himself through his own death. His own suffering and death" (576). Apparently, Sophie has not forgotten since she attempts to redeem herself in the same way.

(through his gifts of expensive clothing and elaborate period costumes); and many of the pleasures for which she has longed (from the exotic meals that nourish her sickly body to the phonograph and records that nourish her soul). He even moves into a palace with her, the "Pink Palace," Mrs. Zimmerman's progressive boarding house. "Like a redemptive knight from the void," Nathan appears "and restore[s] her to life" (380); and Sophie "felt an immediate blessing like showering light – resurrection from the dead" (388).

The blessing, however, is short-lived. Even as he keeps weaving his spells over Sophie, Nathan sinks more deeply into madness. Soon he begins degrading and humiliating her, until their relationship falls into what for Sophie is a predictable pattern of subservience and abuse: his delight in her beauty and his physical desire for her alternate with an obsessive jealousy that manifests itself in physical harm. Realizing she can neither live with Nathan's continuing violence and threats nor live without him, Sophie makes her most existential choice yet – to die with him. Their suicide – ironically, to the sounds of Bach's redemptive *Jesu, Joy of Man's Desiring* – is their ultimate flight not simply from reality but also from faith. Yet, notes Rhoda Sirlin, "their joint suicide makes total psychological sense; both are unable to bear the burden of their knowledge and experience" (24).

Stingo is also a questing hero; the initial object of his quest is Sophie herself. The moment he meets her, he falls "if not instantaneously, then swiftly and fathomlessly in love with her" (54). Though Sophie is disconsolate over Nathan's angry departure and his insulting parting words to her, Stingo's sole desire is to take her to bed. "I mean it," he writes, "when I say that no chaste and famished grail-knight could have gazed with more slack-jawed admiration at the object of his quest than I did at my first glance of Sophie's bouncing behind" (437). As he befriends Sophie over the next few weeks, his priapic impulses only increase; but he also strives to know her better, to understand the nature of her sadness and the sense of doom that hangs over her and Nathan and that binds them as intimately as their raucous lovemaking. An understanding of Sophie's doom and sadness, in fact, is essential to Stingo's eventual understanding of the deaths of his first love, Maria Hunt (by suicide), and of his mother (from a ravaging cancer), in which he holds himself complicitous.

At first, Stingo feels like a spectator in the magical, blissful world of Sophie and Nathan's creation. A latter-day Lancelot in a love triangle torn by conflicting affections for his dearest friend and his friend's wife, Stingo feels an overwhelmingly carnal desire for Sophie at the same time that he loves Nathan as a supportive "older brother" (141) and "generous, mind-and-life-enlarging mentor" (227). After Nathan accuses them of infidelity ("Guess what ol' Stingo's up to with his best friend's wife!" [543], he wonders aloud) – an infidelity so far only imagined – Stingo takes Sophie away with him to his own Joyous Gard, an inherited peanut farm in Virginia, where "the

.

ancient chivalry still prevailed" (51). En route, Sophie and Stingo finally consummate their relationship. But while Stingo delights "in clasping in my arms at last the goddess of my unending fantasies" (603), Sophie feels only "Gilt" [sic] and terrible "Despair about Nathan," to whom she knows she must return, "for whatever that mean" (607). And return she does – to die alongside Nathan in their bed, the very spot that circumscribed so much of Stingo's experience of the pair.

Furious at Sophie's desertion, Stingo decides to travel on alone to Virginia. The "extravagant nightmarishness," however, of the wasteland he passes through – "the dreary suburbs, the high-rise penitentiaries, the broad Potomac viscid with sewage" (612) – reinforces his feelings of loneliness and hastens his return to Brooklyn. He arrives too late for anything other than the opportunity to deliver a bedside (and later graveside) farewell to his friends. Nevertheless, the memory of Sophie and Nathan – and of all the other lost and "beaten and butchered and betrayed and martyred children of the earth" (625) – provides both a catharsis for his conflicted emotions and an end to his "quest for some unnameable prize taking me to unknown destinations" (442). On the sands of Coney Island, his tears spill forth; and he awakes the next morning, still on the beach, "blessing [his] resurrection" (626).

Interestingly, even the most depraved characters in *Sophie's Choice* seek – albeit unsuccessfully – a redemptive Grail. Von Niemand, the doctor in charge of selection at Auschwitz, had been "a failed believer seeking redemption, groping for renewed faith," but "cracking apart like bamboo, disintegrating [like Höss] at the very moment that he was reaching out for spiritual salvation" (591–92). Sophie's profession of religious faith on the railroad platform prompts him to ask about her trust in Christ the Redeemer – and then to give her the chance to "redeem" one of her children, at the cost of damning herself and the other child. Rather than being the agent of her salvation (and possibly his own – since he "still retained a potential capacity for goodness . . . and his strivings were essentially religious" [590]), he forces her to commit the unpardonable sin, thus sealing his own doom as well as hers.[18] Rudolf Höss, another failed believer who "used to have faith in Christ" but who had since "broken with Christianity" (277), worships the Führer as "his lord and savior" (324). Sophie nevertheless believes that he can be the agent of her (and her son Jan's) redemption; and she hopes for "the magic moment into which the Commandant, like some soul-eaten Tristan, had had the infirmity to allow himself to be lured" (344). That moment seems imminent on her last day in Höss's employ.

---

18 In this respect, von Niemand is much like Walker Percy's Lancelot. "Was it not supremely simple, then," wonders Stingo of von Niemand, "to restore his belief in God, and at the same time to affirm his human capacity for evil, by committing the most intolerable sin he was able to conceive? Goodness could come later. But first a great sin" (593). In *Lancelot*, Lancelot himself believes that "In times like this when everything is wonderful, what is needed is a quest for evil." And so he "set out, looking for something rarer than the Grail. A sin" (138, 140).

Sophie flirts with him and moves him to confess his attraction to her. But just as Höss speaks – in almost Grail-profaning words – of wanting "to deposit [his] seed within such a beautiful vessel" (343), he is interrupted by his adjutant; and afterwards, no longer distracted by Sophie's charms, he fails to honor his promise to reunite Sophie with Jan or to place the boy in the Lebensborn repatriation program. In a world as absurd as Sophie's, even Hitler himself, whose portrait she glimpses at the Höss's home, is described as "a Knight of the Grail in armor of Solingen stainless steel" (272).

In that absurd world, Nathan – a latter-day prophet made mad by the larger madness around him – punishes himself and Sophie for their survival; he uses the very chemicals employed by the Nazis to achieve his end. Potentially a "redemptive knight" (380), Sophie's "savior" becomes her destroyer as well as his own, his death serving as a reminder that one the great tragedies of the twentieth century claimed more than just its immediate victims. Sophie, seeking expiation for her own guilts and for the sins that destroyed her family, finds her salvation, ironically, through her damnation. The suffering she tries so hard to internalize not only redeems her self-confessed "badness" but also forces her to examine the faith she professes to have lost. And her inevitable death helps Stingo to understand and deal with his own familial guilts. For while Stingo tried to save Sophie from Nathan as well as from herself, in the end it is Sophie who saves him, not just from his adolescent fantasies but from the inherited genocidal guilt over slavery that plagues them both. Though Sophie and Nathan fall prey to the dark gods, Stingo's book – the story of Sophie – manages to resurrect and, in turn, to redeem them. As in Walker Percy's fiction, the Grail imagery of medieval romance thus finds in *Sophie's Choice* not simply a parallel in the strong Southern chivalric tradition but also a hope for redemption in the wasteland of the modern world.

Another contemporary novelist who uses the Grail and other Arthurian themes is Jerzy Kosinski, a writer who experimented with many forms in his fiction, from the *Bildungsroman* and the picaresque in his acclaimed first novel, *The Painted Bird* (1965), to "auto-fiction" in his ninth and final novel, *The Hermit of 69th Street* (1988). Yet certain archetypes and myths, including the Arthurian, underlie all of his work and, in most instances, suggest the great disparity between heroic ideals and the lack of actual heroism in the contemporary world.

Kosinski's first specific reference to the Arthurian legends occurs in his innovative second novel, *Steps* (1969), winner of the National Book Award. In one of that novel's early episodes, the narrator describes a game he remembers from his army days. About twenty or twenty-five "Knights of the Round Table" would sit around a table, each with a long string tied to his organ. One man called "King Arthur," without knowing who was at the other end of each, would hold all of the strings. Then, at intervals, King Arthur "would select a string and pull it, inch by inch, over the notched markings on the table top" (24), as the soldiers scanned each other's faces for signs of suffering. While bets were made to see how many notches the string would pass over before he cried out and revealed his identity, the victim would try to conceal his pain and maintain a regular posture. "Some soldiers ruined themselves for life by sitting out the game just to win the prize money" (24).

The game, however, proves not to be an honest test of strength or endurance. Conspiring with King Arthur, one of the men ties the string around his leg rather than his genitals and consequently seems to withstand more pain than the others. Of course, he and King Arthur succeed in pocketing large sums of money from the betting. When "the cheated knights" discover the conspiracy, they secretly select the punishment they think is fitting. "The guilty men were grabbed from behind, blindfolded, and taken into the forest. There they were stripped and tied to trees. The knights, one after another, slowly crushed each of the victim's parts between two rocks until the flesh became an unrecognizable pulp" (24–25). "The game," as Jack Hicks has noted, "enacts the arbitrary power – indeed, the fate – of social control and the individual's stoic yielding to it, and that force is brought home when the cheaters are discovered" (230) and the symbolic castration of the game is made real in the punishment. But the game also has another dimension: by inverting the term "knight" and the sexuality ordinarily associated with it, the participants appropriate knighthood for themselves despite their limitations of character and position. Paul Bruss writes: "The fact that the participants should be willing to risk their sexual well-being in a contest of physical risks may or may not reflect a lack of satisfactory experience elsewhere, but it surely indicates the importance, for these knights, of achieving a grand sense of manliness that will at least momentarily separate them from the realities of their everyday experience. As they conceal their pain in masks of manliness, they enact a strategy of displacement that allows them the grace of achieving the ground of a generally unavailable heroism" (188–89). Yet, Kosinski implies, that heroism is ultimately as false as the rules of the game.

It is, however, Kosinski's seventh novel, *Passion Play* (1979), that is his most overtly Arthurian work. Like Percy's *Lancelot* and Styron's *Sophie's Choice*, *Passion Play* is the story of a perverse or unholy quest. Whereas for medieval writers the Grail was an apparition, a means for salvation to be achieved outside of oneself, in Kosinski's world the Grail has become an industry – Grail Industries, to be precise, a business conglomerate presided over by the Stanhope family, its unworthy keepers. The nation's largest electronics manufacturer, Grail Industries is not the embodiment of the spiritual ideal of the Grail but rather its antithesis, as false a representation of the original as Duessa was to Una in Spenser's allegory. Kosinski's modern-day knight errant Fabian, who engages in various acts of love and combat typically found in the medieval romances, recognizes that the real quest must be for something more sacred than profane, for something that can only be found within. So, throughout the novel, Fabian embarks on a quest for the self, both the awareness of his own self and the realization of the self of those around him; and he strives to become the knight who is "the salvation, not only of one kingdom but of many" (the knight to whom Cervantes refers, in the passage used by Kosinski as an epigraph).

A self-proclaimed "existential cowboy," an aging polo player and some-time equitation teacher, Fabian had discovered his aim as a boy. Astride a farm horse at full gallop, he would play peasant games and send a ball the size of an apple across the meadow to strike a target no larger than a pumpkin. Polo, however, is traditionally a team sport, with the roles of its four players clearly delineated: always forward, number one sets up the shots; number two acts as the driving force of the attack; number three, the pivot man and often the captain of the team, links attack with defense; and number four stands guard at the team's back. No one of these roles fully consumes Fabian's ability to strike and to score – and to do so unaided. Like the medieval knight, his greatest challenges and greatest triumphs are achieved as an individual. So, while the confrontation of opposing teams, each attempting to score a higher number of goals, is the core of the game, for Fabian polo becomes essentially a one-on-one contest in which two players fight for possession of the ball. His disregard of the other three players on his team antagonizes and humiliates them, and early in his pro-fessional career he gets a reputation as a maverick. Others refuse to play with him; dropped from one team after another, he resigns himself to traveling around the country in search of one-on-one engagements, usually with wealthy opponents, during which he can fight for supremacy and submit to rules that both contestants obey, without an umpire, away from the fickle-ness of a public that might choose favorites.

Like the Grail knight, however, Fabian is sometimes diverted from the real goal of the exploration and enhancement of the self. One such lapse occurs when he is hired by Fernando-Rafael Falsalfa, the unchallenged autocrat of a Latin American republic, to serve as his occasional polo partner. Falsalfa (a "false self") sets Fabian up by threatening to frame him for the murder of a controversial political columnist. But Fabian learns a very valuable lesson from his experience with the dictator: that in life he must create and direct his own scenarios rather than act out the scripts that others provide for him. Later, for example, when Vanessa Stanhope, the young woman whom he has loved since she was a girl, offers him a million dollars to marry her, he balks at the implications of such financial security and refuses to be tempted from his quest by her gift. His thoughts "unreeled the lucid image of himself, of his life and the shape of it. The reel accelerated, and he saw himself free from the chance and desperation of snaring a one-on-one game, the panic before the contest allayed, the tension of the game slackening, the easy drifting away of all that was absolute in him, all that defined the elusive order of his nature" (249). Fabian realizes that Vanessa's money is not simply a gift of life, but of a life defined both by the very nature of the gift and by the memory of the giver. To accept would be to experience transformation in the most negative sense, to lose the integrity that is most dear to him and to all true questers. Thus, he declines Vanessa's offer.

Kosinski suggests, however, that Fabian's decision is difficult to make. Vanessa was always special to him, different from his other adolescent equitation students; as if to preserve that unique bond between them, he had never violated her youthful virginity. Years later, when he re-enters her life, he appears as a knight on a white horse, offering her a rose as a token of his love; she, like the pure maiden who is the object of such devoted and courtly love, a woman like the one Palamede dreamed of in Erskine's *Tristram*, has in turn saved herself for him. Inevitably yet somewhat reluctantly, Fabian consummates their love, but that consummation leads him to a growing awareness of his own physical deterioration and a realization of Vanessa's possessiveness.

Fabian's decision to reject the million dollar check is therefore meant to be a way of helping Vanessa to preserve her integrity as well. Like the narrator of Kosinski's second novel *Steps*, who engages the woman in several acts of demystification and then finally leaves her so that she can achieve a new level of the self, Fabian heightens Vanessa's awareness to the degree that she is "finally free of him, free of herself" (225). Having played many roles in her life – as mentor, as father, as lover – Fabian must ultimately leave and allow her to create her own dramas, her own plays of passion, without him. And, in the novel's final pages, he apparently succeeds: Vanessa quite literally takes off on her own. Fabian, again on horseback, rushes to catch up to her plane; but just as it is about to ascend, Fabian feels freed from his despair by the exhilaration that comes from the speed of his mount. He forgets Vanessa and returns to his struggle for the freedom of his self, like a knight "in combat with an enemy only he could see" (271) – the final image bringing a powerful conclusion to a novel that successfully uses medieval motifs to describe the struggle of a modern knight errant against a society that constantly besieges his selfhood.

The encounter with Vanessa, while not as physically dangerous as that with Falsalfa, is nonetheless threatening. Fabian's face-off with Eugene Stanhope is, however, the ultimate literal one-on-one. Fabian's friend and his chief source of income, Eugene is the wealthy heir to Grail Industries. Through Eugene's assistance, Fabian is able to purchase his VanHome, a kind of castle on wheels that allows the contemporary knight a place to prepare for his combats, to recover from his wounds, and to transport his steeds. Yet after Eugene's girlfriend Alexandra seduces Fabian and lies about it (a perversion of the medieval courtly love triangle), Eugene challenges him to a stick-and-ball game, one-on-one, during which Fabian's shot fells and kills his former friend. By all accounts, Fabian acquits himself well in the combat, not because he has injured his opponent but because he has

observed the code of the game. Like Hemingway's heroes, he has performed
with a certain grace under pressure. Still, Fabian is pained by the loss of his
friend and by the lingering doubts that others have that Eugene's death was
not entirely accidental.

Two years later, at the Grail Industries Stanhope Polo Tournament, Fabian
meets Alexandra again. She is with Costeiro, a handsome young player, and
again she – like Morgan le Fay tempting Accolon to oppose King Arthur –
contrives a match in which she is sure Fabian will be bested. As he prepares
for his combat with Costeiro, Fabian feels more like a paltry clown in a
carnival play than the gallant knight in a tournament of passion. Nevertheless, as did Nick Adams in Hemingway's "Big Two-Hearted River," he
measures each of his motions in what becomes a rite of purification. Once on
the field, Fabian smashes a ball near Alexandra, a proper shot that nevertheless disturbs Costeiro's concentration and causes him to lose the match. By
again observing both the code of the game and the rituals that define it,
Fabian is victorious in his combat. One of the few occasions on which he is
not victorious occurs near the end of the novel; Fabian, riding Vanessa's
horse at Madison Square Garden, is distracted by Alexandra from completing the final jump. Yet the fault is as much his as it is hers: by competing only
for Vanessa's sake, by compromising his principles for the Stanhopes, Fabian
cannot help but fail in his attempt.

Numerous motifs from medieval romance, such as the repeated testing of
the knight errant, undergird Kosinski's narrative; certain episodes, however,
have even more specific connotations. At one point in the novel, for instance,
Fabian arrives in Florida to play polo at the estate of a rich and powerful
businessman. He stops first at a local stable, where – overcome by the fierce
southern heat, his exhaustion from the flight, and the medication he has been
taking – he passes out. In an episode that reads like a parody of Elaine of
Astolat's tending of the wounded Lancelot, a salesgirl comes to his assistance
and offers to take him back to her apartment until he is able to move on.
Fabian stays with her for several days; becoming her lover – by accepting
more favors than Lancelot did from Elaine – as well as her patient, he is
struck by her incredible passivity. Overweight and sloppy, she spends all of
her free time virtually glued to her television set. Fabian thinks of her as a
refugee from some nameless war, "forgotten, still in futile wandering, searching for a place she might call her own" (143).

As soon as he recovers, he leaves her and is installed at the home of his
millionaire host. The girl, however, shows up uninvited one night to see him.
Unnerved and agitated, Fabian insists that she go away. Claiming that she
has no life apart from him, but without the romance of Elaine's inability to
live with Lancelot, she refuses to leave and mindlessly repeats that she wants
to be with him. And she continues to pursue him even though he shouts that
"I'm not your TV, you can't turn me on when you want to" (151). Finally he
abuses her, both physically and verbally, and tells her that she has nothing to

give, that her emotions are as crude as her body, and that she is deserving only of the company of her television. Later she is found hanging from a boundary post on the edge of the estate, the victim of her own failed imagination. Her death, lacking the tragic dignity or even the true passion of Elaine of Astolat's, emphasizes the waste of mind and life that makes the modern world literally a land of waste.

What the unnamed girl lacks is precisely what Fabian seeks and ultimately achieves: a sense of self, his elusive but very contemporary Grail. Through his various involvements – with the transsexual Manuela (they are "each an embodiment of the other's quests" [119]); with Stella, the black woman posing as white, whom he sets free and allows to reclaim "awareness of her self"; with his young saddle brides, whom he initiates into sex as well as equitation; and, of course, with Vanessa, whom he liberates of both inhibitions and ties to the past (when he makes love to her one last time in her hometown, aptly named Totemfield, he tries again "to impel her back to herself" [265] so that she can discover her own identity) – he attempts to restore some heroic values to a society that devalues heroism as it celebrates an almost mindless conformity. Opposing the ignoble values of Grail Industries by fighting one-on-one for principles that he alone defines, Fabian proves himself to be both a true knight errant and Kosinski's modern mythic hero.

Another important contemporary treatment of the Grail theme occurs in Bobbie Ann Mason's award-winning first novel *In Country* (1985), a story about the national conflict effected by the Vietnam War. Unlike the majority of writers who deal with the war in their fiction, Mason does not focus on the soldier, for whom the horrors of combat are made tolerable by easy camaraderie and genuine closeness (Durham 45); she focuses instead on the Southern working class, the class that was most profoundly affected by the war, and on the dislocations felt by the multi-generational members of that class as they struggle to cope with the psychological and social changes in American culture that were the repercussions of Vietnam. What gives *In Country* its special resonance are the multiple mythic structures upon which Mason builds, from the Homeric search for the father to the heroic naming ritual in which Samantha ("Sam") Hughes must engage in order to discover her own identity. Among the most significant of those myths – the one most popular with Malamud, Kesey, Styron, Kosinski, and many other contemporary writers as well – is that of the Fisher King.

In Mason's novel, it is Sam's uncle, Emmett Smith, who is a type of the Fisher King. As a veteran of an undeclared war – a war whose purpose he never quite understood, in a country whose very topography was horrifyingly alien to him – Emmett returns to Hopewell, Kentucky, a wounded and broken man who simply does not fit into the society he had so recently left. At first, Emmett appears to be one of the lucky ones; less fortunate boys like Emmett's brother-in-law Dwayne Hughes never make it home alive. But

Emmett's wounds, though less obvious, are no less real or serious than Dwayne's.

Sam suspects that Emmett has been sexually maimed, that his manhood was destroyed by some kind of physical injury suffered in Vietnam; and she raises the question of Emmett's wounding with all of her friends and family. Emmett's exposure overseas to Agent Orange, she tells her best friend Dawn, could cause him to have children with birth defects. "Maybe," concludes Dawn, "that's why your uncle never married" (41). To her boyfriend Lonnie, Sam wonders "if something could have happened to Emmett in the war, like a wound or something, that means he can't have girlfriends," to which Lonnie responds, "You mean could he have had his balls shot off?" (186). At Grandma Smith's, Sam admits, "Mom always blamed everything on the war. Do you think he [Emmett] could have had a wound – you know where?" (150). Grandma "never heard tell about it" but suggests an even stranger possibility: perhaps, when he was stricken with mumps at the age of eleven, the mumps "fell on him – [in his] balls" (149). Still curious, Sam asks her mother Irene directly, "Did he get wounded in the war? . . . I thought maybe some reason like that was why he never had any girlfriends" (169). Irene confirms only that "not long after that [returning from Vietnam], Emmett flipped out for a while, and then you probably remember that time he lost the feeling in his legs. The doctors said he was identifying with the paraplegics, but he didn't even know anybody like that then" (234). And after Sam tries to have sex with Emmett's friend Tom Hudson, who proves to be impotent ("There ain't nothing wrong with me," he claims. "It's just my head" [128]), Sam applies the same diagnosis to Emmett. "Then it occurred to her that Emmett might have the same problem as Tom. It seemed so obvious now. . . . Maybe Emmett even had an actual wound, nerve damage of some kind" (130).

Emmett does have an "actual wound," but that wound – like Nick Adams' – is more psychic than physical. It is a survivor's guilt, a gnawing pain over the fact that he lived while his buddies died, that he survived by pretending that he too was dead, by hiding all night and all day under their corpses, until the smell of their blood in the jungle heat felt "like soup coming to a boil" (223) and until he, the lone survivor, felt more dead inside than they. That pain festers and grows: many years later, he still sleeps poorly, hears his buddies' voices calling out to him on stormy nights, and feels other strange sensations inside his head. Despite his father's prodding, he holds no job, because "ain't nothing worth doing" (45); and – apart from Sam – he has nothing or no one to distract him from his painful past.

Like the Fisher King in his blighted land, Emmett lives in a dilapidated house with a cracked foundation. "The house was damp and musty, and the humidity exaggerated ancient smells in the house. The wallpaper was coming unglued . . . like some repressed life that wanted to emerge" (106). Even "the floor was rotting" (65), as were the joists; and "all kinds of things could be breeding" (73) in the basement, in which were stored several years' of unbundled newspapers intended for the Scouts, "swollen and mushy" stacks of *Reader's Digest* magazines, a trash can filled with liquor bottles, and numerous plants that finally "had given up seeking the light. She [Sam] couldn't remember what year they died. The dead stalks in the tub . . . were oppressive, something useless and ridiculous" (152). As if to maintain a modicum of order in his crumbling kingdom, Emmett obsessively digs a ditch around the frame of the house hoping to contain the collapsing walls.

Emmett's memories of Vietnam are also of a blighted land – of napalm disintegrating the palm trees and of other toxic chemicals contaminating the water. "Once," Emmett tells Sam, "we came across this place that had been defoliated. And I remember thinking, This looks like winter, but winter doesn't come to the jungle. It's always green in the jungle, but here was this place all brown and dead" (95). The sole object of beauty he recalls there was an egret so white it was almost ghost-like. "That beautiful bird just going about its business with all that crazy stuff going on over there." Once, a grenade hit some trees and caused an entire flock to take wing. It was such a remarkable sight, Emmett recalls, that "we thought it was snowing up instead of down" (36). Back in Hopewell, Emmett searches everywhere for egrets, in the hope that finding such a sign of life, beauty, and vitality might restore some joy to him and some life to the wasteland around him.

Emmett is eccentric in other ways as well. From the skirts he wears around the house because they are "healthier" than pants to the government loans he refuses as a point of honor to repay, from his unwillingness to seek regular employment to his inability to sustain traditional relationships with women, his behavior demonstrates his lack of convention. Yet it is too facile to dismiss that behavior simply as "crazy," as some Hopewell residents do: many of Emmett's actions deliberately mock more typical male behavior. In rejecting convention, by acting in a fashion perceived to be outside the norm, he consciously challenges the means by which society defines the norm at the same time that he insulates himself from painful interaction with that society, which in fact has rejected and displaced him. And he creates a way to preserve his shattered sense of self until such time as he is ready to reintegrate socially and to be healed.

Just as the Fisher King's wound is reflected in the wounded land around him, Emmett's behavior is microcosmically a mirror of the social upheaval that took place during the Vietnam era. Even Grandma Smith recognizes that fact. "Everything started to change," she says, soon after Emmett came home; and she sees the reverberations of those changes in the world around her: "Hopewell used to be the best place to bring up kids, but now it's not" (147). Yet she too has changed as a result: when Pap, complaining about Emmett's laziness, asserts that he can still "pull himself up and be proud," Grandma blames Pap's (and, by implication, society's) conventional thinking for causing Emmett's problems in the first place: "You were all for him going [to Vietnam]!" she accuses him. "You said the Army would make a man out of him. But look what it done" (149). Sam's other grandmother is also cognizant of the postwar social changes: when Sam asks Mamaw if, given the chance to go back in time, she would have let Dwayne go to Vietnam or sent him to Canada, Mamaw can only say sadly that people "don't have choices" like that (197); she implies, however, that the choices – even *her* choices – would be different today than they were two decades ago. In ways such as these, suggests David Booth in "Sam's Quest, Emmett's Wound: Grail Motifs in Bobbie Ann Mason's Portrait of America After Vietnam," *In Country* "reenacts Eliot's lament for the spiritual weariness of England in a lament for America in the aftermath of Vietnam" (100).

If Emmett is the Fisher King, then – in an interesting gender twist – Sam is the Grail knight who eventually restores him, and those around him, to health. To be sure, it is not an easy process, for Sam bears wounds of her own from Vietnam. As the daughter of a father who conceived her in the month of marriage before going overseas and who died a month before she was born, she must first come to terms with her past, a past of which she, like the rest of her generation, is mostly unaware; engage in a ritualistic process that involves remembering and then celebrating – in part by reenacting – her history; and ultimately find a mechanism for interweaving memory and imagination, the real and the idealized, in a way that will open the past to the present. Like the traditional questing knight, she must ask the questions that will effectuate the healing of the wounded land. After all, as David Booth observes, the wasteland can only be restored by "a reintroduction of the woman who in turn forces the wounded generation of men to come to terms with itself" (109).

Sam's quest begins when she graduates from high school, a symbolic and cultural rite of passage from childhood to adulthood. The commencement speaker preaches to her graduating class about keeping the country strong, words that make Sam "nervous" and cause her to "start thinking about war, . . . [thoughts that] stayed on her mind all summer" (23). Afterwards, when she unrolls her diploma, she discovers only a blank page inside; "the real diplomas were mailed later" (200). The blank piece of paper that she has received is like the legacy of the Vietnam War; and, as Katherine Kinney notes, "until she can fill in the imaginative space occupied by her father and the war, her education will remain incomplete" (40).

So Sam embarks on a journey, first metaphorical, later literal, to complete that education. But, virtually from the outset, she is discouraged in her pursuit and repeatedly admonished by others that the war does not concern her. Her mother Irene, now living in Lexington with her second husband and baby, has a new life; it has taken Irene years to break away from the unhappy memories of her former home in Hopewell and the burdens of war, including her early widowhood and her responsibility for her brother Emmett; Irene sees no purpose in dredging up the past. "Don't fret about this Vietnam thing," she tells Sam. "It had nothing to do with you" (57). Sam's boyfriend Lonnie is a sexually charged adolescent whose interest in Vietnam is as limited as his knowledge of it. When Sam tells him that, contrary to her mother's advice, the war "had *everything* to do with me" (71), Lonnie tries to silence her by saying, "Hush . . . people are looking." Grandma Smith, who can't comprehend Sam's preoccupation with Agent Orange, changes the subject whenever it is raised: "Sam, don't think that way" (148). Emmett's ex-girlfriend Anita concedes that the experience of Vietnam, like that of the Dark Ages, was "something you're not supposed to know" (64). Even Emmett, a surrogate father closer to Sam than her real father ever was, refuses to discuss Vietnam with her. "Women weren't over there," he snaps. "So they can't really understand" (107). When Sam presses him to "tell me something that happened [in Vietnam]," he deflects her request: "You don't want to know all of that" (54).

But that is exactly what Sam does want to know. Insistent upon learning about "what it was like" (94) and frustrated by Emmett's non-responsiveness, she grows "curious about the veterans he hung around with," men whom "she had known for years" but never "thought much about . . . as vets" (46). Yet they too talk about Vietnam primarily among themselves, because – according to one – "nobody else could ever know what you went through except guys who have been there" (78). Pete, the vet with a map of western Kentucky tattooed on his chest, advises Sam explicitly to "stop thinking about Vietnam. You don't know how it was, and you never will. There is no way you can ever understand" (136). Another suggests she "just stop asking questions about the war. Nobody gives a shit" (79).

Reminded by Irene of Dwayne's letters from Vietnam, Sam finds them in her mother's old room, arranges them chronologically, and reads them with great care. The letters, however, reveal little about her father beyond his delight over Irene's pregnancy and his desire to be home again; still, they help to create the first tangible bond between father and daughter. She discovers for the first time something about her own name: Dwayne had picked it out. His favorite name was Samuel; "If it is a girl," he wrote Irene, "name it Samantha" (182).

This is an especially vital bit of information for Sam, who had mused since childhood that "If she couldn't know a simple fact like the source of her name, what could she know for sure?" (53). Names and naming, moreover, assume increased significance throughout the novel and underlie part of the ritual that Sam must perform in the quest for her father, for her own identity, and for the answers that will ultimately heal Emmett, her surrogate father. The newfound knowledge that Dwayne, though dead by the time she was born, had been responsible for giving her a name, in fact his *favorite* name, prompts Sam to visit his parents, the Hughes, for more clues to the past. At Sam's urging, Mamaw locates Dwayne's diary, which she dismisses as nothing more than scribblings about "troop movements and weapons and things like that" (200). But, as Mamaw hands the notebook to her, Sam is instinctively aware that she is getting closer to the object of her search. "Sam remembers reaching just this way at graduation when the principal handed her the rolled diploma" (200). At graduation, however, the paper was blank and her name was missing; now Sam is beginning to fill in some of those blanks, to complete her education – and to pass another test that brings her closer to the achievement of her quest.

The diary does not prove as ennobling as Sam anticipates: contrary to Mamaw's idealized version of the war, Sam reads about Dwayne's making "gook puddin" (204) and his taking teeth from dead men as good luck; she learns that her father not only had killed Vietcong but also had enjoyed the experience, facts that upset her enormously. Afterwards, she is overwhelmed by a sense of rot and decay; the wasteland images described by her father – his own shriveled feet, his dead buddy, the dead V. C. corpse, the sickly-sweet smell of banana leaves – reverberate in the equally sickly reality of the Hughes' home that she has just left, with its smell of manure-sodden farm clothing, decaying bathroom mat, mangy dog and clip-eared cat, Donna's ugly baby, and Mamaw's rusty pea bucket. Sam "had a morbid imagination, but it had always been like a horror movie, not something real. Now everything seemed suddenly so real it enveloped her, like something rotten she had fallen into, like a skunk smell" (206).

The connection with her father that Sam makes through the diary is also a connection with the animal fact of the deaths he caused and of his own death; it is a connection so intimate yet so profound that it scares and repulses her. Unable to confront Dwayne and to direct at him the anger she feels about his conduct, she races home to confront Emmett instead. Emmett, however, is not there; having just released a series of flea bombs, he has left the house until the chemicals subside. Sam, her imagination inflamed by her father's description of Vietnam, associates Emmett's killing of the fleas with Dwayne's murder of the Vietnamese, and she leaves the diary on their kitchen table with the accusatory note, "Is that what it was like over there? If it was, then you can just forget about me. Don't try to find me" (207). She then runs away to Cawood's Pond, where she intends to "hump the boonies" and thus to discover the purpose men believe they have in going to war.

Alone in the swamp, like the Grail knight keeping his solitary vigil, she spends the night "walking point" (211), observing "first watch," and imagining the face of the V. C. in every raccoon she sees and their presence in every sound of nature she hears. Like Nick Adams in "The Big, Two-Hearted River," Sam ritualizes each of her actions. But it is not until morning, when Emmett – haggard and frightened over her absence – finds her that she gives voice to her anger, an anger simultaneously toward her father for his inability to live up to the image she has formed, toward herself for being capable of the same kind of brutality, and toward Emmett for his unwillingness to share with her the ugly truth of Vietnam. Sam's profession of hatred toward

Dwayne is so intense that Emmett tries to defuse it by admitting that Dwayne "could have been me. All of us . . ." (222); and, overcome by emotion, he reveals his long-held secret of how he survived by hiding for hours under the bodies. Sam's disappearance, says Emmett, duplicated for him the horror of that event; it was "like being left by myself and all my buddies dead" (225).

The confrontation that Sam has forced allows Emmett to begin his healing. Having uttered the unutterable, having spilled his long-held secret, he can begin to expiate his guilt and, as a result, to heal from his wound. The moment, which binds them more closely than ever before as family, therefore proves cathartic for both, and it marks the beginning of a kind of transcendence (symbolized by the recurring references to the egret and to other birds) that they ultimately achieve in Washington, DC, where they travel with Mamaw Hughes.

At the Vietnam Veterans' Memorial, the three generations – Sam, the fatherless daughter; Mamaw, the childless mother; and Emmett, the surrogate father to Sam and surrogate son to Mamaw – find Dwayne Hughes's name at the top of the black granite wall. Though distanced from Dwayne by accident and time, they realize that they are nonetheless inextricably linked: a father dead before he ever became a father and a daughter, now almost the same age as her father was when he died, very much alive and coming of age, who has at last found her father and – in finding him – has found herself; a brother, which Dwayne was to Emmett by marriage as well as by circumstance, finally grieving for himself and his dead comrades, all of whom were brothers-in-arms; a mother, at last able to offer a proper farewell to her lost child. As Mamaw clutches Sam's arm and speaks of the despair she felt when she first saw the wall but the "hope" she now finds in its symbolism and as Emmett bursts into a smile that indicates his reconciliation with the past,[19] Sam goes to the directory to view her father's name once again. And there, running her finger along all the different Hughes names listed there, she finds her own: SAM A HUGHES. Locating it on one of the wall's granite slabs, she discovers, "It is the first on a line. It is down low enough to touch. She touches her own name. How odd it feels, as though all

---

19 Ellen A. Blais writes that the final image of Emmett sitting on the ground in front of the names of his buddies on the wall "becomes the iconic equivalent of Sam's recognition of herself in the Vietnam veteran who bears her name" (117). Robert H. Brinkmeyer, Jr., sees in Emmett's posture "a profound, almost phoenix-like rebirth . . . In finally confronting the terrors of his past, Emmett is ready to forge a new life, something he has been resisting since his return from Vietnam" (31). Thus, as Sam does, Emmett gives birth to himself at the wall. Thomas Morrissey, in "Mason's *In Country*," also comments on the concluding image of Emmett as phoenix; Morrissey contends that it is the culmination of numerous bird images throughout the novel. Even the memorial itself, which Mason describes as a "black wing embedded in the soil," is – according to Morrissey – "a fallen bird . . . [that] has nevertheless unburdened the survivors so that they can rise from the ashes of war and sorrow to meet their own destinies" (63–64).

the names in America have been used to decorate this wall" (244–45). While
Sam Hughes, the Vietnam soldier whose name is etched on the wall, is dead,
another Sam Hughes, the young woman who imagined herself to be a
soldier in order to understand Vietnam, is alive and, by this experience, possessed "of a deeper knowledge of the dark complexities that shadow all
human experience [and an understanding of] the nature of growth and
regeneration" (Brinkmeyer 30).

Sam and Emmett's shared experience, which allows them to make their
separate peace with the war and to move beyond the painful memories and
the often violent legacy of the past, is portrayed by Mason in very gender-
specific imagery that suggests the cycle of rebirth and regeneration inherent
in the vegetation myths of the Fisher King and the Grail quest. At
Cawood's Pond, where Sam forces Emmett to face the ghosts of his dead
comrades which haunt him, Emmett breaks down sobbing and crying; he
admits his desire to be a father, especially to Sam; and, having given birth
to his sorrow and guilt, he leaves the swamp looking "like an old peasant
woman hugging a baby" (226). By facing his terror, he can forge a new life
(suggested by the image of the baby), something he has been unable to do
until now; and that new life begins with his taking a job, paying off his
debts, preparing Sam to go away to college, and undertaking the journey of
reconciliation to Washington. A comparable image is evoked later in the
novel, at the Vietnam Veterans' Memorial. Against the sexual imagery of
the Washington Monument, "a big white prick" (238), and the Memorial, a
deep "black gash in the hillside . . . a giant grave . . . a hole" (239) – imagery
reminiscent of the Grail legend's spear and cup – "Sam doesn't understand
what she is feeling, but it is something so strong, it is like a tornado moving
in her, something massive and overpowering. It feels like giving birth to
this wall" (240). Katherine Kinney writes that "In this revisionary image the
daughter gives birth to the father, the future to the past, the living to the
dead – but the relationship between destruction and regeneration is no
longer horrific" (48). Indeed, by locating Dwayne's name on the wall, Sam
brings the missing father to life, just as her cathartic confrontation with
Emmett at Cawood's Pond brings him to life; and, in the course of her
search for Dwayne, Sam metaphorically gives birth to herself, as evidenced
by her discovery of the name "Sam A. Hughes" on the wall. The name
absent from her diploma at the beginning of her journey and hidden away
from her on the documents in the Hopewell courthouse is now etched
forever, not only in Sam's personal and family history but also in the
national consciousness. The powerful closing image of Sam, Emmett, and
Mamaw thus fuses the simultaneous shame and hope of a family and of a
nation and offers a sense of shared identity, at once personal, familial, and
national, and of reconciliation that transcends generational boundaries. It is
also, as Owen Gilman suggests, "a paean to remembrance . . . [that is]
tightly linked to southern customs [and that] celebrates the spirit of memory

[by demonstrating] the absolute necessity of finding the past and coming to terms with it" (*Southern Imagination* 47).[20]

The Vietnam War, which created deep political and philosophical divisions in this country, left scars not only on the young men who fought there but also on the society that they left behind. Sam's quest to understand the meaning of Vietnam is as noble as any quest in medieval literature, and its achievement helps to heal the war-wounded Emmett and others around her as well. Moreover, in its patterns of rebirth, and especially of the rejuvenation of Emmett, the injured contemporary Fisher King, *In Country* suggests the national need for healing, for returning vitality and honor to the country and to the notion of America itself. Through the use of the Grail legend to undergird her very contemporary tale, Mason thus makes a noteworthy contribution to the American Arthurian tradition.

While Malamud, Kesey, Percy, Styron, Kosinski, and Mason use the Grail legend and other Arthurian motifs to provide a mythic framework for one or more of their novels, another major contemporary American novelist, Thomas Berger, actually sets his Arthurian story in medieval Camelot, which becomes for him an analogue of contemporary America. Berger has noted that, as a boy, he "preferred the pleasure of the imagination to those of experience" and read incessantly (Hughes 24); he mentions with great fondness his "own boyhood King Arthur . . . the work of one Elizabeth Lodor Merchant," a gift from his father at Christmas 1931 (Landon 6–7). That childhood reading no doubt inspired Berger to write one of his most popular novels, *Arthur Rex* (1978). On the dust jacket, in fact, Berger describes the novel as essentially his "memory of that childish version [of *Le Morte d'Arthur*] as edited and expanded according to the outlandish fantasies (and even some of the droll experiences) he has had in the years since." On another occasion, Berger expressed a similar sentiment: "I chose to make my contribution to the [Arthurian] theme," he wrote, "because I had always adored the Arthurian stories as a child, and in my career I sooner or later strive to give permanency to each of my childhood fantasies" (Berger, Letter to Alan Lupack, Dec. 8, 1980).

Called by critics "the Arthur novel of our time" (Romano 62), "in many ways the most impressive" modern ironic fantasy (Thompson 155), *Arthur Rex* is indeed a complex and clever retelling of the timeless Arthurian tales.

---

20 Robert H. Brinkmeyer, Jr., finds links also to Southern literary tradition. He writes that "this final scene is significant not only as a strong and fitting conclusion to a fine novel but also as a revealing statement on the state of contemporary Southern fiction." Likening it to Allen Tate's "Ode to the Confederate Dead," another work in which a character stands "at a graveyard memorial, struggling to come to terms with himself/herself and with society at large by meditating upon history," Brinkmeyer suggests that the conclusion of *In Country* "transposes a crucial paradigm of the Southern literary renascence – that to understand the present, including oneself, one explores the past – into a contemporary setting. In doing so, Mason maintains the integrity of the paradigm but alters its thrust and direction" (31) – much as she does with the Arthurian legend itself.

Yet, as Brooks Landon observes, while the characters "struggle to meet their own self-perceived responsibilities, [*Arthur Rex*] – like all of Berger's novels – reveals his own sense of responsibility to literary tradition" (48). In this case, the obvious sources are Malory and the line of other tellers who have made the Arthurian legend the Matter of Britain. Michael Malone has recorded Berger's resentment at coming across an Arthurian screenplay written by someone who had apparently read "none of Malory, Chrétien de Troyes, Wolfram von Eschenbach, Alf Tennyson, Dick Wagner's *Tristan* and *Parsifal* and the many other forerunners whose works I ransacked (including two books for children which were my principal sources) . . . . This unbelievably trashy practitioner," Berger exclaimed, "had *invented* his own Arthurian narrative!" (Malone 24; cited in Landon 48).

Berger found in Malory and in other works within the Arthurian tradition not only a wealth of source material but also a clear and certain moral focus. As he wrote in a foreword to a volume of *German Medieval Tales*: "Medieval narratives are not devious in their means . . . . In the Arthurian tales the reader is seldom in doubt as to the virtues, or lack thereof, of the principal figures: Sir Galahad is not secretly a rascal, nor is Mordred, underneath it all, a decent chap whose only problem consists in being misunderstood by his father the king" (Berger, cited in Landon 48–49).

Yet, at the same time that Berger demonstrates a great admiration for the legend of Arthur as told by Malory and others, he modernizes, at times parodies, and radically revises it. Although subtitled "A Legendary Novel," *Arthur Rex* never slips into nostalgia for a lost world of simple heroism and gallantry. And, while Berger would concur with his narrator that without legend "the world hath become a mean place" (433), he urges his readers to contemplate not so much "the realm of legend [in which] deeds are counted" (427) but rather the enduring complexities of the transitory joy and tragedy of the Round Table, "the paradoxes at the heart of the Arthurian legend, and the paradoxes implicit in the history of its telling." Among those paradoxes is the very influence of the legend, which appeals "first to the child in us, then inexorably reminds us of the world of adult consequences, a world in which the child is father to the man and not always to happy effect" (Landon 53–54).

Like the legend itself, Berger's novel is full of paradoxes and ironies. For instance, after Arthur pulls the sword from the stone and assumes the throne, he quickly discovers the burden of kingship. One of the first of those discoveries is that a monarch has fewer liberties than his subjects do. "Captive of many laws, ordinances, traditions, customs, and moreover, prophecies," all of which conspire to guarantee that he "is never free to do his will" (65), Arthur feels that he is "fundamentally a slave" (78).

Kingship reveals to Arthur other unpleasant realities, such as the fact that doing good may in fact lead to evil.[21] His marriage shatters in large part because of his own selfless actions. Arthur extols Launcelot's virtues to

Guinevere and assigns Launcelot not to the quest, for which he longs, but to the queen's side as her protector and defender. As Berger writes, out of his admiration for his friend and his desire that his wife "be at one with him in his enthusiasms . . . King Arthur took every opportunity to bring Guinevere and Sir Launcelot together" (217). What makes the love triangle of king, queen, and knight so curious is that they each have only the deepest affection for each other; "and all throughout their lives Arthur and Guinevere and Launcelot did love one another, though each pair in a different way" (153). Moreover, the dissolution of Arthur's household mirrors the dissolution of his fabled Order, a noble concept that leads ultimately to war and to the deaths of every Knight of the Round Table. "For this," according to Berger, "was the only time that a king had set out to rule on principles of absolute virtue, and to fight evil and to champion the good, and though it was not the first time that a king fell out with his followers, it was unique in happening not by wicked design but rather by the helpless accidents of fine men who meant well and who loved one another dearly" (447).

In fact, as Suzanne H. MacRae demonstrates, throughout the novel, for Arthur as for others, "Good intentions regularly 'gang a-gley.' Pellinore's obsession with his noble quest blinds him to his daughter's needs, and she commits suicide. Perceval's innocence leads him to fornication, but he is chastised not for the sexual offense but for being ignorant of what he did. His naive piety elicits people's outrage, and many lesser knights challenge him in battle, only to die at his hand" (91). Launcelot's sincere attempts at modesty have unwitting, often deleterious consequences: because of Launcelot's "gentle prevarication" (179), Kay actually believes that he has slain a ferocious enemy and briefly contemplates engaging other superior knights in like combat. Another time, fearing that undertaking the adventure with the Green Knight might be a vain and self-aggrandizing gesture (even though Arthur encourages it), Launcelot forces his beloved comrade Gawaine to volunteer and thereby places him in considerable jeopardy. Gawaine's actions have similar consequences. Out of his deep love for Elaine, Gawaine tells her what she wants to hear – that Launcelot does indeed reciprocate her affection; but his well-meaning consolation only hastens Elaine's demise and contributes to Launcelot's unhappiness as well as his own. Even Gareth's willingness to assume additional kitchen duties is greeted with scorn, and he is punished by the great cook for having "introduced a disorder here" (232).

Conversely, the renouncing of evil does not necessarily lead to good, as illustrated by the example of Sir Meliagrant. Enamored of Guinevere, whom he has detained and imprisoned, the notoriously wicked knight decides to change himself in order to win her affection. But "whereas he had been

---

21 Even as a child, Arthur would sometimes worsen his relationship with Kay because of a good intention gone awry. When his foster-mother Olwen gave him a larger portion of food, "Arthur might well try surreptitiously to exchange his greater quantity with the lesser plate of Kay, thus earning his brother's despite once again" (20).

fearsome when vile, he was but a booby when he did other than ill" (174). The newly-reformed Meliagrant is soon robbed and wounded by a beggar (who, insultingly, purchases the weapon he uses against Meliagrant with the gold that the knight had earlier given to him in charity) and then is killed in a fight with Launcelot. Before he dies, however, Meliagrant concedes – with some understatement – that "This honor can be a taxing thing" (175).

Honor is a taxing thing, especially since virtually every knight of Camelot strives for it. Yet it is a theme, perhaps *the* theme, of *Arthur Rex* that extreme adherence to moral rules can be more damaging than lapses in morality. This is not to suggest that Berger finds the desire to be better and to make things better wrong. But in Berger's novel, the desire to make things *perfect* without admitting human failings usually causes more trouble than outright imperfection does.

Interestingly, Berger's female characters seem best able to articulate this notion of the pursuit of the dangerous ideal. Late in the novel, for instance, when Launcelot says that his war with Arthur is not the result of any hatred between the two, Guinevere thinks to herself, "Nay, it hath happened because of men and their laws and their principles!" (442). In effect, she implies that idealism itself is responsible for many of the world's problems. This notion is echoed by Morgan la Fey, Arthur's half-sister and his greatest nemesis. Throughout the novel, Morgan repeatedly seeks to undermine Arthur's kingdom, especially by counseling Mordred on the "remarkable satisfaction" of bringing pain to others and on the significance of evil as a way of "serv[ing] Life" (224), advice that registers all too easily and too well on Arthur's bastard son. Finally, however, Morgan enters the Convent of the Little Sisters of Poverty and Pain, for after a long career in the service of evil she comes to believe that corruption "were sooner brought amongst humankind by the forces of virtue, and from this moment on she was notable for her piety" (453). She even becomes Mother Superior of the convent that Guinevere eventually joins.

Similarly, the Lady of the Lake, who serves as the antithesis to Morgan's villainy, tells Arthur and his knights that no quest should be conducted blindly. The principles of chivalry, she suggests, must admit some alteration; otherwise, those principles become mere abstractions. And the knights – even the kings – who grow obsessed with "adherence to the letter" (312) stop being men and become instead "abstract example[s] for-argument's-sake" (431). To have a noble purpose is good, she says; "but to be so intent upon it as to see only its end is folly. Never to be distracted is to serve nothing but Vanity" (105).

In a later episode, the Lady of the Lake teaches the same valuable lesson to Gawaine, who is detained at Liberty Castle, a mysterious place where "the freedom of [the] guest is absolute" (201). In keeping with this directive, the castle – Berger's version of the Gothic castle in the great medieval poem *Sir Gawain and the Green Knight* – is full of luxuries and pleasures, including scantily clad young women (or young men, for those so inclined) and exotic foods like "lark's eyes in jelly," "coddled serpent-eggs," and "pickled testicles of tiger." Gawaine tries nobly to resist the temptations by rejecting sexual pleasures and preferring, in good British fashion, "cold mutton and small beer" (203) to the unusual delicacies.

At last, however, he succumbs to the advances of the woman he believes to be his host's wife. Since the terms of his bargain with the host require the exchange of whatever each has won during the day, Gawaine decides to lie: he chooses to say that he gained nothing that day rather than return to a man the pleasure he received from a woman. Whereas in the medieval poem Gawain tries to save his own life by keeping a green girdle presumed to have magical powers, for Berger the issue is preserving one kind of virtue by yielding another. The dilemma that Gawaine faces – lying *to* his host rather than lying *with* his host – highlights the moral complexity of Berger's tale of the Green Knight in particular and of *Arthur Rex* as a whole.[22]

The Green Knight, whom Gawaine encounters after leaving Liberty Castle (and who turns out to be the Lady of the Lake, in another of her disguises), recognizes that Gawaine's failing is small and so gives him, as in the earlier poem, a small nick on the neck rather than the beheading Gawaine expects. At the same time, she explains to him that "a knight does better to break his word than, keeping it, to behave unnaturally. And a liar, sir, is preferable to a monster." Not only does the Lady of the Lake illustrate rather graphically to the young knight the danger of rigid adherence to abstract ideals defined by others; she also sanctions his conclusion that "sometimes justice is better served by a lie than by the absolute and literal truth" (215).

The lessons of the Lady of the Lake serve Gawaine in good stead. Her tutoring, Berger implies, helps turn Gawaine from a notorious lecher into Arthur's "best knight" and allows him to engage in his most noble act of all, his marriage to Lady Ragnell and his subsequent acknowledgment of her sovereignty. In refusing to exercise the rather conventional power of husband as "lord and master" over his wife – "Thou art not an object which I possess like unto a suit of armor" (325–26), he declares – Gawaine not only breaks the spell Morgan la Fey cast on Ragnell but also, and perhaps more importantly, himself gains an even greater power.

The Lady of the Lake appears again to instruct the wounded king on the battlefield at Salisbury Plain. When Arthur wonders if he could have ruled more wisely, she reassures him, "Thou couldst not have done better than thou didst. . . . Thine obligation was to maintain power in as decent a way as would be yet the most effective, and a Camelot without Guinevere, a Round Table without Launcelot, were inconceivable, as would be an Arthur who

---

22 For a fuller discussion of the ways in which Berger adapts and modifies *Sir Gawain and the Green Knight* in Chapter IX of *Arthur Rex*, see Klaus P. Jankofsky, "Sir Gawaine at Liberty Castle: Thomas Berger's Comic Didacticism in *Arthur Rex: A Legendary Novel*."

put to death his best friend and his queen. All human beings must perform according to their nature" (484). Because of her affirmation of his efforts, writes Klaus P. Jankofsky, Arthur "is able to console Bedivere that rather than weep at his king's mortality and the disintegration of his realm he should 'thank God in joy that for a little while we were able to make an inter-regnum in the human cycle of barbarism and decadence' " (390).

Yet the recognition, and ultimately the appreciation, of the dangerous ideal is not restricted to the women in Berger's novel. Merlin, for one, is quite aware of it, especially as he instructs and assists Arthur in the early chapters. The young king, with the zeal of youth, wants to burn the "strumpet residents" of a nearby brothel called the Nunnery of St. Paul's and have the "trollops [sent] to a proper convent"; but Merlin "cast a spell upon Arthur, in which he seemed to see smoke and flames arising from the stews" (33). Just as Malory's Merlin uses a spell to save Arthur in a battle with Pellinore, here Berger's Merlin uses a spell to save Arthur from a moral battle that will bring him only harm. In another instance, when Arthur dis-covers corruption among officials of the Church, he commands that the bishops be flayed alive and the Archbishop of Canterbury be "quartered, then burned." Arthur rationalizes that "our purpose shall be solely to serve the Right, by destroying the Wrong." Once again Merlin controls Arthur's incendiary inclinations and convinces him of the political expediency of having the Church's support; he even advises Arthur to have the Archbishop crown him, with great pomp and ceremony. "Once seated firmly on the throne you may do as you wish, but first you would be wise to do what others expect. Precedent may be mostly rubbish, but timorous mankind look with less fear on that which is oft repeated, even if evil, than on the new, even if good" (34–35). Arthur shrewdly follows Merlin's advice, and within twelve months "the old caitiff" is indeed excommunicated, just as Merlin had promised. Later, after defining his principles of chivalry ("A code for, a mode of, knightly behavior, in which justice is conditioned by generosity, valor shaped by courtesy. . . . The vulgar advantage is declined. Dignity is preserved, even in a foe" [42]), Arthur expresses his concern about wielding the enchanted sword Excalibur against his enemy King Ryons, who is armed with only a "conventional weapon." Merlin says it is "never justice, but rather sentimentality, to deal mildly with intruders" (39–40). He tries to impress upon Arthur that "each king must fashion his own [scale for gauging moral differences], and determine for himself where pride becomes mere vanity, where apparent generosity is real meanness, where justice is not held in equilibrium but is overweighted towards spite or cowardice" (39). And Merlin warns Arthur against lapsing into childish conceptions of chivalry, as did Uther (who lacked altogether the capacity to elevate "to a noble idea" [26] the simple sense of Britain as a land to preserve and defend) or into contemptuous attitudes towards knightly values, as does Ryons (who rails against chivalry as "shitful rubbish" [42]).

Arthur himself echoes Merlin's advice when he tells Kay not to seek perfection at arms, either in himself or in others. But immediately afterward
Arthur hears of Launcelot's prowess and "must have him." When Guinevere
reminds Arthur of his warning about perfection-seeking to Kay, he says, "As
we know, absolute perfection is found only in Heaven. But if 'tis gallant to
seek it as a vassal, it is obligatory to seek it as a king. We know at the outset,
if even the Christ Himself did die as man, that we shall necessarily and ultimately fail. But we can fail gloriously, and glory doth come only from a quest
which is impossible of attainment" (95–97). Arthur's taking of Launcelot into
the Order of the Round Table is part of his quest for the perfection of which
he speaks. So too is his marrying Guinevere. In fact, Arthur decides to wed
Guinevere before he has even seen her, so that he will be "protected from
illicit desire" of the type that led to his affair with Morgawse (78). Thus it is
Arthur's ideals and principles that bring Launcelot and Guinevere together
and lead ultimately to the glorious failure of the realm. For while Arthur is
able to appreciate the sensibility of Merlin's advice, he is – by his very nature
and because of his very human nature – unable to follow that good counsel
so far as to avoid the dangerous idealism that creates but also undermines
Camelot. Only when it is too late does he realize that "to the profound vision
there is no virtue and no vice, and what is justice to one, is injustice to
another" (461).

Like the theme of the dangerous ideal, Berger's use of Arthurian characters is central to the success of his retelling. In *Arthur Rex*, Berger employs
characters in several interesting ways: by recontextualizing some of the most
familiar ones, such as Merlin, who in Berger's version harks back not to
British Arthurian tradition but to earlier American literary treatments; by
recasting others, such as Galahad, whom Berger allows to achieve perfection
without ever embarking on the Grail quest; by giving fuller, richer, more
original roles to minor figures, such as Ygraine, as well as major figures, such
as Guinevere, who has a life apart from Arthur and Launcelot; and by establishing nontraditional juxtapositions between traditional characters, such as
Launcelot and Gawaine, and character types (e.g., fathers and sons). Berger
also creates a new character, the narrator, who assumes not only an authorial
voice but also a distinct persona in the novel.

Berger's Merlin, for instance, tries to limit Arthur's idealism and adapt it
to the practical necessities of the real world. He thus belongs to the American
tradition, which originates with Twain, of questioning the possibility of
achieving perfection in a fallen world. Although not a villain, Berger's
Merlin – unlike the romantic Merlin of Tennyson and other British writers –
is realistic and practical. The Lady of the Lake understands the essence of
this wizard; after sealing him forever in his "cave of alchemy," she tells him:
"Thou hast provided great aid to King Arthur in his gallant experiment to
make noble that which hath ever been mean. But now thy time has come to
leave him, for in the irony that so characterizes human affairs, it is thee who

art the realist, while he will go ever further into the legendary" (109). And, while he is neither the central character, as he is in Robinson's poem, nor central to the book's main conflict, as he is in *Connecticut Yankee*, Merlin is important in laying the groundwork for the novel's main themes, especially the theme of the dangerous ideal, which defines virtually all of the action in *Arthur Rex*.

If Berger's Merlin has some antecedents in American literary history, his Galahad does not. Especially at first glance, Berger's Galahad is anything but the perfect knight he is usually perceived to be; rather, he is a sick young man whose singular distinctive battle deed is the accidental killing of his father, Launcelot. Galahad, who as Jay Rudd contends "has never been much more than a personified abstraction, the emblem of perfection as it might exist in human form," is therefore the character who receives the most thorough reworking in Berger's novel. Whereas in Malory Galahad is introduced as an ideal to be admired – "passynge fayre and welle made . . . seemly and demure as a dove, with all manner of goode features" (Malory 2: 854) – in Berger he is an effeminate, frail, "slight youth and pale to the point of looking quite ill" (422). Moreover – as Rudd details – throughout his retelling Berger continues to present Galahad's career in sharp contrast to tradition. In Malory, Galahad arrives triumphantly at court, sits in the Siege Perilous after pulling the sword from the stone, embarks on the quest for the Holy Grail, which he ultimately achieves, and performs numerous other miraculous feats before his death, which begins the series of calamities that culminate in the dissolution of the Round Table. In Berger, however, Galahad does not even start his career until after the table has been split. He is already dying before he leaves the sheltered castle in which he has lived all of his life with his mother; and when he arrives at Camelot, it is deserted, since most of the knights are fighting at Joyous Garde. Feeling faint, Galahad falls into the nearest chair, which happens to be the Siege Perilous. But it is no glorious event, and only his companion Percival is witness. Eventually Galahad rides out to Salisbury Plain, where he is knighted by Arthur just before the final battle. Then Galahad, exhausted by the excitement and by his own exertion, falls asleep and misses most of the fighting; and when he awakens, he mistakes Launcelot for the enemy and kills him, dying himself with the effort. Yet, despite his physical weaknesses, Galahad enjoys a power that comes from perfection; and "that perfection explains why Galahad does not need to search for the Holy Grail in Berger: being perfect, he has always been in its presence" (Rudd 98). There is, nonetheless, a grim irony in Galahad's one overt knightly act, the killing of Launcelot, a man whom he mistakenly supposed was "a vicious enemy of virtue" (489) – a man, moreover, who had wanted to die from the beginning of the novel and who finally gets his wish at the hands of his son. Berger's markedly unfamiliar approach to the familiar character of Galahad suggests his interest is not so much in the tradition itself as in the very human drama that underlies his story.

Berger is also surprisingly sensitive to other human dramas, especially the often "confine[d] . . . feminine principle" (109); and he generally assigns the women of the legend roles that are much fuller and richer than those they play in other contemporary novels (apart, of course, from the recent popular fantasy and feminist novels of writers like Marion Zimmer Bradley and Persia Woolley, in which women are central). Ygraine, for instance, is typically cast as Gorlois's unfortunate widow, who is deceived, seduced, and impregnated by Uther Pendragon. Berger's Ygraine, however, takes a much more active role in the Arthurian story. Infatuated with Uther, she is as much seducer as seduced: when Gorlois leaves the castle at Terrabil to take up the fight with his rival, Ygraine schemes, albeit subtly, to facilitate Uther's entry. She dismisses the guards, leaving only a solitary porter at the castle gate; kennels the dogs; even marks her bedroom doorway with an appliquéd sign of the Pendragon. And, after Merlin's spell wears off and Uther appears in his own form, she is wholly unsurprised to see him; in fact, she greets him warmly as "my dragon!" (13) and immediately disrobes for his pleasure.

Even when Berger draws on more traditional Arthurian characters and character types, he succeeds in portraying them in nontraditional ways. The details of the episodes in his novel are familiar, but Berger often gives them a new twist. For instance, Launcelot not only appears to fight on Arthur's side at the last battle but, despite earlier wounds inflicted upon him by Mordred and Gawaine, he slays hundreds of enemy soldiers. Berger also shifts the emphasis from the particulars of the contests or battles to the personal conflicts that lead up to those encounters. Especially illustrative of this shift – and especially significant – is the recurrent motif of fathers and sons. Arthur, anxious to understand his father Uther, ultimately reenacts his father's sin – and with even more tragic consequences: he sleeps with his half-sister Margawse, a queen (like Ygraine) who is another man's wife, and begets by her a son who proves to be his undoing. Mordred, in turn, hopes to re-create his father's incest by killing Arthur and taking Guinevere as his queen. The eventual battle between the evil Mordred and the idealistic Arthur, in which both men are killed, is paralleled by the battle between two other knights, the righteous Sirs Galahad and Launcelot, also son and father, who unwittingly take each other's lives. The latter combat is reminiscent of Gawaine's honest fight with another knight of the Round Table, King Pellinore, who had killed Gawaine's father, King Lot – a fight that, precisely because of its honesty, Sir Lamorak, who is both Gawaine's colleague and Pellinore's son, chooses not to contest or avenge; nor does Pellinore's other son, Sir Percival. Later, when Gawaine enters his final battle with his close friend Launcelot, his thoughts are of his own six sons; he feels that honor dictates that he fight, "for what would my sons think of a father who forsook his duty?" (455). Even the wickedness of Meliagrant is tempered by his father Bademagu, a dotty old man who feels only pride for his "pious" and "saintly" son and who continues to hail him as a hero even after his death.

Berger also focuses on other symbolic relationships. The affectionate friendship of Launcelot and Gawaine, for example, serves to gauge the moral health of the kingdom. Their initial combat tests their knightly mettle; afterwards they seal their friendship by vowing never to fight against each other again. That friendship is so dear, in fact, that Gawaine – in a love triangle that serves as a foil for that of Arthur, Launcelot, and Guinevere – refuses to profess his own feelings of affection for Elaine of Astolat. Moreover, he promotes Launcelot to her – albeit with tragic consequences. Gawaine even defends "the noble Launcelot" (438) to Arthur after his half-brother Mordred accuses Launcelot of treason with the queen. When the two knights finally engage in the combat that claims Gawaine's life, it is because honor demands it – Launcelot has unwittingly killed Gawaine's brothers and allowed Mordred to accede to power – and not because Gawaine doubts Launcelot's bravery or generosity or decency; their fight, friend against friend, signals the end of Arthur's realm. An especially tragic contest in which neither wants to be the victor, it confirms Arthur's observation that "our obligations do oft war on each other" (392).

Another interesting character – and certainly Berger's most original character – is the unnamed narrator of *Arthur Rex*. "It is through this narrator," according to Landon, "that Berger pays homage to Malory while refusing to make his own the limits of Malory's vision, and it is through this narrator that Berger creates, not just another version of the Arthurian story, but a comment on the traditions of its telling" (55). Insofar as the obligations to various narrative traditions conflict, the narrator uniquely mirrors the dilemma of the characters in his story. And, while his telling celebrates Malory and strives to be true both to the spirit of Malory and to the larger tradition of Arthurian legend, Berger's narrator, as Landon demonstrates, "differs from his masters" in several respects: by undercutting the conventions of narrative piety with much pragmatic assessment and critique of Christianity as a system of belief; by redirecting attention from the norms of knightly conduct to the realities of power; by consistently revealing his chauvinistic subscription to the conventions of the age's conception of women while even more consistently portraying the women in the Arthurian legend as the only characters deep enough and realistic enough to understand its meanings; and finally by commenting, both implicitly and explicitly, on the language and literature of the Arthurian story. In his smug but often wise asides, the narrator also "judges the motives of everyone from God to King Leodegrance's gardeners and heroically attempts to observe all of the hierarchical proprieties that weave and snarl the Arthurian legend"; and, in his observations (for instance, that churls die from plague and "other maladies of the common folk" while knights "perish only in battle and ladies from love"), he comments on Arthurian conventions at the same time that he balances humorous self-reflexivity with serious insights (Landon 55–56).

In addition to innovative characters and character types, Berger introduces some uniquely American qualities to his story. For example, finding no relief from her problems in religion, Ygraine turns to food and develops an eating disorder; striding from Guinevere's room in "his velvet house-coat and slippers" (418), Launcelot becomes the very image of comfortable domesticity; and Gawaine settles so fully into married life that he spends his spare time gardening and, twice monthly, getting together with the in-laws. But it is Berger's use of the central theme of the dangerous ideal that most explicitly links his book to a tradition of American literature that explores the quest for perfection and examines the notion of the American Dream.

Arthur Rex was not Berger's first reworking of mythic material; he had already examined the great American myth of the frontier in his most celebrated novel, *Little Big Man* (1964). Both *Arthur Rex* and *Little Big Man*, as Landon has remarked, are explorations of a "vital national myth" and represent the central traditions of their respective literary histories (Landon 30). The two novels share other similarities as well, perhaps best expressed in Walker Percy's observation that Arthurian literature is popular "for the same reason (partly) that the Western is popular – perennial appeal of loner, chivalry, combat as ritual, simple good *vs* simple evil etc." (Percy, undated letter to Alan Lupack).

Arthurian motifs are more evident in *Crazy in Berlin* (1958), *Reinhart in Love* (1962), *Vital Parts* (1970), and *Reinhart's Women* (1981), the four novels that comprise Berger's Reinhart series, which chronicles the adventures of Carlo Reinhart over a period of more than thirty years. Berger himself noted the significance of the Arthurian references throughout that series. "Reinhart's quest," he stated in an interview, "is for the Holy Grail" (Hughes, quoted in Landon 47). And, indeed, it is the nature and duration of his quest that define Reinhart, whom Ihab Hassan has called "a clowning knight errant, pure of heart – that is, a custodian of our conscience and our incongruities" (4).

The Reinhart of *Crazy in Berlin* is a blond 21-year-old US Army medic corporal in Allied-occupied Germany. His own life, it appears, is as crazy and chaotic as life in postwar Berlin, where he is stationed; by the novel's end, in fact, Reinhart is so convinced of his own mental illness that he admits himself to a psych ward, where he confesses his literal belief in the Arthurian stories. But because "believing in the actuality of King Arthur turned out to be quite O.K. mentally" (428), he is soon released to continue his own quest.

That quest, as Landon writes, is his attempt to understand a range of paratactic ideologies, represented by the various characters whom he encounters; it is, above all, an "enduring quest . . . for freedom, a definition of self free from the experiences and opprobrium of others," the visual model for which is the knight in Dürer's etching *Ritter, Tod, und Teufel*. Reinhart admires the knight, a man who has "served his time in the gully of death and the devil" and who now rides alone, needing "no helpless victim to give him respect" (360, 361). With his "wonderful tough face, sure of itself," the Knight looks "not at the airy castle or horseshit Death or the mangy Devil, because they'll all three get him soon enough, but he doesn't care. He is complete in himself – isn't that what integrity means? – and he is proud of it, because he is smiling a little" (360–61). Even more fascinating to Reinhart than Dürer's knight, however, are Arthur's knights and comrades – Launcelot, who exchanged "ethereal admiration . . . with King Arthur's wife" (361) yet who *"let them say what they would, and straight he went into the castle, and tied his horse to a ring in the wall; and there he saw a fair green court, and thither he dressed himself, for there him thought was a fair place to fight in"* (362); Sir Servause, who *"had never courage nor lust to do battle against no man, but if it were against giants, and against dragons, and wild beasts"* (361); and the Fisher King ("Having confessed, he had awaited the question of a pure-hearted fool, which, the old legends promised, would heal his wound" [366]).[23]

In *Reinhart in Love*, Reinhart returns from the wasteland of postwar Berlin; he moves from the rubble of Germany "to the bustle of postwar American business, from an economy of scarcity – whether of material goods or of the spirit – to an economy of excess, from the nightmares of the German past to the absurdities of the American dream" (Landon 22). Discharged from the army, in which he had been quite content, Reinhart must face civilian life, which he finds infinitely more dangerous. His continuing quest for identity is often described in medieval and Arthurian imagery: at the time of his discharge, for instance, Reinhart is wearing an Army coat that is likened to "chain mail" (3). When the object of his courtly love, his friend Splendor ("Gallant") Mainwaring's sister, shoots him a look of amused contempt, he thinks that "even a stable-knave with his feet in horse manure can look upon a lady" (51). Speaking to Genevieve, the woman who tricks him into marriage, Reinhart calls her "Guinevere" (then he "caught himself; whenever he tried to make himself understood, he thought irrelevantly of King Arthur" [183]). Later, when he makes love to the new Mrs. Reinhart (in their tin-roofed bower of bliss, a Quonset hut he believes to have been gotten through "wizardry" [200]), "the conviction that for the first time in his life he was doing what everybody everywhere approved, gave him the endurance of Galahad, who had the strength of ten because his heart was pure" (204). Reinhart's Arthurian interest, the reader learns, dates back to "a dog-eared copy of *King Arthur*, with 'Carlo R. age 10' in a childish mess on the flyleaf" (207),[24] a book much like the one Berger himself recalls receiving as a gift from his father when he was a boy.

---

23 Even from the beginning of the novel, Reinhart is described in romance terms: "kingly," "like a monarch" (14), ready to take up the gauntlet (31), anxious for the quest (or, as his friend Schatzi puts it, "the qvest" [194]). That quest, at one point, is described as a "quest for a villain to save someone from" (325).

24 Other Arthurian images appear as well. When Splendor retells – plagiarizes, actually – Melville's story of Bartleby, he renames the long-suffering main character "Arthur"; Reinhart then titles the "original" story "Arthur" and submits it to *The Midland Review* (220–222, 231). There are also allusions to other Arthurian characters, such as Tristan and Isolde (345).

By *Vital Parts*, Reinhart has changed considerably; he is an overweight, middle-aged man of forty-four, with a failing marriage and a string of failed business ventures behind him. Against the cultural turmoil of the late sixties, he battles a variety of personal demons, which include a rebellious son who hates him and a fat, innocent, utterly helpless daughter who adores him; begins an affair with a young girl; and contemplates cryonics, both as a business proposition and as a solution to his own problems. Trying to comprehend how his life went so terribly wrong, he reasons, for instance, that he should have been his son Blaine's best friend, especially since they share the same sensibilities. "Underneath [Reinhart's aging skin] throbbed the questing mind of a philosopher-king, vitalized by the blood of a poet's expansive heart. His own parents had never had a clue to his true character. Why cannot they see me as a prince? he had asked in vain for the last time, and joined the Army at eighteen. He was careful not to have the same failing with Blaine. Had read him King Arthur when the boy was six or seven" (242). At the time, "Blainey's favorite was Sir Galahad, the pure, the dedicated, whose strength was that of ten because his heart was squeaky clean." But Reinhart had considered Galahad too sexless, priggish, obsessive compulsive; he preferred Launcelot, "who carried about him an aura of stain even in the bowdlerized versions for children." Both, Reinhart now realizes, "were water over the dam . . . except that Blaine wore his hair like the Perfect Knight, which may have been one of the leavings, and there was also the possibility, now that Reinhart thought about it, that Blaine believed his own morality to be Galahadic" (242–43). Yet Reinhart, too, shares some of his son's Galahadic morality. When his estranged wife Genevieve chronicles his failures as a husband, he responds simply, "Don't try to impress me with your filthy talk. I'm clean as Sir Galahad" (257).

By *Reinhart's Women*, Reinhart is, if not as clean as Galahad, at least respectable again. Fifty-four years old, in relatively good physical condition, Reinhart is living with his daughter, now a thin and beautiful model, and still trying to reach accommodation with his son, now a snobby, successful stockbroker; and Reinhart has a new passion in his life: cooking. With reminiscence to "armor" (90) him, his same "sacred principles" (94) and "courtesy" to guide him, and the "moral bravery" (139) that comes with age to embolden him, he forges a new life for himself. Even when Genevieve wants a reconciliation, he refuses to be seduced again, professing to have "taken a vow of chastity" (103); and the novel ends with Reinhart's achieving, in some small measure, the quest for understanding he has sought for so long, a sort of secular Holy Grail that he had glimpsed over the years but that had until now eluded his grasp.

And that understanding – in the Reinhart series, an understanding of the ongoing quest for self-definition that parallels the Arthurian Grail quest to which Reinhart often alludes; in *Arthur Rex*, an understanding that Gawain learns from the Lady of the Lake, that Percival possesses inherently, and that both Launcelot and Arthur achieve only before dying – is perhaps Berger's true Grail.

Another intriguing retelling of the Arthurian story – though one less ambitious and successful than Berger's *Arthur Rex* – occurs in Donald Barthelme's last novel. Posthumously published, *The King* (1991) is both a parody of medieval myth and a political allegory that conflates a familiar legend with modern history, both factual and imaginary. Like so much of Barthelme's earlier fiction, the novel consists of fragments seemingly associated at random; but it is precisely the seeming randomness of those fragments that forms the pattern and ultimately reveals the meaning of the work. "Only trust the fragments," Barthelme advised his readers; and in *The King*, it is the fragments of the Arthurian legend that provide the novel's main structure.

Those fragments, however, are intercut with numerous references to people and events of World War II. The news of Guinevere's adultery with Launcelot and later with the Brown Knight, for instance, is spread not by court gossip but by Lord Haw-Haw in his radio broadcasts from Berlin. Mordred's shortcomings, particularly his inability to govern, remind the Yellow Knight of "this fellow Churchill [who] seems less than competent" and whom Launcelot agrees has "not done very well by us thus far, that's a certainty" (55). There is fear that "the invincible forces of the Reich are advancing on all fronts. Dunkirk has been completely secured. The slaughter is very great. Gawain has been reported captured – " (3). And the quest is no longer for the sacred cup but for the ultimate weapon, a bomb that will "chastise and thwart the enemy" and "that will end the war with a victory for the right" (76).

This intercutting of Arthurian matter and modern history not only deflates the traditional mythic notions of chivalry and courtly love but also links the medieval conflicts with the modern. Charles Molesworth suggests that, in fact, the main ideas of this clever, fragmentary novel "are something like this: wars never seem to be concluded, since they express mythic longings and are thus constantly reenacted as tragedies ('legend requires a tragic end,' as Guinevere puts it – *but*, significantly, the novel ends without one); romance – the realm where the wish is parent to the fact – also never ends because of the same mythic longing; and these two ever-renewed sources of action are what keep history from being merely an unshapeable succession of events ('Well, it was one damn thing after another,' says Arthur, alluding to one of the most famous definitions of history as nonsignifying)" (106). *The King* is indeed about war and romance and history. Like *Snow White*, perhaps Barthelme's best known work, it comments on the fact that kings and princes and other mythic heroes no longer exist because they have been driven out of existence precisely by daily life.[25] Like the narrator of

25 Richard Gilman argues this point most convincingly. One of Barthelme's major premises,

"The Glass Mountain," who scales the mountain, approaches the "beautiful enchanted symbol" that resides at the top in "a castle of pure gold," and then tosses it to his rather crude companions below, Barthelme's characters are attracted by the hopefulness of myth and fairy tale yet are ultimately too modern to believe in either. And while they still seek enchanted symbols, it is largely for the purpose of disenchanting those symbols once they find them.

The knights in *The King* seek a Grail – the atomic bomb – that will ostensibly destroy the very notion of the quest. But unlike the enchanted symbol that can be disenchanted, the "Grail-as-bomb" (79), once achieved, can never be unachieved; it will remain, as inescapable as "a volcano in the parlor" (142), its very existence denying the need for knights ever again. As the highwaywoman Clarice observes, "All you good and worshipful knights out of work. On the dole. Not a pretty picture" (142).

Arthur is quite aware that this new quest works against the "Round Table as an institution," and although his comrades advise him to develop the bomb before his enemies do, he refuses. As he tells Kay, "the essence of our calling is right behavior, and this false Grail is not a knightly weapon" (130). Arthur's opposition is so strong, in fact, that he destroys the three equations – the first of which appears in a box of Girl Guide cookies, the second attached to the leg of a hanging man, and the third inside a box along with the mace Launcelot left in the men's room of the Lamb and Flag pub – that comprise the mathematical formula for making the bomb. Yet part of the very real sadness in this darkly comic novel arises from the fact that, contrary to all of Arthur's good intentions, his enemies *do* get the bomb, the Round Table as an institution *is* destroyed, and the need for knights or reason for quests in the modern world *is* indeed eliminated.

Correspondingly, throughout *The King* the characters undercut their own mythic significance by contrasting their current circumstances with the "old days." Guinevere admits to Varley that "this is not my favorite among our wars. . . . Once upon a time the men went out and bashed each other over the head for a day and a half, and that was it. Now we have ambassadors hithering and thithering, secret agreements with still more secret codicils, betrayals, reversals, stabs in the back – " (4–5). Sir Kay, lamenting the accumulation of unanswered correspondence that reduces him to a secretarial role, recalls that "in the old days, we'd have made the messengers eat the letters. Including the seals" (10). Arthur rejects Kay's advice to strike preemptively because bombing civilian populations is a violation of the social contract. "We're supposed to do the fighting, and they're supposed to pay for it." That, Kay reminds Arthur, is how it *used* to be: "Those were the days" (12). Launcelot

he writes, is "that princes no longer exist, in a crucial double sense. As a figure in reality . . . he has been driven out of existence precisely by daily life . . . and as a literary figure, the hero, he can have no stature because the reality he has been abstracted from no longer sustains the values necessary to his creation" ("Barthelme's Fairy Tale" 31).

remembers that "once upon a time, one could have a love affair in decent quietude. . . . Now one can't pop open a French letter without it being plastered all over the hoardings" (16). When the Brown Knight tells Guinevere the bombing losses per raid are "very close to acceptable" – using a formula that changes daily, to cover all possible situations – Guinevere remarks again that this is "a ghastly way to fight a war. I much prefer the old ways" (45). The Black Knight and the Blue Knight exalt "former times [in which] bombing had some military purpose – taking out a railyard, smashing the enemy's factories, closing down the docks, that sort of thing. Today, not so. Today, bombing is meant to be a learning experience. For the bombed. Bombing is a pedagogy" (79).

One of the main differences between the "old days" for which the characters long and the current times is the inherent value of the causes that they espouse and the principles that they defend. The unnamed Pole who represents unhappy workers in the shipyards and on the railways is fighting not for a higher purpose (as Walesa's Solidarity did) but for higher wages; the workers want "more money" (6), which the King is glad to give – that is, after "rais[ing] the tax on a pint commensurately" (10). Launcelot and the Black Knight listen as the pilgrim Walter the Penniless makes a strong case for the dissolution of the chivalric order by pointing to the king's strange recent behavior and asking if he has become "just too noble and grand to answer for his actions." Afterwards, the two debate not the merits of Walter's argument but their own response – whether to "brast his pate or give him a few pennies." Launcelot advocates the latter, since he believes that it would "deprive [Walter] of his rationale"; and the episode ends with "the knights showering money on Walter the Penniless" (40) – a gesture that, ironically, gives greater credence to Walter's arguments.

Knightly ideals are not the only things that are diminished in *The King*; even dreams reflect the characters' frustrations. Arthur, who knows that dreams are always prophetic, recalls a recent dream for Kay: on the street, a beautiful woman gives him a first look, then a second look; soon they are in bed together. But, knowing that Arthur is married, the woman leaves – "quite properly so" (122). In a second dream, however, Arthur is in bed with a big hairy male bear: "the bear was a king too. Spoke Latin and smelled bad." Though Arthur's Latin is weak, he thinks the bear says to him "something to the effect that 'when there are bears on the boulevards, then the state is tottering' " (122). And, unfortunately for Arthur and his Order, it is the second dream that proves more prophetic than the first: though no bears are sighted on the streets, the kingdom is definitely in ruin. By contrast, Kay – on whom the affairs of state register more lightly – dreams "of cheese. Toasted, mostly" (123). Like Arthur's, Launcelot's dreams are intense and sadly touching. On the novel's final page, and in the novel's final image, Launcelot lies sleeping. Observers wonder if he is dreaming "that there is no war, no Table Round, no Arthur, no Launcelot!" (158). But his dream is actually about Guinevere – her "softness," "sweetness," "brightness," and "sexuality" – who, like a latter-day Grail maiden, "enters the dream in her own person, wearing a gown wrought of gold bezants over white samite and carrying a bottle of fine wine." The fact that all of this takes place "under an apple tree . . ." (158) at first suggests a certain hopefulness and promise: Launcelot as a kind of Adam may yet find happiness in a new world with his Eve (just as Walker Percy's Lancelot, another Adamic figure, may find happiness in a new world with his Eve, fellow mental patient Anna). But the apple tree – borrowed from another myth, Genesis – also implies the sad end of that hope and the corruption of Adamic innocence and trust. Barthelme's Launcelot, after all, does not achieve his quest; and even his dreams ultimately serve to mock his ambitions. (An earlier episode in the novel foreshadows this final scene: Launcelot loses his way in the dark woods and mistakes a tree for "a golden cup or chalice" [92].)

Perhaps because most of the major characters in the novel fall so short of the mythic stature of their medieval counterparts, they are preoccupied with how they appear to others. In particular, they share a very modern obsession with their own press. Guinevere feigns nonchalance as she listens to Lord Haw-Haw's radio broadcast from Berlin, in which he accuses "the false and miscreant king" of languishing "conspicuously alone" (3) at Dover and Guinevere of spending "all her time drinking sloe gin while dallying with one of the king's chief advisers" (4). But rather than ignore the filth, Guinevere insists that her assistant Varley switch the station to Ezra Pound's broadcast so she can hear what he might be saying about her. As a monarch, Arthur understands the benefit of meeting regularly with reporters; such proximity to the press allows him, on occasion – as with the matter of the alleged flaying off of his beard – to put his own spin on events. Yet even he worries about what kind of obituary he will get from *The Times*: "How many pages? How many photographs? Of what size?" (12). The Black Knight also wonders "what sort of play the press will give the story when I depart" (18). Launcelot, more realistic than his medieval counterpart, admits that he "took the precaution, some time ago, of sitting down with the chap who does *The Times* obits" (18) to ensure that the reporter understood the "peculiar circumstances" of Launcelot's birth, class, and history.

As different in form and language as *The King* is from more conventional American Arthurian literature, it has some important links to those other works. Not least is the preoccupation in *The King* with the notion of democracy and the downplaying of kingship. Chivalry is obsolete, according to Walter the Penniless; he announces to Launcelot that "the old order is dead. Finished. We don't want the extraordinary, as represented by you gentlemen and your famous king, any longer. It is a time for the unexceptional, the untalented, the ordinary, the downright maladroit. Quite a large constituency" (37). Even Arthur, as he tells the reporter from the *Spectator*, believes that the concept of king is "fundamentally an absurd idea. Has to do with dogs, dog breeding, really, dogs and horses." He concedes that not being king "might be quite grand." He welcomes the pleasure of being inconspicuous, "a fudge in the crowd" (81) who does not have to fret about royal problems like the correct seating of baronets at state functions, the setting of appropriate amounts of taxation, and the ever-increasing costs of ermine.

Ironically, the most noble of all ventures – the quest for the Holy Grail – becomes in Barthleme's novel one of the most democratic. For all the knights' talk about achieving the "Grail-as-bomb," the only actual Grail in *The King* is an opera called *The Grail*, which attacks the king. In the opera, written by Sir Percy Plangent, "the Grail is [literally] a bomb that will make everyone happy forever." In Act One, that bomb, consisting of a compound of europium and eurekium, is discovered; in Act Two, it is refined; and in Act Three, it explodes. "In the first act, everybody denounces Arthur for not having a wonderful bomb like this. In the second act, everybody decides that something must be done. In the third act, the bomb goes off!" (101). The bomb itself is purportedly "a metaphor for the unhappiness of those groaning under the yoke" (101). What makes Barthelme's Grail – or, more precisely, *The Grail's* Grail – so unusual is not just the form it assumes but its accessibility to commoners, "the folk . . . under the yoke" (101). No longer simply a spiritual ideal to be achieved by the purest and most noble knight or knights, as in traditional accounts, this Grail represents (as do Walter and Clarice) the very real hopes and frustrations and fears of the majority. (In "The Educational Experience," a story in the volume *Amateurs* [1976], museum-visiting students also "quest" after the truth; but complicating their task is the fact that the Chapel Perilous has been turned into a bomb farm; the Fisher King is "fishing, hopelessly, in a pool of blood"; and "The world is everything that was formerly the case." So the students are advised "to get back to the bus" [127–28].)

Barthelme's Arthurian world in *The King*, in which Arthur gets called to jury duty, King Unthank produces porno films starring his wife, and brazen knights actually wear brown armor with black horses, is – to be sure – quite modern. But it is also mythic, almost postmythic, the way Barthelme's fiction is sometimes labeled postmodern. Yet Barthelme's use of Arthurian motifs suggests that for him, as for so many other contemporary American novelists, the legendary world provides an excellent vantage point from which to survey and to parody contemporary events. And his Americanizing of the characters and democratizing of the Grail places Barthelme squarely in the tradition of American Arthuriana that – despite its obvious contemporaneity – reaches back to Lowell's Launfal.

Most of the contemporary novelists who incorporate Arthurian motifs and imagery in their fiction set in modern times draw on the myth of the Fisher King and the Grail. John Updike, however, finds inspiration elsewhere – in the story of Tristan and Isolt. His novel *Brazil* (1994), in fact, updates and reinterprets the legend by transforming the lovers into a modern Brazilian couple who find their fate and their life's purpose in the passion they feel for each other.

Tristão Raposo, a nineteen-year-old black child of the Rio slums, meets Isabel Leme, an eighteen-year-old upper-class white girl, on the beach at Copacabana; approaching her with tremendous "courtliness" (7), he offers her a stolen ring, a gift that instantly binds them as husband and wife. Afterwards, in the nearby apartment of Isabel's affluent Uncle Donaciano, they make love, Isabel's virginal blood leaving on the sheets a chalice-shaped stain as symbolic testament to the sanctity of their union. Both families, however, disapprove of the relationship and force them to take flight: Tristão's whoring mother Ursula considers the two "pure crazy," curses them, and dismisses Isabel as "trash" (34, 40); blind old Granny smells their "bad luck" (42); and Euclides and Chiquinho, thinking that Isabel's attraction to their brother is some kind of "trap" (40), betray the couple by disclosing their whereabouts to the thugs hired by Isabel's father. Yet Isabel remains devoted to her "knight" (49), whom she loves for his "gallantry" (13) and "chivalrous impulse[s]" (19), and Tristão in turn longs to act as Isabel's "defender" (53); believing that fate brought them together, they continue to "*Keep faith*" (64–65), even as circumstances seem to pull them farther and farther apart.

Over the next few years, their love is repeatedly tested and renewed. Tristão and Isabel move from Rio to São Paolo, where they live blissfully for a time at the "Hotel Amour"; to Brasília, where they are reunited despite her father's vow that "she will not see Tristão again" (73); to Serra de Buraco, in Brazil's interior, where they stake a claim to a small plot and struggle for four years – Tristão, laboring each day to exhaustion in the mine; Isabel, prostituting herself with local men and caring for her two young children (neither one by Tristão); to the Mato Grosso, where they encounter anew Isabel's father's henchman, whom Tristão must kill in order to evade. They take flight again, but their troubles continue. After being set upon by Guaicuru, who murder their loyal retainer and kidnap Isabel's children, the lovers are "rescued" by Antonio Peixoto. Captain of a "*bandeira* of brave and pious Paulistas" (166), Antonio forces the "nigger" Tristão into shackled slavery and takes the blonde Isabel as his third wife, whose "service" produces a limp, spiritless, amber-eyed son named Salomão, after Isabel's father. For three years, Isabel complies with Antonio's demands; but when one of his other wives, Ianopamoko, hints that a shaman can relieve her sorrow and restore her loss, Isabel seizes the opportunity.

As in the best tradition of South American magical realism, which is an obvious influence on Updike's novel, at this moment the story assumes an almost fairy tale quality. Isabel journeys for seventeen days before finding the shaman, to whom she offers a bejeweled cross stolen from her uncle. He asks instead for the ring with which Tristão had originally pledged his love and then makes clear that "for every gain, there is a sacrifice, somewhere else" (186). After Isabel agrees "to change [her]self, to sacrifice," for Tristão, the shaman's magic transforms her from a pale beauty into an ebony-skinned warrior woman, while – unbeknownst to her – in a simultaneous transformation, Tristão sheds his handsome blackness for a blond whiteness.

At this point, it is as if Updike decides to retell the first part of the novel, only this time in reverse. Persons, places, and events in the novel are transformed accordingly. Isabel and Tristão, together again after Antonio flees the encampment, rediscover their passion; yet, in their sexual relationship, they reverse roles – suddenly, "she was the cock and he the hen" (205). The two retrace their journey through the Mato Grosso, returning to Brasília, where this time Isabel's father welcomes them and – as Tristão had wished many years before – treats Tristão as he would any white gentleman, which of course Tristão has now become. Giving them his blessing, Isabel's father even offers to copy for Isabel the ring that was Tristão's first gift to her. (Now an object of rarity and great value, the ring was originally thought to be a mean trinket.) The couple ultimately arrives in São Paolo, the site of their earlier privation, where they achieve financial success and social standing, and where Isabel gives birth to three more children (as before, none by Tristão). On a visit to Uncle Donaciano, in whose apartment they first consummated their relationship and with whom relations are again warm, they reminisce about Isabel's childhood. From Donaciano, Isabel learns the truth about her "bad mother," whom she had believed for years to be a kind of saint, which creates a new bond with Tristão – though now he denies his whoring mother's neglect. Meanwhile, bored by the conversation, unable to sleep, Tristão leaves the apartment to revisit the beach where he and Isabel met; there he is assaulted by several dark street boys, who so resemble his younger self that they could pass for his own sons. Though he tries to convince them that "I am one of you" (254), the boys rob the blond stranger and stick him with a razor, much like the one Tristão himself used to carry; and they leave him to die in his grey suit, stripped of his Rolex watch and his wallet, lying in the saltwater.

When Isabel, accompanied by her uncle and several police officers, finds Tristão, he is "face down, his flawless teeth bared in a polite snarl, his hand curled near his chin in the childish way he had when he slept. . . . *Fidelity*, his stiff body said, clinging there to the beach" (258). Remembering from their early and lonely days at the mining shack the story of "a woman, long ago, who, her lover dead, lay down beside him and willed herself to die, and did" (259–60), Isabel tries to do the same. But "there would be no miracle today" (260), so she staggers to her feet and lets her uncle lead her home. Thus ends the contemporary tale of Tristão and Isabel.

Not simply a South-Americanizing of the Tristan and Iseult romance (the Joseph Bédier version of which, Updike notes in his "Afterword," gave him the "tone and basic situation" of his novel), *Brazil* is also an Americanized and democratized retelling of the familiar tale. The fact that Tristão is a black youth from the lower classes (and that Isabel, after her transformation, has the experience of a lower class black as well) suggests that, for Updike, as for so many other American writers who treat the Arthurian legends in their fiction, nobility is a quality of the real "self within the outer selves" (189). The young black Tristão is a bold man who knows what he wants and how to get it. The older white Tristão, distanced from his humble roots, loses some of his "instinctive chivalry" (205) and becomes "an artificial man" (237). No longer the "knight errant" (224) he perceives himself to be, Tristão develops an increasing sense of class consciousness: "he took up the status-appropriate activities – tennis, jogging, squash, wind-surfing – and excelled in all, with his limber grace and latent ferocity. He even seduced a few of his middle-management colleagues' wives, when it became clear that this, too, was a game" (234). Yet, commuting between favored restaurants in São Paolo and their beach house in Ubatuba, "he was forever getting lost" (234). The new life of affluence to which he had long aspired is, in reality, far less fulfilling than the life he left behind; "he thought back nostalgically upon the emptiness of the Mato Grosso, when he and Isabel had first traversed it, with its faint woody tang of some spiritual heartwood . . . [and] he thought of how in their worst extremity" Isabel's pale body had served as "the food of love" (235). Unlike Isabel, who experiences real liberation after assuming the blackness of a slave in a riches-to-rags transformation, Tristão realizes – too late – that he was richest when in poverty.

Updike further deromanticizes Tristão and Isabel by depicting the stark realities of their daily life. Whereas, in most medieval versions, love is enough to sustain the couple, enough even to turn their wildest surroundings into a pleasant pastoral, Updike's lovers need more. When their stake produces no gold, they grow hungry and gaunt. Tristão feels "too bone-weary, generally, to minister to Isabel" (127); dust-covered, exhausted, virtually defeated, he rarely wants to make love anymore. Isabel, at first conscious only of Tristão's comfort and pride, soon "falls into a kind of doze when he left her alone in the shack, with the babbling of the poisoned creek behind, and the dangers of the desolate sunstruck street outside" (128); and, "to satisfy a ravenous thirst for some world other than this one" (129), a world of good foods and pretty clothing, she begins prostituting herself with local men. "Romanticism," writes Updike, "is what brings a couple together, but realism is what sees them through." So, when Isabel surprises Tristão with a lavish meal of bacon and fish and pineapple, he mutely accepts the bounty and seats "himself at the unusually loaded table with the constrained formality of a king whose sceptre is hollow" (130).

Early in their relationship, during their enforced separation, both Tristão and Isabel had taken other lovers. Yet even after their reunion they are not monogamous. Isabel, especially, keeps sleeping with other people, from Antonio's young wife Ianopamoko to the jeweler Olympio. She never bears a baby by Tristão; all six of her children are by other men. The couple nonetheless continues to "keep faith," albeit in a way that only realists, not pure romantics, could. Unlike their medieval counterparts, who – in some versions of the tale – resort to elaborate ruses to keep from consummating marriages to their respective spouses, Tristão and Isabel accept infidelity as routinely as they do beatings or poverty; it becomes part of the fate that binds them to each other.

Nowhere is the realism of Updike's reinterpretation more evident, however, than at its conclusion, which strips the original legend of its most magical moment. As Isabel lies on the sand beside her lover and waits "to ride [his] body like that of a dolphin into the submarine realm of death," a bitter seaweedy taste "already flavored his skin. The crowd sensed the grand thing she was attempting, and grew reverentially hushed" (260). But no mystical metamorphosis occurs. Instead, Isabel's closed lids get burned by the rising sun; the crowd grows bored and begins to disperse; and Donaciano, embarrassed by his niece's "vulgar display of Brazilian romanticism" (260), helps her to her feet. No symbolic vine attesting to the permanence of their passion springs up on the spot where Tristão died. Just the opposite: the waves quickly erode all signs of their footprints, utterly erasing "Tristão's deep, spongy steps" (258) along with Isabel's.

Updike first retold the tale of Tristan and Iseult almost three decades earlier in "Four Sides of One Story," an epistolary short story originally published in the *New Yorker* and collected in *The Music School* (1966). As the title indicates, the story consists of four letters, one from each of the protagonists of the tale. As Michael Harry Blechner notes, "Each letter is meant to reflect not only the writer's personality, but also his or her place in the myth as Updike understands it. Tristan is the Grand Lover seeking the meaning of passion and of life; Iseult the Fair eschews meanings and seeks rather a kind of emotional fulfillment; her counterpart, Iseult of the White Hands, is the ordinary person beset by problems she can feel but not fully understand; and Mark, Tristan's counterpart, is the cool rationalist who thinks he has everything under control" (31–32).

The first and longest letter, from Tristan, is addressed to his beloved, Iseult the Fair. To escape his obsession with her – and to avoid the divorce suit her husband has initiated – Tristan has booked passage on an ocean liner to some unknown destination; from on board, he attempts to rationalize his conduct. "We are in love," he writes. "The only way out of love is marriage, or some sufficiently pungent piece of overexposure equivalent to marriage. I am prepared to devote my life to avoiding this death. As you were brave in creating our love, so I must be brave in preserving it" (93). Though Tristan admits that he often denied Iseult's pain, "cheated it of dimension and weight," his justification is that he did it for her: "Whatever sacrifices you offered to make, whatever agony you volunteered to undergo for me, I permitted. In the limitless extent of my willingness to accept your love, I was the perfect lover" (91). Tristan's quickness to abdicate any real responsibility for his actions – and his insistence on ascribing guilt to others – comically under-cuts the nobility of the traditional Tristan character.

Tristan's wife, Iseult of the White Hands, apparently possesses a sensibil-ity as modern as her husband's. In her letter to her brother Kaherdin, she complains about their three bratty children, bemoans her own lack of dignity in Tristan's ongoing affair, and explains her conflicting emotions about the other Iseult. "I've never much liked her, which oddly enough offends him, but I really do sympathize with what he must have put her through" (95). Her sex life with Tristan was good, she writes, although the better she was in bed, the more "he took it as a reproach" (96). But it was the "real action," the ordinariness of married life, that terrified him the most. Now that he has left – "again" – all she has is "a house, . . . a bank account, and a ghost" (94), and a lot of Noilly Prat to help her get through the day.

Iseult the Fair, on the other hand, has more pressing concerns: a husband who is ready to divorce or commit her. "Nothing matters" (98), she con-cludes in her brief but rambling unsent letter to Tristan, imploring him to return. In his absence, she is trying to teach herself to love Mark, the king whom she acknowledges they have "brought low" (97, 98); but images of the flowers and books Tristan gave her recur, and she wishes it was his knock at her door, not Mark's.

The final letter, "dictated but not signed" (100), is from King Mark to his retainer Denoalen. The legal proceedings against Tristan and Iseult, Mark advises, should be temporarily halted: "confronted with the actuality of marriage, the young man bolted even sooner than we had anticipated," leaving Iseult "accordingly disillusioned and satisfactorily tractable" (99). Their affair, he concedes, was only to be expected: Iseult, after all, is "a woman of Irish blood" and Tristan "a man whose upbringing was entirely Continental" (100). At the moment, though, the queen is a political asset; should her therapy fail, there is always commitment. Either way, Mark believes that he is "fully in control of matters at last" (100) – although his self-confidence is as dangerously hollow as Tristan's philosophic posturing.

Updike's story includes all of the major elements of the traditional myth, from Tristan and Iseult's drinking of the magic potion to Mark's jealousy, from Tristan's bravery in battle to his subsequent betrayal of his wife. Yet, as in *Brazil*, the characters in "Four Sides of One Story" are as contemporary as they are timeless: Iseult of the White Hands drinks too much and explains her husband's frequent absences as "business trips"; Iseult the Fair loses weight from stress, takes pills, and is in treatment; Mark photostats incrimi-nating correspondence from his wife's lover to use in his divorce case; and Tristan complains about the tattered copies of Paris *Match* in the ship's library and the poor service he receives from an arrogant waiter. Updike, however, gives the traditional story itself a very clever, contemporary twist, a twist that is not fully revealed until all four sides of the story are told: Mark's suit against Tristan and Iseult, which would leave Iseult the Fair free to marry Tristan, is just a ploy. Mark knows – as Iseult of the White Hands can attest – that Tristan loves love but hates marriage, a fact Tristan confirms by running away from both Iseults. The suit, therefore, is Mark's way of forcing Tristan's hand and evincing his cowardice and inconstancy. With Tristan on the run and out of the picture, Iseult tries to patch things up with Mark – precisely what Mark originally intended – while the other Iseult, unable to bear the gossiping, begins to re-evaluate her marriage. It is a very modern situation indeed, and an interesting variation on the original tale, with which it is juxtaposed.

In *The Afterlife* (1994), Updike returns yet again to the legendary lovers. In his story "Tristan and Iseult," Tristan is a dental patient, and Iseult is his new hygienist; the threat of pain that adds "mystical spice to these liaisons" (148) heightens the intimacy of their encounter. Like a courtly lover, "Tristan" dares not glance directly at the eyes of "Iseult" but rather gathers their "spiritual, starlike afterimage" (150) in her safety goggles. "Enwrapped, protected" by her paper mask, she reveals herself to him slowly: by her "pricking and probing" attentions and "tactful" touches, by her forgiveness of his damaging dietary excesses, by her easy acceptance of a side of himself that he normally manages to keep hidden (an angle on the self "more loathsome than in his humblest moments he had dreamed" [151]), and by her faintly more aggressive invasion of his flesh. "She was made for him," he announces happily, "of the same imperilled and fallible substance, yet also woven of Heaven, unpossessable, timeless, inviolate" (151).

Once Tristan's teeth have been cleaned and polished, the relationship changes; "without the threat of pain, their encounter became small" (152). Iseult, however, recommends an additional procedure, a bleaching process to retard staining. Tristan believes that this is her way of trying to extend their encounter; yet he is aware that she will not be witness to the shining result. Since she is a stranger to him and since he knows it is unlikely that he will find himself in her chair again, Tristan concludes that "the principle lay between them like a sword. Otherwise, it wouldn't be sublime" (153).

By recasting the ill-fated lovers as a hygienist and a dental patient, Updike punctures the traditional myth. The patient's immediate recognition of the new hygienist as "a rare one, one he could trust not to hurt him more than necessary" (148), lampoons the romantic notion of instant, undying love, as does his realization that the sublimity of their engagement lies in its fleetingness and utter impossibility. Nevertheless, in his brief but witty "Tristan and Iseult," as in his other two treatments of the Tristan and Iseult story, Updike offers his readers a new version of the old myth, a version that – while it retains numerous elements of the original – is more contemporary, more realistic, and more adapted to modern sensibilities and concerns.

To be sure, other important writers apart from Malamud, Kesey, Percy, Styron, Kosinski, Mason, Berger, Barthelme, and Updike treat Arthurian themes or incorporate Arthurian motifs in their fiction. Saul Bellow, for instance, employs the quest theme extensively in his fiction; and although that quest is largely non-Arthurian in nature, in works like *Henderson, the Rain King* (1959) he draws on ritual aspects of Grail and wasteland mythology. Similarly, in *A Bad Man* (1967), Stanley Elkin depicts a modern day wasteland presided over by a warden named Fisher, who describes himself as a fisher of bad men. Feldman – a "felled man," as his name suggests – is nevertheless a kind of knight errant, who experiences "a grapple of grail" (327) and restores some life to Fisher's wasteland. He even rejuvenates his friend Dedman (another "dead man"). And Kurt Vonnegut, whose wonderfully comic novels satirize familiar myths and stories, weaves numerous Arthurian allusions into his fiction. In an early work, *Mother Night* (1961), for example, he depicts some of the adventures – and misadventures – of Howard W. Campbell, Jr., a Nazi by reputation and a former US counterintelligence agent in fact, who himself can no longer tell if he is a hero or a traitor. At one time, Campbell had been a playwright who wrote about romantic topics such as love and knights. One play, "The Goblet," found in a trunk in Berlin at the end of the war, tells the story of the Holy Grail, which is guarded by a blindingly pure young maiden who will surrender it only to a knight as pure as herself. "Such a knight comes along, and is pure enough to win the Grail." But, by winning it, he causes the girl to fall in love with him, and he falls in love with her. They begin having impure thoughts about each other, "tending, involuntarily, to disqualify themselves from any association with the Grail. The heroine urges the hero to flee with the Grail, before he becomes unworthy of it. The hero vows to flee without the Grail, leaving the heroine worthy of continuing to guard it." Apparently the hero makes their decision for them, since they both have become impure in thought. The Holy Grail disappears. Stunned by this unanswerable proof of their depravity, the lovers confirm what they firmly believe is their damnation with a tender night of love. The next morning, "confident of hell-fire, they promise to give each other so much joy of life that hell-fire will be a cheap price to pay." At that moment, the Grail appears to them, signifying that Heaven does not despise love like theirs. "And then the Grail goes away again, forever, leaving the hero and heroine to live happily ever after" (147–48).

The Grail – or at least the allusion to it – recurs in other of Vonnegut's novels, such as *Deadeye Dick* (1982), in which the protagonist's father assumes that all of Dick's friends are familiar with the legends of King Arthur (38), the protagonist's mother assumes that seeking the Holy Grail is "clearly a man's job" ("she already had a cup that overflowed and overflowed with good things to eat and drink anyway" [216]), and the protagonist's acquaintance Mr. Barry assumes that "Sir Galahad was a Jew" (154). ("According to Fred T. Barry, a Jew named Joseph of Arimathea took Christ's goblet when the Last Supper was over"; brought the goblet to the Crucifixion, where some of Christ's blood fell into it; was arrested "for his

Christian sympathies" but survived in prison because the goblet fed him; traveled to England, where he founded the first Christian church – at Glastonbury; and had children, who inherited "the goblet, which came to be known as the 'Holy Grail.' " But "sometime during the next five hundred years, the Holy Grail was lost. King Arthur and his knights would become obsessed with finding it again – the most sacred relic in England. Knight after knight failed. Supernatural messages indicated that their hearts weren't pure enough for them to find the Grail. But then Sir Galahad presented himself at Camelot, and it was evident to everyone that his heart was perfectly pure. And he did find the Grail. He was not only spiritually entitled to it. He was legally entitled to it as well, since he was the last living descendant of that wandering Jew, Joseph of Arimathea" [154–55].) Grail imagery also appears in *Bluebeard*, when the novel's protagonist, artist Rabo Karabekian, describes his quest for Marilee Kemp, the mistress of his mentor Dan Gregory. As Gregory is "working on a new edition of *Tales of King Arthur and His Knights*" and Marilee is posing as Guinevere, Rabo decides he must make himself worthy of her: "I would bring her the Holy Grail" (182). Years later, he is still in no position to make her his own: a military man, his pay was low, and "There were no Holy Grails for sale at the Post Exchange" (207). When they meet again, after the war, it is not Rabo but Marilee – now a wealthy widow – who seems to have found the Grail in a nurturing sisterhood of abused women she literally supports in her palazzo. And in Vonnegut's most popular novel, *Slaughterhouse-Five* (1969), Billy Pilgrim, like Percy's Lancelot and Barthelme's Launcelot a kind of American Adam, survives the firebombing of Dresden, perhaps the biggest contemporary wasteland of all, in order to deliver to Earthlings the healing knowledge he gains from the Tralfamadorians.

Even Norman Mailer, whose fiction (most recently in *The Gospel According to the Son*) retells a variety of myths, used the Arthurian legend to parallel part of the plot of one of his earliest works. In *Barbary Shore* (1951), originally titled *Mrs. Guinevere* (Manso 158), the character of Guinevere was apparently based on a real person, the landlady of a boarding house in which Mailer rented a room in the summer of 1947. The details of *Barbary Shore*, however, are more than just "a facsimile of life"; the novel – as Carl Rollyson has observed – is "a parody of an Arthurian romance, with Guinevere, a former burlesque queen, the center of everyone's attention" (67).[26] But the symbolic value of the name Guinevere, as Barry H. Leeds notes, is underlined not only by her previous position but also "by devices as '. . . the hem of her purple velvet wrapper swished luxuriously along the floor.' It is an indication of the sordid state of our times and our society as Mailer sees it, if Beverly Guinevere is to represent our royalty" (*Structured Vision* 66). Leeds also

26 Carl Rollyson writes of Mailer that he was "utterly serious" about his fiction, "with the novel . . . in magisterial reign . . . as sacred mission, as icon, as Grail" (80).

highlights other important Arthurian parallels in the novel: Arthur is not McLeod, Guinevere's real husband, but "*Leroy*, the king, Hollingsworth, inheritor of a new world where mediocrity, expedience, and narrow-minded ignorance rule."[27] Guinevere's lover is Lannie, "too close to Launcelot to be ignored as coincidence," who performs a dual role in the Arthurian pattern: a submissive figure of somewhat ambiguous sexual identity whose love is unrequited and who is ultimately deserted, Lannie suggests not only the character of Launcelot but also of Elaine of Astolat, particularly as represented by Tennyson in "The Lady of Shalott" (*Structured Vision* 85). This connection to Elaine is strengthened both by Mailer's mirror imagery and Lannie's statement to Guinevere late in the book: "And that is why you love me, for I would be a mirror to you, and we escape only when we follow our mirror and let it lead us out of the forest. I can let you see your beauty, and so you will love me for I adore you and unlike the others want nothing but to lie in your arms, the mirror" (259).[28]

The number of contemporary writers – from fabulists to black humorists,[29] from parodists to Southern existentialists, from traditionalists to modernists and postmodernists – who focus on Arthurian themes and who treat Arthurian motifs in their fiction is indeed considerable. Their interest attests to the enduring appeal of the Arthurian legend in American literary culture, a fact confirmed by the prominence of Arthur in many aspects of American popular culture as well.

27 In fact, as Barry H. Leeds notes, Guinevere says of Hollingsworth, whom she takes as a lover and with whom she betrays her husband, "Sometimes I think he's the son of a prince" (66).
28 Critics have argued that there are Arthurian motifs in other of Mailer's novels. Rollyson, for instance, suggests that "the characters in *Tough Guys Don't Dance* relate to each other as in an Arthurian romance" (334), but he offers little evidence, apart from the plot involving an unfaithful wife, to support his argument. Perhaps the names of the characters – Regency and Lareine – allude to the king and his unfaithful queen; but such evidence is too flimsy to characterize the novel as Arthurian.
29 In *Wampeters* (108), Vonnegut wrote a bit dismissively that "Black humorists' holy wanderers find nothing but junk and lies and idiocy wherever they go. A chewing-gum wrapper or a used condom is often the best they can do for a Holy Grail."

8

The Arthurian Tradition and American Popular Culture

From the Las Vegas Excalibur, one of the largest resort hotels in the United States, to Excalibur vacuum cleaners and toilet brushes; from Avalon restaurants to the town of Avalon on the island of Catalina and the riverboat, the Belle of Louisville, originally called the Avalon; from "Camelot" design china and Camelot kitchen cabinetry to Camp Camelot,[1] a summer program for overweight teenagers, and the "meet-a-millionaire" Camelot Women's Club; from Merlin phone systems to Merlin electronic games; from the "Guinevere Robe" by Victoria's Secret to the Guinevere bed linens in the Medieval Collection by Ralph Lauren – it seems clear that the Arthurian legends have permeated not just American literary tradition but its popular culture as well.

Even some of America's most iconic figures have been influenced by the legends. Acquainted with the "image of the historic bard" through "Richard Hovey's charming masque," America's foremost architect Frank Lloyd Wright named his own homes, Taliesin East and West, after the Arthurian "singer" (*Wright* 172). Famed aviator Charles A. Lindbergh, inspired by the heroism of twentieth-century "knights of the air," determined to join their fellowship. In his *Autobiography of Values*, Lindbergh explained his admiration for such modern knights: "Attacking enemy fighters, bombers, and balloons in mortal combat, he [the aviator] represented chivalry and daring in my own day as did King Arthur's knights in childhood stories" (62). Even Elvis Presley, when writing pseudonymously to one of his girlfriends, adopted the name of the most legendary lover of all: "El Lancelot."

And, of course, "Camelot" has become virtually synonymous with the brief tenure of John F. Kennedy, America's thirty-fifth president. Actually, the identification between Kennedy and Camelot first occurred soon after JFK's death, when Jacqueline Bouvier Kennedy urged her friend, reporter and historian Theodore H. White, to label her late husband's historical myth in specifically Arthurian terms. In a chapter of his memoirs entitled "Camelot," White recalls, "she urged my using the word 'Camelot' to describe it all. And her message was his message – that one man, by trying, may change it all"

---

1 Michele Friedman, one of the directors of Camp Camelot, writes that "The concept of the name originated because 'Camelot' was a place where dreams come true – and we [at Camp Camelot] have that kind of environment. In addition, I was a great admirer of President Kennedy, and Camelot was a place he aspired to as well!" (Letter of Jan. 21, 1994, to Barbara Lupack).

(538). Jackie subsequently repeated the Arthurian association in interviews with *Life* magazine, in which she reminded Americans that "For one brief shining moment [when Kennedy was in office] there was Camelot"; "There'll be great Presidents again," she was quoted as saying, "but there'll never be another Camelot." Apparently, as she was watching her own personal Camelot vanish, she was creating the public one for history (Knight 28). Rose Kennedy, the President's mother, endorsed the myth-making. Pleased that Jackie "had taken Camelot as a small, personal, private symbol of their romantic and glorious life together," she recalled Jack "in his boyhood reading and rereading his copy of *King Arthur and the Round Table* [by A. M. Hadfield]" (112). And, indeed, over the years, presidential historian William Manchester and others increasingly associated Kennedy with the legend of Arthur – so much so, in fact, that "The New Frontier" was perceived as an analogue of Arthur's dream and the Peace Corps as a "group of Kennedy's knights who went on their individual quests, fighting the dragons of poverty and helping populations in distress, enduring hardships for noble causes in strange and foreign lands," while assassin Lee Harvey Oswald emerged as "the Mordred of the piece" (Knight 31).

The appeal of the Arthurian legends in America, moreover, is as esoteric as it is broad. One of the newest New Orleans Mardi Gras krewes, for instance, is Arthurian in theme and concept; members, or krewe knights, are named for traditional characters like Lancelot, Galahad, and Gawain.[2] Like Arthur's knights, the wizard Merlin has gained a popular following in recent years, in large part due to the contemporary spiritualist and best-selling author Deepak Chopra. In various works, including Chopra's novel *The Return of Merlin* (1995), his self-help book *The Way of the Wizard: Twenty Spiritual Lessons for Creating the Life You Want* (1995), and the tapes and videos based on both, Merlin has emerged as a New-Age healer and a curative force for the ills of modern life; by awakening Merlin's magic through love and forgiveness, argues Chopra, people can transform the wasteland of their lives. The Arthurian legends are also a cornerstone of the New Age theology of Elizabeth Clare Prophet, founder of the Church Universal and Triumphant and the "Aquarian-age community" named Camelot. Prophet, who believes herself to be the reincarnation of Guinevere, has "recorded" *Mysteries of the Holy Grail* (1985), a book allegedly written by the Archangel Gabriel, which "unlocks a mystery of self" by explaining the Grail journey and applying the Holy Grail "to present problems." The Archangel's insights, claims Prophet in the book's front matter, explain everything from "the Supreme Court" to "what makes a Jim Jones tick."

While media mogul Ted Turner and his wife Jane Fonda take refuge in the

---

2   Predating the establishment of the Arthurian Mardi Gras krewe was the annual Arthurians' Ball in New Orleans, held at "Arthur's Winter Palace." Among the rituals at the ball: after "Arthur" arrives, Merlin taps ladies with his magic wand to select them as the annual Guinevere and her court (*The New Arthurian Encyclopedia* 363).

sanctuary of his plantation named Avalon, even ordinary citizens – as the ads for products like Camelot paving bricks promise – can turn their homes into castles. And those castles can be landscaped with a variety of Arthurian-named plantings, such as "Camelot" and "Avalon" daffodils, "Camelot" roses, "Lancelot" hostas, "Black Knight" butterfly bush, day lilies (including "Tristan," "Isolde," "Lancelot," "Quest for Excalibur," "Guiniver's Gift," and "Merlin's Magic"),[3] and delphiniums in the Arthurian series ("Astolat," "Guinevere," "King Arthur," "Galahad," "Black Knight," and "Connecticut Yankee"). Potential home owners can take up residence in builder's models like "King Arthur" and "Avalon" or move into neighborhoods with Arthurian names like "Camelot Village," which are springing up all over the country. In Rochester, New York, alone, for example, there are two housing developments with Arthurian-themed street names such as Lancelot Lane, Tristram Court, Astolat Road, Galahad Drive, and Gareth Way. And businesses with Arthurian names, both local and national (e.g., Round Table Pizza, Camelot Music), abound.

Examples of Arthurian art grace some of America's loveliest and best known buildings, both private and public. At Princeton University, for instance, the Chapel's Milbank Choir contains stained glass windows depicting the four Christian epics of Bunyan, Milton, Dante, and Malory. Designed in the 1920s by the architectural firm of Cram (author of the play *Excalibur*) and Ferguson and executed by Boston stained glass artist Charles J. Connick, *Le Morte d'Arthur* is located in the central bay of the north wall. Scenes organized thematically rather than narratively are grouped into three tiers, with *The Vision of Christ* surmounting all. The Bottom Tier, "Life and Death of King Arthur," suggests "the atmosphere of early legend and war that surround the history of Arthur and the story of the sword Excalibur that is bound up with it" (Stillwell 61). In the lower left-hand corner of the window panels is Malory, shown writing *Le Morte d'Arthur* in Newgate Prison. Large figure portraits (running left to right at the top of the tier) depict Queen Morgan le Fay, Sir Mordred the Traitor, King Arthur of England, and the Lady of the Lake. The remaining panels (reading left to right) include "The Birth of Arthur," "Arthur is Crowned King," "The Winning of Excalibur," "The Marriage of Arthur and Guinevere," "The Fight Between King Arthur and Accolon of Gaul," "Mordred and Arthur Fight to the Death," and "Excalibur is Returned to the Lake." The Middle Tier, "Aspirations of Chivalry," uses as its central symbols the fellowship of the Round Table and romantic love as revealed in the championships of the tournament. The large figures (left to right) at the top in this tier depict Sir Tristram of Lyonesse, King Arthur with eight knights, Queen Guinevere, and Sir Launcelot du Lac.

3   Other day lilies with Arthurian names include the following: "Astolat," "Camelot Gold," "Camelot Green," "Camelot Rose," "Galahad," "Little Wart," "Lyonnesse," "Maid of Astolat," "Morgan," "Pink Camelot," "Round Table," "Sir Galahad," "Sir Lancelot," and "Sir Modred."

The other panels combine the adventures of the "most famous" knights and the eight virtues that Caxton noted in his preface: "Frendshyp" (Launcelot and Tristram), "Veray Gentylnesse" (Linet and Gareth), "Noble Actes" (Dinadan rescuing a lady), "Quest" (Launcelot and Guinevere), "Feythfulnesse" (Tristram and Isoud), "Curtosye" (Lamorack and Belliance), "Mercy" (Pelleas sparing Gawaine and Ettard), and "Prowesse" (Launcelot rescuing the Queen). The Top Tier, "The Quest for the Holy Grail," depicts portraits of the four "great companions," treated as medieval symbols of spiritual aspiration: Sir Bors de Ganys, Sir Percival, the Sister of Percival, and Sir Galahad the Good Knight. The panels (reading from the bottom up) include "Temptation of Bors," "Bors to the Rescue," "Percival Tempted by a Fiend," "Percival Tempted by a Lady," "The Sacrifice of Percival's Sister," "Galahad's Knighting by Sir Launcelot," and "Galahad in the Siege Perilous and the Appearance of the Grail." The Tracery above the Top Tier symbolizes the achievement of the Grail, with the dominant piece devoted to the Grail itself, the Christ of the vision of Carbonek. Richard Stillwell, in his study of *The Chapel of Princeton University*, writes that "here [in the Tracery] is symbolized the Mediaeval Christ as distinct from the visions offered by the other Epics. The four Angels of the Passion, St. Joseph of Arimathea, the Twelve Holy Doves, stars and clouds of Heavenly Vision complete the design" (75). Although neither as elaborate nor as distinctive as the Malory windows in the Milbank Choir, another large series of panels highlights an alcove in Princeton University's Proctor Hall. Also designed by Charles J. Connick in the early twenties, that series portrays the Grail legend.[4]

Like Connick, artist and craftsman Louis Comfort Tiffany produced several stained glass windows with Arthurian themes, including the 1902 Ogden Cryer Memorial window in St. Andrew's Dune Church, Southampton, New York, copied from Frederick Watts' painting *Sir Galahad* (1862), and the 1917 three-panel composition of the *Red Cross Knight* (after Spenser's *Fairie Queene*) in the National Headquarters of the American Red Cross, Washington, DC.[5] And one of the church windows in Rutland, Vermont, has a less distinguished but no less significant pedigree: the money to finance its creation and installation was raised as part of a project by members of the area's Arthurian youth group, a castle of the Knights of King Arthur.

In the Delivery Room of the Boston Public Library at Copley Square is another remarkable work: a series of murals, "The Quest and Achievement of the Holy Grail," by Edwin Austin Abbey. Installed in 1895, the frieze

---

4   For a brief comment on the Malory windows, see *NAE* 370. For a full description of the portraits and panels and a discussion of the relationship of the Malory windows to the windows in the other epics represented in the Milbank Choir, see Richard Stillwell's *The Chapel of Princeton University* (especially pp. 59–75).
5   Other American firms produced Arthurian windows, notably J. Gordon Guthrie (a "Galahad" window) and Willet Stained Glass Studios (a "Quest for the Grail," in the Fort Lincoln Cemetery, Washington, DC, and a "Parsifal," after Wagner's opera, in the Allegheny Cemetery, Pittsburgh) (*NAE* 429).

consists of fifteen panels, beginning with "The Vision, or The Infancy of Galahad," in which Galahad's mother is visited by a dove carrying a golden censer and an angel carrying the Grail, and "The Oath of Knighthood," in which Galahad receives his spurs from Sir Lancelot and Sir Bors. In the third panel, "The Round Table of King Arthur," Galahad takes his seat in the Siege Perilous before embarking, in "The Departure," on the quest with the other knights. In "The Castle of the Grail," he encounters the wounded Amfortas but fails to ask the question that might heal him, a failure for which he is assailed in "The Loathely Damsel." The next three panels – "The Key to the Castle," "The Conquest of the Seven Deadly Sins," and "The Castle of the Maidens" – depict other adventures leading up to the wedding of Galahad to Blanchefleur, whom he leaves (in "Galahad Parts From His Bride: Blanchefleur") to return to the Grail castle, where he finally asks the question that heals Amfortas and allows him to die (in "The Death of Amfortas"). In "Galahad the Deliverer," "The Voyage to Sarras," and "The City of Sarras," Galahad passes from the land onto Solomon's Ship, which bears him to Sarras; and, in the final panel, "The Golden Tree and the Achievement of the Grail," he is made king and builds a golden tree. When the tree is complete, Joseph of Arimathea appears, Galahad's kingly trappings fall away, and his spirit – along with the Grail – ascends to Heaven. Inspired by Tennyson, Abbey depicts Galahad as the ideal Grail knight, although Abbey's striking reinterpretation combines elements from the medieval stories of both Galahad and Percival.

Not all applications of the legend, however, are so lofty. In print, radio, and television advertising, for example, the legends are often put to far more mundane use. Arthur and Guinevere debate the merits of garage doors and remote-controlled openers; Merlin serves as spokesperson for a wide array of products ranging from Christmas tree lights to phone systems; Excalibur is featured in promotional ads for television's Learning Channel as well as in recruiting materials for the Marines; and Camelot is a place from which the now-departed Joe Camel once pitched cigarettes to his young audience.

In merchandising as in advertising, Arthurian connections evidently enhance sales. Guinevere wedding gowns, Morgan le Fay capes, Knights of the Round Table menswear, Avalon wood stoves, Excalibur knives and letter openers, to name but a few, entice buyers into the Arthurian world, while promotional items like Wendy's 3-D Arthurian comic book and *Quest for Camelot* toys and McDonald's *Sword in the Stone* figures draw in even younger consumers. And Arthur serves as a profitable minor industry for the Franklin Mint, a true barometer of popular taste, which continues to make and market various types of Arthurian wares, from pewter goblets and bowls to sculptures of the mounted king and replicas of his faithful sword.

Arthurian-inspired items have even found their way into American supermarkets. In addition to imported foodstuffs such as British King Arthur Toffees and Canadian Avalon spring water, shoppers can choose from brands that include Excaliber [sic] Pizza, Excalibur dessert pies, Chef Boyardee's Sir Chomps-A-Lot canned pastas for children, Quest sparkling water, Grail Ale, and King Arthur Flour. The last of these products has a particularly rich and strikingly American heritage. Introduced in 1896 by Sands, Taylor, & Wood, King Arthur Flour was the first domestically produced flour for the Boston-based company, which announced the debut in a rather spectacular way: by having a lone figure dressed as King Arthur in chain mail atop a black stallion ride through the streets of the city. The event was no doubt orchestrated to evoke Paul Revere's famous ride through the same streets more than a century before to announce an earlier emancipation from Britain. From that day in 1896 forward, according to the company's promotional materials, "all of Camelot [was] reborn on bag and barrel" with products that included Round Table Pastry Flour, Queen Guinevere Cake Flour, Merlin Magic Doughnut Mix, and a variety of bread flours (Squire, Page, Sir Kay, Excalibur). "King Arthur" rode the streets again, in 1927, to visit towns and cities in Massachusetts; the following year, a truck outfitted with a calliope and an enormous wood carving of the mounted king was dispatched to New York in an effort to expand the market. By the 1930s, radio audiences tuned in to the "King Arthur Coffee Club" and "King Arthur Round Table of Song" and learned of new products like King Arthur Coffee, Tea, and Wheat Germ – some of which were being distributed to the poor through the Knights of King Arthur, as one of the designated charitable acts performed by the boys' clubs. And, while King Arthur Flour has since turned to print and television advertising for promotional purposes, the tradition of its radio broadcasts continues with the popular weekly program "King Arthur's Kitchen."[6]

Arthurian motifs and characters are also prevalent in toys, games, and comic books. Among the earliest Arthurian board games was Parker Brothers' *Chivalry* (1887), reissued with the new title *Camelot* in 1930 (*90 Years of Fun* 11), which consisted of charging knights and slower moving footmen, or "men at arms," who seek to become "castled" on the opponent's end of the board either by "canters" over friendly pieces or "jumps" over enemy pieces. A favorite of company founder George S. Parker, *Camelot* combined the concept of checkers with some of the intricacies of chess. Although the company produced other medieval or Arthurian-themed games, including *King's Castle* (1903–1904), *The Knight's Journey* (1928–1930), *King Arthur and the Knights of the Round Table* (1930–1936), and *King's Men* (1937–mid-1940s),

---

6 "King Arthur's Kitchen" is a weekly radio show on "Radio New England Magazine," broadcast to more than eighty stations throughout the Northeast. And, on the 200th anniversary of the parent company, King Arthur Flour's "King Arthur" returned again on horseback, to launch the company into its third century and to celebrate King Arthur Flour as "the King Arthur of Flours" in the American food industry. For more particulars, see *King Arthur Flour Cookbook*, which provides a history of the company as well as a variety of recipes for its current products.

little is known about them today.[7] *Camelot*, however, proved to be one of
Parker Brothers' greatest successes and was manufactured until 1968.

Entering production in the 1950s were a number of similar games that tied
in to – and promoted – early television programs. The Lisbeth Whiting Company's board game, *Adventures of Sir Lancelot*, for example, was based – as the
box announced boldly – "on the exciting new NBC TV series" and marketed
as "The Official Game" of that popular show. Depending upon the color of
their game pieces, players assumed the roles of Sir Lancelot, the Green
Knight, Merlin the Magician, or King Mark; and as they attempted to capture
either Camelot or Westbury Castle, they encountered hazards such as the
"Spear Pit," the "Dragon Trap," the "Bow and Arrow Trap," and the rather
anachronistic "Alligator Pit."

In 1978, Parker Brothers, acknowledging the increasingly sophisticated
tastes of young people, launched a sell-out product that helped to move the
company as well as its competitors into a more high-tech entertainment world.
Merlin, an "electronic wizard," was a programmable music-player that also
featured five "ingenious" games of logic, strategy, skill, memory, and chance.
Named for the "wizard . . . Merlin" (Wojahn 83), it soon became the industry's
number one toy and a $100 million bonanza, which rapidly spawned
numerous, less successful imitators. Meanwhile, growing interest in fantasy
fiction led to the development of various role-playing games, from the
extremely popular *Dungeons & Dragons*, which listed Arthurian names among
the game characters, to more exclusively Arthurian ones like *Knights of the
Round Table* (1978), designed by Philip Edgren, and *King Arthur Pendragon*
(1985/new editions, 1988 and 1993), designed by Greg Stafford, also the force
behind *Prince Valiant, the Storytelling Game* (1989) and board games like *King
Arthur's Knights* (1978) and *Merlin* (1980),[8] as well as to solo fantasy gamebooks
(*The New Arthurian Encyclopedia* [hereafter cited as *NAE*] 175).

Unlike some of the earlier games, the fantasy-adventure games were
geared as much to adults as to young people. In *Merlin* (Heritage USA, 1980),
for instance, Merlin represents good against the evil of Morgana le Fey; their
battles involve not only the Knights of Camelot but also "the hosts of the
undead, even the Angels of Heaven and the Demons of the Dark Regions."
In *Knights of Camelot* (TSR Games, 1980), players assume the role of gallant

7 "I have been through our archives," writes Carol Steinkrauss, Public Relations Manager
   of Parker Brothers, "and unfortunately background information on our games is very
   limited, let alone any written documents on George Parker's game development interests" (Letter of Jan. 24, 1994, to Barbara Lupack).
8 Stafford, president of Chaosium, Inc., has also compiled five game supplements, *The
   Pendragon Campaign* (1985), *Noble's Book* (1986), *King Arthur Pendragon* (1990), *Knights
   Adventurous* (1990), and *The Boy King* (1991); he has also co-authored three adventure
   modules, *Tournament of Dreams* (1987), *Savage Mountains* (1991), and *Blood and Lust* (1991).
      Still other recent board games include *Knights of Camelot* (1980), designed by Glenn and
   Kenneth Rahman, and *King Arthur and His Knights of the Round Table* (1988), designed by
   Matthew Hill et al. (*NAE* 606, 175).

knights who travel across the land in the name of chivalry and virtue. "Knights" search for the Grail as well as for treasure they can bring back to Camelot in *Grail Quest* (Metagaming, 1980); in that game, however, they observe such unusual chivalric rules as "Knights NEVER use poison! . . . Potions, bombs, and molotails are not knightly." And *Hidden Kingdoms* (New Rules, Inc., 1983) offers a complete campaign that allows players to strategize "around two polarized world-views as they existed in the Age of Arthur: (1) the existing Pagan Order and (2) the insurgent world-view of Christianity."

Increasingly sophisticated games have since brought Arthur into the age of video and CD-ROM. In *Artura* (Arcadia, 1989), for example, in which players are encouraged to "hack and smash [their] way to glory," the quest is to rescue Nimue, beautiful apprentice to Merdyn the Mage, who has been kidnapped by Artura's evil half-sister Morgause. *Conquests of Camelot: The Search for the Grail* (Sierra, 1989) purports to restore the mystic rituals and passions of the original legends, not "the soft and toothless fairy tales most commonly seen today," by emphasizing the love between Guinevere and Launcelot and the struggle for supremacy between Christianity and the ancient Roman warrior-god Mithra. In *Spirit of Excalibur* (Virgin Games, 1990), the Knights of the Round Table fight to defend medieval Britain from Morgan and the Shadowmaster, Lord of Demons, whom she has summoned; after Morgan's death, however, the Shadowmaster begins working his own will by imprisoning the king, kidnapping Nineve, stealing Excalibur and the newly-recovered Grail, and turning Britain into a new wasteland. The Knights must follow the demon lord to medieval Spain, and in the companion game *Vengeance of Excalibur* (Virgin Games, 1991) they must cope with Moorish enchantments, greedy mercenaries, and unending feuds between Christian kings and Moslem Caliphs. The young Gawain, about to be ordained into the Order of the Round Table, is both the hero of *Chronicles of the Sword* (Psygnosis, 1996) and the identity that game players must assume; his quest is to find and destroy Morgana before she destroys Camelot and all that Arthur has created. Also popular are those games that interactively spin off films like the Indiana Jones series or *Monty Python and the Holy Grail*.

Like games, Arthurian comics have generated great interest and introduced the legends to generations of readers. One of the earliest and still among the best is Harold R. (Hal) Foster's durable weekly strip *Prince Valiant*, dating back to 1937 (and drawn, since 1980, by Cullen and John Cullen Murphy), which recounts the exploits of the exiled young prince as he arrives at Arthur's court, becomes a squire to Gawain, embarks on a series of worldwide adventures, and participates in other traditionally Arthurian episodes. Foster's creation of Prince Valiant, which led to numerous related books, games, movies, and television series, has been followed by the introduction of still more comic book knights of the Round

Table, including the Shining Knight[9] and the Knights of Pendragon (in *The Knights of Pendragon* and *Knights of Pendragon*).

Over the years, in fact, almost all of the major comic book characters – Spider-Man, Spider-Woman, Superman, Superboy, Batman, Iron Man, Swamp Thing, Demon, The Mighty Avengers, Dr. Strange, the Fantastic Four – have had Arthurian adventures, as have some more nontraditional ones, including Uncle Scrooge, the Little People, the Three Stooges, and Pinky and the Brain. In turn, various Arthurian characters, from Modred (*Modred the Mystic*) and Parsifal (*Star*Reach*) to Guinevere (*Lady Pendragon*) and the ever popular Merlin (*Merlin, Merlin Realm in 3-D*), have been featured in their own comics or comic series, with the Arthurian world itself figuring prominently in *Arthur, King of Britain* and *Camelot Eternal*. Some comics, like *Lancelot and Guinevere, Indiana Jones and the Last Crusade*, and *King Arthur and the Knights of Justice*, are based on films or television shows; others, like the bawdy and erotic adventures of King Arthur (in the X-rated comics *Arthur Sex, King Arthur Uncensored*, and *Camelot Uncensored*), are entirely original. And still others, like Mike Barr and Brian Bolland's *Camelot 3000* (1982–1985), in which Arthur and his knights return in the year 3000 to save Britain from invasion from outer space, and Matt Wagner's *Mage* (1984), in which an ordinary man drawn into magical struggles between good and evil turns out to be a reborn Arthur, offer particularly original handlings of the Arthurian theme.

The continuing interest in Arthuriana – an interest due in large part to the youth groups that led so many people to read about the legends, to enact them in their lives, and to pass their Arthurian interests on to their children – is, however, perhaps best reflected in the wealth of American popular literature, much of which introduces specifically American elements that democratize the legend, either by downplaying the notion of kingship that is central to British versions of the story or by implying that the qualities of knighthood are moral rather than physical or social and thus can be achieved by anyone who aspires to them. Furthermore, some popular fiction brings the legends to America by literally setting plot lines in the United States or by creating American characters who interact – and often contrast – with the more traditional Arthurian ones.

The scope of American popular Arthurian literature is suggested by the many perspectives from which the stories of Arthur and his knights are told: historical, science fiction, fantasy, feminist, trilogies and other series, romance, mystery, and juvenile, among others. Yet, even within these broad and sometimes overlapping categories, there is considerable diversity. The historical novelists, for example, who set their works in fifth- or sixth-century Britain and who look to the early chronicles of Arthur's life, sometimes combining them with traditional literary accounts like Malory's, take a variety of approaches to the familiar stories. Gil Kane and John Jakes retell

9   For more on the treatment of Arthurian themes in comics, see *NAE* 97–98.

the "stirring saga" of Arthur and his "mighty sword" as a typically American fast-paced adventure, an approach consistent with Jakes's many best-selling tales of the Wild West. Even the cover of *Excalibur!* (1980) suggests the connection: "Here," it announces, "is the dazzling epic of England's past . . . the birth of the nation that gave America birth." Kane and Jakes's Guinevere and Lancelot are lovers before, but not after, her marriage to Arthur – although their "forbidden love" continues to pose a threat to the stability of Arthur's new kingdom; Modred poisons Arthur and fights him with Saxon troops; and the questing Galahad discovers the Grail: England itself. Other popular historical novelists, like Douglas Carmichael, focus on the psychological motivation of the characters about whom they write. In *Pendragon* (1977), for instance, Carmichael eschews magic for rational explanations as he re-creates the twelve battles that Artorius, aided by Myrddin and Lanceolatus, fought to consolidate his kingdom.[10] Original twists enhance Marvin Borowsky's *The Queen's Knight* (1955), which employs a kind of Connecticut Yankee theme in reverse. Arthur, a slow-witted oaf brought to the throne as a puppet-king by Merlin and Mordred, uses his Yankee-like ingenuity, peasant's good sense, and dream of peace to earn the kingdom's respect. Unfortunately, his efforts are insufficient to bring lasting unity. Edison Marshall's *The Pagan King* (1959) begins rather conventionally, in fifth-century England, a time when the country – beset with Picts on the north, the wild men of Eire on the west, and Saxon pirates on the east and south – desperately needs a strong leader like Arthur, the pagan king, to turn the tide of barbarism. In telling Arthur's story, Marshall tries to infuse some humanity into what he calls the often bloodless characters of myth: Arthur's half-brother Modred, for instance, emerges as a complex, fascinating figure, not merely the representative of unmitigated evil, and Merdin is not simply a wizard but a shrewd kingmaker and last of the great Druids. But the plot becomes contrived, especially towards the end, when Arthur gives up the kingship so that he can wander as a bard – a downplaying of kingship similar to that in Cram's *Excalibur* and in other earlier American works.

Unlike the historical novelists, whose fidelity to their Dark Ages context limits the extent of the liberties they can take, some popular novelists incorporate aspects of the legend into a High Middle Ages or even contemporary time frame. Barbara Ferry Johnson, whose sentimental novel *Lionors* (1975) is based on a passage in Malory, tells the story of the Earl Sanam's daughter, who bore Arthur a child. Dorothy James Roberts' three Arthurian novels, also based on Malory, offer modern perceptions into theme as well as character. In *The Enchanted Cup* (1953), Roberts examines the conflict between love and duty in the tragic romance between Tristram and Isoud. Love is again the subject in *Launcelot, My Brother* (1954), in which Bors, here Launcelot's

10 Carmichael is also the author of an Arthurian short story, "The Grievous Stroke," an account of Balin's maiming of Pellam.

brother rather than his cousin, tells of Launcelot's love for Guinevere and of the ensuing demise of the Round Table. *Kinsmen of the Grail* (1963) shifts the focus to the quest, specifically to the Grail quests of the sheltered Perceval and the world-weary Gawin, and the search for the meaning of life.[11]

Of the novelists who employ contemporary settings, among the most interesting is Babs H. Deal. In *The Grail: A Novel* (1963), she cleverly reveals – as F. Scott Fitzgerald before her had – a correspondence between modern sports and medieval warfare by transposing the Arthurian story to the world of American college football. Arthur, Guenevere, and Launcelot are transformed into Coach Arthur Hill of Castle University, his wife Jennie, and his star quarterback Lance Hebert; the Grail is a perfect season with no losses. The coach – hailed as "king" for his career successes – seems well on the way to achieving his dream, until Lance falls in love with Jennie and disrupts the unity of the team, which loses its final game. Virtually all of the traditional characters appear in the novel, usually as players and their sorority girl-friends. The guitar-playing fullback Buck Timberlake, for instance, is Tristan the harpist; twin linebackers Wayne and Dwayne O'Hara are Gawain and Gareth. "Even the feud with Lancelot is recalled," notes Raymond H. Thompson; "Wayne abandons his earlier support of Lance after the quarter-back strikes Dwayne for challenging him about his affair with Jennie" (*Return* 24). Deal's use of the sports and Grail motifs in combination is also reminiscent of Bernard Malamud's *The Natural*, in which Roy Hobbs becomes a modern-day Percival in search of a contemporary Grail, winning the World Series. But ultimately, despite its witty premise, *The Grail* lacks the sustained and darker vision that makes *The Natural* a much more effective work. In *Guinever's Gift* (1977), the best-selling novel by Nicole St. John (pseudonym of Norma Johnston), the Arthur-Guinever-Lancelot relationship is again transposed into a modern setting, this time as a Gothic romance with many of the familiar conventions: a dark house that contains untold mysteries, a crippled aristocratic owner obsessed with the past, and an innocent heroine whose life is threatened.[12] What makes St. John's story even more

11 In some novels, the Arthurian background is more peripheral. Anya Seton's *Avalon* (1965), for instance, is the story of Rumon, a descendant of Charlemagne and King Alfred, who has visions of King Arthur's Avalon, and Merewyn, a lonely but courageous girl descended from King Arthur. After a shipwreck off the Cornish coast, the two find that their lives are entwined. The novel spins out their stories against a broad historical background, which includes Iceland, Greenland, North America, and England.

12 Of the relationships in *Guinever's Gift*, Nicole St. John writes: "Referring back to the synthesis between rational/irrational within the individual (which many writers refer to as the masculine and feminine within each of us) and Eastern myths, I see in the Guinevere/Lancelot/Arthur triangle the universal myth of Isis/Osiris/Horus and its various forms (some Christian writers see this as Father, Son and Holy Spirit!) . . . the immortal Earth Mother, and the dying/rising godlike-king . . . Shakespeare's 'Phoenix and the Turtle.' You will, of course, have recognized that the plot of Guinever's Gift is essentially that of the Fisher King/Sleeping Beauty story, with the difference that Guinever as well as Lancelot is on a quest for Self. I see Guinever as, at different stages, all the dimensions of the Feminine (what Medievalist Madeleine Pelner Cosman calls, in the words of the

interesting, as Thompson points out, is the fatal triangle that occurs not once but twice. The first time, the heroine Lydian Wentworth's mother and father represent Guinever and Arthur, while the young Lord Charles Ransome is Lancelot. Later, Charles (a scholar whose historical specialty is King Arthur) takes on the Arthurian role, while Lydian, now his wife, and Lawrence Stearns, his archeological assistant, are cast as the lovers. Charles's cousin "serves as a fusion of Elaine of Corbenic and Morgause, and she bears him an illegitimate child who functions as Mordred. The crippled Charles also evokes elements of the Fisher King legend" (Thompson *Return* 25). Another romantic tale, Will Bradley's *Launcelot and the Ladies* (1927), published half a century earlier than *Guinever's Gift*, finds the protagonist, an American dreamer named David, reliving scenes from the love triangle of Launcelot, Guenevere, and Elaine (a fusion of the two Elaines); when he must make a comparable choice in his own life, he marries the younger, single woman.

More popular and more original in their handling of the legends than either the historically-based or the more realistic (non-fantasy) novels set in the High Middle Ages or in contemporary times are the works of Arthurian science fiction and fantasy. Andre Norton, perhaps the best known science fiction author to treat Arthurian themes, explained her ongoing interest in the legend in terms of its relevance to modern American life. "The story of an intrepid leader fighting with a small force against odds," she writes, "has been important all through history – such men are the cherished folk leaders of all time – Arthur, standing against the black night of the fall of civilization, is as important to our fears and hopes now he was in his own day." Moreover, his "defeat because of a flaw in his own following" ensures that "we can understand such a man."[13] In Norton's *Merlin's Mirror* (1975), Arthur is indeed the once and future king, sealed by the "half star-born" Merlin in a chamber until future space travelers are able to heal him. Merlin, meanwhile, is the product of cross-breeding with aliens; his powers are the result of extra-sensory perception. Both Arthur and Merlin figure again in Norton's juvenile fantasy, *Steel Magic* (1965), in which three children enter Avalon to recover three stolen magic talismans of power, Arthur's sword Excalibur,

Middle Ages, 'beast/bitch/saint/virgin' . . . and some branch or other of myth studies termed Eve/Helen/Mary/Sophia). And Lancelot/Arthur as all the dimensions of the Masculine, dichotomized into young and old, with the two of them (like Osiris/Horus?) being essentially the same man in different stages." Referring to "the Great Mother figure [dichotomized] between Mary, Lilith and Magdalen," St. John concludes, "I see Guinever as being that dichotomy synthesized" (Letter of Dec. 18, 1980, to Alan Lupack).

13 Andre Norton explains her own conception of Arthur in a letter of December 31, 1980, to Alan Lupack. She writes, "I, myself, went back as well as I could to the historical Arthur in my own writing – as did Mary Stewart and other writers of this era – brushing aside the pagentry of Mallory [sic] who fitted the old legends into the pattern of his own time. It is this earlier Arthur, who faced terrible odds and went down to defeat because of a flaw in his own following, who appeals to us at this day and age – we can understand such a man. . . . My Arthur is not a 'knight' but a man holding out against all odds and trying to keep a fragment of civilization intact."

Merlin's iron ring, and Huon's silver horn. (Huon is the subject of an earlier work, *Huon of the Horn* [1951], Norton's adaptation of a portion of the Charlemagne cycle; in that novel, Huon and Arthur – in anticipation of King Oberon's passing – amicably resolve the rule of the Land of Faery.) Artie Jones, a young boy, is transported to historical Britain in order to participate in the rise, fall, and secret burial of Artos in "Pendragon: Artos, Son of Marius," a tale from *Dragon Magic*, a companion volume to *Steel Magic* (1965). The Siege Perilous transports another protagonist, Simon Tregarth, from a post-World-War-II world to a magical and matriarchal realm where he can discover his destiny in *Witch World* (1963), a novel in Norton's most extensive and familiar series.

Among the recurring and related devices employed by Norton and other writers of American Arthurian science fiction are the use of time travel and parallel universes, the "return" of Arthurian characters to modern society, and the introduction of aliens and other strange beings into the Arthurian world. Time travel, in particular, has become a kind of staple of the genre: a wounded soldier awakens as Ogier the Dane and encounters Morgan le Fay in Poul Anderson's *Three Hearts and Three Lions* (1961);[14] a reborn Arthur, with Merlin's help, must keep the evil Morlocks from using the time machine to invade nineteenth-century England from the distant future in K. W. Jeter's *Morlock Night* (1979), a sequel to H. G. Wells's *The Time Machine*; the twenty-third-century hero of Steve White's *Legacy* (1995) is rescued from imprisonment by time travelers, also from the distant future, who send him back to Arthur's day. Such travel often involves parallel worlds, which figure prominently in juvenile literature, discussed below, as well as in adult fiction like Victoria Strauss's *Worldstone* (1985), in which the realms of magic and technology are no longer united after Arthur's death. Strauss's novel describes a quest to return the worldstone (Grail), originally stolen by Percival, to the world of Mindpower from the modern world of Handpower.

Of the traditional Arthurian characters, one common time traveler is Merlin, who moves backward – albeit in his dreams – in a work like *Merlin and the Dragons of Atlantis* (1983), by Rita and Tim Hildebrandt, which is set millennia in the past and which suggests that Merlin's skills – like the dragons' – are products of highly developed but lost sciences in Atlantis and Lemuria, and forward in Fred Saberhagen's *Dominion* (1982), where Merlin finds himself in modern-day Chicago trying to fend off Nimue's diabolical plan for world control.[15] Arthur himself makes similar journeys in time – though far less often than his wizard. As Norris Lacy and Geoffrey Ashe

14 In another of Anderson's works, *A Midsummer Tempest* (1974), King Arthur and the Knights of Avalon appear among the Royalist forces to turn King Charles's last stand, on Glastonbury Tor at Midsummer, into Cromwell's utter defeat.
15 In Saberhagen's *Merlin's Bones* (1995), in which Merlin's spirit plans to return to rebuild Camelot in the otherworld of Logres, the characters move backward, from the twenty-first century to the time of Vortigern.

note, Arthur is *supposed* "to return from Avalon, where he is sleeping. [Yet] surprisingly, novelists have treated his return less frequently than Merlin's and that of other Arthurian characters" (*The Arthurian Handbook* [hereafter cited as *AH*] 211). In one of his most inventive reappearances, after centuries of sleep Arthur Pendragon awakens as "Arthur Penn," to campaign success- fully for mayor of New York City in Peter David's *Knight Life* (1987). Though Penn – aided by Merlin, ever his best political adviser – hopes eventually to run for president, he must first cope with his resurrected adversary Morgan. In Molly Cochran and Warren Murphy's novels, *The Forever King* (1992) and *The Broken Sword* (1997), Arthur is reincarnated as a twentieth-century boy, Arthur Blessing; aided by Merlin and Hal Woczniak, an alcoholic former-FBI agent (and eventually by the once-blind Beatrice, whose sight is restored by a vision of the Grail), he takes possession of Excalibur, begins a quest, and tries to restore the old order of Camelot. Irving E. Cox follows a different charac- ter; his "Lancelot Returned" tells a story of 1950s Hollywood, as Lancelot comes to rescue a young girl from an "evil enchantress," her actress mother. And, in the short story "Excalibur and the Atom" (1951) by Theodore Sturgeon (pseudonym of Edward Hamilton Waldo), a private eye who is hired to locate a cup with the power to render H-bombs useless, last known to be in the possession of a shepherd named Percival, "remembers" that he was formerly Galahad. The return theme occurs even in poetry, such as Richard Huemer's book-length poem *Dragon on the Hill Road* (1958), which offers an unusual variation on the theme by taking Lancelot into twentieth- century Tennessee. And in one of the finest modern Arthurian poems, "The Naming of the Lost" by Valerie Nieman Colander, Merlin and Nimue reappear and are reunited in twentieth-century West Virginia. Like Merlin, Arthur, Lancelot, and other characters displaced from their traditional Arthurian realm, aliens (e.g., the mind-controlling "intelligent form of slime" who invade Annwn, a world ruled by Arthur's descendants, in George Henry Smith's *Druid's World* [1967]) and mutants provide additional oppor- tunities for intriguing juxtapositions and satirical commentary.

Among the finest science fiction treatments in contemporary American fiction are those by Roger Zelazny and C. J. Cherryh (pseudonym of Carolyn Janice Cherry). Zelazny's Prince of Amber series incorporates various legends, including the Grail quest and wasteland themes. The strongest Arthurian parallels occur in *The Guns of Avalon* (1972), in which Lancelot appears briefly, just as Merlin does in the fifth novel, *The Courts of Chaos* (1979), and Parsifal and Excalibur do in a later humorous fantasy, *Bring Me the Head of Prince Charming* (1991), co-written with Robert Sheckley. But it is in "The Last Defender of Camelot" that Zelazny most adroitly handles his Arthurian subject. In that story, Lancelot forms an alliance with Morgan le Fay in order to prevent a re-awakened Merlin from imposing his will upon a new age. Zelazny's Lancelot is Camelot's last defender because he prevents Merlin from creating a new Arthur and from conferring on this new leader a power that would be dangerous in the modern world. Cherryh's *Port Eternity* (1982) imagines a marooned spacecraft, the *Maid of Astolat*, owned by wealthy Dela Kirn and staffed by androids, or "made people," modeled on the characters from Tennyson's *Idylls of the King*: Elaine, Dela's beautiful, loyal maid and the narrator of the novel; Lancelot, Dela's programmed lover and household manager; Vivien, the efficient keeper of the accounts; Gawain and Lynette, the pilots; and Percivale and Modred, the engineers. At the beginning of the journey, they "play out the old game" (12), with Dela acting as a kind of Guinevere and drawing in some of the "born men" like Griffin, the novel's Arthur figure. But as soon as the ship gets stranded in an alien dimension, the made people begin asserting their personalities and living out their Arthurian roles, even to the point of a final battle, in which they are overwhelmed by the alien "Beast" and giants. Yet, like their Arthurian counterparts, they experience an almost legendary triumph in their defeat. Although the plot is not seamless, *Port Eternity* nonetheless integrates the Arthurian element more successfully than any other science fiction novel except perhaps Norton's *Merlin's Mirror*.

Like science fiction, fantasy novels also feature imaginative uses of Arthurian subjects. In *Silverlock* (1949), John Myers Myers sends his protagonist on a picaresque journey through a land filled with memorable literary characters, including Nimue and Gawain, who teach him a fuller appreciation of life. A sequel, *The Moon's Fire-Eating Daughter* (1981), chronicles a similar journey: a university science professor, guided by supernatural beings like Merlin and Morgan le Fay, develops his literary talents as he encounters famous poets and authors, including Taliesin. As Myers did, Robert Nathan merges the Arthurian and literary/academic worlds. His entertaining novel *The Elixir* (1971) takes place in modern Britain, where an American professor touring Stonehenge and other nearby sites encounters Anne (Niniane) and Myrdin.[16] A long-lived Merlin, again in a contemporary setting, uses his talents in a somewhat different capacity in Linda Haldeman's *The Lastborn of Elvinwood* (1978), as he brings together a fairy groom and a mortal bride needed to save Oberon's dwindling race.

Not surprisingly, the Tristan legend holds a special appeal for writers of romantic fantasy.[17] As early as 1938, Mary Ellen Chase had incorporated

16 Robert Nathan is the author of two other novels with a nominally Arthurian connection: *Sir Henry* (1955), which recounts the comic adventures of an aging knight, and *The Fair* (1964), about the journey of a young Celtic girl and an angel, set in the period following Arthur's defeat by the Saxons.
17 Like Dorothy Roberts in *The Enchanted Cup* (1953), discussed earlier in the chapter, Joyce Carol Oates (writing under the pseudonym Rosamond Smith) retells the Tristan story. In *You Can't Catch Me* (1995), a suspense novel in which bibliophile Tristram Heade is tricked into helping a beautiful young woman, Fleur, with whom he is infatuated, to escape her unhappy marriage. Tristram realizes that he has been betrayed when he sees a photograph of Fleur with her new lover at a performance of *Tristan and Isolde*. And numerous other novels (e.g., Douglas Carmichael's *Pendragon*) draw on the legend for subplots.

aspects of it in *Dawn in Lyonesse*, in which the narrator's reading of an old romance of Tristram and Iseult gives her insight into a comparable situation between her husband and a friend, and in Chase's "A Candle at Night" (1942), it leads Mary Penrose to forgive her friend Susan Glover for falling in love with her fiancé. Ruth Collier Sharpe's *Tristram of Lyonesse* (1949) addresses the legend more directly. While attempting to treat the story in its entirety, Sharpe places it in a "disconcertingly anachronistic setting that recalls the 18th century" (*NAE* 417) and transforms it into a tediously long and sentimental Gothic melodrama with a convoluted plot and a happy ending, with Mark giving Ysolt a "Bill of Divorcement" that allows her to become Queen of Lyonesse. Dee Morrison Meaney's *Iseult: Dreams That Are Done* (1985), narrated by Iseult herself, also uses much of the traditional material. Meaney's changes, however, are significant: the lovers are never trapped by enemies, and it is they who decide that Tristram should leave court. Both, moreover, love – and continue to love – the noble-minded Mark. Later, when Tristram dies of a wound, Iseult arrives too late to bid farewell; so, instead, she expires at his side. It is not Iseult (here called Esseilte) but her cousin Branwan, daughter of Morholt, who is the narrator of Diana Paxson's *The White Raven* (1988).[18] Branwen describes the love between Drustan (Tristan) and Esseilte, for which she acts as a go-between, and recounts the story of how she took the latter's place in the marriage bed with the noble King Marc'h. Only after Esseilte's death does Branwan reveal her love for the king with whom she shared a special and symbolic bond and her shame in his betrayal.

Another significant fantasy motif is the quest. In *Excalibur* (1973), Sanders Anne Laubenthal skillfully introduces Arthurian characters into a modern setting, where they fulfill Arthurian quests as they search for Excalibur, brought to the New World by Prince Madoc and now hidden in Mobile, Alabama.[19] Andrew M. Greeley's *The Magic Cup: An Irish Legend* (1979) tells an equally unusual version of the Grail quest – an Irish version (though with democratic elements that resonate with American readers), in which Cormac MacDermot, the young king destined to lead Ireland from paganism to

---

18 Paxson has also written other works with Arthurian themes, including a masque in verse, "The Feast of the Fisher King" (1992), based on Chrétien de Troyes, and "The God-Sword" (1995), about the origins of the holy sword Excalibur before it passes into Arthur's hands.

19 "I had been familiar with the Arthurian story, in many versions, for most of my life," writes Laubenthal. "I had also long been familiar with the Prince Madoc legend, and I had read somewhere that the royal house of Gwynedd claimed descent from Arthur. One summer evening in what must have been 1963, I was standing on the back porch of our house in Mobile, looking eastward into darkness and a thick tangle of trees. Out of sight, the land fell away towards the city and the bay; and I was pondering on the beauty, the differentness, the mystery of that old and then much smaller city. Suddenly, out of nowhere, an image came to me: the image of Excalibur thrust into the stone, in an underground place full of fiery, golden light. From that image the whole book evolved, over a period of almost ten years" (Letter of Jan. 18, 1981, to Alan Lupack).

Christianity, accompanied by Brigid, the pagan slave girl, and the wolfhound Podraig, seeks the princess who will lead him to the magic cup that confirms his right to be the Irish High King.

To be sure, one of the most successful and influential fantasy novels is Marion Zimmer Bradley's *The Mists of Avalon* (1982), which relates the Arthurian story from the viewpoint of the women in the legend: Igraine, the wife of Gorlois; Morgaine, their daughter and the central figure and primary voice of the novel; Morgause, Igraine's half-sister, and later the wife of King Lot; Viviane, Igraine's half-sister and Lady of the Lake, who is a priestess of the Holy Isle of Avalon and mother to Lancelet; Niniane and Nimue, Viviane's descendants; and Gwenhwyfar, queen and wife of Arthur.

The popularity and the influence of the book rest largely on the central roles of its women. Though the *Mists* draws heavily on Arthurian tradition, "Arthur is no longer in the focus of the novel's interest" and "the important events are not initiated by him" (Volk-Birke 411). Throughout the novel there are feminist overtones in keeping with the focus of the women, as when Igraine says she will not have Morgaine "brought up to feel shame at her own womanhood" (79); or when Morgaine herself criticizes the Christian foes of Avalon for being "overfond of that word *unseemly*, especially when it relates to women" (288); or when Viviane asks, "What woman would betray a fellow woman" by exposing her adultery? (473), a question that foreshadows Niniane's refusal later in the book to assist Mordred in trapping Gwenhwyfar with Lancelet. "Am I to help you by betraying a woman who has taken the right the Goddess has given to all women, to choose what man she will?" Niniane asks (851), a stance for which she is killed by Mordred.

Though *The Mists of Avalon* is usually read as a feminist tale, not all of the women are admirable. For most of the book Gwenhwyfar is a nagging agoraphobe who tries to inflict her religious beliefs on everyone around her, including Arthur and therefore the people of his realm. First seen as a weeping child lost in the mists of Avalon, she dutifully marries Arthur and with her uncompromising piety draws him, and all of Britain, under the powerful sway of the Christian priests. She even believes in making "such laws as would keep my people from sin" (420). It is she who insists that Arthur abandon the Pendragon banner because of its ties to the ancient religion of Britain. Instead she has him carry a Christian banner and will not permit a compromise – either the carrying of both banners or allowing one of Arthur's captains to bear the symbol of Britain while Arthur fights under the banner depicting the Virgin Mary and the cross of Christ that Gwenhwyfar has made for him. By failing to fight under the Pendragon banner, Arthur breaks the vow he made to Viviane as Lady of the Lake when she presented him with the sword Excalibur and its scabbard, crafted by Morgaine and enchanted so it will prevent him from bleeding while he wears it.

This struggle between a matriarchal Avalon and a patriarchal Christianity becomes the central conflict of the novel. Sabine Volk-Birke rightly sees the "juxtaposition of the two concepts of Avalon and Christianity" as essential to the understanding of the book. This is in part because Bradley's joining of "the age-old tale of the Round Table and the grail with the Neo-Pagan monomyth" (Fry 339) gives her a framework for her feminist approach to the legends. But the contrast between Avalon and Christianity is symbolic of something more important to the book than the feminist theme. As Raymond Thompson has noted, "The basic conflict is waged between tolerance and intolerance" (*Return* 132), which is couched primarily in terms of the struggle between the natural and liberating Goddess worship of Avalon and the restrictive and constrictive rules of Christianity. Throughout the novel, those who practice the religion of Avalon are generally tolerant of Christianity and object mainly to its attempt to declare all other religions heresy. A basic principle of the religion of Avalon is that "all the Gods are one" (779), a notion that echoes throughout the *Mists*. It is preached by Taliesin, the first of two "Merlins" – here a title rather than a name – who appear in the book, and by his successor, Kevin, who tries to accommodate the new religion in ways that seem to Morgaine such a betrayal that he must be put to death. It is a similar sacrilege by Arthur, using Excalibur as a cross on which to swear an oath to the Saxons, that prompts Morgaine to give the sword to Accolon, her lover (and the son of her husband Uriens), to use against Arthur, who is himself more interested in peace in his realm and in his marriage than in doctrine.

More important, however, than the discord between Morgaine and Kevin or Morgaine and Arthur is that between Gwenhwyfar and Morgaine. Morgaine is initially a priestess who is possessed of the Sight. She is also a tormented woman, torn, as Gwenhwyfar is, by love for Lancelet and her failures as a mother, sister, and wife; and it is her tragic and heroic fate to bring down Arthur, her brother, lover, and foe. Against this continuing conflict, Bradley tells the traditional story – of Arthur's conception; his fathering of Mordred by his half-sister; his marriage to Gwenhwyfar; his establishing of the Round Table; the love between Gwenhwyfar and Lancelet; the affair between Lancelet and Elaine and the resulting birth of Galahad; the Grail quest, including Galahad's achieving of it; and Arthur and Mordred's final battle – albeit in an often untraditional way. For example, Lancelet's love for Gwenhwyfar is tinged with homosexual desire for Arthur; and the half-sister and mother of Mordred, whose birth name is Gwydion, is not Morgause but Morgaine. And Morgaine, as Lee Ann Tobin demonstrates, is "a vision of female power rather than an evil manipulator," just as Gwenhwyfar is an example of the way in which "women lost power in Western culture" (147). By such "reinscrib[ing of] power for female characters" and by decentering "such Arthurian commonplaces" as chivalry, concludes Tobin, Bradley accomplishes a "specifically feminist revisionary act" (147) that gives her novel a distinctive voice and makes it a cult classic.

But even this rivalry is softened by a natural bond between women.

Morgaine recognizes that "in spite of all old enmities, there was love too" between her and Gwenhwyfar (725). And in the end Gwenhwyfar can think of Morgaine "with a sudden passion of love and tenderness" (864). Though it takes most of the book for this to happen, both of them become a little more forgiving of each other and of what each represents. Through her love for Lancelet, a love she chooses and not a relationship that is thrust upon her, Gwenhwyfar finally overcomes her fear of being out in the open, which is really a fear of life. Just as she learns to love her newfound freedom, however, she realizes that because of the love she has for Lancelet and the obligation, paralleling Morgaine's, that she has to Britain, she must forego her chance for personal happiness and retire to the nunnery at Glastonbury. The sense of enclosure in the cloister, which had once made her feel "so safe, so pro-tected," now almost overwhelms her as she feels the walls "closing her in, trapping her" (864). But she is willing to endure the maddening sense of imprisonment because her sacrifice will prevent the kingdom from being torn apart as Troy was because Helen "had all the kings and knights of her day at strife over her" (862). Though Gwenhwyfar is still sacrificing her happiness for others, it is now her choice to do so, a mature sacrifice for a higher good rather than a frightened child's acquiescence to authority figures.

Morgaine too matures, as does her view of the worship of the Goddess as the feminine principle in the world. As Avalon fades more and more into the mists and Morgaine feels that it might be lost forever to the outside world, she brings to Glastonbury cuttings from Avalon's thorn tree, which grew originally from the staff of Joseph of Arimathea, so that something of Avalon will remain. There she learns that nuns pray for Viviane, to whose burial at Glastonbury rather than Avalon Morgaine had objected. Once thought to be an evil sorceress by the Christian priests, now Viviane, or at least her memory, is treated with respect by the nuns of Glastonbury, who also drink from the Chalice Well so important to the old religion and pray to Brigid as a saint though she is in fact "the Goddess as she is worshipped in Ireland" (875). Morgaine realizes that the nuns know "the power of the Immortal" (875) and that the Goddess is not only within those who worship her but within the world as well. Her ability to accept the nuns of Glastonbury as representa-tives of the Goddess is a broadening of her awareness of the presence and power of the divine force she worships. With this new awareness, she under-stands that "I did not fail. I did what she had given me to do. It was not she but I in my pride who thought I should have done more" (876).

In a sense the very feminism of Bradley's book, especially as it is subsumed into the larger theme of religious tolerance (reminiscent of that found in an earlier novel, William H. Babcock's *Cian of the Chariots*), marks it as very American. In the *Mists*, the notion that a king is not the highest authority is made clear. Both Viviane and Morgaine, for instance, challenge Arthur when he breaks his vow to Avalon. And, as in other American Arthurian works, the role and power of the king are downplayed. Viviane tells Morgaine that the "High King is a leader in battle – he does not own the lives of his subjects . . ." (494). Arthur himself says, "I command no man's conscience, King or no" (331); and, in a sentiment like that expressed in Sallie Bridges's poem "The King and the Bard," Arthur recognizes that "such music as [Kevin's] is not to be commanded, even by a king" (681). Similarly, Elaine, the mother of Galahad, says of her son that "even if he was to be king one day, he must be brought up to a simple and modest manhood" (603). Bradley's modern, feminist retelling is perhaps the best known and most widely read Arthurian novel since T. H. White's *The Once and Future King*; and, as such, it has had tremendous influence on other novelists and on readers who now take for granted that approaching the Arthurian legend through the women characters is as acceptable as approaching it through the men who have traditionally been more prominent.

Bradley's recent novel *Lady of Avalon* (1997), which spans the creation of Avalon and foreshadows the birth of Arthur, also offers a strong feminine presence. Three holy women steer the fortunes of Roman Britain as they struggle with their own destinies: Caillean retreats to Avalon, where she and a small band of priestesses establish a sisterhood to serve the Great Goddess, raise the heir to the mystic royal line, and veil the island from a hostile world in its everlasting mists; Dierna guides Avalon through difficult political times; while Ana gives birth to a baby girl who will be the mother of the future king. Ana's beautiful older daughter Viviane, however, is the woman destined for true greatness, as the Lady of the Lake and the guardian of the Grail.

Though little known, Mary J. Jones's *Avalon* (1991), described by the publisher as a "lesbian Arthurian romance," is also a noteworthy contribution to feminist fantasy fiction. Gwenhyfar's child Argante ("brilliant one"), who grows to womanhood with her soul-friend Elin and becomes the fabled Lady of the Lake, is a Daughter of the Goddess whose duty it is to watch over the Celtic Realms of Ireland, Britain, and Gaul. But her foe, Annis the Hag, the fearsome dark sister of the Goddess Mother and Queen of the Wastelands, wants dominion over the Celtic Realms; and so Argante and the Daughters of Avalon must do battle. The novel reworks the legends in radically feminist ways: for example, it is Morgant, not Merlin, who moves the huge stones to Salisbury; and Morgant is Nimue's lover. The male characters, in large part secondary, are easily corrupted: Balin, for instance, is seduced by Annis.

Some of the most fascinating and extended treatments of Arthurian topics occur in fiction series.[20] The early but fine sword-and-sorcery novels of H.

20 The series have many different focuses. Science fiction and fantasy author Robert N. Charrette, for instance, portrays the clash between magic and technology in *A Prince Among Men* (1994), *A King Beneath a Mountain* (1995), and *A Knight Among Knaves* (1995). Courtway Jones's projected "Dragon's Heir Trilogy," including *In the Shadow of the Oak King* (1991) and *Witch of the North* (1992), is a series of historical romances, while Gael Baudino's Dragonsword series – *Dragonsword* (1991), *Duel of Dragons* (1991), *Dragon Death* (1992) – is set in the alternate world of Gryylth and contains numerous Arthurian parallels.

Warner Munn, like much American Arthurian literature, bring the legends to the New World. Munn's heroic fantasy *King of the World's Edge* (1939) traces the odyssey of Ventidius Varro, Arthur's former centurion, and Myrdhinn (Merlin) in Arthur's ship Prydwenn after the battle of Camlann; the two – and a handful of other survivors of the last battle – arrive in North America, where they forge new alliances among the native peoples. In *The Ship from Atlantis* (1967), published together with *King of the World's Edge* as *Merlin's Godson* (1976), Gwalchmai (Gawain) learns the customs of his father Varro and of his godfather Myrdhinn, who gives him a magic ring with the power to defend against various enemies and to defy the passage of time. In the final book, *Merlin's Ring* (1974), Gwalchmai, who enjoys an enduring romance with the immortal Corenice from Atlantis, travels over centuries and across continents before returning to Britain. There he finds Arthur's sword in a faery mound and restores it to the king, who lies sleeping in a cavern beneath St. Michael's Mount in Cornwall.

Gwalchmai (the "Hawk of May") appears again as the narrator of *Hawk of May* (1980), the first book in Gillian Bradshaw's popular series. After witnessing the horrifying rituals of his mother Morgawse, the boy escapes to the Isles of the Blessed; when he returns years later, he seeks service with her adversary, his uncle Arthur, from whom he learns the dark secret of Medraut's (Mordred's) incestuous origins. In *Kingdom of Summer* (1981), which starts nine years later, Rhys ap Sion, Gwalchmai's servant, tells the story of his master's ill-fated love affair with Elidan and his ongoing struggle with Morgawse, the Queen of Darkness. In the end, Morgawse is beheaded by Agravain, and Gwalchmai finds Elidan. But, receiving no forgiveness from Elidan, Gwalchmai leaves without learning that Gwynn, a Percival-like character, is his son. *In Winter's Shadow* (1982) shifts the focus to Gwynhwyfar, whose first-person narrative, a gripping and convincing account of her passion for Bedwyr, her love for Arthur, her fear and hatred of Medraut, and her guilt and shame for her part in the breakup of the "Family," is written years later from the convent where she is now an abbess.[21] Medraut, whom she has tried to poison, exposes the lovers. Bedwyr, in trying to rescue her, accidentally kills Gwynn. This inspires in Gwalchmai a passion for revenge that leaves the empire vulnerable to Medraut's usurpation and the ensuing tragedy. Bradshaw borrows material "from a variety of traditional sources" and "integrates it with skill" into her trilogy "to produce a convincing, if increasingly somber, vision of the Arthurian legend" (*NAE* 51).

Told in the words of Artorius Pendragon, *Firelord* (1980), the first novel in

---

21 *In Winter's Shadow*, the third novel of the series and "the one where everyone gets killed," is the most realistic. Bradshaw writes, "I do not try, like T. H. White or Rosemary Sutcliff, to mitigate the tragedy. I want it to be very painful. . . . I want it to be a proper tragedy. It's no use having such noble characters if you're not going to use them for a tragedy" (Letter of April 17, 1981, to Alan Lupack).

Parke Godwin's Arthurian "triptych," portrays the king as "a spiritual Everyman" and a visionary Pict who strives to restore life and purpose to a mighty nation.[22] After Arthur's death at the hands of his son Modred (by Pictish wife Morgana, the earthy ruler of Prydn, the Faerie-folk), Guenevere – her husband's equal in strength and character – comes into her own. In *Beloved Exile* (1984), she tries to retain control of the society she and Arthur forged, though it means forming odd alliances and even living for a while in servitude and captivity by the Saxons, whose values she learns to appreciate. Guenevere's experience, which in many ways parallels Arthur's, provides a nice symmetry between the two novels. *The Last Rainbow* (1985) goes back in time, to the life of St. Patrick before he became a saint. Living among British pagans, he meets Dorelei, the Prydn ruler who teaches him the powers of the earth and the pleasures of love; in turn, he offers her and her people a new god and savior. The Arthurian element occurs later, when Patrick meets Ambrosius Aurelianus, who has begun his struggle for British autonomy. Godwin's narrative techniques and attention to modern concerns, especially to the role of Guenevere and other women within their respective societies, no doubt account for much of the novels' success.[23]

The increasing emphasis in American fiction on the legend's female characters is reflected in several other series that focus on those figures often minimized or overlooked in more traditional accounts. For instance, as suggested by the titles *Guinevere* (1981), *The Chessboard Queen* (1984), and *Guinevere Evermore* (1985), Sharan Newman's trilogy examines the queen's protected childhood and her troubled marriage. But Newman also infuses the familiar Arthurian world with otherworldly elements like the Unicorn; features uncommon depictions of Merlin, Gawaine, and Arthur as youths; and introduces original characters such as Alswytha, the Saxon maid, and Gaia, a lonely woman who is the victim of self-condemnation. Persia

22 "After everybody and his brother was coming out with a version" of the Arthurian story, Godwin "determined the only way to do it was *my* way." So, writes Godwin, "I made Arthur a universal type, a spiritual Everyman so that his joy and sorrow echoed eternal truths about the human condition. And to do this, I needed him downstage, immediate, talking *directly* to the reader, even referring to the reader as 'you' quite often. The other main choice was the treatment of Merlin. This bloody old bore has irritated me since I first read Tennyson. I resolved instead of a remote and all-wise Druid tripping over his beard and omniscience, that I'd make him Arthur's genius, his alter-ego. This way, growing with Arthur, he carries the nobility and 'legendary' qualities that an immediate 'now' character like my Arthur has to leave off." Godwin views Modred and Morgan Le Fay as "a beleaguered minority . . . sort of like emergent third-world people . . . a modern relevance" (Letter of Jan. 19, 1981 to Alan Lupack).
23 In at least three of his short stories, Godwin explores Arthurian themes. "The Lady of Finnigan's Hearth" (1977) moves Isolde from the afterlife in heaven to modern life in America; "The Last Rainbow" (1978) tells a story of the Grail; and "Uallannach" (1988), anthologized in *Invitation to Camelot: An Arthurian Anthology of Short Stories*, a volume of original tales edited by Godwin, describes the fatal encounter from Modred's perspective.

Woolley's Guinevere trilogy, *Child of the Northern Spring* (1987), *Queen of the Summer Stars* (1990), and *Guinevere: The Legend in Autumn* (1991), also begins with Guinevere's description of her youth and marriage to Arthur; continues with her idyll with Lancelot at Joyous Gard; and concludes with the quest for the Grail and the fall of the Round Table. Though Woolley draws heavily on Malory for details, she offers a host of psychological insights into her characters' motives that makes the story more accessible and understandable to modern popular audiences. Patricia Kennealy's projected nine-book Keltiad includes three novels, *The Copper Crown* (1984), *The Throne of Scone* (1986), and *The Silver Branch* (1988), known as the Aeron trilogy, in which Aeron, queen of the Kelts, must recover the Thirteen Treasures that disappeared with Arthur after the battle of Camlann (here a "space battle"). The continuation of the series, the Tales of Arthur trilogy, includes *The Hawk's Gray Feather* (1990), *The Oak Above the Kings* (1994), and *The Hedge of Mist* (1996), the last two written under the name Patricia Kennealy-Morrison. In these novels, Taliesin recounts Arthur's early wars to restore the High Kingship, his marriage to Gweniver, and the growing danger posed by his half-sister Marguessan (Morgause). As she did in the first part of the series, Kennealy simultaneously employs and radically transforms traditional elements like the Grail and the love story of Tristan and Isolde by framing them in the distant star-realm of Keltia. Even Joan Wolf's otherwise undistinguished historical-romance series – *The Road to Avalon* (1988), *Born of the Sun* (1989), and *The Edge of Light* (1990), all but the first only marginally Arthurian – puts some of the women in unusual situations; Morgan, for instance, is both Mordred's mother and Merlin's daughter as well as Arthur's aunt and his ongoing lover. In Quinn Taylor Evans's "Merlin's Legacy" romance series, which suggests a possible new direction for popular Arthurian literature, Merlin has not just one but three daughters: the second-sighted visionary Vivian of Amesbury in *Daughter of Fire* (1996), the changeling Brianna of Scotland in *Daughter of the Mist* (1996), and the healer Cassandra of Tregaron in *Daughter of Light* (1997).

Another noteworthy series is Stephen Lawhead's Pendragon Cycle, originally planned as a trilogy but now consisting of five books: *Taliesin* (1987), which describes the bard's origins, religious conversion, and marriage to a princess of Atlantis; *Merlin* (1988), the autobiographical story of Taliesin's son, who prepares for Arthur's coming in much the same way that Taliesin prepared for his; *Arthur* (1989), the tale of the High King and Pendragon of the Island of the Mighty who tries to bring about the Summer Kingdom, a reign of peace and prosperity foreseen by Taliesin; *Pendragon* (1994), in which Arthur, the Bear of Britain, battles to keep alive his cherished dream of Summer; and *Grail* (1997), the account of Arthur's miraculous renewal by the sacred relic, which mysteriously vanishes and must be recovered by the king and his Dragon Flight. Although a religious message underlies Lawhead's cycle, the novels nonetheless use their Welsh and Celtic source material to tell a thoroughly engrossing story.[24]

Simon Hawke (pseudonym of Nicholas Yermakov) employs the Arthurian material in a less traditional but even more inventive way than Lawhead does. His "Wizard" books are all set in the future, a fantastic time in which magic reigns supreme, characters "die" but send their essences into the bodies of others, and spirits offer assistance. Joining forces against the Dark Ones in the various novels – *The Wizard of 4th Street* (1987), *The Wizard of Whitechapel* (1988), *The Wizard of Sunset Strip* (1989), *The Wizard of Rue Morgue* (1990), *The Samurai Wizard* (1991), *The Wizard of Sante Fe* (1991), *The Wizard of Camelot* (1993), and *The Wizard of Lovecraft's Cafe* (1993) – are Morgan le Fay, her son Modred, two descendants of her sisters Elaine and Morgause, Merlin, the spirit of Gorlois, the descendants of Gorlois's three daughters, a punk rocker named Billy (whose body, at one point, is shared by the spirits of Gorlois and Merlin), and a policeman named John Angelo (into whose body Modred sends his dormant essence). The international adventures, which span London, Los Angeles, the sewers of Paris, Tokyo, Santa Fe, Camelot, and New York City, involve opponents like a werewolf and a Jack the Ripper-style murderer enlisted by the ubiquitous Dark Ones, who have escaped their imprisonment.

Robert Monaco's two series are almost as long as Hawke's but considerably less engaging. Loosely based on Wolfram von Eschenbach's *Parzival*, Monaco's Grail books present an especially grim and bloody version of the Arthurian world, a realm full of savagery, rapes, murder, even cannibalism and other gratuitous horrors. In *Parsival* (1977), *The Grail War* (1979), *The Final Quest* (1980), and *Blood and Dreams* (1985), the holy fool Parsival searches for the Grail in a rationalized and despiritualized quest that leads ultimately to emptiness, while the demonic Clinschor devastates the country in his own ruthless pursuit of the vessel. The novels, in which the behavior of the aristocracy is generally deplorable and even typically noble knights like Lancelot and Lohengrin kill without a second thought, are "all anti-romances of the most extreme sort." Parsival, in particular, "continually rejects his role as Grail savior, first in extreme knightly brutality, and then in his turning to family life for comfort from the horror of a harsh, feudal, plaguey, hungry, and war-torn world – a true wasteland" (*NAE* 326). But nothing brings the unknightly knight any real balm. Monaco's second Arthurian fantasy series seems almost as gloomy and as full of treacherous misconduct as his first: *Runes* (1984) treats the adventures of Arthur's parents, Bita, a British slave, and Leitus, the son of the gladiator Spartacus, while *Broken Stone* (1985) continues their story and introduces the young

---

24 Lawhead's publisher Crossway, which typically publishes work with a religious orientation, also published Donna Fletcher Crow's *Glastonbury* (1992), a sentimental religious novel about the holy site, Joseph of Arimathea, and Arthur as historical Christian king.

Arturus to his half-sister Morga. Although the brutality in Monaco's work, according to Raymond H. Thompson, recalls the world of sword and sorcery fantasy and "provides an ironic contrast to the high-minded ideals of chivalric romance and the Holy Grail" (*Return* 145), ultimately it is hard to look "below all the ugliness . . . on the surface" (*Parsival* 335). Consequently, the most memorable aspects of both series are their confused plots and repetitious scenes of butchery and violence.

The Arthurian stories have also provided the basis for interesting and innovative American mystery fiction,[25] some of which is set in Camelot during Arthur's day. In Maxey Brooke's short story, "Morte d'Alain: An Unrecorded Idyll of the King" (1969), for instance, a knight is murdered at King Arthur's court. Merlin's apprentice describes how his master, the magician, solves the mystery, not through any supernatural "power of darkness" (271) but by the time-honored art of following the killer's footprints, and how he forces the killer to confess. Merlin solves another crime at court by deducing who destroyed financial records and assaulted his assistant in Brooke's "Morte d'un Marcheant" (1992). Phyllis Ann Karr also sets her *Idylls of the Queen* (1982) in Camelot. Based on a short episode in Malory about Sir Patrise, who is killed after eating a poisoned apple at a banquet given by the queen, Karr's novel is narrated by Sir Kay, who discovers the truth about the crime and clears Guinevere of suspicion. A medieval gumshoe, Kay makes other unusual discoveries about people at the court, especially about those traditionally dismissed as villains. He realizes that Mordred is an intelligent man who is embittered not only by the circumstances of his birth but by the prophecy that dooms him as well as his father, and that Morgan feels true concern for the kingdom. Unfortunately, Kay is not accorded the full or proper credit for his successful detective work; Lancelot, who defends the Queen in trial by combat, and Nimue, whose magic corroborates the murderer's guilt, receive more praise than the hapless seneschal does. "This resolution," writes Thompson, "comments upon the Arthurian world, where valor and sorcery are more highly prized than intelligence" (*Return* 123). Yet the plot line, in which a lesser figure achieves what more prominent characters cannot, is quite compatible with the more democratic tradition of American Arthuriana. (Sir Kay reappears – though not as a detective – in a later short story by Karr; in "Two Bits of Embroidery" [1988], a scullery maid's love for Kay is counterpointed with the story of Elaine of Astolat's tragic love for Lancelot.)

More common are mysteries set in the modern day that draw, often obliquely, on Arthurian legend. Typically, those novels involve a quest for a

25 See the entry by Daniel Nastali on "Mystery and Suspense Fiction" in *NAE* 339–40. Nastali concludes that "Even the best of these [Arthurian mystery and suspense] novels can scarcely be considered genuine developments of the Arthurian tradition; they represent, rather, adjuncts to it. But they also serve as illustrations of the extent to which the tradition has become part of our common literary currency" (340).

specific legendary artifact like the Grail. Such is the case in Richard Ben Sapir's *Quest* (1987), in which the hero, worldly-wise Detective Arthur C. Modelstein – "Artie" – rises to untypically chivalrous stature in the pursuit of the gold, gem-encrusted saltcellar that incorporates the Holy Grail and that was originally created for Queen Elizabeth I to celebrate the victory over the Spanish Armada. Artie's quest inside the criminal world of international gem dealers takes him from New York to Cairo, to Paris, to London, and to Geneva. In Nelson DeMille's *The Quest* (1975), characters with analogues in the Arthurian stories seek the holy cup, which is hidden in an Ethiopian monastery, whereas Alice Campbell's *The Murder of Caroline Bundy* (1932) sets the mystery in Glastonbury and James Goldman's *The Man from Greek and Roman* (1974) at Cadbury Hill. The Grail in James P. Blaylock's *The Paper Grail* (1991) is not even a cup but a nineteenth-century Japanese sketch that had once been shaped into a cup used to gather blood. Northern California museum curator Howard Barton discovers the "paper Grail's" mystery and eventually succeeds Michael Graham, the novel's Fisher King, as its keeper.

The Grail, however, is not the only mysterious or coveted artifact. In Jo Anne Stang's *Shadows on the Sceptred Isle* (1980), it is the discovery of the leaden cross from Arthur's grave that motivates the wealthy industrialist Sir Edmund Littell to conspire to restore Britain's national purity in Arthur's name and forces the heroine, Elizabeth Kendall, the American on sabbatical in England, to untangle the mysteries at Thorn Hill Manor. And an ancient iron ring is at the heart of Elizabeth Peters' *The Camelot Caper* (1969), in which the owners of an old manor in Cornwall try to create an Arthurian archaeological site by salting it with fifth-century objects.

Among the most widely-read versions of the Arthurian legend are those works written for a juvenile audience. Inspired by the youth movements of the late nineteenth and early twentieth centuries, writers like Sidney Lanier and Howard Pyle retold the popular stories for younger readers, an important trend that has continued throughout the century with the contributions of increasing numbers of new and prominent writers.

Whereas the retellings by Lanier and Pyle were based largely on *Le Morte d'Arthur*, Allen French, in his early juvenile romance *Sir Marrok* (1902), uses only a brief passage in Malory as the basis of his story. French's noble knight Marrok is sent by King Uther, at Merlin's suggestion, to restore peace and justice to Bedegraine, "a fertile land laid waste" (7) and rife with witches, robbers, and other violent and unholy people, and then by the new king, Uther's son Arthur, to fight the kings who oppose him. Before going to war, Marrok sets his affairs in order and leaves the welfare of both his son and his new kingdom of Bedegraine in the hands of the duplicitous Lady Irma, a member of the council of Morgan le Fay. In Marrok's absence, Irma "began new ways" (85); and, upon his return, she uses her magic to transform him from man to beast, forcing Marrok to roam the woods for more than seven years in the form of a gray wolf. Yet, even in his altered state, Marrok continues to protect his vassals and to turn adversity into opportunity. He defends Lady Agnes, daughter of the good Sir Simon, against the men of Sir Morcar; delivers his retainer Andred from robbers; assists the swineherd Blaise; saves the monk Norris; protects Father John from harm until he is made abbot; and brings a peasant child home, on his back, in the middle of a brutal snowstorm. Even those whom Irma tries to enlist to kill the wolf – Wat, Pellinore, Tristram – soon come to respect and admire his dignity. Ultimately, by using a secret passage to the castle that Merlin had long before advised him to build, Marrok destroys the magic wolfen image of himself, is restored to his former shape as a man, and frustrates Irma as she tries to work a similar evil transformation on his son Walter. Within six months, Walter and Irma's good daughter Gertrude are married; "and all the land of Bedegraine was happy, except that the peasants lamented that they saw the great gray wolf no more" (280). French's didactic tale, which reminds younger readers not to be deceived by appearances, underscores the virtues of strength, devotion, and loyalty that Marrok displays even in the most difficult circumstances.

Still other juvenile novelists draw not on characters from traditional sources like Malory but instead use Arthur's court as a historical background for their own original characters, oftentimes young people the same age as their intended audiences, and for their own original American "rags-to-riches" stories, in which the achievement of knighthood depends on moral qualities rather than circumstances of birth. In Catherine Owens Peare's *Melor, King Arthur's Page* (1963), for instance, the youthful Melor learns from the mistakes he keeps making and eventually redeems himself by saving Arthur from a huge boar named Troynt. In *Page Boy for King Arthur* (1949), the first of two delightful novels by Eugenia Stone, Tor, a peasant boy rescues Sir Lancelot and is rewarded by being made a page to Sir Galahad. In Stone's *Squire for King Arthur* (1955), Tor rescues the son of Pellinore from the Saxons, warns Arthur of a Saxon invasion, and is made Pellinore's squire. The hero of Clyde Robert Bulla's *The Sword in the Tree* (1956) performs similar brave acts. After his father Lord Weldon reportedly dies in quicksand and his uncle Lionel usurps the family's castle, Shan runs away with his mother and eventually travels to King Arthur's court, where – on a "special day" – he asks the king for a boon: assistance in reclaiming the property that is rightfully his. With Sir Gareth's help, he returns to his castle; retrieves his father's sword, which he had hidden in an old oak tree; and frees his father, who has been imprisoned in the dungeon by Lionel. Since the story Shan told King Arthur is true, Gareth suggests that "the king *will* call [him] to Camelot some day" (95) to train as a page, a squire, and ultimately a knight. Maturation and elevation to knighthood are also the subject of Gwendolyn Bowers' *Brother to Galahad* (1963), in which Hugh of Alleyn leaves his ancient castle of Brannlyr; travels to Glastonbury, where he learns that he is descended from the line of Joseph of Arimathea; becomes Galahad's squire on the Grail quest;

witnesses Arthur's defeat; and realizes his need to embark on his own quest back to Alleyn, where he is most needed. Galahad's words ring in Hugh's ears: "For you too follow the Grail – by another road" (186). Another Hugh, this one a lame young monk whose treacherous father slew Thomas Beckett, is cured by a vision of the Grail during a fire that destroys Glastonbury Abbey in Eleanore Myers Jewett's *The Hidden Treasure of Glaston* (1946). The orphaned Wulf, protagonist of another of Bowers' books, *Lost Dragon of Wessex* (1957), makes an important discovery as well: he learns that he is a descendant of Arthur's bard Taliesin and fulfills Merlin's prophecy by presenting a dragon-shaped armring that originally belonged to Arthur to another great king, Alfred. Young men are not alone in proving their nobility through their deeds. In Donald J. Sobol's *Greta the Strong* (1970), set in the lawless years following Arthur's reign, it is a strong but sensitive heroine who embarks on a quest to recover the lost Excalibur. Eventually, however, she learns that there are better ways to achieve justice than by the sword.[26]

Also popular are the juvenile novels of fantasy, particularly those involving time travel, in which characters journey back to Arthur's day or Arthurian characters travel to contemporary time – or sometimes in both directions, as in British-American author Susan Cooper's immensely popular "The Dark Is Rising" series. Three young American boys go back to Camelot, where they defeat the Black Knight and save the kingdom from both a giant and a dragon in Jon Scieszka's illustrated *Knights of the Kitchen Table* (1991), whereas Merlin travels to modern times in Tom McGowen's clever fantasy *Sir MacHinery* (1971), in which he teams up with a scientist named Arthur and his knightly robot to help the brownies defeat the demon dwarves led by the evil Urlag. In the fantasy series by Pamela F. Service, Britain – after five hundred years of nuclear winter – is still in a new Dark Age that is again the setting for a conflict between Arthur and Merlin and their old enemy Morgan La Fay. In Service's *Winter of Magic's Return* (1985), Merlin revives in the body of a teenager and, with the help of two schoolfriends, Wellington Jones ("Welly") and Heather McKenna, embarks on a quest to find Arthur, who is "needed again" (97). After confronting Morgan and her consort Garth, a werewolf, at Stonehenge, the three teens build a boat held together by magic; arrive in Avalon, a contrast to the wasteland they have left behind; and enlist the aid of Arthur, who wonders "Is there anything here worth fighting for?" (191). In Service's *Tomorrow's Magic* (1987), the trio supports Arthur in his struggle to reunite the feuding kingdoms of Britain against Morgan and her horde of mutant invaders. Merlin, however, realizes that his powers are waning: simple spells still work, but the important aspects of magic escape him; and even with his Bowl of Prophecy he has difficulty

---

26 Although *Greta the Strong* is his only explicitly Arthurian work, Sobol is the author of the very popular Encyclopedia Brown detective series for younger readers. In that series, there are occasional references to Excalibur.

seeing into the future. When Morgan uses Heather's amulet to entrap him and then taunts him for his weakness in needing to "be loved," Merlin responds, "your powers are nothing! They're tattered, dying relics. . . . Your amulet, my bowl – they are *things*, cold, lifeless things. . . . The strongest new magic comes from people, not things" (181–82). And, after Morgan hurls Merlin through the crack that she had wedged in time and he finds himself – along with Welly and Heather – back on the very day that the Devastation began, Merlin indeed calls on Heather's "new power" (185) to defeat Morgan's evil by "build[ing] a world of hope" in which the vision of the nuclear winter that they have experienced will prevent "this ultimate horror" (190) from ever actually transpiring.[27]

As in adult science fiction and fantasy, the crack in time is a familiar device: it occurs not only in Service's novels but also in other works, such as L. J. Smith's juvenile Arthurian fiction, in which Smith creates an elaborate new – and often convoluted – Arthurian mythology. After the Weerul Council, the supreme ruling body of Findahl (Wildworld), decrees that the Wildfolk be evacuated to their own world and the passages to Stillworld (Earth) be sealed, the sorceress Morgana Shee protests because she has fallen in love with a young Native American boy, a dreamsinger, who lives on the other side. Morgana argues that, because her mother was a Quislai (fairy) and her father a human, she is entitled to spend half her time in the Wildworld and half in the human world. Thia Pendriel, a magistrate of the Council, opposes the plan; but the Council allows a single "Passage" to remain through which Morgana can move. That passage can be opened only by an amulet, which – against the Council's directive – Morgana eventually shares with her new husband, the dreamsinger. But when he uses it to follow Morgana to the other world, Thia has him put to death; and Morgana herself is exiled to Earth, never to return to Wildworld, where she now has numerous enemies. In Smith's *The Night of the Solstice* (1987), Morgana still guards the sole gate to the parallel universe of the Wildworld, a mirror located in her contemporary suburban California mansion, Fell Andred, built directly on the Great Coastal Passage. When Morgana is betrayed and imprisoned in the Wildworld by her former friend Cadal Forge, now a sorcerer who wants to enslave the earth, Morgana's familiar (a vixen who has the powers of speech) recruits the four Hodges-Bradley children to find her. The rescue must be accomplished before December 21, the night of the winter solstice, the one night that Cadal Forge can travel through the mirror to Stillworld. The adventures continue in *Heart of Valor* (1990), which is set a year and a half later. Although, by the end of the first novel, Morgana and the children had managed to close the last gateway to Wildworld, a California earthquake now threatens to re-open the passage. As Morgana goes

27 In a more recent work, *Wizard of Wind and Rock* (1990), a children's book illustrated by
    Laura Marshall, Service recounts Merlin's youth.

searching for the quake's epicenter, the children are left to battle Morgana's archrival Thia Pendriel, who has the power of the stolen Forgotten Gem, the Heart of Valor of the novel's title. By their combined efforts, including Janie's skill at sorcery and Claudia's ability to talk to animals, they succeed – in time for June 21, Midsummer Eve, the summer solstice. Whereas Smith's Morgana is largely a sympathetic character, it is a more traditional and evil Morgan who is defeated in Jane Curry's *The Sleepers* (1968), a novel in which four children discover Arthur and his knights sleeping underground in the Eildon Hills. With the help of Myrddin (Merlin), they foil a plot by Morgan and Medraut to destroy the Sleepers and capture the thirteen Treasures of Prydein (Britain).[28]

Merlin, one of the most popular characters in juvenile Arthurian fiction, is also the central character in several books by the prolific author Jane Yolen.[29] In *Merlin's Booke* (1986), a collection of tales for younger as well as older readers, Yolen tells of the magician as a boy, as a man, and as a centuries-old legend. The thirteen stories and poems (about half previously published) describe a series of separate events from the sorcerer's birth to his entrapment and, ultimately, to the discovery of his grave in the twenty-first century. In *The Dragon's Boy*, Merlin – known to most as Old Linn, the apothecary – is revealed to be the dragon whom Artos (Arthur) encounters in a dark cave and who teaches him the game of wisdom and imparts the knowledge he needs to become a man and a warrior. Drawing very loosely on Geoffrey's twelfth-century *Vita Merlini* and the few other early accounts of his life, "The Young Merlin Trilogy" traces Merlin's unusual and generally unhappy childhood. In Book One, *Passager* (1996), Merlin, as an eight-year-old boy, is abandoned in the woods; after a year of sleeping in the trees and foraging for food, he is captured by a falconer, who tames him as he would a passager, an immature bird caught in the wild, and who helps the boy relearn the things that he has forgotten. Among the falconer's hawks and merlins, the boy finally remembers his own name and begins reclaiming his magical identity. After his adoptive family is destroyed by fire in Book Two, *Hobby* (1996), Merlin is orphaned again. Assuming new identities as "Hawk" and "Hobby" (the name of a small falcon), the birds that recur in his dreams, he joins a company of traveling performers that includes Viviane and Ambrosius, who help him to explore his new powers, especially the dreams that come true "on the slant" (82). In *Merlin* (1997), the now twelve-year-old boy falls into the hands of another band of outcasts – the *wodewose*, or wild folk – and begins to come into his magic. His dreaming, however, continues to mark

---

28 Though set not in the contemporary day but in sixteenth-century Cornwall, Nancy Faulkner's *Sword of the Winds* (1957) also tells the story of the sleeping King Arthur and his knights. The young hero who discovers them helps Arthur to use his power against the Spanish Armada.

29 Merlin also appears in a number of the stories in *Camelot: A Collection of Original Arthurian Stories*, edited by Jane Yolen.

him as an outsider; and his survival seems to lie in the "cub" he meets –
Artus, or "bear-man" – for whom some of Merlin's dreams, like that of a
table round, eventually materialize. Even in Yolen's beast fable, *The Acorn
Quest* (1981), in which King Eathor the owl sends four of his knights – Sir
Tarryhere the turtle, Sir Belliful the groundhog, Sir Gimmemore the rabbit,
and Sir Runsalot the mouse – to save the creatures of Woodland from starva-
tion, Merlin appears as the wizard Squirrelin, on whose advice Eathor initiates the quest for the golden acorn.

The quest underlies another novel, Katherine Paterson's *Park's Quest*
(1988), a juvenile work that uses the Arthurian legends in a truly innovative
and interesting way and that is reminiscent of Bobbie Ann Mason's adult
fiction *In Country*, in which a young woman quests for similar answers.[30]
Paterson's Parkington Waddell Broughton the Fifth – "Park" for short –
embarks on a quest to learn about his father, who died in Vietnam when he
was just a baby. Park's quest takes him first to the Vietnam Memorial in
Washington, DC, and then to the farm where his father was raised, where he
discovers the family secrets that his mother has withheld from him – that she
divorced his father just before his second tour of duty in Vietnam, during
which he was killed; that his grandfather, a career military officer called
simply "the Colonel," had suffered his first stroke when he heard the sad
news. And Park learns the deepest secret of all: that Thanh, the strange and
scrappy Vietnamese girl who lives on the farm, is actually his half-sister. The
very contemporary Park is therefore much like the traditional Percival,
whose mother kept him ignorant of chivalry, which she blamed for his
father's death; who, learning of the existence of knights, ignored his
mother's grief and left for court; who, in a strange castle, is witness to a
strange procession but, as advised, never questions what he sees; and who
eventually asks the question that cures the infirm Fisher King. Park's
mother's refusal to discuss his father and her attempts to shelter him from
the Colonel and the rest of the family, whose military associations date back
centuries and whom she somehow holds responsible for the Vietnam War
and the loss of her husband, impel Park to find things out for himself. But,
upon the advice of his mother and out of his own fear of seeming forward or
impolite, he rarely asks the necessary questions; when his uncle Frank picks
him up at the bus stop, for instance, Park realizes "he had used up his one
question" (43). After several visits to the farm's springhouse, where Thanh –
a kind of modern-day Grail maiden – not only gives him water but also
guides him to various self-discoveries, he is able at last to speak to his grandfather. His questions – "What's the matter?"; "Does something hurt?"; "Do

30 The quest is also at the heart of Robert Newman's juvenile Arthurian novels. In the
humorous fantasy *Merlin's Mistake*, three questing youngsters – Brian, a sixteen-year-old
squire; Tertius, a boy gifted with special sight; and Lianor, disguised as a crone – end up
at Nimue's castle. The situation is more serious in *The Testing of Tertius*: to keep England
safe and to rescue Merlin and Blaise, the three must face Nimue and the evil wizard Urlik.

you miss him?" (147) – cause the old man to break down in tears that bring healing to both of them. When Thanh reappears, she holds in her hands a coconut shell full of clear water for the two men to drink. "Then they took the Holy Grail in their hands and drew away the cloth and drank. . . . And it seemed to all who saw them that their faces shone with a light that was not of this world. And they were as one in the company of the Grail" (148). In entwining the Grail theme with a young boy's odyssey to understand Vietnam and discover his heritage, *Park's Quest* tells a powerful story that is at once traditionally Arthurian and uniquely American.

The continuing use of Arthurian motifs, in plays such as Margery Evernden's *King Arthur's Sword* (1959) and Keith Engar's *Merlin's Tale of Arthur's Magic* (1982) and in juvenile fiction, particularly the recent illustrated series by Hudson Talbott (*King Arthur: The Sword in the Stone; King Arthur and the Round Table;* and *Excalibur*) and Robert D. San Souci (*Young Guinevere, Young Lancelot, Young Merlin,* and *Young Arthur*), indicates that, for children as for adults, the magic of the legends is stronger than ever.

The Arthurian legends have also had a deep and pervasive influence on American film. As Kevin J. Harty, who has written extensively and incisively about Arthurian cinema, notes, "since at least 1904 the major names in the film industry both before and behind the camera have been associated with Arthurian film" (*Cinema Arthuriana* [hereafter cited as *CA*] xvi). *Parsifal* (1904), the earliest American Arthurian film and the most ambitious and costly film Edwin S. Porter made while working for Edison, was Porter's attempt to capitalize upon the successful New York production of Wagner's opera at the Metropolitan Opera House in New York in late December, 1903. Unusual for its length as well as for its elaborate sets and trick photography (action shot from the audience's point of view and exaggerated acting to suggest that the actors are actually singing), *Parsifal* had to be withdrawn from circulation because of copyright problems (Harty, *CA* 4).

Other American Arthurian silent films followed. *Launcelot and Elaine* (Vitagraph, 1909; dir. Charles Kent), based on Tennyson's poem from the *Idylls of the King*, was hailed for its artistry in blending action with narration and for innovative cinematic techniques that included shots inside a dark cave and close-ups of the tournament in which Launcelot fights to win the Queen's favor (Harty, *CA* 5). Another Vitagraph film, *The Lady of Shalott* (1915; dir. C. Jay Williams), starring Flora Finch, Constance Talmadge, and William Shea, also drew on Tennyson's poetry for inspiration.[31] Little is known today about *King Arthur, or Knights of the Round Table* (New Agency, 1910), but a later film, *Knights of the Square Table, or The Grail* (Edison, 1917; dir. Alan Crosland), reflects the attempts by Robert Baden-Powell, the

---

31 According to Einar Lauritzen and Gunnar Lundquist in *American Film Index: 1908–1915* 333, *The Lady of Shalott* was released on March 15, 1915. The scenario, written by Cecilie B. Peterson, was "inspired by the poem by Tennyson." The cast included Flora Finch, Kate Price, William Shea, Jay Dwiggins, and Constance Talmadge.

founder of the scouting movement, to model the organization in part on the fellowship of the Round Table. With a screenplay written by the National Field Scout Commissioner James A. Wilder, *Knights of the Square Table* tells parallel stories of two groups of boys, one a gang of delinquents, whose leader's prize possession is a book recounting the quest for the Holy Grail, and the other a group of Scouts. After the leader of the delinquents is wounded in a robbery in which he is forced to participate, the Grail knight appears and cures him; afterwards, he and his gang join up with the Scouts (Harty, *CA* 6). In *The Light in the Dark* (Hope Hampton/AFN, 1922; dir. Clarence L. Brown), another "spiritually moving film,"[32] Lon Chaney stars as Tony Pantelli, a gangster in love with a girl who is restored to health through the powers of the Holy Grail and who, in the end, returns to her regenerated millionaire boyfriend. The film, shot in black and white, was dyed using beautiful tints of blue, purple, and grey for the Holy Grail subplot, which took the form of a flashback. But perhaps the most interesting film of the period is one that was never made: D. W. Griffith's *The Quest of the Holy Grail*, a spectacle to be based on the murals painted by Edwin Austin Abbey for the Boston Public Library's Delivery Room (Harty, *CA* 6).

Unsurprisingly, the most popular Arthurian films made in America were those based on the most American retelling of Arthurian material: the Connecticut Yankee transported to King Arthur's court. Drawing, often very loosely, on Mark Twain's classic *A Connecticut Yankee in King Arthur's Court*, published in 1889, those films attempted to copy the novel's humor and convey the remarkable inventiveness of the Yankee. But virtually all failed to evoke the darkness of the ending of the novel and the disturbing aspects of Hank's character.

The popular silent film, *A Connecticut Yankee at King Arthur's Court* (Fox, 1920; dir. Emmett J. Flynn), followed the adventures of wealthy young Martin Cavendish (played by Harry C. Myers). One night, while reading a book about chivalry, Martin is knocked unconscious by a burglar and dreams that he travels to Arthur's court. There he encounters Sir Sagramore, who captures him (and whom he later bests in the lists); Morgan le Fay, whose amorous advances he must resist before rescuing the imprisoned Alisande; and Merlin, whom he must outwit in Twain's famous eclipse scene. Relying on cowboy devices such as a six-shooter and a lariat and other all-American technology, including telephones and plumbing, in order to survive in Camelot, Martin re-awakens in time to elope with the woman he loves rather than marry Lady Gordon, the woman his socialite mother wants him to wed. More than mere slapstick, the first adaptation of Mark Twain's novel was an intelligent comedy whose screenplay included numerous "touches of

---

32 According to Robert Connelly in *The Motion Picture Guide: Silent Film, 1910–1936* 149, *The Light in the Dark* was an 8-reeler based on a story by William Dudley Pelley. The cast included Lon Chaney, Hope Hampton, E. K. Lincoln, Theresa Maxwell Conover, Dorothy Walters, Charles Mussett, Edgar Norton, Dore Davidson, and Mr. McClune.

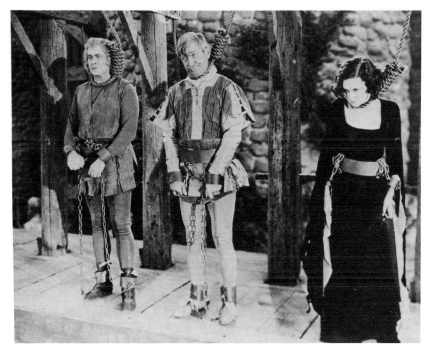

Figure 9. Hank, King Arthur, and Sandy about to be hanged, from the 1931 film *A Connecticut Yankee* starring Will Rogers (dir. David Butler; Fox).

contemporaneity . . . [like references] to the Volstead Act, Tin Lizzies, and the Battle of Argonne"; whose subtitles relied heavily upon American slang and colloquialisms; and whose action featured an army of knights arriving not on bicycles, as in the novel, but on motorcycles (Harty, *CA* 6–7).

The success of Flynn's silent version of Twain's novel led naturally to other adaptations, including a sound picture, *A Connecticut Yankee* (Fox, 1931; dir. David Butler), starring Will Rogers as Hank Martin, Maureen O'Sullivan as Alisande, and Myrna Loy as Morgan le Fay. Hank, a "radio man," must deliver a battery to one of his customers, an eccentric who believes that – when atmospheric conditions are right – he can tune in to voices from the past; in fact, when Hank calls at the house, he is receiving a transmission from King Arthur's court. After being knocked out by a suit of armor, Hank himself is transported to Camelot, where he is imprisoned alongside Clarence, a young man of less than noble birth whose crime is daring to love Alisande, daughter of King Arthur. By invoking the "Yankee curse" to blot out the sun, Hank saves them both and, as Sir Boss, begins a successful re-organization of the kingdom. When Morgan, with Merlin, plots against Arthur, Hank tries to intercede. While the final battle is being waged, however, falling debris from Morgan's castle knocks him out again, and he wakes up in Connecticut, to discover that the broadcast from Camelot he had heard earlier was only a weekly radio program and not the real thing. The film nevertheless ends on an upbeat note, with Hank's assisting two young lovers, Clarence and Alisande, to find a preacher so that they can wed.

In many significant ways, Rogers' Hank Martin is the most American Connecticut Yankee of all, from his distinctly American accent and drawl to his cowboy heroics. (Not only does he ride a cowpony in the tournament; he also wears chaps, a kerchief, and a cowboy hat and knows how to use a gun, as he demonstrates in Morgan's dungeon.) Hank's Yankee ingenuity seems boundless: he initiates a Camelot switchboard, which he staffs with lovely ladies of the court; employs a pretty stenographer to take dictation in his office; opens an assembly-line service station to oil and repair armor, with the knights still in it; establishes the *Camelot Courier* and live broadcasts from chivalric contests; and even introduces the selling of hot dogs and tournament programs. At the same time that Hank is the most enterprising of the many cinematic Yankees, he is also the most democratic. After Clarence and the other knights ride in – with a fleet of automobiles, tanks, and bomber planes – to rescue him, Arthur, and Alisande just seconds before they are to be hanged at Morgan's castle (a surprisingly dark and realistic scene), Hank refuses to leave until all of the prisoners in the torture chamber have been freed. A common man himself, he respects other common men. Even when Hank's family tree suggests that he is descended from nobility, specifically from one of the Knights of the Round Table, his ancestor turns out to be Clarence, who is not noble born but who, at Hank's instigation, is knighted as a reward for his bravery. The motif of nobility as defined by actions and not by circumstances of birth, in fact, underlies the film and recurs in later Arthurian films like *The Black Knight* and the recent *First Knight*. It also underscores Hank's Americanness, as do the numerous allusions to contemporary American culture, including references to President Coolidge, "Mr. Toastmaster and Bróther Lions," daylight savings time, farm relief, flea powder, and the Ku Klux Klan.

The 1949 musical remake, *A Connecticut Yankee in King Arthur's Court* (Paramount; dir. Tay Garnett), starring Bing Crosby as Hank, Rhonda Fleming as Sandy (Alisande), and Sir Cedric Hardwicke as a dotty King Arthur, proved to be a welcome postwar fantasy of escapism as well as an archetype of the time-travel romance (Wachhorst, cited in Harty, *CA* 9). The film is actually a story-within-a-story: while touring Pendragon Castle, Hank meets a descendant of King Arthur and describes to him his own incredible adventure in Camelot. A New England blacksmith, Hank had been riding his horse during a storm when he was struck and knocked unconscious by a tree branch; awakening in Camelot as the prisoner of Sir Sagramore (whose first name is Clarence), he keeps from being burned at the stake by using the wizardry of a match and a magnifying glass. After Hank – "Sir Boss" – is awarded a little blacksmith shop, he pursues Arthur's niece Alisande (Sandy); bests Sandy's betrothed, Sir Lancelot, in a tournament by using various cowboy skills; and tries to suppress Mordred's rebellion and re-establish Arthur's rapport with the peasants. But, as Hank rides in to Merlin's Tower to rescue the kidnapped Sandy, he is again knocked on the head and re-awakens to find himself in Connecticut. Amused by the tale, the lord of Pendragon Castle directs Hank to a garden below his window, where the Yankee encounters his host's niece – Sandy. Largely a vehicle for the popular crooner Crosby (who, as Hank, manages to change the tempo of the king's orchestra to a forties big-band beat), *Connecticut Yankee* nonetheless offers its own brand of Yankee inventiveness, especially as Hank turns out guns and bullets in his blacksmith shop, teaches Sandy how to wink, and shows Galahad how to offer the three-fingered scouts' salute.

While the 1949 Bing Crosby version remains the most accessible and therefore most familiar to viewers, Twain's *Connecticut Yankee* continues to be retold cinematically, often with some new twists. Only three years after Garnett's film, Westinghouse Studio One produced an original, made-for-television version, *A Connecticut Yankee in King Arthur's Court* (1952; dir. Franklin Schaffner) starring Boris Karloff as King Arthur and Tom Mitchell as a middle-aged Hank Martin. A nineteenth-century inventor, avid reader of almanacs, and superintendent of an arms factory, Hank is hit in the head by a crowbar wielded by one of his angry workers, a blow that sends him back to Camelot; he saves himself from execution by using the traditional Yankee wizard's magic – blotting out the sun, lighting a cigar with a match – and introduces Arthur to various inventions, including a security system (a bell for his chamber door), telephones, switchboards, and guns. The story – well acted, for early television – is rather standard fare, except that the evil knight plotting to take over the kingdom and crown himself king is Sir Sagramor and not Mordred, who is not part of the film's small cast of characters. An early television movie, the Westinghouse production was soon followed by *A Connecticut Yankee* (Kraft Theatre/ABC-TV, 1954; dir. Fiedler Cook), with Edgar Bergen and Carl Reiner; *A Connecticut Yankee* (NBC-TV, 1955; dir. Max Liebman), a restaging of Rodgers and Hart's 1927 musical, with Eddie Albert as Martin Barret and Boris Karloff, reprising his earlier role as King Arthur; *Tennessee Ernie Ford Meets King Arthur* (Ford Startime, 1960; dir. Lee J. Cobb), in which Ford, trapped inside a time machine, brings his homespun wit to Camelot; and *A Connecticut Yankee in King Arthur's Court* (Once Upon a Time, 1978; dir. David Trapper), one of the few adaptations "to nod in the direction of its source's dark conclusion" (Harty, bibliography of "Arthurian Film").

Walt Disney Productions provided an even more interesting spin on the familiar story by sending robotics engineer Tom Trimble (Russ Mayberry), the victim of a NASA malfunction, to Arthur's court in *Unidentified Flying Oddball* (1979; dir. Dennis Dugan), released in Britain as *The Spaceman and King Arthur*. Upon arriving in Camelot, Tom is captured, condemned to be burned at the stake (but saved by his flame-retardant space suit), and forced to fight Sir Mordred. Just before the fight, however, Tom substitutes his look-alike robot Hermes, who is hacked apart in the contest but later repaired. Although he wins a seat at the Round Table, Tom – whose "magic" includes a copy of *Playtime* magazine as well as such devices as a laser gun ("the magic candle"), a radio transmitter by which he communicates with Hermes, a Polaroid camera, a lunar rover, a jet pack, and a NASA spacecraft complete with rocket engines, thrusters, and magnetic fields – is anxious to return to the present, but not before turning his spacecraft around for one last stop in Camelot to pick up Alisandre.

A 1989 made-for-television Christmas special transformed the Connecti-cut Yankee into a saccharine and precocious Connecticut kid, Karen Jones, played by Keshia Knight Pulliam from television's *The Cosby Show*. Knocked off a horse at an after-school equitation class, she is revived in Camelot as the prisoner of Sir Lancelot. Conveniently, Karen's backpack survives the fall as well as the time travel; its contents – a "lightning box" that traps people "in flatness" (a Polaroid camera); a Walkman; a tape recorder – make "Sir Boss" (a.k.a. "Lady Boss," "Grand Diva," and "Head Honcho") so powerful that Arthur improbably grants her both a blacksmith shop and the position of Prime Minister and accedes to her request for one percent of all revenues. As if that is not enough, within days of her arrival Karen lectures the women of the court on the evils of carving ivory (and directs their energies instead to needlepointing "Save the Elephants" pillows for each knight); teaches Guinevere and her ladies-in-waiting the twin arts of aerobics and of self-defense; devises a plan by which to improve personal hygiene while ridding the kingdom of poverty (peasants will manufacture and sell toothbrushes, which knights will advertise on their shields); and impresses upon Arthur the fundamentals of feminism and equality. Having saved Camelot from the machinations of Merlin and the evil Mordred, bowdlerized for a younger audience into Arthur's nephew, Karen floats away from Camelot in a hot air balloon that her young friend Clarence has copied from one of her textbooks.

Karen Jones is not the only young person to make the backward journey in American Arthurian films. In *A Kid in King Arthur's Court* (Walt Disney Pictures, 1995; dir. Michael Gottlieb), thirteen-year-old Calvin Fuller (Thomas Ian Nicholas), who plays for a Little League baseball team called the Knights, falls through an earthquake crack during a game and ends up in King Arthur's time. Mistakenly fetched by Merlin, who needs a knight to restore Camelot to its former glory, Calvin wins the trust of King Arthur, played by the veteran actor Josh Ackland; brings a certain kind of California cool to the court by teaching the princesses Sarah and Katey to rollerblade and by introducing them to rock and roll via a CD player and to the wonders of a Swiss army knife; and provokes the evil Lord Belasco, who wants to marry Sarah and assume Arthur's throne. After helping the Black Knight (who is actually Princess Sarah in disguise) defeat Belasco, Calvin – now "Sir

Calvin of Reseda" – returns to the twentieth century with a new sense of self-confidence, in time to hit a home run for his team. The Arthurian story, however, is far better told in another 1995 Disney film, *Four Diamonds* (The Disney Channel; dir. Peter Werner), a made-for-television cable release about Chris Millard, a fourteen-year-old boy who died in 1972. Based on an original short story Millard wrote soon after he was diagnosed with cancer, the film concerns a young squire at King Arthur's court in search of knighthood who must earn the four diamonds – courage, wisdom, honesty, and strength. But the film actually tells two stories, the fantasy that Millard writes to distract himself from his disease and his own life story; and, accordingly, the princi- pal actors play dual roles (Tom Guiry, for example, is both Chris and Sir Millard, the squire; Jayne Brook is both Chris's mother and the Wise Hermit). As Kevin Harty noted in a review of the film, *Four Diamonds* uses "one of the key tropes of the Arthurian legend, the return to Camelot – a return, in this case, for healing. The real Chris Millard – already at age twelve familiar with stories of King Arthur in which knights overcome seemingly overwhelming obstacles – taps into this trope by finding in the world of Arthur an almost allegorical universe parallel to his own. In the Arthurian universe, Sir Millard is successful against all foes and meets all challenges. He also finds the virtues that Chris needs to live in his other, real world" (Harty, Rev. of *Four Diamonds* 117). As a reinterpretation of the Arthurian story, *Four Diamonds* is as powerful as *A Kid in King Arthur's Court* is predictable.

Although not strictly a retelling of Twain's novel, *Arthur the King* (CBS, 1985; dir. Clive Donner), released in England as *Merlin and the Sword*, tells a similar tale, albeit in a uniquely silly and sophomoric way. Katherine Davidson (Dyan Cannon), a modern tourist to Stonehenge, falls into the cave where Merlin and Niniane have been imprisoned since Arthur's day and from where she watches the happy love that develops between Gawain and Ragnell, the doomed love between Guinevere and Lancelot, and other events at Camelot. Although at first Katherine cannot change anything that she observes, she gets Niniane to confess why she betrayed Merlin and caused their mutual confinement – something, in over a thousand years together, Merlin and Niniane apparently have never before gotten around to discuss- ing – and encourages the wizard to leave his "physical self" and use his "astral body" to save Lancelot from the dragon that Morgan has conjured to destroy him. After Merlin vanquishes the creature and impales Morgan with Excalibur (which Mordred had stolen after stabbing Arthur), he returns to the cave, where Katherine informs him that he has always possessed the power to end his confinement. "Love," she says, "cancels all curses; love breaks all spells." As Merlin and Niniane float magically away, Katherine falls on a rock and awakens back at Stonehenge, with only Merlin's fading voice and a piece of fabric from his robe to attest to her adventure. There are weak and laughable attempts in the film to introduce feminism into the familiar story. Guinevere, for instance, tells Arthur she wants to use her talents to help him rule; and later Arthur pays what he believes is a great compliment to his wife, admitting to Merlin that she has "the body of a woman, but the mind and will of a man." And Ragnell shapes her own destiny by offering to lead Gawain out of the Castle of Enchantment if he will take her along. The film, however, is memorable mostly for its unintentional humor.

Besides the remakes of *Connecticut Yankee*, other popular and well-received Arthurian films were released in the fifties and sixties. One of the most unusual was *The Black Knight* (1954), produced by the British company Warwick but distributed by Columbia, with an American director (Tay Garnett), screenwriter (Alec Coppel), and star (Alan Ladd). Unlike the other films of the period, *The Black Knight* had little basis in tradition. Although Arthur resides at Camelot, his knights gather at the Round Table, and a few familiar characters appear, the film – as the *Monthly Film Bulletin* reviewer observed – "is gleefully disrespectful of history and tradition. . . ." John, a blacksmith in the service of the Earl of Yeonil, loves the earl's daughter Linet but is told by the earl that no relationship can ever develop because of the difference in their stations. The threat to John's personal happiness is paralleled by a threat to Camelot: as John learns, Palamides and his Saracens, who are in league with King Mark's Cornishmen to take over Arthur's kingdom, have been masquerading as Viking raiders, creating panic and instability in Britain. In order to prove his accusation of treason against Palamides, John must acquire the skills of a knight as well as a secret identity as the Black Knight. Ultimately, through his innate ability and with a sword he has forged with his own hands, John saves both the woman he loves and the kingdom from the foreign threat; and, as a result, he is knighted and is granted the hand of Lady Linet in marriage.

The unprecedented plot of *The Black Knight*, with pagans about to sacrifice Christians at Stonehenge and Saracens attacking Camelot, seems strange indeed. But Tay Garnett, who had directed the Crosby musical remake of *Connecticut Yankee* five years earlier, was creating something different in *The Black Knight*: not just a thoroughly Americanized version of the Arthurian legends but a version that reflects perennial American values and ideals as well as specific American concerns of the 1950s. John's rise from rags to riches, after all, is the very basis of the American Dream. The question of John's station is therefore central to the movie. Although Linet realizes that "a birthright's an accidental thing, no more," it is precisely John's birthright that makes him unacceptable to her father. Sir Ontzlake, on the other hand, has more democratic notions than his friend, the earl; he tells John: "You made spurs here [in your blacksmith shop]; apply them to yourself. You have ambition; fashion it like a suit of armor."

In the opening sequence, John had been forging a sword as a gift for the earl – a process the viewer observed in quick, successive stages, and a process important to the story line since the manner in which John obtains

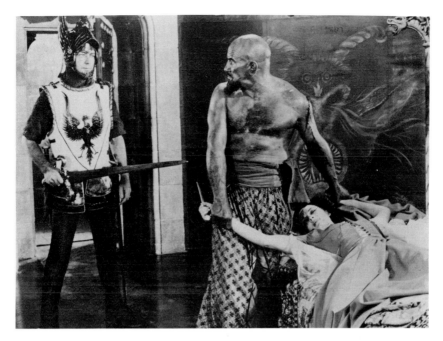

Figure 10. John the blacksmith as the Black Knight rescues the damsel he loves from a servant of Palamides, the wicked, foreign knight who threatens Arthur's kingdom. From the 1954 film *The Black Knight* (dir. Tay Garnett; Warwick-Columbia).

his sword becomes as significant as how he uses it later. Because John is dismissed from the earl's employ, he never has the opportunity to present his gift, which Ontzlake urges him to keep. "You made it with your own hands," Ontzlake says; "now let it make you." And so John begins to shape his destiny as he had earlier shaped the sword. He trains with Ontzlake in the use of several weapons, including sword, lance, and knife (another series of quick scenes that parallel the making of the sword); and he chooses a striking visual image to wear as his heraldic device – an eagle with wings displayed (the position of the eagle on the dollar bill) – that marks him not just as hero but as an all-*American* hero.

If, however, John is symbolically representative of American values, there is a challenge to those values, indeed to the stability of Arthur's kingdom, from several sources: from a foreign invader, from treason within, and from an attack on Christianity. Given that combination of forces and the mood of America in the fifties, the threat to Camelot may be perceived as a thinly disguised allegory for the Communist threat. Ironically, it is Palamides who says, "Certainly there is an enemy in our midst." And John is the first to recognize that enemy's nature. When the Earl of Yeonil's castle is sacked and burned, John follows one of the pillagers, Palamides' servant Bernard, to Camelot. But, since the raiders were disguised as Vikings, John is not believed; and it is he whose life is placed at risk until he can prove his accusation.

In *The Black Knight*, Arthur's kingdom is undoubtedly Christian. Early in the film, for example, as Sir Hal is being knighted, he must promise to be a Christian gentleman. And John, like his father, proves himself to be a supporter of the church. In contrast, the hostile forces are intent on destroying Christianity (just as Communism, according to Nora Sayre in her book on cold-war films of the fifties, was seen as "a peril to Christian civilization" and Communists sought "to destroy Christianity and morality" [10–11]). The raiders burn the abbey, rip the crosses off the necks of monks, and wonder – as Palamides does aloud – "Are Christians invincible to arrows?" Mark, the other enemy within, is "a baptized Christian king," though apparently only "to deceive Arthur." Actually, Mark believes that "there's danger in this Christianity," an echo of Marx's well-known statement that "religion is the opiate of the masses." An advocate of a debauched style of paganism, Mark wants to install the high priest of Stonehenge as the religious leader of Britain.

John, the Black Knight, defends against both enemies. After Linet, along with the abbot and some of his monks, is brought to Stonehenge to be ritually sacrificed, John arrives just ahead of Arthur and his knights to save her from the sword. And the Black Knight appears again to rescue Linet, from the other enemy within, as she is about to be tortured at Palamides' castle by the evil, dark-featured, and foreign Bernard. Whereas John wields his trusty hand-wrought sword, Palamides – also dark and distinctly foreign-looking – employs an unusual and exotic weapon, a scimitar. That scimitar, like the room in his castle in which Linet is held captive (a room decorated with a mural of a demonic hell-mouth), marks him not just as a villain but as a non-believer, an agent of the devil himself – and as the antithesis of the hero.

The treacherous Saracens, almost literally a "red horde" in their red tunics as they launch a mass assault at the film's end, and the pagan religion of the Cornishmen suggest the combined threat of the "Other" – and, as Peter Biskind writes, in fifties films, "The Other was clearly Communism" (186). When *The Black Knight* is seen as an allegory for the triumph of American values over a Communist threat, its strange and untraditional elements make perfect sense. Forming a familiar pattern, those elements mark *The Black Knight* as a work in the tradition of Lowell's *Vision of Sir Launfal* and Twain's *A Connecticut Yankee in King Arthur's Court*, a work that departs radically from standard Arthurian story to create a tale that is thoroughly a product of its time and thoroughly American.

Other American films of the period like *Knights of the Round Table* (MGM, 1953; dir. Richard Thorpe) retained the spectacle of *The Black Knight*. The first MGM production filmed in CinemaScope, *Knights* purported, in the opening credits, to be "based on Sir Thomas Malory's *Le Morte D'Arthur*"; and indeed many of the traditional characters are featured in the film, though often in some untraditional situations. Morgan le Fay, for example, supports Modred, whom she wants to install as king and with whom she plots to destroy her half-brother. Here, Arthur is an adult, not a boy, when he first pulls the sword from the stone; and, after fighting for many months to prove with deeds rather than words his right to rule, he draws Excalibur from the stone again, this time at "the ring of stones," before the council of lords. Here, Elaine is not only the sister of Sir Percival but also the wife of Sir Lancelot (Robert Taylor), who marries her, at the suggestion of Guinevere (Ava Gardner), to quell the gossip at court. Together, Lancelot and Elaine move to the north country, where he grows genuinely fond of her, and they live happily for a time, until she dies giving birth to their son Galahad. After Elaine's death, Lancelot returns to Camelot, where Modred exploits and exposes his rather chaste affection for Guinevere; and, although Arthur banishes him, Lancelot returns again to fight at the king's side against Modred – and even, at Arthur's request, to cast Excalibur into the sea. The film ends with Percival and Lancelot at the now-empty hall of the Round Table, where the former sees the Grail and the latter is told in voice-over to take comfort because "nothing is lost": Lancelot's own sins have been forgiven and his son Galahad will be the greatest knight of all. Like *The Black Knight*, *Knights of the Round Table* depicts Camelot as a Christian kingdom, in which the knights cross themselves at the mention of the Holy Grail and at the sound of the bells on Christmas day. But perhaps the film's greatest debt is to the Western, a genre to which Arthurian film is sometimes compared and from which it seems to have borrowed a number of familiar plot devices.[33] In fact, the most enduring relationship in the film is between Lancelot and his faithful horse, who rescues him during the fight with Modred by pulling him out of quicksand – a staple scene in the Western – and for whom Lancelot professes aloud his love.

Like *Knights of the Round Table*, *Prince Valiant* (Twentieth-Century Fox, 1954; dir. Henry Hathaway) used CinemaScope to offer audiences a variety of spectacular effects, including a climactic scene in which the castle held by the enemy Vikings is destroyed by fire. Yet, as Kevin Harty notes, whereas *Knights of the Round Table* presents "a sort of *Classics Illustrated* version of the legend of Arthur, in which the good guys wear white armor and the bad wear black. . . . with *Prince Valiant*, Hollywood turned from the *Classics*

33 In his essay "The Outlaw," André Bazin writes that "we see clearly drawn in the western. . . the obvious quest for the Holy Grail" (*What Is Cinema?* 2: 164). The influence of the Western is obvious not only in Arthurian films of the fifties and early sixties (e.g., *Knights of The Round Table* and *The Black Knight*) but also in the fifteen-part serial, *Adventures of Sir Galahad* (Columbia, 1950), an Arthurian cliffhanger with a convoluted plot in which Galahad must retrieve Excalibur and rescue the queen. For his acts of bravery, Galahad is rewarded by being made a Knight of the Round Table. According to Kevin J. Harty, despite the medieval setting, "the armor and the swordplay, the characters [in *Adventures of Sir Galahad*] are really nothing more than cowboys chasing each other across medieval versions of the Great Plains of the Old West" (*CA* 10).

Illustrated to the comics, as Henry Hathaway filmed a version of Hal Foster's long-running strip" (*CA* 11–12). Overthrown and driven into exile, the king of Scandia has gone into hiding with his wife and son, Prince Valiant (Robert Wagner). As a young man, Valiant goes to Arthur's court, where he is befriended by Sir Gawain, who trains him to become a knight; falls in love with a beautiful princess, Alita (Janet Leigh); and faces the treachery of Sir Brack (James Mason), the illegitimate son of Uther and one of the knights of the Round Table, who has assumed the guise of the Black Knight in order to betray Valiant's family and usurp Arthur's throne. By his brave acts, Val restores his father's kingship and receives his own knighthood – and, of course, wins Alita's hand in marriage. His story illustrates the lesson about nobility and knighthood that underlies *The Black Knight* and other Arthurian films of the period and to which King Arthur alludes when Valiant first arrives in Camelot: "Knighthood cannot be had for the asking. It is not enough to be high born. Knighthood must be won," with deeds of moral courage. And, like *The Black Knight* and *Knights of the Round Table*, *Prince Valiant* champions Christian values, from Val's promise to restore the cross of Christ to the Vikings to Arthur's description of his fellowship of knights as "our most Christian order." Also, as in *The Black Knight*, there are echoes of the McCarthy era: one of the evil Vikings, for instance, tries to get Valiant to name the Christian Vikings at the court of the pagan Sligon. Moreover, as did *Knights of the Round Table*, the film recalls the Western, particularly in such plot devices as the trusty weapon (in this case, a singing sword), the faithful horse who warns its owner of impending danger, the rope tricks (*Valiant* uses his mattress roping as a lasso, hitching one end to a turret and then scaling the castle wall), and the barroom-style brawling.

The lessons about nobility and knighthood central to some of the films of the early postwar period are integral to more recent American Arthurian films as well. In the cult classic *Knightriders* (United Films/Laurel Entertainment, 1981; dir. George Romero), the Arthur-like Billy Davis (played by Ed Harris) is king of a motley troupe of entertainers who travel throughout Pennsylvania staging medieval tournaments on motorcycles. Although their performances often involve bloody violence – the motto "Fight or Yield" is emblazoned on the van in which they carry their equipment – the troupe actually espouses rather old-fashioned, even utopian, values: loyalty, integrity, community. Their code of modern chivalric conduct involves various rituals, including the method by which the king is determined; and, although they utilize the latest biker technology, they resist the crassness and commercialism of much of contemporary life. Billy, for instance, refuses a young boy's request to autograph a photo of him that appears in a biker magazine, which he feels devalues his performance and misconstrues the troupe's purpose. And when a corrupt deputy ignores the permit that the group has obtained and comes looking for a kickback, Billy again refuses to comply, despite the fact that – as Morgan points out – it would be more expedient simply to pay off the officer and be rid of him. But principle is paramount to Billy and to the society that he has created, and he feels compelled to fight any challenge to that order. "It's real hard," he reminds the members of his court, "to live for something you believe in."

It is precisely such idealism that links Billy to the legendary Arthur, a connection made clear at the beginning of *Knightriders*, as Billy rises naked from lovemaking in the woods with the queen, bathes (and flagellates) himself in the nearby river, kneels before the sword he has stuck in the ground, and dresses himself in armor to prepare for combat. It is only as he rides off on his motorcycle, with Linet behind him, that the viewer realizes the setting is not sixth-century Britain but rather late twentieth-century America. Like Arthur's fellowship, however, Billy's fellowship soon begin to crumble. A disgruntled Morgan, the would-be king, signs on as a solo star with a promoter who promises to book him in Vegas; other members of the group are lured away by prospects of profit and fame; and Alan (the Lancelot figure in the film), Billy's good friend and staunchest supporter, rides off with a young woman (a latter-day Elaine) whom he picks up at a tournament. Although Morgan and the others eventually return, Billy realizes that his dream of an ideal society is tarnished. He concedes his crown to Morgan; allows Linet, his queen, and Alan, his best knight, a chance for happiness together; sets matters right with both the autograph-seeking boy and the corrupt deputy; and takes off on the open highway, where he is crushed by a truck – although not before being transformed into a medieval knight on a charger riding against an unseen enemy. Like Arthur, Billy holds on to his vision of an ideal kingdom (and of a kingdom of ideals) until the very end; and, by accepting his defeat with integrity, he provides an example to the society of misfits that he has created and a reason for them to endure. Even his funeral, attended by the entire troupe, reaffirms the principles of fellowship and solidarity for which he lived. Thus *Knightriders*, in its strong assertion of a distinctly American theme – that anyone, even a tattooed black man or a motorcycle-riding misfit, can become a heroic or knightly figure on the basis of his or her moral qualities – is a significant contribution to the tradition of American Arthurian film.

The defining of nobility according to moral and not social stature recurs in another recent film, *First Knight* (Columbia, 1995; dir. Jerry Zucker). Contrary to tradition, the itinerant Lancelot is not born noble; his lack of hereditary nobility, in fact, allows him to empathize with the peasants in the villages who are victimized by the evil Sir Malagant, just as he and his family were brutalized before "the wars" by other oppressors. When Lancelot rescues Guinevere after her party is ambushed by Malagant's men en route to her wedding in Camelot, she asks him, "Doesn't it please you to know that you have saved the life of a lady?" Since birthright means little to him, he replies, "I'd be just as pleased if you were a dairy maid." He survives by fighting for money in the town squares, a criticism that one of the other knights is quick to raise when Arthur proposes to make Lancelot a member of the Round Table as a reward for his bravery in rescuing the queen a second time. "Sire," says the knight, "we don't know anything about him." But Arthur recognizes Lancelot's innate virtues: and while Lancelot has "no wealth, no home, no gold," he possesses "the passionate spirit that drives [him] on." That spirit, moreover, is what Arthur increasingly values, as he confirms by his dying wish that Lancelot serve as "First Knight" of Camelot and that he take care of Guinevere. In the democratic tradition of other American Arthurian films, Lancelot thus rises from low-born outsider to a position of privilege – in this case, to the helm of Arthur's kingdom – by earning his rank through deeds of moral courage and bravery.

Like the notion of the American Dream – of the common man able to achieve distinction through his actions – the search for the Grail provides another interesting motif in American Arthurian films. The little-seen independent production *To Parsifal* (Canyon City Co-op, 1963; dir. Bruce Bailie) transports the Grail myth into a technological world. Bailie, however, treats the myth indirectly: the legendary Parsifal never appears in the film, which is divided into two sections, representing sterility and regeneration, and which features music from Wagner's *Parsifal*. And the notion of a wounded Fisher King is evoked, for example, by a fish cut with a knife (Lacy and Ashe 278). A more popular and accessible Grail film is *The Fisher King* (Tri-Star Pictures, 1991; dir. Terry Gilliam), in which Jack Lucas, a Howard Stern-type disk jockey, is partly responsible for the death of the wife of Henry Sagan, a professor of medieval history, who goes insane and believes himself to be on a quest for the Holy Grail. "I'm a knight on a special quest," Henry (who now calls himself Parry) tells Jack, "and I need your help." But, in fact, it is Jack – like Parry, both a Fisher King and Grail knight figure – who needs Parry's help. After retrieving from a Fifth Avenue apartment a trophy cup that Parry thinks is the Grail, Jack is able not only to heal his friend but also to assume responsibility for his own actions, to resurrect his career, and to rebuild his personal relationships. More popular still was *Indiana Jones and the Last Crusade* (Paramount, 1989; dir. Steven Spielberg), the third installment of the Spielberg trilogy that takes archaeologist Indiana Jones (Harrison Ford) on a new search, first for his father (Sean Connery), an old-world archaeological scholar who has disappeared while tracking the hiding place of the Holy Grail, and then for the Grail itself.[34] Alerted by wealthy collector Walter Donovan to his father's disappearance and guided by the elder Jones'

34 The popularity of the films, in fact, led George Lucas (Lucasfilm) to license a series of novels based on the character of Indiana Jones. A number of those novels have Arthurian connections: Rob MacGregor's *Indiana Jones and the Last Crusade* (1989) is based on the filmscript by Jeffrey Boam; MacGregor's *Indiana Jones and the Dance of the Giants* (1991) features an excavation of Merlin's dwelling and a brief appearance by him at Stonehenge; and Martin Caidin's *Indiana Jones and the White Witch* (1994) involves King Arthur's sword Caliburn and its protective scabbard, now in the white witch's possession (*NAE*, 599, 583).

notebooks on the sacred vessel, Indy travels to Venice, where Dr. Elsa Schneider leads him to a knight's tomb – and to another clue to the Grail's location – and then to a German castle, where he rescues Dr. Jones from the Nazis who are holding him captive. But both Donovan and Elsa turn out to be Nazi sympathizers, and the notebooks are sent to Berlin, where the Joneses must infiltrate a Nazi rally in order to retrieve them. Eventually, everyone ends up at the temple of the Grail. Although only Indy and his father possess the knowledge to survive the three lethal obstacles, Donovan mortally wounds Dr. Jones, forcing Indy to lead him to the Grail, which alone can save his father. Greeted by the last surviving protector of the Grail, they must choose the real Grail from among scores of goblets. Donovan chooses poorly and dies; Indy chooses well and restores his father to health; Elsa and the Nazis try to remove the Grail from the temple, against the knight's advice, and fall to their deaths. The film is full of high adventure and remarkable special effects, especially as Indy passes the Grail tests; its ending, with the Joneses riding off into the sunset, reinforces yet again the connection between Arthurian film and the American Western.

Whereas *The Fisher King* and *The Last Crusade* updated and reinterpreted the Grail myths, two American films, altogether different in content, tone, and targeted audience, drew their subject matter and inspiration from T. H. White's tetralogy, *The Once and Future King*. Yet, as Alice Grellner demonstrates, both remained "true to at least one aspect or dimension of White's vision, while eliminating or downplaying much of the novel's multifaceted, ambivalent, misogynistic, often contradictory, and darkly pessimistic view of human nature" (71). *The Sword in the Stone* (Walt Disney Productions, 1963; dir. Wolfgang Reitherman), based on the first book in the tetralogy, focuses on Merlin's education of Wart, the young Arthur, and culminates in Arthur's drawing the sword from the stone and accepting, reluctantly, the kingship for which the wizard has been preparing him. Though the film falls quickly into a predictable pattern of chases and transformations, it is nonetheless an example of the outstanding animation for which Disney is rightly famous. Arthur's childhood is also recalled, passingly, in *Camelot* (Warner Brothers, 1967; dir. Joshua Logan), the film version of Lerner and Loewe's musical, which starred Richard Harris, Vanessa Redgrave, and Franco Nero. Based on White's later Arthurian books, the film concentrates largely on the tragic effects of the love between Guinevere and Lancelot. There is, to be sure, a magical element to that relationship – Lancelot wins Guinevere's love by performing a miracle – but in the end the magic cannot be sustained, especially as the wicked Mordred, like a serpent in the garden, exploits their affection (as well as Arthur's affection for them) and corrupts their Eden. As Grellner notes, the film managed to draw on contemporary events, such as "the one brief, shining moment" that came to be associated with the presidency of John F. Kennedy, and it provided a fantasy "escape from the disillusionment of Vietnam, the bitterness and disenchantment of the antiwar demonstrations, and the grim reality of war on the evening news" ("Two Films That Sparkle" 75). Yet there was something very dated and decidedly unliberated in the depiction of Guinevere as a woman wondering rather petulantly why the man she encounters in the woods – her future husband Arthur, though she is not aware of his identity at the time – has no intention of abducting or ravishing her and in the oversimplification of other of the characters. Nevertheless, despite its flaws, *Camelot* is memorable for its pageantry and, of course, for its enduring music and lyrics.[35]

A very different portrait of the queen emerges in *Guinevere* (Lifetime Productions, 1994; dir. Jud Taylor), another film inspired by popular litera- ture. The made-for-cable movie, based on the feminist novels of Persia Woolley, depicts Guinevere (Sheryl Lee) as a woman whose education in the cult of the goddess and whose skills in riding, fighting, and ruling the kingdom are equal to any man's. Raised, after her mother's death, by the High Priestess Morgan le Fay, Guinevere eventually incurs Morgan's wrath by refusing her order to wed her adopted son Lancelot (Noah Wylie) and to fight alongside her against her incestuous half-brother, the High King. Com- pelled to escape Morgan's sanctuary, Guinevere meets Lancelot again later, after she has agreed to marry Arthur, Morgan's nemesis, in gratitude for his defense of her father's kingdom of Camelot; but the lovers ultimately part, soon after Lancelot rallies his army to support Guinevere in her rescue of Arthur from his capture by Malagant. In addition to the heavy-handed feminist overtones – Morgan refers to the sword in the stone as the "fabled phallus" and complains "Where are the women in Pendragon's world?" while Guinevere, who insists on ruling as Arthur's equal, proves to be superior to the often weak and simpering king – the film departs from tradi- tion in other ways. Guinevere, for example, gives birth by Arthur to a daughter, whom Merlin helps to hide from Morgan – a daughter who will, presumably, become the Once and Future Queen. And, after Merlin's death and Lancelot's departure from Camelot, Guinevere and Arthur "endure" as husband and wife and co-rulers of Camelot, which becomes "a beacon to all people in all lands for all times." For some inexplicable reason, neither Morgan nor the "seed" she bears after bringing Arthur magically to her bed pose any further threat. A prettified, surprisingly sanitized, and often outright incoherent version of the Arthurian story, *Guinevere* is certainly con- sistent with the trend in popular Arthurian literature of giving voice and power to the legend's female characters.

The more recent *Merlin*, a four-hour television miniseries (NBC-TV, 1998; dir. Steve Barron), attempts to do for Arthur's wizard what *Guinevere* did for his queen. Told in Merlin's voice, the miniseries recounts most of the major

35 Another film of *Camelot* (HBO; dir. Marty Callner), starring Richard Harris, was released in 1982, when Home Box Office filmed the Broadway revival of the Lerner and Loewe musical.

events of Merlin's life, including the circumstances of his birth (a "half-human" with no "mortal father"); his enduring love for Nimue, whom he rescues from a patch of quicksand and from the scorching breath of the great dragon to whom she has been sacrificed; his role as advisor and wizard to a succession of kings – Vortigern, Uther, Arthur; and his ongoing struggle with Queen Mab (Miranda Richardson), a practitioner of the "old ways" who hopes to enlist him in her own battle against the new Christianity, which threatens to destroy her legacy. The miniseries incorporates many elements of the traditional legend: Merlin (Sam Neill), for instance, foresees the defeat of the red dragon (Vortigern) by the white dragon (Uther); assists Uther in consummating his passion for Igraine; and recognizes Arthur's error in choosing Guinevere for his wife and queen. But the miniseries also takes liberties with the familiar story: it is Merlin, for instance, who – disappointed by Uther's unwise use of Excalibur – plunges the sword into a stone until Arthur can reclaim it; Uther, after fulfilling his desire for Igraine, eventually goes mad and kills himself; and Elaine, here the wife of Lancelot, combines the roles of the two Elaines, as mother of Galahad and broken-hearted lily maid borne by barge to Camelot.

Significantly, many of the women in the miniseries suffer from regrettable and often gratuitous deformities – Morgan (Helena Bonham Carter) has an annoying lisp and an exaggerated lazy eye, Nimue (Isabella Rosselini) a severely burned face and neck, Mab an irritating screech for a voice – that hint at their ultimate weaknesses. Morgan, insecure over her physical appearance, allows herself to be manipulated by Mab; and, once her son Mordred has been raised to evil manhood, she suffers a convenient and fatal fall at Mab's hands. Nimue, anxious for Mab's magic to restore her beauty (her beauty having earlier been stolen, indirectly, by Mab, who urged Vortigern to sacrifice her to the dragon), agrees, at least initially, to Mab's plan for Merlin's confinement. And even Mab realizes her greatest fear, as her powers wane and her voice is ultimately "forgotten." More interesting than the women is Mab's oversized, shape-shifting gnome Frik (Martin Short), who tutors both Merlin and Morgan and who eventually shifts his allegiance from Mab to Merlin. Effective as well are some of the recurring images, such as the mirrors through which Mab plies her magic (e.g., the bedroom mirror at Joyous Gard by which Elaine glimpses Lancelot's adultery with Guinevere). And, of course, the miniseries is full of remarkable special effects worthy of a big-budget theatrical release, including malicious griffins, nest-making fairies, a talking man of the mountain, and an ethereal Lady of the Lake adorned with a necklace of live fish.

Elements of the Arthurian story also appear in a number of non-Arthurian films, such as *Little Miss Marker* (Paramount Pictures, 1934; dir. Alexander Hall), based on the Damon Runyon story.[36] A little girl, left by her

36 *Little Miss Marker* was remade as *Sorrowful Jones* (Paramount, 1949; dir. Sidney Lanfield),

father as a marker for a gambling debt and soon orphaned by his suicide, is taken in by a bookie, his nightclub-singing girlfriend Bangles, and their associates. From the moment she meets them, "Markie" (Shirley Temple) gives each of her new friends an Arthurian name – Bangles becomes Lady Guinevere, the scowling bookie is Sir Sorry and later Sir Galahad – that she bases on the Arthurian stories from Lanier that her late mother used to read to her. But the association with such proverbial low-lifes begins taking a toll on Markie's manners and speech; and so, to help prevent further corruption of the youngster's innocence and in the hope of restoring her childish won-derment, Bangles and company dress up as members of the court of King Arthur and throw her a party, complete with her own castle cake and charger (the racehorse at the center of both the fix and the intense betting that was responsible for her father's death). When Markie is thrown from the horse and requires a transfusion to survive, even the hardest-hearted hoodlums get soft, offering to be tested and then waiting for news of her recovery by the operating room door. After his prayers seem to have been answered by Markie's optimistic medical prognosis, the bookie decides to go straight, marry the singer, and give Markie the new family she deserves. *Little Miss Marker* thus reworks the familiar theme in Arthurian films, that even the most common – and, in this case, corrupt – people can become knights if they aspire to high moral values.

Arthurian elements are evident as well in films like *7 Faces of Dr. Lao*, a fantasy about a Western town brought to its senses by parables performed by a mysterious traveling circus, whose players include Merlin. The influence of the legend is also apparent in *Avalon* (Tri-Star, 1990; dir. Barry Levinson), a nostalgic look at immigrant life in Baltimore. The "Avalon" of the film's title is an old, turreted apartment building in which the large Krichinsky family lives and holds court for many years, before family tensions and new tech-nologies like automobiles and television cause their old way of life to dis-appear. And, of course, there are strong echoes of myth, Arthurian and otherwise, in the most successful films ever, the *Star Wars* trilogy, noted for brilliant and futuristic special effects. Yet, as various critics have pointed out, the *Star Wars* series actually has more in common with films like *The Knights of the Round Table* than with space-age adventures like *2001*. Unaware of his true identity, Luke Skywalker (Mark Hamill) is a young Arthur figure. Obi-Wan "Ben" Kenobi (Alec Guinness), the film's wise Merlin character, informs "Sir Luke" that he is the son of a Jedi Knight; and, after giving Luke his father's sword (an Excalibur-like laser blade), Ben tutors him in its use. And use it Luke does – especially when Ben and Luke challenge Darth

with Bob Hope and Lucille Ball, and as *Forty Pounds of Trouble* (Curtis Enterprises/Uni-versal, 1963; dir. Norman Jewison), with Tony Curtis, Suzanne Pleshette, and a good cast of character actors. It was also remade as *Little Miss Marker* (Universal, 1980; dir. Walter Bernstein), with Walter Matthau as the bookie, Sara Stimson as the little girl, Julie Andrews as the love interest, and Tony Curtis as the heavy.

Vader, quite literally a black knight, and his crew in a final battle.

The Arthurian legends are also familiar television fare. In *Squareheads of the Round Table* (1948), a classic episode of the Three Stooges set in the "Days of Old," Moe, Curly, and Shemp are three troubadours on their way to King Arthur's court, where they help reunite Cedric the blacksmith with his beloved Elaine and defeat the evil Black Prince, who covets her father Arthur's throne. In *Mr. Merlin* (1981–1982), Barnard Hughes starred as Merlin, a garage owner and mechanic with a teenaged apprentice, Zachary Rogers, to whom he tries to teach a responsible brand of his magic. The short-lived Aaron Spelling series *The Round Table* (Sept. 18 – Oct. 16, 1992) featured a group of twenty-something young people, largely lawyers and law enforcement officers, in Washington, DC, who meet regularly at a bar called "The Round Table" and who, in the title credits, sport "Round Table Knights" sweatshirts that suggest their fellowship. (The series lasted only a few episodes, so how much further it might have pursued its Arthurian analogues is uncertain.) Arthurian characters have also been incorporated in episodes of numerous popular television shows, from *Highway to Heaven, The Twilight Zone,* and *MacGyver* to *Quantum Leap* and *Babylon 5.*

The world of Camelot is re-created regularly in cartoons and animated series. In the cartoon *Bugs Bunny in King Arthur's Court* (Chuck Jones Enterprises, 1977), the rascally rabbit burrows his way into Camelot, where he performs some Twain-like magic by blotting out the sun, founds an armour works, and draws the sword from the stone to become the new king, "Arth-Hare." The three nephews of Scrooge McDuck, along with their friend, the "gadget-man" Gyro, get caught in a time machine and travel back to King Arty's Quackalot Court in *Sir Gyro de Gearloose* (Walt Disney, 1989), an episode of Disney's *Duck Tales.* After encountering Moreloon the wizard, the nephews and Gyro are forced to come up with inventive ways to battle fiery dragons and evil knights like Sir Lessdred. *Arthur! And the Square Knights of the Round Table* (UAV, 1992) finds King Arthur engaging in "amazing" (and anachronistic) adventures. In the various episodes, Morganna and the Black Knight plot to steal Excalibur and gain power in Camelot; Lancelot escapes from his own wedding ceremony and later rescues Guinevere from a giant; Merlin gets a head cold and loses some of his magical powers, to Morganna's delight; Arthur and Lancelot use a mouse to win back Camelot from an Eastern emperor and his elephant; and Merlin and Lancelot join forces to retrieve Arthur's crown and sword from an octopus before Morganna does. In *The Legend of Prince Valiant* (1992), a production for the Family Channel, the characters from Hal Foster's strip deal with modern issues like the conflicting demands of conservation and commercial development.[37] *King Arthur*

37 *The Legend of Prince Valiant* was produced in France and Korea by the Sei Young Animation Company and developed for television by David J. Corbett, with Dianne Dixon as story editor (*NAE* 608).

and the Knights of Justice (Bohbot Entertainment, 1992) are actually members of a football team, the Knights, headed by a player that sportswriters call Arthur the King. After suffering a bus accident outside of New York, they are transported to "Castle Camelot" in Arthur's time. In order to return home, the Knights (who have names like Lance – and Lug, Trunk, Darren, Wally, and Brick) must find the Keys of Truth. *Princess Gwenevere and the Jewel Riders* (New Frontier Entertainment, 1995), with its strong female heroine, is interesting in part because it is designed primarily for girls. In the series, Avalon is a magical kingdom controlled by Merlin "for the good of all." When the outlaw Lady Kale imprisons him, he scatters the Seven Crown Jewels she needs to rule. Only the Jewel Riders, a heroic band of youngsters and forest animals led by Princess Gwenevere, can counter Lady Kale's "antimagic," recover the jewels, rescue Merlin, and ultimately save the kingdom. Similarly, in *Quest for Camelot* (Warner Bros., 1998), a full-length animated feature film, it is up to the young Kayley to rescue Excalibur and save Camelot from the evil Sir Ruber, who wants to be king. Ruber, who ten years earlier had killed Kayley's father, the good knight Sir Lionel, is assisted by the beastly Griffin and the awesome Ogre. But Kayley, who wants to be a knight, persists in her quest; and, with the aid of the blind hermit Garrett and several creatures from the Forbidden Forest, including Ayden the falcon and the two-headed dragon Devon and Cornwall, wins back Excalibur and restores Arthur's kingdom. As a reward for her heroism, Kayley is dubbed a lady and – along with Sir Garrett – made a knight of the Round Table. Based very loosely on Vera Chapman's novel *The King's Damosel*, *Quest for Camelot* demonstrates that even animated children's versions of the Arthurian story are beginning to take a less traditional and more democratic approach to the legends.

From cartoons and television shows to movies, from toys and games to comic books and fantasy and science fiction novels, from art and architecture to advertising and merchandising, it is clear that the legends of King Arthur have permeated American popular culture. Yet it is equally clear that, by reworking and often democratizing those legends, Americans have adapted the Matter of Britain to American concerns and made it their own. This widespread use by Americans of the Arthurian material is due in part to the proliferation of the legends in the nineteenth and early twentieth centuries through youth groups – which were themselves a popularizing of the legends – and through the widespread popularity in America of the Arthurian works of writers like Lowell, Twain, and Tennyson. The prevalence of Arthurian material in American popular culture, which makes the legends accessible to everyone and which promotes the ideals of the Arthurian realm as attainable by anyone who cultivates the right values, is in fact the ultimate democratization of the Arthurian tradition.

Bibliography

Abbott, Charles D. *Howard Pyle: A Chronicle*. New York: Harper, 1925.

Abdoo, Sherlyn. "Woman as Grail in T. S. Eliot's *The Waste Land.*" *The Centennial Review* 28 (Winter 1984): 48–60.

Adams, Oscar Fay. "Aristocratic Drift of American Protestantism." *North American Review* 142 (1886): 194–99.

———. *Post-Laureate Idyls*. Boston: D. Lothrop and Co., 1886.

———. *Sicut Patribus, and Other Verse*. Boston: Printed by W. B. Jones for the Author, 1906.

Adams, Richard P. "Sunrise Out of The Waste Land." In *Critical Essays on The Sun Also Rises*. Ed. James Nagel. Boston: G. K. Hall & Co., 1995. 53–62.

Adeler, Max. "The Fortunate Island." In *The Fortunate Island and Other Stories*. Boston: Lee and Shepard, 1882.

Adkins, Nelson F. "Emerson and the Bardic Tradition." *Publications of the Modern Language Association* 63. 2 (1948): 662–77.

Agosta, Lucien L. *Howard Pyle*. Boston: Twayne, 1987.

Aiken, Conrad. "Three Reviews." In *Edwin Arlington Robinson: A Collection of Critical Essays*. Ed. Francis Murphy. Englewood Cliffs, NJ: Prentice-Hall, 1970. 15–28.

Allen, William Rodney. *Understanding Kurt Vonnegut*. Columbia: University of South Carolina Press, 1991.

Anderson, Poul. *A Midsummer Tempest*. Garden City, NY: Doubleday, 1974.

———. *Three Hearts and Three Lions*. Garden City, NY: Doubleday, 1961.

Anspacher, Louis K. *Tristan and Isolde: A Tragedy*. New York: Brentano's, 1904.

The Arthurian Revival: Essays on Form, Tradition, and Transformation. Ed. Debra N. Mancoff. New York: Garland, 1992.

Astro, Richard, and Jackson J. Benson, eds. *The Fiction of Bernard Malamud*. Corvallis: Oregon State University Press, 1977.

———. "Phlebas Sails the Caribbean: Steinbeck, Hemingway, and the American Waste Land." In *The Twenties: Fiction, Poetry, Drama*. Ed. Warren French. Deland, FL: Everett/Edwards, 1975.

Audhuy, Letha. "The Waste Land Myth and Symbols in *The Great Gatsby*." *Etudes Anglaises* 33 (1980): 41–54.

Babcock, William H. *Cian of the Chariots: A Romance of the Days of Arthur Emperor of Britain and His Knights of the Round Table, How They Delivered London and Overthrew the Saxons After the Downfall of Roman Britain*. Ill. George Foster Barnes. Boston: Lothrop Publishing Co., 1898.

———. *The Two Lost Centuries of Britain*. Philadelphia: J. B. Lippincott, 1890.

Baetzhold, Howard G. " 'The Autobiography of Sir Robert Smith of Camelot': Mark Twain's Original Plan for *A Connecticut Yankee*." *American Literature* 32.4 (Jan. 1961): 456–61.

———. "The Course of Composition of *A Connecticut Yankee*: A Reinterpretation." *American Literature* 33.2 (1961): 195–214.

Baker, Carlos. *Ernest Hemingway: A Life Story*. New York: Charles Scribner's Sons, 1969.

———, ed. *Hemingway and His Critics: An International Anthology*. Introduction by Carlos Baker. New York: Hill and Wang, 1961.

———. *Hemingway: The Artist as Writer*. Princeton: Princeton University Press, 1956.

Banks, Albert Louis. *Twentieth Century Knighthood: A Series of Addresses to Young Men*. New York: Funk & Wagnalls, 1900.

Barnard, Ellsworth. *Edwin Arlington Robinson: A Critical Study*. New York: Macmillan, 1952.

———, ed. *Edwin Arlington Robinson Centenary Essays*. Athens: University of Georgia Press, 1969.

Barrett, Deborah J. "Discourse and Intercourse: The Conversion of the Priest in Percy's *Lancelot*." *Critique: Studies in Contemporary Fiction* 23.2 (1981–2): 5–11.

Barthelme, Donald. *Amateurs*. New York: Farrar, Straus & Giroux, 1976.

———. *The King*. Wood Engravings by Barry Moser. New York: Harper and Row / An Edward Burlingame Book, 1990.

Bates, Milton J. "Men, Women, and Vietnam." In *America Rediscovered: Critical Essays on Literature and Film of the Vietnam War*. Ed. Owen W. Gilman, Jr. and Lorrie Smith. New York: Garland, 1990. 27–63.

Baudino, Gael. *Dragon Death*. New York: ROC, 1992.

———. *Dragonsword*. New York: ROC, 1991.

———. *Duel of Dragons*. New York: ROC,1991.

Baumbach, Jonathan. *The Landscape of Nightmare: Studies in the Contemporary American Novel*. New York: New York University Press, 1965.

Bazin, André. *What Is Cinema?* 2 vols. Trans. Hugh Gray. Berkeley: University of California Press, 1967.

Beard, Dan. *Hardly a Man Is Now Alive: The Autobiography of Dan Beard*. New York: Doubleday, 1939.

Bédier, Joseph. *The Romance of Tristan and Iseult: Drawn from the Best French Sources*. Trans. Hilaire Belloc. Ill. Robert Engles. London: George Allen, 1903.

———. *Tristan et Iseut: Pièce en trois actes, un prologue et huit tableaux*. Paris: Inpr. de l'Illustration, 1929.

Bellamy, Gladys Carmen. *Mark Twain as a Literary Artist*. Norman: University of Oklahoma Press, 1950.

Bennett, Mary Angela. *Elizabeth Stuart Phelps*. Philadelphia: University of Pennsylvania Press, 1939.

Benson, Jackson J. "Patterns of Connection and Development in Hemingway's *In Our Time*." In *Critical Essays on Ernest Hemingway's In Our Time*. Ed. Michael S. Reynolds. Boston: G. K. Hall, 1983.

———, ed. *The Short Stories of Ernest Hemingway: Critical Essays*. Durham: Duke University Press, 1975.

Berger, Thomas. "Arthur Rex." *Playboy* Sept. 1978: 102–105, 110, 232–34, 236.

———. *Arthur Rex: A Legendary Novel*. New York: Delacorte Press / Seymour Lawrence, 1978.

————. *Crazy in Berlin*. New York: Delacorte / Seymour Lawrence, 1958.

————. "Foreword." *German Medieval Tales*. Ed. Francis G. Gentry. New York: Continuum, 1983. vii–x.

————. *Little Big Man*. New York: Dial Press, 1964.

————. *Reinhart in Love*. New York: Delacorte / Seymour Lawrence, 1962.

————. *Reinhart's Women*. New York: Delacorte / Seymour Lawrence, 1981.

————. *Vital Parts*. New York: Delacorte / Seymour Lawrence, 1970.

Berkove, Lawrence I. "The Reality of the Dream: Structural and Thematic Unity in *A Connecticut Yankee*." *Mark Twain Journal* 22.1 (Spring 1984): 8–14.

Berman, Ronald. *The Great Gatsby and Modern Times*. Urbana: University of Illinois Press, 1994.

Berthold, Dennis. "The Conflict of Dialects in *A Connecticut Yankee*." *Ball State University Forum* 18.3 (Summer 1977): 51–58.

Bicknell, John W. "The Waste Land of F. Scott Fitzgerald." *Virginia Quarterly Review* 30 (Autumn 1954): 556–572. Rpt. in *F. Scott Fitzgerald: A Collection of Criticism*. Ed. Kenneth E. Eble. New York: McGraw Hill, 1973, 67–80.

Bigelow, Otis. *The Giants' Dance: A Play*. New York: Dramatists Play Service, 1965.

Bishop, Farnham, and Arthur Gilchrist Brodeur. *The Altar of the Legion*. Ill. Henry Pitz. Boston: Little, Brown, and Co., 1926.

Biskind, Peter. "Pods, Blobs, and Ideology in American Films of the Fifties." In *Invasion of the Body Snatchers*. Ed. Al LaValley. New Brunswick, NJ: Rutgers University Press, 1989. 185–97.

Blais, Ellen A. "Gender Issues in Bobbie Ann Mason's *In Country*." *South Atlantic Review* 56.2 (May 1991): 107–18.

Blaylock, James P. *The Paper Grail*. New York: Ace, 1991.

Blechner, Michael Harry. "*Tristan* in Letters." *Tristania* 6.1 (Autumn 1980): 30–37.

Blotner, Joseph. *Faulkner: A Biography*. 2 vols. New York: Random House, 1974.

Board, Marilynn Lincoln. "Art's Moral Mission: Reading G. F. Watts's *Sir Galahad*." In *The Arthurian Revival: Essays on Form, Tradition, and Transformation*. Ed. Debra N. Mancoff. New York: Garland, 1992. 132–54.

Boardman, Phillip C. "Arthur Redivivus: A Reader's Guide to Recent Arthurian Fiction." *Halcyon* 2 (1980): 41–56.

Booth, David. "Sam's Quest, Emmett's Wound: Grail Motifs in Bobbie Ann Mason's Portrait of America After Vietnam." *Southern Literary Journal* 23.2 (Spring 1991): 98–109.

Borowsky, Marvin. *The Queen's Knight*. New York: Random House, 1955.

Bowers, Gwendolyn. *Brother to Galahad*. New York: Walck, 1963.

————. *The Lost Dragon of Wessex*. New York: Walck, 1957.

Bradley, Marion Zimmer. *Lady of Avalon*. New York: Viking, 1997.

————. *The Mists of Avalon*. New York: Knopf, 1982.

Bradley, Will. *Launcelot and the Ladies*. New York: Harper and Bros., 1927.

Bradshaw, Gillian. *Hawk of May*. New York: Simon and Schuster, 1980.

————. *In Winter's Shadow*. New York: Simon and Schuster, 1982.

————. *Kingdom of Summer*. New York: Simon and Schuster, 1981.

————. Letter to Alan Lupack. 19 Jan. 1981.

Bridges, Sallie. *Marble Isle, Legends of the Round Table, and Other Poems*. Philadelphia: J. B. Lippincott, 1864.

Brinkmeyer, Robert H., Jr. "Finding One's History: Bobbie Ann Mason and Contemporary Southern Literature." *Southern Literary Journal* 19.2 (Spring 1987): 22–33.

———. "Walker Percy's *Lancelot*: Discovery Through Dialogue." *Renascence: Essays on Value in Literature* 40.1 (1987): 30–42.

Brodeur, Arthur G. *The Art of Beowulf*. Berkeley: University of California Press, 1960.

———. *Arthur, Dux Bellorum*. Berkeley: University of California Press, 1939.

———, trans. *The Prose Edda*. New York: The American-Scandinavian Foundation, 1916.

Brooke, Maxey. "Morte d'Alain: An Unrecorded Idyll of the King." In *Rogues' Gallery: A Variety of Mystery Stories*. Ed. Walker Gibson. Garden City, NY: Doubleday, 1969. 265–73.

———. "Morte d'un Marcheant. In *The Camelot Chronicles*. Ed. Mike Ashley. New York: Wing Books, 1995. 243–52.

Brookhouse, Christopher. "Imagery and Theme in *Lancelot*." In *Edwin Arlington Robinson Centenary Essays*. Ed. Ellsworth Barnard. Athens: University of Georgia Press, 1969. 120–29.

Brooks, Cleanth. "The Image of Helen Baird in Faulkner's Early Poetry and Fiction." *Sewanee Review* 85.2 (Spring 1977): 218–34.

———. *William Faulkner: The Yoknapatawpha Country*. New Haven: Yale University Press, 1963.

Brooks, Van Wyck. *New England: Indian Summer 1865–1915*. New York: Dutton, 1940.

Broun, Heywood. "The Fifty-First Dragon." In *Modern Essays*. Selected by Christopher Morley. New York: Harcourt, Brace, 1921. 338–51.

Bruccoli, Matthew J. *Some Sort of Epic Grandeur: The Life of F. Scott Fitzgerald*. New York: Harcourt Brace Jovanovich, 1981.

Bruss, Paul. *Victims: Textual Strategies in Recent American Fiction*. Lewisburg: Bucknell University Press, 1981.

Bryer, Jackson R., ed. *The Short Stories of F. Scott Fitzgerald: New Approaches in Criticism*. Madison: University of Wisconsin Press, 1982.

Bugge, John. "Arthurian Myth Devalued in Walker Percy's *Lancelot*." In *The Arthurian Tradition: Essays in Convergence*. Ed. Mary Flowers Braswell and John Bugge. Tuscaloosa: University of Alabama Press, 1988.

———. "Merlin and the Movies in Walker Percy's *Lancelot*." *Studies in Medievalism* 2.4 (Fall 1983): 39–55.

Bulla, Clyde Robert. *The Sword in the Tree*. Ill. Paul Galdone. New York: Thomas Y. Crowell, 1956.

Cabell, James Branch. *The Cream of the Jest: A Comedy of Evasions*. New York: R. M. McBride, 1921.

———. *Jurgen: A Comedy of Justice*. New York: Robert M. McBride, 1919.

———. *Something About Eve*. New York: R. M. McBride, 1927.

Caidin, Martin. *Indiana Jones and the White Witch*. New York: Bantam, 1994.

The Camelot Periodicals: Arthurian Fiction from Magazine Appearance. N.p. [Vista, CA]: n.p. [Green Chapel Books], n.d.

Cameron, Kenneth Walter. "The Potent Song in Emerson's Merlin Poems." *Philological Quarterly* 32.1 (1953): 22–28.

Campbell, Alice. *The Murder of Caroline Bundy.* New York: Farrar and Rinehart, 1932.

Campbell, Harry Modean, and Ruel E. Foster. *William Faulkner: A Critical Appraisal.* Norman: University of Oklahoma Press, 1951.

Carlsen, Chris. *Berserker: The Bull Chief.* London: Sphere Books, 1977.

Carmichael, Douglas. "The Grievous Stroke." *The Round Table* 5 (1989): 25–34.

———. *Pendragon: An Historical Novel.* N.p.: Blackwater Press, 1977.

Carpenter, Frederic Ives. "Tristram the Transcendent." In *Appreciation of Edwin Arlington Robinson: 28 Interpretive Essays.* Ed. Richard Cary. Waterville, ME: Colby College Press, 1969. 75–90.

Carter, Everett. "The Meaning of *A Connecticut Yankee*." *American Literature* 50.3 (Nov. 1978): 418–40.

Cary, Richard, ed. *Appreciation of Edwin Arlington Robinson: 28 Interpretive Essays.* Waterville, ME: Colby College Press, 1969.

Casey, Roger. "Hemingway's El(l)iot." *American Notes & Queries* 4.4 (October 1991): 189–93.

Cawein, Madison J. *Accolon of Gaul with Other Poems.* Louisville: John P. Morton & Co., 1889.

———. *The Poems of Madison Cawein.* 5 vols. Boston: Small, Maynard & Co., 1907.

Charrette, Robert N. *A King Beneath the Mountain.* New York: Warner Books, 1995.

———. *A Knight among Knaves.* New York: Warner Books, 1995.

———. *A Prince among Men.* New York: Warner Books, 1994.

Chase, Mary Ellen. "A Candle at Night." *Collier's* (9 May 1942): 17, 74–77.

———. *Dawn in Lyonesse.* New York: Macmillan, 1938.

Cherryh, C. J. *Port Eternity.* New York: Daw, 1982.

Chopra, Deepak. *The Return of Merlin.* New York: Harmony Books, 1995.

———. *The Way of the Wizard: Twenty Spiritual Lessons in Creating the Life You Want.* New York: Harmony Books, 1995.

Cinema Arthuriana: Essays on Arthurian Film. Ed. Kevin J. Harty. New York: Garland, 1991.

Ciuba, Gary M. "Lancelot's New World of Language." *Notes on Mississippi Writers* 20 (1988): 1–7.

———. "The Omega Factor: Apocalyptic Visions in Walker Percy's *Lancelot*." *American Literature: A Journal of Literary History, Criticism, and Bibliography* 57.1 (1985): 98–112.

Clemens, Cyril. *Mark Twain and Franklin D. Roosevelt.* With a Foreword by Eleanor Roosevelt. Webster Groves, MO: International Mark Twain Society, 1949.

Clemens, Will M. *Famous Funny Fellows: Brief Biographical Sketches of American Humorists.* Cleveland: William W. Williams, 1882.

Cochran, Molly, and Warren Murphy. *The Broken Sword.* New York: TOR, 1997.

———. *The Forever King.* New York: TOR, 1992.

Colander, Valerie Nieman. "The Naming of the Lost." *The Round Table* 5 (1989): 4–10.

Colby, Merle. *Handbook for Youth.* New York: Duell, Sloan & Pearce, 1940.

Coles, Robert. *Walker Percy: An American Search.* Boston: Little, Brown and Company, 1978.

Collins, Carvel. "Introduction." In William Faulkner. *Mayday.* Notre Dame: University of Notre Dame Press, 1978. 1–41.

Collins, William J. "Hank Morgan in the Garden of Forking Paths: *A Connecticut Yankee in King Arthur's Court* as Alternative History." *Modern Fiction Studies* 32.1 (Spring 1986): 109–14.

Connelly, Robert. *The Motion Picture Guide: Silent Film, 1910–1936*. Chicago: Cinebooks, 1986.

Cornellier. Thomas. "The Myth of Escape and Fulfillment in *The Sun Also Rises* and *The Great Gatsby*." *Society for the Study of Midwestern Literature Newsletter* 15.1 (Spring 1985): 15–21.

Couturier, Maurice, and Regis Durand. *Donald Barthelme*. London: Methuen, 1982.

Cowan, Michael H. *Twentieth Century Interpretations of The Sound and the Fury*. Englewood Cliffs, NJ: Prentice-Hall, 1968.

Cowley, Malcolm. "Nightmare and Ritual in Hemingway." In *Hemingway: A Collection of Critical Essays*. Ed. Robert P. Weeks. 1962; Englewood Cliffs: Prentice-Hall, 1965. 40–51.

Cox, Don Richard. "The Vision of Robinson's Merlin." *Colby Library Quarterly* 10.8 (Dec. 1974): 495–504.

Cram, Ralph Adams. *Excalibur: An Arthurian Drama*. Boston: Richard G. Badger, 1909.

Crow, Donna Fletcher. *Glastonbury: The Novel of Christian Britain*. Wheaton, IL: Crossway, 1992.

Crowley, J. Donald, and Sue Mitchell Crowley, eds. *Critical Essays on Walker Percy*. Boston: G. K. Hall, 1989.

Crowley, J. Donald, and Sue Mitchell Crowley. "Walker Percy's Grail." In *King Arthur Through the Ages*. Ed. Valerie M. Lagorio and Mildred Leake Day. 2 vols. New York: Garland, 1990. 2: 255–77.

Curry, Jane Louise. *The Sleepers*. Ill. Gareth Floyd. New York: Harcourt, Brace & World, 1968.

Daiker, Donald A. "The Affirmative Conclusion of *The Sun Also Rises*." In *Critical Essays on The Sun Also Rises*. Ed. James Nagel. Boston: G. K. Hall & Co., 1995. 53–62.

David, Peter. *Knight Life*. New York: Ace Fantasy Books, 1987.

Davis, Charles T. "Robinson's Road to Camelot." In *Edwin Arlington Robinson Centenary Essays*. Ed. Ellsworth Barnard. Athens: University of Georgia Press, 1969. 88–103.

Davis, J. Madison. "Walker Percy's *Lancelot*: The Shakespearean Threads." In *Shakespeare and Southern Writers: A Study in Influence*. Ed. Philip C. Kolin with a Foreword by Lewis P. Simpson. Jackson: University Press of Mississipppi, 1985. 159–72.

Deal, Babs H. *The Grail: A Novel*. New York: McKay, 1963.

De Bellis, Jack. *Sidney Lanier*. New York: Twayne, 1972.

Dell, Floyd. *King Arthur's Socks and Other Village Plays*. 1916; rpt. New York: Alfred A. Knopf, 1922.

Delving, Michael. *Die Like a Man*. New York: Unibook, 1970.

DeMille, Nelson. *The Quest*. New York: Manor Books, 1975.

Desmond, John F. "Sign of the Times: Lancelot and The Misfit." *The Flannery O'Connor Bulletin* 18 (1989): 91–8.

———. "Walker Percy and T.S. Eliot: The Lancelot Andrewes Connection." *The Southern Review* 22.3 (1986): 465–77.

Donaldson, Susan V. "Tradition in Amber: Walker Percy's *Lancelot* as Southern Metafiction." In *Walker Percy: Novelist and Philosopher*. Ed. Jan Nordby Gretlund and Karl-Heinz Westarp. Jackson: University Press of Mississippi, 1991. 65–73.

Douglas, Ann. "Art and Advertising in *A Connecticut Yankee*: The 'Robber Baron' Revisited." *The Canadian Review of American Studies* 6.2 (Fall 1975): 182–95.

Dowell, Bob. "A Note on John Steinbeck in King Arthur's Court." In *The Arthurian Myth of Quest and Magic: A Festschrift in Honor of Lavon B. Fulwiler*. Ed. William E. Tanner. Dallas: Caxton Modern Arts, 1993. 71–74.

Drake, David. *The Dragon Lord*. New York: Berkley/Putnam, 1979.

Drew, Elizabeth. *T. S. Eliot: The Design of His Poetry*. New York: Charles Scribner's Sons, 1949.

Du Bose, Horace M. *The Gang of Six: A Story of the Boy Life of Today*. Nashville, TN: Publishing House of the M. E. Church, South; Smith & Lamar, Agents, 1906.

Ducharme, Robert. *Art and Idea in the Novels of Bernard Malamud*. The Hague: Mouton, 1974.

Durham, Marilyn. "Narrative Strategies in Recent Vietnam War Fiction." In *America Rediscovered: Critical Essays on Literature and Film of the Vietnam War*. Ed. Owen W. Gilman, Jr. and Lorrie Smith. New York: Garland, 1990. 100–10.

Durham, Sandra Bonilla. "Women and War: Bobbie Ann Mason's *In Country*." *Southern Literary Journal* 22.2 (Spring 1990): 45–52.

Eble, Kenneth E., ed. *F. Scott Fitzgerald: A Collection of Criticism*. New York: McGraw-Hill, 1973.

Eggers, J. Philip. *King Arthur's Laureate: A Study of Tennyson's Idylls of the King*. New York: New York University Press, 1971.

Eigner, Edwin M. "The Loathly Ladies." In *Bernard Malamud and the Critics*. Ed. Leslie A. Field and Joyce W. Field. New York: New York University Press, 1970. 84–108.

Eliot, T. S. *The Waste Land and Other Poems*. 1922; rpt. New York: Harvest Books, 1963.

Elkin, Stanley. *A Bad Man*. New York: Random House, 1967.

Ely, Kathleen. "Transforming the Myth: The Use of Arthurian Material in the Church Universal and Triumphant." In *Popular Arthurian Traditions*. Ed. Sally K. Slocum. Bowling Green: Bowling Green State University Popular Press, 1992. 132–43.

Emerson, Ralph Waldo. *The Journals and Miscellaneous Notebooks of Ralph Waldo Emerson*. 16 vols. Ed. A. W. Plumstead, William H. Gilman, and Ruth H. Bennett. Cambridge, MA: The Belknap Press, 1975.

———. *Letters and Social Aims*. Boston: James R. Osgood and Co., 1876.

———. *Poems*. 1904; rpt. New York: AMS Press, 1968.

Engar, Keith. *Merlin's Tale of Arthur's Magic Sword*. New Orleans: Anchorage, 1982.

Erskine, John. *The Delight of Great Books*. Indianapolis: Bobbs-Merrill, 1928.

———. *Galahad: Enough of His Life to Explain His Reputation*. Indianapolis: Bobbs-Merrill, 1926.

———. *Tristan and Isolde: Restoring Palamede*. Indianapolis: Bobbs-Merrill, 1932.

Evans, Quinn Taylor. *Merlin's Legacy: Daughter of Fire*. (Book 1 of Merlin's Legacy.) New York: Zebra Books, 1996.

———. *Merlin's Legacy: Daughter of Light*. (Book 3 of Merlin's Legacy.) New York: Zebra Books, 1997.

———. *Merlin's Legacy: Daughter of the Mist.* (Book 2 of Merlin's Legacy.) New York: Zebra Books, 1996.

———. *Merlin's Legacy: Shadows of Camelot.* (Book 4 of Merlin's Legacy.) New York: Zebra Books, 1997.

Evernden, Margery. *King Arthur's Sword.* Chicago: Coach House, 1959.

Excalibur: A Tale for American Boys. Philadelphia: King & Baird, 1865.

Faulkner, Nancy. *Sword of the Winds.* Garden City, NY: Doubleday, 1957.

Faulkner, William. *Absalom, Absalom!* 1936; rpt. New York: Vintage Books, n.d.

———. *Go Down, Moses.* 1942; rpt. New York: Vintage Books, 1973.

———. *The Hamlet.* New York: Random House, 1940.

———. *Mayday.* Introduction by Carvel Collins. Notre Dame: University of Notre Dame Press, 1978.

———. *Mosquitoes.* New York: Liveright, 1927.

———. *Pylon.* New York: Harrison Smith and Robert Haas, Inc., 1935.

———. *Soldier's Pay.* 1926; rpt. London: Chatto & Windus, 1930.

———. *The Sound and the Fury.* 1929; rpt. New York: Vintage Books, 1954.

———. *The Town.* New York: Random House, 1957.

Fawcett, Edgar. *The New King Arthur: An Opera Without Music.* New York: Funk & Wagnalls, 1885.

Federman, Raymond, ed. *Surfiction: Fiction Now and Tomorrow.* Second ed., enlarged. Chicago: Swallow Press, 1981.

Fenton, Charles A. *The Apprenticeship of Ernest Hemingway: The Early Years.* 1954; New York: New American Library/Mentor Books, 1961.

Fiedler, Leslie A. *No! in Thunder: Essays on Myth and Literature.* Boston: Beacon Press, 1960.

Field, Eugene. "The Vision of the Holy Grail." In *John Smith, U.S.A.* Chicago: M. A. Donohue and Co., 1905. 103–06.

Field, Leslie A., and Joyce W. Field, eds. *Bernard Malamud and the Critics.* New York: New York University Press, 1970.

The Figure of Merlin in the Nineteenth and Twentieth Centuries. Ed. Jeanie Watson and Maureen Fries. Lewiston: The Edwin Mellen Press, 1989.

Fisher, John Hurt. "Edwin Arlington Robinson and Arthurian Tradition." In *Studies in Language and Literature in Honour of Margaret Schlauch.* Ed. Mieczyslaw Brahmer, Stanislaw Helsztynski, and Julian Krzyzanowski. Warsaw: PWN – Polish Scientific Publishers, 1966. 117–31.

Fitzgerald, F. Scott. *Afternoon of an Author: A Selection of Uncollected Stories and Essays.* Ed. Arthur Mizener. New York: Scribner's, 1957.

———. "Babylon Revisited." In *The Short Stories of F. Scott Fitzgerald: A New Collection.* New York: Scribner's, 1989. 616–33.

———. *The Beautiful and The Damned.* 1922; rpt. New York: Scribner's, 1950.

———. "The Bowl." *The Saturday Evening Post.* 21 January 1928: 6–7, 93–94, 97, 100.

———. *Correspondence of F. Scott Fitzgerald.* Ed. Matthew J. Bruccoli and Margaret M. Duggan, with the assistance of Susan Walker. New York: Random House, 1980.

———. *F. Scott Fitzgerald in His Own Time: A Miscellany.* Ed. Matthew J. Bruccoli and Jackson R. Bryer. Kent: Kent State University Press, 1971.

———. *The Great Gatsby.* 1925; rpt. New York: Scribner's, 1953.

———. *The Last Tycoon: An Unfinished Novel. Together with The Great Gatsby.* 1925; rpt. New York: Scribner's, 1951.

———. *The Letters of F. Scott Fitzgerald.* Ed. Andrew Turnbull. 1963; rpt. New York: Laurel, 1966.

———. *The Notebooks of F. Scott Fitzgerald.* Ed. Matthew J. Bruccoli. New York: Harcourt Brace Jovanovich, 1978.

———. "O Russet Witch!" *Tales of the Jazz Age.* New York: Scribner's, 1922. 234–72.

———. "Outside the Cabinet-Maker's." *Afternoon of an Author.* 137–41.

———. "Six of One – ." *The Short Stories of F. Scott Fitzgerald: A New Collection.* Ed. Matthew J. Bruccoli. New York: Scribner's, 1989. 667–79.

———. "The Spire and the Gargoyle." *The Apprentice Fiction of F. Scott Fitzgerald: 1909–1917.* Ed. John Kuehl. New Brunswick: Rutgers University Press, 1965. 105–14.

———. *Tales of the Jazz Age.* New York: Scribner's, 1922.

———. "Tarquin of Cheepside." *The Apprentice Fiction of F. Scott Fitzgerald: 1909–1917.* Ed. John Kuehl. New Brunswick: Rutgers University Press, 1965. 118–23.

———. *Tender Is the Night.* 1933. New York: Scribner's, 1962.

———. *This Side of Paradise.* 1920. New York: Scribner's, 1960.

Fitzgerald, F. Scott, and Zelda Fitzgerald. *Bits of Paradise: 21 Uncollected Stories by F. Scott and Zelda Fitzgerald.* Selected by Scottie Fitzgerald Smith and Matthew J. Bruccoli with a Foreword by Scottie Fitzgerald Smith. London: The Bodley Head, 1973.

Fitzgerald, F. Scott, and Maxwell E. Perkins. *Dear Scott/Dear Max: The Fitzgerald-Perkins Correspondence.* New York: Scribner, 1971.

Fitzgerald, Zelda. *Save Me the Waltz.* 1932; rpt. London: The Grey Walls Press, 1953.

Flint, Kate. *The Woman Reader 1837–1914.* Oxford: Clarendon Press, 1993.

Folsom, James K. *Man's Accidents and God's Purposes: Multiplicity in Hawthorne's Fiction.* New Haven: College and University Press, 1963.

Fontenrose, Joseph. "*Tortilla Flat* and the Creation of a Legend." In *The Short Novels of John Steinbeck.* Ed. Jackson J. Benson. Durham: Duke University Press, 1990. 19–30.

Forbush, William Byron. *The Boy Problem: A Study in Social Pedagogy.* Intro. by G. Stanley Hall. Boston: The Pilgrim Press, 1901.

———. *The Coming Generation.* New York: D. Appleton, 1912.

———. *Guide Book to Childhood.* Philadelphia: American Institute of Child Life, 1913.

———. *The Queens of Avalon.* 4th ed.; Boston: The Knights of King Arthur, 1925.

———, compiler. *Songs of the Knights of King Arthur.* Detroit: The Knights of King Arthur, 1911.

Forbush, William Byron, and Dascomb Forbush. *The Knights of King Arthur: How to Begin and What to Do.* Oberlin, OH: The Knights of King Arthur, 1915.

———. *The Knights of King Arthur: The Merlin's Book of Advanced Work.* Oberlin, OH: The Knights of King Arthur, 1916.

———. *The Merrye Yeomen of King Arthur: A Happy Church Organization for Junior Boys.* Oberlin, OH: The Knights of King Arthur, 1916.

Forbush, William Byron, and Frank Lincoln Masseck. *The Boys' Round Table: A Manual of the International Order of the Knights of King Arthur.* 6th ed., rewritten. Potsdam, NY: Frank Lincoln Masseck, 1908.

Ford, Robert. *American Humourists: Recent and Living*. London: Alexander Gardner, 1897.

Foster, Edward. "*A Connecticut Yankee* Anticipated by Max Adeler's *Fortunate Island*." *Ball State University Forum* 9.4 (Autumn 1968): 73–76.

Fowler, D. C. From "*The Waste Land*: Mr. Eliot's 'Fragments.' " *College English* 14 (January 1953): 234–35. Rpt. as "What the Thunder Said." In *The Waste Land: A Collection of Critical Essays*. Ed. Jay Martin. Englewood Cliffs, NJ: Prentice-Hall, 1968. 34–36.

Franchere, Hoyt C. *Edwin Arlington Robinson*. New York: Twayne, 1968.

Frank Lloyd Wright: Writings and Buildings. Selected by Edgar Kaufmann and Ben Raeburn. 1960; rpt. New York: Meridian, 1974.

Frazer, Sir James George. *The Golden Bough: A Study in Magic and Religion*. New York: Macmillan, 1956.

Freese, Peter. "Parzival als Baseballstar: Bernard Malamuds *The Natural*." *Jahrbuch für Amerikastudien*. Heidelberg: Carl Winter Universitätsverlag, 1968. Band 13. 143–57.

French, Allen. *Sir Marrok: A Tale of the Days of King Arthur*. New York: Century, 1902.

French, Warren. *John Steinbeck*. New York: Twayne, 1961.

———. *John Steinbeck's Fiction Revisited*. New York: Twayne, 1994.

———. "Steinbeck's Use of Malory." In *Steinbeck and the Arthurian Theme*. Ed. Tetsumaro Hayashi. Steinbeck Monograph Series No. 5. Muncie, IN: The John Steinbeck Society of America, Ball State University, 1975. 4–11.

Freshney, Pamela. "The Moviegoer and *Lancelot*: The Movies as Literary Symbol." *The Southern Review* 18 (1982): 718–27.

Friedman, Michele (Co-Director, Camp Camelot). Letter to Barbara Tepa Lupack. 21 Jan. 1994.

Froula, Christine. "Eliot's Grail Quest, or, The Lover, the Police and *The Waste Land*." *The Yale Review* 78.2 (Winter 1989): 235–53.

Fry, Carrol L. " 'What God Doth the Wizard Pray to': Neo-Pagan Witchcraft and Fantasy Fiction." *Extrapolation* 31.4 (Winter 1990): 333–46.

Gardiner, Jane. " 'A More Splendid Necromancy': Mark Twain's *Connecticut Yankee* and the Electrical Revolution." *Studies in the Novel* 19.4 (Winter 1987): 448–58.

Gardner, John. "The Quest for the Philosophic Novel." In *Critical Essays on Walker Percy*. Ed. J. Donald Crowley and Sue Mitchell Crowley. Boston: G. K. Hall, 1989. 58–61.

Gealy, Marcia. "A Reinterpretation of Malamud's *The Natural*." *Studies in Jewish American Literature* 4.1 (Spring 1978): 24–32.

Geoffrey of Monmouth. *History of the Kings of Britain*. Trans. Sebastian Evans. Rev. Charles W. Dunn. New York: E. P. Dutton, 1958.

Gerogiannis, Nicholas. *Ernest Hemingway: 88 Poems*. New York: Harcourt Brace Jovanovich, 1979.

Gerstenberger, Donna. "Steinbeck's American Waste Land." *Modern Fiction Studies* 11.1 (Spring 1965): 59–65.

Gilman, Richard. "Barthelme's Fairy Tale." In *Critical Essays on Donald Barthelme*. Ed. Richard F. Patteson. New York: G. K. Hall, 1992. 29–35.

———. *The Confusion of Realms*. New York: Random House, 1969.

Gilman, Owen W., Jr. *Vietnam and the Southern Imagination*. Jackson: University Press of Mississippi, 1992.

Gilman, Owen W., Jr., and Lorrie Smith, eds. *America Rediscovered: Critical Essays on Literature and Film of the Vietnam War*. New York: Garland, 1990.

Girouard, Mark. *The Return to Camelot: Chivalry and the English Gentleman*. New Haven: Yale University Press, 1981.

Gladstein, Mimi Reisel. "*America and Americans*: The Arthurian Consummation." In *After The Grapes of Wrath: Essays on John Steinbeck in Honor of Tetsumaro Hayashi*. Ed. Donald V. Coers, Paul D. Ruffin, and Robert J. DeMott. Athens: Ohio University Press, 1995. 228–37.

Godwin, Parke. *Beloved Exile*. New York: Bantam, 1984.

————. *Firelord*. Garden City, NY: Doubleday, 1980.

————. "The Lady of Finnegan's Hearth." *Fantastic* (Sept. 1977): 50–71, 122–24, 131.

————. *The Last Rainbow*. New York: Bantam, 1985.

————. "The Last Rainbow." *Fantastic* (June 1978). Rpt. in *The Fire When It Comes*. Garden City, NY: Doubleday, 1984. 112–45.

————. Letter to Alan Lupack. 19 Jan. 1981.

————. "Uallanach." In *Invitation to Camelot: An Arthurian Anthology*. Ed. Parke Godwin. New York: Ace. 1988. 83–107

Goldman, James. *The Man from Greek and Roman*. New York: Golden Apple Publishers, 1985.

Goodman, Jennifer R. *The Legend of Arthur in British and American Literature*. Boston: Twayne, 1988.

Goodrich, Peter H. "Modern Merlins: An Aerial Survey." In *The Figure of Merlin in the Nineteenth and Twentieth Centuries*. Ed. Jeanie Watson and Maureen Fries. Lewiston, NY: The Edwin Mellen Press, 1989. 175–97.

Gordon, Andrew. "*Star Wars*: A Myth for Our Time." *Literature/Film Quarterly* 6.4 (Fall 1978): 314–26.

Gordon, Lois. *Donald Barthelme*. Boston: Twayne, 1981.

Graham, Sheilah. *The Real F. Scott Fitzgerald: Thirty-Five Years Later*. New York: Warner Books, 1976.

Graham, Sheilah, and Gerold Frank. *Beloved Infidel: The Education of a Woman*. New York: Henry Holt, 1958.

Gray, Phoebe. *Little Sir Galahad*. Boston: Small, Maynard and Co., 1914.

Greeley, Andrew M. *The Magic Cup: An Irish Legend*. New York: McGraw-Hill Book Co., 1979.

Grellner, Alice. "Two Films That Sparkle: The Sword in the Stone and Camelot." In *Cinema Arthuriana: Essays on Arthurian Film*. Ed. Kevin J. Harty. New York: Garland, 1991. 71–81.

Gretlund, Jan Nordby and Karl-Heinz Westarp, eds. *Walker Percy: Novelist and Philosopher*. Jackson: University Press of Mississippi, 1991.

Griffin, Peter. *Along with Youth: Hemingway, the Early Years*. Oxford: Oxford University Press, 1985.

Gurko, Leo. *Ernest Hemingway and the Pursuit of Heroism*. New York: Thomas Y. Crowell, 1968.

————. "Hemingway and the Magical Journey." In *Hemingway: A Revaluation*. Ed. Donald R. Noble. Troy, NY: Whitston Publishing Co., 1983. 67–82.

Gwynn, Frederick L., and Joseph L. Blotner. *Faulkner in the University*. Charlottesville: University of Virginia Press, 1959.

Haldeman, Linda. *The Lastborn of Elvinwood*. Garden City, NY: Doubleday, 1978.

Hall, G. Stanley. *Adolescence: Its Psychology and its Relations to Physiology, Anthropology, Sociology, Sex, Crime, Religion and Education*. 2 vols. New York: D. Appleton, 1904.

Hall, John Lesslie. *Old English Idyls*. Boston: Ginn & Co., 1899.

Halsey, Francis Whiting. *Women Authors of Our Day in Their Homes: Personal Descriptions & Interviews*. New York: James Pott, 1903.

Hamilton, Ian. "The Waste Land." In *Eliot in Perspective: A Symposium*. Ed. Graham Martin. London: Macmillan, 1970. 102–11.

Hansen, Chadwick. "The Once and Future Boss: Mark Twain's Yankee." *Nineteenth-Century Fiction* 28.1 (June 1973): 62–73.

Hardy, John Edward. *The Fiction of Walker Percy*. Urbana: University of Illinois Press, 1987.

Hare, Amory (pseudonym of [Mary] Amory Hare Hutchinson). *Tristram and Iseult*. Gaylordsville, CT: The Slide Mountain Press, 1930.

Harley, Marta Powell. "Faulkner's Medievalism and *Sir Gawain and the Green Knight*." *American Notes & Queries* 21.7–8 (March/April 1983): 111–14.

Harty, Kevin J. "Arthurian Film" (a bibliography). Arthuriana / Camelot Project Bibliographies. URL: http://www.lib.rochester.edu/camelot/acpbibs/harty.htm.

———. "Cinema Arthuriana: A Filmography." *Quondam et Futurus: Newsletter for Arthurian Studies* 7.3 (Spring 1987): 5–8.

———. "*The Fisher King*: A List of Critical Reviews and Other Discussions." *The Arthurian Yearbook* 3 (1993): 273–76.

———. "*The Knights of the Square Table*: The Boy Scouts and Thomas Edison Make an Arthurian Film." *Arthuriana* 4 (Winter 1994): 313–23.

———. Rev. of *Four Diamonds*." *Arthuriana* 6.2 (Summer 1996): 115–18.

Hassan, Ihab. "Conscience and Incongruity: The Fiction of Thomas Berger." *Critique: Studies in Modern Fiction* 5.2 (1965): 4–15.

Haviland, Mary S. "'Knighthood of Youth'—a New Solution of an Old Problem." *School Life* 12.2 (Oct. 1926): 36–37.

Hawke, Simon. *The Samurai Wizard*. New York: Warner Books, 1991.

———. *The Wizard of Camelot*. New York: Warner Books, 1993.

———. *The Wizard of 4th Street*. New York: Popular Library/Warner Books, 1987.

———. *The Wizard of Lovecraft's Cafe*. New York: Warner Books, 1993.

———. *The Wizard of Rue Morgue*. New York: Popular Library, 1990.

———. *The Wizard of Santa Fe*. New York: Warner Books, 1991.

———. *The Wizard of Sunset Strip*. New York: Warner Books, 1989.

———. *The Wizard of Whitechapel*. New York: Popular Library, 1988.

Hawthorne, Nathaniel. "The Antique Ring." In *The Dolliver Romance and Other Pieces*. Boston: James R. Osgood and Co., 1876. 107–24.

Hays, Peter L. "The Complex Pattern of Redemption." In *Bernard Malamud and the Critics*. Ed. Leslie A. Field and Joyce W. Field. New York: New York University Press, 1970. 219–33.

———. "*Gatsby*, Myth, Fairy Tale, and Legend." *Southern Folklore Quarterly* 41 (1977): 213–23.

———. "Malamud's Yiddish-Accented Medieval Stories." In *The Fiction of Bernard*

Malamud. Ed. Richard Astro and Jackson J. Benson. Corvallis: Oregon State University Press, 1977. 87–96.

Helterman, Jeffrey. *Understanding Bernard Malamud.* Columbia: University of South Carolina Press, 1985.

Hemingway, Ernest. *Death in the Afternoon.* New York: Charles Scribner's Sons, 1932.

———. *For Whom the Bell Tolls.* New York: P. F. Collier and Son, 1940.

———. *Green Hills of Africa.* New York: Scribner, 1935

———. *In Our Time.* 1925; rpt. New York: Charles Scribner's Sons, 1970.

———. *The Old Man and The Sea.* New York: Charles Scribner's Sons, 1952.

———. *The Sun Also Rises.* 1926; New York: Charles Scribner's Sons, 1970.

Heroes Every Child Should Know: Tales for Young People of the World's Heroes in All Ages. Ed. H. W. Mabie. New York: Grosset & Dunlap, 1907.

Hershinow, Sheldon J. *Bernard Malamud.* New York: Frederick Ungar, 1980.

Hicks, Jack. *In the Singer's Temple: Prose Fictions of Barthelme, Gaines, Brautigan, Piercy, Kesey, and Kosinski.* Chapel Hill: University of North Carolina Press, 1981.

Hildebrandt, Rita. *Merlin and the Dragons of Atlantis.* Ill. Tim Hildebrandt. Indianapolis/New York: Bobbs Merrill, 1983.

Higginson, Thomas Wentworth. *Tales of the Enchanted Isles of the Atlantic.* New York: Macmillan, 1898.

Hoben, Alice M. *Knights Old and New.* Intro. John H. Finley. New York: D. Appleton, 1929.

Hoberg, Tom. "In Her Own Right: The Guenevere of Parke Godwin." In *Popular Arthurian Traditions.* Ed. Sally K. Slocum. Bowling Green: Bowling Green State University Popular Press, 1992. 68–79.

Hobson, Linda Whitney. *Walker Percy: A Comprehensive Descriptive Bibliography.* New Orleans: Faust Publishing Company, 1988.

Hodges, Laura F. "The Personae of *Acts*: Symbolic Repetition and Variation." *Steinbeck Quarterly* 12 (Winter–Spring 1979): 20–27.

———. "Steinbeck's Adaptation of Malory's Launcelot: A Triumph of Realism over Supernaturalism." *Quondam et Futurus: A Journal of Arthurian Interpretations* 2.1 (Spring 1992): 69–81.

———. "Steinbeck's Dream Sequence in *The Acts of King Arthur and His Noble Knights.*" *Arthurian Interpretations* 4.2 (Spring 1990): 35–49.

Hoffman, Donald L. "Mark's Merlin: Magic vs. Technology in *A Connecticut Yankee in King Arthur's Court.*" In *Popular Arthurian Traditions.* Ed. Sally K. Slocum. Bowling Green: Bowling Green State University Popular Press, 1992. 46–55.

Hoffman, Frederick J., and Olga W. Vickery, eds. *William Faulkner: Three Decades of Criticism.* 1960; rpt. New York: Harbinger Books, 1963.

Hoffman, Nancy Y. "*The Great Gatsby*: Troilus and Criseyde Revisited?" *Fitzgerald/Hemingway Annual* (1971): 148–58.

Hoffmann, Charles G., and A. C. Hoffmann. " 'The Truest Sentence': Words as Equivalents of Time and Place in *In Our Time.*" In *Hemingway: A Revaluation.* Ed. Donald R. Noble. Troy, NY: Whitston Publishing Co., 1983. 99–113.

Holmes, Lillian. *Little Sir Galahad.* Chicago: David C. Cook, 1904.

Hovey, Richard. *The Birth of Galahad.* Boston: Small, Maynard, and Co., 1898.

————. *The Holy Graal and Other Fragments by Richard Hovey: Being the Uncompleted Parts of the Arthurian Dramas.* Ed. with an Introduction and Notes by Mrs. Richard Hovey and a Preface by Bliss Carman. New York: Duffield & Co., 1907.

————. *The Marriage of Guenevere: A Tragedy.* Boston: Small, Maynard and Co., 1899.

————. *The Quest of Merlin.* Boston: Small, Maynard and Co., 1898. [The play was first published in 1891.]

————. *Taliesin: A Masque.* Boston: Small, Maynard and Co., 1900.

Howard, Leon. *Victorian Knight-Errant: A Study of the Early Literary Career of James Russell Lowell.* Berkeley: University of California Press, 1952.

Huemer, Richard. *A Dragon on the Hill Road.* Ill. Walter Peregoy. Los Angeles: Valley Village Press, 1958.

Hughes, Douglas. "Thomas Berger's Elan: An Interview." *Confrontation* 12 (Summer 1976): 23–39.

Hylton, J. Dunbar. *Arteloise: A Romance of King Arthur and the Knights of the Round Table.* Palmyra, NJ: The Hylton Publishing Co., 1887.

Jankofsky, Klaus P. " 'America' in Parke Godwin's Arthurian Novels." *Arthurian Interpretations* 4.2 (Spring 1990): 65–80.

————. "Sir Gawaine at Liberty Castle: Thomas Berger's Comic Didacticism in *Arthur Rex: A Legendary Novel.*" In *Theorie und Praxis im Erzählen des 19. und 20. Jahrhunderts: Studien zur englischen und amerikanischen Literatur zu Ehren von Willi Erzgräber.* Ed. Winfried Herget, Klaus Peter Jochum, and Ingeborg Weber. Tubingen: Gunter Narr, 1986. 389–404.

Jarman, A. O. H. "The Welsh Myrddin Poems." In *Arthurian Literature in the Middle Ages: A Collaborative History.* Ed. Roger Sherman Loomis. Oxford: Clarendon Press, 1959. 20–30.

Jason, Philip K., ed. *Fourteen Landing Zones: Approaches to Vietnam War Literature.* Iowa City: University of Iowa Press, 1991.

Jay, Gregory. "Eliot's Poetics and the Fisher King." *Yeats Eliot Review* 7.1 & 2 (June 1982): 28–35.

Jeter, K. W. *Morlock Night.* New York: Daw, 1979.

Jewett, Eleanore Myers. *The Hidden Treasure of Glaston.* Ill. Frederick T. Chapman. New York: Viking, 1946.

Jewett, Sophie. "The Dwarf's Quest: A Ballad." In *Persephone and Other Poems: By Members of the English Literature Department, Wellesley College, for the Benefit of the Wellesley Library Fund.* Boston: The Fort Hill Press, 1905. 53–61.

Johnson, Barbara Ferry. *Lionors.* New York: Avon, 1975.

Johnson, Mark. "*Lancelot*: Percy's Romance." *Southern Literary Journal* 15 (1983): 19–30.

Johnston, Annie Fellows. *Keeping Tryst: A Tale of King Arthur's Time.* Boston: L. C. Page and Co., 1906.

————. *Two Little Knights of Kentucky: Who Were the "Little Colonel's" Neighbours.* Boston: L. C. Page and Co., 1899.

Jones, Courtway. *In the Shadow of the Oak King: First Book in the Story of Dragon's Heirs.* New York: Pocket Books, 1991.

————. *Witch of the North.* New York: Pocket Books, 1992.

Jones, Mary J. *Avalon.* Tallahassee: Naiad Press, 1991.

Kahn, Sy. "*This Side of Paradise*: The Pageantry of Disillusion." *The Midwest Quarterly* 7 (Jan. 1966): 177–94. Rpt. in Eble 34–47.

Kane, Gil, and John Jakes. *Excalibur!* New York: Dell, 1980.

Karl, Frederick R. *American Fictions, 1940–1980: A Comprehensive History and Critical Evaluation.* New York: Harper and Row, 1983.

Karr, Phyllis Ann. *The Idylls of the Queen.* New York: Ace, 1982.

———. "Two Bits of Embroidery." In *Invitation to Camelot: An Arthurian Anthology.* Ed. Parke Godwin. New York: Ace. 1988. 31–45.

Kazin, Alfred. *F. Scott Fitzgerald: The Man and His Work.* 1951. New York: Collier, 1962.

Kelly, Lori Duin. *The Life and Works of Elizabeth Stuart Phelps, Victorian Feminist Writer.* Troy, NY: The Whitston Publishing Co., 1983.

Kennealy, Patricia. *The Copper Crown: A Novel of the Keltiad.* New York: Bluejay, 1984.

———. *The Hawk's Gray Feather: A Book of the Keltiad.* New York: ROC, 1990. (Vol. 1 of The Tales of Arthur.)

———. *The Silver Branch: A Novel of the Keltiad.* New York: New American Library, 1988.

———. *The Throne of Scone: A Book of the Keltiad.* New York: Bluejay, 1986.

Kennealy-Morrison, Patricia. *The Hedge of Mist.* New York: HarperPrism, 1996. (Vol. 3 of The Tales of Arthur.)

———. *The Oak Above the Kings.* New York: ROC, 1995. (Vol. 2 of The Tales of Arthur.)

Kennedy, Rose Fitzgerald. *Times to Remember.* New York: Doubleday, 1974.

Kenney, Alice P. "Yankees in Camelot: The Democratization of Chivalry in James Russell Lowell, Mark Twain, and Edwin Arlington Robinson." *Studies in Medievalism* 1.2 (Spring 1982): 73–78.

Kesey, Ken. *Demon Box.* New York: Viking, 1986.

———. *One Flew Over the Cuckoo's Nest.* 1962; rpt. New York: New American Library, 1962.

Kesey, Ken, with Ken Babbs. *Last Go Round: A Real Western.* New York: Viking, 1994.

Kessler, Carol Farley. *Elizabeth Stuart Phelps.* Boston: Twayne, 1982.

Ketterer, David. " 'The Fortunate Island' by Max Adeler: Its Publication History and *A Connecticut Yankee.*" *Mark Twain Journal* 29.2 (Fall 1991): 28–32.

———. " 'Professor Baffin's Adventures' by Max Adeler: The Inspiration for *A Connecticut Yankee in King Arthur's Court?*" *Mark Twain Journal* 24.1 (Spring 1986): 24–34.

Kimsey, John. "Dolorous Strokes, or, Balin at the Bat: Malamud, Malory, and Chrétien." In *The Celebration of the Fantastic: Selected Papers from the Tenth Anniversary International Conference on the Fantastic in the Arts.* Ed. by Donald E. Morse, Marshall B. Tymn, and Csilla Bertha. Westport, CT: Greenwood Press, 1989. 103–12.

King Arthur Flour. *King Arthur Flour 200th Anniversary Cookbook.* Norwich, VT: Sands Taylor & Wood Co., 1990.

Kingsolver, Barbara. "Desire Under the Palms." *New York Times Book Review*, 6 February 1994, 1, 26–27.

Kinney, Arthur F. "The Arthurian Cycle in *Tortilla Flat.*" *Modern Fiction Studies* 11.1

(Spring 1965): 11–20. Rpt. in *Steinbeck: A Collection of Critical Essays*. Ed. Robert Murray Davis. Englewood Cliffs, NJ: Prentice-Hall, 1972. 36–46.

———. "*Tortilla Flat* Re-Visited." In *Steinbeck and the Arthurian Theme*. Ed. Tetsumaro Hayashi. Steinbeck Monograph Series No. 5. Muncie, IN: The John Steinbeck Society of America, Ball State University, 1975. 12–24.

Kinney, Katherine. " 'Humping the Boonies': Sex, Combat, and the Female in Bobbie Ann Mason's *In Country*." In *Fourteen Landing Zones: Approaches to Vietnam War Literature*. Ed. Philip K. Jason. Iowa City: University of Iowa Press, 1991. 38–48.

Klein, Marcus. *After Alienation: American Novels in Mid-Century*. Cleveland: World Publishing Co., 1964.

Klinkowitz, Jerome. *Donald Barthelme: An Exhibition*. Durham: Duke University Press, 1991.

———. *Kurt Vonnegut*. London: Methuen, 1982.

———. *Literary Disruptions: The Making of a Post-Contemporary American Fiction*. Urbana: University of Illinois Press, 1975.

———. *Slaughterhouse-Five: Reforming the Novel and the World*. Boston: Twayne, 1990.

Knight, Stephen. *Arthurian Literature and Society*. New York: St. Martin's, 1983.

Knight, W. Nicholas. " 'Lancer': Myth-Making and the Kennedy Camelot." *Avalon to Camelot* 2.1 (1986): 26–31.

Kordecki, Lesley C. "Twain's Critique of Malory's Romance: *Forma tractandi* and *A Connecticut Yankee*." *Nineteenth-Century Literature* 41.3 (Dec. 1986): 329–48.

Korg, Jacob. "Modern Art Techniques in *The Waste Land*." *Journal of Aesthetics and Art Criticism* 18 (June 1960): 456–63. Rpt. in *The Waste Land: A Collection of Critical Essays*. Twentieth Century Interpretations. Ed. Jay Martin. Englewood Cliffs, NJ: Prentice-Hall, 1968. 87–96.

Kosinski, Jerzy. *The Hermit of 69th Street: The Working Papers of Norbert Kosky*. New York: Henry Holt/Seaver Books, 1988.

———. *Passion Play*. New York: St. Martin's Press, 1979.

———. *The Painted Bird*. Boston: Houghton Mifflin, 1965.

———. *Steps*. New York: Random House, 1968.

Krause, Sydney J. "Steinbeck and Mark Twain." In *Steinbeck's Literary Dimension: A Guide to Comparative Studies*. Series II. Ed. Tetsumaro Hayashi. Metuchen, NJ: The Scarecrow Press, 1991.

Kruse, Horst H. "Literary Old Offenders: Mark Twain, John Quill, Max Adeler and Their Plagiarism Duels." *Mark Twain Journal* 29.2 (Fall 1991): 10–27.

———. "Mark Twain's *A Connecticut Yankee*: Reconsiderations and Revisions." *American Literature* 62.3 (Sept. 1990): 464–83.

Lacy, Norris J., and Geoffrey Ashe. *The Arthurian Handbook*. New York: Garland, 1988.

Lagorio, Valerie M. "Edwin Arlington Robinson: Arthurian Pacifist." In *King Arthur Through the Ages*. Ed. Valerie M. Lagorio and Mildred Leake Day. 2 vols. New York: Garland, 1990. 2: 164–79.

Lagorio, Valerie M., and Mildred Leake Day, eds. *King Arthur Through the Ages*. 2 vols. New York: Garland, 1990.

Lanahan, Eleanor. *Scottie, the Daughter of . . .: The Life of Frances Scott Fitzgerald Lanahan Smith*. New York: HarperCollins, 1995.

Landon, Brooks. *Thomas Berger.* New York: Twayne, 1989.

Lanier, Sidney. *The Boy's King Arthur.* Ill. Alfred Kappes. New York: Charles Scribner's Sons, 1880.

———. *The Boy's King Arthur.* Ill. N. C. Wyeth. New York: Charles Scribner's Sons, 1917.

———. *Knightly Legends of Wales or The Boy's Mabinogion: Being the Earliest Welsh Tales of King Arthur in the Famous Red Book of Hergest.* Ill. Alfred Fredericks. New York: Charles Scribner's Sons, 1893.

Laubenthal, Sanders Anne. *Excalibur.* Introduction by Lin Carter. New York: Ballantine, 1973.

———. Letter to Alan Lupack. 18 Jan. 1981.

Lauritzen, Einar, and Gunnar Lundquist. *American Film Index: 1908–1915: Motion Pictures, July 1908–December 1915.* Stockholm: Film Index, distributed by Akademibokhandeln, University of Stockholm, 1976.

Lavers, Norman. *Jerzy Kosinski.* Boston: Twayne, 1982.

Lawhead, Stephen R. *Arthur.* The Pendragon Cycle, Book Three. Westchester, IL.: Crossway Books, 1989.

———. *Grail.* Book Five of the Pendragon Cycle. New York: Avon Books, 1997.

———. *Merlin.* The Pendragon Cycle, Book Two. Westchester, IL: Crossway Books, 1987.

———. *Pendragon.* Book Four in the Pendragon Cycle. New York: Morrow/AvoNova, 1994.

———. *Taliesin.* The Pendragon Cycle, Book One. Westchester, Ill.: Crossway Books, 1987.

Lawson, Lewis A. "Moviemaking in Percy's *Lancelot.*" *South Central Review: The Journal of the South Central Modern Language Association* 3.4 (1986): 78–94.

———. "Gnosis and Time in *Lancelot.*" *Papers on Language and Literature* 19 (1983): 72–86.

Leavis, F. R. "The Poem's Unity." In *Storm over The Waste Land.* Ed. Robert E. Knoll. Chicago: Scott, Foresman, 1964. 24–38.

Leeds, Barry H. *Ken Kesey.* New York: Frederick Ungar, 1981.

———. *The Structured Vision of Norman Mailer.* New York: New York University Press, 1969.

Lehan, Richard D. *F. Scott Fitzgerald and the Craft of Fiction.* Carbondale: Southern Illinois University Press, 1966. 91–102, 122–23. Rpt. as "*The Great Gatsby* and Its Sources." In *Critical Essays on The Great Gatsby.* Ed. Scott Donaldson. Boston: G. K. Hall, 1984. 66–74.

———. "The Romantic Self and the Uses of Place in the Stories of F. Scott Fitzgerald." In *The Short Stories of F. Scott Fitzgerald: New Approaches in Criticism.* Ed. Jackson R. Bryer. Madison: University of Wisconsin Press, 1982. 3–21.

Leigh, Joseph. *Illustrations of the Fulfilment of the Prediction of Merlin Occasioned by the Late Outrageous Attack of the British Ship of War the Leopard, on the American Frigate Chesapeake, and the Measures Taken by the President, Supported by the Citizens Thereon.* Portsmouth, NH: Printed for the Author, 1807.

Leland, John. " 'The Happiness of the Garden': Hemingway's Edenic Quest." *The Hemingway Review.* 3.1 (Fall 1983). 44–53.

Lerner, Alan Jay, and (music by) Frederick Loewe. *Camelot.* New York: Random House, 1961.

Le Vot, André. *F. Scott Fitzgerald: A Biography*. 1979. New York: Warner Books, 1983.

Lewis, Charlton Miner. *The Beginnings of English Literature*. Boston: Ginn & Co., 1901.

———. *The Principles of English Verse*. New Haven: Yale University Press, 1929.

———. *Sir Gawayne and the Green Knight: A Fairy Tale*. Boston: Houghton, Mifflin and Co., 1903.

Lewis, Sinclair. *Launcelot*. Printed by the Harvard Press for Harvey Taylor, n.d.. (This pamphlet, limited to 1000 copies, contains the text of the short poem "Launcelot," Lewis's first published work, which first appeared in the *Yale Literary Magazine* in 1904.)

Lidston, Robert C. "Malamud's *The Natural*: An Arthurian Quest in the Big Leagues." *West Virginia University Philological Papers* 27 (1981): 75–81.

Light, Martin. "Sweeping Out Chivalric Silliness: The Example of *Huck Finn* and *The Sun Also Rises*." *Mark Twain Journal* 18.3 (Winter 1974–75): 18–21.

Lilly, Paul R., Jr. *Words in Search of Victims: The Achievement of Jerzy Kosinski*. Kent: Kent State University Press, 1988.

Lindbergh, Charles A. *Autobiography of Values*. Intro. by Reeve Lindbergh. New York: Harcourt Brace Jovanovich / A Harvest/HBJ Book, 1992.

Linneman, William R. *Richard Hovey*. Boston: Twayne, 1976.

Lisca, Peter. *John Steinbeck: Nature and Myth*. New York: Thomas Y. Crowell, 1978.

Literary History of the United States. Ed. Robert Spiller et al. 3rd ed.; New York: Macmillan, 1963.

Lowell, James Russell. *The Poetical Works of James Russell Lowell: Household Edition*. Boston: Houghton Mifflin, 1895.

———. *The Vision of Sir Launfal*. Cambridge: George Nichols, 1848.

Lupack, Alan. "Acting Out an Old Story: Twentieth-Century Tristan Plays." In *Popular Arthurian Traditions*. Ed. Sally K. Slocum. Bowling Green: Bowling Green State University Popular Press, 1992. 162–72.

———. "American Arthurian Authors: A Declaration of Independence." In *The Arthurian Revival: Essays on Form, Tradition, and Transformation*. Ed. Debra N. Mancoff. New York: Garland, 1992. 155–73.

———. "The Americanization of Merlin." *Avalon to Camelot* 2.4 (1987): 13–16.

———. "The Arthurian Legend in America: A Moderated Discussion on 'Arthurnet.' " *Arthuriana* 4 (Winter 1994): 291–97.

———. "Beyond the Model: Howard Pyle's Arthurian Books." *The Arthurian Yearbook* 1 (1991): 215–34.

———. "An Enemy in Our Midst: *The Black Knight* and the American Dream." In *Cinema Arthuriana: Essays on Arthurian Film*. Ed. Kevin J. Harty. New York: Garland, 1991. 29–39.

———. "The Merlin Allusions in *Billy Budd*." *Studies in Short Fiction* 19 (Summer 1982): 277–78.

———. "Merlin in America." *Arthurian Interpretations* 1.1 (Fall 1986): 64–74.

———. "Modern Arthurian Novelists on the Arthurian Legend." *Studies in Medievalism* 2.4 (Fall 1983): 79–88.

Lupack, Barbara Tepa. "F. Scott Fitzgerald's 'Following of a Grail.' " *Arthuriana* 4 (Winter 1994): 324–47.

———. *Insanity as Redemption in Contemporary American Fiction: Inmates Running the Asylum*. Gainesville: University Press of Florida, 1995.

————. *Plays of Passion, Games of Chance: Jerzy Kosinski and His Fiction*. Bristol, IN: Wyndham Hall Press/Rhodes-Fulbright International Library, 1988.

Lynn, Kenneth S. *Hemingway*. New York: Simon and Schuster, 1987.

Macdonald, Allan Houston. *Richard Hovey: Man & Craftsman*. Durham, NC: Duke University Press, 1957.

MacGregor, Rob. *Indiana Jones and the Dance of the Giants*. New York: Bantam Books, 1991.

————. *Indiana Jones and the Last Crusade*. Adapted from the screenplay by Jeffrey Boam. Based on a story by George Lucas and Menno Meyjes. New York: Ballantine Books, 1989.

MacRae, Suzanne H. "Berger's Mythical *Arthur Rex*." In *Popular Arthurian Traditions*. Ed. Sally K. Slocum. Bowling Green: Bowling Green State University Popular Press, 1992. 85–95.

Mailer, Norman. *An American Dream*. New York: Dial Press, 1965.

————. *Barbary Shore*. New York: Rinehart, 1951.

————. *Tough Guys Don't Dance*. New York: Random House, 1984.

Malamud, Bernard. *The Assistant*. New York: Farrar, Straus & Giroux, 1957.

————. *The Fixer*. New York: Farrar, Straus & Giroux, 1966.

————. *The Natural*. New York: Farrar, Straus & Giroux, 1952.

————. *A New Life*. New York: Farrar, Straus, and Cudahy, 1961.

Malin, Irving, ed. *Saul Bellow and the Critics*. New York: New York University Press, 1969.

Malone, Michael. "Berger, Burlesque, and the Yearning for Comedy." *Studies in American Humor* 2 (Spring 1983): 20–32.

Malory, Sir Thomas. *The Works of Sir Thomas Malory*. 3 vols. Ed. Eugène Vinaver. 2nd ed.; Oxford: Clarendon Press, 1967.

Mancoff, Debra. *The Arthurian Revival in Victorian Art*. New York: Garland, 1990.

Mandel, Jerome. "The Grotesque Rose: Medieval Romance and *The Great Gatsby*." *Modern Fiction Studies*, 34 (1988): 541–58.

Manso, Peter. *Mailer: His Life and Times*. New York: Simon and Schuster, 1985.

Marovitz, Sabfird E. "The Cryptic Raillery of 'Saint Katy the Virgin.'" In *A Study Guide to Steinbeck's The Long Valley*. Ed. Tetsumaro Hayashi. Ann Arbor: The Pierian Press, 1976. 73–80.

Marquis, Don. *Out of the Sea: A Play in Four Acts*. Garden City, NY: Doubleday, Page and Co., 1927.

————. *Sonnets to a Red-Haired Lady and Famous Love Affairs*. Drawings by Stuart Hay. Garden City, NY: Doubleday, Doran and Co., 1929. (Contains the poems "Tristram and Isolt" and "Lancelot and Guinevere.")

Marshall, Edison. *The Pagan King*. Garden City, NY: Doubleday, 1959.

Mason, Bobbie Ann. *In Country*. New York: Harper & Row, 1985.

————. *Shiloh and Other Stories*. New York: Harper & Row, 1982.

Mathews, Basil. *The Splendid Quest: Stories of Knights on the Pilgrims' Way*. Cleveland: The World Syndicate Publishing Co., 1929.

Maynadier, Howard. *The Arthur of the English Poets*. 1907; rpt. New York: Haskell House, 1966.

McElrath, Joseph R., Jr. "Mark Twain's America and the Protestant Work Ethic." *The CEA Critic* 36.3 (March 1974): 42–43.

McGowen, Tom. *Sir MacHinery*. Chicago: Follett Publishing Co., 1970.

Meaney, Dee Morrison. *Iseult*. New York: Ace, 1985.

Mellard, James M. "Four Version of Pastoral." In *Bernard Malamud and the Critics*. Ed. Leslie A. Field and Joyce W. Field. New York: New York University Press, 1970. 67–83.

Melling, Philip H. *Vietnam in American Literature*. Boston: G. K. Hall, 1990.

Merriman, James Douglas. *The Flower of Kings: A Study of the Arthurian Legend in England Between 1485 and 1835*. Lawrence: University Press of Kansas, 1973.

Meyers, Jeffrey. *Hemingway: A Biography*. New York: Harper and Row, 1985.

———. *Scott Fitzgerald: A Biography*. New York: HarperCollins, 1994.

Michaels, Philip. *Grail*. New York: Avon, 1982.

Milford, Nancy. *Zelda: A Biography*. New York: Harper & Row, 1970.

Miller, Linda Patterson. "Brett Ashley: The Beauty of It All." In *Critical Essays on The Sun Also Rises*. Ed. James Nagel. Boston: G. K. Hall & Co., 1995. 170–84.

Miller, Robert Keith. *Mark Twain*. New York: Frederick Ungar, 1983.

Mitchell, Robin C. "Steinbeck and Malory: A Correspondence with Eugène Vinaver." *Steinbeck Quarterly* 10 (Summer–Fall 1977): 70–79.

Mizener, Arthur. "*The Sun Also Rises*." In Arthur Mizener. *Twelve Great American Novels*. New York: World, 1969. 120–41.

Moddelmog, Debra A. "The Unifying Consciousness of a Divided Conscience: Nick Adams as Author of *In Our Time*." *American Literature* 60.4 (Dec. 1988): 591–610.

Molesworth, Charles. *Donald Barthelme's Fiction: The Ironist Saved from Drowning*. Columbia: University of Missouri Press, 1982.

———. "The Nasciemento Effect and Barthelme's *The King*." *The Review of Contemporary Fiction* 11.2 (1991): 102–07.

Monaco, Richard. *Blood and Dreams*. New York: Berkley, 1985.

———. *Broken Stone*. New York: Ace, 1985.

———. *The Final Quest*. New York: Putnam's, 1980.

———. *The Grail War*. Ill. David McCall Johnston. New York: Wallaby, 1979.

———. *Parsival or a Knight's Tale*. Ill. David McCall Johnston. New York: Macmillan, 1977.

———. *Runes*. New York: Ace, 1984.

Monroe, William. "Performing Persons: A Locus of Connection for Medicine and Literature." In *The Body and the Text: Comparative Essays in Literature and Medicine*. Ed. Bruce Clarke and Wendell Ayacock. Lubbock: Texas Tech University Press, 1990. 25–40.

Moorman, Charles. *Arthurian Triptych: Mythic Materials in Charles Williams, C. S. Lewis, and T. S. Eliot*. Berkeley: University of California Press, 1960.

Moreland, Kim. *The Medievalist Impulse in American Literature: Twain, Adams, Fitzgerald, and Hemingway*. Charlottesville: University Press of Virginia, 1996.

Morgan, Elizabeth. "Gatsby in the Garden: Courtly Love and Irony." *College Literature* 11 (1984): 163–77.

Morris, Robert K., ed., with Irving Malin. *The Achievement of William Styron*. Rev. ed. Athens: University of Georgia Press, 1981.

Morrissey, Thomas J. "Mason's *In Country*." *Explicator* 50.1 (Fall 1991): 62–64.

Morrison, Gail Moore. " 'Time, Tide, and Twilight': *Mayday* and Faulkner's Quest Toward *The Sound and the Fury*." *The Mississippi Quarterly* 31 (1978): 337–57.

Morse, Donald E., Marshall B. Tymn, and Csilla Bertha, eds. *The Celebration of the*

Fantastic: Selected Papers from the Tenth Anniversary International Conference on the Fantastic in the Arts. Westport, CT: Greenwood Press, 1989.

Munn, H. Warner. *King of the World's Edge.* New York: Ace, (1966). (1st book ed.; appeared earlier in *Weird Tales*, 34, nos. 3–6, Sept.–Dec. 1939.)

———. *Merlin's Godson.* New York: Ballantine, 1976. (Combines *King of the World's Edge* and *The Ship from Atlantis.*)

———. *Merlin's Ring.* Intro. Lin Carter. New York: Ballantine, 1974.

———. *The Ship from Atlantis.* New York: Ace, 1967.

Murphy, George D. "Hemingway's *Waste Land*: The Controlling Water Symbolism of *The Sun Also Rises.*" *Hemingway Notes* 1.1 (Spring 1971): 20–26.

Myers, John Myers. *Silverlock.* New York: Ace, 1949.

———. *The Moon's Fire-Eating Daughter.* Virginia Beach, VA: Denning, 1981.

Nagel, James, ed. *Critical Essays on The Sun Also Rises.* Boston: G. K. Hall & Co., 1995.

Nathan, Robert. *The Elixir.* New York: Alfred A. Knopf, 1971.

———. *The Fair.* New York: Alfred A. Knopf, 1964.

———. *Sir Henry.* New York: Alfred A. Knopf, 1955.

Neff, Emery. *Edwin Arlington Robinson.* N.p.: William Sloane Associates, 1948.

Nennius. *British History and The Welsh Annals.* Ed. and trans. John Morris. London: Phillimore, 1980.

The New Arthurian Encyclopedia. Ed. Norris J. Lacy et al. New York: Garland, 1991.

The New Woman and Her Sisters: Feminism and Theatre 1850–1914. Ed. Vivien Gardner and Susan Rutherford. Ann Arbor: The University of Michigan Press, 1992.

Newman, Paul B. "Hemingway's Grail Quest." *The University of Kansas Review* 28.4 (June 1962): 295–303.

Newman, Robert. *Merlin's Mistake.* New York: Atheneum, 1970.

———. *The Testing of Tertius.* New York: Atheneum, 1973.

Newman, Sharan. *The Chessboard Queen.* New York: St. Martin's, 1983.

———. *Guinevere.* New York: St. Martin's, 1981.

———. *Guinevere Evermore.* New York: St. Martin's, 1985.

Nitze, William Albert. *Arthurian Romance and Modern Poetry and Music.* Chicago: University of Chicago Press, 1940.

Noble, Donald R., ed. *Hemingway: A Revaluation.* Troy, NY: Whitston Publishing Co., 1983.

Norton, Andre. *Merlin's Mirror.* New York: Daw, 1975.

———. *Dragon Magic.* New York: Ace, 1973.

———. *Huon of the Horn, Being a Tale of That Duke of Bordeaus Who Came to Sorrow at the Hand of Charlemagne and Yet Won the Favor of Oberon, the Elf King, to His Lasting Fame and Great Glory.* New York: Harcourt, Brace, 1951.

———. Letter to Alan Lupack. 31 Dec. 1980.

———. *Steel Magic.* Ill. Robin Jacques. Cleveland: World Publishing Co., 1965.

———. *Witch World.* New York: Ace Books, 1963.

O'Brien, William James. "Walker Percy's *Lancelot*: A Beatrician Visit to the Region of the Dead." *Southern Humanities Review* 15 (1981): 153–64.

Olderman, Raymond M. *Beyond the Waste Land: A Study of the American Novel in the Nineteen-Sixties.* New Haven: Yale University Press, 1977.

Oliver, Nancy S. "New Manifest Destiny in *A Connecticut Yankee in King Arthur's Court.*" *Mark Twain Journal* 21.4 (Fall 1983): 28–32.

Ornstein, Robert. "Scott Fitzgerald's Fable of East and West." *College English* 18 (1956): 139–43. Rpt. in Eble 60–66.

O'Shaughnessey, Margaret. "Edwin Austin Abbey's Reinterpretation of the Grail Quest: The Boston Public Library Murals." *Arthuriana* 4 (Winter 1994): 298–312.

Owens, Louis. "Camelot East of Eden: John Steinbeck's *Tortilla Flat*." *Arizona Quarterly* 38.3 (Autumn 1982): 203–16.

Parker, Dorothy. *Death and Taxes*. New York: Viking, 1931. (Contains the poems "Iseult of Brittany" and "Guinevere at Her Fireside.")

Parker Brothers. *90 Years of Fun 1883–1973: The History of Parker Brothers*. N.p.: n.p., 1973.

Parry, John J., and Robert O. Caldwell. "Geoffrey of Monmouth." In *Arthurian Literature in the Middle Ages: A Collaborative History*. Ed. Roger Sherman Loomis. Oxford: Oxford University Press, 1959. 72–93.

The Passing of Arthur: New Essays in Arthurian Tradition. Ed. Christopher Baswell and William Sharpe. New York: Garland, 1988.

Paterson, Katherine. *Park's Quest*. New York: Lodestar Books / E. P. Dutton, 1988.

Patteson, Richard F., ed. *Critical Essays on Donald Barthelme*. New York: G. K. Hall, 1992.

Paxson, Diana L. "The God-Sword." In *Excalibur*. Ed. Richard Gilliam, Martin H. Greenberg, and Edward E. Kramer. New York: Warner Books, 1995. 3–28.

———. "The Feast of the Fisher King: A Masque in Verse (with narrative inclusions)." In *Grails: Quests, Visitations, and Other Occurrences*. Ed. Richard Gilliam, Martin H. Greenburg, and Edward E. Kramer. Atlanta: Unnameable, 1992. Rpt. as *Grails: Quests of the Dawn*. New York: ROC / Penguin, 1994. 36–59.

———. *The White Raven*. New York: William Morrow, 1988.

Peare, Catherine Owens. *Melor, King Arthur's Page*. New York: Putnam's, 1963.

Percy, Thomas. *Reliques of Ancient English Poetry: Consisting of Old Heroic Ballads, Songs, and Other Pieces of Our Earlier Poets; Together with Some Few of a Later Date*. 2 vols. Ed. J. V. Prichard. London: George Bell and Sons, 1876.

Percy, Walker. *Lancelot*. New York: Farrar, Straus & Giroux, 1977.

———. *The Last Gentleman*. New York: Farrar, Straus & Giroux, 1966.

———. Letter to Alan Lupack. Undated.

———. Letter to Alan Lupack. 14 Feb. 1987.

———. *Love In the Ruins*. New York: Farrar, Straus & Giroux, 1971.

———. *The Moviegoer*. 1961. New York: Knopf, 1973.

———. "Questions They Never Asked Me (So He Asked Them Himself)." In *Critical Essays on Walker Percy*. Ed. J. Donald Crowley and Sue Mitchell Crowley. Boston: G. K. Hall, 1989. 73–91.

———. *The Second Coming*. New York: Farrar, Straus & Giroux, 1980.

———. *The Thanatos Syndrome*. New York: Farrar, Straus & Giroux, 1987.

Percy, William Alexander. *Enzio's Kingdom and Other Poems*. New Haven: Yale University Press, 1924.

Perosa, Sergio. *The Art of F. Scott Fitzgerald*. Trans. Charles Matz and the author. Ann Arbor: University of Michigan Press, 1965.

Perrine, Laurence. "The Sources of Robinson's *Merlin*." *American Literature* 44 (1972–73): 313–21.

Peters, Elizabeth [pseudonym of Barbara Gross Mertz]. *The Camelot Caper*. New York: Meredith Press, 1969.

Peterson, Richard F. "The Grail Legend and Steinbeck's 'The Great Mountain.' " In *A Study Guide to Steinbeck's The Long Valley*. Ed. Tetsumaro Hayashi. Ann Arbor, MI: The Pierian Press, 1976. 89–96.

Phelps, Elizabeth Stuart. "Afterward." *Independent* 32 (22 July 1880): 1. (Reprinted in *Songs of the Silent World* 59–63 as "Guinevere.")

———. *Beyond the Gates*. Boston: Houghton Mifflin, 1883.

———. *Chapters from a Life*. Boston: Houghton Mifflin, 1897.

———. "The Christmas of Sir Galahad." *Independent* 23 (7 Dec. 1871): 1.

———. "Elaine and Elaine." *Independent* 35 (7 June 1883): 35. (Reprinted in *Songs of the Silent World* 77–78.)

———. *The Gates Ajar*. Ed. Helen Sootin Smith. 1869; rpt. Cambridge, MA: The Belknap Press of Harvard University Press, 1964.

———. "The Lady of Shalott." *Independent* 23 (6 July 1871): 1. (Reprinted in *Sealed Orders* 48–64.)

———. "The New Knighthood." *Independent* 25 (3 April 1873): 417–18.

———. "The Royal Test." *Youth's Companion* 66 (31 Aug. 1893): 424.

———. *Sealed Orders*. 1879; rpt. New York: Garret Press, 1969.

———. *Songs of the Silent World*. Boston: Houghton Mifflin, 1891.

———. "The Terrible Test." *Sunday Afternoon* 1 (Jan. 1878): 49. (Reprinted in *Songs of the Silent World* 92–93.)

———. "The True Story of Guenever." *Independent* 28 (15 June 1876): 2–4. (Reprinted in *Sealed Orders* 65–80.)

———. *Within the Gates*. Boston: Houghton Mifflin, 1901.

Pifer, Ellen. "Malamud's Unnatural *The Natural*." *Studies in American Jewish Literature*. 7.2 (Fall 1988): 138–52.

Pilkington, John. *Stark Young*. Boston: Twayne, 1985.

Pinion, F. B. *A T. S. Eliot Companion*. London: Macmillan, 1986.

Piper, Henry Dan. *F. Scott Fitzgerald: A Critical Portrait*. New York: Holt, Rinehart and Winston, 1965.

Pipkin, E. Edith. "The Arthur of Edwin Arlington Robinson." *English Journal* 19 (March 1930): 183–95. Rpt. in *Appreciation of Edwin Arlington Robinson: 28 Interpretive Essays*. Ed. Richard Cary. Waterville, ME: Colby College Press, 1969. 6–16.

Pitz, Henry C. *Howard Pyle: Writer, Illustrator, Founder of the Brandywine School*. New York: C. N. Potter, 1975.

Pivar, David J. *Purity Crusade, Sexual Morality and Social Control, 1868–1900*. Westport, CT: Greenwood Press, 1973.

Porter, M. Gilbert. *The Art of Grit: Ken Kesey's Fiction*. Columbia: University of Missouri Press, 1982.

Powell, Perry Edwards. *The Knights of the Holy Grail: A Solution of the Boy Problem*. Cincinnati: Press of Jennings & Graham, 1906.

Poulson, Christine. "Arthurian Legend in Fine and Applied Art of the Nineteenth and Early Twentieth Centuries: A Catalogue of Artists." *Arthurian Literature* 9 (1989): 81–142.

Pratt, John C., ed. *One Flew Over the Cuckoo's Nest: Text and Criticism*. New York: Viking, 1983.

Pressman, Richard S. "A Connecticut Yankee in Merlin's Cave: The Role of Contradiction in Mark Twain's Novel." *American Literary Realism* 16.1 (Spring 1983): 58–72.

Prindle, Dennis. "The Pretexts of Romance: Steinbeck's Allegorical Naturalism from *Cup of Gold* to *Tortilla Flat.*" In *The Steinbeck Question: New Essays in Criticism.* Ed. Donald R. Noble. Troy, NY: The Whitston Publishing Co., 1993. 23–36.

Probert, K. G. "Nick Carraway and the Romance of Art." *English Studies in Canada* 10.2 (June 1984): 188–208.

Prophet, Elizabeth Clare (Purported Recorder for Archangel Gabriel). *Mysteries of the Holy Grail.* Recorded by Elizabeth Clare Prophet. Los Angeles: Summit University Press, 1985.

Puzo, Mario. *Fools Die.* New York: Putnam, 1978.

Pyle, Howard. *The Story of King Arthur and His Knights.* New York: Charles Scribner's Sons, 1903.

———. *The Story of Sir Launcelot and His Companions.* New York: Charles Scribner's Sons, 1907.

———. *The Story of the Champions of the Round Table.* New York: Charles Scribner's Sons, 1905.

———. *The Story of the Grail and the Passing of Arthur.* New York: Charles Scribner's Sons, 1910.

Randall, Neil. *Storm of Dust: A Crossroads Adventure in the World of David Drake's Dragon Lord.* New York: Tor / A Tom Doherty Associates Book, 1987.

Ratner, Marc L. "Style and Humanity in Malamud's Fiction." *Massachusetts Review* 5 (Summer 1964): 663–83.

Reynolds, Michael S. "False Dawn: A Preliminary Analysis of *The Sun Also Rises'* Manuscript." In *Hemingway: A Revaluation.* Ed. Donald R. Noble. Troy, NY: Whitston Publishing Co., 1983. 115–34.

———. *Hemingway: The Paris Years.* Oxford: B. Blackwell, 1989.

———. *Hemingway's Reading, 1901–1940: An Inventory.* Princeton: Princeton University Press, 1981.

———. "Signs, Motifs, and Themes in *The Sun Also Rises.*" In *Critical Essays on The Sun Also Rises.* Ed. James Nagel. Boston: G. K. Hall & Co., 1995. 146–60.

———. *The Sun Also Rises: A Novel of the Twenties. A Student's Companion to the Novel.* Boston: Twayne, 1988.

Richman, Sidney. *Bernard Malamud.* New York: Twayne, 1966.

Roberts, Dorothy James. *The Enchanted Cup.* New York: Appleton-Century-Crofts, 1953.

———. *Kinsmen of the Grail.* Boston: Little, Brown and Co., 1963.

———. *Launcelot, My Brother.* New York: Appleton-Century-Crofts, 1954.

Robinson, Edwin Arlington. *Edwin Arlington Robinson's Letters to Edith Brower.* Ed. Richard Cary. Cambridge, MA: The Belknap Press of Harvard University, 1968.

———. *Lancelot: A Poem.* New York: Thomas Seltzer, 1920.

———. *Merlin: A Poem.* New York: Macmillan, 1917.

———. *Modred: A Fragment.* New York, New Haven, Princeton: Edmond Byrne Hackett, The Brick Row Bookshop, 1929. (Limited to 250 copies signed by Robinson.) (A fragment deleted from Robinson's *Lancelot* and published for the first time in this edition.)

———. *Selected Letters of Edwin Arlington Robinson.* New York: Macmillan, 1940.

———. *Tristram.* New York: Macmillan, 1927.

Rohrkemper, John, and Karen L. Gutmann. "The Search for Control: Eliot, Hemingway, and *In Our Time*." *Midamerica* 15 (1988): 59–71.

Rollyson, Carl. *The Lives of Norman Mailer: A Biography*. New York: Paragon House, 1991.

Romano, John. "Camelot and All That." *New York Times Book Review* 12 Nov. 1978: 62.

Rosenberg, John D. "Tennyson and the Passing of Arthur." In *The Passing of Arthur: New Essays in Arthurian Tradition*. Ed. Christopher Baswell and William Sharpe. New York: Garland, 1988. 221–34.

Rothert, Otto A. *The Story of a Poet: Madison Cawein. His Intimate Life as Revealed by His Letters and Other Hitherto Unpublished Material, Including Reminiscences by His Closest Associates; also Articles from Newspapers and Magazines, and a List of His Poems*. Filson Club Publications No. 30. Louisville, KY: John P. Morton & Co., 1921.

Rudd, Jay. "Thomas Berger's *Arthur Rex*: Galahad and Earthly Power." *Critique: Studies in Modern Fiction* 25.2 (Winter 1984): 92–100.

Ruderman, Judith. *William Styron*. New York: Ungar, 1987.

Ryan, Barbara T. "Decentered Authority in Bobbie Ann Mason's *In Country*." *Critique* 31.3 (Spring 1990): 199–212.

Saberhagen, Fred. *Dominion*. New York: TOR, 1982.

———. *Merlin's Bones*. New York: TOR, 1995.

St. John, Nicole. *Guinever's Gift*. New York: Random House, 1977.

———. Letter to Alan Lupack. 18 Dec. 1980.

Salda, Michael N. "William Faulkner's Arthurian Tale: *Mayday*." *Arthuriana* 4 (Winter 1994): 348–75.

Samway, Patrick. "Another Case of the Purloined Letter (in Walker Percy's *Lancelot*)." *New Orleans Review* 16.4 (1989): 37–44.

San Souci, Robert D. *Young Arthur*. Ill. Jamichael Henterly. New York: Doubleday, 1997.

———. *Young Guinevere*. Ill. Jamichael Henterly. New York: Doubleday, 1993.

———. *Young Lancelot*. Ill. Jamichael Henterly. New York: Doubleday, 1996.

———. *Young Lancelot*. Ill. Daniel Horne. New York: Doubleday, 1990.

Sapir, Richard Ben. *Quest*. New York: E. P. Dutton, 1987.

Sayre, Nora. *Running Time: Films of the Cold War*. New York: Dial, 1982.

Schatt, Stanley. *Kurt Vonnegut, Jr*. Boston: Twayne, 1976.

Schictman, Martin B. "Whom Does the Grail Serve? Wagner, Spielberg, and the Issue of Jewish Appropriation." In *The Arthurian Revival: Essays on Form, Tradition, and Transformation*. Ed. Debra N. Mancoff. New York: Garland, 1992. 283–97.

Schmidt, Susan. "Ecological Renewal Images in 'Big, Two-Hearted River': Jack Pines and Fisher King." *The Hemingway Review* 9.2 (Spring 1990): 142–44.

Schulz, Max F. *Black Humor Fiction of the Sixties: A Pluralistic Definition of Man and His World*. Athens: Ohio University Press, 1973.

———. "Mythic Proletarians." In *Bernard Malamud and the Critics*. Ed. Leslie A. Field and Joyce W. Field. New York: New York University Press, 1970. 185–95.

Scieszka, Jon. *Knights of the Kitchen Table: The Time Warp Trio*. Ill. Lane Smith. New York: Viking, 1991.

Scott, Robert Ian. "The *Waste Land* Eliot Didn't Write." *Times Literary Supplement* 8 Dec. 1995: 14.

Service, Pamela F. *Tomorrow's Magic*. New York: Atheneum, 1987.

———. *Winter of Magic's Return*. New York: Atheneum, 1985.

———. *Wizard of Wind and Rock*. Ill. Laura Marshall. New York: Atheneum, 1990.

Seton, Anya. *Avalon*. Boston: Houghton Mifflin, 1965.

Sharpe, Ruth Collier. *Tristram of Lyonesse: The Story of an Immortal Love*. New York: Greenberg, 1949.

Silverman, Kaja. "Dis-Embodying the Female Voice." In Mary Ann Doane, Patricia Mellencamp, and Linda Williams, eds. *Re-vision: Essays in Feminist Film Criticism*. Frederick, MD: University Publications of America / The American Film Institute Monograph Series, 1984. 131–49.

Simmonds, Roy S. "A Note on Steinbeck's Unpublished Arthurian Stories." In *Steinbeck and the Arthurian Theme*. Ed. Tetsumaro Hayashi. Steinbeck Monograph Series No. 5. Muncie, IN: The John Steinbeck Society of America, Ball State University, 1975. 25–29.

———. "The Unrealized Dream: Steinbeck's Modern Version of Malory." In *Steinbeck and the Arthurian Theme*. Ed. Tetsumaro Hayashi. Steinbeck Monograph Series No. 5. Muncie, IN: The John Steinbeck Society of America, Ball State University, 1975. 30–43.

Simpson, Roger. *Camelot Regained: The Arthurian Revival and Tennyson 1800–1849*. Cambridge: D. S. Brewer, 1990.

Sirlin, Rhoda. *William Styron's Sophie's Choice: Crime and Self-Punishment*. Ann Arbor: UMI Research Press, 1990.

Sklar, Elizabeth S. "Thoroughly Modern Morgan: Morgan le Fey in Twentieth-Century Popular Arthuriana." In *Popular Arthurian Traditions*. Ed. Sally K. Slocum. Bowling Green: Bowling Green State University Popular Press, 1992. 24–35.

Sklar, Robert. *F. Scott Fitzgerald: The Last Laocoön*. New York: Oxford University Press, 1967.

Slocum, Sally K., ed. *Popular Arthurian Traditions*. Bowling Green: Bowling Green State University Popular Press, 1992.

———. "Waxing Arthurian: *The Lyre of Orpheus* and *Cold Sassy Tree*." In *Popular Arthurian Traditions*. Ed. Sally K. Slocum. Bowling Green: Bowling Green State University Popular Press, 1992. 96–103.

Smith, George Henry. *Druid's World*. New York: Avalon Books, 1967.

Smith, Grover. *T. S. Eliot's Poetry and Plays: A Study in Sources and Meaning*. 1956; 2nd ed. Chicago: The University of Chicago Press, 1974.

Smith, Henry Nash. *Mark Twain's Fable of Progress: Political and Economic Ideas in "A Connecticut Yankee."* New Brunswick: Rutgers University Press, 1964.

Smith, L. J. *Heart of Valor*. New York: Macmillan, 1990.

———. *The Night of the Solstice*. New York: Macmillan, 1987.

Smith, Rosamond [pseudonym of Joyce Carol Oates]. *You Can't Catch Me*. New York: Dutton, 1995.

Smith, Scottie Fitzgerald. "The Colonial Ancestors of Francis Scott Key Fitzgerald." In *Some Sort of Epic Grandeur: The Life of F. Scott Fitzgerald*. Ed. Matthew J. Bruccoli. New York: Harcourt Brace Jovanovich, 1981. 496–509.

Sobol, Donald J. *Greta the Strong*. Chicago: Follett, 1970.

Spilka, Mark. "The Death of Love in *The Sun Also Rises*." In *Hemingway: A Collection of Critical Essays*. Ed. Robert P. Weeks. 1962; Englewood Cliffs: Prentice-Hall, 1965. 127–38.

Spivack, Charlotte. *Merlin's Daughters: Contemporary Women Writers of Fantasy*. Westport, CT: Greenwood Press, 1987.

———. "Morgan Le Fay: Goddess or Witch?" In *Popular Arthurian Traditions*. Ed. Sally K. Slocum. Bowling Green: Bowling Green State University Popular Press, 1992. 18–23.

Stang, Jo Anne. *Shadows on the Sceptered Isle*. New York: Crown, 1980.

Starke, Aubrey Harrison. *Sidney Lanier: A Biographical and Critical Study*. Chapel Hill: University of North Carolina Press, 1933.

Starr, Nathan Comfort. "Edwin Arlington Robinson's Arthurian Heroines: Vivian, Guinevere and the Two Isolts." *Philological Quarterly* 56 (1977): 231–49.

———. *King Arthur Today: The Arthurian Legend in English and American Literature, 1901–1953*. Gainesville: University of Florida Press, 1954.

———. "The Transformation of Merlin." In *Edwin Arlington Robinson Centenary Essays*. Ed. Ellsworth Barnard. Athens: University of Georgia Press, 1969. 106–19.

Stauffer, Donald Barlow. *A Short History of American Poetry*. New York: E. P. Dutton, 1974.

Steinbeck, John. *The Acts of King Arthur and His Noble Knights*. Ed. Chase Horton. New York: Ballantine / Del Rey, 1977. (Originally published in 1976 by Farrar, Straus and Giroux.)

———. *Cup of Gold: A Life of Sir Henry Morgan, Buccaneer, with Occasional Reference to History*. New York: Covici Friede, 1936.

———. *In Dubious Battle*. New York: Sun Dial Press, 1940.

———. *Steinbeck: A Life in Letters*. Ed. Elaine Steinbeck and Robert Wallsten. New York: Viking, 1975.

———. *Tortilla Flat*. New York: Grosset & Dunlap, 1935.

———. *The Winter of Our Discontent*. New York: Viking, 1961.

Steinkrauss, Carol, Public Relations Manager, Parker Brothers. Letter to Barbara Tepa Lupack. 24 Jan. 1994.

Stern, Milton R. *The Golden Moment: The Novels of F. Scott Fitzgerald*. Urbana: University of Illinois Press, 1970.

Stillwell, Richard. *The Chapel of Princeton University*. Princeton, NJ: Princeton University Press, 1971.

Stone, Eugenia. *Page Boy for King Arthur*. Ill. Rafaello Busoni. Chicago: Wilcox and Follett, 1949.

———. *Squire for King Arthur*. Ill. Rafaello Busoni. Chicago: Follett Publishing Co., 1955.

Stoneback, H. R. "Hemingway and Faulkner on the Road to Roncevaux." In Noble, Donald R., ed. *Hemingway: A Revaluation*. Troy, NY: Whitston Publishing Co., 1983. 135–63.

Strauss, Victoria. *Worldstone*. New York: Macmillan, 1985.

Strychacz, Thomas. "Dramatizations of Manhood in Hemingway's *In Our Time* and *The Sun Also Rises*." *American Literature* 61.2 (May 1989): 245–60.

Sturgeon, Theodore. "Excalibur and the Atom." *Fantastic Adventures* (Aug. 1951): 8–51.

Styron, William. *The Confessions of Nat Turner*. New York: Random House, 1967.

———. *Lie Down in Darkness*. Indianapolis: Bobbs-Merrill, 1951.

———. *Set This House on Fire*. New York: Random House, 1960.

————. *Sophie's Choice*. New York: Bantam, 1980.

————. *A Tidewater Morning: Three Tales from Youth*. New York: Random House, 1980.

Sundermeier, Michael. "Why Steinbeck Didn't Finish His *Arthur – The Acts of King Arthur and His Noble Knights* (1976)." In *Steinbeck's Posthumous Work: Essays in Criticism*. Ed. Tetsumaro Hayashi and Thomas J. Moore. Steinbeck Monograph Series No. 14. Muncie, IN: The Steinbeck Research Institute, Ball State University, 1989. 34–42.

Sylvester, Bickford. "Hemingway's Extended Vision: *The Old Man and the Sea*." *Publications of the Modern Language Association* 81.1 (March 1966): 130–38.

Talbot, Hudson. *Excalibur*. New York: Morrow, 1996.

————. *King Arthur and the Round Table*. New York: Morrow, 1995.

————. *King Arthur: The Sword in the Stone*. New York: Morrow, 1991.

Tarkington, Booth. *Penrod*. Garden City, NY: Doubleday, Page & Co., 1914.

Taylor, Beverly, and Elisabeth Brewer. *The Return of King Arthur: British and American Arthurian Literature since 1800*. Cambridge: D. S. Brewer, 1983.

Teasdale, Sara. "Guenevere." In *Helen of Troy and Other Poems*. New York: Macmillan, 1911. 27–29.

Telotte, J. P. "A Symbolic Structure for Walker Percy's Fiction." In J. Donald Crowley and Sue Mitchell Crowley, eds. *Critical Essays on Walker Percy*. Boston: G. K. Hall, 1989. 171–84.

Tennyson, Alfred, Lord. *Idylls of the King and a Selection of Poems*. Ed. George Barker. New York: Signet, 1961.

Thompson, Raymond H. "The First and Last Love: Morgan le Fay and Arthur." In *The Arthurian Revival: Essays on Form, Tradition, and Transformation*. Ed. Debra N. Mancoff. New York: Garland, 1992. 230–47.

————. "Humor and Irony in Modern Arthurian Fantasy: Thomas Berger's *Arthur Rex*." *Kansas Quarterly* 16.3 (Summer 1984): 45–49.

————. "Morgause of Orkney, Queen of Air and Darkness." *Quondam et Futurus: A Journal of Arthurian Interpretations* 1.3 (Spring 1993): 1–13.

————. *The Return from Avalon: A Study of the Arthurian Legend in Modern Fiction*. Westport, CT: Greenwood Press, 1985.

"370,000 in Child Clubs." *New York Times* 14 Feb. 1934: 24:2.

Tichi, Cecelia. "Women Writers and the New Woman." In *Columbia Literary History of the United States*. Ed. Emory Elliott et al. New York: Columbia University Press, 1988. 589–606.

Ticknor, Frank O. *The Poems of Frank O. Ticknor, M.D.* Ed. K. M. R.. With an Introductory Notice of the Author by Paul H. Hayne. Philadelphia: J. P. Lippincott, 1879.

Tillyard, E. M. W. *The Elizabethan World Picture*. London: Chatto & Windus, 1943.

Timmerman, John H. *John Steinbeck's Fiction: The Aesthetics of the Road Taken*. Norman: University of Oklahoma Press, 1986.

Tobin, Lee Ann. "Why Change the Arthur Story? Marion Zimmer Bradley's *The Mists of Avalon*." *Extrapolation* 34.2 (Summer 1993): 147–57.

Trask, Diana. *Under King Constantine*. 2nd ed.; New York: Anson D. F. Randolph and Co., 1893.

Tsuboi, Kiyohiko. "Steinbeck's *Cup of Gold* and Fitzgerald's *The Great Gatsby*." In *John Steinbeck: East and West: Proceedings of the First International Steinbeck*

Congress Held at Kyushu University, Fukuoka City, Japan in August, 1976. Ed. Tetsumaro Hayashi, Yasuo Hashiguchi, and Richard F. Peterson. Steinbeck Monograph Series, No. 8. 1978; rpt. Millwood, NY: Kraus Reprint, 1980. 40–47.

Tuck, Dorothy. *Crowell's Handbook of Faulkner*. New York: Thomas Y. Crowell Company, 1964.

Turnbull, Andrew. *Scott Fitzgerald*. New York: Charles Scribner's Sons, 1962.

Turner, Frederick W., III. "Myth Inside and Out: *The Natural*." *Novel: A Forum on Fiction* 1.1 (Fall 1967): 133–39. Rpt. in *Bernard Malamud and the Critics*. Ed. Leslie A. Field and Joyce W. Field. New York: New York University Press, 1970. 109–119.

Twain, Mark. "A Connecticut Yankee in King Arthur's Court." *The Century Illustrated Magazine* Nov. 1889: 74–83.

———. *A Connecticut Yankee in King Arthur's Court*. New York: Charles L. Webster, 1889.

———. *A Connecticut Yankee in King Arthur's Court*. With an Afterword by Edmund Reiss. New York: Signet / New American Library, n.d.

———. *Mark Twain's Notebooks & Journals*. Vol. 3 (1883–1891). Ed. Robert Pack Browning, Michael B. Frank, and Lin Salamo. Berkeley: University of California Press, 1979.

Updike, John. *The Afterlife and Other Stories*. New York: Alfred A. Knopf, 1994. (Contains the story "Tristan and Iseult.")

———. *Brazil*. New York: Alfred A. Knopf, 1994.

———. *The Music School: Short Stories*. New York: Alfred A. Knopf, 1966. (Contains the story "Four Sides of One Story.")

Utter, Glenn H. "The Individual in Technological Society: Walker Percy's *Lancelot*." *Journal of Popular Culture* 16 (1982): 116–27.

Vauthier, Simone. "Story, Story-Teller and Listener: Notes on *Lancelot*." *South Carolina Review* 13 (1981): 39–54.

———. "Mimesis and Violence in *Lancelot*." *Delta* 13 (1981): 83–102.

Vickery, Olga W. *The Novels of William Faulkner: A Critical Interpretation*. Baton Rouge: Louisiana State University Press, 1959.

Volk-Birke, Sabine. "The Cyclical Way of the Priestess: On the Significance of Narrative Structures in Marion Zimmer Bradley's *The Mists of Avalon*." *Anglia* 108 (1990): 409–28.

Vonnegut, Kurt. *Bluebeard*. Delacorte Press, 1987.

———. *Deadeye Dick*. Delacorte Press, 1982.

———. *Mother Night*. 1962; rpt. New York: Avon, 1969.

———. *Slaughterhouse-Five; or, The Children's Crusade, a Duty-Dance with Death*. New York: Dell, 1969.

———. *Wampeters, Foma & Granfalloons (Opinions)*. 1974; rpt. New York: Dell, 1976.

Wachhorst, Wyn. "Time-Travel Romance on Film: Archetypes and Structures." *Extrapolation* 25 (1984): 340–59.

Waggoner, Hyatt H. *American Poets: From the Puritans to the Present*. New York: Delta, 1968.

Walden, Daniel. "Bernard Malamud, An American Jewish Writer and His Universal Heroes." *Studies in American Jewish Literature*. 7.2 (Fall 1988): 153–61.

Waldhorn, Arthur. *A Reader's Guide to Ernest Hemingway*. New York: Farrar, Straus & Giroux, 1972.

Warren, Robert Penn, ed. *Faulkner: A Collection of Critical Essays*. Englewood Cliffs, NJ: Prentice-Hall, 1966.

Wasserman, Earl R. "The Natural: World Ceres." In *Bernard Malamud and the Critics*. Ed. Leslie A. Field and Joyce W. Field. New York: New York University Press, 1970. 45–65.

Watson, James G. "Literary Self-Criticism: Faulkner in Fiction on Fiction." *Southern Quarterly* 20 (1981–82): 46–63.

Weeks, Robert P., ed. *Hemingway: A Collection of Critical Essays*. 1962; Englewood Cliffs: Prentice-Hall, 1965.

Weir, Charles, Jr. " 'An Invite with Gilded Edges': A Study of F. Scott Fitzgerald." *The Virginia Quarterly Review*. Rpt. in Kazin. 133–46.

Welsh, Andrew. "Lancelot at the Crossroads in Malory and Steinbeck." *Philological Quarterly* 70.4 (Fall 1991): 485–502.

Westbrook, Perry D. *A Literary History of New England*. Bethlehem, PA: Lehigh University Press, 1988.

Weston, Jessie. *From Ritual to Romance*. 1920; rpt. Garden City, NY: Doubleday Anchor Books, 1957.

Wheeler, Bonnie. "The Masculinity of King Arthur: From Gildas to the Nuclear Age." *Quondam et Futurus: A Journal of Arthurian Interpretations* 2.4 (Winter 1992): 1–26.

Whitaker, Muriel. *The Legends of King Arthur in Art*. Cambridge: D. S. Brewer, 1990.

White, Leslie. "The Function of Popular Culture in Bobbie Ann Mason's *Shiloh and Other Stories* and *In Country*." *The Southern Quarterly* 26.4 (Summer 1988): 69–79.

White, Steve. *Legacy*. New York: Baen, 1995.

White, Theodore H. *In Search of History: A Personal Adventure*. New York: Harper & Row, 1978.

Whitley, John S. *F. Scott Fitzgerald: The Great Gatsby*. London: Edward Arnold, 1976.

Williams, Dakin, and Shepherd Mead. *Tennessee Williams: An Intimate Biography*. New York: Arbor House, 1983.

Williams, James D. "Revision and Intention in Mark Twain's *Connecticut Yankee*." *American Literature* 36 (1964): 288–97.

Williams, Julia. "A Year with The Knighthood of Youth." *The Journal of the National Education Association* 19 (1930): 9–10.

Williams, Mary C. "Lessons from Ladies in Steinbeck's 'Gawain, Ewain, and Marhalt.' " *Avalon to Camelot* (1984): 40–41.

Williamson, George. *A Reader's Guide to T. S. Eliot: A Poem-by-Poem Analysis*. Second ed., with an Epilogue entitled "T. S. Eliot, 1888–1965." New York: Octagon Books, 1979.

Wilmer, Lambert A. *Merlin: Baltimore, 1827: Together with Recollections of Edgar A. Poe*. Ed. Thomas Ollive Mabbott. New York: Scholars' Facsimiles & Reprints, 1941.

Winther, Marjorie. "M*A*S*H, Malls and Meaning: Popular and Corporate Culture in *In Country*." *LIT: Literature Interpretation Theory* 4.3 (1993): 195–201.

Wojahn, Ellen. *Playing by Different Rules*. New York: AMACOM, 1988.

Wolf, Joan. *Born of the Sun*. New York: New American Library, 1989.

———. *The Edge of Light*. New York: New American Library, 1990.

———. *The Road to Avalon*. New York: New American Library, 1988.

Woloch, Nancy. *Women and the American Experience*. New York: Alfred A. Knopf, 1984.

Woolley, Persia. *Child of the Northern Spring*. New York: Poseidon Press, 1987.

———. *Guinevere: The Legend in Autumn*. New York: Poseidon Press, 1991.

———. *Queen of the Summer Stars*. New York: Poseidon Press, 1990.

Wright, Frank Lloyd. *Frank Lloyd Wright: Writings and Buildings*. Selected by Edgar Kaufmann and Ben Raeburn. New York: Meridian / New American Library, 1960.

Wylder, Delbert E. "The Two Faces of Brett: The Role of the New Woman in *The Sun Also Rises*." In *Critical Essays on The Sun Also Rises*. Ed. James Nagel. Boston: G. K. Hall & Co., 1995. 89–94.

Yarborough, Stephen R. "Walker Percy's Lancelot and the Critic's Original Sin." *Texas Studies in Literature and Language* 30.2 (1988): 272–94.

"The Ylle Cutt Mantell: A Romaunt of the Tyme of Gud Kynge Arthur (Done into Modern English from an Authentic Version)." *The Democratic Review* May 1844: 465–76.

Yolen, Jane. *The Acorn Quest*. Ill. Susanna Natti. New York: Thomas Y. Crowell, 1981.

———, ed. *Camelot*. Ill. Winslow Pels. New York: Philomel Books, 1995.

———. *The Dragon's Boy*. New York: Harper and Row, 1990.

———. *Hobby*. The Young Merlin Trilogy, Book Two. San Diego: Harcourt Brace & Co, 1996.

———. *Merlin*. The Young Merlin Trilogy, Book Three. San Diego: Harcourt Brace & Co, 1997.

———. *Merlin's Booke*. Ill. Thomas Canty. Minneapolis: Steel Dragon Press, 1986.

———. *Passager*. The Young Merlin Trilogy, Book One. San Diego: Harcourt Brace & Co, 1996.

Young, Philip. *Ernest Hemingway*. New York: Rinehart & Company, 1952.

Young, Stark. *Guenevere: A Play in Five Acts*. New York: The Grafton Press, 1906.

Zelazny, Roger. *The Courts of Chaos*. Garden City, NY: Doubleday, 1978.

———. *The Guns of Avalon*. Garden City, NY: Doubleday, 1972.

———. *The Last Defender of Camelot*. New York: Pocket Books, 1980.

Zelazny, Roger, and Robert Sheckley. *Bring Me the Head of Prince Charming*. New York: Bantam, 1991.

Zurlo, John A. "Hank's Egomania." *Mark Twain Journal* 21.3 (Spring 1983): 60.

Index

Masseck, Frank 66, 67, 68
Mathews, Basil
  The Splendid Quest: Stories of Knights on the Pilgrims' Way 63n1
McGowen, Tom
  Sir MacHinery 303
Meaney, Dee Morrison
  Iseult: Dreams That Are Done 291
Meliagrance, Meliagrant, Mellegrans
  in Berger's *Arthur Rex* 252–3, 257
  in Lanier's *The Boy's King Arthur* 77, 78
  in Pyle's Arthurian books 83
Melville, Herman 1, 260n24
  "Bartleby the Scrivener" 260n24
Merchant, Elizabeth Lodor 249
Merlin, Myrddin, Merdin 3, 8, 76, 95, 200, 254
  in Berger's *Arthur Rex* 254, 255–6
  in Borowsky's *The Queen's Knight* 285
  in Bradley's *Mists of Avalon* (as title) 293
  in Bridges's "Merlin's Grave" 15
  in Brooke's Arthurian mystery stories 300
  in Cabell's *Something About Eve* 176n61
  in Carmichael's *Pendragon* 285
  in Colander's "The Naming of the Lost" 289
  in Cram's *Excalibur* 102–3
  in Curry's *The Sleepers* 305
  in David's *Knight Life* 289
  in Emerson's poems 6–8
  in Fawcett's *The New King Arthur* 36–7
  in French's *Sir Marrok* 301–2
  in Godwin's *Firelord* 297n22
  in Haldeman's *The Lastborn of Elvinwood* 290
  in Hawke's Wizard series 299
  in Hawthorne's "The Antique Ring" 1–2
  in Hildebrandt, Rita and Tim, *Merlin and the Dragons of Atlantis* 288
  in Hovey's *Quest of Merlin* 104
  in Jeter's *Morlock Night* 288
  in MacGregor's *Indiana Jones and the Dance of the Giants* 320n34
  in Marshall's *The Pagan King* 285
  as model for advisers of youth groups 63–64, 68
  in Myers' *The Moon's Fire-Eating Daughter* 290
  in Nathan's *The Elixir* 290
  in (Robert) Newman's fiction 306n30
  in (Sharan) Newman's Guinevere trilogy 297
  in Norton's *Merlin's Mirror* 287
  in Norton's *Steel Magic* 287
  in Percy's "In the Cold Bright Wind" 232n16
  as prophet 3–4, 7
  in Robinson's *Merlin* 125–8

  in Saberhagen's *Dominion* 288
  in Saberhagen's *Merlin's Bones* 288
  in Service's *Tomorrow's Magic* 303–4
  in Service's *Winter of Magic's Return* 303
  in Service's *Wizard of Wind and Rock* 304n27
  in Steinbeck's *Acts of King Arthur* 204
  in Twain's *Connecticut Yankee* 52, 56, 176n61
  in Wilmer's *Merlin* 4–5
  in Yolen's fiction 305–6
  in Zelazny's *The Courts of Chaos* 289
  in Zelazny's "The Last Defender of Camelot" 289
Merlin (1998 TV miniseries) 322–3
Merlin and the Sword see *Arthur the King* (1985 TV movie)
Milbank Choir windows, Chapel, Princeton University 278–9
Millard, Chris 313
Mitchell, William 139
Modred, Mordred 18, 250
  in Adams' "At the Palace of King Lot" 38–9
  in Barthelme's *The King* 262, 264, 265
  in Berger's *Arthur Rex* 252, 257, 258
  in Borowsky's *The Queen's Knight* 285
  in Bradley's *Mists of Avalon* 292, 293
  in Bradshaw's *Hawk of May* 296
  in Bradshaw's *In Winter's Shadow* 296
  in Curry's *The Sleepers* 305
  in Fawcett's *The New King Arthur* 36
  in Godwin's *Firelord* 297, 297n22
  in Godwin's "Uallannach" 297n23
  in Hawke's Wizard series 299
  in Kane and Jakes's *Excalibur* 285
  in Karr's *Idylls of the Queen* 300
  in Marshall's *The Pagan King* 285
  in Pyle's Arthurian books 82, 87, 90
  in Robinson's *Modred* 118n9
Monaco, Robert
  Broken Stone 299–300
    Arturus 300
    Morga 300
  Grail series (*Parzival, The Grail War, The Final Quest, Blood and Dreams*) 299–300
    Grail 299–300
    Parzival 299
    Runes 299–300
moral knighthood, symbolic knighthood, nobility of character 35, 59–60, 284, 302
  in Du Bose's *The Gang of Six* 70–1
  in *First Knight* 319–20
  in Gray's *Little Sir Galahad* 72
  in Holmes's *Little Sir Galahad* 72–3
  in Johnston's *Keeping Tryst* 74–5

Tristan and Isolt legend
  in American drama 107–9
  in popular fiction 290–1, 298
  in Roberts' *The Enchanted Cup* 285
  in Updike's fiction 266–72
Turner, Ted 277
Twain, Mark 3, 80, 89, 255, 326
  Connecticut Yankee in King Arthur's Court 3, 35, 41, 46–57, 59, 176n61, 186, 316
    abuse of power as theme 48–9, 54–6
    adaptations of 57
    Arthur 51
    Battle of the Sand Belt 113
    Clarence 48
    Cote Male Taile 48
    Dowley the blacksmith 53–4
    films based on 57, 308–14
    Galahad 48
    Lancelot 48
    Merlin 52, 56, 176n61, 256
    Malory used in 46
    Morgan, Hank 42, 44, 46, 48–57, 109
      as American Adam 51–2
      as despot 51–6
      as prototypical American 49–51
      Smith, Bob, as original name for 56–7
    Morgan le Fay 56
    Sandy 48
    satire in 47, 47n2, 49, 54
    Siege Perilous 48
    similarities to Adeler's "The Fortunate Island" 42–4, 46, 49, 51
    as source of the term "new deal" 51
  Twilight Zone, The 325

Unidentified Flying Oddball 311–12. *See also Spaceman and King Arthur, The*
Updike, John 210, 266–72
  Brazil 266–70, 271
    Bédier's version of Tristan story as influence 268
    Donaciano, Uncle 267, 268
    Leme, Isabel 267–70
    magical realism as influence 267
    Raposo, Tristão 267–70
  "Four Sides of One Story" 270–2
    Denoalen 271
    Iseult the Fair 270–2
    Iseult of the White Hands 270–2
    Kaherdin 271
    Mark 270–2
    Tristan 270–2
  "Tristan and Iseult" 272
    Iseult 272
    Tristan 272
  Tristan legend used by 266–72
Uriens, Urience
  in Cawein's *Accolon of Gaul* 111

Urre
  in Bridges's "The Best Knight" 16
  in Lanier's *The Boy's King Arthur* 79, 79n6
Uther Pendragon 76, 257

Verlaine, Paul
  "Parsifal" 114, 117
Vietnam War 211, 321–2
  in Mason's *In Country* 241–9
  in Paterson's *Park's Quest* 306–7
Vinaver, Eugène 202, 203
Vivian, Vivien, Viviane. *See also* Nimue, Niniane
  in Adams' "Thomas and Vivien" 39
  in Bradley's *Lady of Avalon* 295
  in Bradley's *Mists of Avalon* 292, 294–5
  in Fawcett's *The New King Arthur* 36
  in Robinson's *Merlin* 125–8, 129
Vonnegut, Kurt 211
  Bluebeard 274
  Deadeye Dick 273
    Grail motifs in 273–4
  Mother Night 273
    Goblet, The, Grail play in 273
  Slaughterhouse-Five 274
    wasteland in 274
  Wampeters, Foma & Granfalloons 275n29
Vortigern
  in Hall's poems 99–100
Vortimer 100

Waitkus, Eddie 211
Walesa, Lech 264
Washington, George 20n2
wasteland 210
  in Adams' "The Vision of Sir Lionel" 40
  in contemporary fiction 211
  in Eliot's *The Waste Land* 115–16
  in Fitzgerald's *The Great Gatsby* 146–7
  in Fitzgerald's novels and stories 141, 152–3
  in Hemingway's novels 155–6, 157–9, 161–2
  in Malamud's writings 218, 219–20
Watts, George Frederick
  "Sir Galahad" 66, 279
Wells, H. G.
  The Time Machine 288
Weston, Jessie 163, 215n5, 218
  From Ritual to Romance 58, 113–15, 118, 231
White, Steve
  Legacy 288
White, T. H.
  Once and Future King, The 123, 183, 295
    as source for film 321–2
Whittier, John Greenleaf 21
Wilder, James A. 308

ARTHURIAN STUDIES